The American Woman's Gazetteer

The American Woman's Gazetteer

by Lynn Sherr and Jurate Kazickas

Photo Credits

RLI:
VLM 9 (VLR 8-10)
IL 8-adult

THE AMERICAN WOMAN'S GAZETTEER
A Bantam Book / June 1976

All rights reserved.
Copyright © 1976 by Lynn Sherr and Jurate Kazickas
This book may not be reproduced in whole or in part, by
mimeograph or any other means, without permission.
For information address: Bantam Books, Inc.

ISBN 0-553-01041-7

Published simultaneously in the United States and Canada

Bantam Books are published by Bantam Books, Inc.
Its trademark, consisting of the words "Bantam Books" and
the portrayal of a bantam, is registered in the United States
Patent Office and in other countries. Marca Registrada.
Bantam Books, Inc., 666 Fifth Avenue,
New York, New York 10019.

Printed in the United States of America

0 9 8 7 6 5 4 3 2 1

Introduction

This book started out as a feminist travel guide—a proud and unabashedly biased catalog of all the places in America where women made history. No state in the Union is without its female contribution to our national heritage, but you wouldn't know it from reading most standard tour books. Boastful highway markers all over the East point out every bed where George Washington is said to have slept, but not even a discreet plaque identifies the church where the world's first female minister was ordained. Such consistent omissions of sites dealing with women led us to do some traveling of our own, in search of the landmarks that are part of women's history. After reading dozens of books, making countless inquiries, and coming up against a number of dead ends, we found Antoinette Brown's church at South Butler, New York, and fifty states later, we added almost fifteen hundred other locations connected with women in America.

Now you, too can tour the country in the footsteps of the nation's heroines. Start at Athens, Alabama, where Patty Malone, who was born a slave and became a famous opera star, is buried in an unmarked grave. Stroll across the sturdy steel Kate Shelley Bridge in Moingona, Iowa, and ponder the death-defying act of heroism that fifteen-year-old Kate performed on a rickety old wooden railroad trestle in 1881. Walk by the bas-relief of scientist Ellen Swallow Richards at MIT in Cambridge, Massachusetts, and rub the shiny bronze nose of the woman who is said to have pioneered the science of ecology. And venture off the main highway into the old mining camp of South Pass City, Wyoming, where the nation's first female justice of the peace, Esther Morris, made the women of her state the first to vote in the United States.

Like any proper gazetteer, or geographical dictionary, this book is arranged alphabetically, by state and city (and county and occasional mountain), to make it as convenient as possible to retrace the routes of celebrated women around the country. In addition to the few enshrined birthplaces and homes that are now museums, we have also included private homes whose current owners were unaware of their famous former occupants; towering monuments to anonymous pioneer women; courthouses and hospitals where women defied contemporary prejudice in pursuit of new careers; graves that are grandly marked or sadly neglected; and even trails along which heroines on horseback galloped fearlessly, despite enemy fire, to save an entire town.

But two years of research, travel, and writing have turned up more than simply a collection of feminist shrines. We have also discovered distinct regional aspects in the development of American women. The East produced Revolutionary heroines, mill workers and labor organizers, scores of intellectuals and liberal thinkers who believed so strongly in education for women that they opened their own schools. A number of eastern women were also religious dissenters, frequently banished or hanged as witches for their radical notions. Southern women emerged most prominently as a result of the Civil War: Confederate spies; diarists who provided valuable historical accounts of the troubled times; plantation owners who developed such new crops as indigo or silk, or whose passions were so fired by the treatment of slaves that they defied decades of chivalry and tradition and turned into abolitionists. The West, which at one time included everything in that unexplored territory west of the Mississippi, demanded still more of the American woman, who met the challenge by conquering the frontier and homesteading the wilderness despite danger and constant loneliness. The rugged adventure of settling the West also lured women to the mining camps, where gold could be found either in the rocky hills or in the elegant gambling halls. Even further physical endurance was required of the women who settled the frozen frontier—Alaska—while the robust queens of Hawaii got to make their feminist contributions in the heat of the sun.

The natural features of the land also gave rise to some enterprising agricultural successes. It was the women who cultivated the blueberry bogs of New Jersey, the olive groves of California, the rice paddies of the Carolinas, and the pastures of Wisconsin that fed the cows that made the cheese that led to the first dairy co-op in the country.

The land inspired other women to write, some so specifically about the land they knew best that we have used their words to describe it: Christian Reid in North Carolina, Willa Cather in Nebraska, Celia Thaxter in Maine.

But for many women, it did not matter whether they lived in mountain or valley, desert or forest. The earliest American women—the Indians—were everywhere, fighting off the onslaught of European settlers and, when that proved futile, helping keep the peace. Often their less diplomatic brothers retaliated against encroachment of white settlers by abducting colonists. A number of women, the most prized captives, survived their ordeals to write about them, thus creating an entire genre of literature, known as Indian captive narratives, that brought their authors fame and fortune and left valuable records for modern historians.

State lines were no barriers to the precedent-setting women who became the first in the nation to break into all-male professional careers. Iowa nurtured the first female lawyer in the United States; Ohio, the first female dentist; New York, the first doctor; Kansas, the first mayor; Virginia, the first bank president; Nevada, the first to run for the U.S. Senate; Arkansas, the first elected to the U.S. Senate; Oklahoma, the first elected to statewide office. Delaware even claims the first female member of Britain's Royal Astronomical Society; and Connecticut, the first female member of the Massachusetts Historical Society.

The great equalizer, of course, was sex discrimination, which spawned suffrage workers in every state, even as the states were added to the Union. But, although the home of Susan B. Anthony, "the mother of us all," is carefully preserved in New York, and Laura Clay's room bears her own campaign poster in Kentucky, nothing commemorates the lifetime dedication of Marilla Ricker in New Hampshire, Jeannette Rankin in Montana, Clara Colby in Nebraska, or Mary Livermore in Illinois, to name just a few. In fact, most of the historic houses where these and other women were born, lived, and mapped out their lifework, are, we sadly discovered, gone. Many have been replaced by parking lots, skyscrapers, and reservoirs.

Even discovering that disappointing information took so much digging into musty old city records, or, for example, wandering around the countryside in search of a now-flooded ranch, that one sympathetic historian titled us feminist archaeologists.

In some cases, our search paid off—so successfully that we unearthed the same site in different states. The Shoshoni guide, Sacajawea, for instance, is so highly revered that both South Dakota and Wyoming have proudly marked her grave in cemeteries some five hundred miles apart. In the South, at least four different cities in three different states (Georgia, Mississippi, and Virginia) claim that Memorial Day originated there. And all over the country, dozens of colleges tack on minute qualifiers to protect their title as the first institute of higher education for women.

Researching certain women required more hiking than digging. Mary Baker Eddy roamed all over New England in the process of founding the Christian Science Church, and every step she took has been dutifully tracked by her followers. Clara Barton slogged across countless Civil War battlefields, and monuments to her work adorn almost every war zone. Laura Ingalls Wilder's sentimental journey through her childhood that she recorded in books for children has been carefully traced by loyal fans. Indeed, if every woman's life were as well mapped out as these, our job would have been considerably easier.

As it was, we were largely dependent on many hundreds of dedicated local historians, reference librarians, chambers of commerce, descendants of notable women, and friendly passersby, all of whom generously shared their memories and their research with us. Some assured us that suitable monuments were already in the works for certain women; others got so caught up in redis-

covering their native daughters that they promised to initiate a campaign for an appropriate memorial instantly. In fact, just as we were going to press, the citizens of Astoria, Oregon, notified us that they had raised more than one thousand dollars to erect a fine granite monument where previously only a grass-covered pauper's stone had identified the grave of pioneer doctor Bethenia Owens-Adair. "You can take the credit for moving us off our duffs!" they told us. And we did not mind at all having to rewrite that entry at the eleventh hour. To everyone who helped us, and to our own families and friends, who good-naturedly accompanied us on tombstone-readings and on uncharted forays off paved roads, and who patiently waited for us to finish this book and move beyond the nineteenth century, we thank you.

A word about logistics: With a few exceptions (like Jeanette Piccard in Dearborn, Michigan), all of the women we have chosen as subjects had died as of January 1975. The term *site of* indicates that the landmark is no longer standing. And the term *private* indicates that the landmark is currently occupied and is not open to the public, although our experience is that many of the owners are delighted to show off their houses. You can assume that any entry not titled *private* is either open to the public, or accessible for a visit.

One final thought. Although we would be gratified and encouraged to see busloads of tourists stopping off at some of our favorite finds—such as Vergennes, Vermont, to pose in front of the home of the world's first female licensed steamboat captain—or to hear of a pilgrimage to the graveside of Indian chief Nancy Ward in Tennessee, or to learn of a trek along Ann Eliza Webb Young's escape route from her husband in Utah, that is not the only purpose of this gazetteer. You probably don't even have to venture beyond your own city or county line to discover a worthy local heroine. If you find a landmark for her, please let us know.

ALABAMA

Athens

Site of Patty Malone Grave, South Hine Street Cemetery. Born a slave in 1853, Patty was gifted with a contralto voice too beautiful for simply answering orders. Her sympathetic owners encouraged her talent and sent her to music school. Patty became one of the outstanding voices with the famous Jubilee Singers and, with them, she toured Europe, delighting royal audiences. On her return home in 1896, her brilliant career was tragically cut short when Patty was injured aboard a ship during a heavy storm. She died shortly afterwards. There is no tombstone over her grave, but we were told that the County Historical Society has plans to erect a suitable marker to the famed singer.

Athens College. In 1842, the Tennessee Annual Conference of the Methodist Church authorized the building of Athens Female Institute, and in 1843 the state legislature passed an act incorporating the college, "the second of its kind in the world." The school has operated without interruption ever since.

Birmingham

Arlington House, 331 Cotton Avenue, SW. This elegant Greek revival plantation house, built in the 1840s, was used as Union headquarters during the Civil War. Up in the attic, the esteemed poet Mary Gordon Duffee carefully listened to the officers' plans and reported back to her Confederate command.

Mary A. Cahalan Monument, Woodrow Wilson Park. Seated with her customary open book on her lap, Powell Public School's favorite principal is honored with this life-sized Alabama marble statue. When it was dedicated in 1908, with more than five thousand of her admirers in attendance, the monument was said to be the only statue in the world of a female educator. Mary came to Birmingham in 1883 as one of the first two teachers in town, and she served as principal of Powell until her death in 1906.

Grave of Pattie Ruffner Jacobs, Elmwood Cemetery, 600 Montevallo Road, SW. The humble plaque embedded in the grass with only her dates (1875–1935) leaves unrecorded the brilliant career of suffrage leader Pattie Jacobs. Rallying the women of her state, Pattie warned men that "the pedestal platitude appeals less and less to the intelligence of southern women, who are learning in increasing numbers that the assertion that they are too good, too noble, too pure to vote in reality brands them as incompetents."

Blountsville

Murphree Sisters Memorial, Route 26. An historical highway marker, erected in 1964, commemorates the ingenious heroics of twenty-one-year-old Celia Murphree and her eighteen-year-old sister Winnie Mae during the Streight-Forrest campaign of the Civil War in 1863. Celia's grandson, Capt. Eugene Maynor, provided us with the exciting details. It seems that three Union soldiers, in search of horses and medical supplies, raided the house where Celia and Winnie Mae were baby-sitting. The three soldiers rambunctiously insisted on being served mint juleps. Winnie Mae obliged, cleverly spicing the drinks with soporific toothache medicine stirred into the honey. The potent cocktail was so tasty that the soldiers demanded another round and then promptly passed out, enabling the sisters to seize their weapons and turn the Yankees in to the nearest Confederate camp. For their bravery, Celia and Winnie Mae were each rewarded with a handsome mare.

Fort Payne

Grave of Nancy Callahan, Little River Cemetery. "Granny Dollar," who died in 1931 when she was 105, was a familiar and beloved figure. She lived alone in a tiny cabin in the woods, surrounded by a glorious orchard of abundant fruit trees that she nurtured. Dressed in old shabby clothes, barefooted, with her favorite pipe in her mouth, she was a doctor and a midwife whose strange, sweet-smelling potions cured every conceivable ache and pain. Best of all, she liked to tell stories of her happiest days when the Cherokee still owned the land. When her tribe was driven out in the 1830s, little Nancy was one of the few who refused to leave. In her last days, she had carefully saved twenty-three dollars for a tombstone, but the money was stolen days after her death. More than forty years went by before local residents erected the fitting memorial that stands today—a monument with the graceful head of an Indian woman, inscribed "Daughter of the Cherokee."

Gadsden

Emma Sansom Monument, First and Broad Streets. The fearless fifteen-year-old, who guided Gen. Nathan Forrest as he pursued two thousand federal troops in 1863, is honored with this towering marble likeness pointing the way to a secret passage across Black Creek. A bas-relief at the base of the monument shows Emma riding on the back of Forrest's horse, whispering the crucial instructions in the general's ear. As enemy gunfire burst all around them, Emma waved her sunbonnet defiantly at the federals who, in spite of themselves, cheered the spunky heroine. Emma's secret shortcut enabled Forrest to capture the Union forces, and, that night, having asked for a lock of her hair as a cherished souvenir, he sent "his highest regards to Emma Sansom for her gallant conduct." Thirty-six years later, the state legislature voted to give Emma 640 acres of land in "admiration and gratitude." Today a popular ballad tells of her brave deed—beginning and ending with these stirring words:

The courage of man is one thing, but that of a maid is more
For blood is blood and death is death and grim is the battle fore
And the rose that blooms, tho' blistered by the sleet of an open sky
Is fairer far than its sisters who sleep in the hot house nigh.

Guntersville

Site of Creek Path Mission, Route 79. The grave of Catherine Brown, first teacher of Indian girls, her school, and the entire village of Creek Path have been inundated by the waters of the man-made Guntersville Lake. When Catherine, the daughter of an Indian chief, came to open a Christian school for girls here in 1820, a local villager observed, "the most enthusiastic joy was occasioned among the people." Close to fifty Cherokee men assembled immediately to build a schoolhouse which they finished in two days. Catherine taught there almost a year, but she was frail and sickly, and she died in 1823, barely twenty years old.

Hazel Green

In a small cemetery near the site of the old Jeffries house, which burned down several years ago, four tombstones mark the graves of Misters Jeffries, High, Brown, and Routt, the last four husbands of six-times married Elizabeth Dale who lived in Hazel Green from 1833–55. Neighbors, disconcerted by the way Elizabeth kept a top hat of each of these men on a special rack in the hallway, speculated that this strange and aloof woman had murdered all her husbands, but no one dared speak of it. When some of Elizabeth's cattle roamed onto Abner Tate's property, wrecking his cotton crop, Tate published a sensational pamphlet charging that "around the marriage couch of that woman six grinning skeletons are hung." Soon after, Tate was mysteriously wounded, and when her neighbors became increasingly hostile, Elizabeth moved to Mississippi. They still talk about her in Hazel Green, although some now say Elizabeth's only crime was in getting married six times.

Huntsville

Howard Weeden Birthplace, 300 Gates Avenue (private). This two-story brick house with its outstanding entrance fanlight was the 1847 birthplace and the lifelong home of one of the most famous of Alabama's early artists and poets. Her fame rests on four slim volumes in which oil and watercolor portraits of family-owned slaves are accompanied by descriptive verses. In her painting, wrote one contemporary historian, "the negro is not made beautiful but the beauty in him is revealed." Howard's greatest contribution was to record the passing away of the old relationships between slave and master. Although much of her work was intended to show how happy the slaves were, and to show their trusting acceptance of their pathetic servitude, occasionally Howard saw what the condition of slavery really meant, describing the "innate pathos in [the slave's] eyes and words." Joel Chandler Harris described her poems as "little verses that flutter across the page as delicately and shy as the falling yellow leaves of the old mimosa that stood near a dear old lady's window years and years ago."

Livingston

Tutwiler Hall, Livingston University. Through the energetic work of Julia Tutwiler, pioneer educator, this college was the first woman's school to receive state funds (1883). Tutwiler (see *Montgomery*), known as the mother of coeducation in Alabama, came here in 1881 and retired as president emeritus in 1910.

Mobile

Site of Octavia Celeste Le Vert House, Government Street. "In a plain, substantial mansion, combining taste, elegance and comfort," that stood here until it was demolished a few years ago to make way for a parking lot, Octavia Le Vert reigned as queen of Mobile's social and literary circle in the mid-1800s. "Her intellectual accomplishments and the perpetual sunshine of a gay and glad spirit, always amiable, kind and considerate were her charms," wrote an admiring biographer. She was the first Alabama writer to achieve national acclaim with the publication of *Souvenirs of Travel* (1857), a two-volume account of her travels through Europe, "rich in brilliant descriptions and picturesque and flowing in style" and including such anecdotal chapters as "The Ascent and Eruption of Vesuvius" and "Moonlight in Venice." Conversing ably in the several languages she had learned as a child in *Pensacola, Florida,* Octavia met with such celebrities as Napoleon III, the poet Lamartine, Elizabeth Barrett Browning, and Pope Pius IX. The Civil War depleted her fortune, her Northern sympathies eventually alienated her from Mobile society, and she finally moved to New York where she was active in Sorosis, one of the earliest women's clubs. She died in Georgia in 1877.

Augusta Jane Evans Wilson House, "Georgia Cottage," 2558 Spring Hill Avenue (private). The state's first novelist purchased this charming Creole cottage surrounded by moss-hung oak trees with the proceeds from her first book, *Inez: A Tale of the Alamo.* She lived here from 1857–68. During this time, she wrote two more powerful novels. *Macaria,* with its provocative war episodes, was banned by the federal army and caused a flurry of insubordination as soldiers smuggled copies into their barracks faster than the officers could confiscate and burn them. *St. Elmo,* published in 1866 (see *Columbus, Georgia*), was so popular that the state of Alabama named a town after the hero of the title. Wilson was the first woman in America to earn more than $100,000 from her writings.

Site of Kate Cumming Home, Franklin Street, between State and Congress. Believing that "the war is certainly ours as well as that of men," Kate Cumming left Mobile in 1862 with a group of women, none of whom had any nursing training, to help care for the wounded in hospitals throughout the South (see *Corinth, Mississippi*). During her three years as a field nurse and hospital administrator, she kept a vivid diary, which was published in 1866 as *A Journal of Hospital Life in the Confederate Army in Tennessee.* Countering the perennial prejudice against women in the field, Kate always insisted, "A woman's respectability must be at a low ebb if it can be endangered by going into a hospital."

Montevallo

Tutwiler Hall, Alabama College, was named for Julia Tutwiler, whose pioneering efforts on behalf of education for women led to the founding of this school in 1895. (See *Montgomery*.)

Montgomery

Julia Tutwiler Memorial, Department of Archives and History, Washington Avenue. This marble plaque, designed by noted

Alabama sculptor Geneva Mercer and dedicated in 1933, honors the "teacher, poet, prison reformer, patriot, lover of humanity, beauty and truth. Pioneer for Industrial and University Education for Women in America." Her tireless efforts led to the founding of several colleges for women, all of which have named buildings in her honor. One of her lesser known contributions to the well-being of Alabama was Julia's nostalgic poem, written while she was a student in Germany in 1874. It is now the state song.

Russellville

Catherine Sevier Home, Franklin and Gaines Streets (private). In 1836, when she was eighty-two, the legendary and fearless pioneer came here from her home in *Livingston, Tennessee,* to spend her last days with her son in the Alabama countryside. Here, Sevier died shortly after.

Talladega

Betsy Hamilton Birthplace, "Idlewild," Eastabago Road (private). Born here in 1843, the noted author and dialect reader Idora McClellan Moore, who wrote under the pen name of Betsy Hamilton, published dozens of short stories recalling life on the "old time" plantations. In one story about Christmas at the turn of the century, Hamilton wrote, "I long to experience again, for a little while at least, some of those pleasant old-time customs among Southern women when friends were informally invited to 'Come and spend the day, bring your knitting, come early and stay late;' and when ladies would sit together quietly and talk deliberately, and in moderate tones, perhaps about their gardens or chickens or of the accomplishments of their children, and never an unkind word of gossip. Then when the sun was sinking low in the sky, slowly knit to the middle of the needles . . . deliberately put on their bonnets, say the usual parting words, promise to come again soon, kiss and bid goodbye, walk leisurely to the gate, stand and talk a little longer, kiss again, slowly get into the carriage and drive down the lane."

Site of Enfield Joiner House, 103 Brignoli Street. The old family home of the town's distinguished teacher of the deaf was torn down in 1970 to make way for the Telephone Exchange, but an historical marker briefly records some of Enfield's outstanding accomplishments. At the time of her death in 1965, Enfield was considered an authority on the education of the deaf throughout the country, and she had taught in special schools in four different states.

Troy

Site of Ann Love Cabin, Carroll Building, Church Street. As a widow with six children, Ann Love built the town's first log cabin and managed a popular little inn here from 1839 to her death in 1858. With her handy whip and sharp butcher's knife, Ann settled everyone's arguments in the rough frontier town. Every Sunday morning, she rounded up the drunks for services in the Methodist Church that she had helped to found.

Tuscaloosa

Julia Tutwiler Hall, University of Alabama. Already one of the most popular dormitory namesakes in the state (see *Livingston; Montevallo*), Julia was honored again here for her vital role in convincing the state authorities that the university should be coeducational.

Tuscumbia

Helen Keller Birthplace, "Ivy Green," 300 West North Common Street. Born here on June 27, 1880, stricken nineteen months later with a mysterious illness that left her blind, deaf, and

Helen Keller's well

dumb, Helen Keller described herself as a "Phantom living in a world that was no world." But on March 3, 1887, the day that Helen would forever call her "soul's birthday," twenty-four-year-old Anne Sullivan, herself partially blind, arrived to train the child who was nothing more than a small wild animal. Barely a month later, the miracle occurred. Down at the well, Sullivan pumped water on the child's hand, tapping out in alphabet code the five letters of the word *water.* As Helen would later write in *The Story of My Life,* "there was a strange stir within me—a misty consciousness, a sense of something remembered. It was as if I had come back to life after being dead. . . . Thoughts that ran forward and backward came to me quickly—thoughts that seemed to start in my brain and spread all over me. . . . Delicious sensations rippled through me, and sweet strange things that were locked up in my heart began to sing." Soon Helen learned Anne's name—"Teacher"—as she would forever call her, and by the end of a few hours, Helen had learned thirty words. Two years later, after many lessons under the pine trees in the garden, perfumed by the mimosa and musk grapes in the arbor, came the day when Helen could say, "I am not dumb now." This extraordinary partnership of a gifted, sensitive teacher and an eager, intelligent pupil led to the development of the woman whom Mark Twain called the most marvelous person of her sex who existed on the earth since Joan of Arc. Helen was also a great crusader on behalf of woman's rights. She spoke out for birth control—"The incalculable mischief of an uncontrolled birth rate sucks up the vitality of the human race;" the Woman's Party—"(It) stands for Women First. It means an individual allegiance to our ideal—the ideal of sex equality and responsibility;" and suffrage, writing in 1915, "Let us see how the votes of women will help solve the problems of living wisely and well." Until her death in 1968, Keller traveled, lectured, and wrote tirelessly to help those with the same handicaps that she had so courageously overcome. (See *Watertown, Massachusetts.*) Every summer, the play *The Miracle Worker* is performed on the grounds of Keller's home, now a permanent shrine in her honor.

Wetumpka

The historical society sadly informed us that the tombstone of Caroline Bostwick was stolen a long time ago. Inscribed on the granite marker, erected by grateful guests who probably never knew who she really was, were the names "Henry Ritter, Emma Ritter, Demma Ritter, Sweet Potato, Crema Tarter, Caroline Bostwick." The little slave girl was given as many names as errands to run when she worked at the local hotel near here, dying in 1852 from overwork at the tender age of nine.

Julia Tutwiler Prison for Women, Rockford Road. Concerned for the betterment of opportunities for all women Julia Tutwiler (see *Montgomery*) turned her commanding organizational skills to the unfair treatment of prisoners, instigating the passage of the 1880 law to improve conditions in county jails.

Jeannette Nichols wrote the first detailed history of the territory: *History of Alaska* (1924). Senator Ernest Gruening called her book "the authoritative study of Alaska's political history during its first forty-five years after the transfer" into U.S. hands.

Anchorage

Site of Rendezvous Building, Fifth Avenue and D Street. The building that stood here until 1971 was torn down without the approval of its owner, Zula Swanson Wester, due to legal entanglements. The Alabama-born Alaska settler ran a fashionable brothel here in the 1930s. Later it became a bar. She is said to have garnered one-half million dollars in real estate holdings when she died at age 81 in 1973. The obituary listed her clubs as Daughters of the Elks, the National Association for the Advancement of Colored People and the Northern Lights Civic and Social Club.

Juneau

Marie Drake Junior High School, 1250 Glacier Avenue, the first in the capital city, honors the woman who pioneered in Alaska education and wrote the official state song. Marie Drake came to Alaska from Ohio with her husband in the early 1900s. One of her immediate assignments as the first secretary to the newly created Department of Education was to find her own table and chair. The only furniture available was provided for the commissioner. Marie Drake's next challenge was to visit all the territorial schools. Her transportation included boats, dog teams, trains, and planes. Overcoming seemingly insurmountable odds, she created schools, managed to get supplies, and encouraged teachers in the barren wilderness. She was rewarded for her efforts by being appointed assistant commissioner of education in 1934. Marie Drake also wrote a poem, inspired by the newly designed territorial banner, to make Alaska schoolchildren aware of the natural beauties of their country. The verse was later set to music by Elinor Dusenbury and became the official territorial song—"Alaska's Flag"—by act of the legislature in 1955. It became the state song when Alaska entered the Union in 1959. On February 13, just before she died in 1965, Marie Drake learned of a birthday tribute paid her by the governor and more than two hundred Alaskans from the North Pole to the "lower 48." From her sickbed she cooed, "This is the happiest birthday I have ever known."

Baranof Hotel, Second and Franklin. On the piano in the lobby Elinor Dusenbury first played her arrangement of the poem, "Alaska's Flag," for its author, Marie Drake, in 1938. "When I finished there were tears on her face," the musician later recalled. "Fortunately for me, she loved it." So did the entire territory, then state, which adopted it for official use. Elinor Dusenbury had lived at Chilkoot Barracks at Haines with her husband for several years before leaving for a new home in Nebraska. She explained that she set the poem to music "from pure, unadulterated homesickness for Alaska!"

Ann Coleman Room, Juneau Memorial Library, 114 West Fourth Street. "It's been a good hundred years," the Alaska librarian said at her centennial birthday party in 1972. "I'd like to be around for another hundred." The spirit of this hardy Juneau settler will be remembered for more than another century with the children's reading room named in her honor. Ann Coleman came to Juneau in 1913 and served as city librarian until her retirement in the late 1940s. She also grew flowers and vegetables that attracted visitors from miles around, and the nearby Coleman Gardens on her homesite perpetuate her remarkable horticultural abilities.

Winn's Opera House was built to accommodate Anna Snow and her talented husband and children, Juneau's first family of the theater, at the turn of the century. A farm girl whose mother called her the "only decent woman on the stage," Anna Snow joined her husband George on his side-wheel steamer trip to Alaska in 1887. While he searched for gold in the Yukon, Anna raised young Crystal and Monte and entertained the town with songs and dances. Her lovely voice lent itself to the weddings and funerals of the entire frontier settlement. When the elder Snows died, their plucky offspring continued the family tradition. Daughter Crystal Snow Jenne ran the Forget-Me-Not Flower Shop, sat in the Territorial Legislature, and ran the Juneau Post Office for eleven years. Her motto when she was in her seventies: "When you cease to grow you are a potato, and I will never be a potato."

Mount Blackburn

The first woman to climb the rugged and treacherous Mount Blackburn (16,390 feet) was Dora Keen, intrepid leader of an expedition that first conquered the peak in 1912. The experienced alpinist, barely five feet tall, had been forced to turn back from an earlier attempt when her twelve-day food supply was threatened by a thirteen-day journey. The following winter she returned with seven men and nine dogs. "I was going again because I had need of courage and inspiration," she later wrote, "and because on the high mountains I find them as nowhere else." The group took off at 5:00 A.M. on April 22, toting a ton of equipment on eight sleds and trailers. The early spring Arctic air registered eighteen degrees. After a week of rising at one in the morning in unheated tents, traveling by first light at 3:30 A.M., putting on snowshoes when the sun shone to avoid sinking into the softened snow, and stopping by 10:00 A.M. to await a new hard crust, the party reached the main sources of Kennicot Glacier. Dora Keen described it: "In a horseshoe curve above us rose a majestic amphitheatre of lofty snow peaks, jagged ridges, and precipitous walls. Between the ridges tumbled the mighty ice falls of seven great glaciers. We seemed like atoms before these impregnable fortresses as we prepared to pit our human littleness against the pitiless forces of nature."

The rest of the journey meant dodging avalanches and balancing along narrow crevasses; braving six-below-zero temperatures at night and ninety degrees at noon. They sat out one snowstorm in caves chiseled out of a gulch, and they hid under ice cliffs to escape slides. A final severe storm kept them cavebound for thirteen days. Finally, at 8:30 on the morning of May 19, an icy gale whipping at her, Dora Keen stood on the summit with the single man who had not turned back. "There was nothing to impair a view on which our eyes were the first that had ever looked," she reported, "and the panorama seemed limited only by the haze of distance as we gazed a full 200 miles on every side. Probably nowhere except in Alaska, not even in the Himalayas, could mortal man attain to the center of so vast and imposing a stretch of unbroken snow over great glaciers and high snow peaks. . . . The limited snow areas of the Alps, the Canadian Rocky Mountains, even the high Andes, faded into insignificance in my memory." With aching hands, they planted their flagpole, then began the descent. After her return from this experience, the second successful ascent of an Alaska mountain, Dora Keen ticked off the precedents of her four-week climb. They were: "the first to succeed without Swiss guides, the first to live in snow caves, the first to make a prolonged night ascent, the first to succeed on an avalanche-swept southeast side, and the only Alaskan ascent in which a woman has taken part."

Mount Stroller White

Josephine White named this mile-high peak west of Mendenhall Glacier in honor of her late husband in 1930, a tribute to the spirit of both members of the adventurous couple. They came to Alaska with the gold rush of 1898, cutting a notable swath through the Yukon. While he published newspapers, "Josie" earned a reputation as a sure-shot, regularly bagging rabbits and ptarmigan for supper. In Juneau, she achieved some celebrity as the highest-scoring female bowler at the local Elks Club alleys. And mountaintops bowed under her sure footsteps, even when she was past seventy. To the surprise of her neighbors, who were sure she'd live forever, Josephine White died in 1956 at the age of eighty-three.

Point Barrow

One of the few Eskimo women to attain financial prominence in the icy North was Reindeer Mary, owner and operator of a vast reindeer industry. She efficiently built her business despite the difficulties of polar life, which an early issue of *Pioneer* magazine called even harder for women than for Eskimo men: "Eskimo women have to toil early and late. The leather that goes into the footwear and the skin garments for the tribe is always laboriously worked into form by these poor women, most of whom pass their interminably long days chewing the leather so as to soften it for wearing apparel. . . . It is, perhaps, the bleakest, most toilsome life imaginable, the life that these women of the Arctic zone have to live."

Ramparts

The schoolteacher stationed at this remote point sixty miles below the Arctic Circle was, for a time, Isabel Ambler Gilman. Dedicated to the education of native Alaskans, she spent the winter of 1915–16 in sixty-below-zero temperatures as a teacher with the government-sponsored Alaska School Service. The English-born writer described the role of the teacher in the remote homes of nonwhites: "She is census taker, keeper of vital statistics, arbitrator of quarrels, health officer, peace officer, friend and confidant of everyone in distress." Isabel Gilman performed these duties with dispatch and pleaded with political leaders to remove the stigma from nonwhite children and accord them equal educational rights. "The half-breed is a permanent resident," she wrote in 1916. "Alaska is his home."

Sitka

Shortly after the American purchase of Alaska, Emily McCorkle FitzGerald came to this army fort with her husband, the post surgeon, in 1872. Before she arrived on the steamer from Portland, Oregon, that August 16, one baby in hand and another on the way, Emily wrote her sister, "I was horrified and feel doleful" about the prospect of spending time in the isolated northern country. After fixing up a roomy apartment and slipping into her winter flannels, she wrote her mother back home in Pennsylvania: "With a different climate, this would be a lovely spot. . . . It will be dreadfully lonely here; the winters are so long, but I guess we will flourish." Her letters, preserved by her mother and published as *An Army Doctor's Wife on the Frontier,* provide a firsthand glimpse of those spartan days. Russian sables sold for twelve dollars a skin, mink for two dollars, and a young

mother feeling "a little pulled down and tired fussing with the children" needed day care as much as mothers do today. Once Emily observed a powwow nearby: "The Sitka Indians, while out hunting seals recently, shot and killed a squaw belonging to the neighboring tribe, mistaking her for a seal (she being in the water at the time)." The Indians settled for one thousand blankets to compensate for the death of their hefty sister and paddled away in their war canoes. Emily FitzGerald eventually found life very comfortable at Sitka and even admitted before she left in May 1876, four years after she first came, "This is a most wonderful country."

Skagway

Pullen House, a lively old hotel in this once flourishing boomtown, bears the name of its hardy pioneer founder, Harriet Smith ("Ma") Pullen. Born in Wisconsin in 1859, married to a fur trader in 1880, she found herself a penniless widow with four children by 1897. The gold rush lured her to Skagway, which she found "confusing, a conglomeration of tents, log huts, board buildings, and thousands upon thousands of people . . . Afraid? No. I wasn't afraid, for I didn't know enough to be afraid."

Her first enterprise was to set up her stove on the beach and bake dried apple pies for the hungry adventurers. At three dollars a day, she earned enough to open her own restaurant, then to purchase a team of horses and drive her own freighter service along the gold trail. In 1898 she rented this house from Skagway homesteader Capt. Ben Moore and opened her hotel. From the time she bought it outright in 1900, until her death in 1947, she presided over a lively clientele that included President Warren G. Harding. Prominent visitors flocked here to listen to Ma Pullen's tales of the old days. Today, they can view her collection of Alaska memorabilia in the museum she established nearby in Skagway. She is buried in a private plot near Pullen House.

Teller

Elizabeth Davis Nowell steamed up the Alaskan coast with her husband and six-year-old daughter, Dorothy (whom she called "the Small Person"), to spend two years here in the early 1900s. Her first glimpse of the diminutive Arctic village, one hundred miles north of Nome, was from the tug that took them ashore. "I can hardly explain how dismal, dreary and forlorn the tiny town first appeared to me," she wrote in 1911. "It was depressing to my spirits although I soon began to know the Arctic better and to admire and then to love the bleak, storm-ridden land." With her family for comfort and the Eskimos as her new friends, she flourished in the frigid outpost, even helping the minister to build a church.

Unalaska (Unalaska Island)

Holy Ascension Russian Orthodox Church. The priceless icons and crosses of this church were saved during World War II by Anfesia Shapsnikoff, who was in charge of transferring them to southeastern Alaska for safekeeping. A native-born Aleut who had been educated in the last Russian school in Alaska, Anfesia took over her husband's leadership of the church when he was lost in a shipwreck in 1933. From that time on, with the blessing of Alaska's Bishop Alexei, she replaced priests as the church reader, and she single-handedly perpetuated the Orthodox religion on her island. Born at Atka in 1901, she also dedicated her life to maintaining the heritage of her fellow Aleuts. She was an expert basket weaver, and she taught that forgotten art all over the territory. The governor presented her with a special citation for her efforts to keep native arts and crafts alive. Even in her seventies, Anfesia continued to teach music and dancing. And a month before her death at seventy-two in 1973, she was at the University of Alaska recording for historians examples of the Atka and Unalaska dialects.

Orthodox Church, Unalaska, 1935

Wrangell

When Wrangell was still a fort in 1890, Septima M. Collis visited on the steamer, *Queen,* and, in a journal later published as *A Woman's Trip to Alaska,* described the Indians she observed: "The Siwash woman is a beast of burden. If captured in a war, she becomes a slave and a drudge to her captors for the rest of her life; if living with her own tribe, she is none the less a serf to the man whom she calls her husband, and who leads a life of indolence and vice. It is therefore a common habit of these poor wretches to murder their female offspring at their birth, and thus save them the inheritance of a life of toil, shame, and misery. But if a girl escapes being the victim of infanticide, a much worse fate awaits her on her arrival at womanhood; she is often then sold for a few blankets to the highest bidder, and here commences a life which would seem to justify, if anything could, the murderous act of the mother."

First United Presbyterian Church, known as the oldest Protestant church in Alaska, was established by Amanda McFarland in 1879. She had been sent from the Presbyterian Church at Portland, Oregon. The church is featured on navigational charts as a landmark for ships, since an illuminated cross atop the building lights the way for vessels. McFarland, who landed at Wrangell in 1877 dressed in black with a long crepe veil, was the first female missionary here and also established a home for native girls. One of her pupils recalled, after McFarland's death in 1912, "the untiring energy she expended in our behalf . . . [she was] our most devoted, faithful and loving friend and mother."

ARIZONA

Camp Verde

The first schoolteacher at this former army camp on the banks of the Verde River was Jennie Jordan Belle, who arrived in 1866 after training in Maine. The townspeople had promised her the generous annual salary of eighty-five dollars, but they tried to talk her down in price because she was living with her sister. Jennie Jordan Belle pointed out that as a graduate of the Gorham Normal School, she expected even more money.

Casa Grande

Pauline Cushman, long retired from her Civil War espionage activities (see *Shelbyville, Tennessee*), ran a hotel here on the south side of the railroad tracks with her husband Jerry Fryer. Wearing a .45 on her hip and answering to "the Major," Pauline served as unofficial peacekeeper in the lawless new town. Once she interrupted her kitchen work to block a gunfight by stationing herself between the two duelists. A witness wrote, "Bullets whistled past within 15 to 20 feet from where she was standing. At no time did she flinch." Then she returned to her stove.

Florence

Pinal County Courthouse, Pinal Street between Eleventh and Thirteenth. In the rear of this 1891 structure, where license plates are now handed out, Pearl Hart, Arizona's first, last, and only female road agent, was jailed for robbing a stage in 1899. Pearl's escapade—as she tremulously pointed a .38 revolver at equally nervous passengers—appealed to the romantic instincts of many Arizonans, who were so proud of their tiny outlaw heroine in her ill-fitting shirt and white sombrero that they acquitted her when she first came to trial. Her companion, Joe Boot, got thirty years. After a second charge hastily prepared by the angry judge, the jury obligingly voted Pearl a five-year sentence. Six months after the holdup on the Florence-to-Globe stage run, Pearl boarded a train for the Territorial Prison at *Yuma.*

Pauline Cushman Home, Granite Street near Sixth (private). A huge tamarisk tree guards the Uptown Apartments, a ramshackle stucco adobe building where Civil War Union spy Pauline Cushman (see *Shelbyville, Tennessee*) once lived. Married to Jerry Fryer in 1879, after abandoning espionage, she worked with him in *Casa Grande.* They moved into this house when Fryer won the race for county sheriff in 1886. Pauline left him within a few years and moved to *San Francisco, California.*

Fort Apache

Most of the original buildings of this abandoned army fort still stand, a silent reminder of the occupancy of Martha Summerhayes and her husband, Lt. John Summerhayes of the Eighth Infantry Regiment, U.S. Army. In 1874, they came to the Southwest for the first time, crossing the sun-scorched Mojave Desert with the long army train of blue wagons. Martha entered Fort Apache in a bumpy mule-drawn ambulance, the first of many entrances to many camps as her husband was transferred to posts throughout the inhospitable country. Through it all, Martha followed loyally, the perfect army wife in the harsh frontier she once called "that dreaded and then unknown land." Most of her experiences are recorded in her delightful narrative, *Vanished Arizona.* One resigned observation: "In the Army Regulations, wives are not rated except as 'camp followers.' " Although she watched her leather-bound books float downriver during one journey, and endured the horrified stares of customs officials when they discovered that the cigarettes in her trunk were for her own use, Martha Summerhayes grew fond of the area, confiding when she returned from a trip east that she "had really grown to love the desert . . . I was back again in the army; I had cast my lot with a soldier, and where he was, was home to me."

In the summer of 1974, more than two hundred avid historians retraced the 1874 Arizona crossing, from Yuma, across the Mogollon Rim to Fort Apache, on a journey they called the Martha Summerhayes Centennial Trek. Modern vehicles and roads reduced the trip to only a week, and perhaps the travelers agreed with the woman who, long before, blazed the trail and then said wistfully, "The army life of those years is past and gone, and Arizona, as we knew it, has vanished from the face of the earth."

Oatman

This tiny hilltop retirement community, surrounded by breathtaking spires of rainbow-colored lava, was named by gold miners in 1910 for Olive Oatman, a young Indian captive. During the 1850s, Olive lived and worked among the Mohave Indians in a village in the valley of the Colorado River to the west, within sight of this town. She had been captured in 1851, along with her sister Mary Ann, at *Oatman Flat* in southern Arizona. The Indians, probably Yavapai, massacred her father and mother, brothers and sisters, and eight wagonloads of settlers. Olive and Mary Ann were driven ahead with the cattle and forced to lead a life of servitude in a Yavapai rancheria. Soon they were sold to a nearby Mohave tribe, where life was less harsh. Although both Olive and her sister were tattooed with tribal chin marks, neither was sexually abused. The frail Mary Ann, however, soon died from the hard work.

In 1856, Olive's brother—mistakenly left for dead at the scene of the massacre—persuaded a carpenter at Fort Yuma to secure Olive's rescue. She arrived at the army post in 1856, almost unrecognizable and unable to utter any English words. When she did recover, she became, like most Indian captives, an object of great fascination. A California clergyman wrote up her experiences in a lively book. Her own account of the experience, with descriptions of Mohave life, was a favorite on the lecture circuit and is today considered anthropologically sound.

Oatman Flat

A marker commemorates the spot atop a mesa in the wild and gloomy Gila River Valley where Olive Oatman and her family were attacked by hostile Indians in 1851. Today this area on the Gila Bend Indian Reservation is known as Oatman Flat.

Phoenix

Arizona Museum, 1002 West Van Buren. Among the relics of the Arizona frontier is the sidesaddle used by Mary Adeline Gray, the first white woman to join her Indian sisters in the Salt River Valley. She arrived in 1868 with her husband, Columbus Harrison Gray, "Lum," on a trip to California. The grass was eighteen inches high from a heavy rainfall, and, when the Grays stopped to rest their horses, they decided to stay.

Polacca

This Hopi village at the base of First Mesa is the modern home of the descendants of Nampeyo, the great Hopi artist-potter. As a child living atop the mesa in the village now known as

Hano, Nampeyo (or *Num-pa-yu,* "the-snake-that-does-not-bite") learned the dying art of pottery from her grandmother. By 1892, considered the finest potter of her tribe, she got permission from the matriarch of descendants of the extinct tribe of Sikyatki village to adapt their ancient designs—the peak of Hopi pottery. Nampeyo revived the forms of shallow bowls decorated in brown or red on a yellow surface. Her free-flowing fluid designs and her sense of space and expert craftsmanship revitalized the entire pottery industry and won for Nampeyo nationwide praise.

Today, five generations of Nampeyo's female descendants work in this village, carrying on "the old lady's" polychrome and black rhythmic designs. The family name Nampeyo still commands the highest prices.

Prescott

Sharlot Hall Museum Complex, Capitol Drive between West Gurley and Beach Place. The Governor's Mansion, or "Old Capitol," built in 1864 when Prescott was named the territory's first capital, was preserved and restored by Sharlot Hall, poet and onetime state historian. The pioneer writer, who had traveled to Prescott by covered wagon at the age of twelve, once described Arizona as "a huge, desert-scarred nowhere, tacked onto Dona Ana County, N.M. . . . The people who crossed Arizona did so because they wanted to get somewhere else, and Arizona happened to be in the way." In 1929, using her own money and on her own incentive, she began the task of maintaining the then-vacant log house here. She collected such memorabilia from other early settlers as a hand-hewn rocker and original gold scales that can be seen here today. When she died in 1943, added to the collection were her personal possessions, including a copper-link tunic and pocketbook given her by the United Verde Copper Company to wear when she presented Arizona's electoral vote to Congress. In 1934, the federal government built the stone building next door. Named for Sharlot Hall, it houses her library, containing historical documents for researchers. There you will also learn that Sharlot Hall was the first salaried female officer in the territory.

Trinity Presbyterian Church, 630 Park Avenue. The first shovelful of earth for this brick building among the pines was dug by tiny Viola Jimulla, the chieftess of the Prescott Yavapai Indian tribe. She inherited her job when her husband, Chief Sam Jimulla, died in 1940. Viola, as she was known, ruled with a firm but kindly manner. Her sunny nature was attributed to her habit of watching dawn break over her garden every morning on the reservation near here. The baskets she wove are collectors' items; a long dress she wore hangs in the Sharlot Hall Museum. An early convert to Christianity, the chieftess was instrumental in bringing Anglos into this new church—which was an outgrowth of the old Yavapai Indian Mission. When she died at eighty-eight in 1966, hundreds of people from Prescott crowded into this church to honor her memory. Viola's portrait still hangs in the vestibule, and her daughter continues the matriarchal rule.

Springerville

Madonna of the Trail Monument, Main Street. The seventh in the series of statues erected along a dozen main streets all over the country (see *Springfield, Ohio*) was dedicated September 29, 1928.

Tombstone

Nellie Cashman's Hotel, Fifth and Toughnut Streets. Nellie Cashman, "the angel of Tombstone," was an Irish-born mining expert who struck it rich in camps up and down the rocky spine of the West. Leaving a host of miners grateful for her generosity and good luck, Nellie came to rough-and-tough Tombstone in 1881, the year of the gunfight at the OK Corral. She bought this old adobe building known as Russ House and turned it into a hotel, where she was said to serve the best meals in town. She also nursed the sick, staked the penniless, and befriended the lonely. Once, when an entrepreneur was charging $2.50 apiece for seats to watch a public hanging, Nellie spearheaded a drive to tear down the wooden viewing stand. She also befriended the prostitutes of Tombstone—the women known locally as the "soiled doves"—who probably provided more money for mines than any prospector cared to recall. Nellie always said that when she went looking for help with her charitable work, the most came from the red-light district. Fearless and gutsy, Nellie Cashman was described by the editor of the *Tombstone Epitaph:* "The best woman I ever knew . . . she went about doing good." Today, her hotel is an antique shop.

Boot Hill Graveyard, Route 80, is the compleat tourist attraction in the compleat tourist town. This is the place where they died with their boots on in the "town too tough to die." In one corner lies Dutch Annie, one of the scores of prostitutes whose full names were less familiar than their bankrolls. She was buried here in 1883 in the second largest funeral in town. Also here, Mrs. Ah Lun, or China Mary, who died in 1906. She peddled all the narcotics, labor, and flesh from the large Chinese section of town. History has it that she was also generous, when not tied up handling details for the Tong. Boot Hill Graveyard also displays a grave marker that could stand for all the women of every small town in the West: Unknown.

Tucson

Arizona Pioneers Historical Society, 949 East Second Street. The handsome modern building housing the state's priceless documentary background is a far cry from the organization Edith Stratton Kitt discovered in 1925. As first female secretary of the historical society, she found a storeroom office with one spittoon, a pile of old newspapers, and enormous debts. With painstaking care, she set about collecting the letters, narratives, diaries, and dust-covered documents of Arizona history. She conducted interviews, wrote books, did mounds of research in libraries and out in the field. Once she climbed up and down a canyon to find the grass-covered grave marker of a pioneer, and then she arranged to have it fenced in. In 1929, her first fifteen-dollar raise was deposited in a new building fund for the society. A quarter of a century later, this building went up. A plaque in the front lobby proclaims, "It is her dream that has come true."

Yuma

Site of The Great Western Commercial Establishment, southwest corner First and Main Streets. A bustling Thrifty Drug Store stands where, in the early 1850s, Sarah Bowman Phillips, also known as Sarah Bourdette, erected the first house in Yuma. The pioneering entrepreneur came to Fort Yuma after a popular career as cook and camp follower with the U.S. Army during the Mexican War (see *Brownsville, Texas*). An amazonian woman who stood more than six feet tall, she was nicknamed the Great Western after a huge 750-horsepower steamer of the day. One old-timer recalled her twin six-shooters and described her as " a hell of a good woman." Another fondly remembered her "kind motherly ways." In old Fort Yuma she ran her enormously popular restaurant (the first in Yuma) in an adobe building. Of this sun-scorched desert town she used to say, "There was just one thin sheet of sandpaper between Yuma and Hell." The Great Western died here in 1866 and was later reburied in *San Francisco, California.*

Yuma Territorial Prison State Park, Prison Hill. The new prisoner admitted here on November 18, 1899 was Pearl Hart, the amateur stagecoach bandit from *Florence* who had captured the fancy of copy-starved journalists. On the prison record, Pearl listed her alias as Mrs. Joe Boot (he was her ill-fated partner in crime), her age as twenty-eight, her stature as five feet three inches. It was noted that she used tobacco, alcohol, and morphine. And where it said "wife," "husband" was written in with a fine hand. Inside "hell hole," Pearl won over the prison administration as she had the general public. She did fancy handwork in her cell for cigarette money, and she enjoyed special privileges. In 1902 she was paroled, apparently after convincing the warden that she was pregnant. She was not. Today, the prison museum contains a poem she wrote, as well as a pistol with her name on the butt plate that may or may not be authentic.

Pearl was one of two dozen women who comprised the entire female population during the thirty-five-year existence of this maximum-security prison. The other women of note included Elena the Butcher, a Mexican woman who stabbed a man in self-defense when he attacked her, then cut out his heart and threw it in his face. At the prison she was "the life of the party," wearing a bright costume and playing the guitar to entertain her cell mates. There was also Lizzie, the dance-hall artist who blasted an insulting soldier with a blunt-nosed pistol she carried in her bosom. And there was Bertha Trimble, the only woman in the penitentiary sent there for rape.

One other woman figures prominently in the prison's lurid history. Madora Ingalls, wife of the prison superintendent, once helped stop a jailbreak by climbing up to the watchtower and operating a slain guard's Gatling gun. She softened the blow of what she called her "duty" by providing food and special care for the prisoners. And every June 5, the day established by the WCTU as a time for decorating the nation's prison cells, Madora Ingalls brought flowers into the adobe cells and brightened the halls of the dining room with fragrant blossoms.

ARKANSAS

Clover Bend

Alice French House (private). The novelist known by her pen name, Octave Thanet, spent many winters here, on the banks of the Black River, composing books and short stories about her Arkansas surroundings. A New England-born antisuffragist who first visited this area in 1883, Alice French turned her plantation into the "Montaine" of *Expiation* and set almost half her works here. Among her books of local color, one, *We All* (1891), was described by an Arkansas historian as "an accurate picture of rural Arkansas, as seen by a competent observer-writer, who was somewhat pre-occupied with dialect."

Conway

The politically prominent Conway family, for whom the city was named, settled here at the end of the eighteenth century. Ann Rector Conway, wife of Thomas, is remembered by local tour guides as "the mother of more distinguished sons than any other matron in American history." She also had three daughters, but no one has bothered to identify them. Of Ann Conway's talented male offspring, there were two Arkansas governors, one doctor, one Missouri surveyor-general, one state supreme court justice, one congressional delegate who died in a duel with a campaign foe, and one son who let down the family tradition by dying at twenty-two.

Central Baptist College was founded in 1892 to provide for "the separate and exclusive education of females in this State." Boarders were permitted no postal correspondence except with those on a list furnished by their parents. No girl left the campus without a chaperone. The valedictorian of the class of 1896 described her graduating classmates: "The great door of girlhood closes with a noiseless yet relentless swing, and outside, wonderingly yet bravely, stands the 'brown-eyed class of '96!'" Today the college trains young preachers and others interested in Christian leadership.

Eureka Springs

Carry A. Nation House, "Hatchet Hall," 31 Steel Street. The fourteen-room boardinghouse, where the ax-wielding Prohibitionist spent the last three years of her life, was an instant choice after her first visit. "I never saw such beautiful scenery; I never drank such clear, pure, sparkling water, and I never saw so many old people look young," marveled the sixty-two-year-old reformer when she came here. Although wearied from her decade of lecturing, preaching, and acting on the evils of both alcohol and tobacco, Carry Nation still found time to crusade a bit. A local resident recently recalled that "Carry knocked many cigars out of my mouth when I was young." And Carry's grandson, a Texas lawyer, remembered that his bread-baking grandma occasionally spoke in Texas, always trying to raise money by selling copies of her autobiography and little souvenir hatchets. The bargain size cost fifteen cents, and those with mother-of-pearl facing were thirty-five cents each.

Today, Hatchet Hall, along with the nearby cave and natural cold spring Carry Nation helped to excavate, is preserved as an art museum. Eureka Springs was also the site of her last public lecture, January 13, 1911. Among her last words to the public she had tried for more than a decade to protect: "I have done what I could." That sentiment was permanently inscribed on her gravestone in *Belton, Missouri,* when she died in June of the same year.

Fayetteville

University of Arkansas. Although legislation made the school coeducational from the beginning, a female student on opening day, January 22, 1872, didn't believe it. She looked around at the seven young men in her class and ran home crying, telling her mother she would not return as the only girl. Her patient mother wisely convinced the young woman to return, assuring her that others would soon join her. She was right. On the second day another female student showed up. By the time the pioneering pupils graduated in 1876, the men outnumbered the women only five to four.

Fort Smith

Judge Parker's Courtroom, old Fort Smith Barracks, Rogers Avenue between Second and Third Streets. This was the famous "hell on the Border" court presided over by the "Hangin' Judge," Isaac Charles Parker, whose iron hand and swift gavel rid the territory of lawbreakers and established law and order throughout the western district from 1875 to 1896. The first woman ever tried for a major crime in this room—restored now with its original furniture—was Belle Starr of *Younger's Bend, Oklahoma.* Newspaper accounts headlining the "Petticoat Terror of the Plains," the alleged "leader of a band of horse thieves" who was "their queen and guiding spirit," assured a packed courtroom that February 1883. Scores of townspeople watched in fascination as the velvet-gowned Lady Desperado was convicted to a prison term in Detroit with her husband Sam Starr. It was Belle Starr's only conviction, and she served nine months. In those days, no one appealed Judge Parker's sentences.

Belle Starr

Jonesboro

Site of Hattie Caraway House, 208 Warner Street. Hattie Caraway (see *Bakersville, Tennessee*) was living here in 1931 when her husband Thaddeus died and she was appointed to fill his seat in the U.S. Senate. When she handily won the special election the following January, Caraway became the first woman elected to the U.S. Senate (thus furthering the record set by Rebecca Felton's appointment from *Cartersville, Georgia*). Previously known as a reticent, home-loving Senate wife, Hattie Caraway always said she didn't exactly oppose suffrage, she just found that her family responsibilities left her "mighty little time for anything else. . . . After suffrage, I just added voting to cooking and sewing." But as a senator, she threw her plump body, invariably clad in black, into the job with characteristic efficiency. Winning reelection twice, she supported bills for farm relief, flood control, and she designed a bill to supply a parachute for every airline passenger. In 1943 she endorsed the Equal Rights Amendment. Hattie Caraway's Senate career, frequently described by reporters as "conspicuously inconspicuous," was ended in 1944 when she was defeated for reelection by the young J. William Fulbright.

Little Rock

State Capitol Building, Capitol Avenue, contains portraits of several Arkansas governors painted by the noted artist Jennie Delony Rice Meyrowitz. Born in Washington, Arkansas, in 1866, she spent time in Paris and New York, where she gained her most enduring fame for a portrait of Hetty Green, "the witch of Wall Street" (see *Bellows Falls, Vermont*). The critic for the *New York Times* pronounced the face of the painting (showing the nation's richest woman holding a skye terrier under her arm) "a handsome firm-faced visage indeed." A leading portraitist and miniaturist, Jennie Rice Meyrowitz maintained studios in Little Rock and in New York.

"Lady Baxter" Cannon, Old State House Grounds, 300 West Markham Street. This naval gun brought from New Orleans, Louisiana, in 1861 was used by the Confederates to ward off approaching federal gunboats. When the city was evacuated in 1863, the cannon was left behind. Only in 1874 was it resurrected by two rival Republican claimants for governor and placed on the State House grounds by the victor. The source of its name is unknown, but a state historian told us, "it was probably some male chauvinist who felt that guns, being lethal weapons, should be described in feminine gender."

Marked Tree

The first field tests against pellagra, the dread disease that was taking seven thousand lives a year in the South, were made near here in 1927 by Red Cross director William DeKleine and his faithful nurse, Annie Gabriel. DeKleine experimented with the technique of feeding powdered yeast to victims of the epidemic. With Nurse Gabriel at his side, he prescribed the medication to an eighteen-year-old black woman who was a week away from death caused by the sickness. Annie Gabriel then routinely followed each patient's progress, going from hovel to hovel in the poor farm country while DeKleine tended other medical business. Two weeks later, both Gabriel and DeKleine found their patient fully recovered, the first person to be cured of the disease here. Today, little or no trace of the killer sickness remains in the area.

Morrilton

Petit Jean State Park, Route 154. The most popular park in Arkansas is named for a love-struck French woman who cleverly disguised her identity for several months to prove her mettle to the man she adored. Her real name is not known. In the early nineteenth century, when her betrothed, a French nobleman named Chavet, sailed for the New World to explore parts of the Louisiana Territory, he made her stay behind in Paris, fearing the unsettled lands would prove too rugged and dangerous for her. But she knew she was made of sterner stuff. Donning male clothing, she secured a job as cabin boy on the ship Chavet was joining. So skillful was her disguise that no one, not even her Chavet, recognized her on the voyage across the ocean. The sailors took to calling her Petit Jean. When they arrived here, the entire crew—Petit Jean and the imperceptive Chavet included—spent a happy and friendly summer hunting and fishing with the Indians. Only when they were ready to depart, and Petit Jean came down with fever and fell into a fatal coma, was her identity discovered. She confessed her deception and asked to be buried on the mountaintop. When she died, Indians bore her body on a deerskin stretcher to the site overlooking the park. Chavet returned to Paris alone, a victim of his own inability to assess a woman's endurance.

Pine Bluff

In the great tradition of American seamstresses, Willie Hocker of Pine Bluff designed the red, white, and blue flag of the state of Arkansas. She distinguished the banner by giving it not only stars, but a diamond, symbolic of the fact that Arkansas is the only diamond-producing state in the Union.

Russellville

Galla Creek Wildlife Area was established in the nineteenth century as a Cherokee village. Persis Lovely, widow of Indian agent Maj. William Lewis Lovely, was the only white person permitted to remain on the Cherokee land after the treaty of 1817 forced all other non-Indians to vacate the territory. Although her home has long disappeared, her extensive land holdings extended throughout this area.

Benicia.

Site of Young Ladies' Seminary, 153 West I Street. In 1852, this school opened its doors to young women from as far as Hawaii and South America. Under the guidance of the school's principal, Mary Atkins, who came to Benicia in 1854, the students were taught perfect manners and deportment along with science and languages. The Atkins regime was austere. Pupils were warned not to "tarry before a mirror for more than three seconds." In 1855 the school was bought by Sarah and Cyrus Mills who later founded Mills College in *Oakland.*

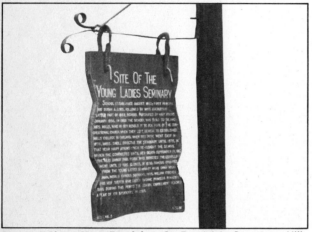

Grave of Sister Mary Dominica, St. Dominic's Cemetery, Hillcrest Avenue. The first American-born woman to become a nun in the order of the Dominican Sisters, Concepcion Arguello, daughter of the Spanish commandant of Monterey, would have rather shared her life with the handsome Russian, Count Nicolai Petrovich de Rezanov, instead of the good sisters. When they met in the early 1800s the count was forty-two, and Concepcion was seventeen, a dark-eyed beauty who was so modest she wanted to cut off her lush eyelashes because they attracted too much attention. Their proposed marriage required approval from the Pope, the king of Spain, and the Russian sovereign, and Nicolai sailed away for the necessary blessings. He fell ill and died in Siberia in 1807. The brokenhearted Concepcion vowed to devote her life to care for the sick and teach the poor. Since there were no convents in California yet, she dressed in her own version of a simple gray habit until the Dominicans came in the 1840s. She was the first to join, soon becoming mother superior. In 1854 Sister Dominica came to Benicia, and she died here in 1857.

Berkeley

University of California. The memory of philanthropist Phoebe Apperson Hearst is perpetuated at various sites on this beautiful campus including the Hearst Mining Building, the Hearst Bridge, and the Hearst Gymnasium where a large portrait of the generous benefactor hangs in the main office. She was one of the first in the state to donate funds for the furthering of female education. Starting in 1891, Phoebe offered five scholarships a year, later upped to eight, to be given to women of "noble character and high aims" who could not afford the tuition fees. She was named the first female regent of the university in 1897. Until her death at seventy-six in 1919, she contributed more than a million dollars for projects as diverse as medical research, archaeological expeditions, and landscaping.

Bodie

One of the most popular and picturesque ghost towns in California still has some of the old shacks from the gold rush days of the 1880s when it was a thriving town of more than ten thousand people. As the gold fever spread, tougher types moved in, and soon Bodie was more notorious for its murders than its mines. A little girl from Nevada who was heading for Bodie was heard finishing up her prayers with "Good-bye God, we're going to Bodie," but the public relations man in town insisted that what she really said was "Good, by God, we're going to Bodie!" Several of the rickety houses in town recall women's names but little of their lives.

Lottie Jahl House. After a brief career in a more lucrative but less challenging profession, Lottie became quite famous in town as a painter. Her home was also the site of the post office where Mary McDonnell sorted deliveries from the Pony Express.

Madame Moustache, a notorious gambler of the day, lived on streets in Bodie named Maiden Lane and Virgin Alley. One day in September 1879 her body was found on the outskirts of town with a vial of poison nearby. Some say she was depressed because a professional gambler had broken the bank in her faro game. No doubt there were other reasons for her tragic suicide, but her last days are still as mysterious as the rest of her shadowy life. (See *Nevada City;* see *Pioche, Nevada.*)

Calico

Legend has it that this ghost town got its name in the 1880s when someone decided that the surrounding mountains were "as purty as a gal's calico pettyskirt. Let's call 'er Calico."

When not working in one of the local hotels, Mrs. Townsend Ricket used to poke around in the hills; one day she struck it silver rich with her mines—Golconda and Alhambra. When a luckless miner tried to jump her claim, Ricket grabbed her gun and gave the scoundrel a souvenir of lead rather than of silver. Another independent Calico resident was Fannie Mulcahy, who broke the sex and speed barrier of the Pony Express as one of its first female letter carriers. Every day in the early morning she would gallop off to Borate, sitting sidesaddle, the mailbags tied securely in back, her long riding cloak flapping in the wind.

Claremont

Scripps College. At the entrance to the campus, a plaque quotes newspaperwoman and philanthropist Ellen Browning Scripps, who founded the college in 1926 when she was ninety-one years old: "The paramount obligation of a college is to develop in its students the ability to think clearly and independently and the ability to live confidently, courageously and hopefully"—exactly the way this extraordinary woman lived her own life (see *La Jolla*). The college, its enrollment consisting of about 560 women, houses the Macpherson Collection, which was originated in 1936 to assemble all available books by and about women—one of the first such collections developed in any U.S. college.

Coloma

Sutter's Mill, Marshall Gold Discovery State Park, Route 49. If it had not been for the unheralded, keen eye of Elizabeth Jane Wimmer, nothing might have panned out for James Marshall and John Sutter. Wimmer, born near the gold mines of

Georgia, knew gold when she saw it, unlike most of the novice miners in California. For weeks, Wimmer insisted that those little flecks in the drinking water at her boarding house were gold, but the men laughed at "Mrs. Wimmer's gold." On the morning of January 24, 1848, Wimmer was making soap, and Marshall showed her the interesting rock he had found. She suggested they put it into the suds, explaining, "If it comes out bright, it is gold." Gold it was. Assured by Wimmer's expert verification, Marshall ran to tell Sutter of his discovery, thus launching the mad California gold rush. Sutter's find, Wimmer's loss—her part in it all disappearing like the soap bubbles.

Death Valley

In this desolate, hauntingly beautiful desert, Juliet Brier, the heroine of the Jayhawker expedition of 1849, crawled on her hands and knees in the starlight looking for oxen tracks to find the way to California and gold. The tiny, delicate Juliet protested a suggestion that she stay at a camp until her husband charted a route and could send for her. "No . . . I have never been a hindrance. I have never kept the camp waiting, neither have my children, and every step I take will be towards California." Her determination was fortunate for the more than thirty-five men in the party, for, without her, no one would have made it across Death Valley. Subsisting only on coffee and beef jerky and, sometimes, no water at all, Juliet managed to find the strength to lift her "athletic" husband from the ground every morning, steady him, and push him on.

Downieville

Site of Hanging of Josefa, Downie River. A beautiful, quiet Mexican woman killed a man in defense of her honor and was brutally lynched here in 1851. When a drunken miner named Fred Canon broke down the door of her tiny cottage and called her a whore, Josefa dared him to say it again, then plunged a knife into his heart. An angry crowd grabbed her, determined to avenge the crime on the spot, but a mock trial was ordered as witness after witness testified against her. More than two thousand men gathered down by the bridge—"the hungriest, craziest, wildest mob standing around that I ever saw anywhere," wrote one reporter. While the scaffold was being constructed, Josefa calmly prayed, then lifted her long black hair and adjusted the rope around her neck. Within minutes it was over, and the sated crowd retreated into the saloons.

Glendale

Site of Root Poultry Ranch, Verdugo Road (private). In 1907 Kara Smart Root came to California for her health and stayed to found one of the most successful poultry businesses in the state. Now, elegant houses stand where her ranch was once located. She won top prizes for her single-comb black Minorcas, homer pigeons, and mammoth white Holland turkeys, which she raised to succulent plumpness, feeding them on barley and clover grown in her garden, in breeding houses of her own invention. One of the first female members of the California State Poultry Association, Root delivered a frequent and popular lecture on the topic, "Poultry as a vocation for women."

Grass Valley

Lola Montez House, Walsh and Mill Streets. The city has assured us that plans are underway to restore the home of the world-famous nineteenth-century dancer and courtesan whose celebrated spider dance seduced, among others, a Russian emperor, a prince of Poland, a king of Bavaria ("I don't know how—I am bewitched," Ludwig cried.), a lord of Ireland, as well as Alexandre Dumas and Franz Liszt. When we visited, the clapboard siding had deteriorated, and huge bushes of weeds choked the dark, dreary house that was listing sadly. Inside, chunks of wood and wallpaper littered the sagging floors. Once

there were tiny-paned french windows with curtains of Belgian lace, sliding doors, mirrors from ceiling to Persian-carpeted floor, and chairs of red and gold brocade next to ebony tables. In 1853, at thirty-five, Lola, weary of center stage, decided to return to this quiet mining town, only to star again as hostess to exquisite parties. Here Lola assembled a household of pets, including dogs, cats, parrots, monkeys, and a large bear named Major that she kept tied with a silver chain to a post on the front lawn. One day Major bit someone, and the next day there was an ad for "an affably inclined bear for sale." But the lure of the stage was too strong, and after teaching some of her favorite dance steps to her little neighbor Lotta Crabtree (see below), Lola left in 1855 for a tour of Australia. Her dancing days behind her, Lola took to the lecture circuit and preached a different kind of feminism than suffrage conventioneers: "One woman going forth in independence and power of self-reliant strength to assert her own individuality . . . will do more than a million convention women to make herself known and felt throughout the world." In her last years she lived in a home for wayward women, repenting her licentious past. She died alone and forgotten on January 17, 1861 in New York.

Lotta Crabtree House, 238 Mill Street (private). Lola Montez's protégée Lotta lived in this unassuming white house where her mother Mary Ann took care of boarders. The tiny, seven-year-

old redhead, an adept pupil, quickly mastered Lola's favorite dances, such as the Highland fling and the sailor's hornpipe. She made her debut weeks later at a mining camp in *Rough and Ready*.

Healdsburg

Hazel Hotchkiss Wightman Memorial, Healdsburg Plaza. The Queen Mother of Tennis is honored in her hometown by this plaque for a feat still unmatched by any female tennis player. For three straight years—1909, 1910, and 1911—Wightman held the triple crown of women's tennis by winning the singles, doubles, and mixed doubles championships. In her formidable career, Wightman won forty-five U.S. titles and a batch of Olympic medals. She was the captain of thirteen Wightman Cup teams for which she provided the silver vase as the prize for the first British-American competition in 1924, the equivalent of the Davis Cup for women's tennis. Wightman, whose protégées have included Margaret Court, Billie Jean King, and Rosie Casals, thoroughly shocked spectators by being the first to wear sleeveless dresses and jaunty head scarfs on the courts instead of the more traditional ankle-length skirts and broad-brimmed hats. By the end of her life, she modestly referred to herself as just "a little old lady in tennis shoes," and she was still giving free lessons to children at her home in Boston months before her death in 1974 at age eighty-eight.

Hemet

Ramona Bowl. Since 1923, Helen Hunt Jackson's novel *Ramona* has been recreated in an annual pageant in this outdoor amphitheater, situated in a canyon on the slopes of Mount San Jacinto, where many events of the novel actually took place. After publication of her book *A Century of Dishonor,* Jackson (see *Colorado Springs, Colorado*) was asked by the U.S. government to prepare a report on the condition of the Mission Indians of southern California (see *San Juan Bautista*). When there was no response to her criticisms and recommendations, she wrote to a friend in 1883, "I am going to write a novel in which will be set forth some Indian experiences in a way to move people's hearts. . . . If I can do one-hundredth part for the Indians what Mrs. Stowe did for the Negroes, I will be thankful." Less than six months later, *Ramona* was completed. It was based on a factual incident in which a white man killed a Cahuilla Indian for horse stealing. Although the novel was reviewed more as a tender love story than as the exposé of Indian persecution that Jackson intended, and although its effects on reform of government policy are uncertain, *Ramona*'s more than three hundred printings to date have at least served to popularize the cause.

Hollywood

Hollywood Boulevard. If it had not been for Mary Penman Moll, this most famous of boulevards would still be named Prospect Avenue or De Longpre Avenue. Hollywood's first schoolteacher, who taught sixty pupils in nine grades in one tiny room in 1887, gathered hundreds of signatures of property owners along the boulevard to have the name officially changed. Her motivation is not known, but in gratitude, as one of the area's earliest settlers, she donated much of her valuable property to the city of Los Angeles to be used for parks.

Jackson

Site of Bordello Memorial, Broadway. The dark square of the sidewalk in front of the small health food store across the street from the police station once contained a heart-shaped bronze plaque which read, "Botilleas Bordellos. World's oldest profession flourished 50 yds. east of this plaque for many years until this most perfect example of free enterprise was padlocked by unsympathetic politicians." The inscription was signed with the acronym formed by the name of the plaque's donators—Envi-

ronmental Resources Enabling Committee to Investigate Our Necessary Services. This dubious tribute was dedicated on Valentine's Day in 1968 and given lavish play by the national media. Negative letters and phone calls, primarily protesting the suggestive initials, came streaming in from all over the country, and, six days later, the plaque was unceremoniously removed.

La Jolla

La Jolla Museum of Art, 700 Prospect Street. This museum has been constructed around the original house, built in 1915, of Ellen Browning Scripps. Born poor in London in 1836, Scripps squirreled away her money to send herself to college, the first woman to graduate from Knox College in Illinois in 1859. Devoted to her younger brothers, especially E. W. Scripps, who called her the main force in his life and career, she helped them in their pioneering newspaper dynasty, wrote a popular column called "Miss Ellen's Miscellany," and reinvested the profits in more newspapers until she was a multimillionaire. Modest and fastidious—she wore white gloves while doing the housework, E. W. recalled—Scripps lived here in La Jolla with her sister, constantly finding new interests that her bulging fortune could help along. When she was ninety-one, she founded Scripps College in *Claremont,* and, at her death five years later, there were still millions left over for her varied projects. A memorial in her honor exists at almost every corner in La Jolla: the Scripps Institute of Oceanography, the Scripps Memorial Hospital, Bishop's School, La Jolla Public Playground, the Woman's Clubhouse, Scripps Field, La Jolla Public Library. On the 129th anniversary of her birth, one California legislator, his sincerity overwhelming his grammar, said, "I know of no other woman in history who has contributed so much of themselves or of their substance to the betterment of mankind."

Lassen Volcanic National Park

Lake Helen, Lassen Park Road, was named for Helen Brodt, the first woman to conquer Lassen Peak (10,457 feet), one of the largest plug dome volcanoes in the world. On August 28, 1864, Helen, her husband Aurelius, and others, including Pierson Reading, reached the peak where they found a crater "sending up vast clouds of sulphurous steam, and making a deafening roar, similar to an immense steam-engine blowing off steam." The party also discovered this lovely jewel of a lake which Reading promptly named Lake Helen.

Lodi

De Force Avenue is named in honor of Laura de Force Gordon, the peripatetic suffragist whose formidable pioneering feminist achievements are almost as long as this two-block street. She was the first to organize a suffrage group in Nevada; the first and only female newspaper owner and editor in Stockton (1874); one of the first two women with Clara Foltz (see *Los Angeles*) to be admitted to the California bar (1879) and to practice before its supreme court (1885); and the first woman to give a public address for equal rights in San Francisco. So eloquent and persuasive were her speeches that Gordon was called the Daniel Webster of Suffrage. Toward the end of her splendid and busy life, Gordon retired to her farm near Lodi where she died in 1907 at the age of sixty-eight.

Los Angeles

Clara Shortridge Foltz House, 153 South Normandie Avenue (private). A widow with five children to support, Clara Foltz was determined to study law even though only "white males" could be lawyers in California. Enlisting the help of Laura de Force

n Browning Scripps at dedication of La Jolla Playground, one of her many donations

Gordon (see *Lodi*), Foltz succeeded in getting the law changed, and she began practicing as the state's first female lawyer in 1878. Shortly after, the same dynamic duo sued the Hastings College of Law in San Francisco for discriminating against women. They won their case and together they were admitted to the bar of the state supreme court in 1879. Whether divorce or murder, Foltz argued all her cases so brilliantly that she was called the Portia of the Pacific. Once when an opposing attorney suggested in court that she ought to be home raising her children, Foltz parried, "A woman had better be in almost any business than raising such men as you." In 1930, at eighty-one, Foltz announced her candidacy for California governor as a Republican and a feminist. Although she was defeated, the more than eight thousand votes she captured convinced her to try again four years later. Tragically, she died before the voters had a chance to elect her.

Site of Agnes Woodward School of Artistic Whistling, Beaux Arts Building, 1709 West Eighth Street. Woodward perfected a natural talent for chirping and tweeting by listening to the birds singing to her from the California treetops. The finest tones in her musical nest were the warbles and trills of the meadowlark and the mocking bird, which she whistled for her many students here in the early 1900s. Hers was the only all-female whistling chorus in the nation, whose cudalees and thrupees, witchas and quittas were praised for their "brilliancy, sweetness, and artistic finish," and were much in demand at conventions and shows. For her thrilling trills, Woodward was honored with a gold medal from the city in 1912.

Hollyhock House, 4808 Hollywood Boulevard. Named for the wild flowers that once covered a nearby hill, this extraordinary house, styled like an Indian pueblo, was designed by Frank Lloyd Wright in 1920 for Alice Barnsdall, theater manager and heir to an oil fortune; she donated it to the city for use as a cultural center. Barnsdall, who died in 1946, spent the last years of her life traveling around the world, and Wright once said that he could never understand why she wanted to build such a beautiful home for herself—"She was a restless spirit."

Angelus Temple, 1100 Glendale Boulevard. "Beautiful Angelus Temple! How I love it," enthused Aimee Semple McPherson, the flamboyant revivalist preacher, after this huge two-million-dollar dome home of her Church of the Foursquare Gospel was built in 1923. It was a far cry from the striped tents where Aimee, after a profound religious conversion at age seventeen, started out preaching her cheery religion. Thousands thronged to the melodramatic sermons (punctuated by booming brass bands) of this charming, gracious woman. With her auburn, sometimes blonde hair, white dress, white shoes, blue cape, and jeweled cross, she was dubbed the Mary Pickford of Revivalism. One day in May 1926, Aimee, wearing a green bathing suit, disappeared into the ocean. Sorrowing followers pelted the Pacific with her favorite white roses and prayed for her deliverance. Her denouncers declared that she had been seen in Carmel on a secret sejour with a married lover. A weary and dusty Aimee appeared a month later in Arizona saying that she had been kidnapped and taken to Mexico. For six months, her mysterious absence was debated, and Aimee toured California, giving such rousing lectures as, "I am Doing a Great Work and Cannot Come Down to Carmel," attracting even more followers. Aimee was indicted on a conspiracy to obstruct justice, but charges were later dropped. She was found in an Oakland hotel room in 1944, dead from an overdose of sleeping pills that was kindly ruled accidental.

Dorsey High School, Farmdale Boulevard. When this school was named in 1937, Susan Dorsey, one of the state's outstanding educators, was the first living person to have a Los Angeles school named in her honor. As the first female superintendent of schools here (1920), Dorsey more than doubled enrollment in her nine-year tenure. She introduced vocational courses and special classes for the retarded and gifted, and she lobbied for higher salaries and sabbaticals for teachers. In 1934, twelve years before her death, Dorsey was named an honorary life president of the National Educational Association, an honor up to then only held by John Dewey.

El Pueblo de Los Angeles Historic Park. The birthplace of modern Los Angeles in 1871, now a popular tourist site, was recreated as a living monument to Mexican and Spanish culture. During a visit in 1926 to the crumbling Old Plaza, Christine Sterling vowed to restore the center to its early splendor, and she dedicated the next thirty-seven years of her life to make El Pueblo the heart of Los Angeles. She once said, "It is not enough that we just remember the pioneer Mothers and Fathers. We must carry forward some part of their work, some definite tangible things to pass on to future generations, and in giving this respect to those who came before us, we earn the remembrance of those who will follow us." The small, humble Avila Adobe was the first home built in Los Angeles, and it was Sterling's home when she died in 1963 at eighty-five.

Malibu

Rindge Mansion, 3401 South Serra Road. This huge white stucco mansion on a level mountaintop in the Malibu Canyon was begun in 1921 by May Rindge, a pioneer settler of the area. Her skillful management of the ranch after her husband died in 1905 made it the most valuable single real estate holding in the United States. When the state decided to build highways and railroads through her property up the coast, Rindge went to court, hired armed guards, and dynamited the roads to intercept determined travelers trying to get to Santa Monica. Rindge died before the fifty-room, half-million-dollar mansion was completed. The Franciscan Friars bought the house in 1942 and use it today for meditative weekend retreats, lighting up dark moments with candles instead of dynamite sticks.

Marysville

This town was named in 1850 in honor of Mary Murphy Covilland, one of the few survivors of the tragic Donner party (see *Truckee*), who later married one of the owners of the town site. She was only twelve during that ill-fated expedition across the Sierra Nevadas, and little is known of her experiences. One diarist recalled that she cut the shoes off the frozen and swollen feet of her poor ten-year-old brother, who finally died in the snow.

Mary Aaron Museum, 704 D Street. This house belonged to one of the early residents of Marysville. Among the period furnishings and memorabilia are a rosary and a tiny brocade coin purse that once belonged to Mary Covilland, as well as an oval framed picture of her sad, calm face.

Napa

Grave of Mary Ellen Pleasant, Tulocay Cemetery, Coombsville

Road. To San Franciscans of the late nineteenth century, she was Mammy Pleasant, a mysterious, beautiful black woman. Some called her a murderer; others, a dedicated worker for her race. But the way Pleasant wanted to be remembered is in the words chiseled on her gravestone: "She was a friend of John Brown," to which friends have added, "Mother of Civil Rights In California." (See *San Francisco*.)

Nevada City

Vingt-et-Un, the blackjack parlor, Eleanore Dumont's first venture into the gambling business, has been run over by the freeway on lower Main Street. In the 1850s, it was an elegant salon with wide wooden rooms decorated with imported paintings of exotic nudes. There were free champagne and string quartets instead of the beer and banjos of less refined bars. However, it seems that Dumont's efforts at French sophistication in the bawdy mining camp did not reach the manners of her patrons. It was here, according to some accounts, that she was nicknamed Madame Moustache for the downy fuzz above her scarlet lips. "She's pretty for sure," a tactless drunk once shouted out, "but look at her moustache." When the hills ran out of gold, and a fire in 1856 destroyed her salon, Madame Moustache moved away to other mining camps (see *Pioche, Nevada*).

Oakland

Mills College, founded in 1871, by Susan and Cyrus Mills, is the oldest woman's college on the Pacific Coast. Its origins go back to the Young Ladies' Seminary in *Benicia* that the Millses purchased in 1865. Although Cyrus was the titular president those early years, Susan made all the faculty appointments, insuring that there were always teachers from her alma mater in the East, Mount Holyoke. She served as president here from 1890 to 1909, endearing herself to students by her discreet offerings of Napa Valley port to nervous or chilly visitors and by her unabashed impatience with tedious guest speakers, once stage-whispering at the lectern, "Your train leaves sooner than you realize. And you'd better make your closing prayer short." She died in 1912, generous to the end: in her will Susan gave away twice as much as she had. She and Cyrus are buried on campus, just behind the faculty houses.

Oroville

Ehmann Olive Products Company, 1795 Mitchell, was started at the turn of the century by the enterprising Freda Ehmann.

She had twenty acres of olive trees and a crude little pickling plant on her back porch. When a local relish expert tasted her first tangy samples, he declared them the best ripe olives he'd ever eaten. A sales trip to New York and Philadelphia, Pennsylvania, brought contracts for nearly fifteen thousand gallons of olives. Freda purchased more land, planted more trees, and built a modern plant. She would spend hours going from vat to vat in the great pickling room, dipping and testing, splashing about in her huge overshoes in temperatures too chilly for even the hardiest male. "I'd rather be here than any place in the world," she once said. "It's something I have created, and no one else can care for these olives just as I do. They are like a child to me." Freda, forever known as the Mother of the Ripe Olive Industry of California, died in 1932, but the Ehmann olive endures as her tasty memorial on supermarket shelves throughout the country.

Pleasanton

Castlewood Country Club and several of the homes on its grounds were all once a part of Phoebe Hearst's magnificent estate, "La Hacienda del Pozo de Verona." (See *Berkeley*.)

Point Loma

Point Loma College. In 1900 this was "White City"—a cluster of magnificent stark-white buildings with cupolas and stained-glass windows—the headquarters of Katherine Tingley's Theo-

sophic community. "It's easy to be good in Southern California," the ebullient Tingley once said, and she gathered devotees around her to try to "understand God through Mystical insight and philosophical speculation." Back down to earth, Tingley encouraged residents of this utopian retreat to cultivate the gardens where exotic orchids bloomed, as well as such new fruits as the avocado and the peach. Between yoga sessions, writers, artists, and poets assembled for cultural seminars and for classical plays held in a small Greek amphitheater—one of the first such theaters constructed in the U.S. Tingley died in 1929 and, without her energetic support, the center gradually disintegrated. Today, Tingley's headquarters at Cabrillo Hall contain Point Loma College's music department. Another residence now contains the administration offices, and the Greek theater is still being used for outdoor plays.

Riverside

The Washington Parent Navel Orange Tree, Magnolia and Arlington Avenues. A sturdy chain fence protects the heroic little tree—from whence billions of juicy seedless oranges have blossomed. A plaque on a boulder, overgrown with ivy, honors Eliza Tibbets and her "good work in planting the first Washington navel orange trees," in 1873. The donors of the memorial have chosen to ignore Eliza's husband, Luther, and the fierce controversy that has raged for more than a century about his role in this historic fruit find. No one knows for sure to whom that precious packet of two newly budded Bahia navel trees was addressed, Mr. or Mrs. Luther Tibbets, a momentous moot

detail that could have easily been avoided if only Eliza had insisted on using her first name for the mail. During the National Orange Show pageants in the 1920s, two decades after Eliza's death, she was the Tibbets the sponsors portrayed as planting the little trees with her own hands and dousing them with nourishing dishwater until they bore their succulent fruit. One contemporary interview does exist, however, where Luther and Eliza in generous marital harmony give each other joint credit for "the world's most valuable fruit introduction."

Mission Inn. Vacationing here in 1909, Carrie Bond (see *Janesville, Wisconsin*) paused to watch the sunset while she was dressing for dinner. "It has truly been a perfect day," the famed composer sighed. As she combed her hair and buttoned her dress, she thought of two stanzas of a poem which she subsequently forgot. About two months later, when she was crossing the Mojave Desert in the moonlight, that same sweet, sentimental feeling stirred her. Remembering her little poem, Carrie hummed the words to a simple tune. "A Perfect Day" became one of the most famous songs in musical history, selling more than five million copies in ten years.

> For mem'ry has painted this perfect day
> With colors that never fade
> And we find at the end of a perfect day,
> The Soul of a friend we've made.

The room on the fourth floor in Writer's Row where Carrie was so fortuitously inspired has been named in her honor. Almost every evening at six o'clock, the carillon bells at this luxurious hotel intone her famous melody.

Rough and Ready

W. H. Fippen's Blacksmith Shop, on the only street in town, is a weathered, ramshackle barn where in 1853, seven-year-old

Lotta Crabtree, encouraged by her celebrated mentor, Lola Montez (see *Grass Valley*), launched her fabulous dancing career. As miners clapped and cheered, Lola hoisted the tiny redheaded imp onto Fippen's anvil where Lotta tap-danced to the beat of a pounding hammer. Lotta began a tour of mining camps in the area, and she refined her act with improvised, slightly risqué songs, friendly banter with the adoring audience, and plenty of high kicks showing just a hint of a bare knee. Garbed in white like an angel, Lotta closed her rousing act with bathetic serenades as the miners made a pedestal of shiny gold nuggets at her silver-shoed feet (see also *San Francisco*). During our visit, the blacksmith's shop was locked and under repair, the precious anvil hidden away for safekeeping. Soon, however, Fippen's will be open to the public with the legendary anvil in place—the tiniest dance floor in the world.

Sacramento

Silvier Pearle Tinsler, the city's first female patent attorney, a former beauty queen, returned from the East for a visit to her hometown in 1925 and patiently explained to a reporter, "Beauty and business are not widely separated and the possession of a few beauty prizes does not bar a woman from succeeding in business. The businessman never sees beauty in the women with whom he has commercial relations anyway."

San Diego

Women of the Mormon Battalion Memorial, Presidio Hill Park. A large granite marker with a drawing of wagons crossing the plains honors the nearly eighty women who, in 1846 and 1847, accompanied a party of soldiers from Council Bluffs, Iowa, to Santa Fe, New Mexico, during the war against Mexico. The leader of the expedition allowed the five companies to bring four laundresses, but many more women insisted on going. "If [my husband] must go, I want to go, too," said Melissa Corey. "Why must women always stay behind and worry about their husbands when they could just as well march beside them." Indeed, laundresses and wives survived the grueling trip better than the men, many of whom became so ill and feeble that they had to form a special sick detachment. The table commemorates the party's arrival in San Diego on January 29, 1847.

Kate O. Sessions Memorial, Balboa Park. On an incense cedar tree, one of Kate Sessions' favorites, a plaque dedicated in 1941 honors the Mother of Balboa Park. During the twelve years Kate worked here, from 1892 on, the pioneering horticulturist introduced hundreds of such exotic trees and plants as the Chinese twisted juniper, the bunya bunya, the Torrey pine, and the pepper tree. She imported trees from as far away as Africa and Asia. A familiar figure in town with her flat-heeled, high-topped shoes, her felt hat, and her bulky brown-tweed suit, clippers and wires poking out from the pockets, Kate treated all of San Diego as her garden. If she spotted scraggly ailing bushes in someone's yard, she stopped by to prescribe unsolicited but always welcome treatment. By the time of her death in 1949, her body was as twisted as a juniper tree from decades of bending down to care for all her plants and flowers.

Site of Kate Sessions Nursery, Pico and Garnet Streets. She once said she "would rather be remembered by one beautiful tree" that she planted "than by all the stone monuments . . . in California." But her devoted friends could not resist erecting this rock with a plaque commemorating her first nursery and the Meyer Medal she was awarded in 1939 by the Council of the American Genetic Association. She was the first woman to be so honored.

Kate Sessions

San Francisco

Site of Birthplace of Isadora Duncan, 501 Taylor Street. A plaque on this building marks the place where that free spirit of love and dance was born on May 27, 1878. She described herself years later as "a child in California, beside the sea, endeavoring to follow in rhythmic movements the rhythm of the waves." By the time she was six years old, Isadora was teaching the neighborhood children her uninhibited, graceful, and sensual style of dance. Throughout her tortured, romantic life, Isadora founded and abandoned schools for her "Isadorables" all over the world. Discarding conventional ballet skirts and ballet thoughts, she danced in a Grecian tunic with ropes of roses around her waist and in her hair. She danced in Greek temples, on roadsides in Turkey, alone in her room, and before enthralled audiences everywhere. Her death at age forty-nine was as flamboyant as her style of dance. Climbing into a sports car for a drive to the countryside of Nice, she flung a six-foot-long red scarf (decorated with yellow birds and blue Chinese asters) around her neck and shouted, *"Adieu, mes amis. Je vais à la gloire."* The fringe of the scarf caught in the wheel and, when the car pulled away, the twisted scarf broke her neck.

The dedication ceremony of this plaque on May 31, 1973 was a "real 'Isadora Happening,'" according to Irma Duncan, who, like many of Isadora's pupils, legally changed her name to that of her beloved teacher. "Young girls in tunics and bare feet [danced] on the sidewalks to music by Schubert, in the roaring traffic. . . . Speeches, cheers, tears. Isadora would have loved it!"

Coolbrith Park, Taylor and Vallejo Streets, was named for California's first poet laureate and favorite librarian. Ina Coolbrith, literary mentor at the Oakland Public Library from 1874–93, gently guided such readers as Isadora Duncan and Jack London to the próper shelves. London said of her, "I loved Ina Coolbrith above all womankind and what I am and what I have done that is good I owe to her." Though her output of poems was small and selective, the fine quality of her lyrics was much admired. Her salon in Russian Hill's Bohemia was a favorite gathering place for the literary elite, including Mark Twain, Joaquin Miller, and Bret Harte. Her magnificent home was destroyed by the 1906 earthquake. But the mountain in the Sierra Nevadas bearing her name—she was the first white child to cross the Beckwourth Pass in 1851—has resisted the ravages of natural disasters, and, like this park, endures in her memory.

Site of Mammy Pleasant Home, 920 Washington Street. A small hospital stands near the same six eucalyptus trees that once shaded Mammy's mansion and her mysterious life. Born Mary Ellen Pleasant, a slave in the South, she arrived in San Francisco in the 1880s and opened a boardinghouse that soon was being visited by some of the city's most powerful businessmen. She practiced voodoo, and no one was sure where she got the money that she was always ready to lend at high interest rates. For all her sinister power, she was a true champion of her race. She is said to have partly financed John Brown's raid in 1858, and, in San Francisco, she rescued slaves from their Southern owners on the docks, badgered merchants to hire blacks for jobs more meaningful than wood and water carrying, and boldly integrated the city's streetcars. Mysterious to the end, she died in 1904 when she was about ninety years old, muttering about a box of jewels hidden somewhere on Octavia Street. (See *Napa*.)

Kate Kennedy School, 1670 Noe Street, is named for the teacher who was one of the first to fight, and win, for equal pay for equal work. When she was made principal of a secondary school, without getting a raise along with the promotion as any man would have, Kate Kennedy fought all the way to the state legislature which in 1874 finally passed a bill permitting women their fair share. In 1887, because of her fearless campaigning and agitation, Kennedy was transferred to a smaller school at less pay. Her devoted students rioted, and Kennedy sued for reinstatement and back pay. After three years of bitter legal struggle, which may have caused her death in 1890, Kennedy won $5,700.75, the largest pay warrant ever issued by the city. That court opinion laid the basis for future teacher tenure decisions.

San Francisco Children's Hospital, 3700 California Street. Originally called the Pacific Dispensary for Women and Children, this hospital was founded in 1875 by Dr. Charlotte Blake Brown and Dr. Martha Bucknell and an all-female board, to provide women with medical aid by competent female physicians and to further the advancement of females in medicine. In 1880, the first nurses training program west of the Rockies was begun here. Mrs. Dr. Brown, as she preferred being addressed in the wards, an innovative medical pioneer, was the first female to perform an ovariotomy and was an early advocate of incubators for premature babies. She died two years before the hospital was severely damaged in the 1906 earthquake. The present buildings have been greatly enlarged and modernized, and the hospital still has an all-female board of directors.

Little Jim's Ward was built with the thousands of dollars that poured in after *San Francisco Examiner* reporter Winifred Black wrote the pathetic story of Little Jim, a poor crippled boy who couldn't find a cot at the hospital. But then, all of Black's stories provoked action. Writing under the pen name Annie Laurie— her mother's favorite song—the intrepid reporter was the first to reach Galveston, Texas, after the 1900 tidal wave disaster; the first woman to cover a prizefight; and the only one who dared hide under a table in a train compartment to land an interview with President Benjamin Harrison. Tough, but proper, Black didn't mind jealous male colleagues calling her anything except "sob sister," the name she and three other female reporters, including Dorothy Dix (see *New Orleans, Louisiana*), were unkindly tagged with for their sympathetic and moving accounts of the woman in the sensational Thaw trial of 1907.

Forever in pursuit of the scoop, at age seventy-two, a year before her death in 1936, Black wrote about her experiences on an airplane flight over Mount Shasta. "The ideal newspaper woman has the keen zest for life of a child, the cool courage of a man, and the subtlety of a woman," she once figured. "A woman has distinct advantage over a man in reporting, if she has sense enough to balance her qualities."

Lotta's Fountain, junction Market, Geary, and Kearny Streets. Dedicated in 1875 in honor of the lovable young dancer (see

Rough and Ready) whose appearance in San Francisco necessitated calling in the army to quell the enthusiastic fans, this fountain, with its cast-iron columns and jutting drinking spigots, has been called the ugliest monument in the city. It is also the most sentimentally beloved one, proving that the magic of Lotta Crabtree's name transcends art.

SAN FRANCISCO NATIONAL CEMETERY, PRESIDIO

Grave of Pauline Cushman. In 1893, the "Federal Spy and Scout of the Cumberland" (see *Shelbyville, Tennessee*) died in a shabby rooming house from an overdose of morphine she'd been taking for rheumatism and arthritis pain, having spent the last years of her life trying to resume the acting career she had practiced most successfully behind the front lines. More than a hundred men in the faded blue uniforms of the GAR marched at her funeral as a bugler played taps, guns fired in tribute, and a minister eulogized her as the Joan of Arc of the Union army. Originally buried at a private cemetery, her body was moved to its present location in 1910.

Grave of Sarah A. Bowman. "The Great Western," courageous cook (see *Brownsville, Texas*) and land developer, died in *Yuma, Arizona* in 1866, but her body was moved here in 1890 with the other heroes of the Mexican War.

Coit Memorial Tower, Telegraph Hill. If this tower resembles the nozzle of a fire hose it is because its donor, Lillie Hitchcock Coit, as the mascot of Knickerbocker Company No. 5 while in her teens, liked to chase fire engines. She had other charming foibles too, such as shaving her hair so her many wigs would fit more snugly, wearing men's suits for a change of costume, and shooting pistols. All of which endeared her to B. Howard Coit who married her (for sentimental reasons, she insisted on adding a No. 5 to her married name) and left her a fortune. After her death in 1924 at age eighty-three, she donated her money to the city. What was left over after financing this tower went for the Volunteer Firemen's Monument in Washington Square.

Donaldina Cameron House, 920 Sacramento. More than two thousand young and innocent Chinese women who were being sold into prostitution and slavery were rescued during forty years of tireless work by Donaldina Cameron, "Lo Mo"—Little Mother—to those grateful children. As manager of the Chinese Presbyterian Mission Home from 1895 on, Cameron would assist the police in their raids on brothels and go to court to prevent the vile traders from reclaiming the women they dishonestly called "their wives." Cameron cared for the women who had no homes, always respecting their culture and educating them in its traditions. Many give credit to Cameron's bold and timely efforts for the passage of the Red Light Abatement Act of 1914 which helped eradicate large-scale prostitution in Chinatown. In 1949, the Presbyterian Church converted her house into a community center.

Rebecca H. Lambert Memorial, Lincoln Park Municipal Golf Park. Duffers near the fifteenth hole can contemplate more profound life goals than a birdie by reading the plaque on this twenty-five-foot bronze monument. It is dedicated to the founder of the Ladies' Seamen's Friend Society as a "landmark of the Seaman's last earthly port and resting place in which he awaits the advent of the great Pilot for his eternal destiny."

San Jose

Sara Winchester Mystery House, 439 Winchester Road. No one really knows what compelled Sara Winchester, the widow to the heir of the rifle fortune, to build this weird house with corridors that lead nowhere and windows that open onto walls. Some say

the impressionable Sara was told by spiritualists that she would be punished for the thousands of deaths the Winchester rifle had caused, and that the only way to insure her own immortality was to start building a house and to keep on building. Such noble intentions may also have been an outlet for her own amazing energy. Every day for thirty-eight years she sketched her design ideas on brown wrapping paper for the sixteen carpenters who followed her instructions to the nail. The result: closets an inch deep, skylights in the floors, doors opening onto other doors, stairways leading to the ceiling—all in all, 160 rooms, 10,000 windows, 2,000 doors, 9 kitchens, and 47 fireplaces. Sara was not without some good ideas though, and she dreamed up such practical innovations as wool insulation for the rooms and washboards molded into the laundry tubs. Although there was enough lumber on hand to build for another year, and the carpenters were busy adding more rooms, the spirits uncooperatively took Sara away on September 5, 1922 when she was eighty-five years old.

San Juan Bautista

Castro-Breen House, Second Street. While compiling her report on the Mission Indians, in June 1882 Helen Hunt Jackson (see *Hemet; Colorado Springs, Colorado*) stayed at this inn (now a museum) which was owned by the Patrick Breen family, survivors of the Donner Party (see *Truckee*). Although Jackson liked the charming city and even considered renting a wing of the house for her writing, she left abruptly when one of the local priests let it be known that he resented her (true) accusations that the Church had neglected its Indian brethren.

San Simeon

The Hearst Mansion. The distinguished Berkeley architect Julia Morgan was hired by William Randolph Hearst in 1919 to design "elegant, yet comfortable" living quarters. The result was La Casa Grande, the most expensive private house ever built, costing the newspaper magnate more than thirty million dollars. The house has more than 100 rooms, an 83-foot assembly hall, 31 bathrooms, two libraries for more than 500 volumes, and a garage for 25 limousines. "Mr. Hearst and I are fellow architects," Morgan once graciously conceded. "He supplies vision, critical judgment. I give technical knowledge and building expertise."

Santa Clara

Site of First School in California, University of Santa Clara campus. In 1846, when Olive Mann Isbell and her husband came from Illinois to the Santa Clara Mission, they found the children running around like little wild dogs and straying outside the mission walls. As much to relieve the worried and overworked mothers as to import culture, Olive decided to start a school. Its exact location is unknown, but she found a room, fifteen-feet square, that once was a stable. She built a fire in the middle of the earthen floor and took some tiles from the roof to let the smoke out and the sunshine in. On December 15, 1846, twenty or more children—"my little scholars," Olive called them—sat on boxes and crude benches, took turns writing at the only table, and learned the alphabet from charcoal letters neatly printed on each child's palm. In this school, the first in California to be taught by an English-speaking teacher, Olive stayed only a few months before moving to Monterey where she began the second school in California.

Santa Paula

Isbell School is named after the first American schoolteacher in California (see *Santa Clara*). Olive Mann Isbell, who died in 1899, is buried on the school grounds where a memorial tablet commemorates her historic classes.

Soquel

Site of Charley Parkhurst's Polling Place, Soquel Firehouse, 4747 Main Street. Near the white fire alarm, a shiny plaque, dedicated in February 1974 by the volunteer fire department in town, honors Charley Parkhurst as the first woman in the world to vote in a presidential election (November 4, 1868). Although it might well be true that this woman who lived as a man all her life voted here for or against Ulysses S. Grant, she is more a legend for her daring exploits as a stagecoach driver in Santa Cruz County. Charley Darkey Parkhurst, born in 1812, dressed up like a little boy to escape from an orphanage and learned how to drive six-horse teams in Massachusetts and Rhode Island before heading west. The floppy cowhides were too comfortable to give up for convention's sake, and it was only when

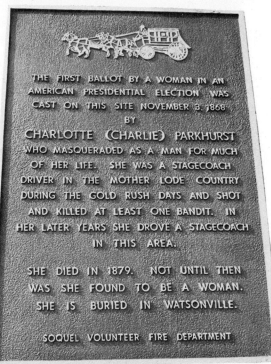

she died in 1870 that it was discovered that this "knight of the road" was a woman. She was buried in nearby *Watsonville*.

Stanford

Stanford University. When their beloved son, Leland, Jr., died in 1884, Jane Lathrop Stanford and her husband said, "The children of California shall be our children," and seven years later they opened the doors of what is today one of the nation's outstanding universities. Although she was a cofounder of the school, Jane was a much more private person than her husband —the man who drove in the golden spike of the transcontinental railroad, a California governor, and a U.S. senator. But after his death in 1893, Jane emerged as an outstanding administrator and a dedicated educationalist. Faced with intolerable financial burdens, and probate lawsuits, she nevertheless refused to close the university. Its first president, Dr. David Starr Jordan, recalled with pride, "The future of a university hung by a single thread, the love of a good woman." She is buried on campus with her husband and son.

Stockton

Site of Harriet Chalmers Adams Home, 605 North Eldorado Avenue. When Harriet wasn't home, she was most likely somewhere in the Andes, the South Seas, or the Near East, exploring remote jungles and studying primitive tribes, traveling more than 100,000 miles into lands never before visited by a white woman. "It seemed incredible that the small, charming woman, gowned in deep red velvet with a long train, could have visited such strange places," recalled Frances Densmore, after a lecture by Adams, who had encouraged the collector of American Indian songs in her work (see *Red Wing, Minnesota*). During one of her exotic explorations in 1926 Adams fell, breaking several vertebrae in her spine, and had to lie still, strapped to a board for two years. But as soon as she could walk, she was off again on an unescorted trip to North Africa. Adams was the founder of the Society of Woman Geographers in 1925, and she wrote and photographed numerous articles for the *National Geographic*. Her piece on Rio de Janeiro in the September 1920 edition is often cited as the "ideal travel article," and it can probably be found in the Central Library now on this site.

Truckee

Donner Lake Memorial, Route 80. This heroic-sized grouping of a man and a woman, anxiously looking west as a child huddles at their feet, stands on a stone base, twenty-two feet high, the height of the snow that trapped a group of ninety emigrants heading for California in October 1846, forcing them to spend a bitter winter of suffering, cannibalism, and death. By the time they were rescued in February 1847, more than half the men had died, but twenty-five of the thirty-five women had survived, each one a heroine. Margaret Breen crawled on her hands and knees in the snow, gathering fir boughs to make a fire to warm her five babies. Margaret Reed caught field mice, boiled strips of hide from the cabin roof, and cut up pieces of the rug for food; mindful of Christmas Day approaching, she hid away little bits of bacon, dried apples, and some beans so that her children could have real food for a holiday dinner. Her daughter Virginia's letter to a cousin about "our trubels getting to California," written after the teen-ager's rescue, is one of the most important records of those miserable four months. "That was 3 died and the rest eat them thay was 11 days without anything to eat but the Dead" was her sole terse reference to the cannibalism that almost all of the survivors resorted to, although several wives, faithful to the end, graciously declined to eat their husbands. The survivors formed a rescue party called "the Forlorn Hope," consisting of ten men and five women, that set out across the mountains for help. Eight of the men perished, but all the women survived. "I expressed my surprise that all the women escaped," wrote California's first governor, Peter Burnett. "I supposed it was owing to the fact that the men, especially at the beginning of the journey had performed most of the labor. They said that, at the start, the men may have performed a little more labor than the women; but, taken altogether, the women performed more than the men. After the men had become too weak to carry the gun, it was carried by the women." A museum at this historic site contains several of the emigrants' personal belongings, including Patty Reed's cloth doll, found years later. A huge boulder in the woods, marking the location of one of the cabins, contains a plaque with the names of these tragic pioneers.

Upland

Madonna of the Trail Monument, Euclid Avenue and Foothill Boulevard. The eleventh and farthest west in a series of twelve identical DAR memorials of homing trails (see *Springfield, Ohio*) bears the inscription, "This trail, trod by Padres in Spanish days became, under Mexican rule, the road connecting San Bernardino and Los Angeles; later, the American post-road."

Watsonville

Charley Parkhurst Grave, Pioneer Cemetery, Freedom Boulevard. Just yards away, traffic piles up on the busy boulevard that once was one of the dusty roads that the fearless driver raced over in her stagecoach with a perfect speed and safety record. Charley, discovered to be Charlotte after her death in 1870, lost an eye while shoeing a horse. She is remembered on this memorial tablet, erected in 1955, as "One-Eyed Charley. . . . noted whip of the Gold Rush Days. . . . and first woman to vote." (See *Soquel*.)

West Covina

Site of Lark Ellen Yaw Home, Lark Ellen Avenue. The town's most famous soprano had an E above high C that soared through tests by tuning forks and pitch pipes. Ellen began singing in 1882 when she was fourteen and delighted audiences all over the world with her incredible voice, whose ethereal quality inspired the name she is remembered by on this street, as well as the name of the hospital that now stands here.

Whittier

Harriet Strong House, Pio Pico Mansion. The adobe house of the last Mexican governor of California has been preserved as an historic monument through the efforts of Harriet Strong, pioneer environmentalist and feminist who lived here from 1867 until her death in 1929. The first female member of the Los Angeles Chamber of Commerce, Strong continuously encouraged women to enter business. She herself acquired a tidy fortune

by growing walnuts and pampas grass and by patenting new methods of irrigation and flood control.

Yosemite National Park

Emerald Pool. In the 1850s this two-acre lake was named Frances, in honor of Jean Frances Neal, one of the first women to enter Yosemite Valley and the first woman to visit the lake. A contemporary newspaper account said that Neal felt "fully repaid" by the splendor of the sight "for all the fatigue she endured in ascending the plateau." The writer added, "Let no one attempt to change the name, but rather add some record of her courage and her love of the beautiful and grand." Despite the admonition, it was later rechristened to honor instead the color of the reflected trees.

Nevada Falls. Jean Frances Neal and Madame Gautier, respectively the housekeeper of the Union House and the first woman to enter Yosemite Valley (1856), were the first women to climb the steep trails alongside this spectacular waterfall, "hugging the ridges as closely as possible, and tugging and pushing [their bodies] up the insecure steep."

Lady Franklin Rock, near the Vernal Falls. Signs along the trail point to a large flat rock where Lady Jane Franklin was carried on a litter in 1863 when she was seventy-one years old and less nimble than in her youth. Here, the doughty explorer was set down for a commanding view of the falls, one of her favorite sights.

Mount Florence. This 12,507-foot peak, situated between Mounts Maclure and Lyell, was named for Florence Hutchings, the first white child born in Yosemite (1864). John Muir, the famous Yosemite explorer who worked in her father's sawmill, described "Floy" in his letters as "that tameless one" and "a smart and mischievous topsy." Floy, who often said she wished she had been born a boy, collected toads instead of dolls, rolled her own cigarettes, and camped alone in the uncharted hills. Barely seventeen years old, the spirited adventurer died after being struck by a rock while hiking.

Yosemite Museum houses a collection of beautiful baskets woven by Lucy Tom Parker Telles, an Ahwahneechee Indian, in the 1920s and 1930s. One exquisite model, more than three feet high and nine feet around, that took four years to make, won first prize at the 1939 World's Fair in San Francisco.

Yreka

Indian Peggy Grave, near Siskiyou County Fairgrounds (private). When Peggy, a Shasta Indian, overheard her tribe's plans to attack the miners, during the mid-1800s, she knew that if the raid were successful, the white men would seek revenge, and her own people would suffer in the end. Even though she knew she would be killed if her treachery were discovered, Peggy warned the miners, advising them to hide in the tunnels with food supplies. When the Indians rode into the village, war paint on their faces, they realized it was futile to wait for the miners to leave their hiding places. A brutal massacre on both sides was avoided by the brave woman's ingenuity. An oval rock, inscribed "Indian Peggy. Born about 1800. Died Oct. 26, 1902. Beloved member of the Shasta tribe. A friend of Indian and whites" marks her grave.

COLORADO

Alma

Mount Silverheels, east face of the Continental Divide. This snowcapped peak (13,822 feet) looks down on the old mining town where a dance-hall entertainer (who favored a custom-made pair of silver slippers) was popularly known as Silver Heels. Legend has it that when a smallpox epidemic broke out, Silver Heels selflessly helped nurse the miners back to health. Years after she had vanished, her face scarred from her own bout with the disease, grateful miners named the mountain for her.

Boulder

High Altitude Observatory, Astro-Geophysics Building, University of Colorado. Dedicated to Mary Converse, navigation teacher during World War II and the first woman in the U.S. to be commissioned a captain in the merchant marines. Converse never succeeded in having the word *he* changed to *she* on the scroll licensing her to command craft.

Boulder Historical Society Pioneer Museum, 1655 Broadway. A hunting costume and some stereo views are among the only reminders of the work of naturalist Martha A. Maxwell, who braved the hardships of the nearby mountains and plains to secure specimens for her scientific work. Her taxidermy, once displayed in a museum she established in Boulder, was noted for its realism—each bird and animal "in his native mountain home—the mountain sheep perched high up the mountainside, free as the brilliant air of his clifflike home, with the elk and beaver below him." Her work was called "a pioneer venture in habitat grouping," and it influenced a change in all museum displays of animal life. Of her outstanding display of birds at the Centennial Exhibition in Philadelphia, Pennsylvania, all that remain are two specimens of screech owl skins (*Otus asio maxwelliae*) at the Smithsonian in Washington, D.C. She collected them at great personal risk.

Brown's Park

Graves of Josie Morris and Queen Ann Bassett, Brown's Park Cemetery. (See *Jensen, Utah.*)

Central City

Central City Opera House, Eureka Street. Almost a century ago, the miners who worked "the richest square mile on earth" piled stone upon stone without benefit of mortar and created this handsome center for minstrels, shows, and entertainment. Even Ann Eliza Webb Young, runaway wife of Brigham (see *Salt Lake City, Utah*), lectured here in 1880 on the evils of polygamy. When the gold veins ran dry, the opera house grew cobwebs. Enter Ida Kruse McFarlane in 1929, an English professor who spearheaded the drive to restore the theater, enlisting the aid of Denver arts patron Anne Evans. The architectural gem reopened in 1932 with a performance of *Camille,* and it is now the site of an annual cultural festival. Among the plaques in its peaceful garden: "You are now 8464.296 feet above sea level—a perfect altitude for health and longevity. Presented by Myrna Loy 1964."

Ida Kruse McFarlane Memorial, top of the hill off Spruce Street. Foundations and a cross are all that remain of the old Saint Aloysius Academy, next to the abandoned Coeur d'Alene mine, now a museum. The cross was saved by Ida Kruse McFarlane, and it remains a towering memorial over Gregory Gulch.

Teller House, Eureka Street. A plaque on the sturdy brick walls of this former hotel (which once quartered President Ulysses S. Grant) reads, "This historic building has been restored as a memorial to Anne Evans whose spirit is an inseparable part of Central City and its festivals." Anne Evans was chairman of the Central City Opera Association (which she helped found). She tempered her gentle ways with a zesty spirit, once saying, "You have to get angry sometimes, or they'll think they can run you, especially if you are a woman."

Anne Evans Promontory, several miles outside the city, is an even more unique memorial. You get there by following a rocky dirt road out past the cemetery, then along the red arrows tacked onto trees. When we visited in the fall, the aspens were at their most golden, and the point was spectacular: a windy clearing overlooking snow-covered peaks to the west. Tall pines guarded picnickers in the bright, chilly sunshine. A peaceful noble spot. Apparently, that thought also struck pioneering Colorado newspaperwoman Frances ("Pinky") Wayne. This was where she had her ashes scattered in 1931.

St. James Methodist-Episcopal Church, Eureka Street. This golden-brown fieldstone building is a monument not only to the hardy settlers of Central City but to the industry and unflagging faith of "Aunt" Clara Brown, a Virginia-born slave. In 1856 she bought her freedom and, after a stay in Kansas, came to Colorado during the gold rush, earning her passage as a wagon-train cook. At Central City she made her living at the washboard. She acquired property and money, and when she heard of the plan to build a church, she donated her time, her money, and her dwelling. The plaque on the church front recalls that "for a while, services were held in the home of 'Aunt' Clara Brown." They were finally held at the church in 1872, where, at the dedication one Sunday morning in July, Aunt Clara's voice joined with others in prayers for the church she had helped build.

Colorado Springs

Helen Hunt Jackson Home, Pioneers Museum, 25 West Kiowa Street. The first time this elegant old gabled and shuttered house was moved was in 1875. Helen Hunt, new bride of William Sharpless Jackson, had the house lifted from its foundations and turned so that she could view the snow-clad Cheyenne Mountains from the front windows instead of from the kitchen. The second move came in the 1960s, when the wrecker's ball threatened, and some sections were brought here to the museum. Through lace-curtained windows you can see the downstairs rooms where Helen Hunt Jackson wrote the popular works that made her Emerson's favorite female poet. A fiery New Englander who came to Colorado for her health, Helen wrote letters to her girlhood friend Emily Dickinson on the old wooden writing desk here. The pile of old Indian baskets reminds us of her lifelong crusade to right the wrongs the American Indians had suffered from whites (see *San Juan Bautista, California*). Also preserved here: the custom-made staircase with the six-pointed stars cut out of the siding, on which she slipped in 1884, breaking her leg in several places. Her leg never healed properly.

Helen Hunt Jackson's Grave, South Cheyenne Canyon, was where she had asked to be buried. To a lofty spot called Inspiration Point, overlooking her adopted town, she was taken after her death in 1885 and interred beneath a pile of rocks. At the Seven Falls, whose tumbling waters helped stimulate her writing, modern signs cheerfully advertise the trail. The first sign is at the base of the mountain: "265 steps. Enjoy your trip. Please use hand rails and take your time." Atop the steep climb, past a fake goat perched on a cliff, another sign warns, "It is one mile to the Grave. The round trip requires at least one hour. Follow white arrows on rocks by the trail." As we followed the babbling brook on the mountaintop, a young man in blue jeans inquired, "Who's Helen Hunt anyway?" The real question is, where's Helen Hunt? Vandals so desecrated the mountain site that, in 1891, her widower left the stones but removed the casket to the less elevated Evergreen Cemetery.

Grace Greenwood Cottage, 801 South Tejon (private). After collapsing during a flood in nearby Manitou Springs in 1893, the building known as "Clematis Cottage" was moved here. Voted the most attractive mountain cottage by the editors of the *Ladies Home Journal,* it was the summer retreat of Grace Greenwood, pen name of Sara Jane Lippincott, a popular if flowery journalist, author, suffragist, and lecturer. About one of her works she said, "I know it's a good book because I wrote it myself."

Colorado Springs Fine Arts Center, 30 West Dale Street. This cultural center, opened in 1936, was donated to the city by heiress Alice Bemis Taylor. Along with music, drama, and paintings, the Taylor Museum contains priceless Navajo rugs, sand paintings, and religious Santos from her personal collection of southwestern folk art. A generous but shy woman, Alice Taylor was the first female trustee of Colorado College, where a building was dedicated to her in 1956, fourteen years after her death.

Pikes Peak (14,110 feet). The first woman to climb this overwhelming crest was suffragist Julia Holmes. Dressed in bloomers, carrying a seventeen-pound pack containing bread, clothing, and her quilt, and accompanied by her husband and two other men, she set out on July 1, 1858 and reached the summit August 5. Here in the cold, cloudy heights, she leaned on a flat stone and wrote to her mother: "I have accomplished the task which I marked out for myself and now I feel amply repaid for all my toil and fatigue. Nearly everyone tried to discourage me from attempting it, but I believe that I would not have missed this glorious sight for anything at all."

That was precisely the sentiment of English professor Katharine Lee Bates, who scaled Pikes Peak by more modern methods on her first trip west in the summer of 1893. The view inspired her to write "America the Beautiful." As she later explained: "It was then and there, as I was looking out over the sea-like expanse of fertile country spreading away so far under those ample skies, that the opening lines of the hymn floated into my mind." Several days later, she penciled the four stanzas into her notebook; it was published in 1895. Today, "America the Beautiful" has been designated the nation's official bicentennial song. (See *Falmouth, Massachusetts.*)

Creede

Site of Carrie Reidmiller Cabin, Wall Street and Creede Avenue. Nothing remains of the hundred-foot-wide cabin or the two-story business house built here by Creede's first resident and pioneer businesswoman. Arriving penniless in 1891, Carrie Reidmiller opened a restaurant—Creede's first—in a nearby cabin. She started with three cups and saucers, a few tin plates, and an old stove. At mealtime, she removed the door from its hinges and nailed it to a butcher block for a table; boxes were used for chairs. In this way she prospered for nearly a year, finally earning $500 a month. She also owned five lots on this site, two of which later grossed her $6,500.

Cripple Creek

The Old Homestead, 353 East Myers Avenue. The only remaining brothel of Cripple Creek's high-living gold camp days, this two-story brick showplace built in 1896 was also its most elegant. The original furnishings included a two-inch thick wooden door with Old Homestead cozily written in script on the glass; a ruby-red hobnail glass chandelier; china spittoons; a light green fainting couch; and a metal bedside foot warmer that is in the shape of, and thus called, a "pig." The grandmotherly women who conduct the tours here treat the old bawdy house with considerably more tolerance than did their forebears from

the "right" side of town. There is even a hint of pride that the Old Homestead was so exclusive. Reported our guide, "It was necessary for a gentleman to write a letter of application. It cost $50 to $100 a visit." Pause. "Or, per trick."

The guide acknowledged the inequities of the trade, even then. She referred to the prostitutes as "working girls," informing us that the police required them to get a bill of health from the doctor every thirty days. "It cost $16 for a working girl, $40 to $46 for a madame. So when you figure there were 350 girls on the street, it was quite a good setup for the police."

The Old Homestead was home to four "working girls" and one madame. They all lived upstairs, where small business cards told who worked inside each tiny but cozy bedroom. Pearl DeVere, who furnished and ran the house, lived in the room to the rear. One June night in 1897, after a rollicking party with imported champagne, she excused herself from the festivities and, complaining of unstrung nerves, took some morphine. Whether by accident or design, the dosage was too much. She died that afternoon, fully clothed, lying across her bed. Pearl's next resting place was just outside of town.

Pearl DeVere's Grave, Mount Pisgah Cemetery. A huge funeral procession accompanied Pearl DeVere's body to the cemetery. At the graveside, the brief sermon was, "Let him who is without sin cast the first stone." After she was buried, the Elks Club band marched back to town, playing "There'll Be a Hot Time in the Old Town Tonight." Today Pearl DeVere's grave is marked by a heart-shaped white marble stone, recently donated and modeled after the original decayed wooden marker.

Cripple Creek District Museum, on Colorado 67, contains the original wooden slab from Pearl DeVere's grave and an old telephone switchboard that was once manned by male operators. Of special note is a photograph of an old saloon here known as Crapper Jack's, with this caption: "When Carry Nation . . . visited Cripple Creek she called it a 'foul cesspool.' It was, she claimed, the most lawless and wicked city to be found anywhere. She warned the people of the Gold camp that Myers Avenue was luring innocent men and women by the hundreds to death and destruction." An additional note names some of the innocent women in the dance hall photo: Dirty Neck Nell, Dizzy Daisy, Tall Rose, Bilious Bessie, Slippery Sadie, and Greasy Gertie.

Isabella Mine, off Gold Camp Road. The weathered headframe still stands over one of the early investments of Mollie O'Bryan, the first female broker on the Cripple Creek exchange. A stenographer who put all her spare money into stocks, she had such "rare good judgment," according to the local newspaper, that "brokers began to defer to her intelligence in making investments." This gold mine was one of her first, a successful venture in the 1890s that soon soared in value. She also became president of several mining companies, including the huge Amalgamated Gold Mining Company, causing the newspapers to rank her "among the leaders of the mining world."

Another venture, whose gold dust has now simply turned to dust, was the Princess Alice Gold Mining Company, a group of

women from Buffalo, New York, who ran the Lafayette Mine and became the first female syndicate to succeed on their own. Their total acreage in Cripple Creek was over ninety acres.

Denver

Frances Wisebart Jacobs Memorial, State Capitol Building, East Colfax. The only woman among the sixteen pioneers honored with stained-glass portraits in the Capitol rotunda was the founder of the Community Chest in Colorado. She is known as the state's Mother of Charities. The philanthropic work of Frances Wisebart Jacobs reached across lines of age, sex, race, and religion, at a time when immigrants flooded into Colorado. After her death in 1892, friends named the new building at Jackson and East Colfax the Frances Jacobs Hospital. It still stands as the National Jewish Hospital and Research Center.

Molly Brown House, 1340 Pennsylvania Street. On stage and screen she was *The Unsinkable Molly Brown,* a nickname acquired when she rowed hysterical passengers to safety aboard Lifeboat No. 6 during the sinking of the *Titanic.* In real life, she preferred the name Margaret despite her flamboyant tastes. In 1890, when her miner husband struck it rich in Leadville, they bought this house. It became an instant showplace. Today, with the sixteen rooms restored to much of their former ornate style,

it is a museum of Victoriana, from the twin white lions outside to the elaborate silver punch bowl in the dining room. Most of Molly Brown's life was devoted to gaining acceptance in the city's social circles. That was guaranteed by her heroism aboard the *Titanic.* After gaining fame as the only woman to row a boat to safety—which she accomplished in 7½ grueling hours—she was admitted to the group of "sacred 36" society leaders. One leader explained that, at a luncheon, she enjoyed Molly's "vivid and chatty conversation" about the tragedy. Another called her "so picturesque in her manner of relating the terrible events of that night."

Catherine Murat Cottage, Ninth Street Historic Park. From this modest cottonwood log cabin—now restored—once known as the Hotel Eldorado, Catherine Murat flew the first American flag in Colorado. She made it from a red flannel petticoat and flew it from the fifty-foot flagpole next to the hotel. It was intended for the First Colorado Regiment to carry in the Civil War. The German-born countess, the first white woman to enter Denver, in 1858, was known as the Mother of Colorado. During her last years, only the smoke rising from a tiny cabin on a hillside above Lake Palmer indicated that the old widow was all right. One day in March 1910, there was no smoke. Countess Murat was dead at eighty-six.

Emily Griffith Opportunity School, 1250 Welton Street. As a frontier schoolteacher at age fourteen, then as a member of the

Denver Public School system, Emily Griffith understood that learning could not be confined to the classroom. In 1915 she decided to start a school without hours, age limits, or rigid schedules, for a working person to "study what he or she wants to learn to make life more useful. . . . I already have a name for that school. It is *Opportunity.*" A year later, her Public Opportunity School opened here, with principal Emily Griffith earning $1,800 a year. The school flourished and became a model for many others. When Griffith retired in 1933, the school was renamed in her honor. Fourteen years later, she was shot in the head by an unknown intruder. Her ashes are buried in Fairmount Cemetery, beneath a headstone shared with her sister and inscribed with the slogan of the school that had educated more than a million students: "For all who wish to learn."

Statue of Dr. Florence Sabin, State Department of Health Building, 4210 East Eleventh Street. This replica of the bronze statue in the Capitol building in *Washington, D.C.,* is a tribute to the pioneering Colorado physician who returned home after a distinguished medical career in the East. At seventy-three, she began a second career, working vigorously for public health legislation in her home state. Most of the bills she introduced, called "Sabin's health laws," were passed, perhaps because of the attitude described by a Colorado governor: "There isn't a man in the legislature who wants to tangle with her."

Rocky Mountain News, 400 West Colfax Avenue. Elizabeth Minerva Sumner Byers arrived in Denver in 1859 with her husband and two babies on a two-seated buckboard. "I felt I was the advance guard of civilization at the foot of the Rocky Mountains," she wrote. With the printing press they'd brought from Omaha, the Byers' set up shop in an office above a saloon and put their new paper to bed at 10:00 P.M. on April 22, 1859. The next day, it beat its rival, the *Cherry Creek Pioneer,* to the streets by one half hour, thus becoming the first newspaper in Colorado. Elizabeth Byers is credited with giving the paper the name it still carries today: the *Rocky Mountain News.*

Pioneer Monument, Colfax and Broadway. Elizabeth Byers led the list of contributors to this traffic island erected June 24, 1911. Here, "at the end of the famous Smoky Hill trail," sits a representative group: Kit Carson; a miner; a hunter; and the pioneer woman, her skirt billowing, a child in her arm, holding a long rifle and facing firmly away from a row of pornographic bookstores on Broadway.

Market Street, 1900 and 2000 blocks. Today this is an industrial area: two blocks of trolley tracks, storage lofts, and warehouses. A century ago, the wares peddled from the houses here were of a different sort. This was Holladay Street (its name now changed at the insistence of indignant members of the namesake's family)—also known as the Row, the Line, the tenderloin—the busy red-light district in the gold-fevered Rockies. The inelegant cribs were at No. 2015, where the American Legion Cathay Post Bar stands today. Verona Baldwin's fancy house was No. 2020. Others lined the block, replaced today by the likes of No. 1937, with its sign: Polar Refrigeration Co. Frigidaire Ice Machines, Walk-In Coolers, and Reach-In Boxes.

Perhaps the house of greatest repute was No. 1942. Here Jennie Rogers opened her House of Mirrors in 1889, a three-story graystone "palace" with five intriguing exterior heads carved from rose stone. Later the site belonged to Martha ("Mattie") Silks, a madame as tiny and plump as Jennie was tall and slim. Mattie dressed like a queen and owned houses in at least four separate locations here until Denver authorities closed down the Row for good in 1915. When Mattie owned No. 1942, she had her name—M. Silks—inlaid in tiles on the front stoop. Today, the tiles are gone, and a loading platform for Bloom Interiors occupies the threshold that was once crossed by untold numbers of amorous souls.

Mattie Silks' Grave, Fairmount Cemetery, East Alameda and Quebec. The Queen of Holladay Street died in 1929 and was buried beneath a simple headstone marked with her married name: Martha A. Ready. When we went to visit the grave, a member of the cemetery staff told us that, two or three times a year, an old man, "all shriveled up," comes to look for Mattie Silks' grave. "He always asks me where it is," she said, "and I'm tempted to tell him that he already knows. He's been coming for several years." Dear Sir, whoever you are: Mattie Silks lies in Section 12.

Estes Park

Estes Park was the destination of English traveler and writer Isabella Bird, the first female Fellow of the Royal Geographical Society (1892), who visited the Rockies in 1873 and later published her own perceptive letters in the delightful book *A Lady's Life in the Rocky Mountains.* Dressed in an ankle-length skirt and full Turkish trousers gathered into her boots, she scaled the mountains and traversed the passes on horseback. Her favorite sight was Longs Peak (14,256 feet), which she called "alone in imperial grandeur. . . . This scenery satisfied my soul. . . . It is magnificent, and the air is life giving." In an area she called "no region for tourists and women," Isabella Bird no doubt owed much of her achievement to her intrepid attitude, appreciated by at least one man she encountered who said, "There's nothing Western folk admire so much as pluck in a woman." Although the Griff Evans Ranch, where she lived, is flooded now by Lake Estes, the timeless peaks and bluffs ascended during her 800-mile journey remain a permanent monument to this courageous adventurer (see *Hanalei Valley, Hawaii*).

Fort Collins

Aunty Stone Cabin, Fort Collins Pioneer Museum, 219 Peterson Street. Elizabeth Hickock Stone crossed the plains in a covered wagon and landed in this small frontier army post in 1864. With her husband Lewis, she built and ran the camp's first officers' mess in this two-story log house. The logs were hand-hewn and hauled to the city from nearby hills on oxteams. Used tent canvas lined the walls. When Lewis died at sixty-four, "Aunty" Stone built a flour mill, then constructed the first brick kiln in this part of the country. The cabin was brought to this location, safely locked behind a wire fence in the museum's backyard, and christened with a bottle of wine in Aunty Stone's presence. When she died in 1895, a year after casting her first vote (from a wheelchair) in the municipal election, the firehouse bell tolled ninety-four times, for each year of her life.

Greeley

Meeker Memorial Museum, 1324 Ninth Avenue. The front parlor of this adobe house was the scene of an emotional investigation in November 1879. Josephine Meeker, an Oberlin graduate, had been teaching young Ute Indians at the White River Agency where her father was Indian agent. Apparently her idealism was better motivated than her father's heavy-handed rule. On September 29 the Utes rebelled against his undiplomatic methods and against their confinement (see *Meeker*). They killed her father and other men, taking Josephine and her mother captive. Like most young women captured by Indians, Josephine suffered indignities—although her captor claimed to have fallen in love with her—until she was rescued a month later. But not until she testified to Gen. Charles Adams, a militiaman determined to find out the facts and punish only the guilty, did the public learn the details of such ordeals. Although most young women captives wrote their memoirs after the fact, with embellished descriptions, Josephine reluctantly gave her candid account to an army stenographer. A brief sampling:

Josephine: Of course we were insulted a good many times; we expected to be.
Adams: What do you mean by insult, and what did it consist of?
Josephine: Of outrageous treatment at night.
Adams: Am I to understand that they outraged you several times at night?
Josephine: Yes, sir.
Adams: Forced you against your will?
Josephine: Yes, sir.

* * *

Adams: Did they seem to think it was very wrong?
Josephine: No; they thought it was a pretty good thing to have a white squaw.

The museum contains Josephine's typewriter, some letters, the dress she made from an Indian blanket, and the book, *Pilgrim's Progress,* that her mother rescued from the burning agency office.

Lamar

Madonna of the Trail Monument, South Main and Beech Streets. The fifth of twelve markers erected by the DAR to show the National Old Trails (see *Springfield, Ohio*) was dedicated September 24, 1928. This commemorates the "Big Timbers"—a thick bank of cottonwoods lining the Arkansas River here, where native and new Americans camped and talked peace.

Leadville

Tabor Cottage, 115 East Fifth Street. The eternal triangle is the classic vehicle that has transported women into the history books. Not our favorite situation, it is a useful reminder of what happens to women trapped by their social roles.

This green clapboard cottage with its yellow and brown trim is where the Tabor triangle all began. Clyde Ducharme, who owns it today, never tires of telling visitors the story: Horace A. W. Tabor was the Silver King, the lucky miner who turned a $17 grubstake into a fortune and bought the bonanza Matchless Mine in 1881 for $117,000. It soon produced up to $100,000 a month. Tabor became the first millionaire in Leadville, while he was married to his first wife, Augusta. She was a long-suffering, respectable New Englander who lived in this cottage when they first settled in Leadville. She still gazes down starkly through oval-frame glasses from a photograph on its walls.

Augusta was the wife Tabor threw over when he struck it rich and fancied the curly-haired, blue-eyed, bubbly Baby Doe McCourt. He married Baby Doe at a lavish wedding in *Washington, D.C.,* in 1883. But Tabor lost his riches as quickly as he'd found them. The financial panic and collapse of silver prices in 1893 wiped him out, and he died a pauper in 1899. His last words to Baby Doe were as ill-advised as his love life: "Hold on to the Matchless," he said. "It will make millions again."

The Matchless Mine, a few miles east of town on Seventh Street, never produced another ounce of silver, but Baby Doe hung on for thirty-six years. At the end of her life she was a recluse living in the small cabin adjacent to the vacant mine shaft. She was, as Clyde Ducharme told us back at the Tabor cottage, an outcast. "They were a divorced couple. All the sympathy was with Augusta."

Some Leadville residents still recall Baby Doe's last years, when she would trudge through blizzards with burlap bags warming her feet, pressing IOU notes into the hands of a local grocer. Her body was found in the cabin frozen to death in 1935, amidst piles of mementos and old newspapers. As Ducharme said wistfully, "This story is one, unlike fiction, that doesn't turn out right."

Meeker

Meeker Massacre Site, three miles west of town, just off Colorado 64. A pink granite slab on a cobblestone base marks the approximate site of the White River Agency, where in 1879 the nomadic Ute Indians rebelled against the confinement of the reservation, killed the stubborn Indian agent, Nathan C. Meeker, and captured his daughter Josephine. Josephine Basin, a wide and shallow clearing to the south, is the area across which she attempted to flee (see *Greeley*).

Montrose

Memorial to Chipeta, Ute Indian Museum. The two most significant figures and peacemakers in Ute history were Chipeta and her husband, Chief Ouray. It was Chipeta who boldly rode overland to order the renegade Utes to release the Meeker captives (see *Meeker*). She then cared for the prisoners. Eugene Field celebrated her heroism in his poem, "Chipeta's Ride." Inside this museum, located on the farm where she once lived, Chipeta is represented in a painting and by her beaded saddlebags, her saddle, and a toy cradleboard she made as a gift. Outside, an eleven-foot rose granite monument honors both Chipeta and Ouray. There is also a stone tepee, a replica of the one they lived in. Her grave is a concrete tomb above the ground. Chipeta died in Utah in 1924, exiled onto a reservation that was not her home. She died sad, blind, and poverty-stricken, in effect as much a victim of rape by the white man as Indian captive Josephine Meeker had been by the red.

CONNECTICUT

Berlin

Site of Emma Hart Willard Birthplace, Norton Road and Lower Lane (private). A boulder marks the farm where Emma Hart, the sixteenth of seventeen children, was born February 23, 1787 and raised on Shakespeare and Chaucer. Nightly philosophical discussions with her father influenced her progressive and determined views on the education of women. "He was fifty years my senior," Emma wrote of him years later, "yet he would often call me when at the age of fourteen from household duties by my mother's side to enjoy with him some passage of an author which pleased him." Her first lesson in female inferiority came when she helped sort the sheep's wool: The best quality went for her father's clothes, the next best for the sons, and, finally, the women could pick out what was not needed for mops, for themselves. In 1802, Emma enrolled at the Berlin Academy and taught there for a while, before moving to *Middlebury, Vermont,* where she opened her own school. (See also *Troy, New York.*)

Bridgeport

Grave of Lavinia Warren Stratton, Mountain Grove Cemetery. When Charles Stratton, also known as Tom Thumb, saw Mercy Lavinia Warren Bumpus, "an accomplished, beautiful perfectly developed woman in miniature," as P. T. Barnum described her, he exclaimed, "I believe she was created on purpose to be my wife." After their much publicized wedding on February 10, 1863, Lavinia was forever called "wife"—on placards and posters, at royal receptions, and finally on her grave, after her death in 1919, having outlived Charles by thirty years. Charles' grave was originally enshrined with a forty-foot Italian marble shaft surmounted by a life-size statue of himself. Lavinia's was a tiny headstone on which she could have easily perched, marked only "Wife." That inadequate headstone still stands, but after vandals destroyed the original monument to her husband, a new one was erected in 1959. Now, in the towering granite, the wife has been given a name.

Grave of Fanny J. Crosby, Mountain Grove Cemetery. Although she lost her sight when she was just an infant, Fanny never stopped hearing beautiful music. She composed more than 2,500 fervent hymns as well as hundreds of popular songs, such as "Proud World, Good-bye I'm Going Home," written years before she finally went—in 1915 at age ninety-two.

Brooklyn

"Friendship Valley," Route 169 (private). In 1838, while she was on trial for her courageous attempts to start a school for black girls in *Canterbury,* Prudence Crandall stayed in this yellow wood house belonging to William Lloyd Garrison's father-in-law. Months later she sought refuge here again with some of her students when her school was being stoned and burned.

Canterbury

Prudence Crandall House, junction of Routes 14A and 169. A gentle Quaker woman, Prudence Crandall opened the Canterbury Female Boarding School in this large white house in 1831 for the daughters of prominent local families. When Sarah Harris (see *Kingston, Rhode Island*), the daughter of a black farmer, applied for admission, Prudence's decision to accept her caused such a furor in the town that she decided to limit attendance exclusively to black women, and she "determined

if possible during the remaining part of my life to benefit the people of color." Her students were so cruelly harassed that Prudence reluctantly retreated to *Brooklyn,* where she was imprisoned for breaking the "black law" that prohibited the teaching of black children. A raging mob assault on the school forced Prudence to close its doors in 1834. The house was empty, rundown and gloomy when we visited, but we were told that the Connecticut Historical Commission is planning to restore it as a museum, with period pieces of Prudence's days, to be open to the public in the summer of 1976.

Fairfield

Site of Edward's Pond, Old Post Road and Beach Road. The pond at the western edge of the green has long since dried up. There, in the mid-1700s the God-fearing folk of Fairfield threw suspected witches who had to prove their innocence by drowning. Since Mercy Disborough and Elizabeth Clawson may have been the only women in town who knew how to swim and float, they were early victims.

Farmington

Miss Porter's School, Main Street and Mountain Road. Sarah Porter, who started the school in 1843, was an intellectual whose scholarly opinions were sought by men all over the state, but she believed that for her "girls" the perfect soufflé was more important than a B.A. Through her sixty-year tenure, until her death in 1900, she emphasized the training of gracious hostesses and homemakers in "docile, amiable and respectful manners." Despite the school's consistent reputation for academic excellence—it was one of the first to introduce science in its curriculum—Miss Porter's name was synonymous with the exclusive pampered life. Maids awakened the girls, shampooed their hair, and served breakfast in bed for those who felt ill that day. Miss Porter, a stern but kindly teacher who liked to take moonlit walks with her students, felt that grades and examinations hindered a spontaneous love of learning. As late as the 1930s, one graduate recalled, "The school was excellent if you wanted to study, but if you didn't, that was okay. If one flunked a course, one had a talk with [the headmaster], but he was very nice and gentlemanly about it."

Glastonbury

The Smith House, 1625 Main Street. The town's most illustrious family lived here in the seventeenth and eighteenth centuries, their talents even more formidable than their names. Zephania Hollister Smith, a preacher and lawyer, and Hannah Hadassah Hickock, linguist, mathematical genius, one of the nation's first abolitionists, were the proud parents of five daughters: Hancy Zephina, Cyrinthia Sacretia, Laurelia Aleroyla, Julia Evelina, and Abby Hadassah, who all lived at home cultivating their numerous and various talents. Some historians say the sisters made a pact never to marry, but most speculate that there was no man who considered himself worthy of any of them. In 1873, Abby and Julia, seventy-six and seventy-one years old, the only ones still alive, were informed that their property taxes were to be raised one hundred dollars. After checking around, the sisters realized it was only themselves and some widows, not one male property holder, who would be surcharged. When Abby and Julia refused to pay, insisting that there could be no taxation without representation, the collectors abducted seven fine Jersey cows (worth about one hundred dollars) that eventually became as celebrated as their doughty owners. In a tedious three-year legal battle that rallied such suffrage leaders as Lucy Stone to their support, Abby and Julia were so piqued by the lengthy proceedings and inept defense attorneys that they started studying to become lawyers. They finally did win their case. By then, only two cows were left. Ever mindful of the promotional possibilities, the sisters named them Taxey and Votey, in the fervent hope that "in a very short time, wherever you find Taxey there Votey will be also." Abby died in 1878. A year later, Julia, aged eighty-seven, married an eighty-six-year-old retired judge who became enamored of her after hearing about her five translations of the Bible from Latin, Greek, and Hebrew. Julia later said it was the only mistake she made in her life. She died seven years later, and in her will she asked to be buried in the family plot near her sisters, with only her maiden name on the grave.

Groton

Mother Bailey House, 108 Thames Street (private). The iron fence that surrounds this lovely 2½-story, white frame, Ionic-columned house was reportedly given to Anna Warner Bailey for her patriotic deed during the War of 1812. When Commodore Stephen Decatur took shelter in New London Harbor as his ships were being pursued by the British, there was an urgent need for old rags to make gun wadding. Anna, one of the few inhabitants of the town who had not fled inland, promptly took off her red flannel petticoat, announcing, "There are plenty more where that came from." Her delicate contribution to the cause, deemed too sacred to be used as gun wadding, was proudly flown as "the martial petticoat" over the fortifications.

Guilford

Agnes Dickinson Lee House, 1 North Street (private). This charming white house, more than two centuries old, was the home of an outstanding Revolutionary War heroine who on several occasions outwitted the Tories. In 1781, Agnes warned the entire town that the British were coming: She fired the cannon in her backyard so relentlessly that the enemy was frightened away. Another time, the Tories, correctly suspecting that the Lee house was the meeting place and armory of the patriots, came to search the place when Agnes was all alone.

"Who's there?" she asked.

"A friend," the crafty Tory replied.

"Yes, friends to King George and the Tories," Agnes shouted, firmly bolting the door.

Hartford

Site of Charlotte Perkins Gilman Birthplace, 36 Main Street. Born here in 1860, Charlotte, who was to become one of the outstanding feminist theoreticians of her day, suffered from a loveless childhood, and throughout her life she was afflicted with weepy bouts of depression. But those unhappy early years formed an independent womanhood. "Self support," she wrote when she was twenty-one, was "a necessary base for freedom." A marriage three years later caused her untold unhappiness. In 1885, after a nervous breakdown, she left her husband and daughter for a trip to California. Alone in the sun, she found that her depression lifted somewhat, and four years later she published her brilliant manifesto, *Women and Economics*, decades ahead in its arguments for communal child rearing and in the redefining of household roles. A suffrage leader once said to her, "I think after all your work will be a help to the movement. What you ask for is so much worse than what we ask for they will give us the ballot to stave off further demands." When she was forty, Gilman married again, happily, and moved to *Norwich* in 1922. St. Elizabeth's Home now occupies the site of her earliest home.

Harriet Beecher Stowe House, "Nook Farm," 77 Forest Avenue. When the famed novelist, who was born in *Litchfield*, bought

this classic nineteenth-century cottage of gray wood and brick in 1873, her momentous novel, *Uncle Tom's Cabin* (see *Brunswick, Maine*), published more than twenty years earlier, had sold more than two million copies. In this blooming cultural center, now restored and open to the public, she entertained such celebrated neighbors as Mark Twain, Isabella Beecher Hooker, and actor Will Gillette, and she worked in her favorite gardens. In the small sitting room near her ten-sided bedroom, Stowe wrote several more novels, essays, and poems. She also painted; her charming watercolor of a snowy owl and her oils of goldenrods and asters are on view in the house along with several original pieces of furniture, including a drop-leaf mahogany table where she wrote parts of her most famous novel. In the years before her death here in 1896, Stowe's gigantic mental powers drifted into childlike simplicity. Mark Twain recalled that she would roam around the grounds, popping up behind visitors with a mischievous "boo."

Keney Memorial Tower, Main and Ely Streets. This red brick tower with a clock that still works was erected in 1898 by prominent Hartford merchants Walter and Howard Keney on the site of their former home. A loving tribute to their mother, the tower is described as the first monument ever built to immortalize a woman solely for her role as a mother, though some have questioned the appropriateness of its shape.

Lebanon

Trumbull House. Faith Robinson Trumbull lived here with her husband John, the governor of Connecticut, during the Revolutionary War. Although Faith is usually only recalled as the mother of extraordinary children including Jonathan, a governor of Connecticut, and John, the famous artist, there were numerous instances of her courageous deeds. It seems only one of them has made the historical record. During the bitter winter of 1777–78, when the Continental army was encamped at Valley Forge, the minister at Faith's church announced a special collection for the impoverished soldiers. Without a moment's hesitation, Faith left her husband's side and walked to the altar where she placed the magnificent cloak she was wearing—a present from the Count de Rochambeau—as her offering. Her generous example inspired the entire congregation, and, that day, Lebanon had a record collection of supplies. Weeks later, Faith's cloak was being worn again as trim on dozens of soldier's uniforms.

Litchfield

Tapping Reeves Law School, South Street and East Street. The first law school in America was established here in 1784 under the tutelage of Judge Reeves, one of the first men in the state to work in the ongoing struggle for more legal rights for married women.

Site of Miss Pierce's Academy, North Street. Opened in 1792, the school, now only noted by a sign on the street and a plaque on a boulder hidden in the bushes, claims to be the first institution in America for the higher education of women. Although it was open only for about forty years, more than three thousand women attended, including the clever Harriet Beecher Stowe. Her essay, written when she was eleven, pondering the question "Can the Immortality of the Soul be Proved by the Light of Nature?" and its concluding "no," was publicly hailed as brilliant.

Site of Harriet Beecher Stowe Birthplace, North and Prospect Streets. A signpost stands on the corner of a wide green lawn marking the place where the author of "the little book that made the big war" was born on June 14, 1812 and grew up in a household of "great cheerfulness and comfort" with sister Catharine and brother Henry. Harriet adored her father Lyman, whose "inspiring talent" turned family apple-peeling sessions

in the kitchen into dramatic narrations of Sir Walter Scott's romantic novels. Years later, Harriet remembered Litchfield as "a delightful village on a fruitful hill, richly endowed with schools . . . with its venerable governors and judges, with its learned lawyers, and senators . . . and with a population enlightened and respectable." (See *Hartford*.)

New Haven

Hester Coster's Lot, Yale University, College and Chapel Streets. This choice piece of land, measuring 205 by 274 feet, once belonged to Hester Coster, who in 1691 willed it to her church. The church's deacons later sold the land to the trustees of Collegiate School, which became Yale College in 1701 and did not admit female students until 268 years later.

Young and brilliant Lucinda Foote tried to apply, but she was turned away with an official proclamation of sex discrimination issued by Yale's president, Ezra Stiles, in 1783: "Let it be known unto you, that I have tested Miss Lucinda Foote, aged 12, by way of examination, proving that she has made laudable progress in the languages of the learned, viz, the Latin and the Greek; to such an extent that I found her translating and expounding with [perfect] ease, both words and sentences in the whole of Vergil's Aeneid, in selected orations of Cicero, and in the Greek testament. I testify that were it not for her sex, she would be considered fit to be admitted as a student . . . of Yale University."

New Haven Colony Historical Society, 114 Whitney Avenue. On view here is the patent model of the cotton gin that every schoolchild has always been taught was invented in 1793 by Eli Whitney. In fact, the idea for a machine that could strip the seeds from cotton balls came from Catherine Littlefield Greene, on whose Georgia plantation Eli was a guest. It was Catherine who provided the young schoolteacher with a basement room where he could tinker on the machine. She fed and encouraged him for six months until one day he showed her a crude model. Some historians concede that Catherine added the final touch to the cotton gin. Eli's model had no means for removing the separated lint, but Catherine instinctively added a tiny brush to the teeth of the machine, and the result is the model you see. Eli never did realize a financial profit from the cotton gin, but, more importantly, his name has been immortalized. Catherine Greene, the inspiration, financier, and perfector of the machine, has never made the history books.

Grave of Delia Bacon. Grove Street Cemetery. A simple tombstone marks the grave of the intellectually fearless woman who in 1857 wrote "The Philosophy of the Plays of Shakespeare Unfolded," a bold analysis that challenged the bard's authorship and concluded that it was Francis Bacon who masterminded those great literary works. (Francis was not a relative of Delia.) Delia was cruelly ridiculed for her interesting theory. She was also criticized for an ensuing romance with a Yale theologian ten years her junior. Although Catharine Beecher defended Delia's love affair in her essay "Truth Stranger than Fiction," and Ralph Waldo Emerson and Nathaniel Hawthorne at times supported her Shakespearean investigations, Delia had suffered too much. After a year in an insane asylum, she died at age forty-eight in 1859.

Troup Middle School, 259 Edgewood Avenue, was named in honor of Augusta Lewis Troup five years after her death in 1920. One of the founders, in 1868, of the New York Working Women's Association—with Susan B. Anthony and Elizabeth Cady Stanton—Troup labored for equal rights within the International Typographical Union whose first liberated move was to elect her their corresponding secretary in 1870. Years later, the union began to admit women as regular members. Troup also devoted much of her time and energy to help Italian immigrants in New Haven, earning the affectionate title of Little

Mother of the Italian Colony, which is inscribed along with other kind words on a plaque in the school's hallway.

Albertus Magnus College, 700 Prospect Street. The first Catholic residential liberal arts college for women in New England was founded by the Dominican Sisters in 1925, its purpose to "rear solid intellectuals and powerful characters of genuine refinement; and these are to become thinkers and leaders and the noble among ladihood of the future."

New London

Hempstead House, 11 Hempstead Street. Mulberry, chestnut, and maple trees shade the leaning chocolate-brown clapboard house, the oldest in New London, built about 1640. This was the twentieth-century home of poet Anna Hempstead Branch. Described as a "minor Christina Rossetti," Branch wrote many of her lyrical and mystical poems in this house. At her death in 1937, she was remembered by the townspeople as one of "God's Prophets of the Beautiful."

Norwalk

Yankee Doodle House, Mill Hill. According to popular tradition, when Elizabeth Fitch saw her brother Thomas heading off to the French and Indian War with a bunch of scraggly soldiers in mix-and-match uniforms, her sense of pageantry was outraged. "Soldiers should wear plumes!" she shouted, and she raided the chicken coops for a bunch of feathers which the men put in their caps. When the British army surgeon Dr. Shuckburgh saw the gaily dressed men arriving at Fort Cralo in Rensselaer, New York, he reportedly exclaimed, "Now stab my vitals, they're macaronis!" using the slang term of the day for "dandy." He then proceeded to write the snappy ditty that became the marching song of the Revolution. A replica of the Thomas Fitch home was under construction when we visited here, but the actual site is on East Avenue, dangerously close to the turnpike and overgrown with wild bushes.

Norwich

Sarah Knight House, Eight Elm Avenue (private). This white wooden house, with its double row of black shuttered windows, was the home and tavern of an adventurous woman who turned a business trip into history. In October 1702, when she was thirty-eight, Sarah Knight, who described herself as a widow, set out alone on horseback from Boston to New York. She kept a diary during the 271-mile journey through wild and unsettled countryside, along perilous roads, tottering bridges, and hazardous rivers—where few men would have dared traverse back then and where the Penn Central Railroad rumbles through today. Each entry in her anecdotal and humorous diary, which was not published until 1825, almost a century after her death, ends with a critical review of the food and lodgings she found in various taverns along the way. It may be the first travel guide in history, although Sarah seems to have encountered little better than half-a-star accommodations throughout her journey. She sharply criticized taverns that served fricassees "contrary to my notion of cooking"; meat that looked like "a twisted thing like a cable but something whiter"; and "barelegged punch" that had "so akward . . . rather awful a sound." She was appalled by rooms furnished "amongst other rubbish" with high beds that had "sad colored linens." Some incidents were just too horrid to write about, as boisterous male travelers with whom she shared rooms kept her awake all night with loud talk "not proper to be related by a female pen." After visiting New Haven and New York, Sarah returned to Boston in March 1705. In 1717, she purchased this house where until her death ten years later she kept "entertainment for travelers" in a tavern that no doubt had edible fricassees, soundless punches, low beds with clean linens, and genteel roommates.

Frances Caulkins Memorial. A marker on the other side of the village green pays tribute to the brilliant town historian, Frances Caulkins, whose scholarly work, published in 1845, brought her national fame. In 1849 Caulkins was elected to the Massachusetts Historical Society, the oldest historical society in the United States, as its first female member and its only woman for a century afterwards. One Albany historian said to Frances in later years, "I imagine there are few in our country, of either sex, whose opinion or accuracy in respect to the past is as good as yours." Her *History of New London,* seven hundred pages long, still stands as the definitive work about her hometown.

Charlotte Perkins Gilman House, 382 Washington Street (private). Freed at last from the terrible household chores that she so despised, the brilliant feminist author lived here from 1922–34 with her second husband (see *Hartford*). When she discovered she had breast cancer in 1932, Gilman purchased lethal chloroform, determined not to let herself be incapacitated by pain. She was able to continue her writing and lectures on "The Falsity of Freud," and she moved to California. When her suffering became unbearable, interfering with her lifework, she inhaled the ether that ended her pain in 1935.

Lydia Huntley Sigourney Home, 380 Washington Street (private). In this large, chestnut-colored house with its gambrel roof and four chimneys, the young poet—born here in 1791—nurtured her creative spirit, reading in the library of the widow Lathrop who employed Lydia's father as a caretaker. Recalling those happy early years, Sigourney wrote in a poem:

> My gentle kitten at my footstool sings
> Her song, monotonous and full of joy.
> Close by my side, my tender mother sits,
> Industriously bent—her brow still bright
> With beams of lingering youth, while he, the sire,
> The faithful guide, indulgently doth smile.

Lydia eventually moved to Hartford, launching her career as the town's "Sweet Singer" in 1811 with the publication of *Moral Pieces in Prose and Verse.* Her marriage to an unenlightened widower with three children—who insisted she busy herself with pots and pans instead of pens—interrupted her career for a while, but, when the family fortune dwindled, Mr. Sigourney suddenly became liberated, and he permitted his wife to be the sole wage earner. Critics characterized her sentimental and lofty poems as "more like dew than lightning," attributing the latter quality to the speed of her output. By the time of her death in 1865, Lydia had compiled more than 46 volumes of her writings as well as 2,000 magazine articles and 1,700 letters.

Old Lyme

Florence Griswold Home, Post Road. The gentle patron of the arts opened her stately old mansion to needy, aspiring artists. "Where," she argued, "could they find more congenial surroundings or richer material than in the lovely hills and shores and river valleys of Old Lyme?" Grateful boarders paid back her generosity by painting signatured masterpieces on panels, walls, and doors of the house. From 1900 until her death in 1937, "Miss Florence" maintained one of the finest summer art colonies in the country, and, today, impressionist paintings are on view by Willard Metcalfe, Childe Hassam, and others whom she encouraged, inspired, clothed, and fed.

Pleasant Valley

Site of Barkhamstead Lighthouse, People's State Forest, Route 181. A bronze plaque once marked the place where Molly Barber lived with her Indian husband Chaugham in the late 1700s, after eloping from her home in Wethersfield. Molly made her rough log cabin in the Narragansett Indian village of Barkhamstead as cozy as possible, filling the windows with lanterns. Sleepy stagecoach drivers, warmed by the sight of Molly's shining house, would call out to their equally weary passengers, "There's Barkhamstead Lighthouse; only five more miles to New Hartford!" Today, the plaque is gone. A granite marker in a large boulder at the edge of the winding road reads, "Site of an Indian Village," with no mention of Molly or her welcoming landmark that cheered lonely travelers more than two centuries ago.

Short Beach

Ella Wheeler Wilcox House, 105 Beckett Avenue (private). Bronze griffins guard the seaside entrance of this lovely house that was built by the celebrated poet as a summer residence in 1891. Dressed in diaphanous evening gowns, a chiffon scarf always in her hand or at her throat, romantic Ella, acclaimed as the Poet of Passion (see *Johnstown, Wisconsin*), welcomed the leading literary figures of the day for her costume balls, soirees, and musicales in rooms decorated with fishnets filled with champagne corks. The daughter of a dance teacher, Ella invented a step called the Ella Wheeler Wilcox glide, although a friend recalled that only Ella could perform "all those rococo turns and twists." But in the middle of all the partying, Ella would slip away to work in her room upstairs—"the poet's corner"—her desk, topped with a quart of ink, overlooking the sea. Expansive and enthusiastic, Ella lived life inspired by her own most memorable verse: "Laugh, and the world laughs with you; Weep, and you weep alone." When critics complained about the platitudes and sentimentality of her poems, Ella airily replied, "It is not art, but heart that wins the wide world over." The world mourned her death in 1919. Ella, who once unsuccessfully petitioned the U.S. Post Office to change the name of Short Beach to Granite Bay because she so loved the granite cliffs in the area, asked that her ashes be sealed in a granite boulder near the house.

South Killingly

Grave of Mary Dixon Kies, Town cemetery, Route 6. A clean white tablet honoring America's first female patent holder stands out among the old tombstones in this country cemetery. Mary was fifty-seven when in 1809 she received a patent for a straw-and-silk weaving machine. Her clever invention brought her fame—Dolley Madison sent her congratulations—but sadly, not much of a fortune. Her children tried to promote the technique, but by 1819 it was already outmoded by the invention of yet another ingenious woman in *Wethersfield*.

Waterbury

Caroline J. Welton Memorial Fountain, Central Green. One of the founders of the Humane Society of Connecticut, Welton left money in her will for this ornamental fountain that was erected in 1888. It is topped by a 2,500-pound bronze figure of her favorite horse, Knight. Welton, an enthusiastic sportswoman, was a familiar sight galloping through the streets of Waterbury on her black charger, no matter what the weather. But a Colorado snowstorm that erupted while she was mountain climbing was too much, causing her to have a fatal heart attack at age forty-two in 1884.

Westport

Lillian D. Wald House, "The House on the Pond," Compo Road (private). The founder of the Henry Street Settlement in *Manhattan, New York City,* bought this white country house surrounded by willow trees in 1917. Here, at the edge of the pond where Wald invited local children to ice-skate in the winter, such famed personages of the day as Albert Einstein and Jane Addams came to see the dedicated social worker. "I always fall under the spell of her personality," admitted Eleanor Roosevelt on one of her visits. In 1937, on the occasion of Wald's seventieth birthday, the citizens of Westport presented a picture book of her life at the House on the Pond, thanking her for making Westport "a better and happier place because you live here."

Wethersfield

Sophia Woodhouse Welles House, 538 Main Street (private). In this magnificent mid-eighteenth-century house that has a lovely view of a small inlet of the Connecticut River, an enterprising young woman perfected a method of using different varieties of grass to make fashionable bonnets and in 1821 was granted a patent for her invention. One of Sophia's creations, made from redtop and spear grass gathered from the riverbanks by her neighbors, won a prize of twenty guineas when it was exhibited at the Society of Arts in London. Louisa Adams, wife of the president, John Quincy, ordered several of these "Wethersfield" hats which John called "an extraordinary specimen of American Manufacturing." Several examples of the bonnets can be seen at the Old Academy Museum in town.

Female Seminary, 133 Main Street (private). Rev. Joseph Emerson started his school in this ruby red wooden house in the late 1820s. One of the twenty-six school regulations was that "young ladies . . . never indulge themselves in saying 'can't' or in any way expressing their inability to perform any exercise required." Mary Lyon, of *Buckland, Massachusetts,* was one of the first eager students.

DELAWARE

Cooch's Bridge

The only battle of the Revolutionary War fought on Delaware soil erupted here, September 3, 1777, as the British were marching northeast. Tradition has it that the new banner stitched up by Betsy Ross of *Philadelphia, Pennsylvania,* was unfurled here for the first time ever in battle.

Dover

Annie Jump Cannon House, 34 South State Street (private). Dover's favorite daughter is Annie Jump Cannon, world-renowned astronomer who learned her love of the stellar world by gazing first at the skies over Delaware. Born in this huge Victorian house December 11, 1863, she eagerly listened to her mother's stories of the constellations and planets, while they watched the stars from a trapdoor in the rooftop. In her first observatory, set up in the attic of the house, Annie made her first planetary identifications, later teaching herself the constellations from a chart in her mother's old astronomy book. She later recalled that her father worried lest her attic candle might set the house afire, "and it was a sigh of relief which he breathed when the evening vigil was over."

It was at this house, also, that Annie grew attracted to the prism, staring in fascination at the rainbows of light reflected through the glass drops in the family candelabrum. Much later, as a staff member of the Harvard Observatory, Annie employed the prismatic technique of telescopic photography and classified more than 400,000 stars, a monumental addition to the Henry Draper Catalog still used by modern astronomers. Her colleague, astronomer Harlow Shapley, said that Cannon's forty years as an astronomer had "enabled her to erect a scientific castle in which man's imagination long can dwell—a structure that probably will never be duplicated in kind or extent by a single individual."

Wesley Junior College, State and Cecil Streets, which Annie Jump Cannon attended when it was still Wilmington Conference Academy, has named a science building for their illustrious graduate; displayed are some of the bedroom furniture from her childhood. From here, the sixteen year old went to Wellesley College, where she studied calculus, observed the Great Comet of 1882 (with its 100-million-mile-long tail), and boycotted chocolate pudding with her classmates.

Delaware State Museum, 316 South Governors Avenue, has an exhibit dedicated to Annie Jump Cannon and the awards she received for important astronomical advances. You can see the cap and gown awarded her as the first woman to receive an honorary degree from Oxford University in 1925. (Britain had earlier made her the first woman—and second person—in its Royal Astronomical Society.) Here also is the Henry Draper Gold Medal she won in 1931 (as its first recipient) from the National Academy of Sciences, along with an assortment of academic hoods signifying honors from four universities. Deeply grateful for the prizes she received, and ever sensitive to the problems of women in science, Annie Jump Cannon donated her prize money to the American Astronomical Society to establish the triennial Annie J. Cannon Prize for an outstanding female astronomer.

Annie Jump Cannon Grave, Lakeside Cemetery, State Street, is marked by a characteristically modest stone. She died in 1941, aged seventy-seven, after more than four decades at the Har-

vard Observatory. At a simple memorial service, astronomer Harlow Shapley eulogized her "as a pure scientist, as an inspiring leader of women scholars, as a human companion . . . in each of her various personalities she was a resplendent example—an illustration in a world that needs comfort and inspiration of just how good mankind can be."

Patty Cannon's Skull, Dover Public Library, 45 South State Street. The only earthly remains of the notorious outlaw from *Reliance* rest in this scholarly hall—in a red wig box lined with red velvet. The library director told us that they take the skull out "for special occasions"—to show to schoolchildren, for instance. Patty Cannon was, after all, a part of Delaware history —a "bad but fascinating" part. (And no relation to Annie Jump.) The skull is on loan from a Georgetown resident whose uncle-by-marriage acquired the grisly relic when it was exhumed for reburial at the turn of the century. The library director pointed out that the soil and the years have taken their toll on Patty's skull. "It's been kind of deteriorating, but I can't get anyone to fix it up." she complained.

Leipsic

Rebecca Snow House, "Snowland," Route 42 (private). This typical sturdy old Delaware brick farmhouse on Little Duck Creek was named by builder Andrew Naudain for his wife, Rebecca Snow. It proved to be her memorial. In 1812, one month after she gave birth to her second son, Andrew, she died here.

Lewes

Fishers Paradise, 624 Pilot Town Road (private). This dormered, house was erected in 1725. The current owner assured us that the legend attached to it, which has for years tarnished the name of one Sarah Rowland, is entirely untrue. Contrary to popular gossip, the fabled postmaster's daughter did not try to intercept the mail of young Caesar Rodney in order to prevent him from riding to Philadelphia, Pennsylvania, to sign the Declaration of Independence. He traveled there by carriage and neatly penned his name. In fact, there may never have been a Sarah Rowland, insists the modern resident, "except in this absolutely false tale." Thus does another woman, however briefly or erroneously noted, fade back into obscurity.

Newark

University of Delaware opened its Women's College in 1914, after a vigorous campaign led by a concerned group of women. Their first resolution, signed in 1910, urged the formation of the college, since, among other reasons, the rates of divorce and infant mortality were decidedly lower among college-educated wives and mothers. Presumably, the all-male legislature could understand these things. By 1913, the women were circulating a pamphlet around the state reading, "Do you know that Delaware is the only State in the Union without some institution for the higher education of its young women?" That situation was ended in the fall term of 1914; today, the Women's College has been merged into the university. Several buildings are named for early women leaders: Robinson Hall, for Winifred Josephine Robinson, first dean of the Women's College; Emalea Pusey Warner Hall, the "guiding light" of the group that promoted the school; and Annie Jump Cannon Hall (see *Dover*).

Reliance

The notorious tavern—run by Lucretia ("Patty") Cannon and her son-in-law, Joe Johnson, in this border town in the 1820s— is long gone, a landmark that no decent citizen of Reliance was sorry to lose. By all accounts, the Canadian-born Patty Cannon was a bold and ruthless outlaw who murdered eleven persons (including her own husband), assisted in killing a dozen others, and led a gang that lured unsuspecting blacks into slavery. The kidnapped free Negroes would be hauled aboard slave ships in the nearby Nanticoke River and sold for duty in the South. Her tavern, a popular way station for slave dealers and more innocent voyagers, was the gang's headquarters, where hapless victims were buried in a secret cellar cave.

The shocking story of Patty Cannon's lurid crimes was finally disclosed in 1829 when she was detected by suspicious neighbors, convicted, and jailed. Three weeks before her scheduled execution, she cheated the hangman and swallowed poison, expiring, as one report put it, "in a most terrible and awful death." The skull of this ill-motivated woman can now be viewed at the Library in *Dover*.

Wilmington

Fort Christina, East Seventh Street and the Christina River, Fort Christina State Park. The first Swedish colonists to settle the state landed here in 1638, at a natural rocky wharf they named after Queen Christina, the young ruler of their country. They also named the river for her. She was an iconoclastic monarch who had herself crowned "king," then abdicated and found men's clothes more suitable to her new way of life.

Site of Elizabeth Shipley House, Fourth and Shipley Streets. The Wilmington campus of the Delaware Technical and Community College occupies the former home of the founders of this city. On a preaching trip in the early 1730s, Quaker minister Elizabeth Shipley rode across Old Brandywine Ford on horseback and saw the hilly landscape of the growing Swedish settlement. Instantly she recognized it as the subject of a recent dream, in which she had been instructed to settle this "new and fruitful land." Elizabeth persuaded her husband to join her, and they lived prosperously in the house they built on this location in 1735. Toward the end of her long and respected life, after the Battle of Brandywine in 1777, Elizabeth Shipley had another prescient vision: The invaders, she predicted, "shall be driven back," and "this nation will secure its independence."

Emily P. Bissell Hospital, 3000 Newport Gap Pike. The funds that made possible the original home for consumptives—Hope Farm—founded here in 1908 were raised by social welfare worker Emily P. Bissell. A year earlier, she hit on a scheme to raise money for treating tuberculosis: Christmas seals to sell for a penny apiece. When the original stamps sold only meagerly at the Wilmington Post Office, she embarked on a national campaign, finally, in 1907, netting about three thousand dollars. That figure multiplied more than fortyfold in 1908, and the anti-tuberculosis Christmas seal in America became an annual addition to the nation's Yuletide mail. The hospital, which opened with eight beds in 1908, was greatly expanded and named for its founder in the 1950s. Today, the administration building of the 200-bed center for treatment of TB and respiratory diseases stands on the site of the original building.

Wilmington has not yet memorialized one of its most remarkable daughters, Mary Ann Shadd Cary, born here in 1829. A mulatto child whose father's family, it is said, was never in slavery, she helped organize schools for blacks in Delaware and Pennsylvania, then went to Canada to help refugees fleeing the Fugitive Slave Act of 1851. There Mary Ann Shadd Cary earned her nickname—the Rebel—for her forthright editorship of the weekly newspaper, the *Provincial Freeman*. She helped found it in 1854 and quickly set its bold policies as a voice for Canadian blacks, thus becoming the first black newspaper editor in North America. Her paper's motto: "Self-Reliance is the True Road to Independence." An editorial in Frederick Douglass's paper, the *North Star,* commended her "unceasing industry . . . unconquerable zeal and commendable ability." Back in the States, Mary Ann Shadd Cary also championed the suffrage cause, telling an 1878 convention in Washington, D.C., that black women would support whatever political party would allow them their rights.

DISTRICT of COLUMBIA

U.S. CAPITOL BUILDING

The Suffrage Monument, first floor crypt. The nation's first statue to women, by a woman, for women's service to women, was dedicated February 15, 1921—Susan B. Anthony's birthday, a year after the suffrage amendment she wrote was passed. But sculptor Adelaide Johnson's eight-ton marble block with portrait heads of Anthony, Elizabeth Cady Stanton, and Lucretia Mott has been subjected to the same kinds of controversy these women endured during their lives. At first one male senator withheld approval because, he said, "The impression it makes is that the subjects are buried alive." Then, in 1922, someone with distinct antifeminist sentiments dipped a brush in yellow paint and obliterated the tributory words on the stone. Today the white marble shines brilliantly in this slightly hidden spot. And a modest wall plaque calls the figures "pioneers of the women's suffrage movement." Unfortunately, some guides still coyly refer to the three busts on their roughhewn base as the "Ladies in the Bathtub."

Frances Willard Statue, Statuary Hall. The first female member of the all-male bronze and marble club in Statuary Hall made her debut here in 1905, the gift of her home state. In 1864, each state was authorized to place in this gallery two statues of famous citizens. For nearly fifty years, that was interpreted as "famous sons"—until Illinois decided to honor the famed feminist and WCTU leader from *Evanston, Illinois.* For more than another fifty years, Willard remained the only woman in the hall, a dignified white marble figure in a prim high-necked dress, sculpted by Helen Farnsworth Mears.

Maria Sanford Statue, Senate connecting corridor north of Statuary Hall. Minnesota presented the second statue of a woman in 1958, a seven-foot stylized bronze of the pioneer educator and civic leader as she looked when she was striding

across the University of Minnesota campus (at *Minneapolis, Minnesota*) where she taught for thirty years. Sculptor Evelyn Raymond unveiled the monument at ceremonies attended by nearly five hundred Minnesotans, who recalled Maria Sanford as the state's "apostle of culture." The inscription on the base calls her "the best known and best loved woman in Minnesota."

Dr. Florence Rena Sabin Statue, Statuary Hall. The third female likeness to enter the grand gallery came from Colorado in 1959. Joy Buba sculpted the noted scientist from *Denver, Colorado,* in bronze, perched on her lab stool with her microscope handy. At dedication ceremonies February 26, 250 guests honored the pioneering researcher and public health reformer, and they heard a telegram from President Eisenhower in which he called her one who "helped to make this earth a better place for all to live." A former student of hers at Johns Hopkins in *Baltimore, Maryland,* said, "She was zippy."

Esther Morris Statue, Statuary Hall vestibule. Wyoming's contribution to the seven statues of women in the Capitol is a tall, spirited bronze of Esther Hobart Morris, who helped make Wyoming the "first government in the world to grant women equal rights." The nation's first female voters (see *South Pass City, Wyoming*) further celebrated Morris by inscribing on the marble base, "A grateful people honors this stalwart pioneer, who also became the first woman justice of the peace." For the all-weather, outdoor version of this statue, see *Cheyenne, Wyoming.*

Be sure to check the locations of all statues, as some have recently been repositioned. Do not neglect the other figures in Statuary Hall just because they depict men. Some have been sculpted by noted female artists.

Anne Whitney (see *Boston, Massachusetts*) created the fine, sturdy marble of Samuel Adams with his arms crossed and his wigged head facing squarely across the hall.

Elisabet Ney (see *Austin, Texas*) carved the statues of her state's two heroes, Stephen Austin and Sam Houston. The tiny (about five feet tall) Austin is in the small House Rotunda just north of Statuary Hall, gracefully dressed in a fringed leather coat. Houston is similarly attired and stands just inside Statuary Hall. Ney made him stand proud and tall, a blanket slung casually over his shoulder. When Washington officials complained that Houston was too tall and Austin too short, Elisabet Ney replied, "God made the two men. I merely reproduced their likenesses."

Belle Kinney sculpted John Sevier, the first governor of Tennessee (see *Nashville, Tennessee*). Blanche Nevil did Peter Muhlenberg. Nellie Verne Walker (see *Keokuk, Iowa*) did Senator James Harlan. And Vinnie Ream created the portly bronze figure of Samuel J. Kirkwood of Iowa and the statue of Sequoyah of Oklahoma, although she is best known for a much larger statue in the Rotunda of the Capitol.

Statue of Abraham Lincoln, west entrance of the Rotunda. The famous life-sized marble of the pensive president was the work of Vinnie Ream, a seventeen-year-old sculptor whose eagerness to produce a likeness of the sensitive leader deeply touched Lincoln. "So she's young and poor is she," he said. "Well, that's nothing agin' her. You may tell her she can come." And so, starting in 1864, the young artist sketched the kind president during half-hour sessions for five months, capturing his moods as he dealt with the waning days of the Civil War. They turned out to be the waning days of his life, as well. The bust she did was so well received that Vinnie Ream was commissioned to do a life study—the first time a woman had received a federal art commission. It earned her ten thousand dollars and opened the way for other female artists. She selected the white Carrara marble herself, and her sculpture was placed here in 1871. (See *Arlington, Virginia*.)

Mary McLeod Bethune Memorial, Lincoln Park, Thirteenth and East Capitol streets. The first statue to a black woman to stand in a public park in the nation's capital was dedicated July 10, 1974, the ninety-ninth anniversary of the birth of the distinguished educator (see *Daytona Beach, Florida*). The large bronze group faces a century-old monument of Abraham Lincoln with a freed slave—across the park—a statue that was repositioned so that Lincoln's back would not be to Bethune. The Bethune likeness is seventeen feet high, a corpulent figure with a broad, beaming face. Her outstretched hand passes her legacy to two young children, the words of her last will and testament now inscribed around the base of the monument: "I leave you love. I leave you hope . . . I leave you racial dignity . . ." (See *Mayesville, South Carolina*.)

Nuns of the Battlefield Monument, Rhode Island Avenue and M Street, NW. On a bronze relief panel set into stone, twelve nuns from as many orders represent the wide array of "Sisters who gave their services as nurses on battlefields and in hospitals during the Civil War." The panel is flanked by two bronze figures: the helmeted male angel representing Patriotism and the female Angel of Peace.

New York City, created this towering monument to the men who died on the *Titanic* nineteen years earlier. Gertrude Whitney lost her own brother on the *Lusitania* when it was sunk by the Germans in 1915.

Statue of Admiral David G. Farragut, Farragut Square, K Street between Sixteenth and Seventeenth Streets, NW. With a federal commission of more than twenty thousand dollars, sculptor Vinnie Ream executed this first capital statue to a naval war hero. The popular young artist began her work on the heroic bronze at the Washington Navy Yard before she was thirty years old. She cast the statue from the bronze of the propeller of the U.S.S. *Hartford,* the flagship of Farragut's Union fleet. While working on the statue, Vinnie Ream met and married Lt. Richard Hoxie, a naval staff officer. However, she lost no time from her sculpting. They lived in a handsome house facing Farragut Square.

Statue of Joan of Arc, Meridian Hill Park, Sixteenth Street and Florida Avenue, NW. The women of France presented this bronze likeness of the heroine of Orleans to the women of America in 1922. The original is at Rheims Cathedral in France.

National Woman's Party Headquarters, 144 Constitution Avenue, NE. This historic three-story brick mansion across the

Future Statue, National Archives Building, Pennsylvania Avenue facade. The twelve-foot figure to the left of the entrance here is an allegorical representation of a female—draped in nondescript neoclassical robes. An open book rests on her lap, and several manuscripts are in her hand. The caption, "What is past is prologue," makes it one of the best federal efforts we know of to support the study of women's history.

Titanic Memorial, Washington Channel Park, Fourth and F Streets, SW. In 1931, sculptor Gertrude Whitney of *Manhattan,*

street from the Capitol has, since 1929, been home to the once-militant arm of the women's movement. The National Woman's Party was founded in the spring of 1913 as the Congressional Union, its one purpose the passage of the federal suffrage amendment. Its fiery founder (and current honorary chairman) was Alice Paul, a New Jersey Quaker whose experience with British suffrage demonstrations, and a stint in jails there, influenced her strategy on this side of the Atlantic. She was responsible for the 10,000-woman suffrage demonstration on March 3, 1913, the day before Woodrow Wilson's inauguration. It was a parade at which "women were spat upon, slapped in the face, tripped up, pelted with burning cigar stubs and insulted by jeers and obscene language too vile to print or repeat," reported a feminist newspaper. Later, this party began a year-and-a-half vigil in front of the White House. One banner pleaded, "How long must we wait, Mr. President?" and one proclaimed, "We demand an amendment to the United States Constitution enfranchising Women." This banner now decorates the first-floor landing of the party headquarters.

introduced the play to America seven years earlier. When the bullets were fired, it was the London-born lead actress who pleaded with the audience "to have the presence of mind and keep your places and all will be well." She also cradled the dying president's head until he was moved across the street.

Willard Hotel, Pennsylvania Avenue. In 1861, abolitionist and poet Julia Ward Howe (see *Boston, Massachusetts*) stayed here after a daylong visit to inspect Massachusetts troops at a

Today the National Woman's Party claims sixty thousand members and also houses Adelaide Johnson's marble busts of women's leaders. You will find the red-velvet upholstered chair that eased the hardworking Elizabeth Cady Stanton; a portrait of Alice Paul that gazes down from one wall; and, in the California Room, an inspiring painting of Inez Milholland (see *Lewis, New York*) astride her white horse as she led the notorious 1913 suffrage parade.

American Red Cross National Headquarters, Seventeenth and Eighteenth Streets, between D and E Streets, NW. The building is dedicated to the women of the Civil War, one of whom was Clara Barton, who founded and first ran the Red Cross organization in this country (see *North Oxford, Massachusetts; Dansville, New York*). Among the items preserved in a basement museum here are a trunk she carted to the front lines of the Civil War; a letter from Florence Nightingale; and a poster advertising a lecture by "Clara Barton, the Heroine of Andersonville."

Jane Delano Monument, in the garden behind the Red Cross Building, honors the founder and first director of the Red Cross Nursing Service. Despite great opposition, Jane Delano insisted on maintaining high standards by including only professionally trained nurses. The idealistic statue, however, represents all nurses, her arms outstretched beneath a draped uniform. (See *Arlington, Virginia.*)

Ford's Theater, Tenth Street, NW, between E and F Streets. *Our American Cousin,* the play Lincoln was watching when he was shot here on April 14, 1865, was produced by Laura Keene (see *Baltimore, Maryland*), an actress and theatrical manager who

nearby army camp. That night, she could not sleep, and, as she later reported in the *Atlantic Monthly,* "the long lines of the . . . poem began to twine themselves in my mind. . . . I said to myself, I must get up and write these verses down, lest I fall asleep again and forget them. . . . I scrawled the verses almost without looking at the paper." Several months later, the poem was published in the *Atlantic's* issue of February 1862, for a payment of four dollars. Almost immediately, "The Battle Hymn of the Republic," sung to the tune of "John Brown's Body," became a Union-wide success. Lincoln is said to have wept when he heard it.

In March 1883, this hotel was the scene of the celebrated wedding between Baby Doe and Senator Horace A. W. Tabor (see *Leadville, Colorado*). President Arthur attended the social event, to which Baby Doe wore an elegant gown now preserved at the State Historical Society in Denver, Colorado. The costly wedding was held here because a delegation of congressional wives, scandalized by the senator's second wedding, refused to attend at the White House.

Daughters of the American Revolution, National Society Headquarters, 1776 D Street, NW. A memorial by Gertrude Whitney to the four founders of this organization—Eugenia Washington, Mary Desha, Ellen Hardin Walworth (see *Jacksonville, Illinois*), and Mary Smith Lockwood (see *Elizabeth, New Jersey*)—stands in an adjacent garden. In many states, only the research of DAR chapters has kept the memory of countless heroines alive. In her recent book, *The Daughters,* author Peggy Anderson tries to sum up the contribution of the organization: " 'I think,' says Sarah Casey, a political liberal and an inactive Daughter, 'that if they ever try to tear down Independence Hall, the DAR is who's going to stop them.' I think Sarah Casey is absolutely right. The Daughters probably wouldn't be the only Americans to cast their bodies in front of the bulldozers, but they would quite likely be the first there and the last to leave."

SMITHSONIAN INSTITUTION
National Air Museum owns the Lockheed Vega monoplane that Amelia Earhart piloted across the Atlantic in 1932; however, it is not currently on view in its "assembled but not restored" condition. This was the record-breaking vehicle that made Earhart

the first female to solo across the ocean (see *Harrison, New York*). It is also the plane that she piloted in the first Women's Air Derby in 1929. Later, fitted out with a 500-horsepower Wasp engine at Teterboro Airport in New Jersey, it easily cruised the Atlantic.

Museum of History and Technology is worth a visit under any circumstances, but particularly to see the original Star-Spangled Banner on the second floor. This giant fifteen-star flag, overwhelming in size and sense of history, hangs dramatically in the alcove known as Flag Hall. Mary Pickersgill (see *Baltimore, Maryland*) made the forty-two-foot banner in 1813, and it flew over Fort McHenry during the British attack in September 1814. This is the flag whose "broad stripes and bright stars" Francis Scott Key noted were "still there" the next morning, inspiring him to write the poem that became the national anthem. Souvenir-hunters tore off the lower section of Mrs. Pickersgill's flag years ago; today, it is protected from human mutilation by law, and by a guard rail.

Descend one floor to the Hall of Medicine to see Linda Richards' uniform, worn by a mannequin in a reconstructed ward of Massachusetts General Hospital as it looked in the 1870s. Linda Richards is acknowledged as the nation's first professionally trained nurse (see *Roxbury, Massachusetts*). Her uniform is a prim high-necked bodice topped by a floor-length white apron.

Scheduled to be on view for the museum's special bicentennial exhibition is a prized relic of the suffrage movement: the round mahogany tea table on which the Declaration of Principles was written for the first woman's rights convention in *Seneca Falls, New York,* in 1848. The table stood for years in the parlor of Mary Ann McClintock, who helped write the revolutionary trea-

tise at *Waterloo, New York*. Then, at the urging of feminist Helen Hamilton Gardner (see *Ithaca, New York*), it was included in the Smithsonian's collection where a museum specialist admits it is now "one of our treasures." Other similar treasures: Susan B. Anthony's famous red shawl, and the gold pen that signed the woman suffrage amendment.

District of Columbia Teachers College, 1100 Harvard Street, NW, is the descendant of the Normal School for Colored Girls, founded in 1851 by New Yorker Myrtilla Miner. The first school to train young black girls as teachers, it was the target of continuing bigotry—fires, racial slurs, mob violence. Yet it endured, growing from six pupils to forty, and gaining financial aid from such abolitionists as Harriet Beecher Stowe, who contributed one thousand dollars from the royalties of *Uncle Tom's Cabin*. But most of the backbone came from Myrtilla Miner herself, who shunned her frail health, stood up, and declared, "There is no law to prevent my teaching these people, and I *shall* teach them, even unto death." She maintained the school until 1860; later it became the Miner Teachers College, then in 1955 was merged to become the D.C. Teacher's College.

Washington College of Law, Nebraska and Massachusetts Avenues (American University), was founded in 1898 by Ellen Spencer Mussey and Emma Gillett, two successful Washington lawyers who had been refused admission to other capital law schools because "women did not have the mentality for law." Ellen Mussey became its first dean—and the first woman in the world to hold such a post—guiding the coeducational school through a period that brought it high prestige and wide acceptance. When Mussey retired in 1913, Emma Gillett took over the job, strengthening the school's stature even further. Ellen Mussey did not restrict her activities to the school. She wrote the law that gave D.C. mothers equal rights and authority over their children and that gave women control of their own property and financial interests. Just before she died in 1936, Mussey told a reporter, "We said ladies then and we said lady lawyers, but I think woman is a beautiful word, and probably less stilted than lady."

Howard University. An absence of barriers because of sex or race made this school a mecca for female and black lawyers in the late 1800s. Emma Gillett attended night school here. Charlotte Ray, the first woman to practice law in the capital and the first black woman admitted to the bar, received her degree from Howard Law School in 1872, after graduating from Myrtilla Miner's school earlier. The *Woman's Journal* reported that she was "a dusky mulatto" and that she possessed "quite an intelligent countenance." Biographer Phebe Ann Hanaford added, "She doubtless has also a fine mind and deserves success."

Black sculptor Edmonia Lewis' *Born Free* is displayed at the Fine Arts Building. And several dormitories are named for women active in black causes.

Trinity College, Michigan and Franklin Streets, NE. This school, the first national Catholic college for women, was founded in

1900 by Sister Julia McGroarty, a determined educator who watched young women being rejected from the nearby all-male Catholic University. Despite objections to Rome from traditionalists that the school might be coeducational (it would not) and that women should not receive higher education (they should), Sister Julia persevered, enrolling twenty-two women during the first academic year. Today, enrollment stands at about seven hundred. When a recent president, Sister Margaret Claydon, took her post in 1959, she was, at age thirty-six, the youngest college president in the country.

CONGRESSIONAL CEMETERY, Eighteenth and E Streets
Anne Newport Royall Grave, site 194, range 26. In 1911, "a few men from Philadelphia and Washington" erected this memorial stone "in appreciative recognition" of the journalist and adventurer who died in 1854. A pioneering traveler and writer who supported herself with the tales of her wanderings, Anne Royall became a powerful crusading Washington newspaperwoman, publishing her own papers, *Paul Pry* and *The Huntress.* She is popularly, although erroneously, credited with sitting on the clothing of President John Quincy Adams, while he was skinny-dipping in the Potomac, until he granted her an interview. Anne Royall didn't need to use such tactics. She interviewed thirteen presidents, including John Quincy Adams, who called her "a virago errant in enchanted armor." Despite her lively, accomplished career, she died a pauper at age eighty-five. This stone, erected belatedly, quotes the last words she used in closing her newspaper, *The Huntress,* in the pre–Civil War era: "I pray that the union of these states may be eternal." (See *Sweet Springs, West Virginia.*)

ANNE ROYALL
PIONEER WOMAN PUBLICIST
1769 —— 1854
"I PRAY THAT THE UNION OF
THESE STATES MAY BE ETERNAL"

Belva Ann Lockwood Grave, site 296, range 78. The first woman admitted to practice law before the Supreme Court of the United States (in 1879 after a five-year struggle) shares a headstone with the family of her daughter. Belva Lockwood took her law degree from the new National University Law School after being turned down by Columbian College (later George Washington University) because "her presence would distract the attention of the [male] students." She was instrumental in bills giving equal pay to female government employees and in securing more property rights for married women in the District. After supporting Victoria Woodhull, the first female candidate for president, Mrs. Lockwood ran for the office herself on the Equal Rights Party ticket in 1884 and 1888, becoming the first woman to run as a major party candidate. She won 4,449 votes the first time. She also attended every suffrage convention in Washington from 1870 to 1900. She once wrote, "I do not believe in sex distinction in literature, law, politics, or trade; or that modesty and virtue are more becoming to women than to men; but wish we had more of it everywhere."

Grave of Marion Ooletia Kahlert, near the Seventeenth Street gate. A grim distinction enabled this ten-year-old girl in high-button shoes and lace-collared dress to be memorialized in marble. She was the first person to die in an automobile accident in Washington, D.C., in 1904.

Marian Adams Monument, Rock Creek Cemetery, Rock Creek Church Road and Webster Street, NW, is so popular with visitors that it is located on the cemetery map. Henry Adams commissioned sculptor Augustus Saint-Gaudens to memorialize his wife—a pioneering photographer as well as the hostess of cultural salons in Boston and Washington, D.C.—whose tragic suicide at age forty-two in 1885 ended her brilliant career. The bronze figure, hooded, contemplative, and peaceful, seated against the wall of an outdoor sanctuary designed by architect Stanford White, is popularly known as *Grief.*

Mabel Boardman Memorial, crypt, Chapel of Joseph of Arimathea, Washington Cathedral, Mount Saint Alban, Wisconsin and Massachusetts avenues, NW. A plaque marks the grave of the woman who ran the Red Cross from 1905 to 1915. Distressed by Clara Barton's growing disorder in handling organization business (she said the founder still ran it as if it were the small group she began), Mabel Boardman outmaneuvered Barton for the leadership of the American Red Cross and turned it into a prestigious national force.

FLORIDA

Apalachicola

Sarah Orman House, Fifth Street (private). Ardent secessionist Sarah Orman used the roof of this two-story frame house as a signal post for Confederate troops returning to Apalachicola during the Civil War. If Union soldiers were in town, she dragged a large keg atop the house to warn the boys returning home on furlough.

Cross Creek

Marjorie Kinnan Rawlings House, Route 325. At an old wooden table on the screened front porch, Marjorie Kinnan Rawlings wrote her Pulitzer Prize–winning novel, *The Yearling,* in 1939. Its vivid description of a young boy's growth in the big scrub country of what is now the Ocala National Forest was just one of her many works depicting the people and places of Cross Creek. The land and its natives inspired Marjorie Rawlings from the day she first glimpsed Florida. "Let's sell everything and move South," she urged her husband impulsively. "How we could write!" That is precisely what she did in 1928, moving into this rambling "Cracker" farmhouse on a sunny citrus grove that was surrounded by lavish birds and deep swampland. But along with the excitement, her first view of the three low buildings connected by porches and bridgeways gave her "some terror, such as one feels in the first recognition of a human love, for the joining of person to place, as of person to person, is a commitment of shared sorrow, even as to shared joy." Marjorie Rawlings shared all her emotions and created her finest works while living here; when she died in 1953, her body was buried on the grounds. Today the house has been restored and furnished with the author's own cowhide chairs and coffee table, and an old wooden stove like the one she used. Some of the trees and shrubs she wrote about with great enthusiasm for the verdant tropics are being planted in front of the house.

Daytona Beach

Bethune-Cookman College, Second Avenue between McLeod and Lincoln Streets. On October 3, 1904 in a shabby four-room cottage, her little son the only boy among five girls, Mary McLeod Bethune opened her school, using the charred splinters of logs as pencils, mashed elderberries for ink, a packing case for a desk, and cornsacks filled with Spanish moss as mattresses for her growing number of boarders. Within two years, she had 250 pupils. With money raised from selling sweet-potato pies and ice cream she bought a nearby dumping ground called Hell's Hole. Buildings sprouted with regularity through generous donations of prominent millionaires whose names Bethune picked out of the papers for a personal fund-raising plea. She concentrated most of her teaching efforts on women —"I felt that they especially were hampered by lack of educational opportunities"—but in 1922 her school merged with Cookman College, the first in the state for the higher education of black males. In the early 1940s, as president of the combined college, which had more than a dozen modern buildings and an enrollment of sixteen hundred, she wrote, "When I walk through the campus, with its stately palms and well-kept lawns, and think back to the dump-heap foundation, I rub my eyes and pinch myself. And I remember my childish visions in the cotton fields." (See *Mayesville, South Carolina; Washington, D.C.*)

Fernandina Beach

The multinational founders of one of the oldest communities in the state chose an egalitarian method of paying tribute to various women in their lives. Amelia Island was named by British soldiers for the beautiful young sister of King George II of England. Spanish warriors, we are told, named Ladies Street for the women who resided there in order to be geographically convenient to the nearby fort.

Fort George Island

Anna Jai House, Kingsley Plantation, Route A1A. This two-story whitewashed building made of frame and tabby (a rare mixture of lime, oyster shell, water, and sand) was the residence of Anna Madgigaine Jai, a Senegalese princess married to plantation owner Zephaniah Kingsley. The wealthy slave trader met the tall, dignified Anna Jai while he was on a buying trip in Africa. Instead of buying her, he married her, at a wedding that took place in Africa according to tribal custom. But tribal custom on this side of the Atlantic would not allow them to live in the same house, so Anna Jai was given this dwelling of her own on the large estate. It is connected to the main house by a covered walkway. Increasing social pressure finally forced Kingsley to move his wife and four children to a plantation in

Haiti, where Anna, as Kingsley told abolitionist Lydia Maria Child, "was very capable and could carry on all the affairs of the plantation in my absence." Eager to protect her from the provincialism of a biased public, he wrote in his will that since he did not "know in what light the law may consider my acknowledged wife, Anna Madgigaine Jai . . . yet she has always been respected as my wife and as such I acknowledge her, nor do I think that her truth, honor, integrity, moral conduct or good sense will lose in comparison to anyone."

Fort Pierce

Zora Neale Hurston Grave, Garden of the Heavenly Rest, Seventeenth Street. When novelist and anthropologist Zora

Neale Hurston died at the Welfare Home here in 1960 at the age of fifty-two, the newspapers said she died in poverty and obscurity. That was also how she began life, but not how she lived it. Born in 1908 in tiny Eatonville, then the only incorporated black town in Florida, she later became the first black recipient of a scholarship from Barnard College. Her long string of best-selling books, including *Tell My Horse* and the autobiographical *Dust Tracks on a Road,* made her a famed literary star of the 1930s and 1940s with an income that rose and fell accordingly. She is credited with dubbing Senator Robert A. Taft "Mr. Republican" in an article she wrote for the *Saturday Evening Post.* Once she turned up as a maid in Miami Beach, saying she took the job to "shift gears." "A writer has to stop writing every now and then and just live a little," she explained and said she was collecting material for a proposed magazine article on the nation's domestic help. The grave of one of Florida's few native-born writers was not marked until 1973, when author Alice Walker made a pilgrimage to the weed-covered cemetery and ordered this plain gray marker erected atop her burial site. It reads: Zora Neale Hurston, "A Genius of the South," Novelist, Folklorist, Anthropologist. Walker chose the phrase, "A genius of the South," from a poem by Jean Toomer. She also located Hurston's house at 1734 School Court Street here in Fort Pierce, but discovered that most of her current neighbors along the unpaved road never heard of the author who had lived there. That is not true of the minister who spoke at Zora Neale Hurston's funeral, which was paid for by dozens of contributions: "The Miami paper said she died poor. But she died rich. She did something."

Mandarin

Site of Harriet Beecher Stowe Memorial, Church of Our Savior. In this tiny one-room chapel that stood on the banks of the St. Johns River, a stained-glass window—paid for with donations from her fans all over the country—gave tribute to the author of *Uncle Tom's Cabin* and her family. The Tiffany Studios in New York executed the magnificent window design, showing a sunset over the river, glimpsed through the moss-covered branches of a live oak—the tree Stowe loved so much. Harriet Beecher Stowe attended services at this church when she started spending her winters in Florida in 1868. Although their house on thirty acres of the Fairbank Grant burned down some time ago, a marker on the Community Building points out that "The move to Florida was due to plans for philanthropy among the Negroes and a desire to benefit her son's health." The best-selling author wrote sketches called "Palmetto Leaves" and "Our Plantation" here, making her a popular attraction for tourists who left their steamers at the river port and filed past her desk to watch her work. (See *Brunswick, Maine; Hartford, Connecticut.*)

Miami

Site of Julia Tuttle House, Lummus Park. The barracks of old

Fort Dallas, now the center of downtown Miami, once sheltered a cow belonging to Julia De Forest Sturtevant Tuttle, one of the earliest and most farsighted landowners of this popular resort city. In 1870, when it was a desolate wilderness, Julia Tuttle purchased 640 acres on the north side of the Miami River from the Bay Biscayne Company. Her pioneering neighbor across the river was Mary Brickell, a businesswoman with a fine reputation who resembled Queen Victoria and generously never foreclosed on a mortgage. The two clever property owners and town promoters led one historian to call the Miami River flowing between them "the river of the mothers."

With Mary Brickell managing the south side, Julia Tuttle planted her fertile fields on the north with juicy oranges, rich vegetables, leafy palms, and fragrant flowers. Her agricultural skills were so adept that her orange blossoms remained unwithered by frost during the severe freeze of 1894–95. With those hardy blooms and her own artful persuasion, in 1895 she helped convince developer Henry M. Flagler to extend his railroad from Palm Beach to the southern part of the state. Julia even transported him to Fort Dallas in a buckboard and deeded him half her holdings so that he could lay out the city of Miami. "This country has wonderful possibilities," Flagler admitted. Tuttle, who opened his eyes to the commercial possibilities of southern Florida, had even bigger plans, once writing, "It is the dream of my life to see this wilderness turned into a prosperous country and where this tangled mass of vine brush, trees and rocks now are to see homes with modern improvements surrounded by beautiful grassy lawns, flowers, shrubs and shade trees." Today, Julia Tuttle Causeway, the thoroughfare named for her, leads to them all.

Amelia Earhart Monument, Miami International Airport. A bronze plaque in the lobby near the main terminal entrance

was dedicated twenty-five years after the ill-fated around-the-world flight that originated from Miami on June 1, 1937. At four minutes before six that morning, Amelia Earhart climbed into

the cockpit of her Lockheed Electra (see *Lafayette, Indiana*) with her navigator, Fred Noonan, and took off into the cloudless sky. The proposed 27,000-mile route took them to Puerto Rico, Brazil, then across Africa, Asia, and the South Pacific. On July 2, 1937 the plane was lost in the South Pacific somewhere near Howland Island. Neither Noonan nor Earhart was ever found. A lighthouse named for her on that tiny atoll commemorates the unfinished trip of the first woman to try to circle the globe by air. The marker at the Miami airport bears her likeness, flanked by Noonan and the plane. The actual point of departure—old Miami Municipal Airport, later renamed Amelia Earhart Field—is currently used by the city of Hialeah as a vehicle-maintenance yard.

Osprey

Site of Bertha Honoré Palmer House, "The Oaks," Tamiami Trail. The remarkable Bertha Palmer of *Chicago, Illinois,* spent the last eight years of her life in an energetic campaign that helped develop the west coast of Florida. "Here is heaven at last," she said of Sarasota Bay. In 1910 she acquired the first of what would total some eighty thousand acres near Sarasota; then she set to remodeling the existing house, naming it the Oaks. Unhesitatingly she threw herself into her latest project— ranching and farming with cattle and citrus in a vast agricultural development. As the wooded land was cleared and the experts were called in, she plunged into exploring and enjoying her Florida investment. She entertained her grandchildren against a backdrop of Monets, speedboats, and fresh-grown grapefruits. She sparked the economy and encouraged civic reforms. And, although not all of her schemes succeeded, so many did so well that by the time she died here in 1918, she could leave a multimillion-dollar inheritance to her family and friends. After a brief period as a tourist attraction, the Oaks was razed, but the house one of her sons lived in, Immokalee (private), still stands.

Pensacola

Dorothy Walton House, 221 East Zaragoza Street. This one-story frame house with its unusual twin chimneys is known by local residents as "the house of the illustrious ladies." One of the first was the fiercely independent Dorothy Camber Walton. Against her Tory father's wishes, she married Revolutionary leader George Walton of Georgia and found herself instantly disinherited. She further charted her own course by refusing to

return to England when war broke out. Instead, she embraced the colonists' cause and was rewarded for her loyalty when her husband signed the Declaration of Independence. Dorothy Walton moved here in about 1822, to live with her son and his family. In the restored living room, she is said to have entertained Rachel and Andrew Jackson and dozens of other Floridians as noted as herself.

Another "illustrious lady," Dorothy Walton's granddaughter, Octavia Walton Le Vert (see *Mobile, Alabama*), described a part of the house when it faced the bay (before it was moved to its present location): "orange and live oak trees shading the broad veranda; the fragrant acacia, oleander and cape jasmine trees which filled the parterre leading down to the beach."

St. Augustine

Henry James once said that Constance Fenimore Woolson's sketches of Florida were her best literary works. Indeed, Woolson's vivid impressions of the Florida that existed in the late nineteenth century (see *Winter Park)* are remarkable. Following is her description of St. Augustine, which she called East Angels in a novel of the same name: "Great trees rose here, extending their straight boughs outward as far as they could reach, touching nothing but the golden air. For each stood alone, no neighbor near; each was a king. Black on the ground beneath lay the round mass of shadow they cast. Above, among the dense dark foliage, shone out occasional spots of a lighter green; and this was the mistletoe. Besides these monarchs there were sinuous lines of verdure, eight and ten feet in height, wandering with grace over the plain. Most of the space, however, was free—wide, sunny glades open to the sky."

Tallahassee

Catherine Murat House, "Bellevue," Big Bend Farm (adjacent to the Junior Museum). Widowed by her extravagant husband, Prince Achille Murat, Napoleon's nephew, Princess Catherine Murat built this modest story-and-a-half house which was then located several miles west of Tallahassee. A generous gift from the French Empire helped erase most of her debts. Then she threw herself into public service, helping to raise three thousand dollars for the purchase of Mount Vernon (see *Mount Vernon, Virginia*), home of her distant ancestor George Washington. Catherine Murat also shored up the Confederate cause, supplying money and food. She firmly declared her Southern sympathies by firing the cannon from the capitol steps, thus announcing Florida's secession from the Union.

Tampa

The only woman who achieved some fame among the handful who landed in Tampa Bay in 1541 with de Soto's expedition was Francisca Hinestrosa, wife of warrior Fernando Bautista. She stayed with the Conquistadores for two years, until she died in a fire set by Indians at the village de Soto had taken from them. One history book reports that the fearless Francisca, who was pregnant, perished when she returned to her hut to rescue her pearls.

Winter Park

Woolson House, Rollins College. This small shrine erected by her niece contains letters and memorabilia of author Constance Fenimore Woolson (see *Mackinac Island, Michigan*), who spent several years in Florida during the late 1800s. One of the first American writers of the "local color" school, she wrote novels that one critic said "dominated the American fiction" of the 1880s. Most of her time in the state was spent in *St. Augustine,* which she wrote about in 1886. Over the doorway to this building, where advanced English classes also meet, is inscribed, "The Dean of Florida Writers."

GEORGIA

Andersonville

Clara Barton Memorial, Andersonville National Cemetery. One of Clara Barton's major activities during the Civil War was to help identify war dead and missing, an undertaking that required strict organization and considerable patience. With the help of a young prisoner from Andersonville, she accomplished that task memorably here during the summer of 1865, marking nearly thirteen thousand graves with identifying headstones. She also raised the first U.S. flag to wave over the prison burial ground. The memorial erected at the prison site in 1915 was the first, apart from one at her birthplace in *North Oxford, Massachusetts,* to honor Clara Barton, and the first in a national cemetery to honor a civilian not interred there.

Athens

Lucy Cobb Institute Building, University of Georgia campus, 200 North Milledge Avenue. The lacy grillwork is still on the hundred-foot veranda of this building that was erected in 1858 to house the Lucy Cobb Institute, one of the earliest colleges for women in the nation. Thomas R. R. Cobb founded it and named it for one of his daughters after he read an article that boldly claimed, "Girls have the same intellectual constitution as men and have the same rights as men to intellectual cultural development." It was signed, "Mother." Cobb agreed with the article and started to raise funds, unaware that the author of the daring proposition was his own sister, modestly maintaining her anonymity. During the Civil War, the women of Lucy Cobb Institute raised $120 to help save the South from bankruptcy. Today, the campus, where young women were carefully chaperoned if they strolled beyond the magnolia trees on the front lawn, is used for police training work.

Mary B. T. Lumpkin House, 973 Prince Avenue. One chilly morning in January 1891, a dozen women with twenty-four green thumbs gathered in the antebellum parlor of this house and organized the first garden club in America. They held fortnightly meetings, heard lectures by leading horticulturists, and exchanged cuttings of prized specimens. Within a short time, they extended membership to "every lady in Athens who might be interested in growing anything, from a cabbage to a chrysanthemum." A year later, they held a flower and vegetable show, the first on record in the country. The daughter of one charter member has written that, although the show was not very grand, "It was a great success, and was attended by virtually the entire community."

Founders' Memorial Gardens, 325 Lumpkin Street. A sunken formal garden below a section of boxwood, entirely interspersed with native Piedmont area trees and shrubs, serves as a memorial to the twelve hardy founders of the nation's first garden club. The Garden Club of Georgia, modern descendant of the Ladies' Garden Club of Athens, maintains its headquarters in the restored antebellum house once owned by a University of Georgia professor. A treasured possession inside is a faded blue ribbon from the pioneering club's 1892 flower and vegetable show. Outside, the greenery would no doubt rack up a winning score based on criteria established at the club's third annual exhibition: "Three points for the best blooms. Two points for mediums. One point for those not so good. One extra point for a very superior bloom. One point taken off for every case of decided badness." And you will find no examples of "A Bad Flower or Rose—Faulty shape, faded color, undersized or confused centre."

Atlanta

Florence Crittenton Home, 3913 North Peachtree Road. Barrett Hall, a dormitory for some thirty young pregnant women, honors Kate Waller Barrett, who founded it as a home for unwed mothers in 1893. She wrote a letter to philanthropist Charles N. Crittenton, who had earlier opened a chain of homes to rescue "fallen women." He sent her a $5,000 contribution and recognized her home as the fifth in the group named for his late daughter. Kate Waller Barrett, who had taken a medical degree to learn more about prostitution, soon became affiliated with the national Florence Crittenton movement and devoted increasing amounts of energy to filling the needs of pregnant young women rather than trying to preach to them. Today, the director told us, the home serves "problem pregnancies. We don't use the term *unwed mothers,* since many of them are already married." They may be minors, or newly separated, she explained, "girls who have some decisions to make about pregnancy."

Frances Newman Typescripts, Price Gilbert Memorial Library, Georgia Institute of Technology. Two leather-bound typescripts of novels that shocked Atlanta socialites in the 1920s (because, we are told, "they were regarded as somewhat risqué") have become part of the collection here. Frances Newman, whose father was a judge and whose mother was a Virginian, worked at this library while turning out two of her most eyebrow-raising titles: *The Hard-Boiled Virgin* (1926) and *Dead Lovers Are Faithful Lovers* (1928). Although *Virgin* was banned in Boston, dedicated Newman readers insist that it is not a dirty book. "The virgin in the novel did go to bed finally with a playwright but found it very boring," one professor explained. "What delighted her most about him was that his play ran a shorter time on Broadway than did hers." H. L. Mencken was also a Newman fan, but Frances Newman's witty satires of the whole range of the Atlanta social scene have not progressed far beyond a display in the library. "Unfortunately, there has been no revival of interest in her," Georgia Tech English professor James Smith told us.

Site of Margaret Mitchell House, 1401 Peachtree Street. A historical marker planted on the grass notes that the modern office building here occupies the site of one of author Margaret Mitchell's childhood homes, where she lived from 1912 until after her marriage in the early 1920s. The loyal Confederate supporter began her mammoth novel in 1926. It was not published until a decade later at the urging of a Macmillan editor. When he asked if it was a story of degeneracy in the South, she replied, "No, it is about tough, hard-boiled people who could take it on the chin." The 1,057-page manuscript dwarfed its five-foot creator and showered her with instant reward. After two years on the best-seller list, it racked up a pair of enviable publishing records: largest sale (50,000 copies) in a single day, and largest total sale (more than 15 million copies to date, as far as the publisher knows) of any novel. Robert Nathan is reported to have said, "The three best novels I read this year were *Gone with the Wind.*" It also won the 1937 Pulitzer Prize for fiction, although Margaret Mitchell modestly told an interviewer, "I know good writing, and I don't think mine good." But she understood the secret of her success even before she got there, telling her brother in this very house, "the story is all that matters. Any good plot can stand retelling and style doesn't matter."

Margaret Mitchell Room, Atlanta Public Library, 126 Carnegie Way, NW, contains memorabilia, bequeathed by her husband, of the best-selling author. Included is her vast library of reference books on the Civil War and the world's most complete collection of editions of *Gone with the Wind*. The novel has been published in twenty-six languages. Also here: the millionth copy of *GWTW*, especially dedicated to the author.

Augusta

Lucy C. Laney High School, 1339 Gwinnett Street. The modern building named for the pioneering black educator stands on the site of the school she founded, the Haines Normal and Industrial Institute. Lucy Laney was determined to provide high-quality private education for black children, and she opened her first school in a church basement in 1886. The first brick buildings went up here a few years later, and Lucy Laney wound up supervising the education of nearly a thousand pupils. One of her early faculty members was Mary McLeod Bethune of *Mayesville, South Carolina,* who gave up the idea of being a foreign missionary because of Lucy Laney's dynamic influence: "From her I got a new vision," the young teacher wrote, "my life work lay not in Africa but in my own country." She later put that vision to use in *Daytona Beach, Florida.* Although Haines Institute was closed and its buildings razed in 1949, this new high school, with an integrated student body, stands in its place. Lucy Laney was buried here in 1933, and her gravestone, which senior students decorate with flowers every April, is visible from the principal's office.

Butler Island

For several months during the winter of 1838–39, British actress Fanny Kemble lived among the live oaks and cypress trees on this island in the Altamaha Delta where her husband, Pierce Butler, owned a vast rice plantation. The glamorous and acclaimed Frances Ann Kemble, who only came to "that dreadful America" when her family's fortunes were reversed, gave up her brilliant stage career to marry the dashing Butler in Philadelphia in 1834. Although they were stormily incompatible from the beginning ("She held that marriage should be companionship on equal terms," Butler wrote indignantly, much later), she agreed to join him with their two small children to oversee the plantations he had inherited here and on *St. Simon's Island.* Fanny quickly saw more than the swampy landscape. Seven hundred slaves worked under the lash on her husband's rice paddies. She saw the squalid shacks they lived in and the meager food they barely existed on. She saw fifteen-year-old mothers and thirty-year-old grandmothers. When she reported the conditions to her husband and told him the slaves were flogged when they complained to her, he replied, "Why do you listen to such stuff? Why do you believe such trash? Don't you know that niggers are all damned liars?" Helpless and disgusted, Fanny Kemble kept a diary of her observations. Nearly a quarter of a century later, when she was back in England and divorced from Butler, she published her *Journal of a Residence on a Georgian Plantation.* In England, it helped combat rising Confederate sympathies during the Civil War. In America, it was called "the best contribution ever made by an individual . . . of the practical working of the slave system in the United States."

Today the slaves and the plantation are gone, and the island where Fanny Kemble was struck by the "profusion of birds" is maintained as a wild bird preserve.

Cartersville

Rebecca Felton House, Routes 41 and 411, about one mile north of cloverleaf (private). While living in this large two-story white frame house from 1853–1905, Rebecca Latimer Felton got the political training that later made her the first female United States senator. Serving initially as her politician husband's campaign manager, then turning to politics and the suffrage cause herself, she went to the Senate in 1922 at the age of eighty-seven when the governor appointed her to fill the seat of a deceased senator. Although some newspapers criticized the appointment as "an empty gesture" by the vote-seeking governor, Felton chose to interpret it as meaning that the "word 'sex' has been obliterated entirely from the Constitution." She received her certificate of appointment at a chilly, damp acceptance ceremony in the local courthouse that October, before a cheering crowd that included her good friend, novelist Corra Harris. Earlier, Harris had modeled her self-willed heroine of *The Co-Citizens* after Rebecca Felton.

Felton's Senate appointment, as the marker here points out, "climaxed a long career in which she gained wide recognition as an orator, newspaper columnist and crusader for woman's rights." When Felton was earlier asked to address the state legislature, the first woman so honored, she was introduced as "the brightest and smartest woman in the state." When she took her seat as junior senator from Georgia, for her brief fifty-one-day term until the newly elected official presented his credentials, Rebecca Latimer Felton told her male colleagues and a gallery full of female fans, "When the women of the country come in and sit with you, though there may be but a very few in the next few years, I pledge you that you will get ability, you will get integrity of purpose, you will get exalted patriotism and you will get unstinted usefulness."

Clayton

Monument to Celestia Parrish, Clayton Baptist Church. A gravestone inscribed "Georgia's Greatest Woman" marks the burial place of the pioneering educator who dedicated her entire life to developing better schools in the South. First committed to helping women earn college degrees despite the barriers of all-male southern institutions, Celestia Parrish soon turned her energies to public elementary schools. In 1903, in Athens, she opened the first progressive Dewey schools in the South. And until her death in 1918, she traveled to rural schools in forty-eight counties in the mountainous north of Georgia for three years in a row, diligently carrying out her position as district state supervisor.

Columbus

Augusta Jane Evans Wilson House, "Wildwood," Wildwood Avenue at Garrard Street. In the Georgian house northeast of the prominent marker, Victorian novelist Augusta Jane Evans Wilson was born May 8, 1835. Although she traveled a good deal as a child and later settled in *Mobile, Alabama,* she got the inspiration for her most successful literary work while on a visit to Columbus. She was paying a call on her aunt at a nearby house when she decided to write a fictionalized account of strong Confederate sentiments—*St. Elmo* was published in 1866. In honor of the novel, that house (now marked at Eighteenth Avenue south of St. Elmo Drive) was renamed "St. Elmo" by its owners in 1878.

Site of First Confederate Memorial Day Service, Second Avenue and Eleventh Street. The Ladies' Memorial Association, formed in the spring of 1866 to honor the Confederate dead, sponsored the first Confederate Memorial Day service at the St. Luke Methodist Church on April 26, 1866. The date was selected as the anniversary of the surrender of Gen. Joseph E. Johnston. Lizzie Rutherford Ellis, secretary of the ladies' group, wrote letters to Southern newspapers urging the adoption of April 26 as an annual celebration, touching off a Southern tradition. (See *Columbus, Mississippi.*)

Ladies' Defender Cannon, Confederate Naval Museum, Route 27 at Fourth Street. The women of Columbus selflessly gave up treasured brass items from their domestic furnishings so that this muzzle-loading cannon could be cast for the Confederate troops. Everything from brass bed frames and cooking tools to jewelry and doorknobs was thrown into the melting pot, self-sacrificing acts of patriotism that reverberated on the artillery field for barely a year. In 1862, the unusual weapon was captured by federal troops at Shiloh and, historians believe, probably turned against the Southern soldiers whose women had created it. In 1904, after an ignominious period of captivity, when it stood on display as a war trophy in Chicago, the cannon was returned to its birthplace by an act of Congress.

Dream Theater, 1030 First Avenue. They used to break the doors down here when blues singer Ma Rainey, the first great exponent of "classic" blues, came to town. Born Gertrude Pridgett in Columbus, April 26, 1886, she made her first stage appearance at the nearby Springer Opera House with a local variety show called the *Bunch of Blackberries.* Later, she took to the road, joining the traveling minstrel show in which her husband was performing. When they started their own road company—during which she discovered jazz great Bessie Smith in *Chattanooga, Tennessee*—Ma Rainey's haunting voice and flamboyant appearance attracted devoted listeners. Originally a star with strictly black southern audiences, Ma Rainey expanded her following when she cut her first record in 1923. After ninety-one known discs that followed, she died in 1939 and is buried in Porterdale Cemetery beneath a stone inscribed simply, "Gertrude Rainey."

Elberton

Nancy Hart Cabin, Nancy Hart State Park. Stones from her original house were used to build the chimney of this reconstructed cabin on the site of the Revolutionary War heroine's original home. Nancy Hart shot her way into the pages of history as a crack markswoman and a loyal American. She was six feet tall, cross-eyed, and big boned. She could cook a pumpkin "as many ways as there are days in the week," according to a reporter. And in this cabin, hung with the antlers of animals she had gunned down and the honeycombs of bees she had uncovered, she held the most heroic dinner party of the Revolution. The story goes that Nancy Hart seethed with fury when a band of Tories burst into her house and demanded that she cook them a turkey—her own—that they had shot. Slyly sending her daughter off to warn the neighbors with a conch shell, the fine chef waited until the Redcoats were enjoying their meal, then snatched one of their rifles from the pile resting against the wall. Nancy Hart shot one intruder, wounded a second, and held the rest at bay single-handedly until some Whig neighbors came in answer to her daughter's call. The remaining Tories were hanged without their supper. Today, you can picnic without fear of Tory intrusion at tables in the park named in the heroic hostess's honor. A swift-running stream adjacent to the cabin is called War Woman's Creek, the Indian's respectful name for the sharpshooting Nancy Hart. She is also immortalized at *Hartwell.*

Fayetteville

Margaret Mitchell Library, Lee Street. The tiny *Atlanta* author who earned her fortune with *Gone with the Wind* charitably shared some of it with this struggling library and made the building possible. On a visit to Fayetteville one day in the 1930s, Mitchell struck up a conversation with a woman who mentioned *GWTW.* "I suppose you have read the new book,"

she said offhandedly. To which the author replied, *sotto voce*, "Don't tell anybody, but I wrote it." When her shocked companion recovered, she invited Mitchell to the library (of which the woman was a founder) for a visit. Margaret Mitchell was so taken with the hardy spirit of the library women—who had lost two book collections in fires and could barely finance their stock—that she started sending them money. Later she brought over a carload of volumes for the new building, which stands adjacent to the site of the original Fayetteville Academy, which Scarlett O'Hara attended. The librarian assured us that, through her brother, they still receive Miss Margaret's annual Christmas donation.

Hartwell

Nancy Hart Monument, Town Square. You cannot pass through the center of Hartwell without learning that it was named for Revolutionary War heroine Nancy Hart. Better yet, Hartwell is in Hart County, which is the only county in Georgia named for a woman. The marker relates the story of Nancy's Hart's patriotic act at *Elberton* and also reports, "Tradition has it that Nancy Hart served as a spy for Gen. Elijah Clarke, sometimes disguised as a man."

Knoxville

Joanna Troutman Monument, Courthouse Square. A bronze plaque set into a boulder commemorates the Knoxville girl who designed the Lone Star flag of Texas. She originally designed it—a single large blue star on a field of white silk—for some Macon boys marching off to war. But it proved such a lucky

banner that the newly independent state adopted it as its own. Today Georgians have only this marker to remember Joanna Troutman; Texans have appropriated her flag and her body, interred at *Austin, Texas.*

La Grange

During the Civil War, a group of militiawomen here organized themselves into a mutual protection society called the Nancy Harts, after the brave patriot of the Revolution from nearby *Elberton*. When a detachment of raiders rode into La Grange in 1865, the sight of the Nancy Harts lined up for action convinced their leader to spare the city from destruction.

Macon

Wesleyan College was founded in 1836 by a group of Macon citizens concerned about the lack of schooling for their young women. One article in the *Georgia Messenger,* urging the creation of Georgia Female College, argued, "Let the young ladies of this republic continue another half century to receive what has, during the last twenty years, been considered a genteel education, and there will not be energy enough in the country, mental or physical, to guide the helm of state or to defend its priceless institutions." It was signed "By a Lady." On December 23, 1836, the college became the first in the world chartered to grant degrees to women. It should be noted that it succeeded admirably despite the attitude of one man who refused to give a contribution, saying, "No, I will not give a dollar; all a woman needs to know is how to read the New Testament, and to spin and weave clothing."

Monument to Women of the Confederacy, Poplar Street Park. One of the earliest memorials to the role of Southern women during the Civil War was unveiled in 1911, the gift of "Their Husbands, Fathers, Sons and Daughters." Two sculptures flank a tall obelisk. One depicts a woman providing water for a soldier. The other shows a woman by her sewing machine, protecting her child.

Marietta

Alice McLellan Birney Memorial, Marietta High School grounds, Winn Street. Every state in the Union sent stones to be incorporated into the monument to the founder of the National Congress of Parents and Teachers, familiar to every schoolchild as the PTA. Alice McLellan Birney was born in Marietta in 1858 and spent most of her happy girlhood here, an early influence in her later decision to begin the organization. While living in Washington, D.C., she felt so strongly that parental ignorance was harming children, that in 1897 she organized a 2,000-mother meeting that grew into the National Congress of Mothers. That group later became the PTA. A sundial in her memory here accurately measures the length of local PTA meetings.

Mount Berry

Martha McChesney Berry House, "Oak Hill," Route 27. From the giant trees on its sweeping lawns to the white columns that frame the wide veranda, everything about the house where Martha McChesney Berry was born in 1855 evokes the mood of a classic Southern plantation. But the wealthy young woman who lived here dedicated her life to educating and assisting the mountain people who lived in rude shacks. One Sunday in the late 1890s, she read some Bible stories to three mountain boys who came by her log shack retreat in the woods. When they returned the following week, she found herself operating a weekly Sunday school. Soon she transferred her classes to the charming wooden Possum Trot Church, where you can still see the biblical mottoes she painted across the walls. When she wasn't there, or here on the plantation, Martha Berry was hitching up her horse and buggy to take the ABCs to the mountain people, a weekly outing that earned her the title the Sunday Lady.

The Berry Schools were the lucky outcome of educator Martha Berry's early decision that the mountain children needed a school of their own. In 1902 she founded the Boys' Industrial School, followed in 1909 by one for girls. Later she jokingly confessed, "If I had known how much more boys could eat, I might have begun with girls instead." The theme was self-help: manual labor in return for vocational, domestic, and later academic schooling. A college was added in 1926. Theodore Roosevelt gave a dinner for Martha Berry at the White House and encouraged donations. Henry Ford gave four million dollars to what he called "the greatest schools in the world." And the woman whose fiancé had left her at the beginning of the century because he disagreed with her plan to open the schools, was able to say, "I married my schools and now I have thousands of children." Martha Berry also said, "The Berry Schools are my life, the red clay hills, my home; the wind in the pines is my song, and when I die, a grave beside the school chapel must be my resting place." She was buried there in 1942.

St. Catherines Island

Indian leader Mary Musgrove Matthews Bosomworth was buried here about 1763, shortly after the island was granted to her by the British governor in one of the great real estate swindles of colonial times. An acknowledged leader of her people, the half-breed Creek had earlier served as interpreter to James Oglethorpe, founder of the Georgia colony, for a fine sum of money. Mary Musgrove enjoyed such respect among both Indians and colonists that she helped maintain the friendship between Creeks and English, and she is credited with saving the settlers from "savage butchery" on a number of occasions. When Oglethorpe left in 1743, in gratitude he presented Mary with a diamond ring and several hundred pounds sterling. But at the urging of her third husband, Thomas Bosomworth—described by one Georgia historian as a man of the cloth with "a very mercenary turn of mind"—Mary tricked her own people and the whites out of this island. First, she convinced the Creeks to deed it to her since she was their rightful "empress." She proved that by donning regal robes. Then, when her husband ran into debt, she threatened the colonists with Indian reprisals if they did not compensate her for past services to the crown. Not until a decade later did the crown come through, granting her this island and a series of payments totaling £2,100. But Mary Musgrove Matthews Bosomworth only enjoyed her property for a few years. Today, the private playground of rich industrialists serves as her graveyard.

St. Simon's Island

Hampton Plantation, Butler Point. The half-buried foundations of the buildings at Pierce Butler's cotton fields have been carpeted with untended foliage, silent evidence of the war and the subsequent neglect of the vacated plantation. When his wife, Fanny Kemble, came here in 1838, a short barge-ride from nearby *Butler Island,* she found a verdant landscape and miles to explore. Frequently she mounted her high-spirited stallion, Montreal, and galloped through the tangled undergrowth and the luxuriant forests of palmettos, pines, and moss-draped oaks. Her goal beyond the fragrant honeysuckles was the old slave hospital, where the ardent abolitionist tried to ease the troubled conditions of the uncared-for island blacks. Fanny Kemble herself was a mystery to the slave population. Often in the evening she penned antislavery letters and kept the record that she would later publish as the *Journal of a Residence on a Georgian Plantation.* "The door of the great barn-like room is opened stealthily and men and women come trooping in, their naked feet falling all but inaudibly on the boards, as they be-

take themselves to the hearth, where they squat on their hams in a circle, like a ring of ebony idols, watching me writing at the other end of the room."

Savannah

Juliette Gordon Low Birthplace, 142 Bull Street. The impish little girl who developed a reputation for saucy remarks always enjoyed the fact that she was born on Halloween (1860). Today, October 31 is celebrated as Founder's Day by the Girl Scouts of America, and endless troops with shined shoes and pressed uniforms make annual pilgrimages to the birthplace of their benefactor. This mecca for patrols of green-garbed girls is a three-story Regency town house restored with all the crystal and brocaded finery that surrounded young "Daisy" Gordon. She lived here until she was married in 1886, sleeping in the canopy bed on the second floor and sipping early-morning tea out of a cup painted with violets. The house is full of her handiwork: her sculptures, paintings, and poetry; her ornate Victorian paper dolls; and the wrought-iron gates she designed for her estate in England. At the end of the tour, a museum here sells a "Daisy pin" that can be worn only on the uniform of genuine Low Birthplace visitors.

Juliette Gordon Low House, 329 Abercorn Street. On one of her many trips to England, Juliette Gordon Low met Gen. Sir Robert Baden-Powell, founder of the Boy Scouts, and she was inspired to organize several troops of Girl Guides in Britain. When she returned to Savannah after her husband died, it was in the carriage house of this residence (where she had moved after 1866) that she founded the first patrol of the Girl Guides in America. Eighteen troopers from Savannah were enrolled on March 12, 1912. By 1915, she had established the nationally based Girl Scouts of America, and she served as its first president. She wore a khaki uniform, Norfolk jacket, and campaign hat; the girls wore wide black bloomers, white middy blouses, and black stockings. As the movement grew, the uniforms were fashioned from blue serge, then the popular green.

In 1927, Juliette Gordon Low died in an upstairs bedroom of this house. Girl Scout Troop 12 of Savannah served as an honor guard at her funeral, and she was buried in the family plot at

Laurel Grove Cemetery. Her house now serves as national Girl Scout headquarters.

Toccoa

Mary Jarrett White House, "Historic Traveler's Rest," Route 123. The last private owner of this wooden frame residence was Mary Jarrett White, the first and only woman to vote in Georgia in 1920. She made her historic trip to the polls that May, and she was found to be a legal voter since she had registered six months earlier in compliance with the law. How Mary Jarrett White managed to register before the Nineteenth Amendment was passed still baffles the Georgia Election Board.

Washington

Sarah Hillhouse House, East Robert Toombs Avenue (private). The first occupants of this historic house were Sarah Porter Hillhouse of New England and her husband David. Sarah Hillhouse wrote her way into Georgia's archives by taking over her husband's *Washington Monitor* when he died in 1803 and becoming the first female newspaper editor in the state. She also became Georgia's first state printer, when she ran off

Juliette Gordon Low (right) and Girl Scout Troop #1

copies of the *Journal* of the Georgia House of Representatives in her printshop. So successful was Hillhouse in her business career that when she turned over the printing presses of the *Monitor* to her son in 1810 (or 1811), she also gave him ten thousand dollars. Although few copies of her pioneering publication survive, a portrait here of Sarah Hillhouse, quill in hand, attests to her writing talent.

Site of Barclay Poplar, West Robert Toombs Street, near the Pope Home. The first woman to be hanged in Georgia once swung from a poplar that has vanished along with all documentation. Polly Barclay was arrested in 1806 for the murder of her merchant husband, John H. Barclay, who was found shot to death. Legend has it that the comely widow was found guilty and, despite her pleas to the sheriff "not to hang so beautiful a woman," was sentenced to the gallows. On May 30, we are told, Polly Barclay rode to the execution in her finest silk dress, sit-

ting atop her coffin. The most colorful version of the story then reports that the accommodating sheriff fixed the noose so that she would not die instantly. She was cut down, pronounced dead, revived by a physician, and she lived to be an old woman, free because the state had carried out its sentence. No grave bearing her name has ever been found in Wilkes County.

Robert Toombs House, East Robert Toombs Avenue. When federal troops came to this Doric colonnaded house to arrest the Confederate general in April 1865, his wife successfully saved his life but imperiled her own. Mrs. Toombs, whose first name has not been widely recorded, stalled the soldiers on the front porch so her husband could slip out the back. When the Union officers promised not to burn her handsome house if she would deliver the general to them, Mrs. Toombs straightened up and announced, "Burn it then." Instead, they evicted her, making another homeless and temporarily husbandless war heroine.

Site of Eliza Frances Andrews Home, "Haywood," north of Town Square. Wilkes Academy now occupies the family plantation where Eliza Frances Andrews watched the last days of what she called "our poor, doomed Confederacy." Deeply saddened that her tiny village would soon be overtaken by federal troops, Fanny kept a lively diary and published it in 1908 as *The War-Time Journal of a Georgia Girl*. Among the revealing portraits of the South under siege was that of Varina Davis (see *Natchez, Mississippi*), wife of the defeated Confederate president. "The poor woman is in a deplorable condition," Fanny wrote when she met her after church, "no home, no money, and her husband is a fugitive." She also heard the men "all talking about going to Mexico and Brazil," and concluded that "if all emigrate who say they are going to, we shall have a nation made up of women, negroes and Yankees." One Thursday in May 1865, Fanny "sat under the cedar trees by the street gate nearly all the morning, watching the stream of life flow by," and heard the sobbing townspeople paying their last calls on Jefferson Davis, just before he signed his last official paper as Confederate president. She reported with a literary sigh of disappointment, "this, I suppose, is the end of the Confederacy."

Site of Washington's First Public School, Hudson Street. A signpost identifies the place where Eliza Frances Andrews taught after the Civil War. The new problems of independence took their toll on the writer and botanist, who never knew how to make a living until her father's fortune disappeared. Suddenly she found herself wearied by the household chores her slaves used to perform. She complained that her "legs ached as if they had been in stocks." Still, she became a fine teacher and a widely published author.

Mary Willis Library, Liberty at Jefferson Street. The first free lending library in the state was founded in 1888 by Dr. Francis Willis in memory of his daughter Mary, of whom it was once said, "to know her was a 'liberal education.'" The admirable young woman was well read and well loved, but apparently she had trouble sleeping. She died when she fell down a flight of stairs in a sleepwalking trance.

Watkinsville

Jeannette Rankin Home, Mars Hill Road (private). Between her two terms as congresswoman from Montana (see *Missoula, Montana*), Rankin bought this small frame house in 1935. She lived here, when not marching in antiwar protests or speaking for woman's rights, until her death in 1973.

The odd-looking cement house on a nearby hill, shaped like the round stone barns of the Shakers, represents Rankin's attempt to start a "kibbutz, Georgia style" so that elderly, poor women could live and work together. None showed up, and in her will Rankin bequeathed it to be used as a home for unemployed workers. Today it is vacant.

HAWAII

"The island life offered a liberal and amiable existence," wrote poet Genevieve Taggard, who spent much of her girlhood here with her missionary father, developing a deep love of the polyglot island culture and an equally deep hatred of racism. From her considerably more academic vantage point of a New England town she later explained in 1934, "My parents hardly knew that they had become mild internationalists . . . we [the children] dressed as children dress now in the summer, as children did not dress in 1910. And we were accustomed to an intense enjoyment in every day of our life." Her parents, she wrote, "at 25 had rejected the small town and all its values; now as middle-aged people they knew how right they had been to reject it."

Hanalei Valley (Kauai Island)

"The atmosphere and scenery were so glorious that it was possible to think of nothing all day, but just allow oneself passively to drink in sensations of exquisite pleasure," wrote British traveler Isabella Bird to her sister in 1873 after a solitary horseback trip through these lush hills and verdant forests. "It was a joyously-exciting day, and I was galloping down a grass hill at a pace which I should not have assumed had white people been with me." She especially liked the fact that the natives laughed at her madcap frolics and threw flowers, calling her *paniola,* or "one who lassoes cattle," and thus, "Hawaiian cowboy." In January 1873 the forty-one-year-old Victorian voyager had stopped in what were then called the Sandwich Islands. Rejecting the easy resort life of the lone hotel on Oahu, she set out for the other islands and roamed freely and exuberantly for seven months. She even gave up the traditional (for ladies) method of riding sidesaddle and learned to gallop astride, wearing a MacGregor tartan flannel riding costume of full Turkish trousers with a tunic reaching to the ankles. This "Hawaiian riding-dress" would later serve her at *Estes Park, Colorado.* Here on the islands, it was accessorized with boots, jangling Mexican spurs, a pine-seed lei, and a broadbrimmed Australian hat to keep off rain or sun. Isabella felt herself "quite Hawaiianised." It was a delicious, exciting sojourn, but she tore herself away from Honolulu on August 7, bound for San Francisco, sad but determined to leave the land where she had earlier written, "I don't know what day it is, or how long I have been here, and quite understand how possible it would be to fall into an indolent life, in which time is of no account."

Hilo (Hawaii Island)

Kilauea Volcano, Hawaii Volcanoes National Park. The first person to confront Pele, the dread fire goddess who spewed forth molten lava in anger, was Kapiolani, high chiefess of Hawaii. One day in December 1824, Kapiolani hiked nearly one hundred miles to this 4,000-foot peak on the slopes of Mauna Loa, then she descended 500 feet into the crater. Despite the frightened pleas of her husband and other superstitious companions, she defied the wrath of Pele by refusing to back off from a steaming lake of red-hot lava. "I fear not Pele," she announced calmly amidst the noisy hissing and bellowing of volcanic gases. And then she hiked back across the island. Kapiolani's bold disregard of the feared pagan idol greatly aided the newly arrived missionaries in their effort to introduce Christianity to the islands. An early and zealous convert herself, Kapiolani faced an even greater challenge nearly two decades later. When cancer was detected in her breast, she underwent a mastectomy without benefit of anesthesia. Although this act of medical heroism went largely unnoted, Tennyson wrote a poem about her de-

scent into the volcano. Today, a park attendant assured us that —perhaps in awe of the fearless Kapiolani—"all is quiet" with Kilauea Volcano.

Liliuokalani Park, Banyan Drive, contains a banyan tree planted by aviator Amelia Earhart when she visited here before her unprecedented solo flight to California in 1935 (see *Honolulu*). The bronze plaque marking the pilot's tree was recently replaced after the original was stolen by vandals.

Honaunau (Hawaii Island)

Restored Hale-o-Keawe, City of Refuge National Historical Park. The first females to break the sex taboos at the old *heiau* ("temple") here were missionary Laura Fish Judd (see *Honolulu*) and Kapiolani (see *Hilo*), along with Kapiolani's husband, Naihe. "It was then surrounded by an enclosure of hideous idols carved in wood," Judd wrote, "and no woman had ever

been allowed to enter its consecrated precincts. Our heroic Kapiolani led the way, and we entered the enclosure. It was a sickening scene that met our eyes. The dead bodies of chiefs were placed around the room in a sitting posture, the unsightly skeletons mostly concealed in folds of kapa, or rich silk. The blood-stained altar was there, where human victims had been immolated to idol gods. Fragments of offerings were strewed about. Kapiolani was much affected and wept, but her husband was stern and silent. I thought he was not quite rid of the old superstition in regard to women.

"A few months after our visit Kaahumanu [see *Honolulu*] came and ordered all the bones buried, and the house and fence entirely demolished."

Honolulu (Oahu Island)

Iolani Palace, 364 South King Street. The only royal palace in the United States housed Hawaii's last reigning monarch, Queen Liliuokalani. When she succeeded to the throne in 1891 after her brother died, a Chicago newspaper reporter observed that "her manner was dignified and she had the ease and the authoritative air of one accustomed to rule." She also had a strong will, and she sought to restore the royal power of the waning monarch. This show of strength threatened many residents, especially Hawaiian businessmen already angry over economic problems and a U.S. tariff that made American sugar two cents cheaper than Hawaiian sugar. The opposition deposed her in 1893 and set up a provisional government to run the islands. A future mayor of Honolulu later observed, "For two cents a pound in the price of sugar a queen beloved by her people was overthrown." Liliuokalani served a comfortable imprisonment for nine months on the second floor of this imposing building, in a corner room facing Kawaihao Church. After Hawaii was formally annexed to the United States in 1898—a development Liliuokalani had fought vigorously—with ceremonies on the front steps of the palace, the former queen moved to Washington Place (see below). Today the palace is being restored, we are told, "to its Monarchy period appearance," complete with portraits of the queen and of Kapiolani (see *Hilo*), who lived here with one of her husbands, Kalakaua. Among the untarnished reminders of royal rule are the twin seabird-feather kahilis (symbols of royalty that resemble giant feather dusters) in Liliuokalani's colors, flanking two regal thrones in the Throne Room. The basement, where there was a billiard room and servants' quarters, the scene of a lively luau that the queen held shortly before her forced resignation, has been converted to more workaday offices.

Washington Place, 320 South Beretania Street. When she left her throne and royal residence at the public's insistence, Queen Liliuokalani lived here, in the charming white house built by her late husband's father. This was her home when officials arrested her in 1895 and reinstalled her briefly at the palace as a prisoner. When she returned here as a private citizen, Liliuokalani was accorded the respect of a retired monarch. The legislature voted her a $4,000 annual pension. Diehard royalists continued to flock around her, and the queen entertained visiting dignitaries—beneath her symbolic, tall kahilis—in her living room. She also spent time at her piano, a gift from the public that still stands in the living room where she no doubt ran through the popular Hawaiian melody she composed, "Aloha Oe." The song is inscribed in bronze in front of the house. After the queen died here in 1917 at seventy-nine, Washington Place became the official executive mansion of the territory. A portrait of the robust ruler reminds the current governor of the previous royal inhabitant.

Queen Liliuokalani Children's Center, 1300 Halona Street, was founded with a living trust she set up in 1909 "for the benefit of orphan and other destitute children . . . in the Hawaiian Islands, the preference to be given to Hawaiian children of pure or part aboriginal blood." The modern headquarters building in the ancient Kauhale style of architecture occupies part of Liliuokalani's original estate and serves nearly 3,500 children.

Queen Emma House, "Hanaiakamalama," 2913 Pali Highway. This white clapboard mansion in the cool Nuuanu Valley was the summer home of anglophile Queen Emma (who was married to Kamehameha IV and barely missed ruling herself when her brother was chosen instead). During Kamehameha IV's monarchy (1854–63), the royal couple contributed to the religious and educational growth of the island, largely under the queen's influence. Emma lived in this six-room house after her husband's death in 1863. The exhibits here include her huge Victorian bed carved of Hawaiian wood, her son's infant cradle, her silver service, and a wardrobe of gowns and jewels from court days, including her own wedding dress, tiny by Hawaiian royalty standards.

Bernice P. Bishop Museum, 1355 Kalihi Street, houses a famed collection of Hawaiian and Polynesian artifacts and cultural information. Upstate New Yorker Charles Bishop founded it in 1889 to perpetuate the memory of his late wife, Bernice Pauahi Bishop, a Hawaiian high chiefess and last in the Kamehameha line of the royal family. Many of her personal possessions, such as jewelry, books, and diaries, are on display. Bernice Bishop donated most of her enormous fortune to educational and cultural causes, both when she was alive and in her will.

Kamehameha Schools, Kapalama Heights. With a generous bequest after she died in 1884, Bernice Pauahi Bishop established these academically superb schools for boys and girls of Hawaiian descent. The royal benefactor made this the sole outlet for her money, and the schools that began in 1887 with 37 pupils today enroll more than 2,500 young people on a 500-acre campus. The students decorate Bernice Pauahi Bishop's grave at Mauna 'Ala, and each December 19 they honor her with a schoolwide ceremony that includes several songs she wrote.

St. Andrew's Cathedral, Queen Emma Street, was built with money raised by Queen Emma, the widow of Kamehameha IV, on a trip to England in 1865–66. The ruling couple had earlier been responsible for the introduction of the Episcopal Church to the islands—the first in the U.S.—and Queen Victoria noted about her royal visitor, "Nothing could be nicer or more dignified than her manner." Queen Emma also devoted many hours to the St. Andrew's Priory, a school for Hawaiian girls. One of the regular churchgoers in a front pew at this cathedral was Queen Liliuokalani.

Royal Mausoleum, 2261 Nuuanu Avenue, contains the tombs of six queens and five kings who ruled Hawaii, including Liliuokalani, Kapiolani, Emma, and Bernice Bishop.

Kaahumanu, who was reburied here several decades after her death in 1832, was a highly influential and respected early ruler. As the favorite wife of Kamehameha I, Kaahumanu helped lead the islands into Western ways. When the king died and his son took over, Kaahumanu ranked as a coruler, sharing some of the council duties with the new king's mother, Keopuolani. The two women persuaded the young ruler to dine publicly with them in 1819, thus shattering the traditional taboos against women's place and weakening the power of the old gods. Kaahumanu further broke down antifeminist barriers in *Honaunau* with missionary Laura Fish Judd, who wrote that the "tall, stately and dignified" queen was "an Amazon in size and could dandle any one of us in her lap, as she would a little child, which she often took the liberty of doing." Following the lead of Keopuolani, the islands' first Christian convert (1823), Kaahumanu turned to Christianity in 1825, undergoing such a zealous conversion that she was called the "New Kaahumanu." She was later responsible for introducing the first code of laws to her people.

Queen's Medical Center was named for Queen Emma, who personally urged King Kamehameha IV to solicit funds for this two-story building, the first public hospital in Hawaii and the first in the United States founded by royalty. It opened in 1860.

Kawaiahao Church, 957 Punchbowl Street, commemorates some of the royal Christian converts who helped change the face of Hawaii. One bronze tablet repeats the words that Queen Kaahumanu, the missionaries' greatest success story, is said to have uttered at her death in 1832: *"Eia No Wau, e Iesu . . . E Nana Oluolu Mai"* ("Lo, here I am, O Jesus, Grant me Thy gracious smile").

Honolulu Academy of Arts, 900 South Beretania Street. Anna Cooke, whose parents and in-laws stretched back to a long line of missionaries, donated the construction money and fine art collection to this handsome gallery. A series of display rooms around open courts, topped by a pitched roof, when the gallery opened in 1927 on the site of Anna Cooke's home, it was clear that it would remain a vital and flexible center for international works. "We wish to avoid the stiffness and formality of an institution," Cooke insisted. "We wish to make the building a pleasant place where people shall be welcome." Art patron Anna Cooke hoped that the treasures from both East and West would help promote racial equality on the islands where she had chosen to live.

Mission Houses Museum, 553 South King Street. Three small structures display memorabilia relating to the influence of Christian missionaries on Hawaii. The first missionaries arrived in 1820, and among their legacies to the islanders was the Mother Hubbard dress that turned into the Hawaiian muu-muu. Early female missionaries included Lucy Goodale Thurston, Maria Loomis, and Laura Fish Judd (see *Honaunau*), who wrote in 1861, "The great national want is not a standing army nor a foreign loan to meet State expenses, nor more ample provision for the support of English schools, to urge on the *forcing process,* nor more liberty, nor better laws, nor a lighter taxation; but a generation of uncontaminated Hawaiian mothers, with their Bible in their own language, their family altar, unambitious for foreign accomplishments and luxury, and willing to perform with their own hands the humble but elevating duties of the household."

Amelia Earhart Memorial, Diamond Head Road, view point east of the lighthouse. A bronze tablet set into a boulder points out that the plucky pilot from *Atchison, Kansas,* was the "first person to fly alone from Hawaii to North America, January 11, 1935." The adventurous Pacific crossing began at 4:30 P.M., as Earhart took off from the navy's Wheeler Field in her new Lockheed Vega that was painted red to facilitate a sea rescue. Barely avoiding a string of westbound tropical squalls, she flew over this point at five thousand feet, then nudged her plane even higher into the clear skies over the ocean. Throughout the starry night, she navigated with her compass and gulped down malted-milk tablets and hot chocolate from a thermos. Eighteen hours and fifteen minutes later, she touched down near Oakland, California, just after noon, to a cheering reception of ten thousand people. It had been her longest flight, and she was exhausted. After flashing her famous grin to the crowd, she went to take a long nap.

Kailua (Hawaii Island)

Hotel King Kamehameha occupies the royal land on the Kona coast where Queen Kaahumanu lived with her famous husband, for whom the hotel is named. On precisely this spot, the ancient laws forbidding women to dine with men were broken by Kamehameha II (son of the Great) at the urging of his mother, Keopuolani, and of one of his deceased father's other wives, Kaahumanu (see *Honolulu*). Here, too, the two courageous widows shattered the traditional ban against cooking food for both sexes in the same oven and against women's eating such foods as banana, coconut, or ulua fish.

Hulihee Palace, Alii Drive, the century-old seaside residence of Kaahumanu's little brother (who named it *Hulihee* or "Turn Soft-Heart" for her when she converted to Christianity), contains a remarkable collection of royal memorabilia. Among the most curious: Kapiolani's seven-foot-long koa wood trunk that she took to visit Queen Victoria; the peacock-feather hat she wore to call on the queen; a portrait of the ample Kaahumanu; and an ample armchair for the equally large Princess Ruth.

Kauiki Head (Maui Island)

Birthplace of Kaahumanu. A plaque on a boulder on the ocean side of this cinder cone near Hana identifies the little cave above it as the place where the great Queen Kaahumanu was born in the late eighteenth century. The regal maternity ward was probably chosen for its isolation, to prevent abduction. Kaahumanu was unmistakably a queen: a courageous, effective warrior and administrator who was admired as much for her girth as for her fearless dismissal of the old deities at *Kailua*. She encouraged the unifying rule of her husband,

served as *kuhina nui* ("premier," or "coruler") for his son, and served as regent for yet another. Then she married the ruler of Kauai, bringing that kingdom in with the others. (See *Honolulu*.)

Laihana (Maui Island)

Queen Keopuolani Grave, Waiola Church Cemetery. One of Kamehameha the Great's wives, who proved her own mettle by defying the traditional taboos (see *Honolulu*), is buried here next to Kalakua, the woman with whom she shared her husband.

Waimea (Kauai Island)

Waimea Foreign Church, Makele Avenue, was begun in 1846 and relentlessly supported by Queen Deborah Kapule, a Christian convert who defied the old idols by keeping cows in the *heiaus* ("temples"). Her six-foot, 300-pound frame, standard for Hawaiian royalty, was a constant presence at the construction of the stone church. Queen Deborah was the last reigning sovereign of Kauai, and a pageant honoring her is celebrated at the Coco Palms Hotel in Wailua, in the shadow of her grave, every August 26, the anniversary of her death in 1853.

IDAHO

Ashton

Grand Tetons, Routes 20, 191. Viewing the enormous range to the southeast, technical-minded American mountain men named the peaks Pilot Knobs. But French trappers in the early 1800s took a more lascivious look and named them *Trois Tetons* ("the three breasts"). (See *Grand Teton National Park, Wyoming*.)

Boise

Ann Morrison Park, Sixteenth Street, dedicated in 1959, with picnic sites, flower gardens, and an illuminated fountain, was named in honor of one of the town's leading citizens. Ann Morrison was called "the first lady of construction" for her concern for and generosity to the employes of her husband's huge building company. At her death in 1957, Morrison was hailed as "a true Idahoan and an outstanding example of the sturdy, industrious and generous-hearted people who helped build her state."

Mary Ann Chapman O'Farrell House, Fifth and Fort Streets. Now a pioneer museum, the first log cabin in Boise, built in 1863 on a sagebrush plain, was the home of an Irish immigrant. Mary Ann is remembered for her numerous good works and the seven orphans she cared for along with her own seven children and her husband John, the first miner to discover gold in Colorado. The first Catholic service in town was held here when Mary Ann, spotting two dust-covered riders on horseback, instinctively figured they were priests and invited the two French missionaries to celebrate mass. The cabin was quickly converted into a makeshift chapel, and, years later, Mary Ann donated land for the construction of a real church.

Bonanza

Grave of Lizzie King, Boothill Cemetery. This ghost town's most notorious saloonkeeper lies in an unmarked grave now, but once there was a sign, "Agnes Elizabeth King, native of London, England. Died July 26, 1880." In fact, Lizzie died six days later, when she and her husband were mysteriously murdered. The date of her wedding to a poker player was July 26, but as far as Charles Franklin, her jilted lover, was concerned, that was the day Lizzie ceased to exist. Townspeople suspected Franklin as the murderer when he carved that symbolic date over her grave and then bolted out of town.

Cottonwood

St. Gertrude's Convent has a small museum with numerous items belonging to Polly Bemis (see *Grangeville*), including two earrings, a brooch, dresses, a sunbonnet, and a tiny pin—showing a pick, shovel, and pan—that Polly made to sell to the miners.

De Lamar

Jean Heazle House, south side of main road, west of town boardinghouse (private). Jean Heazle, the last permanent resident of this tiny fading town, died in 1949. She is generally credited as the first Idaho woman to wear pants. Some say this Irish-born rancher once caught her long skirt in the spokes of a wagon wheel and, from then on, put convenience—and safety—ahead of fashion. Others say she was already in slacks when, alone and unprotected, she crossed the country in 1883 to visit relatives here. "She was one of a kind, that's for sure," Ben Panzeri, who now owns Jean's ranch a few miles outside of

town, told us. "I was only seven or eight then, but I remember her. She was a dried-up little woman with no teeth. But very tough, very strong." When the men got together to match wits and strengths, Jean often beat out everybody in the woodcutting and nail-driving contests. "There was nothing genteel about her," said Panzeri. "She really wanted people to think she was a man." Alone, she managed a dairy and cattle ranch, adding to her legendary feats when, during the winter before her death at age seventy-one, this hardy pioneer spent three weeks in the deserted, snow-locked town looking after her two hens and a couple of cats. "I guess it took a lot of determination to live alone like that," Panzeri figured. "Why did she live that way? Maybe just because she liked it."

Grangeville

Abigail Scott Duniway (see *Portland, Oregon*) spent a day here in June 1881, collecting money and subscriptions for her paper, the *New Northwest,* "with the poorest imaginable results." She then headed for Mount Idaho in "a rattling and uncertain lumber wagon, with a lock formed by a rope and a pole, a load of wood for ballast and a load of flour for cargo."

Polly Bemis Grave, Prairie View Cemetery. Lalu Nathoy was a slave girl, brought to Grangeville from China when she was nineteen, and won by Charles Bemis, who aced out her Chinese master in a poker game. Bemis protected "Polly" from the burly miners in the dance hall where she worked, and, when he was shot in the eye after a poker quarrel, Polly nursed him back to health. After they were married, Polly lived on a ranch near the Salmon River where she grew plums, pears, grapes, and cherries and raised chickens and cows. "She was gentle and kind to all and had many friends," we learned from Sister M. Alfreda Elsensohn, who has collected many of Polly's memorabilia at the convent in *Cottonwood*. Polly, who died in 1933 when she was eighty years old, is buried here. A tiny pagoda is carved on her tombstone.

Idaho Falls

First Baptist Church, 665 John Adams Parkway. Widowed and impoverished, all her belongings taken from her by law, Rebecca Brown Mitchell suddenly "awakened and took in the legal restrictions of my sex, which has been as a fire shut up in my bones, permeating my whole being and making me what I am along the lines of independent thought." Despite the prejudice against female ministers, impelled as much by a need for self-support as by a desire for salvation, Rebecca founded this church in 1884. Appropriately enough, for she later became the first president of the local WCTU, it was located in an old saloon, and she used beer bottles as candle holders. "Willing to endure hardness, that citizenship for women might be won," Rebecca argued for suffrage outside the polling booths. Through her persuasive appeal, women won the vote in Idaho in 1895. "Not for myself did I care so much, for I had learned to

labor and wait," she wrote, "but for womanhood was the victory dear to my heart." Her portrait hangs in the entranceway of the church.

Irene Welch Grissom Home, 237 Twelfth Street (private). Idaho's poet laureate, appointed in 1923, for more than a quarter of a century, wrote most of her lyrical and inspirational poems on a nearby farm on the Snake River, but she lived here in her later years. A local reviewer once said, "The only person who does not like Mrs. Grissom's poetry is one that has never read it." She wrote often about the early settlers of Idaho:

> Life's chosen ones are these who dare
> To storm the wild and wrest their bread
> From out the grasp of frontier plains. . . .

But her favorite poem was "Pioneer Woman":

> Go tell the world that the women give
> In an equal share with man!

Kate Curley Park, Ninth and North Emerson Streets, was dedicated in the 1940s in memory of the city's pioneer settler, organizer of its first study club, and founder in 1897 of the Village Improvement Society.

North Lewiston

Grave of Jane Silcott, Old Cemetery near the Snake River. The Sacajawea of Lewiston was sixteen years old when in 1860 a band of white men came looking for a guide to help them find the gold the Indians said they saw in the mountains, "shining like the eyes of the Great Spirit." As excellent a scout as her Shoshoni sister (see *Salmon*), Jane, the daughter of a Nez Percé chief, led E. D. Pierce and seven men to Alpowa where, in August, gold was found, causing a rush that in the next year brought more than seven thousand miners to the lucky spot. After the expedition, Jane married John Silcott and settled near here to operate a ferry. As fond of the bottle as her husband was, Jane fell into a fireplace when high on spirits, and she burned to death in 1895. Her grave is marked, but souvenir-hunters, anxious for treasured relics of the legendary gold scout, have pilfered all her bones.

Preston

Pioneer Women Monument, Route 91. A roughhewn obelisk of colored rocks commemorates the heroic work of the women who cared for the victims, both Indian and white, of the ferocious Battle of Battle Creek, 1863.

First School House, City Park. Heated by a large fireplace at the east end, with a dirt floor and a dirt roof that leaked so badly that classes were canceled on rainy days, the first school in Idaho opened in the fall of 1861. Although the teacher then was a man, Hannah Comish is honored as the first teacher in the state because for months before she had held classes in her own home, which no longer stands.

Rocky Bar

A post office, a general store, and a tavern are all that remain of the days when miners worked their claims in the hills; but there is still talk of brave Pegleg Annie Morrow. In March 1898, Annie, who had been working in a bordello in Atlanta on the other side of the mountains, decided to attend a dance here. She equipped herself with snowshoes and, with her friend Emma, started out on the sixteen-mile hike. A wild blizzard suddenly swept the mountain and trapped the two women for three days. When the miners finally found them, Annie was half naked, crawling on her hands and knees, babbling crazily. Her first question was about Emma, who was found dead the next day covered with Annie's clothes. Annie's frozen feet were amputated with the only instruments available—a hunting knife and a meat saw. For the next twenty years she lived happily with the man who provided her with her peg legs, saving the money earned from the rooming house she managed here, only to be deceived by the scoundrel when he disappeared with all her savings. But her sisters did not forget her, and they cared for their courageous friend until her death in 1934. She is buried in Boise, with a tiny stone marker bearing her real name, but there is no reference to her heroic deed.

Ruby City

No one knew what to make of the small, shy tenderfoot who came riding into the mining town in 1868. Joe Monahan, a "strange little person," kept to himself, away from the saloons, built up a fine cattle ranch, and gained a reputation as the best broncobuster in town. When Joe died in 1903, his celibate life was explained. Joe was really Johanna Monahan, an orphan who had escaped from the dreary East to live free and unbothered in the wild plains. What really motivated Jo will always be a mystery, but some say that at least Jo should get credit for being the first woman to wear pants in Idaho. (See *De Lamar*.)

Salmon

Site of Sacajawea Birthplace, Route 28. A mighty boulder marks the general location of the Lemhi Indian village where, sometime around 1786, the famous Indian heroine was born. Her capture by the enemy Hidatsa a few years later (see *Three Forks, Montana*) started the chain of events that eventually led to her significant role in the momentous Lewis and Clark expedition that explored the West.

Soda Springs

Grave of Mary Christofferson Anderson, Old Cemetery. The epitaph on the gravestone donated by her children is about nine hundred words long, summarizing the story of the Morrisite Massacre of 1862 and the subsequent trials of a group of Mormons who had seceded from the official church of Brigham Young. Neils Anderson, called the Father of the Anti-Mormon party in Idaho, and his wife Mary survived the massacre, though Mary's chin was shot off by a cannonball. She was able to continue her religious work despite the handicap until her death in 1928.

Spalding

Spalding Mission, Nez Percé National Historic Park. Seeking relief from the mosquito-infested village of Lapwai, two miles away, Eliza Hart Spalding and her husband Henry moved to their new mission in 1838 with their one-year-old daughter Eliza, the first white child born in Idaho. In this shaded grove on the banks of the Clearwater River, the Spaldings built their house, a school, and a printing shop whose sites are marked with boulders and signs. Here, Eliza taught the Indian women to sew, weave, and knit and to read "the white man's Book of heaven" that she illustrated on charts six feet long and translated into Nez Percé. The Indians were kind to her, but it was a difficult life for the quiet, sickly Eliza, who missed her good friend Narcissa Whitman—120 miles away in *Walla Walla, Washington*—with whom she had shared the exciting trip as the first white women to cross the Rockies (see *South Pass, Wyoming*). The two arranged to have simultaneous prayer sessions every morning at nine o'clock, to be together in spirit at least. When Narcissa and her husband Marcus were massacred in 1847, the Spaldings, fearing reprisals from the Indians,

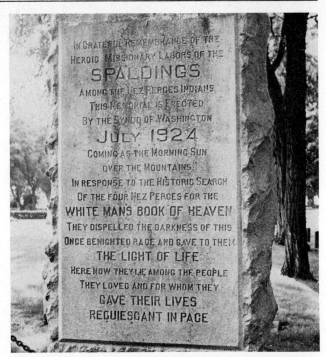

moved to Oregon, where Eliza died four years later at age forty-three. She and Henry are buried here. A huge boulder over their grave calls them "pioneers, missionaries, and founders of Industry, Education, Religion and Christian Citizenship, coming as the morning sun over the mountains. . . . In themselves their greatest monument."

Twin Falls

On a high bluff overlooking the Snake River Canyon, near the Blue Lakes Ranch, Lyda Southard poisoned two husbands in the early 1900s. In all, America's Female Bluebeard killed four husbands, a brother-in-law, and, most horridly, an infant daughter named Lyda, to collect the insurance—a sinister way to become self-supporting and independent. By the time the authorities caught on, Lyda was living in Hawaii with husband number five whom she had urged to take out $10,000 worth of life insurance. Paul Southard refused to believe the allegations against Lyda and staunchly supported her during her trial here in Twin Falls. Only after she was sentenced to ten years in prison did Southard consider divorce. Lyda escaped from prison but was eventually caught in Denver, Colorado, where she was involved in another deadly courtship.

Wallace

May Arkwright Hutton Home, 304 Cedar Street (private). May arrived from Ohio in 1883 and opened a fine, successful boardinghouse for the miners. She continued to manage it after her marriage to Lou Hutton, a railroad engineer. A 3/32 interest in the Hercules Mine, which cost them about $2,284, made May a millionaire, with dividends growing from $750 a month in 1902 to a whopping $568,750 in 1918. While living in this huge eight-bedroom cream-colored house, May wrote her book, *The Coeur d'Alenes: A Tale of Modern Inquisition in Idaho,* an impassioned attack on mineowners and a justification of labor unions which proved to be somewhat of an embarrassment when the Huttons became successful mineowners themselves. But it was May's labor involvement that enabled her to get the support of male workers for suffrage in Idaho. Her success here led to the major part of her lifework on behalf of equal rights in the state of Washington, where she moved in the early 1900s. (See *Spokane, Washington*.)

ILLINOIS

Andover

Jenny Lind Chapel, Route 81. When Swedish Pastor L. P. Esbjorn told touring opera star Jenny Lind of his financial difficulties with his new Augustana Church, she donated $1,500 so the tiny white structure could be built.

Cedarville

Jane Addams Birthplace, Mill Street (private). Stephenson County's most famous citizen was born in this two-story white frame house September 6, 1860. (Her older sister Sarah, who became a banker in *Girard, Kansas,* was born here too.) Here, the future social reformer received all the girlhood benefits of the well-to-do, including schooling at the seminary in *Rockford* and a trip to Europe. It was on the other side of the Atlantic that Jane Addams first was awakened to the plight of urban poverty, later recalling, "I gradually became convinced that it would be a good thing to rent a house in a part of the city where many primitive and actual needs are found, in which young women who had been given over too exclusively to study, might restore a balance of activity along traditional lines and learn of life from life itself; where they might try out some of the things they had been taught." She put that plan into operation in *Chicago.*

Jane Addams Grave, Family Burial Plot, Mill Street. About twelve hundred feet from the house where she was born, Jane Addams was buried in 1935. The international reputation and acclaim that had followed her settlement work in *Chicago* is simply recorded on a small stone beneath a towering shaft: "Jane Addams of Hull House and The Women's International League for Peace and Freedom."

Chicago

Old Water Tower, Michigan and Chicago Avenues, marks the northern limits of the 1871 fire that made Catherine O'Leary the nation's most famous female dairy farmer. The blaze started in her barn on DeKoven Street. But the story that her cow kicked over the lamp that caused the conflagration that cost hundreds of lives and $200 million was not confirmed by the official inquiry. And despite newspaper accusations that Mrs. O'Leary herself had carried the lantern into the barn, she was never prosecuted. In fact, Catherine O'Leary was starkly aware that the fire that wiped out her own five cows and scanty possessions had taken a rough toll. "Rough!" she exclaimed to a newspaper reporter, "Why, my God, man, it was a terror to the world."

Site of Northwestern Sanitary Fair, Bryan Hall, 89 Clark Street (now 502 Clark). The momentous meeting in October 1863 that took place in the building located on this site was inspired and arranged by Mary Livermore, tireless Civil War relief worker who reorganized the Chicago Sanitary Commission into a formidable group. Along with her friend and coworker Jane Hoge, Livermore visited army outposts from Cairo, Illinois, to Vicksburg, Mississippi, entering Vicksburg with General Grant and keeping the soldiers supplied with fresh vegetables, dried fruit, and hospital needs. The great Sanitary Fair, which raised nearly $100,000 for the cause and inspired dozens more in cities all over the country, featured orator Anna Dickinson (see *Manhattan, New York City*) and offered for sale the original draft of Lincoln's Emancipation Proclamation. It sold for $3,000. The fair also awakened Mary Livermore to the sorry state of

woman's rights, and she plunged into the suffrage movement with vigor. Drawing on her early journalistic career (she was the only woman reporter present at Lincoln's inauguration), she established *The Agitator,* her own suffrage newspaper, and edited it until she moved to Boston, Massachusetts, to help Lucy Stone with the *Woman's Journal.* While her Civil War work and her suffrage (and temperance) activities occupied her with lectures and writing until her death, Mary Livermore made an even more valuable contribution in 1893. With her friend Frances Willard (see *Evanston*), she edited the colossal *Woman of the Century,* an encyclopedia of American women, with nearly fifteen hundred sketches of notables. That book is a lively and invaluable contribution to the history of American women.

Site of Bertha Honoré Palmer House, 1350 North Lake Shore Drive. The elegant million-dollar mansion that financier and hotel owner Potter Palmer completed for his family in 1885 was the most fabulous fortress of the Windy City. Here Bertha Honoré Palmer, acknowledged Queen of Chicago society, reigned over the city's artistic and social life. At first known only as a fashionable hostess, she supported Jane Addams' Hull House and various trade union groups, and she crowned her achievement as an influential woman when she acted as chairman of the Board of Lady Managers during the 1893 World's Columbian Exposition. The towered castle she lived in—where she entertained princes, suffragists, and welfare leaders, wearing her famous diamond tiara and rope of pearls—contained the first passenger elevator in a private Chicago house, no outside locks, and a three-story octagonal entrance hall covered with tapestries, mosaics, and fine oil paintings. Although she continued to maintain the house even when she moved to *Osprey, Florida,* the mansion was destroyed in 1950 to make way for an apartment house.

Site of Woman's Building, World's Columbian Exposition, Jackson Park. "When our palace in the White City shall have vanished like a dream, when grass and flowers cover the beautiful spot where it now stands," observed Bertha Honoré Palmer as she presided over the closing ceremonies at the Woman's Building in 1893, "its memory and influence will still remain with those who have been brought together within its walls." Thanks to Mrs. Palmer, that memory is a noble one even for those of us who were born too late to visit it. In spirit, it was meant to "present a complete picture of the condition of women in every country of the world . . . and more particularly of those women who are breadwinners." And it was designed by a woman: twenty-two-year-old Sophia G. Hayden, the first female architecture graduate of MIT, who won the $1,000 prize in a nationwide competition. Her three-story white Italian Renaissance-style structure, with its delicate arches and columned terraces, took shape quickly on the north end of the lagoon that was here. When it was completed—the first building on the fairgrounds—Mrs. Palmer praised its "delicacy, symmetry and strength" and told the immense crowd at the dedication, "Even more important than the discovery of Columbus, which we are gathered together to celebrate, is the fact that the General Government has just discovered women." The building proved to be one of the most popular attractions at the exposition. At Mrs. Palmer's indefatigable urging, forty-seven nations sent displays: Impressionist Mary Cassatt sent a mural; New Jersey fisherwomen sent nets; the queen of Belgium sent fine lace. Even the Infanta Eulalia of Spain arrived in a panoply of pomp and circumstance. And through it all, Bertha Honoré Palmer presided with rare poise and efficiency. Her leadership built a sturdy pavilion and a spectacular event, where it was established without question, as she observed earlier, that "Freedom and justice for all are infinitely more to be desired than pedestals for a few."

staff who later became famous: Julia Lathrop, who became first head of the Federal Children's Bureau, followed by Grace Abbott (see *Grand Island, Nebraska*) and her sister Agnes; Dr. Alice Hamilton, first female assistant professor at Harvard Medical School; and Florence Kelley, founder of the Consumers' League. Jane Addams united and led them all, from the Hull House octagonal office on the first floor or from her own sitting-room office upstairs, both of which have now been restored to show visitors how welcoming they looked.

Also on view here is the Nobel Peace Prize Jane Addams won in 1931 (the first female recipient), a tribute to her founding role and first presidency of the Women's International League for Peace and Freedom. She was a pacifist, a reformer, and a suffragist (hosting a 1907 luncheon for suffrage leaders here). When Jane Addams died in 1935, tens of thousands viewed her body as it lay at Hull House for two days. The settlement had by then grown into thirteen buildings covering a city block. Jane Addams's body was returned to her birthplace in *Cedarville* for burial.

Ida B. Wells-Barnett House, 3624 South Martin Luther King, Jr., Drive (private). This three-story gray-stone residence with its

Hull House, 800 South Halsted Street. Jane Addams once defined a settlement house as "an institution attempting to learn from life itself," an apt description of the organization she made into the foremost settlement house in the world. With her *Rockford* classmate, Ellen Gates Starr, Addams founded Hull House in September 1889. What began as a purely local effort to aid the immigrant population of Chicago's Nineteenth Ward—with schooling, day nurseries, playgrounds, medical care, and guidance—soon influenced settlement house work all over the nation. Jane Addams' magnetic supervision and creative approach attracted scores of financially well-endowed but socially conscious young women as workers. Among her Hull House

old-fashioned cupolas was the home of the crusading newspaperwoman and social reformer from about 1919 to 1928. One of her pet projects here was the Negro Fellowship League, a community center she organized on State Street to provide young men an alternative to the neighborhood bars. Her daughter, Alfreda Duster, still living in Chicago, told us that she remembered the house as a center for reformers, when "all those people interested in agitating for justice would find their way to my mother's parlor." Ida B. Wells-Barnett had earned her spurs fighting lynchings in the South (see *Memphis, Tennessee*). She was also a crusading clubwoman, founding a number of organizations for black women. Her Alpha Suffrage Club was the first such group for blacks. Mrs. Duster remembers marching in suffrage parades with her feminist mother, both clad in white, a big yellow flower pinned on her mother's dress. Although this house serves as a memorial to Ida B. Wells-Barnett, her daughter feels that the best monument is the Ida B. Wells Housing Project at 454 East Pershing. It was the first federal housing project in Chicago, built in 1940, and Alfreda Duster assured us it was still one of the finest.

Provident Hospital, 426 East Fifty-first Street, was established by Fannie Barrier Williams and her husband as an interracial institution. Fannie Williams was also influential in pointing out the need for a black nursing school, making Provident the first to train black nurses in 1891. A prominent clubwoman and lecturer, who broke an impressive array of barriers to racial justice —first black woman in the Women's Club of Chicago, first black on the Chicago Library Board—Fannie Barrier Williams early observed, "Certain it is that colored women have been the least known, and the most ill-favored class of women in this country." Still, she maintained her fight and wrote in 1904 that despite the "dark and painful past" of slavery, "I believe that the colored women are just as strong and just as weak as any other

Women's Building, Columbian Exposition *Courtesy Chicago Historical Society*

women with like education, training and environment."

Chicago Board of Education elected Ella Flagg Young as superintendent in 1909, making her the nation's first woman to lead the school system of a major city. A dedicated educator who began her career in Chicago in 1862, Ella Flagg Young introduced such radical notions as giving teachers more say in the curriculum, teaching boys (as well as girls) how to sew, and instituting a program of sex education. A protégée and close associate of John Dewey, she so impressed him that he admitted he often failed to see "the meaning or force of some favorite conception of my own till Mrs. Young had given it back

to me." In 1910, she became the first female president of the National Education Association, continuing her extraordinary expansion and transition of the Chicago school system despite a spate of controversy over her independent policies. After she died in 1918, her portrait was placed in the Teachers Room at the Chicago Public Library.

Buckingham Memorial Fountain, Grant Park. The largest fountain in the world, made of pink Georgia marble, was donated by Kate Sturges Buckingham in 1927 to honor her brother Clarence. The independent-minded and generous heiress had the fountain made as an enlarged version of "Latona" at Versailles.

Elsah

Principia College. The collegiate extension of the school founded by Mary Kimball Morgan in *St. Louis, Missouri,* helps promote the cause of Christian Science. Morgan lived here from 1935—three years after it was established—until her death in 1948, turning over the job of president to her sons.

Evanston

Frances Willard House, "Rest Cottage," 1730 Chicago Avenue. When Frances Willard moved here from *Janesville, Wisconsin,* to attend the North Western Female College, a town ordinance

prohibited the sale of alcoholic beverages. It was a clear omen of the young woman's future course. Starting in 1874, she threw herself into the temperance movement, first as a state officer, then as national president of the Woman's Christian Temperance Union (WCTU) in 1879, spearheading a coast-to-coast movement that made liquor more than just a friendly enemy. Willard coined the WCTU slogan, "For God and Home and Native Land," and under her leadership the white ribbon of purity and the rallying cry, "Home Protection," were adopted. She turned the genteel ladies of the antialcohol brigades into "an army, drilled and disciplined," she wrote proudly. And she combined her crusading antitemperance oratory with relentless suffrage demands, becoming one of the most effective advocates of woman's rights to share the platform with Susan B. Anthony. Her unflinching motto: "Do everything."

Today, the house where she lived until her death in 1898 is restored with her furnishings, and it serves as national WCTU headquarters. Included among the mementos on display are her yellowed family Bible, in which everyone signed the temperance pledge; her desk, where she penned her famous Polyglot Petition for worldwide prohibition; and the bicycle she learned to ride at age fifty-three.

Forest Park

Emma Goldman Grave, Forest Home Cemetery, 863 South Desplaines Avenue. The first woman in the nation to speak out publicly on birth control, and coeditor of *Mother Earth,* a radical New York newspaper (its motto: "No Gods, No Masters"), died in exile in 1940 while living in Canada. Only then was Red Emma's desire to return to America granted, more than two decades after she had been deported on the transport, the *Buford,* for her anarchist activities (see *Home, Washington*). Her body was buried in the Dissenter's Row of this cemetery, near the monument to the four victims of the 1887 Haymarket labor incident that had helped spark Emma's own rebel activities. The bronze portrait over her grave, sculpted by her friend Jo Davidson, carries the quotation, "Liberty will not descend to a people, a people must raise themselves to liberty."

Freeport

Townspeople of Freeport told us they generally accept the legend that Elizabeth Phoebe Baker named the new community as a wry tribute to her husband's generosity. When William ("Tutty") Baker eagerly shared all his meals with passersby, his wife is said to have suggested the town be named Freeport, "for that is what it will be if you run it." But one historian assured us that Elizabeth herself was "a brave, helpful and generous woman." Once she unselfishly fed a new settler her only remaining corn and part of a catfish, unconcerned that her husband might not return for some time with new supplies. The lucky diner was nourished well enough to serve, years later, as the man who introduced Abe Lincoln at the Freeport Debate.

Stephenson County Historical Society Museum, 1440 South Carroll Avenue, contains a Jane Addams Room with pictures, letters, and the infant cradle of the woman born in nearby *Cedarville.* They also have her college records if you want to examine the undergraduate days of a successful career woman.

Galesburg

Mary Ann Bickerdyke Statue, Courthouse Square. "Mother" Bickerdyke was probably the best-known Civil War relief worker in the Northern army. Starting in 1861 at the Union Hospital at Cairo, Illinois, she spent four selfless years ranging all over the battlefield and making "her boys" a little more comfortable. At first on her own, then employed by the Sanitary Commission, she cooked food, washed uniforms, and delivered supplies. On one occasion, she dressed a young man's wounds with the lace from her nightgown. On another, she brewed barrels of coffee and made mush for 312 soldiers in one day. A soldier at Chattanooga, Tennessee, said simply, "She is a power of good." This statue of Mother Bickerdyke giving a wounded soldier a drink of water perpetuates another example of her influence. An army surgeon complained to his commander that Mother Bickerdyke had fired him. The officer's response is inscribed on the base of the statue: " 'She outranks me.'—General Sherman."

Knox College has always admitted women as students, but before 1870 they got only a high school education and had to sit on the other side of the room from the men. As a Knox official explained to us, "The Female Collegiate Institute was designed to offer women students the type of courses theoretically best suited for them—courses such as china-painting and so forth." The trustees' decision to admit women on an equal basis thus saved the nation from a great excess of hand-painted dinnerware.

Godfrey

Monticello College Foundation, Route 67, perpetuates the charter of the women's college founded here in 1835 by Captain Benjamin Godfrey. The retired Cape Cod seafarer began his Female Seminary specifically to provide a better education for his eight daughters. Assisted by educator Theron Baldwin and counseled by Mary Lyon of *South Hadley, Massachusetts,* Godfrey opened the school in 1838 with sixteen pupils. It was one of the earliest institutions of higher education for women, and the neighbors clucked their tongues over such folly. Several years later, Baldwin explained that the school tried to prepare its graduates "not for any imaginary state of existence—but for the sober realities and duties of actual life." Although the college was closed in 1971, the foundation that continues grants funds to promote women's education.

Harvey

Site of Amanda Smith Industrial Home for Girls, 147th Street and Jefferson Avenue. A raging fire early one evening in 1918 destroyed the brick orphanage established here in 1899 by Amanda Berry Smith. The ex-slave and popular evangelist opened her orphans' home with profits from her autobiography, published six years earlier, and with public contributions. It was the only such Protestant shelter in Illinois for black children. Under her guidance, as many as thirty resident children grew their own vegetables in a vacant lot to the east of the school and learned trades to support themselves. Amanda Smith died several years before the fire that took the lives of two of the twenty-two children asleep on the second floor. The others were rescued and placed in different orphanages, but the home was not rebuilt.

Jacksonville

Site of Ellen Hardin Walworth Birthplace, Philip Morris Building, South Main and College. A bronze marker indicates the location of the brick house where one of the founders of the DAR was born October 20, 1832. An eager clubwoman, Ellen Hardin Walworth cut her teeth on a project to preserve and mark various sites on the Revolutionary battlefield at Saratoga, New York. Several years later, in 1890, her home was the meeting place of the fledgling society (see *Washington, D.C.*) that she organized along with two other women.

Jacksonville State Hospital, 1201 South Main, was opened in 1851, partly at the urging of reformer Dorothea Dix. A decade later, Elizabeth Packard entered as a patient, and, as the current librarian reminded us, "She was our most famous case." Angry that the three-year confinement engineered by her husband was entirely within the limits of the law, Packard embarked on a crusade to grant married women their legal rights and to protect patients at mental hospitals. After a jury found her sane in 1864 and prevented her husband from again having her committed, she wrote a number of books and took up lobbying for her causes. Her legislation affected four states and aided countless numbers of women, but it antagonized physicians who were seeking more, not less, public confidence in mental hospitals.

Mendota

Helen Hokinson House, 906 Michigan Avenue (private). Cartoonist Helen Hokinson grew up here in the early 1900s, first applying her satiric pen to paper with a group of caricatures for her high school yearbook. Later she created the familiar plump clubwomen who paraded through the pages of the *New Yorker* with a delightful lack of understanding of the modern world. The chatty matrons were prone to malapropisms, virtuous moralizing, and helpless naïveté, characteristics that brought their creator both fame and wealth from a constantly chuckling audience. Many of her original drawings are displayed in museums here in Mendota, where she was buried in 1949.

Mount Olive

Grave of Mother Jones, Union Miners Cemetery. Before her death at age one hundred in 1930, the colorful union organizer said, "I hope it will be my consolation when I pass away to feel I sleep under the clay with those brave boys." She was referring to the miners killed in the 1898 massacre at Virden, Illinois, and she rests next to them today. Her gray metal casket, blanketed with white carnations and purple (her favorite color) chrysanthemums, was placed on a special railroad car that traveled from Washington, D.C., along the same route that took Lincoln's body to Springfield. Mother Jones spent almost fifty years of her long, peripatetic life organizing strikes to improve the working conditions of miners (see *Pratt, West Virginia*). "No matter what your fight, don't be ladylike," she once said, and she lived accordingly. Above her simple headstone is a twenty-two-foot pink granite monument showing her kindly face in bas-relief flanked by two life-sized statues of miners in full working gear.

Nauvoo

Emma Smith House, Joseph Smith Historic Center. This expanded log cabin familiarly known as the Joseph Smith Homestead was the first residence of the Mormon prophet and his wife, Emma Hale Smith, when they came here in 1839. Since the Mormon leader had early told Emma of his revelation to "Let thy soul delight in thy husband," her prominence in church affairs was somewhat restricted. Still, she emerged as the leading woman of Mormonism, in 1842 becoming president of its Female Relief Society. While living in this house she was a constant hostess. As her eldest son recalled: "There was scarcely a Sunday in ordinary weather that the house and yard were not crowded—the yard with teams and the house with callers."

Emma Smith is also buried on the grounds on the river side of the house.

The Mansion House was Emma and Joseph Smith's residence from 1842. When they added a wing and turned the house into a hotel, Emma assumed the duties of innkeeper of the Nauvoo Mansion for most of its twenty-six years in business. Emma was living in this handsome building in 1844 when the bodies of Joseph and Hyrum Smith were brought in, martyred victims of religious persecution. Most of the Mormons then trekked to *Salt Lake City, Utah,* under the leadership of Brigham Young, but Emma Smith chose to remain in Nauvoo. One reason was her unshakable hostility toward polygamy. Joseph Smith had accorded her the dubious title of the sect's first plural wife, but she always refused to acknowledge it, maintaining against all evidence (including dozens of Mrs. Joseph Smiths) that he had married her alone. Several years later, Emma Smith remarried a non-Mormon. Her son, Joseph Smith III, became president of the nonpolygamous Mormons who remained in Nauvoo.

Emma Smith House, "Nauvoo House," was the third and last Nauvoo residence of the First Lady of the Mormon Church. She moved in with her new husband, Lewis Crum Bidamon, in 1869, and she died here in 1879. Among the items she owned that can be seen today: her walking stick, blanket chest, and washstands.

Oregon

Ganymede's Spring, a rivulet of mineral water at the edge of Rock River, was named by the distinguished Margaret Fuller when she visited here in 1843. The celebrated author came west from *Boston, Massachusetts,* and found the countryside "enchanting beyond any I have ever seen." In *At Home and Abroad* she wrote, "Here the eye and the heart are filled." The cosmopolitan literary star further complimented the Rock River Valley residents by observing after a week of rowing, climbing, and driving, "I do believe Rome and Florence are suburbs compared to this capital of Nature's art." Seated beneath a red cedar tree on the edge of a high bluff above the stream, Fuller

wrote her poem, "Ganymede to His Eagle." She was so inspired, she named the cliff Eagle's Nest Bluff and the water, Ganymede's Spring. The grateful citizens of Oregon reciprocated by naming a spot of land in the river Margaret's Island and erecting a tablet to her memory in 1880. Today, a county historian lamented with us that the tablet has been removed and the spring, whose pure mineral waters used to fill the jugs of picnickers, is "still flowing, but contaminated." As Margaret Fuller concludes one of her poems, "And so farewell,—a grateful, sad farewell!"

Park Ridge

Park Ridge School for Girls, 733 North Prospect Avenue, was founded a century ago to provide a home for orphaned children of the Civil War. The seed money was the $500 balance belonging to the Illinois Women's Centennial Committee when the Centennial Exposition closed in Philadelphia. A pioneer in the cottage plan—rather than the institutional dormitory-style buildings of most homes—in recent years the school has shifted its emphasis to helping troubled teen-aged girls. Several of the original cottages founded with the feminist money are still in use.

Peoria

The stage on which opera star Emma Abbott made her debut in 1859, strumming her guitar and singing to an audience of coal miners, has long been gone, but Peoria proudly boasts that she spent her childhood and launched her career here. Family history attests to such poverty in the Abbott family that Emma had to walk barefoot to her first recital. Later, properly shod and reaching the peak of her enormously successful life (see *Spokane, Washington*), she is said to have invented the chaste "Abbott kiss." An observant Peoria newspaper reporter described it some years ago as "a dignified form of osculation for stage purposes, intended to give the audience the idea but not the sensation."

Bradley University was opened in 1897, the gift of eighty-one-year-old Lydia Moss Bradley. The philanthropic Peorian, described by a trustee as "a plain woman of the plain, common, real people," opened the school on the site of a cornfield as a memorial to her husband and deceased children. One unique feature of the school in the early days was horology—the study of watchmaking and repair. Lydia Moss Bradley purchased the only school of horology in the nation and had it moved by train from La Porte, Indiana, to this site. It is estimated that nearly fifteen thousand young watchmakers were graduated before time ran out on that aspect of the Bradley legacy in 1961.

Petersburg

Grave of Ann Rutledge, Oakland Cemetery. A wrought-iron fence surrounds the granite gravestone beneath which Abraham Lincoln's legendary first sweetheart lies buried. Ann Rutledge's death in 1835 is said to have deeply affected the future president. Her epitaph, composed by poet Edgar Lee Masters, reads, "I am Ann Rutledge, who sleep beneath these weeds. Beloved of Abraham Lincoln, wedded to him, not through union but through separation." Historians generally believe that Ann and Abe were simply good friends and that their romance was a legend perpetrated by Lincoln's law partner, who never got on with Lincoln's wife, Mary Todd.

Rockford

Rockford College has inherited the legacy of its forerunner, Rockford Female Seminary, whose most famous graduate was Jane Addams. She was the first Rockford student to receive a degree, in 1822, a year after her graduation. Here Jane Addams met Ellen Gates Starr, with whom she would found Hull House in *Chicago*. Today, the college has moved to a bigger campus, but the fireplace from Jane Addams' student room has been dismantled and preserved. We are assured that it will be reassembled in an appropriate setting when the new administration building is built and named after its illustrious alumna.

Springfield

Mary Todd Lincoln House, Eighth and Jackson Streets. Mary Todd first attracted Abe Lincoln's attention on the dance floor, as he marveled at the skill she had learned back home in *Lexington, Kentucky*. After an interrupted romance, they were married in 1842 at the Edwards House four doors north of here, and Mary slipped on a ring inscribed, "Love is Eternal." Two years later they moved here, into the only house Abe Lincoln ever owned. Here he practiced law and learned politics, and she bore three sons. He called her Mother and she called him Mr. Lincoln. Although her grueling housework for the impoverished, lanky Lincoln generated migraine headaches and occasional lapses of hysteria, Mary enjoyed a comfortable, loving homelife here. An astute politician herself, she once talked Abe out of accepting an appointment as governor of the new Oregon Territory and convinced him to remain in Springfield. Thus, at the end of that decade, he was available for the presidential nomination when the Republican gentlemen called on him in this house in 1860. Their next residence was the White House.

Mary Todd Lincoln Grave, Oak Ridge Cemetery. Mary Lincoln did not return to Springfield after her husband was killed in 1865. A victim of press abuse and popular misunderstanding, she traveled abroad, stayed in Chicago, then came back almost two decades later to live here with her sister Lizzie. By then Mary Lincoln was an emotionally and physiologically broken woman. She had been falsely accused of Southern sympathies and of insanity. When she died in 1882, the public began to make its amends, but the former First Lady had foreseen her own solace. "When I again rest by *his* side," she wrote to a friend in 1865, "I will be comforted." Mary Todd Lincoln was buried next to the grave of her husband.

Urbana

Monument to Katharine Sharp, University of Illinois Graduate School of Library Science. The pioneering librarian, head of the first library school in the Midwest and later head librarian here, is memorialized with a bronze bas-relief portrait by the famed sculptor Lorado Taft. The plaque cites her turn-of-the-century role as founder and director of the Illinois Library School and pays tribute to her "nobility of character and grace of person" and her "intellectual vigor and scholarly attainments. She inspired her students and associates with sound standards of librarianship and ideals of service."

Vandalia

Madonna of the Trail Statue, Gallatin Street. The eighth of the dozen identical monuments marking the nation's old highways was dedicated October 26, 1928. Vandalia marks the western terminus of the Cumberland Road (see *Springfield, Ohio*).

Wilmette

Archange Ouilmette, a Potawatomi Indian, once owned the land now occupied by this exclusive residential community. The American government gave her the land in gratitude for her husband Antoine's help in arranging a treaty between whites and Indians. Archange Ouilmette's two square miles of valuable property remained in her possession until she moved west in 1838. Then, unfamiliar with the value of real estate, she simply gave it up.

INDIANA

Beech Grove

Sarah T. Bolton Home, "Beech Bank," 103 South Seventeenth Avenue (private). The famed poet, who grew up near *Vernon* and later managed a tavern in *Indianapolis,* moved to her final residence here in 1871 after a brief sojourn in *Canton, Missouri.* One of the earliest literary stars of the Mississippi Valley, Sarah T. Bolton continued to produce her sentimental verse until her death. A sketch published in 1893, just before she died, reported that "Mrs. Bolton is in poor health, but her pen is not idle." A historical marker identifying the tree-filled estate in this Indianapolis suburb calls her "A pioneer poet of Indiana . . . crusader for women's rights." Just at the top of the back hill, a grove of trees overlooks the Sarah T. Bolton Memorial Park on South Thirteenth Avenue, occupying part of the land once belonging to the Beech Bank estate.

Benton County

Somewhere in this county, according to the indefatigable compilers of the American Guide Series volume on Indiana, rests a weary body beneath a tombstone inscribed:

> Thirteen years I was a virgin
> Two years I was a wife
> One year I was a mother
> The next year took my life.

Although county historians have been unable to pinpoint the tombstone, the sentiment deserves attention.

Evansville

Clara Barton Memorial, corner of Iowa and Mary Streets. From this site in 1884, Clara Barton supervised relief efforts for victims of the great Ohio River flood. It was the first organized disaster relief work conducted in America, and the founder of the American Red Cross (see *Dansville, New York*) did not stay on dry ground during the flood. She sailed up and down the river on the steamer *Josh V. Throop,* the first Red Cross relief boat to float on American waters, as it sounded its bell and whistle to announce help for the washed-out residents. This historic corner of land was made the site of the Protestant Deaconess Hospital. Today, Clara Barton Hall across the street houses students of nursing.

Fountain City

Levi and Catherine Coffin House, 115 North Main Street. This two-story brick house was the Grand Central Station of the Underground Railroad, devotedly operated from 1827–47 by North Carolina Quakers Levi and Catherine Coffin. Among the two thousand slaves they are said to have sheltered on their escape route to Canada was Eliza, the heroine of *Uncle Tom's Cabin*. "Aunt Katy" Coffin is said to have given Eliza her surname of Harris after her perilous flight across the ice-covered Ohio River. The Coffins were also in the book, fictionalized as Simeon and Rachel Halliday. In his own book, Levi Coffin singled out his wife's special knack for dealing with the dangerous occupation they pursued: "Very often the slaves would lie concealed in upper chambers for weeks without the boarders or frequent visitors at the house knowing anything about it. My wife had a quiet, unconcerned way of going about her work as if nothing unusual was on hand, which was calculated to kill suspicion of those who might be watching."

Geneva

Gene Stratton Porter House, "Limberlost," Sixth and Williams streets. The famed Hoosier author and photographer named her fourteen-room residence after the swamplands to the south, a wilderness she later made famous in her books and essays. Gene Stratton Porter lived here from 1895–1913, using the natural life around her as subject matter for the six novels, four nature books, and many magazine articles she wrote while sitting on her broad porch. Her original furnishings and some photography are on view, and visitors can see "Freckles' window" (from her *Freckles*), "the Dream Girl's porch," and other sites mentioned in *A Girl of the Limberlost* (the first American book translated into Arabic) and *The Harvester*. Some of the mounted moths she collected while wading through the underbrush in knee-length khaki skirt and high leather hiking boots are also here. When the swamp was filled in, she chose to find other unspoiled surroundings near *Rome City*.

Graysville

Jane Todd Crawford Grave, Johnson Cemetery, northeast of Graysville (where Hopewell Presbyterian Church once stood). A simple marble slab marks the final resting-place of Jane Todd Crawford, the word's first successful ovariotomy patient. In 1809, at age forty-six, she unflinchingly endured a surgical operation on her ovary, in *Danville, Kentucky,* that saved her life and made medical history. She lived in excellent health to tell about it until she died at her home near here in 1842.

Greencastle

DePauw University was where Arabella Babb Mansfield, the nation's first female lawyer (see *Mount Pleasant, Iowa*), served on the faculty from the 1880s until 1911. She was dean of the School of Art and of Music, and she taught history and aesthetics. When she died in 1911, a former president of DePauw called her "the strongest and truest woman I have ever known . . . a brave, patient, effective worker." The building bearing her name burned down in 1933.

Indianapolis

Sarah T. Bolton Memorial, Indiana State Capitol, Washington Street and Capitol Avenue. A plaque in the rotunda honors the unofficial poet laureate of Indiana, author of that paean to self-sufficiency, "Paddle Your Own Canoe." Bolton (see *Beech Grove* and *Vernon*) penned that familiar poem in 1851 while helping her husband, custodian of the State House, refurbish an earlier building that served as the capitol. On her own, she purchased, pieced, and hand sewed the carpeting for the house and senate chambers, upon which governors of the western states then trod for a conference. Her poem, which became a favorite of schoolchildren and their parents, concludes:

> Nothing great is lightly won:
> Nothing won is lost;
> Every good deed, nobly done,
> Will repay the cost.
> Leave to Heaven, in humble trust,
> All you will to do:
> But if you succeed, you must
> Paddle your own canoe.

Madame C. J. Walker Manufacturing Company, 617 Indiana Avenue. This four-story brick building still producing her cosmetic products is the modern descendant of the factory where Madame C. J. Walker (Sarah Breedlove) first produced the

pomades and creams that straightened and softened kinky hair and made her a millionaire. Here, starting in 1911, the nation's foremost black businesswoman ran the hairdressing empire known as the Walker System, a highly successful enterprise that was promulgated largely by door-to-door saleswomen known as Walker Agents. Like Madame Walker herself, the people who run the plant today shy away from the term hair straighteners. "We do press the hair, but that's different from straighteners," the chairman of the board told us. "We call it hair culture; we preserve the hair." (See *Manhattan, New York City; Irvington, New York*.)

Indiana Women's Prison, 401 North Randolph Street, was the nation's first penal institution managed exclusively by women, for women. It opened in 1873, after a group of Quaker women, horrified by the degrading treatment of female prisoners at the State Reformatory at Jeffersonville, urged the state legislature to construct separate facilities for women. The Quaker reformists had become especially outraged over the open-air baths the female prisoners were forced to take, stripped naked and callously observed by whip-cracking male guards. The men in charge also enjoyed paying the women inmates nocturnal visits with prison-issued keys. When the first of seventeen prisoners was transferred to the new prison here, her manacles were removed, and the new superintendent planted a kiss on her forehead, saying, "I receive thee as a daughter—let us pray and ask Heaven to help us." Her early decrees included a ban on the "unwomanly use of tobacco" which brought instant "gloom and sadness" to the criminals. Soon a work-study program was initiated, and a second superintendent was able to boast after 1884 that "visitors from abroad are amazed and delighted to find women in charge and able to maintain discipline without guards, firearms or other similar appliances of prison management."

The Propylaeum, 1410 North Delaware Street. This four-story brick-and-limestone mansion with its peaked dormer windows and irregular roof lines houses the women's club that was founded in 1875. May Wright Sewall was one of its charter members. A relentless organizer who applied her fine administrative hand to the State Suffrage Society and to the International Council of Women in 1885, Sewall was equally content to supervise civic projects. She founded and headed the Indianapolis Girls' Classical School in 1882 and cofounded the Indianapolis Art Association. It was she who designed the first meetinghouse of the club in 1891, and the silver trowel with which she laid the cornerstone is on display here, in the second clubhouse, purchased in 1921, a year after her death.

Lafayette

Earhart Hall, Purdue University Campus. A women's residence hall completed in the late 1960s stands as a monument to Amelia Earhart, who was a visiting member of the Purdue faculty from 1935–37. About one week out of every four, she left her husband at their home in New York (see *Harrison, New York*) and flew here to act as counselor and adviser for the female students. The role of role model suited the gutsy, grinning aviator, who imparted her feminist philosophy to the students during informal talks. She advocated pacifism, working women, and an end to "the complete dependence of the female" on the male in marriage. One of her rewards for teaching here was a new airplane from the Purdue Research Foundation. The Lockheed Electra, outfitted with the latest navigational equipment, became hers on July 24, 1936. It would, she hoped, escort her around the world. (See *Miami, Florida*.)

Site of Annie Ellsworth House, Seventh and South Streets. In her family home here in 1844, a seventeen-year-old girl chose the text of the world's first telegraph message. The young girl was asked to select the historic words by inventor Samuel F. B. Morse, who was grateful for her speedy relay of the news, in 1843, that the U.S. Congress had passed the bill authorizing construction of the first telegraph line. Annie returned to her home here and, with her mother, worked out the message from the Bible: "What hath God wrought!" She stood at Morse's side in Washington, D.C., a year later, while he transmitted the words in dots and dashes to the terminal station in Baltimore, Maryland, in a few record-breaking seconds. Today, a church building stands on the site where Annie chose her momentous biblical passage.

Helen Mar Jackson Gougar Grave, Springvale Cemetery, 2580 North State Road 25. The prominent suffrage and temperance leader went to her grave in 1907 before women won the vote she worked so long to obtain. In 1894 Helen Gougar decided to beef up her approach. She tried to vote in a state election. When forbidden, she sued the election board, arguing her own case in 1895 as a newly admitted member of the bar. Although she presented her arguments "with deadly effect," according to the editors of *History of Woman Suffrage,* she lost the case. She also lost the appeal, becoming in the process the first female lawyer to appear before the state supreme court.

Lincoln City

Nancy Hanks Lincoln Grave, Lincoln Boyhood National Memorial, Route 162. So little is known of the early life of the mother of the nation's sixteenth president that the National Park Service, who runs this shrine, merely tells us she was "a shadowy figure of obscure lineage." That turns out to be the bureaucratic euphemism for what is assumed to be her illegitimate birth, a fact of nature that never stopped her son from declaring, "All that I am or hope ever to be I get from my mother, God bless her." Nancy Hanks Lincoln died here of "milk sickness" in 1818 in the log cabin where Abe had grown to a nine-year-old boy. Years later, her nephew Dennis wrote, "She knew she was going to die and called up the children to her dying side and told them to be good and kind to their father—to one another and to the world." Abe Lincoln took his mother's advice, but no one marked her grave until 1879.

New Harmony

Twenty-five of the original buildings remain at the colony founded by a group of Rappites in 1815 and sold to Welsh philanthropist Robert Owen in 1825 as an experiment in communal living. Reformer Frances Wright spent some time here after her own antislavery project at Nashoba in *Germantown, Tennessee,* collapsed. At New Harmony, Fanny Wright joined Owen in urging political and economic equality for women, and she founded what is considered the first women's literary club in the country. Her career next moved to the lecture podium. Although the experiment ended in 1827, scientists and educators continued to do research here. From this community was developed an early public school, offering equal education for the sexes.

Fauntleroy Home, West Street, erected in 1815 by the Rappites (members of the Harmonist Society), has been restored to its original handsomeness. In this parlor, just to the right of the large entrance hall, in 1859 Constance Owen Fauntleroy organized the Minerva Club, the nation's first women's club with a written constitution. She modeled it after the literary group founded by Frances Wright, colleague of her grandfather Robert Owen. Pictures of each member of the Minerva Club line the wall, and the original book of minutes is available for visitors to read.

Peoria

Frances Slocum Grave, Bowman Road, Frances Slocum State Forest. More than a decade after she was abducted by Delaware Indians from her home in *Wilkes-Barre, Pennsylvania,* in 1778, Frances Slocum was married to a Miami chief, given the name Maconaqua ("Little Bear"), and settled into a happy, prosperous village near the present town of Peru. She raised several children and a hundred head of livestock. In 1837 she was found by her white brothers and sisters, but the sixty-four-year-old woman, her red hair turned to gray and her skin wrinkled with age, refused to leave her Indian land or ways. Speaking through an interpreter, she told of the kindly treatment by the Delaware family who had adopted her, and of the pleasant life she now led. Disappointed, her white family returned east without her. In 1847, Frances Slocum died, and the White Rose of the Miamis was buried in her beaded leather leggings next to her Miami husband and two young sons. More than a century later, when the site was scheduled to be flooded by the Mississinewa Reservoir, the graves were carefully removed to this spot at the edge of the park named in her honor. Reinterred with her 192-year-old bones were the pottery, china, and pipe with unsmoked tobacco that were found in the original grave.

Philadelphia

Mary Alice Smith Gray House. The woman who worked in the home of poet James Whitcomb Riley, and inspired his "Little Orphant Annie," moved here after she married a farmer. As a fourteen-year-old orphan, Mary Alice Smith moved into the Riley homestead in the late 1800s. For two years she shooed the chickens from Riley's back porch and dusted the walnut stairway—all visible in the Riley home at Greenfield today. She was there, as the poem records, to "earn her board-an'keep," and she has been immortalized in numerous anthologies.

Richmond

Madonna of the Trail Monument, East Main Street. The ninth link in the chain of twelve identical statues erected across the nation by the DAR was dedicated October 28, 1928 (see *Springfield, Ohio*). Richmond was chosen as a place to commemorate the hardy women of the wagon trains because the first tollgate in Indiana stood near this site on the national road.

Rockport

Aunt Lepha McKay House, Lincoln Pioneer Village. This unadorned one-room cabin (Cabin No. Eleven) standing on the land she once owned commemorates Aunt Lepha McKay, who pioneered in the education of black children in the region. At her own expense and on her own initiative, she instructed many of the free blacks in the area before regular schools existed.

Rome City

Gene Stratton Porter House, "Wildflower Woods," Route 9. At this house on the shores of Sylvan Lake, the naturalist and author who had begun her career in *Geneva* continued to produce novels, nature stories, and a children's book. Gene Stratton Porter designed the two-story residence herself, and she had it constructed of Wisconsin cedar logs to suit the wild surroundings. Two carved limestone owls at the gate are also her design. From 1914 until the early 1920s, she flourished amidst the unspoiled environment of flowers and birds. Here she saved trees, transplanted shrubs, grew vegetables, wrote, photographed nature with her forty-pound camera and ten-pound tripods, and laid out her own books, until ill health forced her to move to California. There she supervised the filming of some of her books. It is estimated that some fifty million readers have enjoyed her works, translated into seven languages and set in Braille.

Terre Haute

Amalia Kussner Coudert House, Ohio Street between Second and Third Streets. Today this huge Doric building that houses war relics is called Memorial Hall; nearly a century ago, it was the childhood home of artist Amalia Kussner Coudert. Early on, she expressed an interest in the thoughtful countenances of adults. Her first notable commission, through a Terre Haute woman, was Lillian Russell. Among the other well-known faces she immortalized in her miniatures on ivory were those of King Edward VII then Prince of Wales; the czarina of Russia; and Cecil Rhodes. A contemporary newspaper columnist noted with approval, "It is said that our Terre Haute girl does not confess to a feeling of awe or timidity when in the presence of Royalty."

Vernon

Sarah T. Bolton Room, Our Heritage Museum, is furnished with objects once owned by poet Sarah Bolton of *Beech Grove.* The memorabilia include her antique Chickering piano, on which

she no doubt played the music to which her famed poem, "Indiana," was set. One verse ends with these lines:

> The winds of heaven never fanned
> The circling sunlight never spanned
> The border of a better land
> Than our own Indiana.

Vevay

Mary Wright's Piano, Switzerland County Historical Museum. This dusty, one-pedaled Muzio Clementi piano, the first piano brought into Indiana, once reverberated with the plaintive music of a heartbroken woman. Mary Wright came to Vevay in 1817, the daughter of an aristocratic English family that had fallen on hard times. Mary herself had been jilted by her Engish fiancé. Among the household goods floated on a raft down the Ohio River was the piano, a prized instrument fashioned like a clavichord with 5½ octaves. But even the verdant, rolling hills of Vevay failed to lift Mary Wright's gloom. Her only solace for years was to play her piano. The log cabin concerts for her pioneer neighbors proceeded like clockwork: Mary would descend on an outside ladder from her second-floor seclusion, dressed in the gown and jewels she had worn to court. She would bow, run through her classical repertoire, then return wordlessly to her loft. Although the jewels tarnished and the piano wires loosened, the concerts continued. No one ever saw Mary Wright except at the piano, or on her solitary moonlit walks. They found her dead in her room in 1874, and her body had to be lowered with ropes. Mary Wright's death left an enormous void in Vevay's cultural life.

Vincennes

Site of Madame Godare House, Third and Church Streets. A historical marker identifies this spot as the place where the Betsy Ross of the Northwest Territories was living in 1778 when George Rogers Clark conducted his forays against the old French Fort Sackville to remove the British who were then in control. At the urging of patriotic neighbors, Madame Godare fashioned a flag to replace the Union Jack when Clark marched through. She used 3¾ ells of green serge and 5 ells of St. Marion's red to make her banner. It flew over the fort in 1778, and today, a replica with its thirteen red and green stripes is on exhibit at the nearby fort rotunda.

Site of Alice Roussilon House, Second and Barnett Streets. They called her Alice of Old Vincennes, and Maurice Thompson wrote about her in a novel of the same name. When the British took the fort from the French, Alice grabbed the French tricolor from its staff and hid it, determined to keep it from falling into the British general's possession. Her concerned act made her a town heroine. Later, when George Rogers Clark marched in to claim Fort Sackville as American territory, he honored Alice by asking her to hoist the new flag that was designed by Madame Godare.

IOWA

Amana

Amana Colonies were established in 1854 by Barbara Heinemann and her husband, refugees from religious persecution in Germany, who had earlier experimented with a community in Erie County, New York. Barbara Heinemann moved here in 1861, later becoming the leader of this spiritual community until her death in 1883. The principles of the village were communal ownership, farming, and renunciation of worldly goods. The colony flourished on its 25,000 acres until 1932, when it was replaced by the current order that permits free enterprise in the seven villages.

Arnolds Park

Abigail Gardner Cabin, Monument Drive. This restored log cabin on the shores of West Okoboji Lake was the scene of a violent attack—known as the Spirit Lake Massacre—by renegade Sioux Indians. Although most historians sympathize with the famine of the severe winter and the tribal antipathies toward whites for chasing the game away, this incident has been described as "the bloodiest episode in the annals of Iowa."

On the morning of March 8, 1857, nine members of an outlaw band, led by the feared Inkpaduta, entered the tiny Gardner cabin and slaughtered most of the family. Fourteen-year-old Abigail watched in terror as they shot her father, clubbed her mother and a neighbor to death, scalped them, and beat three small children to a pulp. Abigail was taken captive and forced to witness a continued destructive rampage. Then began a 2½-month march north in the bitter cold. In her narrative of the captivity, Abigail described the attitude that helped her survive: "My tearless acquiescence and willingness to die seemed to fill them with wonder, and even admiration, as they thought it a sign of great bravery, a quality they highly appreciate but which they did not suppose the white woman to possess."

On the last day of May 1857, Abigail was ransomed to some friendly Yankton Sioux for two horses, twelve blankets, two kegs of powder, twenty pounds of tobacco, 32 yards of blue squaw cloth, 37½ yards of calico and ribbon, and other small articles. When her captors traded her, they presented her a handsome Indian warbonnet with thirty-six large eagle feathers "as a token of respect for the fortitude and bravery I had manifested." Abbie was reunited with a sister and, that August, got married. Although deeply affected by her bloody experience, Abigail Gardner Sharp recovered sufficiently to publish her narrative (a best seller in nine editions). She returned to this cabin and opened a small but profitable souvenir shop. Here she told her gory tale to visitors and sold color postcards printed in Germany, showing the cabin, herself, and the nearby stone monument to the victims of the massacre. After she died in 1921, the cabin was turned into a museum.

Cedar Falls

Jacob Hoffman Cabin, Overman Park. This is a replica of the original twelve-by-twenty-foot cabin built more than a century ago by pioneer Jacob Hoffman, prototype of fictional hero Wayne Lockwood in Bess Streeter Aldrich's novel *Song of Years.* The model for Jeremiah Martin in the same book was the writer's grandfather, Cedar Falls pioneer Zimri Streeter. Bess Streeter Aldrich was born here in 1881 to pioneer parents who had crossed the plains by oxteam and covered wagon. She once described their influence on her writing: "I was steeped in an atmosphere of reminiscence of river floods, storms, drought, ox-team trails, log cabins, snow drifting onto beds—all of the harsh experiences which I had escaped by arriving at the tag end of the family of eight after it had moved to town." When she later told her mother how sorry she was that she'd had to endure such a hard life, her mother replied, "Save your pity. We had the best time in the world!"

Cedar Falls also turns up as "Cedartown" in *Lantern in Her Hand.* (See *Elmwood, Nebraska.*)

Cedar Rapids

Cherry Sisters Graves, Linwood Cemetery. A shared headstone inscribed "Cherry Sisters" over the graves of Addie and Effie Cherry is the only memorial to the famous vaudeville team

billed as "The world's worst sister act." Around the turn of the century, along with their sisters Ella, Jessie, and Lizzie, Addie and Effie Cherry developed a routine that was considered so bad it was good. "You'll roll out of your seat!" screeched the billboards. Frequently performing behind a wire screen to protect themselves from tomatoes and eggs hurled by enthusiastic members of the audience, the Cherry Sisters also ran through their act once in a courtroom, to prove they had been maligned in a newspaper. When the judge saw their act, he upheld the newspaper report. When they returned to Cedar Rapids in 1917, they opened a bakeshop, and Effie ran for mayor twice. Like their comeback efforts, the political campaigns flopped.

When two young students visited this grave site recently, they wondered who had placed two plastic roses there. These young men have also written a musical called *Cherrysh!* based on the Cherry Sisters' lives, an effort to show the women as "human beings." The authors noted that they wanted to know, "Were the Cherry Sisters actually smart and shrewd performers, or didn't they really know how bad they were?"

Charles City

Carrie Chapman Catt House, south of town (private). A bronze plaque on a boulder marks the two-story brick farmhouse where the strong-willed Carrie Lane (see *Ripon, Wisconsin*) started to forge her feminist principles. At age thirteen, she wondered aloud why women could not vote in the 1872 presidential election. When a schoolboy friend told her that men voted and fought, while women took care of the house, she got angry. Her father said, "She'll never get married, I'm afraid." In fact she married twice, and she voted. With her second husband, George W. Catt, a civil engineer entirely sympathetic to the women's movement, she signed a premarriage contract guaranteeing her two months off in the spring and two months in the fall for suffrage work. (See *New Rochelle, New York.*)

Clarinda

Goldenrod School, Page County Fairgrounds. While teaching in this tiny school in 1901, Jessie Field Shambaugh, "the Mother of 4-H," first developed the principles that spread into a nationwide movement. She worked with rural children outdoors and in their homes, and then she devised a three-leaf clover pin to reward those who performed well in everything from growing corn to sewing hems. In time, the innovative clubs reached out to farming areas in all fifty states. The insignia became a four-leaf clover, its motto derived from Jessie Field Shambaugh's original one: Head, Heart, Hands, and Health (although Shambaugh's fourth leaf stood for Home). Despite her contribution to the education of the nation's farm youth, she never took credit for founding 4-H. "It was the boys and girls of Page County who took ahold of the parents who backed them up that made 4-H a success," Jessie Field Shambaugh modestly insisted. Today, her historic Goldenrod Schoolhouse has been moved here and turned into a 4-H museum.

Clinton

Nothing reminds visitors that Clinton was the home of two remarkable women.

Judith Ellen Foster, a suffragist, temperance worker, and lawyer, became the first woman in Iowa to be admitted to the bar of the state supreme court in 1872. Unlike her forerunner Arabella Mansfield (see *Mount Pleasant*), Foster actually practiced law and later used it as a springboard for her political activities.

The child born Helen Leonard here in 1861 grew up to be the flamboyant musical star Lillian Russell. The popular, buxom actress inherited her mother's attitude toward feminism, and she energetically marched and lectured in support of suffrage. Once proclaimed "the most desirable woman in America," she joined one mammoth parade down Fifth Avenue in 1915 and elicited a reporter's awe: "Even Lillian Russell, who was accustomed to riding in hansom cabs, walked the long route for the glory of womanhood."

Council Bluffs

Amelia Bloomer Grave, Fairview Cemetery, Lafayette Drive. A stone seven feet high marks the grave of the "Pioneer of Women's Emancipation," whose name is immortalized in the ankle-length pants and tunic she wore and publicized (see *Seneca Falls, New York*). In 1855 Amelia Bloomer and her husband moved here and stayed for the rest of their lives. In response to a minister who delivered a sermon on the "Subordination of Woman," she once prided herself that she "completely demolished the flimsy fancies of the gentleman." Until she died in 1894, she pioneered the votes-for-women drive in Iowa, becoming president in 1871 of the Iowa Woman Suffrage Society. When she presided, the *Des Moines State Register* reported that the convention was run "with a spirit and in a manner after which men might well pattern [themselves]. . . . the ladies who took the lead, showed themselves better posted in general information, in all matters of deliberation, than men."

Today, according to a city official, the conservative nature of Council Bluffs has kept Bloomer from being recognized as an important local figure. The same official told us, "The average citizen would say, 'Oh, yeah, she's the woman who wore baggy pants, right?' Sad, but true."

Ruth Anne Dodge Memorial, Fairview Cemetery, Lafayette Drive. This bronze fountain depicting an angel on the prow of a boat was sculpted by Daniel Chester French as a memorial to Ruth Anne Dodge from her daughters. The figure is modeled after a recurring vision of immortality that Mrs. Dodge described to her children before her death. Since the statue darkened soon after it was erected in 1918, it is known locally as the "Black Angel." That title has not entirely pleased some Council Bluffs residents, who point out that the angel of Mrs. Dodge's dreams was originally clothed in a shining white garment and carried a bowl with the water of life. Despite suggestions that range from treating it with acid, lemon oil, and paint, it has remained black. Margaret Cresson, daughter of the sculptor, has suggested that the statue be gilded; then it could be called "the Golden Angel."

Davenport

Iowa Annie Wittenmyer Home, 2800 Eastern Avenue, was originally organized in 1865 as the Iowa Soldiers' Orphans Home, to care for the children of men killed in the Civil War. Noted relief worker Annie Wittenmyer, who founded the first free school in *Keokuk* a dozen years earlier, fulfilled her promise to dying soldiers she had tended on the front lines by opening a home for their children in Farmington in 1864. It was the first such home in the world. Annie collected funds from sympathetic Iowans by tugging at their heartstrings with the reminder that fallen soldiers had left this legacy: "The little eyes at home have looked and wept for the soldier that shall never return. The windows are darkened, the hearthstone has lost its warmth, and the little bare feet must start out on life's thorny and perilous way alone."

When the original group of twenty-one orphans swelled to ninety-seven, a new home was created in the deserted army barracks on the present site. By 1867, when Annie Wittenmyer left her post as matron, two other branches had been established in the state. This home was renamed in her honor in 1949.

Des Moines

Suffrage Memorial, Iowa State Capitol. Iowa sculptor Nellie Verne Walker (see *Keokuk*) executed this bas-relief honoring the "Pioneer Suffragists and the long procession of workers who helped to secure the final enfranchisement of women." In 1936 Carrie Chapman Catt (see *Charles City*) unveiled this panel of goddesslike figures clad in draped garments.

Iowa Soldiers and Sailors Monument, State Capitol grounds, was sculpted from a design by Iowa artist Harriet A. Ketcham. The noted sculptor won the commission over forty-seven other artists in a competition. When she died soon after, Danish artist Carl Rohl-Smith was selected to execute her sketch.

Fairfield

Auntie Woods Monument, Fairfield Cemetery. An eleven-foot-high granite gravestone recounts the accomplishments of Mehitable Ellis ("Auntie") Woods, who carried supplies and gave tender care to Iowa soldiers in the Civil War. Driving her own commissary wagon and bearing the title of major, Auntie Woods made thirteen trips south and carried nine cargoes of goods, frequently dodging red tape and cannonballs to minister to her boys in blue. She always traveled alone and unannounced, answering all questions that her destination was "to see my sons, all of whom are in the army." In peacetime, Auntie Woods was Fairfield's most charitable resident. She collected clothing and food for cyclone victims in Grinnell. She gathered supplies for Kansas farmers whose crops were chewed to destruction by grasshoppers. When she died in 1891, at age seventy-eight, two days after presiding at the annual banquet she gave for the Ellis Hose Company—named in her honor—Auntie Woods was buried here in a funeral accompanied by brass bands and hundreds of soldiers. Every vehicle in Fairfield was mobilized for her funeral procession. And the firemen who helped carry her bier presented a pillow emblazoned with the words, "Our Mother."

Fort Madison

Grandmother Brown House, Seventh Street and Avenue E (private). Once a red-brick cottage with white trim, now painted pale green, this was the home of Maria Brown, whose daughter-in-law, Harriet Connor Brown, related Maria's life in *Grandmother Brown's Hundred Years.* The book told the story of the Ohio-born pioneer whose first taste of country living came in 1856, after a steamboat ride and an overland trip. "The drudgery was unending. The isolation was worse," she said of farm life. "Oh, those were busy days! Besides the everyday routine of cooking, cleaning, washing, ironing, and baby tending . . . I looked after the chickens, eggs and butter." And made all her clothes, and her candles, soap, and socks. "Someone told me that in Ireland it was the men who did the knitting, the women the sewing. That seems to me like a fair division of labor." Harriet Connor Brown, who won the *Atlantic Monthly* prize for biography for the book in 1928, wrote in her introduction that she did the book to rescue Grandmother Brown from the oblivion common to such women. "To read of her may comfort other women who, passionately and devotedly, but more or less rebelliously, are doing the duty that Nature points them to, the kind of work which the man-world, despite all its fine talk about the glory of womanhood, holds so lightly."

Rebecca Pollard Home, 825 D Street (private). The educator and author spent her last years in this Georgian colonial home of her son Joseph. She was best known for developing the science of phonics, a method of sounding words out to learn to pronounce them. Thousands of schoolchildren studied her *Pollard's Synthetic Readers and Spellers* and learned to connect diphthongs and identify consonants. Her pioneering textbooks were introduced in the 1880s and provided the mainstay of teachers' tools for most of the country. Rebecca Pollard died in this house in 1917, at age eighty-six. For the next two decades, six-year-olds in nearby Keokuk used her Pollard system of learning to pronounce.

Iowa City

Vinnie Ream Hoxie House, "Vinita," 310 South Lucas Street (private). At the turn of the century, the famed sculptor of Lincoln and Governor Kirkwood (see *Washington, D.C.*) spent many summers here, greeting visitors on the spacious lawn where her husband kept a number of caged doves. At a ceremony in Iowa City after she died, two songs she had composed were sung. The first, "I Love Thee," included lyrics by a Cherokee Indian who fell in love with Vinnie when she was a young girl. (He also named *Vinita, Oklahoma,* for her, and she in turn named her house for the town.) The second song, a poem by Joaquin Miller, was called "My Ship Comes In."

Institute of Child Behavior and Development, University of Iowa, is the outgrowth of the Iowa Child Welfare Research Station (the first in the nation) founded in 1917 by Cora Bussey Hillis. She once said that her deep interest in child welfare work was aroused when she realized that everything in her home—shrubbery, dogs, chickens, material goods—had a standard of quality. Everything but her children. " 'Why give scientific study to material things and utterly neglect the child?' I asked . . . But how to go about doing this? Then came the vision: establish an accredited child welfare research laboratory where facilities should be available to the parenthood of the land. I realized that help of a dependable character could come only through applied science based on study of the normal child, the most valuable asset of this or any other nation!"

Keokuk

Site of Estes House, Fifth and Main Streets. The bronze marker describing the days when this hotel was a Civil War hospital neglects to mention the Keokuk woman who became one of the most noted relief workers of the entire war. In 1861, Annie Wittenmyer focused her attention on the wounded here, then used her own money and courage to travel to the front. While shells exploded around her and troops fell at her feet, she worked as Iowa Sanitary Agent and transported some $136,000 worth of relief supplies to federal soldiers from Pittsburg Landing to Vicksburg. During her four years of service, she was Iowa's Angel of the Civil War. Once at a Missouri hospital she came across her feverish brother, who had just turned away the standard breakfast tray: "a tin cup full of black, strong coffee; beside it was a leaden looking tin platter, on which was a piece of fried fat bacon, swimming in its own grease, and a slice of bread." She immediately resolved to nurse soldiers back to health with proper food, and in 1864 she established her Special Diet Kitchens as an alternative to army rations. Untold numbers of military men praised her dietetic innovations while they recovered from both battle wounds and military menus.

Iowa congressman, Fred Schwengel, who had the orphans' home in *Davenport* renamed for her in 1949, called Wittenmyer "the greatest woman in America in her time."

Trinity United Methodist Church, 2330 Plank Road, is the modern successor of the Chatham Square Methodist Episcopal Church founded at Seventh and Morgan streets in 1857. Annie Wittenmyer was one of its motivating forces, and many of the hymns she later wrote were sung here. Among the notable personages who lectured here: Frederick Douglass, P. T. Barnum, and temperance reformer Frances E. Willard (see *Evanston, Illinois*). Prohibition was also a favorite cause of Annie Wittenmyer's after she moved to Philadelphia, Pennsylvania, in the 1870s. She became the first president of the WCTU and continued lecturing on temperance until the day she died, at eighty-three, in 1900.

Statue of Chief Keokuk, Rand Park. The heroic bronze statue, marking the burial place of the Sac and Fox Indian chief, was sculpted by Nellie Verne Walker, an Iowa-born artist who learned her craft in her father's marble shop. She made her name as a sculptor of monumental works, such as this larger-than-life figure of the muscular chief overlooking the Mississippi River. A blanket is draped over his shoulder, and eagle plumes crown his warbonnet. The diminutive Nellie Verne Walker once told an interviewer that she liked her statues "large rather than small. I do like things monumental rather than the more playful sculpture."

Le Mars

Le Mars probably broke all existing records in 1869 when it took its name, not from one wife or sweetheart of a founding father, but from six female visitors. Each lent the initials of her first name for the new settlement. For the record, the women were Lucy Underhill, Elizabeth Parsons, Mary Weare, Anna Blair, Rebecca Smith, and Sarah Reynolds.

Moingona

Kate Shelley Bridge, on the main line of the Chicago and North Western Railroad, four miles north of town. One of the highest and longest double-track railroad bridges in the country spans the Des Moines River just north of the village where its namesake—Kate Shelley—became an Iowa heroine in 1881. Late on the night of July 6, while a torrential rainstorm drenched the rugged countryside and swelled the creek, fifteen-year-old Kate Shelley watched from her widowed mother's cottage as an oncoming train engine plunged helplessly off the Honey Creek Bridge. Disregarding the violent winds and relentless rain, she climbed a bluff, inched her way across the rickety wooden trestle, and ran a mile to the Moingona Station to report the accident. Although railroad spikes tore her clothing and bloodied her hands, and the soaking storm extinguished her little lantern, she arrived just in time. Thanks to her warning, the station operator flagged down the midnight express and saved all its passengers from a watery grave beneath the washed-out bridge. A year later, the Iowa legislature, in recognition of the teen-ager "whom neither the terror of the elements nor the fear of death could appal in her efforts to save human life," voted her a two-hundred-dollar reward and a three-inch Tiffany gold medal embossed with a girl carrying a lantern. Poems about her and tributes to her poured in, but Frances Willard of *Evanston, Illinois,* came through with the more practical college scholarship that gave Kate a year of education. When her impoverished family needed her at home, Kate Shelley returned to Moingona, where she served as station agent. When she died in 1912, the train company sent a special railroad car to her home to convey family and friends to the funeral.

Montrose

Kalawequois Grave, Route 61. The DAR has placed a small monument next to an unlettered stone marking the grave of the Sac Indian, Kalawequois. After she died of consumption in 1837, she was buried by moonlight in a funeral that long echoed with her mother's plaintive cries. A newspaper account of the ceremony so moved poet Lydia Sigourney (see *Sigourney*) that she further memorialized the two Indian women in a poem. Her touching tribute, "The Indian Girl's Burial," begins:

> A wail upon the prairies,
>   A cry of woman's woe,
> That mingleth with the autumn blast,
>   All fitfully and low.
> It is a mother's wailing!
>   Hath earth another tone,
> Like that with which a mother mourns
>   Her lost, her only one?

Mount Pleasant

Mount Pleasant Union Block, Mount Pleasant Square. In a second-floor law office now occupied by an insurance agency, Arabella Babb Mansfield began the studies that would make her the nation's first female lawyer. After two years of poring over statutes and law books, the Iowa Wesleyan graduate and her husband both applied for admission to the bar, June 15, 1869. Belle was admitted at once. At a time when other women were being denied that privilege for the "disability" of being a wife and mother (like Myra Bradwell of Chicago, Illinois), Belle Mansfield's accomplishment was praised by the local newspaper, which added the warning, "she must expect to be stared at, and remarked about upon all occasions, for you know, a female lawyer in the State of Iowa is something new." As it was also something new for the nation, it was cheered by suffrage leaders. But Belle Mansfield denied herself a chance for higher glory when she decided not to practice. Instead, she devoted her life to teaching, first at nearby Iowa Wesleyan (where a $1,000 scholarship for a female prelaw student and a room in the library are named for her), then at DePauw University in *Greencastle, Indiana.*

Sigourney

An early settler of the seat of Keokuk County decided to name it after his favorite poet, Lydia Huntley Sigourney. Although the popular writer (see *Norwich, Connecticut*) never traveled here, she frequently embroidered western themes with her prolific and flowery prose (see *Montrose*). Lydia Sigourney was so flattered by the town being named in her honor that she donated a row of trees to be planted in the courthouse yard. Dutch elm disease has leveled most of them.

Sioux City

Pearl Street, the city's first business thoroughfare, was named for a black cook on the steamboat *Omaha* who was enormously popular with the early settlers. Today the street extends to the hills, where it is more grandiosely named Grandview Boulevard.

Apparently black female cooks were all the rage in the young region. One, known only as Aunty Woodin, is singled out in the county history books as serving such delicious opossum dinners that business persons actually vied for invitations to them.

Wapello

This is the seat of Louisa County, which was thought for many years to have been named for one Louisa Massey, who avenged her brother's death by shooting and wounding his murderer. The bold young heroine appealed to the imagination of early settlers in the wild and woolly days of Iowa, but late records indicate that the county was actually named for Louisa County, Virginia, which was named for Queen Louisa of Denmark, who is not known to have shot anyone.

KANSAS

Argonia

Susanna Medora Salter House, Garfield and Osage Streets. The nation's first female mayor was elected to office April 4, 1887, the year Kansas granted women the right to vote for, and hold, municipal office. Susanna Salter, a twenty-seven-year-old WCTU leader, was as surprised as the rest of the town when she won the election. Until she walked into the polling place, she didn't even know that some antitemperance pranksters had put her name on the ballot as a joke. With a two-thirds majority making her mayor-elect, the joke was on the "wets." Mayor Salter got the news while up to her elbows in wash suds on her back stoop. She ruled efficiently, then declined to run for a second term. She lived in this two-story brick house, which proud Argonians now maintain as a museum, from 1892 to 1893. Earlier, Mayor Salter attended a state suffrage convention at Newton, where Susan B. Anthony is said to have slapped her on the back and said, "Why, you look just like any other woman."

Atchison

Amelia Earhart Birthplace, 223 North Terrace (private). The world's most famous female pilot was born in this two-story frame Victorian house July 24, 1897. She spent much of her childhood here with her sister Muriel and her grandparents. The current owners showed us the southwest bedroom where Amelia was born and the enormous front porch where the two girls made a museum for moths and tadpoles rather than playing with dolls. They also chose rifles and footballs over ruffles and ribbons. The owners pointed out the spot where the youngsters built a chute to the Missouri River below, sliding down in pursuit of the exciting sensation that made the precocious young Amelia squeal with joy, "This is just like flying!" (See *Harrison, New York.*)

Atchison County Museum, 1440 North Sixth Street. In a brown trailer, Marshall Warren displays a charming collection of Amelia Earhart memorabilia. Among them are her needlepoint dancing shoes, a sampler she made in 1905, and her 1906 report card (with marks of Excellent in Reading and English, Very Good in French and Sewing). From her flying days: a fashionable beige suede and knit flying jacket; a copy of the song "Amelia, Queen of the Air"; and a gray and white beaded dress she is said to have worn in Paris in 1932. Mr. Warren told us he remembered Amelia as "a very freckled little girl, with the most wonderful smile. She liked to climb trees." Other townspeople told us they thought this memory has perhaps grown in proportion to the interest in the famed pilot.

The Atchison County Historical Museum also has Earhart memorabilia.

Amelia Earhart Memorial Airport, Route 73. A stone marker commemorates Atchison's favorite daughter at an airport that didn't exist when she was born. Among the fliers who land here are members of the Ninety-Nines, an organization of female pilots that Earhart helped found.

Chanute

Martin and Osa Johnson Safari Museum, 16 South Grant Avenue. In the heart of the southeast Kansas town where she was born in 1894, this unique museum displays photographs and artifacts from Osa Johnson's pioneering South Seas and African expeditions. Together with her husband Martin, between

1910 and 1937 she made five photographic safaris to Africa and three to Polynesia, enduring the equatorial sun and the tropical rains, to capture on film the beasts of the wild. On their first trip to the South Seas, the Johnsons were captured by a cannibal tribe, but after their release they charmed the natives into friendship with the pictures they had taken. In Africa, they flew sixty thousand miles in two amphibious airplanes, one painted to look like a giraffe and one named *Osa's Ark* for all the wounded animals she nursed back to health. Of her intrepid adventures as an explorer, including time as a motion-picture consultant after her husband died, Osa Johnson once said, "The dangers of the jungle are trivial compared with the danger of civilization. Nature made one, man the other. I have implicit trust in Nature's goodness."

Clay County

During the Populist party crusade of 1890, the first speaker at a rally following a three-mile procession here was Mary Elizabeth Lease. She held the huge crowd's attention for more than two hours, a common achievement in her year of making 160 speeches throughout Kansas. They called her the cyclone of Kansas, or Mary Yellin', tributes to her powerful contralto oratory as she stumped the state on behalf of the new political movement. Mary Elizabeth Lease came to Kansas to teach at Mother Bridget Hayden's Osage Mission (see *St. Paul*), but she found her real career stirring up the cause of the debt-ridden farmers. As one of the earliest lecturers for the Farmers' Alliance, the tall, lean orator is said to have urged farmers to "raise less corn and more hell."

Council Grove

Madonna of the Trail Monument, Union and Main Streets. The third in the series of twelve statues erected by the DAR to mark the nation's pioneer trails (see *Springfield, Ohio*) was dedicated September 7, 1928. Council Grove marked the meeting point for freighters along the old Santa Fe Trail.

Delphos

Grace Bedell Billings Monument, Town Square. The town that prides itself as the home of Lincoln's Littlest Correspondent pays tribute to the young girl who changed the face of the U.S. presidency. As an eleven-year-old, Grace Bedell wrote to candidate Abe Lincoln in Springfield, Illinois, and told him she thought his chin was too scrawny. She suggested he might look "a great deal better" with a beard. "All the ladies like whiskers," she assured him. Honest Abe wrote back within a few days, telling the "Dear little Miss. . . . As to the whiskers, having never worn any, do you not think people would call it a piece of silly affectation if I were to begin it now?" And then he let the whiskers grow. These handwritten letters now rest behind vaulted doors in the State Bank at Delphos. Bronze reproductions of them adorn the granite monument. Grace Bedell Billings died at eighty-seven in 1936, after refusing a $5,000 offer for Lincoln's letter and then insuring it for that amount.

Emporia

Peter Pan Park was donated by William Allen White and his wife in memory of their daughter Mary, who died in a horseback riding accident in 1921. Publisher White's most enduring monument to his daughter was the editorial he wrote in his *Emporia Gazette,* included in most high school English anthologies and permanently reprinted here on a bronze plaque. In it he explained that she was an expert rider who died of a blow from an overhanging limb: "She used the horse to get into the open to get fresh, hard exercise, and to work off a certain surplus energy that welled up in her and needed a physical outlet. . . . But the riding gave her more than a body. It released a gay and hardy soul. She was the happiest thing in the world. And she was happy because she was enlarging her horizon." White loved his daughter deeply, and admired the fact that she refused to exchange her pigtails for a more sophisticated hairdo. "The tom-boy in her, which was big, seemed to loathe to be put away forever in skirts. She was a Peter Pan, who refused to grow up."

Fort Riley

Elizabeth Custer House. When Elizabeth Custer accompanied her husband George to his frontier army post in 1866, they lived in this limestone officer's quarters. The windy plateau proved problematic to her billowing skirts. In her own description, the dresses "measured five yards around, and were gathered as full as could be pressed into the waist-band." One walk across the gusty parade ground, and Elizabeth Custer's fancy skirt was blown high above her well-coiffed head, leaving her modesty somewhere down around her ankles. Her husband, then second-in-command to the newly formed Seventh Cavalry, found a way to preserve his officer's dignity, without creating much comfort for Elizabeth. He instructed her to sew strips of lead into her hems. "Thus loaded down," she reported, "we took our constitutional about the post, and outwitted the elements, which at first bade fair to keep us perpetually housed."

Girard

Sarah Alice Addams Haldeman House, 215 East St. Johns Street. The residence of the state's first female bank president (see *Cedarville, Illinois*) is a rest home now, but you can still see the huge carriage stone that once helped travelers alight; its chiseled identification—HALDEMAN. Her office was the Girard State Bank, whose title is carved on a limestone facade beneath the wooden signpost of the Crawford County Abstract Company (107 East Prairie Street). She took over from the bank's president, her husband, in 1905. A printed placard in the door advised patrons: "Bank closed on account of the death of Dr. H. W. Haldeman, which occurred at 5 o'clock a.m. Bank will be continued after funeral under the management and control of Mrs. S. Alice Haldeman." Two years later, apparently unaware of Maggie Walker in *Richmond, Virginia,* Sarah Alice Haldeman told a reporter she was "the only woman bank president in the country, or at least I have been called so without contradiction. I see no reason, however, why women should not be bankers." The bank was described by a financial reporter as "one of the most solid financially in the state."

Hiawatha

Sarah and John M. Davis Memorial, Mount Hope Cemetery. This marble and granite record of a perfect marriage was erected by retired farmer John Davis with his entire $100,000 fortune. Eleven life-sized statues, placed like figures in a house, depict the various stages of his fifty years with his wife Sarah: at first, the newlyweds, sitting discreetly at opposite ends of a love seat; in between, the middle years; at the end, an aged couple seated on marble versions of their plump parlor chairs. The last grouping shows John alone, an old man seated on his armchair beside an empty one which is inscribed, "The Vacant Chair." Martha preceded him to the grave where he now rests as well, beneath one of the most convincing arguments in all of Kansas for giving up the single life.

Independence

Site of Little House on the Prairie, off Route 75. Children's author Laura Ingalls Wilder is believed to have lived on this high prairie south of Walnut Creek from 1868–70. The books she later wrote about this period of her life recall the malaria epidemic (fictionalized as a fever and ague) in July 1869. Dr. George Tann, who treated the Ingalls family, is buried in Mount Hope Cemetery in Independence. Several years ago, the schoolchildren of Rutland County placed a plaque on the courthouse in recognition of "our rich frontier heritage," as perpetuated by Laura Ingalls Wilder. A bas-relief of her log cabin is the only visible reminder of the Little House, except, of course, for the enduring stories. (See *Mansfield, Missouri.*)

Kansas City

Huron Cemetery, Minnesota Avenue, between Sixth and Seventh Streets. This historic burying ground for the Wyandot Indians, where many of its chiefs were laid to rest in the nineteenth century, was saved from destruction by three sisters in the early twentieth century. In 1906, Lena, Lydia, and Ida Conley, daughters of a New York father and a Wyandot mother, heard that the federal government was planning to break its treaty with the Indians and sell the cemetery to business interests. They instantly padlocked the gates and erected a small fortified house ("Fort Conley") on the grounds. Lydia traveled to Washington, D.C., and defended the cemetery before the Supreme Court of the United States. Although Kansas City historians claim that she was the first female lawyer to appear before the high court, Belva Lockwood (see *Washington, D.C.*) actually beat her to the bench. Nonetheless, popular sentiment aroused by the Conley sisters saved the cemetery. They are now buried here.

Site of Constitution Hall, Second Street and Nebraska Avenue. "Probably fully four-fifths of the women of Kansas have never heard of Clarina Howard Nichols," lamented the editors of *History of Woman Suffrage* in 1886. Today that statement seems equally true, since no monuments commemorate the woman who gained Kansas women their first rights. In the building that once stood here, the first constitution of the state was framed in July 1859, under Clarina Nichols' concerned feminist eye. As Elizabeth Cady Stanton put it, "with her knitting in hand, she sat there alone through all the sessions, the only woman present, watching every step of the proceedings, and laboring with members to . . . make all citizens equal before the law." A veteran of woman's rights victories in *Brattleboro, Vermont,* Nichols secured educational and property rights for Kansas women. Although she did not obtain suffrage before she died in 1885, she did, in Stanton's words, make "the idea . . . seem practicable."

Kiowa

Carry A. Nation first experimented with her militant temperance approach at a saloon here in 1900. Setting out from her home in nearby *Medicine Lodge,* she picked up some bricks and stones and applied them with force to the local whiskey emporium. Pleased with the results, she refined her techniques even further in *Wichita.*

Liberal

For the last quarter century, the women of Liberal have paid homage to a housewife across the seas in Olney, England, who, rather than leave her kitchen work behind, took it with her. It all began on Shrove Tuesday, 1445, the day before Lent. The Englishwoman got so involved with her last-minute baking that she forgot, until she heard the carillon tolling, that she was due in church to be "shriven" of her sins. Not one to leave a project unfinished, she dashed off to church wearing her apron and carrying her skillet and pancakes. That was the origin of the Olney Pancake Race. Five hundred years later, women from Liberal made it an international race, competing against time with women from Olney. Today, the races are run simultaneously, starting at 11:55 A.M. Kansas time, over a 415-yard, S-shaped course that starts at the town pump and winds up at the church. In Olney, they race over cobblestones. In Liberal, over asphalt. Each woman wears an apron and scarf and carries a griddle with pancakes, so she can flip the cakes twice during the race. Winners receive a kiss and a prayer book and get their names engraved on the official race Griddle.

In 1974, the star of the Olney runners was a fifty-two-year-old grandmother who had been the first Kansas participant in 1950. She finished next to last and said with a flip of her skillet, "I'm delighted I managed to finish at all."

Manhattan

Augusta Tabor Monument, Tabor Valley Rural School, Tabor Valley. Before he moved on to *Leadville, Colorado,* and became the world-famous Silver King, Horace A. W. Tabor settled here with his wife Augusta; Horace worked, entirely without controversy, as a stonemason. In 1955, when local citizens decided to mark those early years, some townspeople protested that a man who had struck it rich and disposed of his loyal wife to marry the younger, more fetching Baby Doe (see *Washington, D.C.*) was not the sort of man they wanted to commemorate. As a compromise, this gray granite marker now adorning an abandoned one-room schoolhouse was erected to Augusta Tabor, "A pioneer mother who, with her husband H. A. W. Tabor, settled here in 1856 and gave this beautiful valley the name, Tabor Valley. In 1859 they moved on to the Rocky Mountains and found the riches of Golconda and their history will be a legend in Colorado forever."

Medicine Lodge

Carry A. Nation House, 211 West Fowler Avenue. When Carry Nation followed her minister husband David here in 1889, moving into this one-story gray house, Kansas was legally "dry" but practically a drinker's paradise. Having watched her first husband drink himself to death, Carry Nation picked up the temperance banner and helped found a local chapter of the WCTU in 1892. She began to pick up more potent weapons in the summer of 1899. Along with a handful of sympathetic Prohibitionists, Carry Nation started leading prayer meetings and songfests outside the town's taverns. She lectured to the cattlemen and farmers on the evils of the bottle. Then, hoisting her big black umbrella like a staff, she would storm the door of the targeted tavern. It was an act that drew standing-room-only audiences and prompt results. Soon the seven-tavern town was as dry as the law. Carry Nation, in her own words, had experienced "the birth pangs of a new obsession." Although she sallied forth from Medicine Lodge to new tavern territory in *Kiowa* and *Wichita,* she kept this house until about 1902. When she sold it for $800 (at a $1700 loss) the money went for a home in Kansas City for wives and mothers of drunkards. The home was closed in 1910 for lack of occupants. Today this house in Medicine Lodge is a museum, run, naturally, by the WCTU.

St. Paul

Site of Osage Mission. St. Francis Catholic Church stands on the site of the nineteenth-century mission and school whose girls' department under Mother Bridget Hayden was known as "the best school in the Indian country." An Irish immigrant who joined the Sisters of Loretto in Missouri, Sister Mary Bridget came to the frontier outpost with three other nuns in ox-drawn lumber wagons in October 1847. Just across the highway here, she taught the three Rs and homemaking, and she threw in some much-needed nursing and mothering of the Osage Indian girls. By 1870, with many of the Indians moved by treaty to Oklahoma, the school was used mostly for white children, and its name was changed to St. Ann's. Mother Bridget instructed girls of both races in science and art, language and math. In her blue glasses with octagonal frames, she was a popular schoolmarm. In 1895, five years after she died, the entire mission burned down. Today, the bodies of Mother Bridget and the other sisters rest in the cemetery of this church.

Topeka

Shortly after addressing a state temperance convention here in 1901 and receiving their gold medal, inscribed, "To the Bravest Woman in Kansas," Carry A. Nation of *Medicine Lodge* set out in the snow to uphold her reputation. Leading her band of hymn-singing temperance crusaders, she stormed the Old Senate Saloon, a favorite wateringhole of the state legislators. On this occasion, the leader of the Hatchet Brigade carefully aimed her famous weapon and let it fly at the plate-glass window. The glass was demolished along with the entire bar. A newspaper reporter wrote that day, "I am putting my money on Carry Nation—besides having humor, she is morally and fundamentally right." (See *Guthrie, Oklahoma.*)

Kansas State Historical Society, Tenth and Jackson Streets, preserves a number of relics of Carry Nation's "hatchetations." You can see a piece of the mirror broken in the famous Senate Saloon raid, as well as the broad hatchet she used on another saloon on lower Kansas Avenue. Although the shredded paint-

ing of Cleopatra in the buff (see *Wichita*) is not on hand, they do have a painting of *Custer's Last Stand,* mutilated in 1904 by Blanche Boies, a Carry Nation colleague, because it bore a label showing it had been presented by a Milwaukee brewing company. The collection here also includes a number of hatchets and war clubs used by the famed Home Defender. One of our favorite bits of memorabilia is a piece of mirror she broke in an early Topeka bar raid, lovingly framed on a doll dresser that a Kansas father constructed for his two-year-old daughter.

Pioneer Woman Statue, Capitol Square. This bronze by Merrell Gage depicts the dedicated mother guarding her infant and kneeling child, a long rifle across her lap.

Walker

Elizabeth Custer Monument, near the site of old Fort Hayes (old Fort Fletcher) was erected in 1931 by a local rancher to honor the wife of the notorious general. In 1867, Elizabeth nearly died when a flood rampaged through the army fort here. The four-foot pillar was placed at the little hill where Libby Custer's tent stood on the north side of Big Creek where she saw seven soldiers swept away by the waters. Devoted to her husband and his army, she was the only officer's wife who followed the regiment all through the state during their five-year tour of duty in Kansas (see *Fort Riley*). Later, she again avoided certain death by remaining behind at *Mandan, North Dakota,* while the general marched on the Little Big Horn.

Wichita

Site of Hotel Carey Barroom, East Douglas. Encouraged by her successes in drying up *Medicine Lodge* and *Kiowa,* Carry A. Nation tackled Wichita in December 1900. On the day after Christmas, she paid a visit to the bar of the old Hotel Carey. She emptied the contents of a bottle of "demon rum" on the floor, then scolded the bartender for working within sight of an enormous nude painting, *Cleopatra at the Bath.* The bartender shrugged. The next day, Carry brought her real season's greetings. Dressed in a black alpaca dress that reached to her ankles, a poke bonnet, and sensible shoes, she pulled herself up to her nearly six-foot height and wrecked the bar with great dispatch. A hotel employee recalls that she did it with her parasol full of rocks, smashing bottles and shattering the mirrors while she cried, "Glory to God and peace on earth, good will to men." Then, with a cane concealed under her voluminous skirts, she reduced the immodest Cleopatra to a ripple of torn canvas. The bartender and the few customers fled from the once-luxurious mahogany bar. The police appeared. Carry A. Nation was arrested, but, better yet, she was making headlines. Suddenly the world knew about her attacks on intoxicants, forays that would later be called "hatchetations."

Today the Hotel Carey has turned into the Hotel Eaton, and there is no barroom at all. But Carry Nation's portrait, with her hatchet at her side and her Bible open, ceremoniously hangs in the lobby to glare down at intemperate visitors.

Carry A. Nation Fountain, Cowtown, was erected in 1918 by sympathetic WCTU members to commemorate Carry Nation's Christmas binge at the Hotel Carey (now Eaton) in 1900. It first stood at Union Station Plaza, a prim drinking fountain of pure cold water, a hatchet carved into one side and a Bible on the other. But in 1945 it was knocked down by a beer truck. The driver insisted it was accidental. Not until twenty-five years later did anyone raise the $400 to resurrect it at this location.

Wichita Art Museum, 619 Stackman Drive, was made possible, in large part, by a bequest from art patron and interior designer Louise Caldwell Murdock. Just before she turned fifty, she studied interior design in New York and returned to change the faces of many Wichita buildings. As the first interior decorator in Kansas, she introduced Persian rugs to a banker's home and commissioned the sunflower windows in the town library. The museum also houses the Roland P. Murdock Collection (named for Louise's husband) of American art, financed by a trust she established.

KENTUCKY

Boonesboro

Fort Boonesborough State Park. On a riverbank where modern tourists are urged to relax without worry, Jemima Boone, Daniel's daughter, and her cousins Elizabeth and Mary Callaway were kidnapped in July 1776 by Shawnee Indians angry over white settlers' encroachment on their lands. Daniel and a party from the fort tracked them for three days, guided by a trail of broken twigs, torn clothing, and footprints boldly and cleverly left by Betsy Callaway. When the girls were rescued, Betsy was so taken by one member of the party, Samuel Henderson, that she married him a month later at the first settler's wedding in Kentucky.

Bryantsville

Carry A. Nation Birthplace, off Fisher Ford Road near Pope's Landing (private). This frame house on Herrington Lake was the first home of hatchet-wielding Carry Nation, the self-appointed enemy of Demon Liquor. Born here Carry Moore on November 25, 1846, the oldest of six children, she moved about frequently with her family and did not begin her sharp-edged attack on the nation's saloons until she moved to *Holden, Missouri*.

Danville

McDowell House, 125–127 South Second Street. This two-story clapboard house belonging to Dr. Ephraim McDowell, with its adjoining brick apothecary shop, was the site of the world's first successful ovariotomy, performed on the heroic Jane Todd Crawford in 1809. The pioneering surgeon had diagnosed her condition, marked by agonizing pains and an enlarged abdomen, on a visit to her home in *Greensburg*. It was an ovarian growth, and Dr. McDowell promised to remove it, in a frankly experimental and perilous operation, if she would come to Danville. Despite her pain, the forty-seven-year-old woman made the sixty-mile journey on horseback a few days later. The operation took place here on Christmas Day. Since anesthesia had not yet been discovered, the brave patient went under the knife fully dressed and entirely conscious. Dr. McDowell's assistants held down her arms and legs for twenty-five minutes while he removed a 22½-pound tumor. Jane Todd Crawford passed the time reciting psalms. Within five days, she was up making her bed. Three weeks later, according to Dr. McDowell, "she returned home as she came, in good health." She left behind, along with her unwanted tumor, the medical experience that paved the way for a new epoch in abdominal surgery.

Jane Todd Crawford Memorial, rear garden of McDowell House. This white monolith was moved here from McDowell Park when vandals performed their own surgery on it. The stone was erected in 1935, the first concrete memorial ever given by the medical profession to a patient. Her real grave, which was not needed until thirty-three years after the successful operation, is in *Graysville, Indiana*.

Greensburg

Jane Todd Crawford Memorial Hospital is named for the woman who fearlessly underwent surgery without benefit of anesthesia in *Danville* in 1809, becoming the first successful ovariotomy patient in the world. Although her house on Route 61 has long been gone, the fine paved highway—over which she traveled on horseback, when it was a primitive road, to brave the opera-

tion—has been renamed the Jane Todd Crawford Trail. County historian Sam W. Moore told us that when the highway was dedicated in 1932, five hundred trees and four thousand flowers were planted along the roadside. "This may have been the first highway beautification project in the U.S.," he pointed out, thus further expanding the medical pioneer's contribution to American progress.

Harlan County

Pine Mountain Settlement School was founded by Katherine Pettit on two hundred acres of fine land nestled against Pine Mountain. Landowner William Creech donated the site, saying, "There being lots of whiskey and wickedness in the neighborhood where my grandchildren must be raised was a very serious thing for me to study about. My idea was if we could get a good school here it would help moralize the country." The logical organizer was Katherine Pettit, who in 1913 left her first successful venture at *Hindman* to set up a similar center for social, academic, and health work here. Her proven curriculum of farming and cooking along with reading and writing did equally well at Pine Mountain, and one former student wrote her admiringly, "You always did hit straight from the shoulder, Miss Pettit." When she resigned her post in 1930, Katherine Pettit returned to "free-lance" social work, walking through the hills and valleys, dispensing packets of flower seeds and valuable educational advice to the local people. She helped those on welfare get jobs, and she brought orders—and money—for their handmade chests, tables, and quilts. She showed them how to be independent, and she knew every village and villager in the mountains. She died in 1936, shortly after writing to an old friend and colleague, "This has been a glorious world to live and work in—I am eager to see what the next will be."

Harrodsburg

Anne McGinty Cabin, Old Fort Harrod, has been constructed as a memorial to the woman who brought the first spinning wheel over the Alleghenies. Inside her cabin in the old fort (this one is a reconstruction), Anne McGinty is said to have spun the first linen in the West. She also wove buffalo wool and the lint of wild nettles into a coarse but warm cloth. Eager to brighten up the drab colors of natural materials, Anne used nuts and barks to make some of the earliest known dyes.

Hindman

Hindman Settlement School was founded by Katherine Pettit and May Stone to fulfill a request by eighty-two-year-old resident Sol Beveridge that they "come to larn the young 'uns." The school grew out of summer sessions, or "industrials," when the two women pitched a tent on a hill overlooking Troublesome Creek and taught local residents everything from sewing to carpentry to arithmetic. The Knott County folks called them "quare women" but attended every class. The school opened in August 1902, with 162 pupils, under the auspices of the WCTU. Soon the sturdy little school in the Cumberland Hills outgrew its original sponsorship, and it turned into the most effective institution in the area. Cofounders Pettit and Stone brought doctors to treat trachoma, they set up a circulating library, and they scheduled square dancing. Their purpose, as May Stone put it, was "not to educate the child away from his home but back to it." In 1913, Pettit left to start a sister school in *Harlan County*.

Hyden

Frontier Nursing Service Hospital. This twenty-five-bed modern hospital forms the core of the platoon of medical workers established by Mary Breckenridge a half century ago to deliver health services to the mountain people of southeastern Kentucky. A registered nurse who had lost her own two children, in 1925 Mary Breckenridge found this territory "a vast forested area inhabited by some 10,000 people. There was no motor road within 60 miles in any direction. Horseback and mule team were the only modes of travel. Brought-on supplies came from distant railroads and took from two to five days to haul in. . . . There was not in this whole area a single state-licensed physician—not one. . . . From the beginning we needed a rural hospital, and within three years we had it—with a medical director." At first on horseback, now in rugged jeeps, the nurse-midwives care for eighteen thousand people in a thousand-mile area. Their patients, with an average annual per capita income of $1,000, are served at this center or in regional nursing outposts at places like Flat Bed and Wolf Creek. It is still the only hospital in the area.

Lancaster

Site of Thomas Kennedy House, Walker Pike. Not even the foundations remain of the plantation said to have been an inspiration for Harriet Beecher Stowe's *Uncle Tom's Cabin* (see *Washington;* see *Brunswick, Maine*). Nancy Kennedy Letcher, daughter of the slave owner Thomas, is thought to have been the prototype for Little Eva; Lewis Clark for the slave George Harper.

Lexington

Mary Todd Lincoln House, 574 West Main Street. This two-story brick colonial residence of the woman who would be the future wife of Abraham Lincoln was, when we last checked, more or less boarded up and in need of repair. Mary Todd lived here with her family from 1832–39. As Mrs. Lincoln, she made three visits to this house with her husband. Although she was born

in a house on West Short Street that no longer stands, Mary spent most of her adolescent years here, playing with her large family on the grounds of this once-elegant mansion. She became an astute observer of politics and a lifetime enemy of the slavery she watched around her. From this house she set out for boarding school, where she became such an accomplished dancer that when she left to live with a married sister in *Springfield, Illinois*, she attracted Abraham Lincoln's attention at a ball.

Site of Ward's Academy, Second and Market Streets. A plaque on the Dr. Frederick Ridgely building notes that young Mary Todd attended classes here run by the Reverend Mr. John Ward. Since he believed that little minds functioned best in the early hours, Mary and her friends trudged through snow and darkness to be at school by five every morning. Here Mary proved herself a bright student and a nimble knitter.

Henry Clay House, "Ashland," two miles south of town on Richmond Road. The home of the great statesman and senator has been preserved and operated by a foundation set up partly by Madeline McDowell Breckenridge, Henry Clay's great-granddaughter. Her portrait hangs here, and a tour guide reminds visitors that she also lived here when her family moved into the estate in 1882. Social reformer Madeline McDowell Breckenridge left a lasting and loving mark on the entire state of Kentucky. Here in Lexington, she was instrumental in establishing a school, a park, a health clinic, and care for the needy. She ran a weekly page for women in her husband's *Lexington Herald.* And she served as a statewide leader in bills for juvenile labor laws and the judical system. As the mainstay of the Kentucky Equal Rights Association, she once attacked the governor for his inaction on suffrage. "Kentucky women are not idiots—even if they are closely related to Kentucky men," she argued. "You can't ignore them and treat them as if they were kindergarten children, and when work is needed expect them to do a man's share—or a woman's, as you please to state it."

Her cohesive logic in a round of speaking engagements (see *Pikeville*) led the fight against southern tradition and male chivalry that finally culminated in the women's vote in 1920.

Bryan Station Memorial, Bryan Station Road. An octagonal stone wall surrounds the spring that saved the men in August 1782, while Canadians and Indians secretly attacked. When the patriot defenders found themselves emcompassed with the threat of a long siege and not enough water, they sent the women out to feign nonchalance and fill their pitchers. Jemima

Johnson, mother of five, led the female water brigade on their perilous mission in the hot summer sun. The extra supply of water they fetched kept the fort from drying out until help arrived. This story has been disputed.

London

Sue Bennett College, opened in 1897, was named for the woman who first devised a plan to bring education to the people of southeastern Kentucky. Methodist missionary worker Belle Harris Bennett laid the cornerstone of the school after completing the work of her late sister, Sue, and dedicating it as a memorial to her. Originally a high school, Sue Bennett is now a two-year coeducational accredited junior college.

Louisville

Even without markers or memorials, the private kindergarten here where educator Patty Smith Hill and her sister Mildred taught will long be remembered at the nation's celebrations. Along with their pioneering teaching work, the two women collaborated to write a song for their young students: "Good Morning to You." Copyrighted in 1893, the song gained instant fame with different words: "Happy Birthday to You." It is not known how much money in uncollected royalties the clever Hill sisters have been denied.

The Cabbage Patch Settlement, 1413 South Sixth Street, is a social settlement named for the popular book, *Mrs. Wiggs of the Cabbage Patch,* by Alice Caldwell Hegan Rice. She set the story of the poor but cheerful Mrs. Wiggs in a nearby area stretching west of Central Park along the railroad tracks. Once it was used as a cabbage field; later, squatters settled there with such leftovers from the city dump as the old cans on Mrs. Wiggs' roof.

Paris

Anne Duncan House, Public Square. When Maj. Joseph Duncan died about 1800, leaving his widow with six small children, she wisely leased out the adjoining twenty-room Duncan Tavern and built this house next door. On her own, she raised one newspaper publisher, one court clerk, one war hero, one governor (of Illinois), and one lawyer-doctor. Those were her five sons. Of her daughter, we know only that she probably attended a seminary here in Paris.

Pewee Valley

Annie Fellows Johnston House, "The Beeches," Central Avenue (private). This handsome white frame structure with its wide porch was the home of author Annie Fellows Johnston from 1911 until her death in 1931. The quiet village of Pewee Valley was the Lloydsboro Valley of her popular *Little Colonel* stories for children. A neighbor's daughter, Hattie Cochran, who did a charming imitation of her Confederate colonel grandfather, was the prototype for the Little Colonel; the house Annie Fellows Johnston lived in became "The Locusts" in fiction. The books have enchanted several generations of children in English and foreign languages, and they have sold well over a million copies.

Pikeville

When Madeline Breckenridge of *Lexington* spoke here on July 4, 1919 on behalf of female suffrage, a mountain man remarked, "By God, that's the best I ever heard, man or woman, and I'm for her!"

Pippa Passes

Alice Lloyd College was founded in 1917 by Radcliffe graduate

Alice Geddes Lloyd at the request of a barefoot mountaineer who asked her to educate his children so that they would be "not liken the hog but unliken the hog." She had come to the eastern Kentucky mountains to seek relief for the partial paralysis of her right side that had come from spinal meningitis. She stayed in this rocky little pocket of Appalachia to see the construction of more than fifty log and stone buildings, complete with a library and theater. Today, the two-year junior college clings to the slopes that straddle Caney Creek. One of the school's aims is to preserve the Appalachian way of life. Students learn academic subjects and skills so that they can return to work in the surrounding region. One Alice Lloyd graduate who returned to practice medicine nearby said of the college founder, who died in 1962, "She was a shining light unto the hills . . . she gave us confidence in what we could accomplish in life. She was a wonderful person."

Pleasant Hill

Shakertown, a Shaker village settled in 1805, disbanded in 1910, and now restored for visitors, affords a firsthand view of the religious spirit and principles of sexual equality espoused by founder Mother Ann Lee in *Watervliet, New York.*

Prestonsburg

Jenny Wiley State Resort Park, Route 23, is named for the woman who managed to escape from her Indian captors without harming anyone. In 1787, Jenny Sellards Wiley was taken prisoner by some Cherokee and Shawnee Indians who tomahawked her brother and three other children at nearby Walker's Creek. Jenny's own infant baby was also slain. After nearly a year of captivity, one day she let rainwater drip on the rawhide thongs binding her. When the leather stretched, she freed herself and then slipped away. The small stream she crossed while making her escape was later named for her.

Richmond

Laura Clay Birthplace, "White Hall," Route 7. In a second-floor bedroom still furnished with her silver pen and inkwell and her

windup singing canary on a gilt stand, feminist Laura Clay was born February 9, 1849. Overshadowed in childhood by her illustrious father, Cassius Marcellus Clay, Laura went into politics herself when she left this 2,500-acre estate as a young woman. She was a founder and first president of the Kentucky Woman

poetry—including the historical novel, *The Great Meadow* (1930)—not only brought to life her rich surroundings, but it was among the most successful literature to explore the inner consciousness of women. Other noted titles: *The Time of Man* (1926) and *Black Is My True Love's Hair* (1938).

Suffrage Association. She even ran for the state legislature, and one of the campaign posters from that unsuccessful venture greets visitors in her room here. But although Laura Clay, along with her three sisters, lectured, lobbied, and wrote about the need for votes, she was also dedicated to the principle of states' rights. She felt so strongly about it that ultimately she opposed the federal suffrage amendment when it reached the legislature at *Nashville, Tennessee.* National suffrage leader Carrie Chapman Catt was so distressed by the prospect of fighting her former allies, Clay and Kate Gordon of *New Orleans, Louisiana,* that she wrote before ratification, "Even if we win, we who have been here will never remember it with anything but a shudder."

Springfield

Elizabeth Madox Roberts House, 510 North Walnut Street (private). Born in nearby Perryville, novelist Elizabeth Madox Roberts grew up and spent most of her life here, writing about the farm people of this region of Kentucky. Her prose and

Washington

Mary Marshall Grave, grounds of Federal Hill. Mary Randolph Keith and her husband, Col. Thomas Marshall, Sr., lived here in "the House on the Hill" with their son, Capt. Thomas Marshall, Jr. Another son, John, became the first chief justice of the United States. Fourteen other children pursued various occupations. But the unassuming Mary Keith Marshall directed that this inscription be placed on her tombstone when she died in 1809, a modest description of her earthly accomplishments: "Good, but not great, useful but not ornamental."

Marshall Key House (private). While visiting this home of a schoolmate in 1833, Harriet Beecher (later Stowe) went to the nearby courthouse and saw slaves being sold from the block that still stands in the town center. The auction later appeared in graphic detail in *Uncle Tom's Cabin* (see *Lancaster; Brunswick, Maine.*)

LOUISIANA

Baton Rouge

Sarah Morgan was twenty-one when the Union army first propelled its gunboats to the shores of Baton Rouge. She recorded the occupation in a diary published after her death, a remarkable eyewitness account of wartime. In May 1862 she observed a handsome young federal soldier come ashore from the *Iroquois* carrying the Stars and Stripes over his shoulder. "If we girls of Baton Rouge had been at the landing instead of the men," she wrote in outrage, "the Yankee would never have insulted us by flying his flag in our faces! *We* would have opposed his landing except under a flag of truce." Nearly three months later, after fierce shelling and forced evacuation, she returned to her ruined family plantation, walking past unburied bodies and bloodied earth. Although "satisfied" to see her home again, she poignantly described one effect of war on a young girl: "I went to my room. Gone was my small paradise! Had this shocking place ever been habitable? The tall mirror squinted at me from a thousand broken angles. It looked so knowing! I tried to fancy the Yankee officers being dragged from under my bed by the leg. . . . My desk! What a sight! The central part I had kept as a little curiosity shop with all my trinkets and keepsakes of which a large proportion were from my gentlemen friends; I looked for all I had left. . . . Precious letters I found under heaps of broken china and rags; all my notes were gone, with many letters. . . . Bah! What is the use of describing such a scene?"

Cloutierville

Kate Chopin House, Route 1. In 1880, when their family business failed in New Orleans, author Kate Chopin moved with her husband and six children into this typical two-story "Louisiana-type" house. Three years in the bayou country made a deep impression on the talented young woman. In 1883, after her husband died during a swamp fever epidemic, she moved back to St. Louis, Missouri, to be with her mother. There, five years later, at age thirty-seven, she first put pen to paper. Drawing on the cultural strains of her Creole mother and her Acadian neighbors, Kate Chopin turned out a series of stories remarkable for regional characterization and for her insights into the sensibilities of women. Her 1899 novel, *The Awakening,* astutely depicted a young mother's growing awareness of her own sexuality and of her artistic nature. She shocked contemporary critics with her bold discovery that she was not one of the "mother-women . . . women who idolized their children, worshipped their husbands, and esteemed it a holy privilege to efface themselves as individuals and grow wings as ministering

angels." A rare first edition of an earlier collection of her short stories, published in 1894 as *Bayou Folk,* is prominently displayed in the Bayou Folk Museum, housed in this building where Kate Chopin derived so much inspiration from the simple folk who called at her husband's general store. Although modern levees and drainage canals have erased many natural features of the bayou country, Kate Chopin's stories preserve the people and the culture of these surroundings.

Delta

On a plantation near this northern Louisiana town, Sarah Breedlove was born December 23, 1867. When her farmer parents died several years later, she moved to Mississippi, then to *St. Louis, Missouri,* where she first dreamed up the hairdressing idea that would make her one of the nation's first black millionaires.

Lake Charles

Episcopal Church of the Good Shepherd still plays the choral music composed by Kathleen Blair, who came to Lake Charles on vacation after supporting herself as a teahouse pianist in New York. She met her second husband here and decided to stay. Blair was the first in Lake Charles to organize musical groups, or "fetes," where her own and others' music was played. With her husband, she instituted the first community concerts, bringing many famous artists into the area. Among her published songs: "Love Never Faileth," "As the Heart Panteth," and "Thou Wilt Light My Candle."

Melrose

Melrose Plantation, Isle Breville. The 13,000-acre plantation that once flourished on the banks of the Cane River was built by the strong will and equally hardy labors of freed slave Marie Therese Coincoin. "She was probably the most famous woman in this area," a historian from nearby Natchitoches assured us, and a glance at the recorded story of her life explains why. Born a slave in 1742, she was twenty-six and the mother of four when a Frenchman named Claude Thomas Pierre Metoyer took a liking to her. Despite the indignant and semisuccessful efforts of the local Spanish curé to break up what he called "the two partners in concubinage, from which ensues a great scandal and damage to the souls," Metoyer and Coincoin set up house and together produced seven mulatto children. In 1778, he bought her freedom. The couple continued their partnership until 1786, when, after nearly two decades together, they succumbed to age and boredom, and they split up. As they were not married, divorce was not necessary. Metoyer had, however, deeded Coincoin substantial land holdings, and the forty-four-year-old woman threw herself into their care with renewed vigor. Soon she had one of the most envied and well-cultivated fields of tobacco and corn. Her wild bear grease (from animals she trapped herself) was exported to Europe. She raised cattle and grew cotton. And with the profits from her land (an area that had increased with a grant from the king of Spain), she bought or arranged for the freedom of all her children. By the time she died, after 1816, the property was adequately subdivided for her offspring. Today, the plantation that suffered with the fortunes of bad business and the Civil War—and went, according to a recent saying, from "shirt sleeves to shirt sleeves in three generations"—is being restored. You can see the remarkable buildings Coincoin erected, such as Yucca House (of hand-hewn cypress) and African House (a mushroom-

shaped building, the only authentic Congolese architecture in America). The descendants of the famed matriarch still refer to themselves simply as "the people."

Monroe

Saunders Monument, Old City Cemetery, 900 De Siard Street. Ann Livingston Saunders erected this granite and marble tombstone over her husband Sidney's grave in 1889 to squelch town gossip about their marital status. A life-sized statue of her deceased husband (she was his second wife) stands atop the pedestal, his handlebar moustache reaching to his jawline, dressed in his wedding-day cutaway coat and proudly holding an unfurled scroll that is their marriage license. Annie Livingston and Sidney W. Saunders were "joined in holy matrimony," it proclaims to the doubting world. The giant stone statue guards a vault containing the tombs of Sidney and her son Willie, who died several years earlier. Old-time Monroe residents told us that Annie used to take her sewing machine into the vault and stitch away in the company of her departed men; the compartment used to be filled with toys for little Willie. Although it has not been confirmed that Annie was also entombed here after her death, the stone is embellished with flowery poetry promising that she will meet Sidney again in heaven: "For that alone your faithful, loving wife prays, watches and waits."

New Orleans

Ursuline Convent, 1114 Chartres Street. The oldest building in the Mississippi Valley was completed in 1734 to house the first nuns who came to the New World. A handful of the Ursulines had arrived from France seven years earlier to "relieve the poor and sick and provide at the same time for the education of young girls." One of their goals for the French orphan girls they brought over was to help them find husbands and to populate the Gulf Coast. That venture began at *Ship Island, Mississippi.*

Madame John's Legacy, 632 Dumaine Street. A short work of fiction entitled " 'Tite Poulette" by George Washington Cable is responsible for the name of this Louisiana colonial-style house with its aboveground basement and double-pitched roof for protection against the frequent hurricanes. The celebrated heroine of Cable's story was 'Tite Poulette's mother, Madame John, a beautiful quadroon who inherited and lost this house. In real life, the owners were pirates, privateers, and bejeweled widows.

Pontalba Apartments, St. Ann and St. Peter Streets, Jackson Square. The twin block-long red brick buildings flanking Jackson Square were designed and built by Baroness Micaela Almonester Pontalba to dress up downtown New Orleans. The strong-willed, vivacious baroness, a woman as intricate as her ornamental monogram—AP—entwined in the lacy cast-iron grillwork here, modeled her sturdy row houses after the Palais Royal in Paris. She had grown up in New Orleans, the child of Spanish and French parents. She met the groom of her pre-arranged marriage when he came from France to wed her; they were divorced just after a stormy silver wedding anniversary in France, when her father-in-law tried to kill her. By all accounts, the redheaded baroness was an energetic and clever entrepreneur. She supervised the construction of her buildings with an iron hand, dismissing architects and bargaining down builders with professional persistence. From the time ground was broken in 1849, she was on the scene almost daily, climbing ladders and poking into apartments, wearing a pair of pantaloons of her own design. When the first building was completed in 1850, she and her two sons were its first tenants, moving into Number 5 (now 508) St. Peter Street. Shrewdly aware of the value of public relations, Baroness Pontalba furnished another apartment for the month-long visit of opera star Jenny Lind when Lind appeared in New Orleans in 1851. After the Swedish Nightingale left, the baroness auctioned off Jenny Lind's furniture and returned to France for the last time, her striking legacy completely occupied. Today, after a period of neglect that saw fires, fights, and even a full-grown cow ensconced in these apartments, they have been restored and boast a long waiting list for occupancy.

Adelina Patti House and Courtyard, 631 Royal Street. The renowned operatic soprano lived here in 1860, making her debut in this city in *Lucia di Lammermoor.* Her successful sojourn on the New Orleans opera stage followed her debut in New York and directly preceded a dazzling concert at Covent Garden in London that made her the new singing sensation of Europe.

Site of Marie Laveau House, 1022 St. Ann Street. The famed Voodoo Queen of the nineteenth century is said to have lived here and practiced her black magic with great financial success. Although the house was torn down in 1903, Marie Laveau's reputation with charms and ceremonies was so fine that current residents still point out the site of her residence.

Margaret Haughery Statue, Margaret Park, Camp and Prytania Streets. The plump figure of Margaret Haughery, a sweater buttoned on for warmth and her arm protecting a small child, sits on a chair atop a seven-foot base, a gift of the people of New Orleans to the self-made businesswoman and philanthropist who gave so much to them. An Irish immigrant who lost both her husband and her young daughter by her early twenties, she first supported herself as a laundress. Soon she was giving away her meager income to the Sisters of Charity; in time, she purchased a few cows and expertly developed a prosperous dairy numbering forty cows. As Margaret Haughery earned more money, she gave more away. Her contributions funded nearly a dozen asylums for orphans and the aged. In 1858, when she came into possession of a bakery in repayment of a debt owed her, Margaret applied her practiced executive talent and enlarged it, instituting the first steam bakery in the South and making it one of the city's leading commercial industries. She also maintained her charitable habits, even defying the tyrannical federal general, Ben Butler, who threatened to hang her if she continued to distribute her baked goods to starving and needy people. The Bread Lady of New Orleans was not hanged. When she died of illness in 1882, her will stipulated that some $41,000 in cash and property go to a variety of homes and asylums. This statue, paid for with public funds, was unveiled in 1884. And every year since 1958, February 9—the anniversary of her death—is celebrated in New Orleans as Margaret Day.

H. Sophie Newcomb Memorial College, 6823 St. Charles Avenue, was established in 1886 by Josephine Louise LeMonnier Newcomb in memory of her late daughter, Harriot Sophie. The $100,000 gift accompanied Josephine Newcomb's specification that the college be established within the existing (male) Tulane University, thus making Newcomb College the nation's first coordinate college for women. Further gifts from Josephine Newcomb came during the college's early years and at her death in 1901. Her legacy of almost three million dollars—evidence of her excellent business sense in substantially increasing her deceased husband's fortune—made the school the most heavily endowed women's college at the time. Today, after years of semiautonomy, Newcomb shares all of its courses with the men at Tulane but retains its own faculty, degree requirements, and admission processes.

Site of Roza Solomon Da Ponte House, "Roselawn," 3512 St. Charles Avenue. Nothing remains of the turreted Moorish mansion that was built by the fabulous Roza Solomon Da Ponte in the late nineteenth century. The inlaid floors, strange carvings, and Dutch iron stove were outdone only by the red plush theater she built on her luxurious estate. It was the first little theater in the country, and the glamorous widow often appeared in her own performances before hosting an elaborate buffet supper at her home. Earlier, her glamour nearly earned her a permanent but unwilling starring role in the harem of the sultan of Egypt. On a visit to Cairo, she was spotted by some of the sultan's emissaries and kidnapped off the streets as a new addition to the sultan's collection. Only her husband's frantic appeal to Queen Victoria, who interceded in her behalf, returned Roza Da Ponte, unharmed, to her spouse.

Kingsley House Settlement, 914 Richard Street. The head resident here in 1901 and its dedicated administrator for three decades following was Eleanor McMain, social reformer credited with "taking the harshness out of institutionalism." Among her firsts in the field of settlement work in New Orleans were the city's first vacation school, its first free clinic, its first public playground, a Day Nursery Association, and the Women's League, of which she was the first president. When she died in 1934, services were held here in the heart of the Irish Channel section of the city to which she devoted her life. Today, the settlement house she developed into an entire city block is "never closed," according to its current director. An Eleanor McMain Award is a coveted prize for volunteer workers. Once when McMain accepted an award, she said, "I have done what I best love to do. I live and share my life with the dear people of the neighborhood."

Sara Mayo Hospital, 625 Jackson Avenue, was named for the doctor who helped found it and who devoted her life to developing it. Dr. Sara Mayo was graduated from the Women's Medical College in *Philadelphia, Pennsylvania,* but she found that Victorian New Orleans was no more prepared to accept women as physicians in its hospitals than any other major city. A clinic at Kingsley House Settlement convinced volunteers of the need for a women's dispensary. So, like other undaunted female doctors around the country, in 1905 Dr. Mayo and some colleagues opened their own, calling it the New Orleans Hospital and Dispensary for Women and Children. Within a few years, they had their own building, a familiar structure replaced in 1972 with this modern, five-story, 178-bed hospital. It took Dr. Mayo's name after her death in 1930.

Gordon Sisters Memorial, New Orleans Sewerage and Water Board, City Hall. For a time, the most prominent memorial to civic-minded Jean and Kate Gordon was the bronze plaque erected in 1919 to commemorate the Era Club, "through which the role of taxpaying women helped to secure the great public necessities of water, sewerage and drainage." When the Sewerage and Water Building was razed in 1957 that marker was removed and now lies, safe but hidden, in a vault in City Hall. The most enduring monument to these sisters is the New Orleans water and sewerage system itself, obtained only by their whirlwind campaign in 1899. Not only was it a victory for sanitation, but it paved the way for full suffrage for women in Louisiana years later.

Deeply disturbed by the city's inadequate water supply and by the lack of any sewerage system, Kate Gordon became the president of the newly formed Woman's League for Sewerage

TO THE
ERA CLUB OF NEW ORLEANS
WHICH ORGANIZED
THE WOMEN'S LEAGUE
FOR
SEWERAGE AND DRAINAGE
AND THROUGH THE VOTE OF
TAX PAYING WOMEN
HELPED TO SECURE
THE GREAT PUBLIC NECESSITIES OF
WATER, SEWERAGE AND DRAINAGE

and Drainage. Along with her sister and a number of prominent suffrage leaders, she took advantage of the only voting right women had (taxpaying women could vote on tax matters) and rounded up enough signatures on a petition to force a municipal election on the issue. Both male and female voters turned out for the special election, and the new sanitation system was overwhelmingly endorsed.

One first-time voter that day was seventy-five-year-old state suffrage leader Caroline Merrick. "It was only for sewerage and drainage," she told the reporter in a sweet voice, "but then it was for the protection of the home from the invasion of disease, the better health of our city, the greater prosperity of our commonwealth and I am satisfied . . . our votes will soon be wanted in other praiseworthy reforms." That was the hope and unwavering goal of Merrick, Gordon, and all members of the Era Club (for Equal Rights Association), until woman suffrage got in the way of states' rights (see *Richmond, Kentucky*).

Gordon Sisters Memorial, First Unitarian Church (Children's Chapel), Jefferson Avenue and Dannell Street. A stained-glass window based on the theme "'Charity Never Faileth'" pays tribute to the philanthropic work of Jean and Kate Gordon. The memorial at this church that they attended was dedicated in 1932, after both sisters had died within a year of each other. Jean Gordon made her mark by spearheading the drive to pass child labor laws and by becoming the city's first factory inspector in 1906. She also dedicated her time to mentally disturbed children. Kate Gordon joined her sister's reform work and was particularly active in the establishment of a tuberculosis hospital in 1926.

METAIRIE CEMETERY, 5100 Pontchartrain Boulevard
Once a racetrack, this cemetery contains a number of graves worth visiting either because they are important or simply because they are curious.
Dorothy Dix Grave. The prolific and witty columnist who dis-

pensed advice to millions took her pen name to her grave when she died in 1951. Her will prevented anyone from writing a "Dorothy Dix" column ever again. And nothing on the family tomb indicates that Elizabeth Meriwether Gilmer was the author of all those logical solutions to the nation's problems. She enjoyed her privacy. Starting in 1894, in Pearl Rivers' *Picayune* (see below), Gilmer adopted the familiar by-line because she liked the name Dorothy (it was "musical but not mushy"), and she respected a servant whose wife called him Mr. Dicks. For a half century, she told the lovelorn, the widowed, and the friendless how to go on living. Her special flair in speaking to women was accomplished, she wrote, by "telling women the truth about themselves, lambasting them instead of jollying them." But she revealed that about half the letters she got were from men, because after all, "they really need more advice than women do about handling the opposite sex." So trusted was she with the sentiments of America that she once remarked in amazement, "People tell me things that you would think they wouldn't even tell to God."

Eliza J. Nicholson (Pearl Rivers) Grave. The first female publisher of a major daily newspaper in the South has her by-line printed on a large granite memorial, featuring her *New Orleans Picayune*'s front page preserved in bronze for future readers. "A noble woman, true friend, loving wife, devoted mother and gentle poet," she began life in *Picayune, Mississippi.* She joined the paper's staff here as literary editor for $25 a week and took over the debt-ridden business in 1876. Her pen name was Pearl Rivers; her forte, poetry and fine management. By the time she died in 1896, the paper—to which she had introduced such innovative features as a society column, a telephone action line, and Dorothy Dix—was worth nearly $150,000. "Modern times have developed many good newspaperwomen writers," her friend and employee Dorothy Dix once said, "but Mrs. Nicholson is the only woman who has ever MADE a big paper."

Moriarty Monument. In 1887 Irish immigrant Daniel Moriarty erected this sixty-foot monument to his wife, Mary Farrell Moriarty. Local legend says that Moriarty built the towering tombstone so that the people of New Orleans who had snubbed his wife in life would have to look up to her in death. The granite shaft is surrounded by four female figures: Faith, Hope, Charity, and Mary Moriarty.

Langles Monument. This granite shaft attracts swarms of visitors because of the curious inscription at its base:

Angele Marie Langles
105 La. 39

Both Angele and her mother perished in a shipwreck off Sable Island, near Halifax, Nova Scotia, in 1898. Both women had written wills, but it took a court case to straighten out the details of the instructions for their tomb. When the court decreed that Angele's $3,000 stipulation should be honored (to the dismay of selfish heirs), this monument was erected and inscribed with the citation of the Louisiana legal decision that determined the outcome.

Grace King Grave. New Orleans' own author and historian was buried in her native soil in 1932. Her novels and short stories are remembered as part of the "local color" tradition, combining her French and Creole upbringing to recreate the region's past. She also wrote *New Orleans: The Place and the People* (1895).

St. Joseph

Bondurant House, Courthouse Square. Before this house was relocated to this site to become the rectory of the Christ Episcopal Church, it stood on the plantation, "Pleasant View," where its Civil War mistress carried out one of those daring acts of valor under fire. As Yankee gunboats moving down the Mississippi shelled the house, Mrs. Bondurant set a hundred bales of cotton on fire rather than turn them over to the enemy. Her brush with danger became clear when the house was moved to this location, and cannonballs were found embedded in the timbers.

St. Martinville

Evangeline Monument, St. Martin de Tours Church. A small bronze figure marks the grave of Emmeline Labiche, the real-life inspiration for Longfellow's "Evangeline." The poem is based on an actual romance between Emmeline and her Acadian sweetheart (Louis Arceneaux), a love affair that was interrupted when they migrated here from Nova Scotia to escape persecution. This statue, seated on a marble base, was donated to the city by Delores Del Rio and the cast of the silent film *Evangeline,* made here in 1929.

Evangeline Oak, Bayou Teche, Port Street. This spreading oak shading the landing place for boats from New Orleans is one of the most photographed trees in the world. It is said to be the spot where Longfellow's Evangeline came ashore to find her Cajun sweetheart.

MAINE

Appledore Island

This wild and rugged dot of land in the Atlantic Ocean, one of the Isles of Shoals, was immortalized by author Celia Thaxter in verse and prose. Her cottage among the rocks, where Sarah Orne Jewett and John Greenleaf Whittier were frequent visitors, has burned down; her flower garden has gone to weed; her grave in the family plot (marked with a stone that reads "Celia") is overgrown with sumac and poison ivy. But what remain are her memorable descriptions of the natural life of the island where she spent her girlhood: "Now come delicious twilights, with silence broken only by mysterious murmurs from the waves, and sweet, full cries from the sandpipers fluttering about their nests on the margin of the beaches—tender, happy notes that thrill the balmy air, and echo softly about the silent, moonlit coves." (See *Star Island, New Hampshire*.)

Brewer

Fannie Hardy Eckstorm Birthplace, 159 Wilson Street (private). Born here June 18, 1865 to a family with deep roots and interest in the history of northeastern Maine, Fannie Eckstorm furthered the family tradition and became a leading authority on the wildlife and legends of her state. As a child, she traveled with her father by canoe through the wilderness of the North Woods. On a trip that later turned up in her writings, he taught her to track animals and to understand the woodsmen of the area. Widowed at thirty-four, she returned to this family house to live with her sister and embarked on a highly acclaimed career writing books and scholarly articles on the Penobscot Indians, on the craggy coastline she knew so well, and later on the folk songs and language of the area. She died here in 1946, leaving a written legacy that has helped preserve the natural and cultural phenomena that future generations may never see.

Brunswick

Harriet Beecher Stowe House, 63 Federal Street. When Calvin Stowe accepted a teaching post at nearby Bowdoin College in 1850, he and his wife Harriet moved into this pleasant white frame house. Already exposed to the horrors of slavery from their residence in *Cincinnati, Ohio*, Harriet Beecher Stowe grew even more incensed over the new Fugitive Slave Act and its attempt to make slave-catchers of everyone. She decided, she later wrote, "to exhibit [slavery] in a living, dramatic reality." *Uncle Tom's Cabin*, written in this house from 1851–52, was that reality.

In February, she sat down before the fire and wrote the last chapter first: the death of Uncle Tom. When her husband glanced at the hand-penned sheets of paper, he told her, "You can make something out of this." "I mean to do so," she replied. A month later she began at the beginning, and *Uncle Tom's Cabin* was sold for $300 to appear in serial form in the abolitionist *National Era*. From the summer of 1851 until it was finished in March 1852, tearstained copies of the weekly installments were passed from reader to reader. And when it was bound into a book—*Uncle Tom's Cabin; or, Life among the Lowly*—its searing indictment of plantation life aroused passionate feelings above and below the Mason-Dixon Line. Although the first shots of the Civil War were fired at Fort Sumter in 1861, it has been said that the war really began here a decade earlier.

Today the house is an inn, restored and expanded, with some of Harriet Beecher Stowe's original furnishings in her study.

You can also have a drink in Harriet's Place, an original Victorian saloon. (See *Orr's Island;* see *Hartford, Connecticut*.)

First Parish Congregational Church, Harpswell, Maine and Bath Streets. From the pew now marked with her name, Harriet Beecher Stowe listened while her husband Calvin preached here during their stay at the nearby colonial inn from 1850–52.

Kate Furbish House, 15 Lincoln Street (private). From this pleasant house with its tidy lawn, botanist and artist Kate Furbish set out on the wildlife expeditions on which she plucked, identified, and painted in watercolors the plant life of Maine. A dedicated amateur who won the respect of scores of scientists, she tramped through woods, climbed mountains, slogged through bogs, and floated down rivers of her home state in search of scientific specimens. Acadians called her the Posy Lady, little aware that the posies she was identifying—often risking her life in untrod regions—contributed immeasurably to the botanical knowledge of the state. From this house, too, four thousand specimens of dried plants were crated and shipped to their present home, the herbarium at Harvard. Bowdoin College owns sixteen folio volumes of the wild flowers she painted and five hundred drawings of mushrooms. Two plants were named for her: *Pedicularis furbishiae*, the St. John River wood betony that she first reported in Aroostook County; and *Aster cordifolius L.*, var. *furbishiae*, the common frostweed, named as a tribute from a botanist to honor her "undaunted pluck and faithful brush."

Bucksport

Jonathan Buck Monument, Buck Cemetery, Main and Hinks Streets. The woman's leg outlined on the granite monument to town founder Jonathan Buck has inspired a most interesting group of legends. The most enduring of the tall tales suggests that Colonel Buck was cursed by a woman he had sent to the gallows as a witch. She is said to have promised to leave her indelible mark on his tombstone, so that all passersby would say, "There lies the man who murdered a woman." This satisfying myth of female revenge overlooks the fact that Buck lived long after the witchcraft hysteria, that he was in reality an upright civic leader of his town, and that the stained stone does not even stand over his bones. It was erected in 1852, more than half a century after he was buried under a modest slate gravestone about fifteen feet away. The fault, it turns out, lies in the granite, not the man.

Buxton Lower Corner

Tory Hill Meeting House, half a mile north of Quillcote (see *Hollis*), is the colonial church where Kate Douglas Wiggin set her story "The Old Peabody Pew." Each August the story is dramatized here, in the shadow of the imposing Celtic cross honoring the author. The cross is inscribed with the title of the last chapter of her autobiography, "The Song Is Never Ended."

Camden

Edna St. Vincent Millay Room, Whitehall Inn. The diploma she earned from Camden High, along with photographs and some of her writings, line the walls of this room where Edna St. Vincent Millay recited her poem "Renascence," in the summer of 1912. The young poet (see *Rockland*), first published at age fourteen in *St. Nicholas* magazine, wrote "Renascence" in 1911 as a contest entry. It was later printed in the anthology *Lyric Year,* and drew wide acclaim. When "Vincent" read it to guests at this hotel where her sister was working, one member of the audience was so taken by the verse that she invited the young poet to visit her in *Manhattan, New York.* Caroline B. Dow, head of the National Training School of the YWCA, also helped shape Vincent's career by encouraging her to enter Vassar College and to write more poetry.

Edna St. Vincent Millay Monument, Camden Hills State Park, Mount Battie. On a spot overlooking the seacoast view that inspired the prize-winning "Renascence," Camden residents have placed a bronze plaque to poet Edna St. Vincent Millay. The opening lines of her poem are engraved on the marker. It begins:

> All I could see from where I stood
> Was three long mountains and a wood;
> I turned and looked another way,
> And saw three islands in a bay.

Dover-Foxcroft

Lillian M. N. Stevens Birthplace, 191 South Street (private). A granite boulder on the front lawn marks this white frame house, where the "leader of the Woman's Christian Temperance Union in state and nation," was born March 1, 1844. As founder, then president of the Maine WCTU, then of the national WCTU, Stevens helped enlarge the reformist organization with new branches and growing membership. She is not particularly fondly remembered by some soldiers, from whose military bases she successfully barred the sale of alcoholic beverages in 1901. When she died in 1914, the flag on the State House at Augusta was lowered to half-staff, the first time a woman had been so honored.

Ellsworth

Cordelia Stanwood Birthplace, Route 3. The pioneering ornithologist and nature writer–photographer was born in this Cape Cod–style frame house on August 1, 1865. "Cordelia's Room," with the Multiplex Hammond typewriter on which she wrote her numerous wildlife articles, is carefully preserved, along with the forty-acre woodland sanctuary surrounding the house. Here at "Birdsacre" for the last fifty years of her life, Cordelia Stanwood trained her camera and her pen along the winding trails among towering trees—to record the nesting and migratory habits of birds. She made over six hundred photographs of her feathered friends, many of whom allowed her to feed them by hand or carry them on her shoulder. Although she died in 1958, the wildlife refuge and a nonprofit foundation named in her honor remain as a living memorial for contemporary nature lovers.

Farmington

Lillian Nordica Birthplace, Holley Road. The famed operatic soprano was born Lillian Norton on December 12, 1857 in this modest farmhouse built by her father. Although she only lived here for six years, moving to Boston with her family and beginning the vocal training that later made her a star, this house has been turned into a museum with a splendid display of her furnishings, photographs, music scores, and mementos. A dazzling gown room contains the heroic costume and feathered helmet she wore as Brunnhilde, a favorite role during her career as the prima Wagnerian soprano with the Metropolitan Opera. In a tiny passage in the house hang crimson ribbons from her triumphal bouquets, emblazoned with *Giglia Nordica* ("Lily of the North"), the name her Milanese voice coach gave her to

facilitate pronunciation for Italian fans. The exhibition also includes a picture postcard of Nordica in the role of Aïda. It is addressed to British suffrage leader Emmeline Pankhurst in London. Nordica was an ardent suffragist, once singing the "Star-Spangled Banner" to a sea of San Franciscans at a 1911 suffrage rally at Union Square. That was shortly after her only return visit to this house. Three years later she died while on a concert tour abroad. One of the lotus blossoms—her favorite flower—that adorned her casket at her funeral in London was carried here by Nordica's manager. It was framed and now hangs in this museum.

Gardiner

Ellen Swallow Richards Grave, Christ Church Yard. The first woman to graduate from MIT (see *Cambridge, Massachusetts*), who pioneered in the fields of nutrition and environment, and who, according to her biographer, founded ecology, died in 1911, shortly after dictating a speech for her alma mater's fiftieth anniversary. The flags at MIT were lowered to half-mast. Her ashes are buried in this family plot beneath a stone in-

scribed: "Pioneer—Educator—Scientist. An Earnest Seeker—A Tireless Worker. A thoughtful Friend—A Helper of Mankind."

Laura E. Howe Richards House, 3 Dennis Street (private). When author Laura E. Richards moved here with her husband Henry in 1876, this building, known as "the Yellow House," overlooking the Kennebec River became a cultural center for such distinguished visitors as Alexander Woollcott. Here, while she coped with raising seven children, Laura Richards (named by her parents, Samuel and Julia Ward Howe, for Laura Bridgman—see *Watertown, Massachusetts*) became an active force in the civic and literary life of Gardiner. She helped found the library, the nursing service, and charities. And she wrote books, the first one actually "written on the back of my first born." She used the infant's spine as a desk to compose some verses. Along with children's stories (such as *Captain January*), she coauthored, with her sister Maud Howe Elliot, the Pulitzer Prize–winning biography of her mother, *Julia Ward Howe* (1915). Laura Richards outlived her close friend and sister-in-law, scientist Ellen Swallow Richards, by more than three decades. After Laura's death in this house in 1943, she was buried near Ellen Richards in the family plot at Christ Church Yard.

Hampden

Site of Dorothea Dix Birthplace, Dorothea Dix Memorial Park. The future Civil War nurse and crusader for reform in the treatment of the mentally ill was born here April 4, 1802, when Maine was still part of Massachusetts. Although her childhood in Hampden was beset by the problems of caring for an ailing mother and two younger brothers, as a grown woman, Dorothea Dix made her mark on the nation in other cities, earning, as the marker here indicates, "the admiration and reverence of the civilized world." (See *Trenton, New Jersey*.)

Hollis

Kate Douglas Wiggin House, "Quillcote," off Route 4A, Salmon Falls (private). This rambling rural house was where the author and kindergarten educator lived, first as a child, then as a widow in 1899. A fine storyteller with a special talent for holding children spellbound, she achieved lasting fame with her publication of *Rebecca of Sunnybrook Farm* (1903). Its heroine, the irrepressible Rebecca Rowena Randall, delighted millions

Six Little Chickadees, photo by Cordelia Stanwood

of children, first in the book, then the play, and then the movie starring the equally charming Mary Pickford. When Kate Douglas Wiggin died in 1923, her ashes were scattered in the Saco River near this house. (See *Buxton Lower Corner.*)

Kennebunkport

Margaret Deland House, "Greywood" (private). This house on the banks of the Kennebunk River, with a garden that once ran clear down to the water, was, during the early 1900s, the summer home of popular author Margaret Deland. The stone fountain outside the curving wall is dedicated to her husband Lorin, as were all her twenty-five books. Townspeople told us that they remembered her as a large woman, dressed in English tweeds, who made her way around Kennebunkport in an English dogcart pulled by two large, shaggy dogs. They also recall that as a best-selling author she was a prized guest. The summer people who owned large homes along the ocean would send her elegantly engraved invitations. Margaret Deland would turn them over, write "Can't come," and mail them back. Although local authors Booth Tarkington and Kenneth Roberts appear to have outlasted Margaret Deland in popularity, most of her books are in the town library, where a local historian told us, "their circulation is slight, but steady."

Kittery Point

Lady Pepperell House, Route 103. This two-story Georgian mansion was built in 1760 by Mary Sewell Pepperell with the inheritance she received from her late husband, Sir William Pepperell. Since he was the only American created a baronet by the English crown, she was the first American baroness, which, apart from her good taste in architecture, appears to be her only distinguishing achievement. A local resident told us that Lady Pepperell was once described as a woman "of short stature and little wit."

Machias

The first naval engagement of the Revolutionary War might have had a sad beginning without Hannah Weston. The young girl who directed her hostilities toward the British rather than toward the Indians—as her ancestor, Hannah Duston, did at *Haverhill, Massachusetts*—heard about the fighting on June 12, 1775. It is said that Hannah and her younger sister collected fifty pounds of lead and powder from their neighbors in Jonesboro and transported it through the woods to this port. The patriots at Machias used the ammunition to attack and capture the British ship *Margaretta* from the high seas.

Norridgewock

Clarke Sisters House, Route 201 (private). For the last half of the nineteenth century this red brick house with white columns was home to Rebecca Clarke and her sister Sarah, well-known writers who drew on their Norridgewock surroundings for inspiration. Rebecca was by far the better known, an enormously popular children's author who created the mischievous characters of Little Prudy, Dottie Dimple, and Flaxie Frizzle. She wrote under the pen name Sophie May, and the explanation goes that after signing "Sophie" (her own middle name) to her first story in 1861, she added "May," saying, "Well, I may write again and may not." Her sister Sarah was known as the less ambivalent Penn Shirley.

Orr's Island

Harriet Beecher Stowe (see *Brunswick*) set her novel *The Pearl of Orr's Island* here. Written in 1862 after she had left Maine, it inspired Sarah Orne Jewett of *South Berwick* to become a writer.

Poland Spring

Shaker Museum, Route 26, preserves the principles of Shakerism brought to this country two centuries ago by Mother Ann Lee (see *Watervliet, New York*). At the nearby Shaker Village on Sabbathday Lake, fewer than a dozen Shakers still live in their cooperative community, strict adherents to the celibacy that will one day make the sect extinct.

Portland

Site of Sara Payson Willis Parton Birthplace, 24 Franklin Street. The house where the popular and witty author known as Fanny Fern was born in 1811 has been torn down, a sad commentary on her home state, where she said, "the timber and the human beings are sound."

Rockland

Edna St. Vincent Millay Birthplace, 198–200 Broadway (private). The first woman to win a Pulitzer Prize for her poetry was born here February 22, 1892. Vincent, as she was called, moved with her mother to nearby *Camden* in 1904. The plaque that once marked this site was recently removed at the request of the new owners, and it was placed in the public library, where it is locked inside the safe.

South Berwick

Sarah Orne Jewett Birthplace, Route 236. In this fine frame residence built by her grandfather in 1774, novelist Sarah Orne Jewett was born September 3, 1849. Best known for her writings about Maine and its people, she was inspired by Harriet Beecher Stowe (see *Orr's Island*) to use "local color" in her works. She once said, "You must know the whole world before you know the village." The house preserves the Jewett family furnishings and Sarah's bedroom-study, exactly as she arranged it and worked in it. The stories considered her finest are in *The Country of the Pointed Firs* (1896), a gem of regional fiction that Willa Cather called "Magnificent!" Sarah Orne Jewett died in the house in 1909. Among her lifetime distinctions was the first honorary degree from Bowdoin College given to a woman.

Hamilton House, Vaughan's Lane. Sarah Orne Jewett so enjoyed this Georgian house high above the river that she set her novel, *The Tory Lover,* here in 1901.

Waterford

Ralph Waldo Emerson's brilliant but somewhat eccentric aunt, Mary Moody Emerson (see *Concord, Massachusetts*), spent most of her life here, and, although the family farmhouse known as "Elm Dale" has long since burned down, the anecdotes still live on. One nineteenth-century neighbor remembered her in a newspaper article, "trudging about the place clad in a sort of Mother Hubbard robe of white cotton, which looked for all the world like a lady's night robe." Another recalled that, ever prepared, Mary Emerson slept in a bed shaped like a coffin, wearing a shroud for her nightgown.

Winthrop Center

Hannah Bailey House, Route 135. Lipman Brothers Poultry Company has converted this house into a residence for their caretakers, but in the late nineteenth century it was the home of Quaker pacifist and suffragist Hannah Bailey. A temperance worker who also joined with Lillian M. N. Stevens (see *Dover-Foxcroft*) in prison reform, Hannah Bailey was an early opponent of war, violence, and martial toys for children.

Annapolis

Anne Catherine Hoof Green House, Charles Street. As a widow with at least ten children to support and a stack of her husband's bills to pay, Anne Catherine Green took over the publication of the *Maryland Gazette* while living in this now-deserted colonial house. In the April 16, 1767 edition of the paper, Anne announced the death of her husband Jonas, praised his editorial performance, and humbly begged, "I flatter myself that with your kind Indulgence and Encouragement, Myself and Son will be enabled to continue it on the same Footing." Under her skillful direction, the paper became a powerful force in the community, furthering the cause of liberty and the Revolution, although Anne died a year before the Declaration of Independence was signed. In her obituary, her son wrote of his working mother, "She was of a mild and benevolent disposition, and for Conjugal Affection, and Parental Tenderness, an Example to her Sex."

The Chase Home, 22 Maryland Avenue. Hester Ann Chase Ridout, who died here in 1886, provided in her will that this superb Georgian house, built in 1769, be used as a home for indigent elderly ladies "where they may find a retreat from the vicissitudes of life." Today this luxurious retreat with its cantilevered stairway, Palladian window, marble mantels, and crystal chandeliers is home for up to twelve self-supporting women over the age of sixty-five.

Antietam

Clara Barton Memorial, Mansfield Avenue. On the eve of the bloodiest battle of the Civil War, Clara Barton watched the smoke of the two armies' campfires and wrote in her diary, "I was faint, but could not eat; weary, but could not sleep; depressed, but could not weep," and she prayed for the strength to fulfill "the terrible duties of the coming day." As she had feared, September 17, 1862 dawned disastrously, and in the end, 23,000 men were dead or wounded. Through the smoke, fire, and earsplitting noise of war, Barton cleaned wounds, brought lantern light to the surgeons, and prepared gruel for the line of fighting men. When she went back to Washington, D.C., three days later, it was with deep satisfaction, as well as a fever brought on from fatigue. Today her courage is marked by a roughhewn marble slab adorned with a small red cross made of bricks from her birthplace in *North Oxford, Massachusetts.* As the bronze plaque proclaims, Clara Barton's Antietam "act of love and mercy led to the birth of the present American National Red Cross" two decades later. (See *Glen Echo;* see *Dansville, New York.*)

Baltimore

Site of First Post Office, Smith and Baltimore Streets. In 1775, Mary Katherine Goddard was appointed the city's first postmaster in tribute to her commendable speed, efficiency, and accuracy as the city's only newspaper publisher during the Revolutionary War. Mary was responsible for such remarkable scoops as her three-column account of the Battle of Bunker Hill, published less than a month after it happened. She also printed the official copy of the Declaration of Independence, the first with all its celebrated signatures. As postmaster, Mary inaugurated home delivery, a service for which she charged a modest penny a letter. But her position was such a political prize that the postmaster general decided to give the job to one of his cronies, using the feeble excuse that Mary, then more than fifty years old, couldn't be expected to do the strenuous horseback travel involved in the job. Although more than two hundred prominent citizens signed a petition in 1789 on her behalf, and although Mary even asked the help of her good friend George Washington, she was replaced. Mary spent the last years until her death in 1811 using her orderly and efficient skills to manage a bookstore.

Mother Seton House, 600 North Paca Street. In this small red brick house surrounded by a wrought-iron fence, in 1808, Elizabeth Seton (see *Manhattan, New York City*) began a school for Roman Catholic girls, the nation's first free Catholic school. America's first home-born saint, canonized in September 1975,

took the vows of poverty, chastity, and obedience in St. Mary's Seminary Chapel next door in March 1809. Several months later, Mother Seton and four women—in their new habits of black dresses with capes and white caps tied beneath the chin—set out for *Emmitsburg* to begin the work of her new order, the Sisters of Charity of St. Joseph.

Mary Young Pickersgill House, 844 East Pratt Street. This salmon-colored brick building, also known as "The Flag House," was the scene of the nation's most ambitious and patriotic home sewing project. When in 1813 the commandant at Fort McHenry said he wanted "to have a flag so large that the British will have no difficulty in seeing it from a distance," he knew only Mary Young Pickersgill could meet the order. Mary learned her skills with stars and stripes from her mother, who made the first flag of the Revolution, and she was well known in town as "an exceedingly patriotic woman." Assisted by her daughter Caroline, Mary spent six weeks spinning, weaving, and sewing 440 yards of bunting into a mighty banner whose replica now sprawls over a sunlit desk by the window in the upstairs front room. Mary charged a paltry $405.90 for fifteen stars and fifteen stripes that measured 36 feet by 42 feet, and she delivered the flag to Fort McHenry on August 19, 1813. A year later, Francis Scott Key took one long look, and the rest is musical history. The frayed but still magnificent flag hangs in the Smithsonian (see *Washington, D.C.*).

Confederate Women's Monument, Charles Street and University Parkway. In this heroic bronze grouping, erected in 1913, a young soldier lies dying as one woman tries to help him and

another, standing proud and rebellious, clenches her fist with determination to continue the struggle. "In difficulty and danger," reads the inscription, "they fed the hungry, clothed the needy, nursed the wounded and comforted the dying."

Charles Street Theater. In 1853, Laura Keene took over this theater and established herself as one of the first two female theater managers in the country. She directed plays, wrote scripts, designed scenery, sewed costumes, coached actors, and acted herself. However, her most famous role was played offstage. (See *Washington, D.C.*)

Johns Hopkins University. The first woman to receive a Ph.D. from this university (1893) was Florence Bascom, a geologist who learned how to describe and classify rocks before the classic text on petrography was even written. Bascom was also the first female fellow of the Geological Society of America and in 1930 became its first female vice-president. Gertrude Stein came to Johns Hopkins in 1897 as a magna cum laude graduate of Radcliffe. She was a brilliant student with remarkable skill in the dissection of corpses, but she got bored, flunked out, and then found true happiness in writing. Dr. Florence Sabin (see *Denver, Colorado; Washington, D.C.*) was the university's first female full professor (1917) and became the foremost woman of her time in the field of scientific investigation. "All that women need to do to exert our proper influence," Sabin once said, "is just to use all the brains we have."

Elizabeth Gilman Home, 513 Park Avenue. Maryland's first female candidate for governor lived in this yellow brick two-story house, now owned by a construction company, most of her long, colorful life. "Miss Lizzie" was a champion of all the unpopular causes of her day, disdaining Upton Sinclair's gratuitous advice to "get arrested and stay arrested." She demonstrated tirelessly on behalf of Sacco and Vanzetti, striking miners, Spanish leftists, American Indians, and pacifists. Gilman, who decided to tour Europe for two years instead of going to college, found some time between causes to graduate from Johns Hopkins University with a bachelor of science degree at age fifty-five. For many years this house was home to several scholarship students from Johns Hopkins, where Gilman's father was the first president. After her unsuccessful bid for governor on the Socialist ticket in 1930, Gilman tried again and again for the Senate and the mayoralty, but the outspoken firebrand, as well as her innovative proposals such as express bus service, were too radical for the voters.

"Radicals do all sorts of original things," she once proudly observed. "Not because they have been taught that it is the thing to do but because it is the thing that appeals to them. They are good company as well as good citizens." When she died at eighty-two in 1950, her admirers all agreed that Gilman, "as much as anyone established the right of Maryland to be called the Free State."

Lizette Woodworth Reese Memorial, Eastern High School, Thirty-third Street. In a grove of evergreen trees and hawthorns stands a monument of pink Georgia marble, sculpted by Grace Turnbull, that honors the memory of the poet Lizette Reese. When Reese died at age eighty in 1935, H. L. Mencken called her "the most distinguished woman who has ever lived in [Baltimore]." Pairs of sheep cluster around a benevolent shepherd, and the base of the monument is inscribed with the Reese poem, "With a Book of Hymns," that inspired the statue. Another lyrical gem, "Today," stimulated yet another tribute to the poet: Beatrice Fenton's bas-relief design—a graceful figure in a tunic, scattering rose petals—hangs in Baltimore's Enoch Pratt Free Library. A disciplined perfectionist, Reese would sometimes spend up to ten years rewriting the lines that she composed while waiting for a streetcar to take her to Western High School where she taught for twenty years. Her most famous poem, "Tears," which critic George Saintsbury called the third best sonnet in the English language, is inscribed on a bronze tablet in the school's hallway.

Szold Street. This residential street in the northwestern section of Baltimore was dedicated in 1950, five years after the death of Henrietta Szold, lifelong Zionist and the founder of Hadassah. During the 1890s, when Russian persecution of Jews began and refugees came streaming into the city, Henrietta started Baltimore's first night school to teach them English. By the time the city took over the school, more than five thousand immigrants, Christians as well as Jews, had studied here. In 1912, Henrietta started Hadassah, a welfare organization to bring modern medical science to Palestine—where she eventually moved in the 1920s to supervise the building of hospitals, medical schools, and playgrounds open to Jews and Arabs alike. When Hitler came to power, Henrietta was in her seventies, but she never slowed her efforts to evacuate Jewish children from Germany, more than ten thousand of whom were saved and educated under her guidance. She died in Palestine in 1945 and is buried there on the Mount of Olives.

Bethesda

Madonna of the Trail Monument, Wisconsin Avenue. Dedicated in April 1929, this monument is the farthest east and last in the series of twelve identical statues erected by the DAR to mark the old trails used by pioneer settlers. (See *Springfield, Ohio.*)

Cambridge

Grave of Anna Ella Carroll, Trinity Church, Route 16. On the banks of the Little Choptank River, in the slivered shadows of a weeping willow tree, rests "Maryland's Most Distinguished Lady. A great humanitarian and a close friend of Abraham Lincoln," as Anna Ella Carroll is described on the slim marble headstone. Lincoln acknowledged his debt to her for the persuasive political pamphlets she wrote interpreting his constitutional war powers. But no one gave Carroll, a brilliant military strategist, the credit she deserved for her part in winning the Civil War. She devised the Tennessee campaign, called "the greatest military event in the interest of the human race known to modern ages." Its true authorship was kept secret, and when Anna asked for a modest payment and official recognition, she was ignored. Such woman's rights leaders as Matilda Joselyn Gage and the Blackwell sisters spent a frustrating quarter of a century arguing that Anna Carroll was denied due honor because of her sex. Anna, poor, deaf, paralyzed, and in her seventies, kept up the fight until her death in 1893, tragically proving the words of one male believer: "The truth is, your services were so great that they cannot be comprehended by the ordinary capacity of our public men."

Annie Oakley House, 28 Bellevue Avenue (private). After an appearance in Cambridge, where she thrilled audiences with her favorite trick shots—e.g., splitting the thin edge of a card in two—Annie Oakley (see *Nutley, New Jersey*), sharpshooter of the Buffalo Bill Wild West Show, retired briefly and settled here in 1914 with her husband Frank Butler. The four-bedroom house overlooks the lovely Hambrook Bay, which was filled with wild swans when we visited, and no doubt such placid scenes were too peaceful for the energetic fifty-five-year-old Annie. A year later, she left for a fashionable resort in Pinehurst, North Carolina, to give society women shooting lessons. Annie always believed that knowing how to handle a gun increased a woman's self-confidence, nerve, and judgment. She stayed in Pinehurst several winter seasons before going home to *Greenville, Ohio.*

Clinton

Mary Surratt House, Route 381. Her hometown has vindicated the woman who was hanged for plotting with John Wilkes Booth to kill President Lincoln. Over the years, schools and business developments have been named for her but it was not until October 1975 that this nine-room house was restored and dedicated as an historical site. Mary Surratt's troubles began when she leased one of her rooms to John M. Lloyd, a friend of Booth. After the assassination, Booth stopped at this house to care for his broken leg. More circumstantial evidence piled up against her when it was learned that Booth sometimes stayed at her Washington, D.C., boardinghouse. Later Lloyd testified falsely that it was Mary who had provided Booth with the ammunition and guns for his heinous crime. Bewildered and defenseless, she was not even given a fair trial before her execution at age forty-two on July 7, 1865.

Denton

Birthplace of Sophie Kerr, Fifth Avenue and Kerr Avenue (private). The author of many short stories and popular novels, including *The Golden Block* and *Stay out of My Life,* was born in this elegant two-story house in 1880. Its present owners, Dr. and Mrs. Christian Snyder told us that they own several of Sophie's books and one of her dining room chairs, but their prize possession is her old wooden bathtub.

Elkton

Site of Martha Finley Home, 259 East Main Street. After the death of her father, Martha moved here in 1876 when she was forty-eight years old to begin writing the famous children's series of "Elsie" books, whose titles depressingly summarize a woman's fate: *Elsie's Girlhood; Elsie's Womanhood; Elsie's Motherhood; Elsie's Children; Elsie's Widowhood;* and *Grandmother Elsie.* At one point newspaper editors complained, "For God's sake, give us something besides Elsie." But Martha firmly "pursued the even tenor of her ways," calmly replying that she was not writing to please editors but her little friends who couldn't wait for the next installments: *Elsie's New Relations; Elsie's Friends at Woodburne;* and dozens more. Martha's home, described as "pretty and exquisitely neat, comfortable and convenient," has been replaced by a funeral parlor.

Emmitsburg

Seton Shrine Center, U.S. 15. The first Sisters of Charity of St. Joseph, headed by Mother Elizabeth Seton (see *Baltimore*), settled on this rolling farmland in 1809. Their first year was spent in the 200-year-old Stone House where they fetched their drinking water from a stone well and washed on the banks of Toms Creek. Mother Seton soon established a school and later founded hospitals, orphanages, and an institution for lepers. Her small community grew, and, by the time of her death at age forty-six in 1821, there were 50 Sisters of Charity; today there are more than 8,500. Mother Seton was called a saint even in her lifetime, but after three miracles, in the rigorous test for canonization, her sanctity became official in September 1975, two hundred years after her birth. When we visited, dozens of pilgrims were on their way to St. Joseph's Chapel where her sacred relics rest in a small bronze casket beneath the altar.

Frederick

Barbara Fritchie Home, 156 West Patrick Street. The small red brick house is an exact replica of the original, and a flag hangs during the day outside the same dormer window where ninety-five-year-old Barbara Fritchie is said to have waved her Union flag as Stonewall Jackson and his troops marched through town in 1862. The story goes that Jackson was so angered by the sight of the flag that he ordered his men to fire, but the tiny old woman kept right on waving it, so impressing the general that he quickly moved out of town. The truth is that Jackson probably never even came anywhere near town. Barbara was so well known for her exuberant Union loyalty that historians agree that such an act of patriotic defiance would have been just like her. Her courage has inspired dozens of little Barbara Fritchies from coast to coast (see *Middletown;* see *Vancouver, Washington*) who have assured her everlasting fame, as has John Greenleaf Whittier's poem with her bold words: " 'Shoot if you must, this old gray head/But spare your country's flag,' she said." The entire sixty-line poem and a bas-relief of that famous gray head grace the monument over her grave in Mount Olivet Cemetery in town.

Georgetown

Kitty Knight House, Route 213. The plaque near the front door reads, "In honor of Mistress Kitty Knight, Revolutionary Belle and Beauty, a friend of General George Washington. When the British burned Georgetown in 1813 her heroic efforts saved this house which later became her home." It seems that as the soldiers were setting fire to the house young Kitty kept beating out the flames with a broom until the commanding officer, impressed by her dauntless spirit, ordered the house spared. Maryland tourist brochures give Kittty an even larger share of heroic history and tell us she "artfully dissuaded" a British admiral from bombarding Georgetown and its twin, Fredericktown, across the river. Today the house is a hotel and restaurant whose menus provide food for thought with a capsule history of its namesake.

Glen Echo

Clara Barton House, 5801 Oxford Road. The founder of the American Red Cross (see *Antietam*) lived here from 1897 until she died in 1912, when her body was sent to *Oxford, Massachu-*

setts, for burial. This unique building was constructed of lumber salvaged from emergency structures after the Johnstown flood and was designed to resemble a Mississippi riverboat, with railed galleries and a lantern roof. It was the Red Cross Headquarters until Barton's resignation as president in 1904. In this very house, Barton, a lifelong suffrage leader, held a reception for five hundred participants of the 1904 National Woman Suffrage Convention. It was on Honorary President Susan B. Anthony's birthday, February 15, and the delegates marveled at the flags of many nations draped on the walls, gifts to Barton from the world's rulers. At her guests' insistence, the tiny Angel of the Battlefield dug out all the treasures—medals, jewels, pictures—she received from European dignitaries for her distinguished service. Many of these treasures can still be seen in the house.

Ladiesburg

The town got its name in the early 1800s when the entire population consisted of seven ladies and one gentleman. "This is still a small village, population 117," postmaster Ethel V. Sharrer told us, "and it is quite a coincidence that we now have seven widows and one widower living here."

Middletown

Nancy Crouse House, 204 Main Street (private). Even though she lived next door to a Confederate sympathizer, seventeen-year-old Nancy Crouse flew the Union flag every day from the second story of this four-pillared green-shuttered house. One day in September 1862, when sixteen Confederate cavalrymen came to visit Nancy's neighbor, she overheard them planning to tear down "that Yankee rag." Incensed, Nancy rushed upstairs and returned to the front porch defiantly wearing the flag. One of the ruffians pointed a pistol at her head as Nancy shouted, "You may shoot me, but never will I willingly give up my country's flag into the hands of traitors." Hopelessly outnumbered, Nancy watched the Confederate captain tie the flag around his horse's head and ride away. Within hours, however, the rebels were captured and the flag was returned to Nancy as a tribute to her courage. Like her elderly counterpart, Barbara Fritchie in *Frederick,* Nancy and her brave deed were celebrated in an eight stanza ballad:

> Middletown remembers yet
> How the tide of war was stayed
> And the years will not forget
> Nancy Crouse, the Valley Maid.

St. Mary's City

Margaret Brent's Land, "Sister's Freehold," Route 5 (private). The nation's first suffragist, also Maryland's first female landowner, built a small house and a mill on this riverbank property when she arrived here from her native England in 1638. Her historic stand for equal rights came ten years later when Margaret appeared before the General Assembly of the colony, asked to be admitted as a member, and demanded not only one vote, but two—one as an attorney, the other as a landowner. The assembly was amazed at her logic and audacity. "What man would ever have dreamed of such a thing," they marveled and promptly said no. (A large oil painting in the old State House shows Margaret in her historic plea.) Undismayed, Margaret continued buying up all the land and keeping the men of Maryland's first capital city honest by hauling them before the law for any misdealings. She entered court 124 times in eight years, winning every case. The men of the assembly never denied her anything except what she wanted most. It would take almost three centuries for Margaret's followers throughout the nation to get even half of the two votes per woman she sought.

St. Michaels

Amelia Welby House, Mulberry Street (private). "Very few American poets are at all comparable with her in the true poetical qualities," said Edgar Allan Poe about the woman who was born in this modest green house in 1819. Welby's poetic genius was apparent when she was only thirteen, but she hid her poems, written on scraps of paper, in an old drawer. Unfortunately she died a scant twenty years later. Critics agreed that had she been able to complete her life's work, "she might have gained a place second to none in the annals of American poetry."

Stevenson

Hannah More Academy, named for the eighteenth-century author, scholar, and reformer who founded schools for the poor in England, opened in 1834 with the generous donations of Baltimore philanthropist Ann Van Bibber Neilson. In 1873, it became the first Episcopal boarding school for girls in the U.S. Students even spent Christmas at school. After one particularly moving Yuletide service, a member of the class of 1879 was heard to exclaim, "Don't you think if all the world could be here now, all the world would be Episcopalian?" In July 1974 the school merged with nearby St. Timothy's, a boys' school, and Hannah More's name is no more.

Towson

Hampton National Historic Site, Hampton Lane. One of the great post-Revolutionary mansions in America was built from 1783–90 by Charles Ridgely. His wife Rebecca, a devout Methodist, was not enthusiastic about her husband's lavish dream house and worried about the effects on his soul of all this material preoccupation. And rightly so. Ridgely died six months after the mansion was completed.

Westminster

God's Well, Main Street. In the garden of the Carroll County Historical Society sits a windlass structure on the site of this well. According to legend, the well never ran dry. One summer in the late 1880s, Westminster, which had a population of about a hundred and was regularly visited by emigrants, was struck by a terrible drought. Only two wells were working, those of innkeeper Shiller and Squire Winchester, the town's founder. Shiller locked up his well, announcing he would only sell water to villagers at sixpence a bucket. But the squire's elderly daughters, Lydia and Elizabeth, were of more generous spirit. They put up a sign in their garden reading, "Water belongs to God. Free to All." Then came the day when Shiller himself had to beg water from God's well. The sisters did not turn him away, and the well never ran dry. And, according to the Historical Society, "We have every reason to suppose that it continues running deep beneath our garden."

MASSACHUSETTS

Adams

Susan B. Anthony Birthplace, East Road at East Street (private). In this three-story frame house at the foot of Mount Greylock, the future suffrage leader spent the first six years of her life. Born February 15, 1820, into a world where women had few rights and no vote, the young Susan learned at the Quaker meetinghouse she attended with her father that women could be equal. The meetinghouse is still standing in the Maple Street Cemetery. Local historians still talk about the summer of 1897, when the world-famous traveler returned with seventy-nine other relatives for the Anthony Family Reunion, conducting suffrage business at long tables laden with fried chicken and apple pie. The next day, Susan B. Anthony eagerly joined the group that traveled to the summit of Mount Greylock in a six-horse carriage.

Amesbury

Mary Baker Eddy House, 277 Main Street. During her two-year stay in the home of Sarah Bagley (1868–70), Mary Baker Eddy wrote the first draft of "The Science of Man." Her cheerful room on the second floor of this red clapboard house was the scene of a frenzy of writing, as she dropped page after completed page on the floor. (See *Brookline.*)

Amherst

Emily Dickinson House, 280 Main Street. For most of the mid–nineteenth century, this handsome sixteen-room brick house was considerably more visible than the shy, sensitive genius who lived and wrote within it. Emily Dickinson was born here in 1830 and spent almost all of her creative life here. Neighbors knew her only as a figure clad in white, mysteriously moving from room to room. Only to such close friends as Helen Hunt Jackson (who grew up at 249 South Pleasant Street and later moved to *Colorado Springs, Colorado*) and the editor of the *Atlantic Monthly* was it evident that a genius was at work in the second-floor bedroom-workroom. Here, her only real view of the world through a curtained window facing Main Street and a row of tall evergreen trees, she wrote the poems that expressed her deepest sensibilities: "I'm nobody!" and "The Soul Selects Her Own Society." Here too, after her death in 1886, in a box in a dresser drawer, Dickinson's sister found the poems. Only then were they published for the first time. Today, this house is a faculty residence for Amherst College; the bedroom where Emily worked is restored and open to the public. Her chair reposes at Harvard's Houghton Library in Cambridge.

Andover

Abbot Academy was one of the first girls' schools incorporated in New England, February 26, 1829. It gained real impetus when Madame Sarah Abbot contributed a thousand dollars, on the condition that the school be located on School Street, not Main Street, "the place most frequented by Theologues and Academy boys." The "Academy" was Phillips Academy, the nearby boys' school, and, for 143 years, the girls of Abbot kept their distance at Madame Abbot's behest. They remained independent and grew intellectually, being offered a wide range of classes as well as the skeleton of a Prussian mercenary soldier for their anatomy lessons. In September 1972, long after Madame Abbot's death, Abbot's trustees voted to turn over—for one dollar—its assets to the trustees of Phillips Academy. The two are now united as a coeducational school.

Barre

Soldiers Monument, a thirty-five-foot memorial to the soldiers of Barre, started out in nearby *Haverhill* as a twenty-five-foot Italian marble obelisk to honor Hannah Duston for her 1697 escape from Indian captivity. When the outbreak of the Civil War pinched economic resources in Haverhill, and many subscribers failed to honor their pledges, the citizens of Barre purchased it. They removed its ornamental musket, tomahawk, and scalping knife, added ten feet in height, and brought it here.

Boston

(see also *Brookline, Cambridge, Dorchester, Everett, Jamaica Plain, Medford,* and *Roxbury* for Boston area)

Statue of Anne Hutchinson, State House grounds. "She was a woman of haughty and fierce carriage, a nimble wit and active spirit, a very voluble tongue, more bold than a man." Thus did Governor John Winthrop describe Anne Hutchinson, the woman he banished from Boston in 1638 for her audacity in challenging the religious hierarchy of the Massachusetts Bay Colony. The governor was siding with a host of churchly eminences who accused Mistress Hutchinson in a two-day trial. They objected to her biweekly meetings with Boston women. When she maintained her fiery, unrepentant manner, an accuser lashed out with one of the prosecutors' underlying fears: "You have stepped out of your place. You have rather been a husband than a wife, and a preacher than a hearer, a magistrate than a subject." With that, she was excommunicated. Accompanied only by her friend and follower Mary Dyer, she walked out of the church, then traveled to Roger Williams's colony at *Portsmouth, Rhode Island,* and finally settled in the area now known as the *Bronx, New York City.* Long after Hutchinson's public embarrassment, this bronze statue was erected, with a plaque calling her "a courageous exponent of civil liberty and religious toleration."

Statue of Mary Dyer, State House grounds. From the day she sided with Anne Hutchinson, Mary Dyer was also considered a heretic. She too was excommunicated and banished, ultimately converting to the new Quaker faith. Her beliefs led to jail and further harassment and, in 1659, a sentence to be hanged. As she stood on the gallows with the halter around her neck that chilly October day, prepared to die for her faith, a reprieve was announced. Mary Dyer was led out of the colony on horseback. Six months later she returned to Boston, specifically to ask them to repeal the "wicked law" that had convicted her. Again she was sentenced to hang; again she mounted the gallows. The noose closed around her neck in May 1660. As her body swung lifelessly above the crowd gathered on Boston Common, one member of the audience called it "a flag for others to take example by." More than three centuries later, this statue by Quaker Sylvia Shaw Judson, showing the "witness for religious freedom" with a serenely peaceful expression, is the example that remains. The martyred Quaker is quoted on the inscription: "My life not availeth me in comparison to the liberty of truth."

MARY DYER

Statue of Horace Mann, State House grounds. This graceful bronze, which you will encounter between the two religious martyrs, Anne Hutchinson and Mary Dyer, was sculpted by Emma Stebbins (see *Manhattan, New York City*) and installed in 1865.

The Boston Athenaeum, 10½ Beacon Street. The first woman to penetrate the all-male sanctuary of this private club and library was Hannah Adams, pioneering historian whose portrait still looks down sweetly on the men in the Trustees Room. She was granted the extraordinary privilege in March 1829, as

Josiah Quincy put it, "to claim the freedom of its alcoves, and to endure the raising of the masculine eyebrows, provoked by the unaccustomed sight." When the librarian went to lunch, Mrs. Adams (as they called her out of respect for all unmarried women) was locked inside. (See *Cambridge*.)

Granary Burial Ground, Tremont Street. Alongside the bodies of such patriots as Paul Revere, Samuel Adams, and John Hancock lie the remains of Abiah Franklin, mother of Benjamin. A granite obelisk, marking the site where she is interred next to her husband of fifty-five years, calls her "a discreet and virtuous woman." There is also a stone here marked "Mary Goose," which is popularly thought to mark the grave of Mother Goose, the verse writer, who was also known as Elizabeth Foster Vergoose.

King's Chapel Burying Ground, School Street. In the Apthorp family tomb lies the body of Sarah Wentworth Apthorp Morton (1759–1846), a socially prominent poet who wrote under the pen name Philenia and was known as the Sappho of America. She also wrote the second novel ever published in America, in 1789. Also buried here: Mary Chilton (d. 1679), remembered as a "passenger on the Mayflower" on the gravestone she shares with her husband, John Winslow.

Copp's Hill Burying Ground, Hull Street and Snow Hill. Sealed in the Mather tomb with her fiery Puritan minister ancestors is the body of Hannah Mather Crocker, author of the early tract *Observations on the Real Rights of Women* (1818). Although considerably less revolutionary than Mary Wollstonecraft's earlier feminist work in England, this text nonetheless firmly insisted that "the powers of mind are equal in the sexes."

Louisa May Alcott House, 20 Pinckney Street (private). A marker on this three-story red brick building atop Beacon Hill informs passersby in tasteful lettering, "Louisa May Alcott once lived here." However, she spent more time at the family home in *Concord*.

Julia Ward Howe House, 13 Chestnut Street (private). From 1864 to 1879 this handsome residence attributed to Bulfinch was the home of the author of "The Battle Hymn of the Republic" (see *Washington, D.C.*). During this period of her life, as she gained national prominence for her hymn, Julia Ward Howe became active in the women's movement and was an ardent suffragist, founding with Lucy Stone the New England Woman Suffrage Association.

Grave of Phillis Wheatley, Old South Church, Washington Street. When she died in 1784 at age thirty-one, the ex-slave who enjoyed some fame as a poet was too poor to buy a headstone. Today, no marker honors the young woman who stepped off a slave ship in Boston Harbor in 1761 and into the household of a generous couple. Through them Phillis Wheatley was educated and encouraged. In 1773, a book of her poems—with affidavits of its veracity by noted Boston gentlemen—was published. By 1775, one of her poems so attracted the attention of Gen. George Washington that he praised her "elegant lines" and invited her to visit him in Cambridge. Little is known of her later life, except for her death after a troubled marriage. And on the 200th anniversary of her funeral, black women poets finally honored her with a statue in *Jackson, Mississippi*.

Site of Elizabeth Peabody's Bookstore, 13 West Street. Once a sparkling center of Boston's intellectual life, this is where Elizabeth Peabody lived and became Boston's first female bookseller, then publisher. In the book-lined parlor, Margaret Fuller of *Cambridge* conducted her famous Wednesday afternoon Transcendentalist Conversations with local ladies thirsting for knowledge. The topics ranged from Greek mythology to life's problems, and for the first few years of the 1840s they were the most stimulating and talked-about sessions in town. Today, Bostonians still gather here—the site of the West Street bookstore is now a parking lot.

Isabella Stewart Gardner Museum, "Fenway Court," 280 The Fenway. The public was first admitted in 1903 to this Italian-style palace, a treasury of the finest European art collected in the world's capitals under the direction of the free-spirited, witty wife of John Lowell Gardner, known as "Mrs. Jack." For most of the late nineteenth and early twentieth centuries, she was the reigning social and cultural queen of Boston, who once received a letter addressed simply:

> Mrs. Gardner, Esq.
> well known lady in high life
> Boston Mass.

When she completed her showplace of imported Florentine stones and furnished it with the oils of Titian, Rembrandt, and the like, a friend called her "a genius, but I knew that before. . . . A kind of Aphrodite with a lining of Athene." Since her death in 1924, Fenway Court has remained a memorial to her extraordinary taste and delightful eccentricities, a center for music, art, and cascades of bright orange bougainvillea in the courtyard.

First Church of Christ, Scientist, St. Paul, Norway, and Falmouth Streets. The original building was opened December 30, 1894; Mary Baker Eddy, who founded the church, first visited four months later. The famous domed structure that Mrs. Eddy called "our prayer in stone," is still used for special church meetings, although the larger Church Extension now accommodates the regular services. (See *Brookline.*)

Mary Baker Eddy House, 385 Commonwealth Avenue (private). This fifteen-room brownstone was Mrs. Eddy's home from 1888–89. She was here the night before her last address to the annual meeting of her church in Tremont Temple.

Mary Baker Eddy House, 400 Beacon Street, Chestnut Hill. From this pleasant, twenty-five-room house, Mrs. Eddy started the church newspaper—now the internationally famed *Christian Science Monitor.* Memorabilia from her stay here (1908–10) are on display in a second-floor exhibit. (See *Brookline.*)

Boston University was guaranteed its place in American women's history when Anna Howard Shaw of *Ashton, Michigan,* entered its School of Theology in 1876. Determined to become a minister despite her meager finances, she discovered that her forty-two male classmates were offered financial assistance unavailable to her. Undaunted, she sought outside preaching engagements, finally landing a job in Hingham as the congre-

gation's last choice. She graduated in 1878 and later wrote, "Notwithstanding the handicap of being a woman, I was said to be the only member of my class who had worked during the entire course, graduated free from debt, and had a new outfit as well as a few dollars." Eight years later, the Reverend Anna Howard Shaw added "Dr." to her title after earning her M.D. here. She devoted the rest of her life to the suffrage cause. As president of the National American Woman's Suffrage Association from 1904–15, she continued to perform marriages—as long as the women refused "to obey" their grooms. It was her only experience at the altar. Toward the end of her busy life she said, "Thank God, with all my burdens, I have never had a burden of a husband."

Statue of Leif Ericson, Commonwealth Avenue Mall. The colossal bronze at the entrance to the Common was sculpted in 1887 by Anne Whitney, dynamic but publicity-shy sculptor who executed more than one hundred works, some of which can be seen in *Washington, D.C.*

Brookline

Mary Baker Eddy Museum, 120 Seaver Street. With the same care that has gone into preserving the nation's documents at the National Archives, Christian Scientists have maintained the

documents and artifacts of their founder, Mary Baker Eddy. In 1903 philanthropist Mary Beecher Longyear had her stone mansion moved from Michigan to this eight-acre site to house the collection. On display: a little hat with flowers that Mrs. Eddy made herself for two dollars when asked to lecture on temperance in the 1860s; ten of her personal cards with her numerous New England residences; and textbooks and miniatures of Mary Baker Eddy and her work. The main attraction, viewed by about ten thousand visitors each year, is the gold-nibbed fountain pen with which she wrote *Science and Health.* At one end of the formal garden outside stands Cyrus Dallin's larger-than-life bronze of Mary Baker Eddy, an open book symbolically in her left hand.

Buckland

Site of Buckland Female Seminary, Upper Street (private). In the third-floor ballroom of this federal-style brick house built for Maj. Joseph Griswold in 1818, Mary Lyon opened her first school for young women in 1824. It was an innovative step for the zealous young educator who had been born twenty-seven years earlier on a nearby farm. She strongly believed that girls should be educated equally with boys and that woman should teach—a profession she began at age seventeen. During the few winters it functioned—until 1829—Buckland Female Seminary was a success, the precursor of Mary Lyon's greatest achievement in *South Hadley.*

Cambridge

Radcliffe College was opened in 1879 as the nameless-but-nicknamed "Harvard Annex," the brainchild of seven Cambridge women. One, Elizabeth Cabot Cary Agassiz, made the muslin curtains that hung in the first classroom, when twenty-seven young women showed up for instruction. Three years later, when the school was officially titled the Society for the Collegiate Instruction of Women, Elizabeth Agassiz became its first president. She could proudly record later, "We have had as yet no flighty students." It was also Mrs. Agassiz who convinced the legislature to charter the new school in 1894. Radcliffe College was on its own.

An earlier school that Elizabeth Agassiz had founded at her home (gone without a trace from 36 Quincy Street) employed Maria Baldwin, the first black female school principal in the state. When that poised and dignified educator died in 1922, her students honored her with a memorial that called her an "inspiring teacher, wise and beloved Master of this school."

Today, Radcliffe is helping to preserve the records of the nation's women with the Schlesinger Library, a treasure-house of female archives and accomplishments.

Margaret Fuller House, 71 Cherry Street (private). In this three-story white clapboard house, Margaret Fuller was born on March 23, 1810. As a young girl she was educated by her father, who accepted the then-radical notion that girls were the intellectual equals of boys. She learned English, Latin, Shakespeare, Molière, and Cervantes before she was a teen-ager; then she went away to school. From this training Fuller developed into the leading intellectual of Boston, once accurately telling her friend Ralph Waldo Emerson, "I now know all the people worth knowing in America, and I find no intellect comparable to my own." (See *Boston.*)

Mount Auburn Hospital, 330 Mount Auburn Street. The funds for this hospital, originally named the Cambridge Hospital, were raised through the efforts of Emily Elizabeth Parsons, a devoted Civil War nurse whose selfless activities on behalf of the wounded finally impaired her own frail health. One of the forerunners in the movement for female nurses, she won over male prejudice sufficiently to be named supervisor of nurses at

a St. Louis, Missouri, army hospital in 1863. When the war was over, she devoted herself to helping freedmen. Then, unable to "sit down and do nothing," she began collecting money for a new hospital that opened in 1867 in Cambridge. Today, Mount Auburn Hospital uses the original building—named for Emily Parsons—for offices.

Ellen Swallow Richards Memorial, Massachusetts Institute of Technology, Building 4, Massachusetts Avenue adjacent to Killian Court. If you're looking for good luck, the legend goes, stroll by the bronze plaque on the first floor of this old chemistry building and rub your hand over the already shiny nose of Ellen Henrietta Swallow Richards. Then read the words below. They will tell you that Ellen Swallow Richards was MIT's first female graduate (1873); an instructor in sanitary chemistry (1873–1911); and a "leader in the field of public health and pioneer in home economics. She strove for better living conditions as a first step to higher human efficiency." There is no room on the plaque to report what is behind Ellen Swallow Richards's story: She was admitted in 1870 as a "special student" with no tuition fee so that MIT was not obligated to her; and she never received her doctorate of science, according to her husband, because "the heads of the department did not want a woman to receive the first D.S. in Chemistry." Despite these obstacles, she pursued a remarkable scientific career, giving special attention to the new science of *"Oekology,"* an interdisciplinary environmental science she publicly christened in 1892. She was also instrumental in MIT's establishment of a Woman's Laboratory in 1876. (See *Gardiner, Maine.*)

MOUNT AUBURN CEMETERY, 580 Mount Auburn Street
"On Saturday morning . . . I visited Mount Auburn," Susan B. Anthony wrote her family in 1855. "What a magnificent resting-place this is! We could not find Margaret Fuller's monument, which I regretted." Today, the management of this landscaped park has thoughtfully provided maps to prevent having unsatisfied visitors. Following are some of the grave sites to visit:

Mary Baker Eddy Memorial and Tomb, Halcyon Avenue, overlooking Halcyon Lake, is one of the most monumental grave markers here. Eight fluted columns encircle the tomb and garden of pink and white flowers. Carved on the memorial: "Mary Baker Eddy, discoverer and founder of Christian Science. Author of Science and Health with Key to the Scriptures." (See *Brookline.*)

Margaret Fuller Memorial, Pyrola Path. The genius and intellect of this remarkable woman from Cambridge were lost to the world on July 19, 1850 when she, her husband Giovanni Angelo (Marquis Ossoli), and their two-year-old child, Angelo, drowned during a shipwreck in a storm off Fire Island, New York. They were returning from a tempestuous three-year stay in Italy, and only the child's body was recovered. The elaborate marker to all three is adorned with a bas-relief of Fuller's head and a bronze plaque describing her: "By birth a child of New England; by adoption a citizen of Rome; by genius belonging to the world. In youth an insatiable student seeking the highest culture; in riper years teacher, writer, critic of literature and art; in maturer age companion and helper of many earnest reformers in America and Europe."

Hygeia at Dr. Harriot Hunt's grave

Harriot K. Hunt Grave, Poplar Avenue. A simple stone relates the simple facts: Harriot K. Hunt was born in 1805 and died in 1875. "For forty years a physician in Boston. 'She hath done what she could!'" Without much help from the male medical profession. The first woman to practice medicine in the nation (beginning in 1835, after receiving training from an Englishwoman), she was twice refused permission to attend medical lectures at the Harvard Medical School because of her sex. In 1853, after nearly two decades of practice, the Women's Medical College in *Philadelphia, Pennsylvania,* gave her an honorary M.D. One of her biographers said she honored the title more than the title could honor her. But the male establishment that denied her professional equality did not hesitate to tax the considerable fortune she earned from her medical practice. Accordingly, each year Harriot K. Hunt delivered to the city treasurer a protest against having to pay taxes while being denied the vote.

Before she died in 1875, she requested black sculptor Edmonia Lewis to model a statue of Hygeia, the Greek goddess of health. The statue, its nose and hands chipped from a century of New England weather, still stands by the grave.

Hannah Adams Grave, Central Avenue. A lacemaker turned author, probably the first American woman to support herself with her writing, Hannah Adams is remembered with a marble monument that was erected " by her female friends." Citing her highly successful histories—of the Jews and of the Christian sects—the marker also proclaims another of the remarkable Mrs. Adams's accomplishments: "First tenant of Mount Auburn. She died Dec. 15, 1831, aged 76." (See *Boston.*)

Amy Lowell Grave, Bellwort Path. A simple slate marker with her name and dates (1874–1925) stands in stark contrast to her dashing, daring life and her highly sensuous poetry. As a child, Amy Lowell lamented her inability to fit into accepted feminine stereotypes. "I am ugly, fat, conspicuous and dull," she wrote in her diary as a fifteen-year-old. As a woman and a poet, she dominated artistic circles in America and Europe.

Julia Ward Howe Grave, Spruce Avenue, inadequately identifies the famed abolitionist, suffragist, and organizer as "Julia Ward Howe, daughter of Samuel Ward, wife of Samuel Gridley Howe." When she died in *Portsmouth, Rhode Island* in 1910, two years after her election as the first female member of the American Academy of Arts and Letters, four thousand mourners sang her "Battle Hymn of the Republic." In death she lies next to her husband, the man who at first barred her from working, then softened, dying in 1876 and giving her thirty-four years of widowhood to express her creative powers.

Among the other women buried at Mount Auburn are Dorothea Dix (see *Hampden, Maine*); black clubwoman Josephine St. Pierre Ruffin; philosopher Mary Whiton Calkins; physician Lucy Ellen Sewall; art collector Isabella Stewart Gardner; sculptor Harriet Hosmer (see *Watertown*); pacifist Lucia Mead; and actress Charlotte Cushman.

Concord

Louisa May Alcott Home, "Orchard House," 399 Lexington Road. In this handsome buff clapboard house, Louisa May Alcott wrote *Little Women* (1868). An instant success despite her publisher's hesitation, the novel was a literary version of Louisa's own happy homelife. The March family were the Alcotts, with Louisa as the independent Jo, and her mother, Abigail May Alcott, as the strong, warm "Marmee," head of the family during her husband's prolonged philosophical absences. Orchard House preserves many souvenirs of the Alcott Little Women. The dining room was the stage for their innumerable dramas, where "Louisa always preferred the part of a boy," according to the guide. A quick draw of the curtain, and the four young girls would race up the back stairs to change costumes. Louisa's room contains the semicircular shelf-desk (an unusual possession for a girl) where she wrote *Little Women.* Framed on the wall, penned in brown ink in Louisa's graceful

backhand, the understandable arrogance of the successful writer: "Of all sad words/the saddest are these/to an author's ear/'An autograph, please.' Louisa May Alcott, the twenty-eighth appreciation in one week."

In her father's study downstairs hangs a list of the children's hand-printed household duties: "Rise at 5, cold baths at 6; breakfast, housewifery, recreation 9-11; studies; Vigilance, Punctuality, Perseverance. Prompt, cheerful, unquestioning obedience; government of temper, hands and tongue." Despite this rigid schedule, Louisa May Alcott emerged as a talented and highly successful writer. With her profits, she easily supported her parents in their old age. And she retained her independence, never marrying ("I'd rather be a free spinster and paddle my own canoe"), and becoming the first woman to register to vote in Concord with partial suffrage in 1879.

The Old Manse, Monument Street. This historic structure built by the Reverend William Emerson, grandfather of Ralph Waldo Emerson, was home to a distinguished succession of notable women. Sophia Peabody Hawthorne, sister of Elizabeth Peabody of *Boston,* lived here from 1842–46 with her new husband, Nathaniel. She painted in a studio on the first floor while he wrote in a second-floor study. A monument to their loving days here adorns the windowpane of his study, scratched for eternity by Sophia's diamond ring:

> Man's accidents are God's purposes.
> Sophia A. Hawthorne
> 1843.

In 1846, Sarah Bradford Ripley moved here with her husband, the Reverend Samuel Ripley. After he died a year later, she continued to make the house a cultural center through her learned and scholarly discourses with her nephew, Ralph Waldo Emerson, and others. Her portrait remains as a souvenir. Earlier, when she lived in Waltham, Sarah Bradford Ripley taught the boys in her husband's school and tutored some Harvard students in everything from botany to German. The president of Harvard reportedly found her qualified to be a member of his faculty.

Another intellectual connected with the Old Manse was Mary Moody Emerson, born here in 1774, also a distinguished aunt of Ralph Waldo Emerson. Her probing mind was devoted to the education of her nephew, and it was from the seeds of her inspiration that his scholarship and philosophy blossomed. In 1948, under the floorboards of the attic here, repairmen found an 1816 letter from Ralph to his demanding but "dear Aunt," quoting Louis XIV upon hearing a sermon by Massillon: "When I hear others preach I am well please [*sic*] with them, but when I hear you preach I am dissatisfied with myself."

SLEEPY HOLLOW CEMETERY, Bedford Street
Louisa May Alcott Grave, Poet's Ridge. In 1888, two days after the death of her father, Bronson Alcott, the author of *Little Women,* was buried in the literary section of this famous old cemetery. According to a guide at Orchard House, she "once said she hoped her books might become the shabbiest on the library shelves."
Mary Moody Emerson Grave, Poet's Ridge, lies in the Emerson family plot. She died in 1863. An ornate headstone near the grave of her famous nephew, Ralph Waldo Emerson, who was her student, acknowledges her lifetime of learning and teaching: "She gave high counsels—it was the privilege of certain boys to have this immeasurably high standard indicated to their childhood, a blessing which nothing else in education could supply."
Sarah Bradford Ripley Grave, Poet's Ridge. Emerson's other famous and learned aunt is buried a short way down the path. She died in 1867, several years after teaching herself Spanish at age seventy so that she could read *Don Quixote.* Her bronze marker rests between that of her husband and her daughter Ann. Theirs are inscribed in plain English; Sarah's in the more scholarly Latin.

Danvers

Site of Salem Village Parsonage, Centre Street. Only the foundations remain of the house in which one of American history's most shameful periods of bigotry towards women—and some men—had its origins. The year was 1692, and Danvers was still known as Salem Village. Elizabeth (Betty) Parris, nine-year-old daughter of the parson, and her cousin Abigail Williams, age eleven, hung on every word of the tales told by their father's West Indian slave, Tituba. Her stories of devils, voodoo, and hypnotism fascinated, then terrified, the young girls, leading eventually to some unusually overexcited behavior. Unable to diagnose their apparent trances, hysteria, and other fitful actions, the village doctor concluded in ominous tones that the adolescent girls were the victims of an "evil hand." Thus began the witchcraft hysteria that would leave more than twenty dead and dozens more shamed in one nightmarish year. Urged to name their tormentors, the young girls settled on three victims: Tituba the slave and, for no apparent reason, villagers Sarah Osborne and Sarah Good.

Osborne House, 272 Maple Street (private), was the home of the first victim of the persecution, sickly Sarah Osborne. Despite her staunch protestation of innocence, she was jailed several days later, where she died of ill health within two months. Her codefendents fared as poorly. Sarah Good was hanged in July 1692. Tituba remained in jail until she was purchased by another master.

Bishop House, 238 Conant Street (private). The first person actually tried and hanged for witchcraft here was Bridget Bishop, a popular innkeeper whose tavern occupied the kitchen of the old wing of this house. Ensnared by the growing village panic and the continued, unexplained accusations of the young girls, she was tried in a court of oyer and terminer that met in nearby *Salem,* with spurious testimony from vindictive and frightened neighbors. But no proof was needed to condemn the victims of the frenzied villagers. On June 10, 1692, Bridget Bishop became the first accused witch to swing from a rope on Gallows Hill in *Salem.*

Rebecca Nurse House, 149 Pine Street. Few townspeople had the courage to criticize the outrageous witchcraft "trials," fearing the kind of retaliation that ended Rebecca Nurse's life. She was known as a good woman, a religious and charitable citizen, but her denunciation of the hysterical young girls angered villagers. Suddenly the accusing cries of "Witch!" were directed at the aged Mrs. Nurse. Since the local prison was full of accused sorcerers, she was manacled and jailed in a filthy Boston cell. She too protested her innocence; she too refused to confess to a crime she had never committed; she too was hanged on Gallows Hill in *Salem* along with Sarah Good and three other condemned women. Her loyal sons, discontent to leave her body in the traditional unmarked grave, secretly retrieved it in the dead of night and buried it somewhere on the grounds near this beautifully proportioned house. A granite shaft to her memory bears these lines by John Greenleaf Whittier:

> O Christian Martyr, who for Truth could die
> When all about thee owned the hideous lie,
> The world, redeemed from Superstition's sway,
> Is breathing freer for thy sake today.

Page House, 11 Page Street. The gambrel roof of this 1754 brick house is its ticket to immortality. During the Revolutionary War, owner Jeremiah Page patriotically refused to allow tea—highly taxed by the British—to be drunk in his house. His rebellious wife flaunted the edict by inviting her guests to a tea party on the roof. As quoted by Lucy Larcom (see *Lowell*) in an amusing poem, "A Gambrel Roof," Mrs. Page explained, "*Upon* a house is not *within* it."

Dorchester

Site of Lucy Stone House, 45 Boutwell Street, Pope's Hill. Time, neglect, and a recent fire have deprived modern pilgrims of the large, elegant homestead described by Lucy Stone's daughter as "a Mecca to suffragists from all parts of the world." It was to this site overlooking Boston Harbor that Lucy Stone and her husband Henry Blackwell moved in 1869 from *Orange, New Jersey,* with their twelve-year-old daughter, Alice, to run the New England branch of the suffrage movement. Here the plump leader, lace cap on her head, put her farm training to use (see *West Brookfield*) and ran a bustling, happy household, never neglecting either it or her feminist activities. Lucy Stone's lament about her enormous mansion sounds all too modern: "If only the housekeeping would go on without so much looking after!" Here, too, the family all worked on the publication, the *Woman's Journal,* which Carrie Chapman Catt later called the "Voice of the Woman's Movement." (See *Jamaica Plain.*)

Duxbury

Alden House, 105 Alden Street. Jonathan, the son of *Mayflower*

passengers Priscilla and John Alden (see *Plymouth*), built this house in 1653. His parents lived here during their final years, and both are buried in the Old Burying Ground in South Duxbury. Although Priscilla's dates and the details of her life are unknown, she was memorialized in Longfellow's poem "The Courtship of Miles Standish." Perhaps that was the only way a Pilgrim Mother could gain immortality—by rejecting a famous suitor. (See *Little Compton, Rhode Island.*)

Everett

Woodlawn Cemetery, 302 Elm Avenue, contains the graves of two notable women of medicine.

In 1974, Mary Mahoney, the first black professional nurse in America, was honored with a memorial that was sponsored by the American Nurses' Association and Chi Eta Phi sorority. Nurse Mahoney was graduated from the nursing school of the New England Hospital for Women and Children at *Roxbury* in 1879, thus opening the doors to more black women. Her fine performance was widely applauded, and a medal in her honor —for women who have contributed to racial integration in nursing—was established in 1936, ten years after her death. The medal is reproduced on the back of this monument.

Helen Gilson, energetic Civil War hospital worker who began work with the Army of the Potomac in 1862, is also buried here. A frail woman with a deep, low singing voice, she often aided the wounded as much with her soothing songs, sung with her hands clasped, as with her tireless nursing activities. She was present at nearly every major Civil War battle after Bull Run, quietly dressing wounds and raising morale. One member of the Fifth New Jersey Regiment observed, "There isn't a man in our regiment who wouldn't lay down his life for Miss Gilson." Another contemporary described her work at a hospital in Virginia: "It required more than a man's power of endurance, for men fainted and fell under the burden," he wrote. "It required a woman's discernment, a woman's tenderness, a woman's delicacy and tact; it required such nerve and moral force, and such executive power, as are rarely united in any woman's character." When she died in 1868, this monument was erected as "A tribute from soldiers . . . for self-sacrificing labors in the Army hospitals."

Fall River

Lizzie Borden House, 234 Second Street. "Everyone is writing a book about Lizzie," sighed a man who said that pointing out the house was becoming a habit. "It was a gruesome thing. I think generally the consensus is that Lizzie must have done it." The thirty-two-year-old Sunday-school teacher was accused of the ax murders of her father and stepmother in 1892. The celebrated murders took place in this three-story gray structure, now occupied by the Leary Press.

Fall River Historical Society, 451 Rock Street, contains memorabilia of the grisly Borden murders and the subsequent trial at which Lizzie was acquitted. Wearily, a museum custodian ushered us into the Lizzie Borden Room in the rear of the ornate Victorian mansion, insisting that no cameras were permitted to shoot the gruesome relics: photos of the skulls of Andrew and Abby Borden marked with huge gashes brought on by the hatchet; tagged exhibits from the trial; a section of the railing from the courtroom. "The story is that Lizzie never liked her stepmother and thought she was influencing her father," the curator explained. "One current biographer thinks she might have had spells." Several enlightening minutes later, after a full retelling of the story, she insisted that we tour the rest of the museum exhibits—unrelated to Lizzie Borden. "I wish people would leave her alone. I'm so sick of her," she confessed. "We want to be known as the city with one hundred mills."

Falmouth

Katharine Lee Bates Birthplace, 16 Main Street (private). The author of "America the Beautiful" (see *Colorado Springs, Colorado*) was born in this two-story white frame house on August 12, 1859. Although she only lived here until she was twelve, she returned every year to visit her childhood playmate who lived across the street. Falmouth has paid tribute to its poetic daughter by marking her house with a plaque on a boulder, and by naming a street—parallel to Main Street—Katharine Lee Bates Road.

Katharine Lee Bates Grave, Oak Grove Cemetery, is marked with a stone bearing the verse of "America the Beautiful." In addition, a dogwood tree has been planted by local schoolchildren, and a stone bench has been placed by the town to accommodate the hundreds of visitors who travel here each year.

Framingham

Margaret E. Knight House, southwest corner Hollis and Charles Streets. While living here, from the late 1880s until she died in 1914, inventor Margaret Knight took out patents for shoe machinery, a window frame, and rotary engines. As a child in York, Maine, she made kites and sleds that were the envy of all the boys. A real inventor from the age of twelve, when she devised a contrivance to prevent accidental injuries from a steel-tipped shuttle in a cotton mill, she gained her greatest fame from an 1871 machine to fold square-bottomed paper bags. Although the number of her patents has been disputed (from 27 to 87), and although she was not the first American woman to take up inventing (see Mary Kies of *South Killingly, Connecticut*), Margaret Knight was remarkable for her heavy industrial devices—designed by her even though she had little schooling.

Gardner

Site of Lucy Stone's First Feminist Lecture, 55 Green Street. Now it's a tenement; then, it was a church, moved to this location over the years. Lucy's brother, William Bowman, was preaching at the Evangelical Congregational Church in 1847 when Lucy was graduated from Oberlin College in *Oberlin, Ohio*. Although determined to speak out publicly for abolition and "for the elevation of my sex," she was thwarted by the rules at otherwise liberal Oberlin and by her mother's disapproval of her radical notions. Her brother William, however, had written to her, "I wish you to do what you think is your duty. If you violate your sense of duty to please your friends, you will lose more than you will gain." So it was from his pulpit that she embarked on her lifelong crusade to "make the world better" (see *Dorchester*).

Gloucester

Sargent-Murray-Gilman-Hough House, 49 Middle Street. Judith Sargent Murray, the first female occupant of this handsome historic house, was one of the nation's earliest feminists and the first woman born in America to have her plays dramatized by a professional group (1795). With two successive husbands—the second, Rev. John Murray, founder of the Universalist Church in America—she lived here amid the splendor of the Palladian window, paneled mantels, and carved balustrade. Educated only because she insisted on sharing her brother's tutorial lessons for Harvard, she later penned her pioneering 1790 essay demanding schooling for women. It was entitled, "On the Equality of the Sexes," and in it she brazenly asserts, "Yes, ye lordly, ye haughty sex, our souls are by nature *equal* to yours." Her attack broadens as her wit sharpens, questioning the emphasis on women's "domestick employments," and wondering whether a "candidate for immortality" should spend her lifetime contemplating "the mechanism of a pudding." As history would have it, Judith Sargent Murray became a candidate for immortality, not with her feminist essay, but, according to the Sargent genealogy, because of "her beautiful portraits by Copley and Stuart." Photographs of both are in the house, as well as a photo of a Doyle silhouette that makes no attempt to cover her ample double chin.

Groton

Sarah Hartwell Shattuck House, near Wattle's Pond. One of the heroines of Prudence Wright's Guards during the Revolutionary War incident at *Pepperell* lived here after 1872 with her husband, Job. Sarah Shattuck's patriotic spirit was aroused earlier by the Boston Tea Party, which inspired her to join with other local women in burning a batch of tea in front of the town meetinghouse.

Hamilton

Abigail Dodge was born and buried here (1833–96). She further put her hometown on the map by modestly setting aside her own name and writing her witty Washington, D.C., newspaper stories under the pen name Gail Hamilton. A political writer who packed a mighty punch, Gail Hamilton was honored by a contemporary who proclaimed, "Long may she send forth her spicy utterances."

Harvard

Fruitlands, Prospect Hill Road. Bronson Alcott launched his utopian community here in 1843, bringing his entire family along to participate in the transcendental experiment. For Louisa May, then aged ten, it was an exhilarating adventure. According to her diary, "I rose at five and had my bath. I love cold water!" When Bronson forbade his wife Abigail the use of beasts of burden, she pointed out good-naturedly that she was the beast of burden. Within the year, the loving family within this old red farmhouse was experiencing an economic failure, and Mrs. Alcott referred to it as "apple slump." Years later, Louisa would write about this experience, in typically cheery retrospect, in a fictional account called *Transcendental Wild Oats.* As the tour guide here points out, her father's unworkable schemes early forced Louisa to become "the man of the family, making it her constant concern to win bread for them and seek their comfort." She accomplished that goal at *Concord.*

Hatfield

Sophia Smith Homestead, 75 Main Street. As a child, Sophia Smith spent many happy hours here, reading books aloud with her family and entertaining neighbors. It was in this frame house that she planned, at age sixty-five, an institution for the higher education of young women—her means of disposing of a large family inheritance without compromising her ideals. With $400,000, she directed in her will of 1870 that Smith College be founded in nearby *Northampton,* a bold new proposal "for my own sex," with "facilities for education equal to those which are afforded now in our Colleges to young men." This house, Sophia Smith's birthplace, was purchased by the grateful Smith College Alumnae Association in 1915 and restored through the efforts of the class of 1895.

Haverhill

Statue of Hannah Duston, G.A.R. Park. This is the second statue erected in Haverhill to honor the woman who escaped from Indian captivity in 1697 (see *Barre;* see *Boscawen, New Hampshire*). Note the tomahawk in her right hand. It was modeled after the instrument Hannah Duston used to slay and scalp ten of her Indian abductors. The original weapon, or at least one assumed to be the original, is now on exhibit at the Haverhill Historical Society (240 Water Street) along with a crude knife removed from the body of Hannah's Indian master.

The house Hannah Duston returned to is gone, but a huge boulder marks the site of her son Jonathan's home, where she died in 1736.

Hingham

Odd Fellows Lodge, 196 North Street. In 1868, when this building was still the Universalist Church, Phebe Ann Hanaford was ordained as a minister here. She had been inspired to the pulpit by her cousin, Lucretia Mott of *Nantucket,* and by her friend and colleague in suffrage, Olympia Brown of *Racine, Wisconsin.* A talented feminist who began a journalistic career at age thirteen, Hanaford then wrote a biographical dictionary of American women entitled *Daughters of America* (1882). In it she endeavored to prove "that the nation is indebted for its growth and prosperity . . . and for its proud position . . . to its women as well as to its men." Under the section on women as preachers, she modestly listed her own accomplishments: first woman to officiate at the marriage of her own daughter; first woman to serve as chaplain in a state legislature (Connecticut, 1870); first woman minister to give the charge at the ordination of a male minister. One woman still living in Hingham recalls that she was christened by the Reverend Hanaford "about 1897."

Jamaica Plain

Ashes of Lucy Stone, Forest Hills Cemetery, 95 Forest Hills Avenue. A tall copper urn resting in a niche behind a locked iron grate bears a single name engraved in script: Blackwell. Within lie the ashes of Lucy Stone, a pioneer to the last, the first person to be cremated in New England, in 1893. Just before she died at Dorchester, the great woman's rights leader whispered into the ear of her daughter, Alice Stone Blackwell, "Make the world better!" At the cheerful, bright funeral (according to Lucy's instructions), as the procession wound its way out of the church, her husband Henry Blackwell, himself a lifelong suffragist, confided to Alice, "She leads us still."

When Henry, who continued the fight for the women's vote, died in 1909, he chose cremation so that his ashes might be mingled with Lucy's. In 1950, the pioneering family was entirely reunited when Alice Stone Blackwell's ashes were poured atop those of her parents.

Lenox

Edith Wharton Home, "The Mount," south of Route 7. This twenty-nine-room mansion on the shore of Laurel Lake was the home of the famous novelist for the decade after 1902. Here, in her "first real home," which she described as "a spacious and dignified house," Wharton wrote in solitude in the mornings, gardened in the afternoons, and entertained at night on "that dear wide sunny terrace" she hoped her books would finance. One of her most famous literary guests was Henry James, who called her the Lady of Lenox as she presided over what he called "a delicate French chateau mirrored in a Massachusetts pond." The Berkshires surrounding the Mount were the inspiration for one of her most acclaimed works, *Ethan Frome* (1911). The Georgian building now serves as a dormitory for the Foxhollow Boarding School, which is trying to raise money to repair years of neglect.

Lowell

Hamilton Mills, 27 Jackson Street. One of the hundreds of women who flocked to the City of Spindles and to this manufacturing company in 1836 was Sarah G. Bagley, a young mill operative who quickly learned the Lowell regime: at the looms by 5:00 A.M., half-hour meal breaks, and home after 7:30 P.M. to a crowded dormitory where she paid $1.25 of her $1.75 weekly wages for room and board. Bagley became a reformer, organizing women workers all over New England. She helped instigate the ten-hour workday movement, which she promoted in speeches and in print. It did not succeed under Sarah Bagley's leadership, but she later changed careers and broke a different barrier. On February 21, 1846, she took up her post by the signal key in the Lowell Telegraph Depot, becoming the nation's first female telegraph operator. For that unusual chore, she received between $300 and $500 a year.

Lucy Larcom Park, Merrimack opposite Shattuck Street on Canal Bank. This narrow strip of greensward honors the Lowell mill-girl and poet who first displayed her talent in *The Lowell Offering* and in other publications of factory life. When factory regulations prohibited books at work, the budding poet pasted newspaper clippings of poetry all over her window seat. Neither a suffragist nor a reformist, Larcom left one of the best literary accounts of life in the Lowell mills. In *A New England Girlhood,* she wrote of her days changing bobbins on spinning frames: "There were compensations for being shut in to daily toil so early. The mill itself had its lessons for us. But it was not, and could not be, the right sort of life for a child, and we were happy in the knowledge that, at the longest, our employment was only to be temporary. . . . To me, it was an incalculable help to find myself among so many working-girls, all of us thrown upon our own resources, but thrown much more upon each other's sympathies."

Mill Girl Monument, Lowell Cemetery. When Louisa M. Wells died in 1886, she requested in her will that a suitable monument be erected to her career. This enormous marble monolith with carved figures was the result. Its pedestal was inscribed, "Out of the fabric of her daily tasks she wove the fabric of a useful life." Louisa Wells had been one of the original operatives of the Lawrence Manufacturing Company in 1836, boarding at one of the company-run rooming houses. Her dawn-to-dusk working day apparently was satisfying, and Louisa Wells might have agreed with reformist Harriet H. Robinson, who wrote of the early mill-girls: "Their early experience developed their characters . . . and helped them to fight well the battle of life."

Lynn

Lydia E. Pinkham House, 285 Western Avenue (private). In the kitchen of this Victorian house, Lydia Pinkham first brewed the herbal remedies sought by modest friends for their "female complaints." After the financial panic of 1873, at the urging of her sons, Lydia began bottling the mixtures of unicorn root,

MRS. LYDIA E. PINKHAM, OF LYNN, MASS.

Woman can Sympathize with Woman.

Health of Woman Is the Hope of the Race

pleurisy root, and other botanical ingredients, and she put her picture on the label. In 1875, she made the first sales of Lydia E. Pinkham's Vegetable Compound. "Woman can Sympathize with Woman," reads the reassuring label. It promised to cure "all ovarian troubles, Inflammation and Ulceration, Falling and Displacements, and the consequent Spinal Weakness, and is particularly adapted to the Change of Life." Men could use it for kidney complaints. It became one of the most popular elixirs in the world.

Lydia E. Pinkham Laboratories, 271 Western Avenue, continued to produce the famed medicine—with enormous financial success. The kindly face promoting good health and maternal advice found its way into medicine chests and, eventually, into the words of a song. Ladies glowed aftering using the compound, and scores endorsed it, including the WCTU—which didn't bother to scold the 18 percent alcohol content. When Lydia Pinkham died in 1883, the business was worth a fortune. In 1973, however, the business, still run by her great-grandsons, came to an end in Lynn. The huge plant, with its pungent odors of licorice, dandelion, and other exotic herbs, was vacated, and the entire operation was moved to Puerto Rico. But you can still buy Lydia E. Pinkham's medicine, if you don't mind that the alcohol content has been reduced to 13 percent. As it proclaimed on early labels, "Health of Woman is the Hope of the Race."

Mary Baker Eddy House, 12 Broad Street. Using a modest attic room here for her living quarters while she rented out the rest of the house for mortgage money, the founder of Christian Science called this pleasant house her home from 1875–82. The sign outside read, "Mary B. Glover's Christian Scientists' Home," and she completed more of her *Science and Health* here. The small house was considered the very early headquarters of the Christian Science movement. (See *Brookline.*)

Medford

All of Medford was once ruled by the woman known only as the Squaw Sachem of Massachusetts. She was the widow of Nanepashemet, leader of the federation of tribes known as the Massachusetts. At her husband's death in 1619, she took over and led the federation. When she remarried Webcowit, Nanepashemet's second-in-command, she retained power. She died in 1667 and is buried somewhere in Medford.

The last known Medford Indian was Hannah Shiner, who, according to the county historian, "under the civilizing influence of Medford rum, was drowned in the early nineteenth century."

Nantucket

Parliament House, Pine Street. Originally this was the home of Mary and Nathaniel Starbuck. The house was moved here from its location at old Sherborn (elsewhere on the island) in 1820 and given its durable nickname because, in the early 1700s, so much community business was conducted, in the original north section of the present house, under the guidance of prominent citizen Mary Starbuck. A convert to Quakerism who became the island's first minister, she is believed to have spearheaded the colony-wide movement that made most of the colonists here Quakers. Her legendary intellect and administrative abilities gained her various titles, among them, the Great Merchant.

Mary Starbuck's maiden name was Coffin—or Coffyn—a name with timeworn significance for other women of this island. Her mother Dionis was celebrated for the exceptional beer she made at a tavern in Newbury, Massachusetts, in 1653, where she was permitted by court order to charge the exceptional price of threepence per quart.

Miriam Coffin, a successful shipowner born here in 1723, was said to have been tried for smuggling, a most unusual offense for a woman of that era.

Perhaps the best known Nantucket Coffin is Lucretia Coffin Mott, a leading abolitionist, Quaker minister, and suffragist, born here in 1793 (see *Philadelphia, Pennsylvania*). Her mother, Anna Coffin, ran a shop of East India goods and often had to do the trading and purchasing in Boston when her husband was off on long voyages. "The exercise of women's talents in this line," Lucretia Mott wrote years later, "as well as the general care which devolved upon them, in the absence of their husbands, tended to develop and strengthen them mentally and physically."

Maria Mitchell House, 1 Vestal Street. From the "widow's walk" atop this typical island house, the woman born here in 1818 gazed at stars, not whaling ships. As a child, she accompanied her father on his rooftop astronomical studies; at age 12½, she helped him record the time of an eclipse. And in 1847, from the rooftop of a nearby building, Maria Mitchell outspied the trained eyes of all Europe and discovered a comet of her own. It was named in her honor, and she was rewarded with a gold medal from the king of Denmark. Another of Nantucket's fiercely independent daughters, Maria Mitchell was the nation's first female astronomer and the first female professor of astronomy (at Vassar). She was also the first woman elected to the American Academy of Arts and Sciences, a feat so distasteful to one unliberated academician that he insistently called her an "honorary member" instead of a "fellow."

Today, the house and accompanying domed observatory (added after her death), along with a museum and library, form a research center for young scientists. Maria Mitchell's own five-inch Alvan Clark telescope is among the treasures to inspire heavenly contemplation.

Northampton

Clarke School for the Deaf opened in 1867 with pioneering teacher Harriot B. Rogers as its first principal. A bronze plaque in the entrance to Hubbard Hall, the main classroom building, recalls Rogers' devotion to the new "oral" method of teaching speech skills, a radical departure from the traditional—and less satisfactory—manual system. Harriot Rogers was persuaded to combine her newly opened school for five deaf pupils in nearby Chelmsford with the new Clarke School and its fifteen students. Clarke then became the first school in the country to use solely the speech and lipreading method.

Smith College owes its existence to Sophia Smith of *Hatfield,* whose bequest made it the first women's college founded by a woman's money. The college was chartered in 1871, a year after Sophia's death, and it opened in 1875 with fourteen students. It was the first college with entrance requirements as rigid as those for men's colleges. Sophia Smith's instructions, as expressed in her will, were farsighted indeed: "It is my opinion that by the higher and more thorough Christian education of women, what are called their 'wrongs' will be redressed, their wages adjusted, their weight of influence in reforming the evils of society will be greatly increased, as teachers, as writers, as mothers, as members of society, their power for good will be incalculably enlarged." She wanted, not to "render my sex any the less feminine," but to "furnish women with the means of usefulness, happiness and honor, now withheld from them." In 1971, the college reaffirmed her original commitment and barred men from obtaining bachelor degrees at Smith.

North Andover

Anne Bradstreet, the nation's first poet, lived here from 1644 until she died in 1672. That she had given up a patrician life in England for the hardships of the frontier was commendable;

that she was published before any other colonists, notable. But that she wrote several volumes of poetry—some of it even inspired—while raising eight children and fighting frequent bouts of sickness, was extraordinary. Her brother-in-law, who in 1650 sneaked her poems off to London to have them bound, noted in his introduction that "these poems are the fruit of but some few hours curtailed from sleep and other refreshments." The book laid to rest her worst fears, expressed in verse, that "such despite they cast on female wits/If what I do prove well, it won't advance—/They'll say 'tis stol'n or else it was by chance." More of her work was probably burned in the fire of 1666 that consumed their first home. For many years it was mistakenly believed that Anne lived in the house at 179 Osgood Street. Mary Flinn, of the North Andover Historical Society, hastened to correct that frequently printed error, since it (Parson Barnard house) was built in 1715, long after Anne's death. No trace of the Bradstreet house exists, although it is believed to have been somewhere around the land across from the Barnard House.

North Oxford

Clara Barton Birthplace, Clara Barton Road. The "angel" born here on Christmas Day, 1821, would later be known as the Angel of the Battlefield, for her heroic Civil War activities in tending the wounded. Clara Barton's preparation came early, in this house, where as a child she nursed her sickly older brother David for two years. From here, too, at age eighteen, she embarked on her first teaching job—a career that would generate strong feminist overtones at her next residence in *Bordentown, New Jersey.*

North Weymouth

Abigail Adams Birthplace, North and Norton Streets. Abigail Smith was born here in 1744 and spent the first twenty years of her life in this house, now restored and moved several hundred feet from its original location. The living room has been painted her favorite yellow, the fireplace rebuilt with bricks donated by different presidents' wives. Upstairs, the tiny bedroom Abigail shared with two sisters is furnished with a replica fireplace and doll cradle. Here she began to read voraciously—her substitute for no schooling—and to develop the extraordinary letter-writing skills that would make her one of the nation's most celebrated correspondents. Here, too, the young lawyer from Braintree Road courted her, against some haughty neighbors' wishes, and finally won her hand. In 1764 Abigail Smith married John Adams and moved with him to *Quincy.*

Norton

Wheaton College opened in 1835 as a seminary for young women, the gift of Judge Laban Morey Wheaton and the spiritual gift of educator Mary Lyon (see *Buckland* and *South Hadley*). For ten dollars a term, the first thirty-nine female students studied under the educational techniques Lyon had developed at her famous Ipswich academy. They listened as she would admonish them, "Hasten on, young ladies! You are not aware of the habit of lagging you are forming." One of the faculty members here from 1854–62 was poet Lucy Larcom (see *Lowell*), who was especially popular with her students of English for allowing "free discussion" in class. Wheaton graduated from seminary to college in 1912.

Oxford

Clara Barton Grave, North Cemetery. After a lifetime of service and struggle, the founder of the American Red Cross died in 1912 In *Glen Echo, Maryland,* at age ninety-one. A red granite cross caps the tall shaft that marks her grave in the family plot here, several miles from her birthplace in *North Oxford.* The inscription notes her participation in three wars: the Civil War, where she first aided the fallen; the Franco-Prussian War,

where she learned about the Red Cross in Europe; and the Spanish-American War, where she applied her nursing and administrative skills in person, riding mule wagons at the age of seventy-seven.

Pepperell

Site of Jewett's Bridge Skirmish. A covered bridge over the Nashua River has replaced the original open bridge where village women bravely defended their town against Tory invaders in 1775. Several days after the "shot heard round the world" was fired at nearby Lexington and Concord, the women of Pepperell and *Groton* learned that enemy soldiers and spies were moving south from Canada. The women elected Prudence Wright as their commander and assembled from nearby villages, wearing their husbands' clothes and carrying pitchforks and muskets for weapons. In the dark of night, British spy Leonard Whiting approached and was efficiently ensnared by the waiting female ambush. Acting on orders from "Captain Wright," the women searched Whiting and, on finding treasonous papers hidden in his boots, immediately dispatched them to colonial authorities. Prudence Wright died a heroine in 1823, at age eighty-four. Her grave on the Main Street side of the nearby Burying Ground is marked with a plaque honoring her as "The Captain of the Bridge Guard."

Plymouth

Plymouth Rock, waterfront. The first woman from the *Mayflower* to set foot in the New World was Mary Chilton (see *Boston*), vanguard of the first boatload permitted ashore by the men shortly after their arrival in 1620. In all, twenty-five women and young girls made the crossing (financed by at least one woman, Eliza Knight), including Priscilla Mullins (see *Duxbury*) and Desire Minter (the first to return home to England). Earlier, at the first, erroneous landing at *Provincetown*, the women were permitted ashore immediately to do the laundry.

Pilgrim Mothers Fountain, Water Street, was erected by the DAR to honor the women who braved the same dangers as the Pilgrim Fathers in establishing their new colony. It has been said of the Pilgrim Mothers that, in addition to enduring all the handships that the Pilgrim Fathers faced, they also had to endure the Pilgrim Fathers.

Burial Hill, at the head of Town Square, is the final resting-place for many of the Pilgrim women. The body of a woman of another century rests here, also—Mercy Otis Warren, political satirist and influential propagandist of the Revolutionary War. Through publicized letters, she corresponded with her close friends, John and Abigail Adams; through performed plays, she mocked the British government in the colonies, sparing no Tory leader her acid wit. Most of her married life was spent here in Plymouth, as the wife of politician James Warren. When she was criticized as being too brazen for a colonial woman, Mercy Warren wrote, "Be it known unto Britain even American daughters are politicians and patriots, and will aid the good work with their female efforts." (See *Watertown*.)

Provincetown

Mayflower Memorial, Bradford Street, commemorates the five *Mayflower* passengers who died while the ship lay at anchor here, November 11, 1620. One of them was Dorothy Bradford. Here too the men of the *Mayflower* began a deep-rooted American tradition by refusing to allow any of the women to sign the Mayflower Compact.

Quincy

Abigail Adams House, 141 Franklin Street. It was to this compact saltbox that John Adams brought his new bride, one of the

nation's first feminists, after their marriage in *North Weymouth* in 1764. "We think Abigail found this cottage as you see it today," the guide explained. Downstairs, we found such period furniture as a comb-back rocker as well as the enormous pot-filled kitchen with huge iron kettle for making soap. Upstairs are one of Abigail's size-seven dresses (brown silk) and her original dressing table. The room where she bore John Quincy Adams in 1767 has a narrow cradle; the bed she shared with John Adams—when he was not off on colonial business—has ropes instead of springs.

With this house as her creative workshop, while her husband went to Philadelphia, Pennsylvania, to join the Continental Congress, Abigail Adams maintained her extraordinary correspondence with John and other friends. Nearly a year before the patriots drafted their famous Declaration, Abigail declared her own independence from the English: "Let us separate; they are unworthy to be *our* brethren. Let us renounce them." Here too she penned her often-quoted plea that John and his colleagues "Remember the Ladies" in the new Constitution, lest they "foment a Rebellion." Although her pleas fell on deaf ears as far as sexual equality was concerned (John called her "saucy," albeit his "dearest friend"), still Abigail Adams believed she had "helped the Sex abundantly." In this "Humble cottage," she tended house, children, and finances as the war raged around her. She finally left in 1784 to join her ambassador husband in England, becoming the first American woman to be presented at the courts of France and England. From there she wrote in 1787, "I long to return to my native land. My little cottage, encompassed with my friends, has more charms for me than the drawing-room of St. James." She never came back to live in this house.

Abigail Adams Stone Cairn, opposite 353 Franklin Street. Two gray water towers now sit quietly atop the hill where on June 17, 1775, Abigail Adams brought her seven-year-old son, John Quincy, to watch the flaming ruins of Charlestown and to listen to the booming guns of Bunker Hill. In grief, she wrote her husband, "How many have fallen we know not. May we be supported and sustained in the dreadful conflict." But the follow-

ABIGAIL ADAMS CAIRN

ing spring, as she watched more cannons and fighting, she changed her attitude: "The sound I think is one of the grandest in nature. 'Tis now an incessant roar; but oh, the fatal ideas that are connected with that sound. How many of our countrymen must fall."

Adams National Historical Site, 135 Adams Street, was purchased by John Adams in 1787 as a suitable residence after their European sojourn. To Abigail, it was too small, "like a wren's house." After appropriate additions, it became their home—the Old House—where they lived before and after John Adams served as the nation's first vice-president and its second president. Here John and Abigail retired after their eventful lives as hosts in the nation's various capitals; here Abigail Smith Adams died in 1818, just after seeing her son, John Quincy, become secretary of state. Today her body rests next to that of her husband's in a simple tomb in the First Church of Quincy.

Roxbury

Dimock Community Health Center, 55 Dimock Street, is the institution originally known as the New England Hospital for Women and Children. It was opened in 1862 as a ten-bed hospital, largely owing to the guidance of feminist Samuel E. Sewall, whose daughter Lucy Ellen wanted to study medicine. She became the first pupil of Dr. Marie Zakrzewska, an outstanding physician who had left Germany to practice medicine in America without sex bias (see *Manhattan, New York City*). Dr.

"Zak," a familiar figure in her horse and buggy visiting the sick around Boston, became the guiding force of the new hospital as it grew in size and stature and moved here in 1872. In 1870, one of the all-female staff physicians was Dr. Lucy Sewall. Another was Dr. Susan Dimock (see *Washington, North Carolina*) who had been refused by Harvard Medical School. When Dimock died in a shipwreck at age twenty-eight, instead of a monument to her, a free bed here was donated by her family.

In 1872 the hospital also opened the first professional nursing school in the country. Linda Richards (see *Washington, D.C.*), its first graduate, instituted the practice of keeping charts at the foot of patients' beds. In 1879, Mary Eliza Mahoney (see *Everett*), received her diploma and became the first black trained nurse in the country.

Late in the twentieth century, the New England Hospital changed its name and its purpose. Men were admitted to the staff, and it became a community health center, helping the poor as it had helped women a century earlier. Dr. Zak would have approved. She once said, "A millionaire can always get assistance, while it is often not so easy for a poor person."

Salem

The Witch House, 310½ Essex Street. Jonathan Corwin, one of the judges who condemned twenty people to die as witches, lived here and conducted some of the preliminary witchcraft

hearings here in 1692. Within these walls the hysterical accusations of the young girls from *Danvers* indicted both men and women. Today, as then, the site of the testimony draws curious crowds.

Gallows Hill Park. Young Salemites now ski down the slopes that once supported Salem's "Witch Trees," the gnarled old branches from which, according to legend, the condemned victims of the witchcraft delusion were hanged in 1692. Martha Corey (or Cory) of nearby Salem Village—then *Danvers*—and seven others were the last to be executed for this alleged crime on September 22, 1692. Like the many victims before her, Martha Corey swore she was innocent; like them, she was also carted to the gallows in an open wagon. In 1710, eighteen years too late, during a general period of public amends, the verdict against her was reversed.

Salem Witch Museum, 19½ Washington Square North, is the place to relive the hysteria, the passion, the ignorance, and finally the executions of 1692 in "computerized SIGHT AND SOUND." According to the brochure, it is "an experience not to be missed," a statement with which Rebecca Nurse and Martha Corey might strongly disagree.

Site of Sarah Tarrant's Defiance. Only busy Route 114 crossing the North River at North Street marks the site of one of the first

confrontations of the Revolution and the scene of Sarah Tarrant's heroism. A Salem citizen, she earned the title of Barbara Fritchie of Massachusetts (see *Frederick, Maryland*) on February 26, 1775. As a regiment of Redcoats under Col. Alexander Leslie marched toward North Salem to destroy an ordnance depot, a line of minutemen formed to stop them. Amidst the showdown, while a fife corps struck up "Yankee Doodle," Sarah Tarrant leaned out of an open window and berated Colonel Leslie for having the audacity to march on the sabbath. "Go home! Go home!" she shouted. "Fire at me if you have the courage, but I doubt it." She is said to have waved a turkey-wing feather duster as she spoke. The British officer retreated.

Scituate

Local legend insists that teen-aged sisters Rebecca and Abigail Bates, daughters of the lighthouse keeper, heroically saved the lighthouse during the War of 1812. When English sailors aboard a man-of-war threatened to burn the structure, the two girls created a warlike din by beating on a drum and playing the fife. Their cacophonous defense scared the attackers away. In 1880, too old to enjoy it, the sisters were finally granted pensions by Congress.

Sharon

Deborah Sampson Gannett Monument, Rockridge Cemetery. One wing of the memorial to Sharon's war dead is dedicated to Deborah Sampson Gannett, a Fourth Massachusetts Regiment volunteer who flattened her breasts with a bandage and put on a soldier's uniform to defend her country. Enlisting in the Continental army under the name Robert Shurtleff, she marched, fought, and was wounded in several battles. She also, according to her biographer, "preserved her chastity inviolate." Only when a physician attended her for fever was her sex discovered. She was honorably discharged in 1783 and voted a four dollars monthly pension by Congress in 1805, largely at the insistence of Paul Revere. After Deborah died in 1827, her husband was awarded the unusual equivalent of a widow's pension—eighty dollars per year. A small marker by her grave calls her a "revolutionary soldier."

South Hadley

Mount Holyoke College was founded in 1837 by Mary Lyon, the first college for women only, and the first of the group that would be called the Seven Sisters Colleges. It had taken educator Mary Lyon of *Buckland* several years to raise the money for her controversial new school. At first she hoped "benevolent gentlemen" would help with the funding, and she kept a low profile, fearful that too much intrusion would make the men fear "what they will call female greatness." When the gentlemen did not come through, she plunged into fund raising with fervor. Her enthusiasm affected many others. Lucy Stone, in *West Brookfield,* heard the appeal for money while sewing a shirt to raise funds to help educate a theology student. Lucy stopped mid-stitch and decided to educate herself instead. All over the state, sewing societies, small groups, and benevolent women gave from six cents apiece to $1,000. And when the school opened that November day, eighty students from all economic backgrounds converged on the first brick building.

Mary Lyon died twelve years after the college was founded, and she was buried in the shadow of its first building, which has since burned down. Her marble stone, enclosed by an old wrought-iron fence, is engraved: "There is nothing in the universe that I fear, but that I shall not know all my duty, or shall fail to do it."

South Lancaster

Rowlandson Rock, marked by a plaque where a Chevron station intersects Main Street, commemorates the capture by Indians of Mary White Rowlandson and twenty-three other Lancaster residents in February of 1675 or 1676. The captors, participants in King Philip's War, seeking revenge for the land-grabbing activities of the colonists, burned the town and made slaves of the women and children. For nearly three months, the forty-year-old mother trekked along behind the wandering Indians. One of her children died in her arms; others became separated from her. At her suggestion, the Indians, for whom she had developed some affection, finally sold her back to her husband for twenty pounds sterling. On her release, she wrote an account of her adventures which, published in 1682, became the first of a popular genre of Indian captivity narratives written by American women. Her fascinating, fast-paced story was published in more than thirty editions.

Sterling

Mary Sawyer House, Maple Street and Rugg Road. It all began, Mary Sawyer would later recall, in 1815, with a child's love of animals. Her father's ewe gave birth to two lambs, one of which was so weak and sickly that nine-year-old Mary tenderly wrapped it in a blanket and nursed it back to health in this house. One day about two years later, the dedicated pet followed its mistress to her one-room schoolhouse (see *Sudbury*). The students giggled. The rest is poetry. ''Mary Had a Little Lamb'' faithfully recounts the little drama that became part of our national heritage.

According to Mary Sawyer, who penned testimonials until her death at eighty-three, the familiar verses were written by John Roulstone, a twelve year old being tutored for college. But descendants of Sarah Josepha Hale, editor of *Godey's Lady Book,* claim that she composed the poem (and have honored her at

Newport, New Hampshire, for that accomplishment). For years, the disputed authorship kept local historians digging. Finally they turned up a compromise: Young Mr. Roulstone seems to have composed the first twelve lines of the poem; Sarah Josepha Hale added twelve more and brought the poem to national prominence by publishing it for the first time in her volume *Poems for Our Children* (1830). Without Hale's editor's genius for spotting a classic, the town of Sterling might have no reason to honor Mary and her lamb.

Stoughton

Mary Baker Eddy House, 133 Central Street. The founder of Christian Science lived in this pleasant white farmhouse with the Wentworth family from 1868–70. (See *Brookline.*)

Sudbury

Redstone School, Route 20 on the grounds of the Wayside Inn. This is the one-room wooden schoolhouse that catapulted young Mary Sawyer and her pet lamb to fame when they attended class here together in 1817. In 1917, financed by the concerned Henry Ford, the school was moved to this spot to save it from neglect in nearby *Sterling.* The tiny structure is furnished with the same high-back seats under which Mary tried to hide her woolly friend. In front of the room, where Mary was called to recite by her teacher, Polly Kimball, the children's classic is chalked onto the blackboard. Outside, reproduced in bronze, are two pages from *McGuffey's Second Reader,* including Lesson XLVII: the entire poem; a pronunciation guide (''Ma'ry; pa'tient·ly''); and suggested questions: ''What did Mary have? What did the lamb do?''

Redstone School

Swampscott

Mary Baker Eddy House, 23 Paradise Road. While living here during the winter of 1865–66, Mary Baker Eddy (then known as Mrs. Patterson) slipped on the ice on February 1, 1866 and injured her back. Neighbors feared she would never walk again, although that was not a doctor's opinion. Three days later, after intensive reading of Matthew 9:2, she recovered. From this event she dated the discovery of Christian Science and the beginning of the founding of the movement. (See *Brookline.*)

Taunton

Elizabeth Pole Grave, Plain Cemetery, Broadway. A stone slab protected by shatterproof glass marks the grave of Elizabeth Pole (or Pool, or Poole), an English immigrant popularly known as the "foundress" of Taunton. When the township was organized in 1639–40, she was, according to the inscription, "a great proprietor . . . a chief promoter of its settlement and its incorporation." Although she was not one of the original forty-six people who purchased the land from the Indians, she was the first to settle in the wilderness now known as East Taunton, and she was later induced to accept a leadership role in all community affairs. Massachusetts's Governor Bradford sought her counsel; and the town seal honors her as *"Dux Femina Facti,"* the "leader of what was done." The slab was erected in 1771, some 117 years after Elizabeth Pole's death at a virginal sixty-five. Nearly two centuries later, during ceremonies remembering her as the Virgin Mother of Taunton, the stone was removed to this spot and laid flat above her remains.

Watertown

Edmund Fowle House, 28 Marshall Street. A portrait of Mercy Otis Warren of *Plymouth* serves as a reminder that the woman considered to be one of the foremost intellectuals of the American Revolution entertained General and Mrs. Washington here in December 1775. Mercy Warren's description of the future first president of the fledgling nation was sent in one of her delightful and perceptive letters to her good friend John Adams. Washington was, she wrote, "one of the most amiable and accomplished gentlemen, both in person, mind and manners, that I have met with."

Harriet Hosmer Collection, Watertown Free Public Library, 123 Main Street. The largest collection of the works of the famed sculptor is displayed in the library of her hometown. Born here in 1830, Harriet Hosmer was a talented tomboy who became the first successful female sculptor in the world. She collected clay for her first models from the Charles River banks near her home. Then she studied anatomy in *St. Louis, Missouri.* Most of her life she lived and worked in Rome, with her good friend actress Charlotte Cushman. Hosmer was known as an emancipated, creative woman, and the Prince of Wales was among her loyal fans. The collection here includes a bust of *Hesper,* her sculpting tools, various diplomas, and many photographs of her statues.

Perkins School for the Blind, 175 North Beacon Street. The first child admitted to the new school in 1832 was Sophia Carter, aged eight. She made rapid progress under the guidance of Samuel Gridley Howe—husband of Julia Ward Howe—and she was followed by a long line of celebrated pupils. In 1837, seven-year-old Laura Bridgman was enrolled; she later became the first blind-deaf child to be successfully educated. The experience gained from her instruction helped Anne Macy Sullivan, a Perkins graduate, in her triumphant tutoring of Helen Keller at her home in *Tuscumbia, Alabama,* starting in 1887. From 1889–93, Sullivan and Keller resided at Perkins. The measure of the school, it proudly proclaims, is "in its graduates."

Wayland

Lydia Maria Child House, 91 Old Sudbury Road (private). From 1852 until her death in 1880 the dedicated abolitionist and author lived in quiet semiretirement here with her husband. After a celebrated literary career, she devoted most of her writing to the antislavery cause. Her publication of *An Appeal* *in Favor of That Class of American Called Africans* (1833)—the first antislavery tract in book form—caused her reformist friends to salute her and her Southern enemies to denounce her. She also strongly supported woman suffrage. After her husband had just signed her will, she wrote to a friend that it was a legal necessity that incited her "towering indignation. . . . I was indignant for womankind made chattels personal from the beginning of time. . . . The very phrases used with regard to us are abominable. 'Dead in the law.' 'Femme couverte.' How I detest such language!" When she died at seventy-eight, the poet John Greenleaf Whittier said, "O woman greatly loved!" as she was buried at the North Cemetery on Old Sudbury Road.

Wellesley

Wellesley College opened its doors in 1875 with 314 young women, just twenty-four hours ahead of Smith College at *Northampton*. The money and inspiration came from Boston millionaire Henry Fowle Durant, who boldly announced, "Women can do the work. I give them the chance." His wife Pauline, denied an education herself, laid the cornerstone and served on the first board of trustees. At Durant's insistence, women comprised the entire faculty the first year, and Wellesley's presidents have always been female. The second physics laboratory in the country (the first was at MIT) was established in 1878 by Professor Sarah Frances Whiting. Among the college's treasures is a bronze cast of the clasped hands of Elizabeth and Robert Browning, done in 1853 by Harriet Hosmer of *Watertown*. In 1971, Wellesley reaffirmed its commitment to withhold degrees from male students.

West Brookfield

Site of Lucy Stone Birthplace, Coy Hill Road off Route 9. The farmhouse burned down in 1950, and the property has long been out of the hands of Stone descendants, but a strong faction of West Brookfield citizenry is working to restore the brush-covered hilltop. Here the future woman's rights leader was born in 1818—to a mother who had milked eight cows the night before. When she learned the new baby was female, Mrs. Stone lamented, "Oh dear! I am sorry it is a girl. A woman's life is so hard!" For the young farm girl, it was up at dawn to drive the cows, out in the woods to pick berries for college money. And perhaps in reaction to the traditional but loving marriage of her parents, it was in this farmhouse that Lucy Stone married Henry Blackwell in 1855 and signed the pioneering marriage agreement protesting the laws that gave the husband "the custody of the wife's person" and property. Lucy and Henry had to send thirty miles for a minister who would marry them without using the word *obey*. After the ceremony, when the minister delighted that "the heroic Lucy cried, like any village bride!" Lucy Stone retained her own name forever. (See *Dorchester;* see *Orange, New Jersey.*)

West Roxbury

Brook Farm, 670 Baker Street. The only building left of this first transcendental utopian community is the Margaret Fuller Cottage, named for the noted editor of the *Dial* magazine. The communal venture was started in 1841 by such figures as Sophia Dana Ripley (who founded it with her husband George), Nathaniel Hawthorne, Georgiana Kirby, Almira Barlow, and Amelia Russell. Full equality for women was one of the founding principles of Brook Farm. It was disbanded in 1847.

Westwood

Betsey Metcalf Baker House, 955 High Street (private). The oldest house in town once belonged to Betsey Metcalf Baker, who is said to have made the first straw hat—and thus sparked an entire industry—in this area. Betsey fashioned her first bonnet at age twelve, in 1798, copying it from an expensive import she saw in a Providence, Rhode Island, store. She split oat straw, plaited it into a seven-strand braid, bleached it, and lined it with pink satin. The neighbors liked her bonnets, as well as the money they could make from them. Betsey, however, never accepted a penny for her skills. When neighbors suggested she get a patent, "I told them I did not wish my name sent to Congress."

Brook Farm

Worcester

Site of Brinley Hall, State Mutual Building. In this once-famous auditorium, the first national woman's rights convention was held on October 23, 1850, largely at the inspiration of Lucy Stone of *West Brookfield.* Two years after the pioneering local meeting at *Seneca Falls, New York,* this convention made suffrage a national issue for the first time. Among the thousand-plus in the excited crowd: Lucretia Mott, Sojourner Truth (see *Battle Creek, Michigan*), and William Lloyd Garrison. Dr. Harriot K. Hunt (see *Cambridge*) spoke on medical education for women, and Antoinette L. Brown (see *South Butler, New York*) on women's equality in the Bible. The impact of this historic meeting was enormous. Susan B. Anthony is said to have read Lucy Stone's speech in the newspaper in *Rochester, New York;* she then started to shift gears from the antislavery cause to woman's rights. Harriet Upton Taylor, who later wed John Stuart Mill, read the news reports in Europe and wrote a highly laudatory essay, remarking that the American feminist example would soon be followed by Englishwomen.

Abby Kelley Foster House, Mower Street (private). Another speaker at the 1850 woman's rights convention was Abby Kelley Foster, a fiery abolitionist who lived here and lectured in public when it was still considered far beyond woman's sphere. The horrified clergy denounced her as a Jezebel, and even her own Quakers disowned her. According to her friend and disciple, Lucy Stone, "If she had been a weak woman, she would have yielded and fled." Foster, Stone said, "earned for us all the right of free speech."

Fanny Bullock Workman Grave, Rural Cemetery. When she died in 1925, Fanny Bullock Workman's ashes were placed under a headstone she shares with her husband: "Pioneer Himalayan Explorers." An intrepid mountain climber and adventurer, she once transported a Votes for Women banner into the Himalayas. Of her ascents and the books she wrote about them, Fanny Bullock Workman said, "I have what no man or woman can take from me, what is above all price, the satisfaction of my work."

MICHIGAN

Adrian

Laura Haviland Statue, in front of City Hall. A seated likeness of the Quaker abolitionist and educator of freedmen was erected by grateful citizens after Laura Haviland died at her home in Raisin Township in 1898. She was known as the Superintendent of the Underground for her work in helping slaves to freedom. Along with her husband, she founded the Raisin Institute in 1837. Blacks and whites studied together at the school, which also became a center for fugitive slaves. "Aunt" Laura also worked for orphaned children and for imprisoned young girls, but she reserved her strongest sympathies for black victims. In her book, *A Woman's Life Work* (which she holds in this statue), Laura Haviland wrote that she first read of slavery as a child: "The pictures of those crowded slave ships, with the cruelties of the slave system . . . often affected me to tears." Inscribed beneath the water fountain at the base of the statue are the words appropriate to her WCTU work: "I was thirsty and ye gave me to drink."

Ann Arbor

Although more than a dozen different women have been cited as the namesake of Ann Arbor, careful research has settled on Mary Ann Rumsey—the only woman in town when it happened. Town cofounder John Allen spied her seated in a wild-grape arbor one day and asked what she called her pleasant nook. "This is Ann's Arbor; don't you think that is a good name for the place?" she is said to have answered. Allen agreed; thought it a fitting way to remember his own wife, Ann; and got Mary Ann's husband—his cofounder—to second the motion. On May 25, 1824, the new name was officially recorded.

University of Michigan admitted women in 1870 despite some official fears that it would be "ruinous to the young ladies who should avail themselves of it . . . and disastrous to the Institution which should carry it out."

Ashton

Anna Howard Shaw Monument, Frayer Halladay Park. English-born suffrage leader Anna Howard Shaw came to America as a youngster, growing up in a crude log cabin in the woods of nearby Paris, Michigan. When she first came to the frontier with her family in 1859, she found the sorry house built by her father, "its doors and windows represented by square holes, its floor also a thing of the future, its whole effect achingly forlorn and desolate." Her mother "looked slowly around her. Then something within her seemed to give way, and she sank upon the floor." Thus, as described in her autobiographical *Story of a Pioneer*, did Anna early learn to haul wood and tend chores to eke out their spartan existence. One day she heard a woman preach at *Big Rapids,* and Anna determined that she would become a minister. At first practicing her sermons on the trees, she then advanced to the Methodist pulpit. She was seventeen, and a curious crowd filled the room. The bold young orator trembled so violently that the oil from a kerosene lamp at her elbow shook in its glass globe. When it was over, the minister assured her that her first sermon was not a failure. Public reaction was something else. Her family offered to send her to college—and pay the bills—if she would forsake preaching. "I was given twenty-four hours in which to decide whether I would choose my people and college, or my pulpit and the arctic loneliness of a life that held no family circle. It did not require twenty-four hours of reflection to convince me that I must go my solitary way." That way led to Boston University in *Boston, Massachusetts,* and an outstanding life of public service. This monument commemorates the spot where it all began.

Battle Creek

Sojourner Truth Grave, Oak Hill Cemetery, South Avenue and Oak Hill Drive. The first glimpse many women had of the ex-slave, whom Harriet Beecher Stowe dubbed the Libyan Sibyl, was at a suffrage meeting in Akron, Ohio, in 1851. Frances Gage wrote that the all-white crowd buzzed disapprovingly on seeing the "tall, gaunt black woman in a gray dress and white turban . . . march deliberately into the church, walk with the air of a queen up the aisle, and take her seat upon the pulpit steps." But Sojourner Truth's enthralling oratory calling for the rights of women and of blacks won their hearts forever. She ended her stirring speech by facing the feminist leaders squarely and saying, "If Eve, the first woman God ever made, was strong enough to turn the world upside down all alone, these women together ought to be able to turn it back and get it right side again. And now they are asking to do it, the men better let them!" Gage reported: "Amid roars of applause she returned to her corner, leaving more than one of us with stream-

ing eyes, and hearts beating with gratitude. She had taken us up in her strong arms and carried us safely over the slough of difficulty." So it was for the rest of her life. Shortly after that appearance, Sojourner Truth moved to Battle Creek, where a thoroughfare named Truth Street recalls that she lived in a house nearby. From here she carried on her tireless efforts for the vote, for freedmen, for human rights. Her lack of education was no obstacle. "I don't read such small stuff as letters," she said, "I read men and nations." And she brushed aside bigotry with seasoned experience. She took up smoking in self-defense because conductors relegated her back to the smoking car so often, telling Elizabeth Cady Stanton that "she would rather swallow her own smoke than another's."

Sojourner Truth died in 1883, aged about 105, before she fulfilled one of her lifelong dreams: "I must sojourn once to the ballot box before I die."

Kimball House Museum, 196 Capital Avenue, NE, displays a number of items belonging to Battle Creek's famous resident in the Sojourner Truth Room. Included: a dark silk dress said to have been given her by Queen Victoria; some photographs; a copy of the painting of Sojourner Truth with President Lincoln; and the only known autograph of Sojourner Truth, dated 1880.

Mary Wilson Grave, small burial ground east of Memorial Park Cemetery. The simple stone reads "Sister," which may or may not refer to the bold act in the name of sisterhood that Mary Wilson carried off in 1871. The thirty-nine-year-old property owner marched off to the polls one election day and cast her vote for school board officers. When no law could be found to challenge her audacious deed (she was, she insisted, a taxpayer), the vote was counted. Mary Wilson became the first woman to cast a ballot in Battle Creek, and the second, with Nannette Gardner in *Detroit*, in the state.

Ellen G. White House, 63–65 Wood Street. The cofounder of the Seventh-Day Adventist Church lived here with her husband after they moved to Battle Creek from New England in 1855. Along with the Whites came the headquarters for the church they had begun; its new name was conceived in Battle Creek in 1860. Ellen G. White had her first vision in Maine in 1844. From then on, she preached and practiced the new religion, calling herself "a messenger from God." Among her tenets: no coffee, tea, drugs, or alcohol; and a strong emphasis on food and health reform, which led to her role in helping found the first Battle Creek Sanitarium. It was in this house, in an upstairs room, that Ellen G. White wrote the first *The Great Controversy*, one of the fifty books, scores of pamphlets, and thousands of articles she produced. Her publications helped the church expand its influence.

Ellen G. White Grave, Oak Hill Cemetery, South Avenue and Oak Hill Drive. Although she left Battle Creek in 1891, and the base of operations for her Seventh-Day Adventist Church moved to Maryland, Ellen G. White's body was brought back here for burial in 1915. Her gravestone is marked "Mother," and rests next to that of her husband James, thrice president of the General Conference of the church. His stone is marked "Father."

Leila Arboretum, West Michigan Avenue and Twentieth Street, was named for its donor, Leila Post Montgomery, who gave the city ninety acres of land in 1922. Today the arboretum is considered one of the finest plant centers in the country. Leila Post Montgomery also enriched the city and immortalized her lyrical name with Leila Hospital (her choice of nicknames for the Leila Y. Post Montgomery Hospital). The Emily Andrus Home for elderly women bears the maiden name of Leila's mother, who had urged its creation.

Beaver Island

When the lighthouse keeper was drowned in the waters of Lake Michigan during a rescue operation, his widow, Elizabeth Whitney Williams, took over the job. She already knew how to tend the lamps at the top of the winding steps of the stone lighthouse. In her book *A Child of the Sea* (1905), she wrote, "the beautiful lens in the tower was my especial care. On stormy nights I watched the light that no accident might happen." Sometimes trimming the long wicks two and three times a night, she threw herself into her new appointment earnestly. "At first I felt almost afraid to assume so great a responsibility," she wrote, "knowing it all required watchful care and strength, with many sleepless nights. I now felt a deeper interest in our sailors' lives than ever before, and I longed to do something for humanity's sake, as well as earn my living."

Big Rapids

Anna Howard Shaw Monument, grounds of Intermediate School, honors the "Distinguished daughter of the State of Michigan, Pioneer resident of the City of Big Rapids. World Citizen. She cuts a path through tangled underwood of old traditions out to broader ways." It was here in Big Rapids that the young Anna of *Ashton* heard her first woman minister, inspiring her to take her degree in theology. Much later, officiating at a suffrage meeting in Grand Rapids in 1899, Anna Howard Shaw said, "A gentleman opposed to [the] enfranchisement [of women] once said to me, 'Women have never produced anything of any value to the world.' I told him the chief produce of the women had been the men, and left it to him to decide whether the product was of any value."

Dearborn

Jeannette Piccard Monument, William B. Stout Junior High School grounds. The first woman in the world to pilot a balloon into the stratosphere stood by proudly when this marker commemorating her lofty achievement was unveiled in 1965. Dr. Jeannette Piccard made the ascent three decades earlier (from the old Ford Airport located nearby) in a 175-foot-high hydrogen-filled balloon. She was the official pilot. As the marker states, "Accompanying her was her husband, Dr. Jean Piccard, scientific director and observor, who made a study of the cosmic rays." More than forty thousand observers jammed the streets of Dearborn to watch the historic takeoff that October 23, 1934. Finally the big bag was inflated, the gondola packed, and the wind conditions perfect. On signal, pilot Piccard pressed the button and briskly threw off ballast. The balloon soared skyward, carrying its equally elated passengers more than ten miles high and some three hundred miles west. They descended shaken, but unharmed, into the treetops of a hillside near Cadiz, Ohio. "What a rotten landing!" Piccard exclaimed later, lamenting the ragged edges of her torn balloon. "Had I been a mite quicker with the ballast, we would have cleared the trees and landed undamaged in the field." Still, the pioneering balloonist had steered her craft safely and set a record. The only woman who has outdistanced her altitude (57,559 feet) is the Russian cosmonaut Valentina Tereshkova.

Recently Dr. Piccard resumed her heavenly aspirations. She received her divinity degree and joined ten other Episcopalian women in an unprecedented but not uncontested ordination service in 1974.

Detroit

The nationwide suffrage action of 1871–72, in which a number of women challenged the existing ban against female voters, was joined by Nannette B. Gardner in Detroit. The first time she voted was April 1871. The *Detroit Post* reported that her ballot was received and deposited without controversy. "There was no argument, no challenge, no variation from the routine traversed by each masculine exerciser of the elective franchise." She and Mary Wilson of *Battle Creek* were the first women in the state to do so. A year later, Nannette Gardner returned to the polls and again cast her vote. This time, she presented to the alderman of the Ninth Ward—who had first taken her name—a handsome white satin banner trimmed with gold fringe, with the dedication, "To Peter Hill . . . First to Register a Woman's Vote. By recognizing civil liberty and equality for woman, he has placed the last and brightest jewel on the brow of Michigan." That was too much for the city councilmen, who voted to censure the alderman. But they never stopped Nannette Gardner from voting.

Mariners' Church, 170 East Jefferson Avenue. This thick-walled stone church, founded in 1842, was the gift of half sisters Charlotte Ann Taylor and Julia Taylor Anderson. The church was originally located 880 feet west on Woodward Avenue at Woodbridge Street, the site of Julia's home. When Charlotte died, she willed the property to Julia. When Julia died in 1842, she willed the property for the church, to be built as a haven for sailors waiting on shore for their ships to sail across the Great Lakes. The huge edifice was moved to its present location in the Civic Center in 1955.

Pewabic Pottery, 10125 East Jefferson. The big kiln within the timbered walls of this English-tudor ceramic studio once baked the dazzling iridescent and Persian blue glazes created by Mary Chase Perry Stratton. A self-taught ceramist who "loved working with clay but . . . wanted art with color too," she had this charming pottery built in 1907. Much of the tile for its fireplaces, windowsills, and floors was homemade. She named it "Pewabic" after a mine in the Upper Peninsula where she was born, later discovering to her delight that *pewabic* is Chippewa for "clay with copper color." Here she developed the brilliant firing techniques that won worldwide fame for her architectural tiles. Her largest commission came from the Shrine of the Immaculate Conception in Washington, D.C., where she produced the tiles for the crypt and fourteen stations of the cross. Her most unusual commission came from Detroit's Stroh Brewery, where the copper fire-brewing kettles are set in Pewabic tile. Today the cobwebs have been cleared from the rafters and the black soot from the walls, but the creative spirit of Mary Chase Perry Stratton, who died in 1961, continues to inspire the potters who work and exhibit here.

Bonstelle Playhouse, made famous by director Jessie Bonstelle and her repertory group in the 1920s, is now used by Wayne State University for its student productions. *Impresario* maga-

zine decided that, had she seen the Wayne State thespians, "Jessie Bonstelle would have been delighted."

Laura Ingalls Wilder Branch, Detroit Public Library, 7140 East Seven Mile Road. The first library in town to be named after a woman and a living person was dedicated in 1949 to honor the author of the "Little House" books. Laura Wilder, eighty-two at the time and living on her farm in *Mansfield, Missouri,* could not attend the ceremony, where it was said, "In her books, which speak so eloquently of the courage which made our country big and free, of the family solidarity which is its cornerstone, Laura Ingalls Wilder has recorded for all children an enduring intrinsic story of America."

Grand Rapids

St. Cecilia Society, 24 Ransom Avenue, NE. This handsome brick building in Italian Renaissance style was constructed in 1893 to house the first women's music club in the country to have its own recital hall. Nine women under the leadership of Alice Uhl accomplished that remarkable feat, despite rigid zoning ordinances. Today, the building that was erected by women and dedicated to music is used for local music activities, and its 700-seat auditorium, famous for its acoustics, is used for dramatic productions.

Alice Uhl

Constance Rourke Grave, Woodlawn Cemetery, 2530 Kalamazoo Avenue, SE. When author Constance Rourke died in 1941, a civic leader in Grand Rapids called her "our first citizen in scholarship." A nationally respected student of cultural Americana, Constance Rourke wrote about people, customs, and trends in the nation's history. A critic said of her *Audubon* that "she looked at Audubon in somewhat the same way that Audubon looked at a bird." On a visit to her home, Carl Van Doren

autographed a copy of the book Rourke wrote on Benjamin Franklin, "To Constance Rourke, who tops us all." And her brilliant study, *American Humor,* was selected as one of the hundred best books written by women in the last century. Rourke wrote many of her works in Grand Rapids, in the house she shared with her mother. It is said that she never received a rejection slip. Her gravestone is inscribed, "American Biographer, Art Critic, Authority on Folklore."

Jackson

Ella Sharp Museum, 3225 Fourth Street, is located in the farmhouse and on the land where Ella Wing Sharp lived. The family farm, "Hillside," was said to be one of the most impressive rural estates in the state. Ella ran it with her husband. When they wed in 1881, the *Jackson Daily Citizen* reported, "Mr. Sharp is to be congratulated in winning such a charming woman for a wife." Today the museum houses local memorabilia and art exhibits.

Kalamazoo

Ladies Library Association, 333 South Park Street. This ivy-covered two-story brick building with stone facings and tiled cornice was the first in the nation erected exclusively by and for a women's club. It was dedicated in 1879, and within four years the women had cleared all debts from the record. The Library Association, organized in 1852 largely with the help of Lucinda Hinsdale Stone, "the Mother of Clubs," grew out of a neighborhood reading club that three women pursued for their mutual benefit. When the number of readers grew to eight in the village of two thousand, the formal association was formed. It was the first women's club in the state.

Kalamazoo College hired Lucinda Hinsdale Stone as principal of its "Female Department" in 1843, an act that helped elevate the college into a center of progressive education for women. Like her husband who ran the boys' school, Lucinda Stone believed strongly in coeducation—so strongly that she had been laughed at as a young student in New England when she said she wanted to attend college. Such liberal notions, along with her unconventional tendency to teach Byron, *Ivanhoe,* and woman's rights in the classroom, proved too much for some of the conservative Kalamazoo officials. When they talked about replacing her with a male principal, Lucinda Stone resigned in 1863. So did her husband. She did not, however, relinquish the fight for coeducation. One of her students, Madelon Stockwell, became the first female student at the newly liberated University of Michigan in *Ann Arbor* in 1870, and Stone was responsible for the admission of women to the faculty there. In 1890, the woman who had cried when neighbors ridiculed her desire to go to college was awarded an honorary Doctor of Philosophy degree by the University of Michigan.

Lucinda Hinsdale Stone Monument, Bronson Park, Park and South Streets. The bronze tablet on a boulder honors the dedicated "Educator, Organizer, Philanthropist, friend of women." Looking back on her New England girlhood, Lucinda Stone once said, "I used sometimes to wish that I might die, because I thought nobody loved me; but this drove me to my books, and I lived with my books as far back as I can remember."

Litchfield

Rose Hartwick Thorpe Monument, Route M–60. An old fire bell mounted on an eight-foot-high block of fieldstone and cement commemorates the sixteen-year-old Litchfield schoolgirl who wrote the poem "Curfew Must Not Ring Tonight." Rose Hartwick Thorpe was inspired to compose that verse in 1867. She had read the historical account of the English schoolgirl, in the days of Oliver Cromwell, who tried to silence the clapper of a curfew bell with bleeding hands so that it would not toll her lover's intended execution hour at sundown. Unaware of her talent, the Litchfield poet traded her work to the *Detroit News* for a subscription to the paper. Unfamiliar with the need to copyright, Rose Hartwick Thorpe saw her poem pirated by scores of dramatists.

Mackinac Island

"Anne's Tablet," Woolson Rampart, Sinclair Grove, East Bluff, was erected in honor of author Constance Fenimore Woolson, who "has expressed her love of this island and its beauty in the words of her heroine, 'Anne.' " During the mid-1880s the well-known writer (*see Winter Park, Florida*) spent many summers here with her family. Long after she had stopped summering on Mackinac Island, she called it "the most beautiful in the world." *Anne* was her first novel, published in 1882 after *Harper's* had

serialized it. Its realistic portrayal of life on the island at the head of Lake Michigan proved enormously popular. The plaque on this wooded slope depicts the young heroine reaching for a branch. A native fir stands tall in the background. Some lines from *Anne*: "She used to whisper to them to tell them how much she loved them, her old friends. She loved the island and the island trees: she loved the wild larches, the tall spires of the spruces 'bossed with lighter green, the gray pines and the rings of the juniper."

Manistee

Ann Eliza Webb Young Denning House, Third and Sibben Streets (private). Brigham Young's antipolygamous runaway wife (see *Salt Lake City, Utah*) came here to live in 1883 when she married banker Moses Denning. The town gossips had a field day when Denning divorced his first wife (with whom he'd just celebrated a silver anniversary) to marry the beautiful young celebrity. Even the handsome new additions Denning financed for this traditional Michigan farmhouse could not stop the tongues from wagging; nor could they grant Ann Eliza the respectability she craved. As one local historian told us, the house "was not in the 'best' part of town, and in that strait-laced period, the good ladies of Manistee were not inclined to show friendship or even mercy toward one who, in their eyes, had broken up a happy marriage of twenty-five years duration. This, notwithstanding the fact that a couple of years earlier, when she lectured here, they tried to outdo each other in gracious acts toward the celebrated victim and enemy of multiple marriage. Poor Ann Eliza!"

Doubly poor. Monogamy did not prove anymore agreeable to her than polygamy, and she was divorced within the decade.

Pinckney

This small village, named by author Caroline Stansbury Kirkland, served as her home and her chief source of literary material. In the late 1830s, with her husband William, she moved into a log cabin in the Michigan woods, determined to settle the rugged frontier. Her vivid and unromanticized fictional re-creation of the trying life in the backwoods first appeared as *A New Home—Who'll Follow?* (1839). In the novel, Pinckney was turned into "Montacute"; her neighbors were so realistically caricatured with her precise and often unflattering wit that local families are said to hold grudges still. In 1843 the Kirklands left their western outpost since Caroline's literary efforts were proving more financially rewarding than their homesteading. One critic has suggested that publication of the book "had not been conducive to an atmosphere of communal intimacy in Pinckney." Caroline Kirkland defended her sarcastic work in a letter to a friend. "The Western people wish to be flattered. Self-glorification is the order of the day there—but I will not flatter—though I shall be equally careful not to misrepresent. I love the West, and shall be glad to do it good by telling the truth, even if I get the dislike of some."

Port Huron

North American Benefit Association, 1338 Military Street. The two-story Italian Renaissance-style building was erected in 1917 to house the Woman's Benefit Association, founded in 1892 by Bina West Miller. The indomitable schoolteacher and financier opened her first tiny office that October for the unheard-of purpose of selling life insurance to women. A month later she issued her first insurance certificate; a year later, she paid her first death claim. Today the organization that dared to provide coverage for women has more than 100,000 members and assets of almost $80 million. The name was changed in 1966, according to the current president, since "we have been insuring men since 1931, and the change of name, we felt, would make our fine insurance plans more appealing to them."

MINNESOTA

Elk River

Oliver H. Kelley Farm, Routes 10, 52, and 169. The farm he homesteaded in 1850 later served Oliver H. Kelley as his office when he was executive secretary of the National Grange, an organization he cofounded in 1867. It was one of the earliest groups of any kind to operate under the radical principle that women would be full and equal members. Officially established as the Patrons of Husbandry, the fraternal farmers' order aimed to help educate farmers, to combat the monopoly of huge business interests, and "to inculcate a proper appreciation of the abilities and sphere of woman."

Erhard

Hannah Jensen Kempfer represented this territory in the Minnesota state legislature for nearly twenty years. Born on a ship in the North Sea, then orphaned, Kempfer was adopted into a family of poor but loving Norwegian immigrants who prepared her for her career as an independent lawmaker. She was influential in outlawing the use of the cruel steel trap on the state's game lands. A bill to better the lot of illegitimate children succeeded dramatically when Hannah Kempfer stood on the floor of the House and ended all debate by saying, "A child should not be punished for what is no fault of his own. I want to do all I can to improve the lot of these poor children because I am one of them. I am an illegitimate child. I know what it means."

Fairfax

Eliza Muller Monument, Fort Ridgely Cemetery, Fort Ridgely State Park. A stone next to another honoring various fallen soldiers memorializes Eliza Muller for her "valor and her devotion to the care of the sick and wounded soldiers and refugees during and after the Sioux Indian Outbreak of 1862." Working alongside her husband, the fort doctor, Eliza Muller tended the dozen or so whites hurt by the largely superior Sioux force. The Indians rebelled because they were confined to an unspacious reservation and forced to adopt farming instead of their lifelong hunting ways. But the well-trained soldiers and five menacing cannons inflicted more casualties on the Indians than *vice versa*. As for Mrs. Muller, her valor under siege apparently proved unbearable. She went insane and died at the state hospital in 1876.

Hutchinson

When the Hutchinson Constitution was framed in 1855, one of the thirteen articles adopted was, "That it is solemnly decreed that in the future of Hutchinson, women shall enjoy equal rights with men." At another meeting of this liberated assembly, one hundred lots were to be divided among the townspeople for the purpose of building houses. Each woman was to get one lot to show that she had helped in the building of the community.

Minneapolis

Eloise Butler Wild Flower and Bird Sanctuary, Theodore Wirth Park, is named for its founder and first official curator, retired botany teacher Eloise Butler. A showplace of luxuriant wild undergrowth and brilliant birdlife, the twenty-five-acre garden was enlarged and patiently preserved by the dedicated naturalist until her death, in the garden itself, in 1933. At her request, her ashes were scattered over the ground she loved and no doubt helped fertilize the northern pin oak tree, one of her favorites, that was planted in her honor. A bronze plaque nearby reminds nature lovers that in this "sequestered glen . . . her protective spirit lingers."

Loring Park. You can barely see the trees for all the markers to famous women here. Many of the markers are dedicated to officers of the Minnesota Federation of Women's Clubs; and one is dedicated to Maria Sanford. A most interesting memorial on a huge boulder remembers Mary Burr Lewis, founder and leader of the Lewis Parliamentary Law Association. A token of Lewis's efficient manner of keeping order is the miniature gavel sculptured in bas-relief atop her name.

Maria Sanford Hall, University of Minnesota. The first women's dormitory erected here in 1910 was named for the feminist and humanitarian who was the dynamic professor of elocution and rhetoric here from 1880 to 1909. Maria Sanford is probably Minnesota's most widely known and respected adopted daughter (she was born in Connecticut), an inspiring teacher and thrilling orator. When her statue was dedicated in the Capitol in *Washington, D.C.,* the president of the University of Minnesota quoted an earlier president as saying, "The greatest thing I ever did for the University was to bring Maria Sanford here."

Minnesota Man Display, University of Minnesota. The preserved skeleton of the state's oldest archaeological find has been put on exhibit here after several thousand years of obscurity at *Pelican Rapids.* Originally misidentified as the famous Minnesota Man discovery in 1931, the slender, patient bones were properly renamed Minnesota Minnie when their accurate sex was determined.

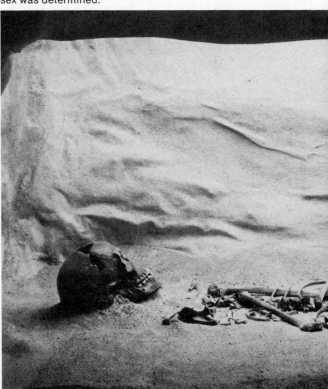

Site of Maternity Hospital, 300 Queen Avenue North. Dr. Martha George Ripley, a Minnesota pioneer who was born in New England, founded the hospital in 1887, first in a private home; then it was moved here in 1896. When her husband was incapacitated by an accident in 1883, the year she received her medical degree, Dr. Ripley set out to support her family. She had a large practice, but she soon devoted herself to medical care for the less fortunate. At first taking young unwed mothers into her own home, she finally created this hospital. The obstetrical care and pediatric service soon gained wide respect, as did Dr. Ripley's suffrage activities. When she died in 1912, her ashes were sealed within the cornerstone of a building erected in her honor. The hospital was closed in 1956 due to lack of funds and today this is an empty lot (see *St. Paul*).

Sister Kenny Institute, 1800 Chicago Avenue, is named for the Australian nurse who revolutionized the treatment of polio and brought her pioneering methods to Minneapolis in 1940. Her demonstration of the techniques she had developed in the remote bush country of her native land so impressed the city that the institute was built in 1942. The Hollywood version of her life starred Rosalind Russell, but Sister Kenny (*sister* is the Australian term for "nurse") was herself idolized—fans rushed to tear buttons from her coat or to take her big Australian hat as souvenirs. Late in 1952, Sister Kenny prayed for a vaccine to abolish the disease she had spent her lifetime trying to combat. She died that year before she heard about Dr. Jonas Salk's discovery.

Betty Crocker Birthplace, General Mills, Inc., 9200 Wayzata Boulevard. The nation's model homemaker isn't a real person. Betty Crocker was created in 1921 by some advertising men who needed a woman's signature to respond to the queries and recipe problems of real female consumers. Rather than hire a new female executive, they made one up. "Crocker" was the surname of a recently retired (male) director. "Betty" struck the midwestern admen as "something sort of cozy and familiar sounding." She has been painted four times, always as a composite with no flaws. Recently she was updated with a new,

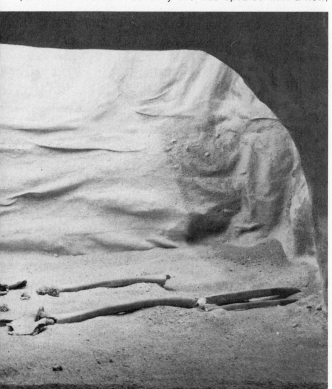

youthful appearance. Crocker seeks no liberation from the kitchen because her kitchens are run by more than seventy people. You are invited to pop in for a visit.

New Ulm

Wanda Gag House, 226 North Washington (private). A marker identifies the childhood home of author and illustrator Wanda Gag, born in New Ulm in 1893. She once wrote that she had grown up "in an atmosphere of old world customs, legends and folk songs," a heritage that inspired many of her drawings and books. Her best known work is the children's classic *Millions of Cats,* which she wrote and illustrated in 1928. An independent artist who abandoned commercial art work to branch out on her own, Wanda Gag explained, "Whether anyone else will like what I do is not important. I'll draw things the way they look and feel to me." Many of her lithographs and engravings, some set in New Ulm, are housed in museums and libraries here.

Owatonna

Mineral Springs Park, the state's first known health resort, derived its reputation from its first cured patient, the frail Indian woman for whom the town is named. The sickly daughter of Chief Wabena, Owatonna was restored to robust good health after drinking the life-enhancing "minnewaucan" waters. Her statue guards the once-bubbling spring, and her grave rests on the hillside overlooking it.

Pelican Rapids

Site of Minnesota Man Discovery, Route 59. The state highway crew repairing the road alongside Prairie Lake dug up a spectacular archaeological treasure here one June day in 1931. The bulldozer uncovered the fossilized remains of a skeleton, approximately nine feet below the surface. Scientists instantly and confidently dubbed the creature Minnesota Man. When it turned out that the bones actually belonged to a fifteen-year-old girl, the identification was adjusted by some to Minnesota Minnie. Although archaeologists disagree as to whether she was 9,000 or 25,000 years old, or maybe even just a century-old Sioux Indian in an unusually deep grave, they do agree that she drowned. It is not known whether she was pushed or fell into the glacial lake. In any event, her much-admired skeleton now rests in appropriate glory at the University of Minnesota in *Minneapolis.*

Pipestone

Pipestone National Monument. This sacred quarry of the Omaha and Yankton Sioux Indians is said to have been rediscovered by Wahegela, an Omaha woman on a buffalo hunt with her Sioux husband. Through neglect, the legend goes, the tribes had lost knowledge of the quarry's location. Wahegela found it again when a "message" directed her to follow a bison to the place where his hooves turned the rocks red. The red pipestone, considered holy by the Indians, was thus turned up by the herds of bison, and Wahegela restored the lands to her tribespeople. Today the stone is quarried for Indian pipes and crafts.

Red Wing

Frances Densmore Birthplace, 729 West Third Street (private). The brilliant student of Indian life and music first heard some Indian songs from her Sioux neighbors across the Mississippi River. "Instead of frightening me with stories of war dances and scalps," Frances Densmore recalled later, "my wise mother said, 'Those Indians are interesting people with customs that are different from ours, but they will not hurt you.' "

From 1893 on, Densmore wrote twenty-two books on Indian music and customs; she recorded, transcribed, and analyzed more than three thousand Indian songs. Using an ancient recording machine with wax cylinders, she captured the moods and lore of tribal life in the authentic voices of the chiefs (including Geronimo) and their followers. Well aware that "there is more to the preservation of Indian songs than winding the phonograph," she tracked down her sources on extensive journeys to reservations all over the U.S. Her research was sponsored largely by the Smithsonian Institution. The Indians called her the Writing Down Woman, since she was always taking notes. Today, twenty years after her death, her work still forms the basis for scholarly research.

Rochester

Pioneer settler Marietta Head, who lived here with her husband George in a log cabin erected in 1854, performed an early feat of showmanship out of zeal for her new town. We learned from Rochester historians that the street now named Broadway was cleared when oxen dragged a log through the prairie brush. Marietta dedicated the new thoroughfare by riding her horse up and down the path for all to see.

Mayo Clinic, 200 First Street, SW. The world-famous treatment center that today draws some 200,000 patients a year was made possible in 1899 by the Catholic Sisters of St. Francis. They built the forty-bed St. Marys Hospital nearby, where the Doctors Mayo tried out their medical and surgical techniques. Sister Mary Joseph, administrator of St. Marys for nearly half a century, and Mother Alfred, who urged the hospital in the beginning, are commemorated with bronze memorials at St. Marys. Edith Graham Mayo, wife of clinic cofounder Horace, was the city's first trained nurse.

St. Cloud

Site of St. Cloud Visiter Office, lawn of Shoemaker Hall, St. Cloud State College Campus. A marker identifies a location a block to the south, near a former boat landing, as the site of the editorial offices run by crusading journalist Jane Grey Swisshelm. After leaving behind her husband and her *Saturday Evening Visiter* (a spelling attributed to Dr. Johnson) in *Pittsburgh, Pennsylvania,* Swisshelm started a paper of the same name here in 1857. Her vigorous antislavery policy did not entirely please some of the local Democrats. One night in 1858 a group of offended readers, led by the Democratic boss, broke into her newspaper office, damaged the press, and hurled much of the type into the Mississippi River. Swisshelm obtained new facilities, continued to publish, and publicly denounced the intruders. When they finally got her to agree not to mention the incident again in the *Visiter,* she simply changed the name of her paper to the *Democrat* and resumed her assault.

St. Paul

Harriet Island, a pocket of picnic grounds and playfields in the middle of the Mississippi River, bears the name of Harriet Bishop, a hardy pioneer who came from New England to the rugged outpost of St. Paul in 1847 to open its first organized school. Her primitive schoolhouse was an old blacksmith's log cabin, chinked with mud to keep out the elements. Starting with a mere handful of curious children, she soon ran a fine school with many grateful pupils. Harriet Bishop was also a suffrage and temperance worker, and she wrote a number of books vividly describing her life on the frontier. In her autobiography, *Floral Home; or, First Years of Minnesota,* she described the community known as "Pig's Eye" (for a one-eyed settler whose eye resembled that of a pig): "Here was a field to be cultivated; a garden of untrained flowers to be tended." She also wrote that a frequent refrain in the new territory was "that a 'unit added to the female population, was virtually of more importance than a whole cargo of the sterner sex.' "

Clara Ueland Monument, State Capitol. A plaque in the west side of the rotunda commemorates the suffragist and reformer who carried on her crusades with "no weakness in her words, no weariness on her brow, no wavering in her loyalties." Clara Ueland helped found the city's first public kindergarten (1897) and was largely responsible for the organizing efforts that gained women the vote in Minnesota in 1919. As first president of the League of Women Voters, she lobbied tirelessly for bills concerning social welfare. The last day of her life was spent here in the Capitol during the 1927 legislative session. As she stepped down from a streetcar carrying her home, she was hit by a truck and killed instantly. The following resolution was adopted by both houses of the legislature on the next day:

"She possessed the respect and confidence of the members of this House to a marked degree . . . an earnest advocate of what she believed to be progressive and remedial legislation for the State of Minnesota and for the United States."

Dr. Martha Ripley Memorial, State Capitol. A plaque in the east side of the rotunda bears a likeness of the pioneer physician and calls her "Fearless in spirit, courageous in action, Champion of righteousness and justice." It notes that she founded the Maternity Hospital in *Minneapolis,* where "she stretched out her hands to the poor."

Taopi

At one point during the 1930s, all the municipal officers of this tiny village were women. In addition, women owned two of the three most important stores, and the official in charge of the post office was a woman. Taopi was named for a famous Santee Sioux chief whose name means "wounded man."

Walnut Grove

Laura Ingalls Wilder, peripatetic author of children's books (see *Mansfield, Missouri*) lived in a dugout along Plum Creek just southeast of here. Her childhood remembrances of the 1870s, including a grasshopper plague and a series of blizzards (during which she aimed snowballs as accurately as the boys), were recreated in her book *On the Banks of Plum Creek.* The old footbridge over the creek and the playground nearby were special places that Laura hated to leave when her family pulled up stakes and moved further west.

Willmar

Guri Endreson Monument, Viktor Lutheran Church Cemetery, pays tribute to a local heroine of the 1862 Sioux uprising (see *Fairfax*), although a local historian told us that she "did nothing more or less than a couple of hundred other women—she protected her men during the uprising." Guri Endreson's deed, which only time can judge, was to load her wounded son-in-law and her neighbor into a cart and bring them to the fort for help. As the Indians were long gone, she was in no apparent danger. The historian maintains that Guri Endreson was the "victim" of a 1905 campaign to find local figures who resisted the uprising, and that other women "did as much, and more."

Winona

Statue of We-no-nah, Main Street. The Sioux woman for whom this city was named is immortalized by the usual love-sick legend that she leaped into the waters rather than enter into marriage with the warrior of her father's choice. In this case, the scene of her demise was Lake Pepin, about sixty miles north of Winona, beneath a high cliff now called Maiden Rock. (They are always called Maiden Rock.) The versions of this story vary to fit the demand (one Winona historian cheerfully told us she could put together one "more elaborate and probably contradictory if you'd like"); nonetheless, the bronze likeness of the independent young Sioux does face decidedly north toward the site of her leap, although she avoids it with a slight easterly glance. The statue was erected in 1902 and sculpted by Isabel Moore Kimball, who did painstaking research to depict accurately the long dress with its buckskin fringe, the sun ornament on her left shoulder, and various decorative items. Kimball did take some artistic license by giving We-no-nah a bow to carry. Indian experts tell us that Sioux women did not hunt with the bow. Had they been allowed to, perhaps it might have curbed the female suicide rate.

College of St. Teresa was founded in 1909 by Mary Molloy, the first woman to receive a doctorate from Cornell University (1907). In 1922 she entered the novitiate and received the name of Sister Mary Aloysius; that is how she was known as president of the College of St. Teresa. Sister Aloysius was the first woman appointed to the executive committee of the college department of the National Catholic Educational Association, and she served as its president in 1947. At the dedication of a library named in her honor after she died in 1954, a St. Teresa faculty member said, "She had characteristics of an aristocrat, a peasant and a drill sergeant."

MISSISSIPPI

Aberdeen

OLD CEMETERY

Mary Points Grave. The last fiery moments of her life have been immortalized on Mary Points's tombstone. Raging flames from an unknown source devour her billowing bouffant skirt, but Mary's face is calm and serene, knowing that she is going out in style. A grieving husband erected this graphic warning to other fashionable women in 1852 with the simple, loving words, "To my Mary in heaven."

Jane Martin Dalton Grave. A replica of St. John's, the church she founded in 1851 three months before her death, has been carved on Jane Dalton's tombstone, with the inscription, "May [the church] long remain a monument to which her surviving friends may fondly point." With a slight change in the roof style, St. John's, located on Commerce Street, remains the oldest ecclesiastical structure in town.

Alice Whitfield Grave. Her relatives have gone to great lengths to deny that Alice, who died in 1854 at age sixty-one, is buried sitting up in her favorite rocking chair, but the story persists. Surrounded by an ornamental wrought-iron fence, this handsome mausoleum, each panel showing two lambs resting under a tree of Spanish hanging moss, certainly has more than enough overhead space for such a comfortable final position from which to depart for one's final reward.

Athens

All that is left of this farming community is the old jail, built in 1845, three years after Athens claims to have organized the first temperance society in the country (April 21, 1842). Twenty-nine women joined seventy men and had "regular meetings, appropriate addresses from time to time, wore uniforms and fought desperately against strong drink," a contemporary historian observed. The temperance society was one of the most active and strongest organizations in the community in years, but it inexplicably folded in May 1846.

Biloxi

Biloxi Lighthouse, Route 90. From 1877 to 1929, this welcome landmark was faithfully operated by Maria Younghans and her daughter Miranda. Several times a night, Maria braved the bitter cold of winter to change the frozen lamps. When Maria was finally too old for the arduous climb, Miranda followed her mother's footsteps up the winding stairs—to shine the light for nine more years, until it was automated.

Sarah Anne Ellis Dorsey House, "Beauvoir," 200 West Beach Boulevard. This raised cottage with a "beautiful view" and a pillared porch over a latticed basement belonged to novelist Sarah Anne Ellis Dorsey (see *Sibley*). She was also the generous benefactor of Jefferson Davis, who lived here during the last twelve years of his life. Without the help and inspiration of this "large-soul'd, noble woman," Davis would not have been able to complete his *Rise and Fall of the Confederate Government* which Sarah helped research for him while at the same time publishing her own fine writings. When she died in 1879, Sarah willed her house to Davis. Ten years later, his widow Varina (see *Natchez*) struggled to keep Beauvoir despite mounting financial problems. She loyally turned down huge offers to turn it into a hotel, accepting instead a smaller donation from the Sons of Confederate Veterans who assured her that the house would be preserved as a Jefferson Davis shrine. Fortunately for women everywhere, so has Sarah Dorsey's name and fame been enshrined.

Cleveland

Nellie Nugent Somerville House, 505 South Victoria Avenue (private). Until her death in 1952 at age eighty-nine, the first female member of the Mississippi House of Representatives (1923), one of the state's leading feminists, lived in this house. Her power was so formidable in the House that her legislative successes were routinely taken for granted—it was bigger news when a bill she proposed failed to pass. A newspaper article in 1904 described her as "a very charming woman; personally she is gentle and attractive, and while having very decided views on the suffrage question, she entirely refutes the idea that a suffragist is not the sweetest and most womanly woman imaginable." The same article concluded that she was "the greatest leader in many lines of woman's work that Mississippi has ever had." Her house is now owned by her daughter, Lucy Somerville Howorth, who followed her mother into the legislature.

Clinton

Sarah Dickey Grave, about one mile north of Northside Drive, is located on the grounds of the Mount Hermon Female Seminary, a boarding school for black girls that Dickey, who died in 1904, founded in 1875. The old school buildings have long since disappeared, but Dickey's grave has been carefully preserved—a tall obelisk, surrounded by oak and dogwood trees and abundant honeysuckle bushes, enclosed by a cyclone fence. (See *Tougaloo*.)

Columbus

Mississippi University for Women. The first state-supported college exclusively for women in the United States was founded in 1884 and accepted 341 students the following year, "fitting and preparing such girls for the practical industries of the age." Today, it is the only state-supported all-female college in the country.

English Lit class, 1912

Site of First Memorial Day Services, Friendship Cemetery. Moved by pity for the more than one thousand federal and Confederate soldiers buried so far from home, a group of women led by Matt Morton (see below) began coming here in April 1863 to remove the weeds around the graves and to place floral wreaths on the simple headstones. The first official Memorial Day took place in April 1886. "First marched in twos the young ladies and girls dressed in immaculate white, each bearing a bouquet ... next came the matrons wearing mourning, typical of the Southern heart in sorrow for its beloved dead ... after these came the elderly ladies in carriages." After "eloquent and elaborate" addresses, the women decorated the graves. "We were pleased to see," wrote one observer, "no distinction was made between our own dead and the Federal soldiers who slept their last sleep by them." There have been several other claims as to the origins of this glorious tribute to war dead, but, as one local historian graciously conceded, "We would not snatch a laurel from the brow of another and accord all honor to the ladies of *Columbus, Georgia*." (See *Petersburg, Virginia*.)

Matt Morton House, "Twelve Gables," 220 South Third Street (private). Matt Morton held a planning meeting here in 1863 to arrange for the care of the neglected graves of the casualties of the Civil War. Her inspiration eventually led to what was possibly the first Memorial Day service in the country.

Corinth

In April 1862 this was the scene of the fierce Battle of Shiloh where Kate Cumming, who had left her home in *Mobile, Alabama*, with no training as a nurse and against the wishes of her family, arrived just in time to help with the wounded. In her diary, she wrote, "Nothing that I had ever heard or read had given me the faintest idea of the horrors witnessed here.... Certainly none of the glories of the war were presented here. ... O, if the authors of this cruel and unnatural war could but see what I saw there, they would try to put a stop to it!" In the midst of unspeakable horrors—amputated limbs piling up in the gardens, starving soldiers, lonely deaths in the night— Cumming endured, staying on longer than most of the other nurses, watching "the same sad scenes—men dying all around me. I do not know who they are, nor have I time to learn."

Flora

Site of Belle Kearney House, Kearney Park Road. Born here on a plantation in 1863, the willful, unconventional Belle found her calling when Frances Willard (see *Evanston, Illinois*) swept her into the WCTU crusade. In 1889, Belle became the organization's state president, trumpeting the cause as "the golden key that unlocked the prison doors of pent-up possibilities. ... the discoverer, the developer of southern woman." But soon recognizing the need for the ballot, Belle lectured with equal passion for suffrage in her "rapid magnetic manner, interspersed with flashes of wit." She once explained her fervor for woman's rights: "There was born in me a sense of injustice that had always been heaped upon my sex, and this consciousness created and sustained in me a constant and ever increasing rebellion." After the passage of the Nineteenth Amendment, Belle was elected Mississippi's first female state senator, serving for two terms at the same time as her equally forceful friend, Nellie Nugent Somerville (see *Cleveland*).

Greenville

Suffrage immortal Anna Howard Shaw (see *Ashton, Michigan*) came here in January 1889 and reported encouragingly, "The dear sisters of the South are beginning to feel the need of the franchise. They find it no less dignified to walk up to the polls and deposit their ballot than it is to stand in the mud all day and button-hole men, and ask them to vote for God and Home and Native Land, with the chance of nine times in ten their voting against it. We find it easier to do a thing ourselves than it is to beg all day for somebody else to do it and then not have it done after all.''

Holly Springs

Sherwood Bonner House, ''Cedarhurst,'' 411 Salem Avenue (private). Katherine Sherwood, born in 1849, destined to become one of the South's most original writers (the first to write stories in southern dialect), lived in this French Gothic house as a child. When she was twenty, she wrote in her diary, ''Marriage is not to sink *me* into a dredge of nonentity, whatever it may do for weaker sisters.'' True to her spirited ideas, she left her husband and child to pursue her literary ambitions in Boston, Massachusetts, where she became the protégée and inspiration of Henry Wadsworth Longfellow. ''I long for life, movement, action. . . . Fancy having written against one's name in the book of fate this:—was born,—married,—died,'' she once said through one of her characters. Sherwood died from cancer at the age of thirty-four, the last eight years of her life spent writing furiously in an attempt to record all the changes that were taking place during the South's transitional years. Her attempts to preserve the black man's dialect and the peculiar expressions of the mountaineers paved the way for Joel Chandler Harris and others. Dorrie Busby Norwood, who wrote her master's thesis on Sherwood, said that although Sherwood did not actively join the suffrage movement of her day, through her books, she ''presented much of the wave of the future woman's world. She portrayed characters much like herself—the girl who wore dresses a little shorter than acceptable, the girl who was interested in politics, the girl who was bored by much of the pretense she saw in Southern life.''

Anne Walter Fearn Birthplace, 331 West Chulahoma Avenue (private). An encounter in San Francisco with the gentlemanly-attired Dr. Mary Walker (see *Oswego, New York*) changed Anne Walter's life, and, even though her family threatened to disown her, she chose the ''dreadful'' career of medicine. Anne, born here in 1865, spent most of her life doctoring in China. She went there in 1893, working so enthusiastically and hard that

the Chinese called her *Tai Foong*, ''the great wind''. Anne married a doctor who worked in another hospital—''we were friendly rivals,'' although he ''felt my independence was unbecoming to a woman.'' During her thirty years in Soochow and Shanghai, Anne conducted her own practice and established hospitals and medical schools—including the Shanghai American School in 1912. After she died in 1939, in California, her ashes were sent to her beloved adopted land as she had requested.

Kate Freeman Clark Memorial Art Gallery, College Avenue. The world's largest single collection of paintings by a single artist is housed in this modern building, provided by funds donated by the artist. Kate signed her more than one thousand paintings ''Freeman Clark,'' so no one would know that a woman had painted the lush landscapes, still lifes, and vivid portraits. She would never permit any of her magnificent works to be sold, dutifully heeding her mother's words: ''It would be like selling a child to sell one of Kate's paintings!'' After the death of her mother in 1923, Kate stopped painting and never again lifted a brush until her death at age eighty-one.

Kate Freeman Clark House, ''Walthall Home,'' 810 East College Avenue (private). Kate's only creative years were spent in New York, and it was not until after her death in 1957 that the town of Holly Springs discovered her vast collection of paintings stored in the attic here. We searched for some clues to explain why this very talented woman did not paint for the last thirty-four years of her life. But all that local residents who remembered her could tell us was that Kate was just one of those people who kept putting things off. ''She kept saying she was going to paint today, but never did.''

Sisters of Charity Memorial, Hill Crest Cemetery. This slender granite monument with a cross at the top was erected a year after the yellow fever epidemic of 1878, in appreciation of the heroic work of six nuns who cared for the hundreds of suffering victims until their own deaths. Sherwood Bonner called the sisters the martyrs of Holly Springs: ''Absolutely fearless, cheerful as though walking among flowers in the sunshine, skilled in the arts of nursing, it was a blessed privilege to have them by the sick bed and when hope was gone their beautiful faith cheered the sufferer.''

Jackson

Monument to Women of the Confederacy, New Capitol grounds, Mississippi Street. This heroic sculpture of Fame, Victory, and a dying soldier was executed by Belle Kinney of *Nashville, Tennessee,* where an identical version also graces the Capitol.

Phillis Wheatley Memorial, Jackson State College. To commemorate the two hundredth birthday of the first book published by a black living in America—the lyrical poems of Phillis Wheatley (see *Boston, Massachusetts*)—this elegant bronze statue by Elizabeth Catlett was dedicated by black female poets at a four-day Wheatley festival in 1973. In celebrating her leg-

acy, poet Alice Walker said, "It is not so much what [she] sang as [she] kept alive in so many of our ancestors *the notion of song.*"

Meridian

Kelly Mitchell Grave, Rose Hill Cemetery, Seventh Street. A granite cross with a crown, inscribed "Queen," marks the grave of Kelly Mitchell, Queen of the Gypsies. She died at forty-seven in 1915, and with more than five thousand faithful in attendance was buried in her most exquisite Romany finery —a bright red robe, trimmed in yellow and green; necklaces of gold Russian and Portuguese coins, some as old as 150 years; and jewels braided into her hair. Her silver-lined coffin was fitted out with casks of wine, combs, and several changes of clothes—in all, a fortune worth close to a million dollars to tide her over in the next life. Although the coffin was wisely covered with concrete and a steel plate, treasure hunters have made determined attempts to cash in on Kelly's journey.

Natchez

Varina Howell Davis House, "The Briars" (private). In her childhood home, Varina married Jefferson Davis in 1845. Shortly after his appointment as secretary of war in 1853, the couple moved to Washington, D.C. "A comely, sprightly woman . . . brimming with zest for life," she was a leader of the social scene, much respected for her learned political opinions. Several months after Mississippi seceded, Varina moved into the executive mansion in Virginia as First Lady of the Confederacy. As one Englishman who visited her declared, "She was the right lady in the right place." She lived briefly in *Biloxi* and after her husband's death moved to New York where she died in 1906, having spent her last years writing, with little financial reward, a defense of her husband and the Civil War.

Oxford

Sarah McGehee Isom House, 10003 Jefferson Avenue. The only female member of the university faculty at "Ole Miss," Sarah Isom was appointed as an elocution teacher in 1885. Her own description of this demanding subject included the study of respiration, vocal culture, orthoepy, gesture, the laws of inflection and emphasis, and analysis of dramatic and practical reading.

Picayune

Incorporated in 1904, this town was named after the *New Orleans Picayune* (nicknamed for the old Spanish coin, picayune, that it sold for), that was saved from bankruptcy when celebrated local resident Eliza Jane Nicholson took over as publisher in 1876 (see *New Orleans, Louisiana*). A marker in front of City Hall honors her fame as a "poet [Pearl Rivers] and pioneer in opening journalism to women."

Eliza Jane Poitevent Nicholson House, "The Hermitage" (private). In this elegant mansion on the banks of the Pearl River, surrounded by pines and moss-hung oaks, Eliza was born in 1849. When she began submitting her poems to newspapers and magazines, Eliza used her favorite river as a pen name. Her first effort appeared in a little sheet called *The South,* and her jealous brothers were so indignant at her success that they stomped on the paper. Ignoring such petulance, Eliza kept writing. Her poetry attracted the attention of the editor of the *New Orleans Picayune,* who offered her a job as the paper's literary editor and later married her. Her daily poetry selections, of course, included her own fine poems. With such a record of capable editorial judgment, Eliza was the logical choice to succeed her husband as publisher. (See *New Orleans, Louisiana*.)

Pocahontas

This Jackson suburb was named for the South's favorite Indian heroine. (*See Jamestown, Virginia*.)

Red Banks

Eliza Moore House, "Maplewood" (private). When federal troops entered this house to search for Confederate soldiers, they barricaded Eliza Moore's husband in a closet, with a burning mattress, under the back stairway. With no thought to her own safety, Eliza rescued her husband and stamped out the flames, as Mr. Moore fled in panic while the federals fired away. Marie Goodman Jenkins, who lives in the house now, told us that, as a child, she remembered seeing the bullet holes in the walls. She also noted that the house, which has been in her family since 1880, has been owned by three women.

Ship Island

Between 1704 and 1728, chaperoned by priests and Ursuline nuns, several groups of young orphaned women called "casquette girls," who were "carefully selected, of industrious habits, skillful at work, of exemplary virtue and piety," arrived here from France on their way to *New Orleans, Louisiana.* There, they were destined to be married "not to gentlemen— but to discharged soldiers, farmers, mechanics." Their humble trousseaux included two skirts and petticoats, six each of laced bodices, chemises, and headdresses, neatly packed into the tiny caskets that gave the prospective brides their macabre name.

Fort Massachusetts. Eugenia Phillips was exiled to an old wooden railroad car on this barren, sandy island when a federal officer accused her of laughing at a passing funeral cortege that passed her home in New Orleans. Previously suspected of being a Confederate spy, Eugenia was wrenched away from her husband and nine children and imprisoned in 1862 with the orders that "she be not 'regarded and treated as a common woman of whom no officer or soldier is bound to take notice' but as an uncommon, bad and dangerous woman, stirring up strife and inciting to riot." Eugenia was served food that had been condemned as unfit for the soldiers, and she was confined to her little cracked shack as the summer storms dumped sand on her mercilessly and millions of mosquitoes relentlessly attacked her. Historian M. James Stevens, who told us about Eugenia's two-and-one-half miserable months of captivity, recalled that despite all the hardships that she recorded in her diary, her letters to her husband and children were cheerful and chatty. "Independent, outspoken . . . she was sometimes laid low by the harsh treatment on the island but maintained her high spirits to the very end" and was grudgingly admired by her captors.

Sibley

Ellis' Cliffs, Route 61 South. The birthplace of noted Mississippi author Sarah Anne Ellis Dorsey (see *Biloxi*) and the home of her governess, Eliza Ann Dupuy, who moved here in the 1830s has long since disappeared. It was here that Dupuy, a chronicler of romantic local history, wrote her most successful novel, *The Conspirator,* about Aaron Burr. Her biographer wrote, "The handsome young governess with her dignified reserve and noble pride was one of the ornaments of Natchez society. . . . everywhere respected and often much beloved."

Toccopola

Grave of Betsy Allen, Old Toccopola High School grounds, Route 334. Lost to history for more than a hundred years, the first native champion of married women's rights was honored with a small granite marker when her grave was rediscovered in 1930. Betsy Allen, a young Chickasaw of independent means, unfortunately married an impoverished, debt-ridden white man whose opportunistic creditors sued Betsy, as was their right under the existing law. But Chickasaw tradition allowed married women the right to separate property, and on the basis that the Allens had married in a Chickasaw ceremony, the Mississippi Supreme Court ruled in 1837 that Betsy's possessions were indeed all her own. This historic ruling led to the passage in 1839 of the first state law in the country giving married women the right to free and separate estates. Sadly, Betsy had already died.

Tougaloo

Sarah Dickey Infirmary, Tougaloo College, was named for the founder of the Mount Hermon Female Seminary (1875), a boarding school for black girls, once located a few miles from here and familiarly called "the Dickey 'stute." "During the next five years," Sarah Dickey wrote, "with never more than one or two helpers, I did a great deal of teaching, about all of the preaching, managed everything, working a great deal with my own hands—in doors and out. . . . on every hand awaiting the failure. But failure never came." Despite threats from the Ku Klux Klan and depressing lack of funds, the school continued for twenty-eight years with an average annual attendance of about a hundred women every session, who graduated and went on to become the finest teachers in the state. (*See Clinton.*)

Vicksburg

"Caves were the fashion—the rage—over besieged Vicksburg. I sat at the mouth of the cave . . . watching the brilliant display of fireworks . . . as [the shells] exploded in the air, the burning matter and the balls fell like large, clear blue-and-amber stars, scattering hither and thither." So wrote Mary Ann Loughborough in *My Cave Life in Vicksburg, with Letters of Trial and Travel,* published in 1864, a year after the bitter forty-seven-day siege. Even though all noncombatants were ordered out of the city, Mary Ann and her small daughter stayed, living in the caves around town that were meant to save them from bombardments. Then, in July 1863, the news came. "It's all over! The white flag floats from our forts! Vicksburg has surrendered. . . . I felt a strange unrest, the quiet of the day was so unnatural. . . . After the surrender, the old gray-headed soldier, in passing on the hill near the cave, stopped, and touching his hat, said: 'It's a sad day this, madam; I little thought we'd come to it. . . . I hope you'll yet be happy, madam, after all the trouble you've seen.' To which I mentally responded, 'Amen.'" So far, only one cave has been identified as an authentic haven of Civil War days—the old Hough cave located on Lovers Lane in the vicinity of the city cemetery.

Civil War relief worker Annie Wittenmyer (see *Keokuk, Iowa*) entered the city on July 4, 1863 with General Grant's army when the Confederate defenders surrendered. She brought food to the famished soldiers and tended the sick and wounded, even at the risk of losing her own life—once by nearly drowning, countless times by shells fired inches away from her. General Grant complimented her this way: "No soldier on the firing line gave more heroic service than she rendered."

Washington

Site of Elizabeth Female College, Route 84. Only a crumbling wall of the original building remains, obscured from the road by trees, vines, and briers. But there are two historical markers across the street. One attests to the location of what claims to be "the first woman's college in America. Chartered on Feb. 17, 1819 to confer degrees on women." The college was named in honor of Elizabeth Roach, who donated the funds for the school. The second marker calls it the Elizabeth Female Academy, "the first girl's school in the United States to have legislative recognition of its authority to confer degrees." Edward Mayes, author of *History of Education in Mississippi,* refers to it as an academy and adds to the controversy and confusion by granting that the academy "achieved the dignity of a college in fact although not in name."

MISSOURI

Belton

Carry A. Nation Grave, Belton Cemetery, Cambridge Road. In June 1911, five months after her last temperance speech in *Eureka Springs, Arkansas,* the nation's Home Defender was buried next to her mother. When alcohol destroyed her first marriage, and her second never quite worked out, Carry Nation reasoned, "Had I married a man I could have loved, God could never have used me." Along with her hatchet-wielding forays against the nation's taprooms, she tried single-handedly to teach Americans that cigarette smoking was hazardous to the health. In the end she reflected, "I can see where I have made mistakes—many of them—but they were mistakes of the head and not the heart." In 1924 the WCTU marked her grave with the granite shaft echoing her own epitaph: "she hath done what she could."

Boonville

Site of Cooper's Fort, off County Route Z. A red granite marker spots the location of the largest and most important fort in the county during the War of 1812. Milly Cooper was its heroine. When the fort was attacked by Indians and badly in need of powder and lead, commanding officer Col. Branxton Cooper agreed to let his teen-age daughter, Mildred, try to slip past the armed circle. As she adjusted her saddle, her father asked, "Milly, is there anything else that you want?" "Only a spur, father," she replied. He gave it to her and ordered the wooden gate drawn open. Mildred spurred her horse on and sped past the surprised attackers, whose war whoops and rifle shots pierced the still air. Several hours later, Milly returned at the head of a rescue party.

Branson

Rose O'Neill Memorial, the Shepherd of the Hills Farm, Route 76. An entire room in this memorial museum exhibits the work of author and illustrator Rose O'Neill. Well known for her drawings and poems in such publications as *Puck, Life,* and *Collier's,* she endeared herself to millions of readers and earned $1.5 million with her 1909 creation of the pudgy little figures known as Kewpies (short for Cupids). The cherubic characters, with their chubby cheeks and perennially perky faces (modeled after her baby brother) were meant, she once wrote, to be "innocent, unsophisticated little souls perpetually amazed at their own exploits and discoveries." They were translated almost immediately from line drawings to salt-and-pepper shakers, buttons, and cutouts. They adorned stationery and soap, curtain fabric and birthday cards. And in 1913 they became Kewpie Dolls—first manufactured in Germany from bisque; then, in America, mass-produced in wood, celluloid, and plastic.

Each year, a loyal gathering of Rose O'Neill's followers hold a "Kewpiesta" in this area, a few miles south of the house at Bonniebrook where she first drew Kewpie and where she was buried in 1944. Festivities at a recent Kewpiesta included a visit to the Rose O'Neill Tea Room at the nearby School of the Ozarks and a trip to gardens frequented by Rose O'Neill, where the visitors were urged, "Please, don't dig up the flowers."

Canton

Site of Sarah T. Bolton Reese House, "Valley Home." The first palatial house built in Canton was constructed by Judge Addison Reese for his second bride, Sarah. The famed poet and author of "Paddle Your Own Canoe" (see *Indianapolis, Indiana*) presided over a sort of salon in this house, which a local historian told us was "the center of the 'cafe society' of that day in Canton." A colleague and poet friend of Sarah Bolton Reese, Missouri Belle Munday, purchased the house from her after the Reeses' marriage dissolved and Sarah returned to *Beech Grove, Indiana.* As Munday shared Sarah's belief in female education, she bequeathed $4,500 to Culver-Stockton College to aid a financially needy student.

Culver-Stockton College, originally founded in 1853 as Christian University, claims to be the first college west of the Mississippi to receive a charter as a coeducational institution. The name was changed in 1917 to honor Mary E. Culver, successful manager of her late husband's iron range company, and her business partner Robert Stockton. Each gave money for the construction of dormitories. Later, Mrs. Culver, who was intensely interested in equal education for the sexes, matched Stockton's gift of a new heating plant by funding a new gymnasium.

The first female graduate of the school, Alice Staples, class of 1870, bested her two male classmates in mathematics. The policy of coeducation was so successful that the class of 1887 contained only women.

Carthage

Site of Belle Starr House, Carthage Square. A stone in the sidewalk on the north side of the square locates the Shirley House, a hotel owned by the father of the girl who was born Myra Belle Shirley in 1848. When the tavern was burned along with the rest of Carthage during an October 1863 Civil War raid, the Shirleys moved to Texas. From there, and later at *Younger's Bend, Oklahoma,* Myra Belle became the infamous Belle Starr, reputed Bandit Queen of the Southwest.

Jasper County Courthouse, Carthage Square, was still under construction when Annie Baxter took office as county clerk. Elected in 1890 but barred from serving when officials argued that women could not hold office, she took the case to the state supreme court. There she won, ably dispatching the duties of county clerk from 1891 to 1895. Carthage history books—apparently overlooking the earlier accomplishment of Lydia Hasbrouck at *Middletown, New York*—proudly claim that Annie Baxter was the first woman in the country to hold elective office.

Columbia

Stephens College, East Broadway and College Avenue, was founded in 1833 as the Columbia Female Academy. Local parents wanted to provide an education for their daughters similar to that arranged for their two sons two years earlier. But they didn't want it entirely equal. Latin and Greek were studied only by the boys. The first preceptress of the academy was Lucy Wales, a local teacher who served until 1840.

Farmington

Site of First Sunday School, Masonic Cemetery, Henry Street. A marble shaft marks the place where Sarah Barton Murphy organized and taught a Methodist Sunday school at her log cabin when she came here in 1803. Hers was said to be the first Sunday school west of the Mississippi. Mrs. Murphy is buried a short distance from the site of the school.

Hannibal

Molly Brown Birthplace, Denkler Alley and Butler Street. The woman who would become renowned as the Unsinkable Molly Brown was born Margaret Tobin in this frame house in July 1867. The future society matron got her start as a waitress at the Park Hotel, where one of her customers, Samuel L. Clemens (Mark Twain), told her of the riches in the Rocky Mountains. Shortly afterwards, Molly Brown headed west and found her fortune in *Denver, Colorado.* As a girl here in Hannibal, Molly learned how to steer a boat on the Mississippi River, a skill that later earned her the "Unsinkable" part of her name when she rowed stranded passengers to safety on a lifeboat from the *Titanic.*

Becky Thatcher House, 211 Hill Street. This two-story frame house is where Laura Hawkins—the real-life model for Mark Twain's Becky Thatcher in *Tom Sawyer*—grew up. It serves as a restored museum and bookshop today. Laura Hawkins was Sam Clemens' boyhood sweetheart. Laura's bedroom, furnished with her towering four-poster bed, looks out on Sam's house across the street. In the book, Tom Sawyer first glimpses Becky in the garden—"a lovely little blue-eyed creature with yellow hair plaited into two long tails, white summer frock and embroidered pantalettes." In real life, when Sam dropped a brick on the finger of his little friend, he cried louder than Laura did.

Holden

Carry A. Nation House, across from the Community Building (private). The first time Dr. Charles Gloyd boldly kissed the girl he had been courting, twenty-one-year-old Carry Moore shrieked, "I am ruined!" Shortly afterward they were married, and they moved into this house. Her early reaction turned out to be prophetic. Gloyd was a habitual drunkard, and the young bride spent most of her days scurrying along the streets looking for him or unsuccessfully trying to keep saloon owners from serving him. Thus awakened to the evils of alcohol by the man she still deeply loved, Carry went home to her parents to have a baby. When Gloyd died of drink in 1868, a year after their marriage, Carry returned here and took teaching courses at nearby *Warrensburg.* She taught school in Holden for four years, until she met her next husband, minister and lawyer David Nation. Although that marriage was not much more successful, it kept her occupied in *Richmond, Texas,* and *Medicine Lodge, Kansas,* until she hit upon a less traditional outlet for her energies.

Kansas City

Pioneer Mother Statue, Penn Valley Park, Pershing Road and Main. You will not see any replicas of this hardy family decorating the trails across the country. Sculptor Alexander Phimister Procter had to agree to destroy the mold once it was cast. His patron, grain broker Howard Vanderslice, wanted to memorialize his mother and his mother-in-law. The statue was dedicated in 1927 and today faces a skyscraper.

Pioneer Mother statue

Union Cemetery, Twenty-eighth Street Terrace and Warwick Trafficway, contains a number of graves of the kind of women depicted by Alexander Procter's statue in Penn Valley Park

At age eleven, Elizabeth Sexton Ferguson served her country nobly, helping her mother mold bullets for the War of 1812.

Elizabeth Porter, an Irish immigrant, was captured by British-aligned Indians in Tennessee during the Revolution and forced to walk with them to their village near Niagara Falls. She was kept prisoner until the following spring, when she came west and settled on a farm here.

Patti Moore served the city as its first police matron and general welfare worker in the late nineteenth century.

Children's Mercy Hospital, Twenty-fourth at Gillham Road, was founded in 1897 by Dr. Alice Berry Graham and Dr. Katharine Berry Richardson, two widowed sisters. Their first patient was a six-year-old crippled girl they found crying on the street. When they cured her, they formed the Free Bed Fund Association for Crippled, Deformed and Ruptured Children, a pioneering effort to treat youngsters regardless of the families' ability to pay. Originally housed in small quarters and staffed by all women physicians (who were subject to the usual ridicule of an unenlightened public), the hospital soon outgrew its early homes. After her sister died in 1913, Dr. Richardson threw herself into a fund-raising drive that produced, in 1917, the three noted Georgian brick buildings at 1710 Independence Boulevard, the hospital's first permanent home. Today, that structure still stands as a reminder of two concerned sisters, although the hospital is now at this location in a thoroughly modern facility that continues its policy of free care. When surgeon Richardson died in 1933, a few days after performing an operation, the *Kansas City Star* wrote, "By doing what should have been done by the entire community, she was Kansas City's first citizen."

Lexington

Site of Elizabeth Aull Seminary, Highland Avenue. Two private residences on a bluff of the Missouri River once housed the school that opened here in 1860. Philanthropist Elizabeth Aull donated the seed money out of concern that educational opportunities for young women were meager and insufficient. The school functioned until 1903. In 1881 an overseer noted, "The health of the institution has been so good, that not a single death has occurred among the boarders or teachers during the 21 years of its existence."

Site of Central Female College, Central Park. An enormous columned building, whose porch stood where the park shelter is now located, once housed the Central Female College, founded in 1869. The curriculum was equal to that of any men's college,

and the philosophy was more progressive than that of many modern institutions. For instance: "Women professors of music, not men, will be teaching young women in this school. Women are as good teachers of music as men. Let us elevate the standard of female education and then, when a lady has attained to a broad and elegant mental culture, and asks for a position in which she may help those of her own sex that are aspiring to the same degree of culture, let us not turn her away and give this place to a man."

Madonna of the Trail Monument, Broadway and Second Street. The fourth in the series of twelve statues erected by the DAR was dedicated September 17, 1928. It stands at the head of Jack's Ferry Road which led to the Missouri River bank and the ferry landing, one of the gateways to the West. (See *Springfield, Ohio.*)

Mansfield

Laura Ingalls Wilder Home and Museum, "Rocky Ridge Farm," Route 60. Although, as poultry editor for some newspapers, she had written a few articles on how to raise Leghorn hens that lay more eggs, Laura Ingalls Wilder never thought of herself as an author. Instead, she worked with her husband on this farm and took pride in her daughter Rose's rising journalism career. One day Rose asked her to write down her childhood memories of the days when she crossed the prairies and settled in *De Smet, South Dakota.* With the subsequent publication of *Little House in the Big Woods* (1932), the story of Laura's birthplace in *Pepin, Wisconsin,* Laura suddenly found herself a famous writer at age sixty-five. Six more books about those pioneer days quickly followed. All were written right here, on lined "fifty-fifty" school tablets that cost a nickel apiece. She published her last book, *These Happy Golden Years,* when she was seventy-six. She died in 1957, three days after her ninetieth birthday. This house, where she spent more than sixty years of her life, is a favorite visiting place for some of the millions of children who have enjoyed her "Little House" books.

Maryville

Mary J. Graham House, 422 South Buchanan Street (private). The first white woman to live within the city limits of the new town—established here in 1848—built this house twenty years later when her husband, Amos, died. In view of the fact that he served as the first county clerk, the first circuit clerk, the first probate clerk, and the first postmaster, and as he built the first log cabin and bought the first lot, it was not surprising that the townspeople chose to name their new settlement after his wife.

Princeton

Site of Calamity Jane Birthplace, near Ollen Owen Corner, Route 36. A small steel plate in the ground marks the site of the log cabin where Martha Jane Cannary was born in May 1848. She grew up to be the legendary Calamity Jane, "Scout of the West, comrade of Wild Bill Hickok, heroine of many thrilling adventures," according to the signboard. Local historians told us that little girls from respectable families were warned not to play with the Cannary girl because "she swore and wasn't nice." So young Martha Jane ignored the sissy girls and joined the boys' games, where she learned how to swim and ride better than any of them. "As a child I always had a fondness for adventure and local exercise," wrote Calamity in her diary. "In fact, the greater portion of my life in those early times was spent in this manner." So was the rest of her life, throughout Wyoming, Montana, and even until her death in *Deadwood, South Dakota.*

St. Charles

Lindenwood College, Kingshighway at First Capitol Drive. Tradition has wrapped a musical shroud around Mary Easton Sibley, cofounder (with her husband) of this pioneering school for women in 1827. Every Halloween, we learned, the ghost of the concerned educator slips away from her tomb in the peaceful cemetery on the college grounds, and, garbed in a sheet, climbs the hill to the chapel in Sibley Hall. There the ghost of Mary Sibley relives her earthly pastime by playing the pipe organ. Her real-life story was no less determined. As a fifteen-year-old newlywed, she traveled by keelboat to nearby Fort Osage with her groom, as well as with the first piano to be transported west of the Missouri River. The first classes for the school were held in their home on the present campus.

The Mother-in-Law House, 500 South Main Street, was built in 1860 by a rich millowner to keep his wife from being homesick for her mother. But his filial devotion stopped at the front door, where he gave his mother-in-law a key and strongly suggested she stay on her own side of the double house. Today the house is a popular restaurant. Reservations are advisable.

St. James

Old City Hall is now a tourist information center, but St. Jamesians are planning a bicentennial restoration that would cheer the spirits of Mayme H. Ousley, Missouri's first female mayor. Elected in 1921 at age thirty-four, Mayor Ousley announced that her first official act would be to clean up City Hall. "The place is dirty just the way city buildings are when men run them," she told a newspaper reporter. "The first thing that will go will be cuspidors." Mayor Ousley won her office by eight votes, after a grueling campaign that took her into every house in St. James. "We certainly had a hot fight," she reported. "Many of the men were opposed to the idea of a woman holding office, especially that of Mayor." They changed their minds sufficiently to reelect "Granny" Ousley three times. A close friend of hers told us that the colorful, dynamic Mayme Ousley was about five feet four inches tall, with a pink and white complexion, and that she was a striking blonde until the day of her death at eighty-four.

St. Joseph

Site of Owen Sisters Homestead, northwest corner of Ninth and Jules Streets. Three remarkable scientist sisters grew up and spent most of their lives in the two-story frame building their father built in 1859. Mary Alicia Owen, the firstborn, was an authority on Indian folklore. Her studies of the Indian holdings around St. Joseph—"the Land of the Road to Paradise"—included fascinating descriptions of the tribal ceremonies on the Court House Hill that once echoed to the sound of sacred drumbeats. The Sac and Fox Indians so respected her work that they granted her tribal membership in 1892 and allowed her to observe their secret societies.

The second sister, Luella Owen, became a renowned geologist, whose studies of the loess soil comprising St. Joseph's hills also made her the only female geologist recognized by the Imperial Chinese government. (Loess soil exists in abundance in the upper reaches of China's Yellow River.) Although Luella spent much of her scientific time in this house, she also traveled the globe (without a passport, as an honored member of the American Geographic Society). A fearless cave explorer, Luella was the only female member of the French Société de Spéléologie. She was also a respected artist, whose motto, "Take the thing that liest nearest thee; shape from that thy work of art," led her to paint some lovely watercolors of her sisters and of herself.

Juliette Owen, the youngest sister, was an ornithologist and botanist who, like Luella, was listed in *American Men of Sci-*

ence. She also painted, completing more than a hundred watercolors of birds and flowers before she died in 1943 in the same room of the old house where she was born. With all the sisters gone, the family homestead was razed in the 1940s to make room for a car sales lot. Today it is a church parking lot.

Juliette Owen

Mary Alicia Owen

Luella Owen

St. Louis

A widow known as Sarah McWilliams was working here as a washerwoman from 1887–1905, supporting herself and her daughter, when she dreamed the hairdressing techniques that would soon make her a fortune. With ingredients she developed in her laundry basins, the future Madame C. J. Walker devised a system of pomade, shampoo, brushing, and heated iron combs that brought shine and smoothness to black women's hair. (See *Delta, Louisiana; Indianapolis, Indiana.*)

Des Peres School Building, 6397 South Michigan Avenue. When this building was a school in 1873, educator Susan Blow founded the first free kindergarten in the state in Room 4. Although a bronze plaque just inside claims that it was the first in North America, official U.S. precedent is given to a kindergarten in *Watertown, Wisconsin.* Still, Blow's pioneering work as an educator (for which she received no pay) did help spread the kindergarten movement all over the United States. The St. Louis model influenced similar classrooms, and Susan Blow's training school prepared the teachers. Today, the old brick building is a supermarket, but blackboards still cover the walls of one old classroom, and Susan Blow's portrait, surrounded by the faces of children, is captioned with her motto, "Let us live for the children."

The Principia, 13201 Clayton Road. This school was founded in 1898 by Mary Kimball Morgan, a Christian Scientist who, owing to the new religion, enjoyed a return to good health after illness had prevented her from attending college in the East. Mrs. Morgan conducted the first classes for her own two sons in 1897 in her three-story brick house. Within a year, she moved to larger quarters and enrolled fifteen pupils. The modest announcement of the venture informed parents, "It will be the aim of the school to teach its pupils how to study, rather than to present numberless things to be studied." Today the school is privately financed and run by Christian Scientists to further the cause of Christian Science. Preschool through twelfth-grade students study at this campus in the suburbs; a four-year college is located at *Elsah, Illinois.*

Old Courthouse, 11 North Fourth Street. The museum in this historic building where the Dred Scott case was tried neglects to display any exhibits of another significant case heard here—that of Virginia Louisa Minor. The suffrage leader and Civil War relief worker charged that her civil rights were violated when a St. Louis registrar refused to allow her to register to vote in the November 1872 election. Along with her lawyer husband, Francis, a staunch supporter of women's rights, Virginia Minor filed a suit, maintaining that the Fourteenth Amendment to the Constitution did not prohibit her from voting. The court found otherwise and was upheld by the U.S. Supreme Court in 1874. Minor's noble effort was part of the nationwide attack on the ballot box that received its most serious setback at *Canandaigua, New York.* When Virginia Minor died in 1894, she was buried in Bellefontaine Cemetery without benefit of clergy, who, she said, had opposed the cause to which she had devoted all her living days.

BELLEFONTAINE CEMETERY, 4947 West Florissant Avenue
Phoebe Wilson Couzins Grave, Vista Avenue, is inscribed with her achievement: "First Missouri Woman Law Graduate 1871." The young suffragist took her law degree from Washington University in St. Louis and was admitted to the bar soon after. Although she never practiced (or if so, only briefly), she was the nation's first female federal marshal, a post she held for two months, succeeding her father when he died in 1887. Phoebe Wilson Couzins was buried here in 1913 with a marshal's star pinned to her chest.
Sara Teasdale Grave, Memorial Avenue, also proclaims her life's work. "American Poet" is etched on the stone, a simple memorial to the woman whose lyric verses ended when she took her own life in 1933.
Kate Brewington Bennett Grave, an ornate Gothic canopy, is probably one of the most instructive burial places for the nation's women. We quote from the story prepared from the cemetery files: "Mrs. Bennett died suddenly in 1855 at the age of thirty-seven, and at the time was regarded as the most beautiful woman in St. Louis, mainly because of her very white complexion. She had been taking small doses of arsenic in order to retain her envied paleness, evidently not knowing that arsenic is a cumulative poison rather than one that is gradually absorbed by the system." The memorial, in exquisite irony, is of pure white marble.

Statue of Beatrice Cenci, St. Louis Mercantile Library, 510 Locust Street. This life-sized figure of a robed woman in repose was presented by sculptor Harriet Hosmer in 1856, probably, as we were told by library officials, the gift of Wayman Crow. Crow had been Hosmer's benefactor when, as a young artist from *Watertown, Massachusetts,* she was forbidden because of her sex to study anatomy anywhere in the East. Crow secured her admission to the anatomical classes at Missouri Medical College and, with the "liberal hand" later acknowledged by Hosmer, helped support her studies in Rome.

Warrensburg

A highway marker on Old Route 50 includes among the names of the town's outstanding citizens, "Carry Moore Nation—1846–1911." The budding temperance worker attended the State Normal School here in 1872 (now Central Missouri State University), while living in nearby *Holden.* She took up teaching in 1874 because her first husband had died a drunk in 1868 and left her penniless. There are probably people in *Medicine Lodge, Kansas,* who would have preferred that Carry Nation had stuck to her teaching.

MONTANA

Armstead

Site of Camp Fortunate, Route 91. In August 1805, Sacajawea was picking serviceberries in the high, dew-covered grass when suddenly she saw some Indians riding toward her. According to William Clark, his brave scout "danced for the joyful sight, and she made signs to me that they were her nation." Sacajawea ran to embrace her brother, Cameahwait, whom she had not seen since she had been captured by the Hidatsa tribe as a child (see *Three Forks*). Through Sacajawea's intercession, Lewis and Clark were able to obtain more horses for their historic westward journey.

Bannack

Site of Lucia Darling's School. "The view was not an inspiring one," wrote Montana's first schoolteacher in 1863 when she saw the mining town's most prominent landmark—the gallows. The territory's first capital, "Bannack was tumultuous and rough . . . lawlessness and misrule seemed the prevailing spirit. But many worthy people were anxious to have their children in school. I was requested to take charge." In October, twenty-four-year-old Lucia began teaching twenty children in a small room in the house of her uncle, Governor Sidney Edgerton, where a fence now surrounds a weedy field. The following year, a small mud-covered schoolhouse was built and furnished with wooden benches and improvised desks made from boxes. Through the windows the children could watch the shoot-outs on the streets and the hangings on the hill. "Bannack," a little boy once remarked, "is a humbug." Today, it is a tourist ghost town.

Billings

Western Heritage Center, Twenty-ninth and Montana. Among the western artifacts and relics in this museum are some of Calamity Jane's favorite things—a pin jar, pearl-handled knives, pewter cream-and-sugar holders, and her infamous diary. The battered and frayed leather book, dedicated to her daughter, was compiled between 1877 and 1903 by the legendary scout and hell-raiser (see *Princeton, Missouri*). In her bold scrawl, Calamity insists she had been legally married to her great love, Wild Bill Hickok (see *Deadwood, South Dakota*). "I am not as black as I am painted," she protests. The diary has generally been discredited, like many of Calamity's claimed exploits. The center's director told us that in his opinion, she "in no way deserves the attention being paid her. Most of her popularity is due to the romantic fiction of the late nineteenth century and not to any greatness in her own right."

Emily Sloan Home, Beta House, 2908 First Avenue. Montana's first female county attorney, admitted to the bar in 1919, lived in this rooming house and practiced in several other buildings in town. In addition to being active in politics, Sloan was a well-acclaimed poet whose finely written ballads earned her the title of official Poet of the Plains.

Black Eagle

Collins School, originally the Hawthorn School, was renamed to honor Fannie B. Collins who served as its principal for thirty-three years before her death in 1950. Aside from one male superintendent, she is the only educator so honored in the city.

Bozeman

Dr. Caroline McGill Home, 320 Ranch, Gallatin Canyon (private). Dr. McGill, the state's first trained pathologist, got her medical degree from Johns Hopkins in 1914, but her practical training in Butte, then the toughest mining camp in the West. Daily she was called to treat victims of stabbings, shoot-outs, and frequent underground mine explosions. She bought this ranch in 1936 and invited her patients here, in the beautiful Land of the Big Sky, to rest and recuperate. After her retirement in her seventies, McGill added to her exquisite collection of valuable antiques which she donated to the Montana State University as the start of their Museum of the Rockies.

Cascade

Mary Fields, in her jaunty cap, a billowing white apron over her generous 200-pound figure, and a large cigar in her mouth, drove the horses through town to collect the mail for the Ursuline School at St. Peter's Mission about twenty miles away. She met every train for eight years, and, if the wagons couldn't get through because of floods or breakdowns, Mary walked. Finally worn out from the rough roads, Mary retired to the northwest part of town (where wild fields have replaced her little shack) and tried to run a restaurant. But tender-hearted "Black Mary" could never turn away a hungry visitor, and eventually she went broke. Dr. R. C. Bellingham, who knew Mary a few years before her death in 1914, told us that the first few times he saw Mary on the street he always said hello, until she finally stopped him and demanded, "Who the hell are you, anyway?" "So I told her, and we were always friendly after that," Dr. Bellingham recalled. "She could drink more whiskey than anyone I ever knew, but if everyone was like Mary in many respects, it would be a better world. She really was a queen."

Custer

Site of Calamity Jane Visit, Route 10. An historical highway marker notes that once Calamity Jane stopped in this "lurid" frontier town to "whoop things up," which usually meant she was up to her old tricks—such as firing her guns at the saloon floor to make the tenderfeet dance.

Ekalaka

This small frontier town, population about 670, was named for the Oglala Sioux girl, who had such charm and power that she inspired David Russell to stay in town and become its first white settler after he married her.

Gilt Edge

One day in 1897, Calamity Jane, oddly attired in a skirt and lacy blouse, sauntered into a saloon here and asked for a drink. "We don't serve ladies," snarled the bartender. "I'm no lady," Calamity is said to have replied. She was promptly served. In the bright afternoon sunshine, her cocktail in her hand, she joined her buddies outside.

When she was not kneading bread, fixing the windmill, threshing the wheat fields, cleaning up the chicken house, or feeding the horses on her ranch near this old mining town, Lillian Weston Hazen would sneak away to write some poems and magazine articles. Massachusetts born, Sorbonne educated, believing that "no honorable profession should be called unwomanly," Hazen, then living in New York, became a writer for the *New York Sunday Herald* in 1888. She soon learned the restrictions placed on her sex. When the Wild West Show came to town, she longed to accept an invitation to ride on the Deadwood Stage, "but being a girl, it would not have been proper for me so I had to sit quietly and watch a man mount the box seat, the place I desired to occupy myself." With visions of that stagecoach seat before her eyes, she eagerly joined her husband for the gold search in Gilt Edge at the turn of the century. She fell in love with the mountains, the fields, and the sunsets. "A sense of unutterable ineffable peace takes possession of me until I happen to glance toward a seventy acre field where grain is waiting to be shocked." Determined to keep up with her writing career, she quickly learned that "country life did not flow on as peacefully and uninterruptedly as I had supposed. Between housework, care of the fowl, four-footed pets and other duties, it took me several days to write even a short story. . . . But the last straw was when my son told me that our hired hand had said that I did the least of any rancher's wife he saw." Hazen's granddaughter, who has written about her life, said there were times in the years before her death in 1949 when Hazen felt her life was unfulfilled. As she wrote in one of her last poems,

> Shorter and shorter grow the hours
> Of work for me . . .
> Blighted are all my youthful dreams
> By Misery . . .

Grass Range

Methodist Church. Belle Carter Harman, who built the original chapel here in the 1920s, was the first woman in the world to be ordained a deacon (1924) and an elder (1926) of the Methodist Episcopal Church. She served as its first resident minister. In her old Ford or on horseback, every Sunday she traveled almost one hundred miles to preach sermons in three churches and nine schoolhouses, where she supervised Sunday-school sessions as the ministry's "first woman circuit rider."

Harlowtown

The Crazy Mountains, Route 12. Legends say that a female emigrant, overcome and enraged by the chores of the wagon train, escaped from the party and was later found, depressed and incoherent, near the mountains visible to the southwest—thus named the Crazy Woman Mountains. The name has been desexed over the years.

Helena

Ella Knowles Office, Masonic Temple, Broadway Street. Ella Knowles came to Montana for a health cure, and, after instigating the passage of a law permitting women to practice law, she became the state's first female lawyer and practiced in this building in 1889. Described as a modest woman "with blue eyes set deep under a fine, full brow indicating rare reasoning power," Knowles was a brilliant orator, hailed as the Portia of the People's Party when she was nominated by the Populists to run for attorney general in 1892. She lost, but she had polled so many votes that the winner named her assistant attorney general and later asked her to marry him. She did not interrupt her career when she married the boss, and later she took on more duties as the president of the Montana Suffrage Association.

Site of Suffrage Convention, Grand Army Republic Hall, 16 North Park. Emma Smith DeVoe, suffrage circuit rider from *Huron, South Dakota,* spent several months preparing the way for the convention that took place here in 1895. The entire area has subsequently been razed. Traveling by "rail, stage, wagon and buckboard through storm and mountain cold," Emma organized suffrage clubs all over the state, using such persuasive arguments that newspapers hailed her as "talented, brilliant and logical." But the suffrage struggle, despite Emma's creditable efforts, would last another twenty-five years. Two months before that fateful election in 1914, suffrage leaders met again. Dressed in the suffrage color, yellow, hundreds of women marched through the streets led by Dr. Anna Howard Shaw (see *Ashton, Michigan*), Jeannette Rankin (see *Missoula*), and an Indian woman representing Sacajawea as "Montana's first suffragist." On November 14, by a vote of 41,302 to 37,588, women won the right to vote.

Blue Stone House, South Warren. Perched on a knobby hill overlooking the town stands a quaint structure; built in 1889 as a husband's wedding present, some say it soon became one of the most popular brothels in town. "There is no documentation to prove that the house was one of ill-repute," the Montana Historical Society told us. But, they added, they had discussed the matter with an eighty-five-year-old Helena resident who remembered delivering papers to the building. "He insists that it was indeed a house of 'assignation,' but not too successful a location as the customers objected to the climb necessary to reach the house."

Site of Chicago Joe's Coliseum, South Main Street. For more than a quarter of a century, Josephine Hensley reigned as queen of Helena's underworld. Dance halls, called "hurdy-gurdy" houses for the hand organs that provided the music, were usually run by men in those days, but the spunky twenty-three-year-old Irish woman, who came to Helena in 1867, soon had one of the finest places in town. Nicknamed Chicago Joe because she imported all her fine-looking "hurdy girls" from her hometown, she was arrested in 1886 and charged with unlawfully operating a hurdy-gurdy house—which the prosecution defined as "establishments wherein men's souls are lured to the shores of sin by the combined influences of wine, women and dance." Her defense was cleverly based on the fact that the music in her establishment was provided by a piano, a violin, and a cornet and was, therefore, not a "hurdy-gurdy" house. She was acquitted. Within a year, Joe opened up the Coliseum, a variety theater with private velvet-curtained boxes where the miners could entertain their hurdy girls, now known as box girls. Joe spent most of her considerable fortune to educate two younger sisters in Chicago who mercifully never asked her what a hurdy-gurdy house was.

La Hood

Sacajawea, Lewis and Clark Expedition Campsite, Route 10. On August 1, 1805, about two hundred yards west of the historical marker here, Sacajawea and the two explorers camped. A week later and farther along, she assured the men that they would soon find her tribe, which they did in *Armstead.*

Livingston

Bozeman Pass Memorial, Route 10. Heading home after their successful trip to the Pacific, William Clark could have gone from Three Forks to the Yellowstone Valley by three different routes. But on July 15, 1806, he turned to his faithful guide Sacajawea and asked her to recommend the best trail. She decisively selected the Bozeman Pass, the most direct route. Later Clark was to write in his journal, "The Indian woman. . . . has been of great service to me as a pilot through this country." Nearby, there is a small recreation park named in honor of Sacajawea.

Loma

Marias River. When Meriwether Lewis saw the "noble river . . . its border garnished with one continued garden of roses," he named it Maria's River for his "lovely fair one," Maria Wood, a beloved cousin who later declined his proposal of marriage. Some time after Lewis lost his sweetheart, the river lost its apostrophe.

Missoula

Site of Jeannette Rankin House, 134 Madison Street. The nation's first congresswoman, its most celebrated pacifist and feminist, grew up in a red brick house that was crowned with a square cupola, built in the 1880s on the same site where Meriwether Lewis camped on his return trip in 1806. A gas station stands here today. Rankin, the eldest of six children, lived at home through her college years, drifting aimlessly in search of a cause and a career. After attending inspiring meetings with such suffrage leaders as Emma Smith DeVoe and Abigail Scott Duniway in Washington State in 1910, Rankin returned home with her lifework ahead of her. "If she could talk personally to every voter in the state, there would be no doubt of suffrage carrying, so great is her charm and so convincing her aruguments," one voter remarked after her lecture. Suffrage did carry in 1914 and, two years later, Rankin was triumphantly elected to Congress where her solitary vote against the war (World War I) stunned the nation. Years later, remembering that historic moment, Rankin said, "I felt at the time that the first woman [in Congress] should take the first stand, that the first time the first woman had a chance to say no to war she should say it." Rankin said no again to World War II in 1941 and again to Vietnam when at age eighty-eight in 1968 she led the Jeannette Rankin Brigade on the march to the Capitol. As the "world's outstanding living feminist," Rankin was made the first member of the Susan B. Anthony Hall of Fame in 1971. She predicted a liberated world "once people get the idea that women are human beings. And that will come when women behave like human beings and stop submitting to everything and everyone." (See *Watkinsville, Georgia.*)

Nevada City

Kate Dunlap's School. Kate Dunlap crossed the plains with her parents in 1863, recording in her diary the details of their hazardous trip. On the sabbath, the horses rested, but "for the women it was wash day, cooking day, and general regulation day." It was the sabbath day times seven when Kate arrived in this busy mining town and soon began teaching school. Her tiny one-room schoolhouse has been restored along with the other neat wooden houses of this tourist ghost town. The sign by the door of the school states that Kate was the first teacher in Montana Territory; that honor accurately belongs to Lucia Darling in *Bannack.* The two started classes within weeks of each other.

Terry

Evelyn J. Cameron, an English Lady, spent more than twenty years on ranches here photographing and writing about her favorite subject, the cowgirl, who, she explained in 1914 to readers of *Country Life* magazine in London, was not a dairymaid but "the feminine counterpart of the cowboy, efficiently performing the same duties." Cameron claimed she had been given credit for dooming the sidesaddle to ancient history and introducing the culotte riding skirt, a hundred-dollar "California riding costume" that she ordered from Chicago in the 1880s. "Although my costume was so full as to look like an ordinary walking skirt when the wearer was on foot, it created a small sensation. So great at first was the prejudice against any divided garment in Montana that a warning was given me

to abstain from riding on the streets of Miles City lest I might be arrested!" The comfortable culottes were soon seen all over Montana, with Dakota quickly following at the initiative of the Marquise de Mores in *Medora, North Dakota.* Cameron took hundreds of photographs of the new prairie fashions worn by her favorite working models, May, Mabel, and Myrtle Buckley.

Three Forks

Site of Sacajawea's Kidnapping, Missouri Headwaters State Monument. As they neared the land of the Shoshoni in July 1805, Sacajawea showed Lewis and Clark the shoal place midriver where as a child she had been captured by the Hidatsa. "She does not show any distress at these recollections or any joy at the prospect of being restored to her country," wrote Lewis in his diary, underestimating with a white man's insensitivity his faithful guide's capacity for sentiment. (See *Armstead.*)

Sacajawea Memorial. Across the street from the Sacajawea Hotel, in a small triangular park spotted by three fir trees, a large boulder was dedicated in 1914 "In patriotic memory of Sacajawea . . . who in acting as guide across the Rocky Mountains made it possible for the Lewis and Clark expedition to succeed."

Townsend

The Courthouse, where Alice Crittenden served in the 1920s as Montana's first female county clerk, has been moved out of town and is now a private home. Crittenden, a Minnesota schoolteacher, was on her way to adventure in Alaska when she stopped in Townsend to visit a friend and stayed for the rest of her life. While serving as county clerk, she was praised for her "exactness, capability and faithfulness to duty" and was reelected more than six times. Only twice did any man even try to run against her.

NEBRASKA

Bancroft

Grave of Susette La Flesche Tibbles, Bancroft Cemetery. The stone marking the grave of the dedicated Omaha reformer and lecturer bears a carved bow and arrow and the English translation of her Indian name, "Bright Eyes." Susette La Flesche made a drawing of the unstrung bow and arrow to illustrate Fannie Reed Giffen's book *Oo-mah-Ha Ta-Wa-Tha (Omaha City)* in 1898, becoming the first American Indian to illustrate a book. She attracted the nation's attention as Bright Eyes in 1879, when she accompanied newspaperman Thomas Henry Tibbles on a lecture tour to publicize the wrongs committed against the Ponca Indians and their chief, Standing Bear. Helen Hunt Jackson (see *Colorado Springs, Colorado*) and Alice Cunningham Fletcher were among the listeners immediately won over to the Indian cause. The lectures also resulted in passage of the Dawes Act, at the time considered a highly progressive step in gaining Indian rights. After marrying Tibbles, Bright Eyes continued to lecture and write, returning here to live on land granted her as a member of the Omaha tribe in 1902. She died in 1903 and was buried on the reservation where she had grown up.

Beatrice

Agnes Freeman Grave, Homestead National Monument. On this grassy elevation overlooking the site of the nation's first homestead, the monument to frontier settler Agnes Suiter Freeman (1843–1931) reads, "A True Pioneer Mother." Together with her husband Daniel, also buried here, Agnes Freeman lived in the first log cabin to be built on land opened by the Homestead Act in 1863. The site of that crude one-room house, originally the only settlement for miles, is visible from the grave site. In that house, Agnes baked biscuits, raised six children, and made friends with neighboring Otoe Indians, learning enough about medicine from her doctor-sheriff-farmer husband to get her own state license as a physician. Never one of the "exploitive leeches," as she called helpless women, Agnes Freeman termed herself "cantankerous" and proudly continued to hitch her own harness and drive her own buggy. When a niece came to visit her more than a decade after they'd homesteaded, asking how her aunt had stood the loneliness that opened the West to millions, Agnes answered, in true pioneer understatement, "It wasn't easy at first, but now it's my home."

Chautauqua Park. One member of the Chautauqua board of directors instrumental in creating this lovely city park was Clara Bewick Colby, who settled here a decade after Agnes Freeman. A devoted worker for woman's rights, in 1883 Colby founded the newspaper, the *Woman's Tribune,* which became the official organ of the national suffrage movement. She also brought leaders of the movement to the new state to speak, one of whom, Elizabeth Cady Stanton, remarked in awe that Clara Colby could "get up a meeting, arrange the platform . . . and introduce a speaker with as much skill and grace as she can spread a table with dainty china and appetizing food, and enliven a dinner with witty and earnest conversation." At one state suffrage convention Colby delivered "a masterly constitutional argument," according to a newspaper reporter, "which demonstrated that women can argue logically."

Crawford

Fort Robinson State Park includes Old Fort Robinson, heart of the U.S. Army forays against the Sioux and the Cheyenne. Regional historian and naturalist Mari Sandoz (see *Gordon*) wrote eloquently about this land and its people in more than a dozen books. One of the best known, *Cheyenne Autumn,* recreates the January 1879 Cheyenne outbreak that resulted in the death of Dull Knife: "At Robinson it was truly the iron hard winter that comes after the swift storms of the Cheyenne autumn. . . . It was a clear, cold night, the moon so large and shining on the snow that it seemed one could see to the horizon. . . . Dull Knife's people were preparing to flee, this time to fight their way through the log walls of a prison house and the soldiers and the winter cold." Here too, Crazy Horse was killed in 1877, the Oglala Sioux chief whom Sandoz profiled, saying, "I have tried to tell not only the story of the man but something of the life of his people through that crucial time."

Elmwood

Bess Streeter Aldrich House (private). In 1909 the Iowa-born writer moved to this two-story red brick house from *Cedar Falls, Iowa,* and embarked on her career, writing her first prizewinning short story in 1911 "while the baby was having her nap."

She wrote novels and stories of the still-present frontier spirit she observed around her. She was inducted into the Nebraska Hall of Fame in 1973, nearly two decades after her death. The resolution proclaiming her membership said that she so "authentically portrayed the life of the settlers who founded the great state of Nebraska and so ably interpreted their characteristics that all are filled with admiration of the pioneers, and are inspired." A marker has been placed in the park across the street here, and her bust now stands in the Capitol at *Lincoln*.

Gordon

Mari Sandoz Grave, off Route 27, lies on a grassy slope overlooking the sandhills region that she brought to life in her writings. Born here in 1896, Sandoz first gained attention with *Old Jules* (1935), the story of her settler father who successfully farmed these frontier hills and grew fruit on them before anyone else. His cabin, immortalized in the book along with the lives of other nineteenth-century homesteaders, still stands in the eastern cluster of ranch buildings here. The Mari Sandoz Heritage Fund, based at nearby Chadron State College, sponsors a tour of her country every other year. Along the roads traveled by Old Jules and his daughters, past Snake Bite Valley and a sod house where Mari boarded, you finally reach Sandoz River Place, which she once described in her foreword to *Love Song to the Plains:* "When I was seven or eight I liked to climb to the top of Indian Hill overlooking miles of the river and beyond, to where I hoped to see far places in the shimmering mirages, perhaps even Laramie Peak, as old-timers promised. The gravel under my bare feet was black from Indian signal fires, and just below me was the place where our father had led a vigilante gang that hanged a man and let him down alive."

Mari Sandoz Museum, Route 27, north of the turnoff for the grave, was built by Mari's sister, Caroline Pifer, who describes it as "mostly a wayside stop on a stretch of fifty-six miles of otherwise deserted road." The modest building houses Mari's apartment just as it was furnished in Greenwich Village, New York, where she wrote her chronicles of the American West. Caroline Pifer encourages visitors to peek in through the windows when the museum is not open. And be sure, she insists, to "have a drink of pure sandhills water from the windmill." While you do, remember that Mari Sandoz's approach to all her books—whether about her father or about the Indians around *Crawford*—began with her surroundings but expanded to encompass the world. She once wrote, "Through the discovery of this one region, this one drop of water, I hope to discover something of the nature of the ocean."

Grand Island

Grace Abbott House, 705 West First (private). In this handsome old wooden house built by their father, social worker Grace

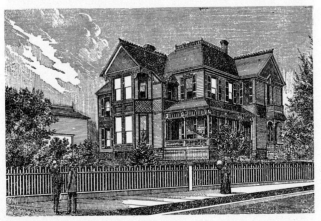

Abbott and her sister, educator Edith Abbott, grew up during the late nineteenth century. Grace was early attracted to reform causes. After her residence at Jane Addams' Hull House in *Chicago, Illinois,* she did valuable work in immigration and children's welfare. She once said that she only left her hometown for career reasons, telling an Omaha reporter, "I was always happy in Nebraska but there isn't much opportunity for a girl in a small city. . . . A boy can come home from college, begin the practice of his profession, and advance rapidly in his home town. But when a girl comes back, what can she do? She can teach, but after she's done that she finds that she has reached the top, that there is nothing more for her." Grace Abbott reached the top in Washington, D.C., heading the Federal Children's Bureau from 1921–34. She is also credited with breaking ground for women who chose to be involved in public affairs. The sisters were reunited in 1934 when Grace taught at the University of Chicago School of Social Service Administration, where Edith served as dean. They are also buried together in the family plot in Grand Island.

Although this house is not yet a registered landmark, there is no lack of memorials to these women. A Liberty ship, a children's hospital, and a park in Grand Island are named for Grace Abbott. And the Edith Abbott Memorial Library on West Second Street was dedicated in 1974, a fitting tribute to the woman whose mother founded the first library in Grand Island with money left over from the Suffrage Society Treasury.

Hastings

Flora Hamilton Cassel Grave, Parkview Cemetery. A white-enameled cast-iron ribbon, tied in a bow, the letters WCTU engraved on its ends, was erected in 1911 to mark the grave of Nebraska's most famous temperance worker and musician. The simple monument represents the white ribbon she and other Prohibitionists wore after signing the pledge to abstain forever from alcohol. Flora H. Cassel was so devoted to eliminating demon rum that she wrote hundreds of hymns and songs on temperance themes. Many of her original lyrics and music appeared in *White Ribbon Variations,* a collection of anti-whiskey songs she published in 1890. She wrote in the introduction: "We trust that the vibrant chords of this little volume may sound in many homes, bringing to every heart cheer, courage and hope." Sample lyrics from "The Curse," designed to cheer:

> See the fatal wine-glass lifted
> For the gay young man's first drink,
> May he pause while he sees a vision
> Of the gulf where the drunkards sink.
>
> See the husband homeward reeling
> To his sad-eyed weeping wife
> Hear the blows and curses falling
> And the moan as she parts from life.

Today, the white ribbon has blackened with age, but a stone marker identifies the grave as Flora Cassel's. She died in Colorado, when a team of runaway horses dragged her across the prairie. Her body was brought back to Hastings for burial, where, at the Baptist Church, they sang two hymns she had written—"The King's Business" and "Loyalty to Christ." They did not sing the hymn found on page 59 of *White Ribbon Variations:* "Hold Your Hosses."

Auditorium Park, Fourth and Denver Avenue, was saved for pastoral purposes, and spared the indignity of a utilities building cluttering the site, by Awana Slaker James, a public-spirited clubwoman who also wrote *The Main Motion,* an important handbook on parliamentary law. She led the fight to keep a water and light building off the parkland in 1924. First she filed an injunction restraining the city, then she went to the state supreme court to uphold it.

Kenesaw

Grave of Susan Hail, alongside the old Oregon Trail, recalls the thousands of unfortunate victims of that rugged route more than a century ago. As many as twenty-five pioneers died along each mile. Susan Hail's grave is one of the few that is marked. The marble stone on the "Lone Grave" was recently installed to replace both the original and a successor, chipped away by souvenir-hunters. It notes that Mrs. Susan O. Hail of Lafayette County, Missouri, died on June 2, 1852, "Aged 34 years 5 months and 12 days." In the impromptu style of the era, her husband is said to have buried her in a coffin made of wagon lumber; then he returned with a marble headstone to immortalize her.

Lincoln

Pioneer Woman Monument, Antelope Park, by Ellis Burman (1935), depicts a refreshingly nonidealized homesteader, her hair swept back, her sunbonnet in hand. No small children crowd near her protective skirts, perhaps an indication that this unconventional woman has decided to contribute something other than offspring to the new frontier.

Bess Streeter Aldrich House, 1000 South Fifty-Second Street (private). The celebrated author of *A Lantern in Her Hand,* and other re-creations of her *Elmwood* life, built this rambling colonial-style house in 1946, so she could be near her daughter. She spent her time doing needlework and continuing to write at a kidney-shaped desk in the upstairs bedroom. As was her usual routine, she did first drafts in longhand, second drafts on the typewriter. This was her home until she died in 1954.

Nebraska Hall of Fame, State Capitol, contains only two female members, both authors.

Bess Streeter Aldrich composed and set her novels in *Elmwood* and in *Cedar Falls, Iowa.* The plaque on her statue recalls that she "gave literary life to Nebraska pioneer memories, honored the trials and dreams of the settlers that all may realize and cherish their heritage."

Willa Cather grew up in *Red Cloud* and wrote of the countryside farmed by sturdy immigrants. "My deepest feelings were rooted in this country," she later explained. "I had searched for books telling about the beauty of the country I loved, and I did not find them. And so I wrote *O Pioneers!*" She also explained what it was like to return to Red Cloud from *Jaffrey, New Hampshire.* "Whenever I crossed the Missouri River coming into Nebraska the very smell of the soil tore me to pieces. I could not decide which was the real and which the fake me."

Carrie B. Raymond Memorial Carillon, First Plymouth Congregational Church, Twentieth and D streets, was dedicated in 1931 to honor the woman who had been the leading musician in Lincoln for forty years. Already a famed organist and choir conductor, Carrie B. Raymond came to Lincoln in 1886 to direct the musical activities at this church. The huge organ she played was once described as "a wonderful instrument with a soul full of harmony and divine melody." She also organized an oratorio society that soon had three hundred faithful members. Never lured away from Lincoln by numerous more lucrative offers, Carrie B. Raymond was especially admired by visitors for her knack of arranging orchestral scores for whatever few instruments were on hand. Although the organ she used was replaced in 1966, the tower houses a forty-eight-bell carillon named for her.

Omaha

In 1856, Amelia Bloomer came to Omaha from her home in *Council Bluffs, Iowa* to deliver a woman suffrage lecture to the state House of Representatives at their invitation. Her speech was cheered and praised, and a contemporary political reporter commented that Bloomer spoke "in a pleasing, able, and I may say, eloquent manner that enchained the attention of her audience for an hour and a half. A *man* could not have beaten it. . . . Her only danger is in asking too much." A few days later, a bill giving votes to women was passed in the lower house. Then, as the reporter had predicted, it was defeated in the senate.

Anna Wilson Grave, Prospect Hill Cemetery, 2235 St. Marys Avenue. An immense polished stone in the dimensions of a king-size bed rests over the double graves of Anna Wilson, a leading Omaha madame, and the only man she ever loved, Daniel B. Allen. The philanthropic proprietor of a series of palatial houses, Anna Wilson bequeathed her famous gabled brothel on Douglas Street to the city when she died in 1911. It became the City Emergency Hospital and for many years served as a venereal disease treatment center. The building has since been razed. It was reported that on the day following Anna Wilson's funeral, by which time she had become rich and generous, and therefore respectable, her little dog died of grief.

Joslyn Memorial Art Museum, 2218 Dodge Street, was donated by Sarah Joslyn, who first came to Omaha in 1879 with her husband George and nine dollars between them. Sixty-one years later, when she died a widow, Sarah Joslyn was called Nebraska's wealthiest woman. Her gift of nearly five million dollars to establish this cultural center was part of the fortune she and her husband accumulated while she managed hotels and he ran a small newspaper business. When he died in

1916, she chose to endow the art memorial over scores of other nationwide possibilities because "Our money was made in Omaha and it will be spent in Omaha." The portrait of Sarah Joslyn hanging in the main foyer was done from available likenesses, since the willful widow refused to sit for the artist. Selflessly, she insisted, "You don't need any portrait of me."

Creighton University, California and Twenty-fourth Streets. Omaha's first university was established with the bequest of $100,000 by Mary Lucretia Creighton, as a memorial to her late husband, Edward. In her will, dated 1875, the year before she died, Mrs. Creighton wrote, "I have selected this mode of testifying to his virtues and my affection to his memory." Mary Creighton's biographer, explaining why she rated only seven pages to her financier husband's thirty, wrote, "If in the lives of most women there is little to chronicle, how much less is there in the lives of those, who by reason of their restricting disposition cultivate the domestic rather than the social virtues! Of this latter class was Mrs. Edward Creighton. Although of charming personality, of refined and winning ways, she cared little for 'society' and preferred the satisfaction of a quiet, friendly conversation to the display of a gay drawing-room."

Osceola

Nebraska's first female attorney, Ada Bittenbender, lived here from 1878–82, passing her historic bar examination in May 1882. Then she moved to Lincoln, where she practiced law in partnership with her husband. A dedicated suffrage and temperance worker as well, she secured passage of a law in 1885 making mothers joint and equal guardians of their children. In 1891 she ran for judge of the state supreme court, receiving 7,322 votes of the total 155,000 cast in the state. It was the largest proportionate vote ever given to the head of the Prohibition ticket.

Red Cloud

Willa Cather Pioneer Memorial Museum, Route 281, is housed in the old Garber Bank building, where her novel *A Lost Lady*

was set. Along with displays of letters, first editions, and other memorabilia of Red Cloud's most famous resident, the foundation that runs this museum also conducts tours of the Willa Cather sites connected with the city and the county. The western half of Webster County has been declared Catherland, a tribute to her realistic depiction of the immigrant spirit that struggled to settle these prairies. Outside of town, a huge plow, like those used by early homesteaders to turn up the soil of the flat plains, marks Red Cloud as the home of Willa Cather. Smaller plow markers identify the numerous places she visited or wrote about. South of town, the Willa Cather Memorial Prairie stands as a living tribute to the woman who sometimes loved it—drifting "along the pale-yellow cornfields, looking for the damp spots one sometimes found at their edges"—and always understood that it could be "one of the loneliest countries in the world." (*See Lincoln.*)

Dane Church, Red Cloud

Willa Cather House, Third and Cedar Streets, was the childhood home of the Pulitzer Prize–winning author. Although she spent only six years here (1884–90), Red Cloud and its surroundings formed the basis for most of her stories and novels of prairie life. This was the place she called Moonstone, Black Hall, and Frankfort in her books. In *The Song of the Lark*, the story of a talented woman (like Willa) and her efforts to rise above her small town's sensibilities, she described this residence as "a low story-and-a-half house, with a wing built on at the right and a kitchen addition at the back, everything a little on the slant—roofs, windows and doors." One of the slanted additions, the lean-to built against the barn, was her personal office. But Willa Cather's favorite room was her attic-bedroom,

which is still covered with the wallpaper she put up. She described it in "The Best Years" as "a story in itself, a secret romance. No caller or neighbor had ever been allowed to go up there. All the children loved it—it was their very own world where there were no older people poking about to spoil things."

Spring Ranche

The only woman ever lynched in Nebraska was Elizabeth Taylor, a landowner whose prosperous ranch, and firm refusal of cattlemen's advances, so infuriated her neighbors that they accused her of stealing horses and damaging their property. Citing entirely unproved charges, a band of armed ranchers whisked off thirty-one-year-old Elizabeth (clad only in a nightgown) and her brother in the middle of a March night in 1885. The two were hanged from a wooden bridge that spanned Pawnee Creek. Even after she was buried at the local cemetery, Elizabeth Taylor was not left in peace. Vandals removed the small marble headstone above her grave, apparently eager for some small token of the incident that one shocked Omaha newspaper called "The Shame of Nebraska." In time, the charges against Elizabeth Taylor were dropped, but it was too late to return her to her ranch.

Walthill

Susan La Flesche Picotte Grave. Like her sister Susette (see *Bancroft*), Susan was the daughter of the remarkable Joseph La Flesche ("Iron Eye"), chief of the Omahas from 1853–64. Susan left the reservation to study at the Women's Medical College in *Philadelphia, Pennsylvania*, becoming in 1889 the first Indian woman to receive a medical degree. Then she returned here, treating more than thirteen hundred members of her tribe. Later she became a leader of the Omahas, in fact if not by title, an unusual achievement for a woman. The hospital she founded here on the reservation was named for her after she died in 1915.

Susan La Flesche Picotte

NEVADA

Austin

Emma Wixom Nevada House, Overland Street (private). Emma lived here as a little girl in the 1860s. Pretending she was a famous opera star, she used to sing in front of cigar-box paintings of Queen Victoria. Twenty years later, Emma Wixom finally performed before the queen, who was so enthralled by her "flute-like" voice that she gave Emma a $100,000 diamond necklace. Gounod hailed her as the Nightingale of Paradise. After triumphant European tours, Emma, who adopted the name "Nevada" because of her undying affection for her home state, always insisted on coming home. The whole town turned out to greet her dramatic arrivals when she came into town by private train.

Carson City

State Capitol. The ornate iron fence surrounding the Capitol grounds was built in 1875 by Hannah Clapp, who won the contract by underbidding the men with her $5,500 fee—submitted by "H. K. Clapp." Clapp supervised the five-year construction in sturdy boots and trousers. That much even the tourist brochures have recorded, but they fail to mention her outstanding work as a pioneer schoolteacher who in 1860 established Sierra Seminary, one of the first coeducational schools in the West. Later, Hannah moved to Reno where she was the university librarian and a leading force in the suffrage movement.

Elko

"The Great What is It" or the "Female Husband," S. M. Pollard, arrived here in 1879 on a sensational promotional tour. The newspapers promised that "one half of the licture will be delivered by him in female attire and the other half will spout forth in male costume." Unfortunately, Sam Pollard's prepared text is unavailable, but it is known that she disguised herself as a man in the mining camps and married a young woman who in a most unsisterly way ran home to mother crying that her husband was female. Irate relatives came looking for Pollard with shotguns. When she was put into jail, the strange case made headlines, assuring the enterprising Pollard packed houses throughout her tour. Years later, she wrote a letter to the editor of the Elko paper saying she had married again and had a baby.

Courthouse Jail Yard. The first and only woman to be executed by due process of law in Nevada was hanged here on June 20, 1890. Elizabeth Potts and her husband Josiah were charged with murder when the charred and dismembered remains of their boarder, Miles Faucett, were found in the cellar of their house, although they oddly insisted his death was a suicide. The sheriff sent out black-bordered invitations to more than fifty prominent town citizens, excluding the women, to watch the gruesome execution. "It is to the credit of Elko, Nevada, that it hangs a woman guilty of murder," editorialized the *San Francisco Daily Report*. "It is a dreadful thing to hang a woman but not so dreadful as to be a murderer."

Fallon

Spudnut Shop, 1350 South Taylor Road. Minnie Nichols Blair started this restaurant in 1949 when she retired from a successful turkey-ranching business, the first in the area, that led to the recognition of Fallon as a center for plump and tender toms. The shop, whose kitchen won a national award for its "Atlasta Beef Sandwich"—roast beef on rye with sour cream, onion soup, and a horseradish dressing—is now run by Minnie's daughter, Helen Milward, who recalled with pride her mother's numerous contributions to community affairs. "She was never too busy to help anyone. She always had time for the downtrodden." Blair, who died in 1973, won the Distinguished Nevadan award from the University of Nevada in 1967.

Genoa

Eliza Ann Middaugh Mott House, Mormon Station. The first white woman in the valley lived in a small log cabin built from abandoned wagon beds after her arrival in May 1852 at this oldest settlement in Nevada. A small museum in the reconstructed house—the original burned in 1910—contains an old photograph of a weary, sad-looking Eliza and other Mormon women of the area, but there is little else to tell us of her hard pioneer life.

Las Vegas

Site of Helen J. Stewart Ranch, Old Mormon Fort, Washington and Las Vegas Boulevards. Only a crumbling remnant of her ranch remains, but once most of Las Vegas belonged to Helen Stewart, the largest landowner in the area's early history. She took over management of her vast properties in 1884, when her husband was murdered. It was said that the independent Helen refused numerous offers of remarriage because she didn't want to change her name, a minor problem conveniently solved in 1903 when she decided to wed her hired hand, Frank Stewart. But it is indeed true, historian Carrie Townley told us, that Helen insisted that Frank sign a premarital agreement assuring her total control over her property. Throughout their marriage, she continued to treat him as her servant, finally forbidding his burial in the family plot. As Las Vegas developed, Helen retired from ranching to become involved in numerous civic affairs. She founded the historical society and the woman's club Mesquite, and she was the first woman elected to the county school board and one of the first female jurors (1916) in the state. Her funeral ten years later was the largest Las Vegas had ever seen.

Maude Frazier Hall, University of Nevada, was named in honor of Nevada's pioneer educator and its first female lieutenant governor. Born in Wisconsin in 1881, Frazier began her teaching career in the mining camps, and in 1921 she became traveling county superintendent of schools. After completing a course in auto mechanics, she tirelessly covered a 40,000-square-mile area alone in her old Dodge roadster. Her nonstop drive from Las Vegas to Goldfield—180 miles in one day—made headlines. When asked if she was afraid of outlaws, Frazier calmly replied, "No, there is an unwritten code of the deserts that insures protection of an unarmed person." She served as school superintendent in Las Vegas for nineteen years, was elected a state senator, and in 1962, at eighty-one, one year before her death, was appointed lieutenant governor, the highest position ever held by a woman in Nevada. The governor said, "I can think of no one more worthy to this office."

Lovelock

Site of Sarah Winnemucca Birthplace, Humboldt Sink. When "Shell Flower" was born here in the mid-1800s, the land belonged to the Paiute Indians. But soon her tribe was forced to move, and Sarah spent her life trying to find a new home for the Paiutes who wandered up and down the Pacific coast. The profits from her book *Life Among the Paiutes* (1883) financed a lecture tour throughout the East. Dressed in buckskin trimmed with shells, a crimson crown in her long hair, she moved audiences to tears with her passionate accounts of the treachery of the Indian agents. Repeated promises were made by the government to return the lands to her people, but at the time of her death in 1891 she knew she had been lied to again.

Pioche

When this frontier town was a booming mining camp, Emma (Eleanore) Dumont ran its finest gambling hall. Here she dealt winning blackjack hands and, in a more costly way, lost her heart to Handsome Jack McKnight. After she married him, they lived for a few years on a ranch until the scoundrel took her money and fled. Legend says that the emotional shock from that traumatic love affair caused Emma's beauty to disappear like her fortune and quickened the growth of the coarse dark hair above her lip that gave her the nickname Madame Moustache. But others say that indelicate title had been bestowed on her long before Handsome Jack went away. (See *Nevada City, California.*)

Pyramid Lake

The Old Lady and Her Basket, a tufa formation, overlooks the northern edge of the lake on the Paiute reservation.

Reno

Site of Anne Martin Home, Mill and Center Streets. A plaque on the bridge near the Holiday Hotel notes the location of her father's house, where Anne Martin lived most of her life after her return in 1911 from Cambridge, England. In England, her fiery dedication to suffrage was kindled by the militant Emmeline Pankhurst, whom she accompanied on numerous demonstrations. Martin once used her champion tennis forehand to hit a bobby on the head with a Nevada Votes for Women sign. Inspired, she returned to Nevada where she traveled more than six thousand miles on foot and horseback and claimed to have spoken to each of the twenty thousand male voters, reaching the most remote men by lowering herself by windlass into the mines in a bucket. Her determined campaigning paid off when the suffrage bill was passed in November 1914. At the Suffrage Association meeting in Nashville, Tennessee, two weeks later, Martin said of her success, "The suffrage victory in Nevada means not only a solid equal suffrage West . . . but a triumph for better government in Nevada. . . . the most 'male' state in America, perhaps the world." In 1918, she ran for the U.S. Senate as an Independent, the first woman in the country to try. She lost and tried again unsuccessfully in 1920. In later years, Martin was an official of the Women's International League for Peace and Freedom and lectured frequently at the University in Reno. She died when she was seventy-six in 1951.

Nevada Historical Society Museum, 1650 North Virginia Street. Included in this fine collection of Nevada memorabilia is the tiny doll buggy of Persia Bowers (see *Washoe City*) and Julia Bulette's fire-chief hat and belt buckle, with the big red number 1 of her favorite *Virginia City* engine company.

Stewart

Grave of Dat-So-La-Lee, Old Burial Ground. The Last of the Basket-Makers, whose designs have been called the most exquisite and artistic in the world, took the secret of her intricate weaving to her grave when she died in 1925, more than ninety-five years old. Each of the more than 300 baskets she made was unique, and contained some 100,000 stitches that took as long as a year to finish. Dat-So-La-Lee wove legends, sacred shapes, and symbols of her Washo tribe into her baskets. With her teeth, she thinned fibers of ferns, willow, and birch trees into thread, and she brewed roots and barks to make her vibrant colors. Some of her baskets can be seen in museums in Carson City and in Pittsburgh, Pennsylvania, and Chicago, Illinois, but the last basket she ever made is buried with her, as she requested. An historical marker outside the cemetery was erected in October 1974.

Virginia City

Piper's Opera House, B Street. In the mid-1800s, when Virginia City was the second largest town west of Chicago with a population of almost thirty thousand, the stage of this reconstructed opera house was graced by such stars as Sarah Bernhardt, Jenny Lind, and Emma Nevada (see *Austin*), whose soulful rendition of "Home Sweet Home" moved the tough miners to tears. Adah Isaacs Menken's act drove them to impassioned frenzy. Her plump thighs squeezed into shocking pink tights, Adah rode through cardboard mountains on horseback in a melodramatic portrayal of the noble Tartar youth in Byron's "Mazeppa." She charmed local theater reviewer Samuel Clemens out of a negative critique of her act.

Julia Bulette Memorial, C Street. "Angel of Miners, Friend of Firemen, and Administrator to the Needy," reads the inscription on a monument set ingloriously and inconveniently in the middle of a parking lot. At the height of her popularity, as undisputed Queen of Sporting Row, Julia charged as much as a thousand dollars a night. But at the sound of the fire bell she would leave her bed and the visitor of the moment to aid the firemen. She was an honorary member of Virginia City Engine Company Number One. Dressed in her purple cape, sable muff, and diamonds and rubies, Julia drove through town in a lacquered brougham emblazoned with her crest of four aces and a lion. She entertained in her "Palace" where the finest French wines were served at tables decorated with fresh flowers from California. "That whore," predicted Eilly Orrum Bowers, the seeress of *Washoe City*, "will come to a bad end." Julia was murdered on January 20, 1867 by John Millian who strangled her for her jewels. Her funeral was the largest the town had ever seen. Hundreds of miners, as well as her favorite fire fighters in their best blue pearl-buttoned uniforms, followed the glass-walled hearse pulled by black-plumed black horses. The Nevada Militia brigade pounded out a mournful dirge but switched to a sparkling version of "The Girl I Left Behind Me" when Julia was safely settled in the hills.

Julia Bulette Grave. About three miles outside of town, shouldered into the side of a bush-covered hill, the rubble of rocks that mark Julia's lonely grave can be spotted through the telescope at Burro Bill's saloon. But it seemed to us a shrine worthy of a more personal sighting. Armed with vague directions to go past the city dump, up the winding rocky road, and down past the marble altar slab, we reached the grave just before sunset —after three unsuccessful attempts. A three-sided wire railing enclosed a crumbling white picket fence around a mound of stones. Julia's name has been carved on the fence, whose two corners strangely resemble ornate bedposts. Most of the fence had been broken off by vandals, though someone's kinder hands had decorated one picket with tiny wreaths of dry flowers.

Washoe City

Bowers Mansion, Route 395. When Eilly Orrum Bowers looked into her crystal ball, she always saw a vision of a most beautiful mansion where she would live in splendor. That was not to be in her native Scotland, she figured, so she converted to Mormonism to come to the United States, where she had two Mormon husbands before divorcing both of them. She opened a boardinghouse in the Gold Canyon near Virginia City. She married miner Sandy Bowers, one of her boarders, and, when he found gold, her dream suddenly became a reality. Construction of the mansion that would cost a half million dollars began in 1860 with granite from the canyon, marble and mahogany from California, and silver chunks for the doorknobs from Sandy's mine. After a two-year tour of Europe, Eilly brought back heavy brocade drapes, marble tables, gilded mirrors, and hand-carved furniture, some of which can still be seen in this magnificent renovated and refurnished mansion. Sandy died in 1868, the mine dried up, and when the creditors besieged her, Eilly shrewdly decided to open her home to weekend visitors for a fee. But she did not make enough to pay the mounting bills, and Eilly was forced to auction off her furniture. A more devastating blow was the death of her precious adopted twelve-year-old daughter, Persia. Eilly moved to California where she spent the last years of her life in a charity home, picking up pennies as a fortune teller, reading happier futures than her own, until her death at age seventy-seven in 1903. She asked to be buried with Sandy and Persia behind the mansion in the tiny plot on the rocky hillside overlooking the placid waters of the Washoe Lake.

NEW HAMPSHIRE

Boscawen

Hannah Duston Monument. This statue, on a tiny island at the confluence of the Merrimack and Contoocook rivers, was erected in 1874, the first permanent monument to a woman in America. Chiseled in Concord granite, Hannah Duston (or Dustin) clutches a tomahawk in her right hand and a handful of scalps in her left, grisly reminders of her celebrated feat here the night of March 30, 1697. Along with her nurse and a fourteen-year-old boy, Hannah Duston, then thirty-nine, led the massacre of ten sleeping Indians who had captured her. (Two weeks earlier in *Haverhill, Massachusetts,* these Indians had brutally slammed her six-day-old infant against an apple tree.) In the predawn hours, threatened with torture and slavery, as a nineteenth-century New Hampshire judge wrote, it was her "steady nerve and unflinching courage that directed the fatal blows and did the sickening mutilation" occasioned by the "vengeance of outraged womanhood." Unfortunately, her outrage never reached the real villain—the power-hungry French governor of Canada who had incited the Indians to attack by promoting high bounties for English scalps. Duston, herself aware of the value of proof of slaughter to colonial minds, carefully collected the hapless Indians' scalps and returned home via *Nashua.* Instantly acclaimed as a heroine, she discovered that in the eyes of the state legislature she was still just a wife with no legal status. Her reward of twenty-five pounds was given to her husband.

Critics of Duston's deed have sought their vengeance on this likeness. In 1952 someone shot off the statue's nose. More recently, a group of Vermont and New Hampshire Indians called Duston a murderer and demanded the removal of the statue. Dr. Arnold George, president of the Duston-Dustin Family Association, which holds annual family reunions to honor their ancestor, explained to us, "We feel that she was a real heroine and deserves historical recognition. Although the Indians have a right to their opinions, we feel that Hannah was justified in everything she did, and we are proud of her."

Bow

Site of Birthplace of Mary Baker Eddy, Route 3A. On July 16, 1821, in a weathered gray farmhouse that was located on this hilltop, the founder of Christian Science was born, the youngest of six children. When she was fifteen, the family moved to *Tilton.*

Canterbury

Shaker Village, Inc. The fifth society faithful to the tenets of Shaker founder Ann Lee (see *Watervliet, New York*) was organized here in 1792. Today it is a thriving cooperative community with four very active sisters welcoming the more than nine thousand annual visitors. Elderly craftworkers make fine furniture and other Shaker products, but they have discontinued making the elegant "Dorothy" cloak, a floor-length cape with a wide collar named for Dorothy Ann Durgun, the first eldress.

Carroll

Crawford Notch, Route 302. Lucy Crawford, an innkeeper in this vicinity, published her *History of the White Mountains* in 1846, a thrilling account of pioneer life. Lucy is remembered for her dauntless courage in facing "fire, flood and much hardship." She is buried in a nearby cemetery.

Charlestown

Susannah Willard H. Johnson House, Old Fort No. 4, Route 11. This reconstructed fort was originally built in 1745 to safeguard the small community of settlers from Indian raids. Nevertheless, Susannah Johnson, her husband, her children, and a sister were captured on August 31. Two days later, Susannah gave birth to a daughter whom she named Elizabeth Captive and, babe in arms, with only a few hours to regain her strength, she made the long march with the Indians through the forests to St. Francis in Canada, where she lived for three years. Eventually ransomed, Susannah published a popular account of her captivity.

Concord

Mary Baker Eddy House, 62 North State Street (private). During the three years she lived here, 1889–92, Mary Baker Eddy brought out the fiftieth edition of *Science and Health;* published *Retrospection* and *Introspection;* and relaxed by adding her fine soprano to home quartet sessions.

Pleasant View, which opened in 1927 as a home for elderly Christian Scientists, was built on the site of Mary Baker Eddy's home from 1892 to 1908—where she watched the phenomenal growth in membership of her church. Here, she published numerous journals, including the beginnings of the *Christian Science Monitor* (see *Brookline, Massachusetts*).

Dover

Site of Cocheco Manufacturing Company, Cocheco Falls. Protesting such loathsome restrictions as a 12½-cent fine for arriving one second after the morning bell, no talking at the machines, and, worst of all, a reduction in wages from 58 cents a day to 53, female employees went on strike here in December 1828. In the first strike to be organized by women in American labor history, more than three hundred disgruntled workers set off fireworks and paraded through the streets with banners and signs. A Boston newspaper called it a "riot." But the protest was not nearly rowdy enough it seems, for the dejected women returned to their jobs before the first of January with none of their demands realized, figuring a miserable job was better than none at all when the millowners began advertising in Dover for three hundred openings.

Marilla Ricker House, 7 Ham Street (private). Marilla opened the New Hampshire bar to women (1890) but did most of her own practicing in Washington, D.C., returning to her home state in the summer. Here, she campaigned for prison reform and birth control, spoke out against organized religion, and, as a superb athlete, galloped into the countryside on her favorite fast horses. An ardent suffragist, Marilla, who lived in this house for two years before her death in 1920, was widely admired for her clever replies to unliberated opponents. "Mrs. Ricker is not given to mincing words," an early biographer wrote. She does "not beat about the bush in search of euphemistic expressions to gild the edge of criticism." Her success with such candid politicking encouraged her to run for governor in 1910. Faced with such a formidable competitor, state officials quickly refused her candidacy on the grounds that women did not have the right to vote. They chose to ignore the fact that forty years earlier, Marilla had been the first woman in the country to register to vote. Under the Fourteenth Amendment, whose fair interpretation suffragists claimed made their vote valid, Marilla cast her vote for a straight Republican ticket. (Eight months later, her good friend Susan B. Anthony also voted a straight Republican ticket in *Rochester, New York,* but she somehow knew, in her case, it would cause "a fine agitation.")

Exeter

Tabitha Gilman Tenney House, 65 High Street (private). Novelist Tenney spent the last years of her life here after assuring her fame with the publication of her best novel, *Female Quixoticism: Exhibited in the Romantic Opinions and Extravagant Adventure of Dorascine Sheldon* (1801), a clever satire about a foolish young woman easily deceived by romantic nonsense—who nevertheless was shrewd enough to stay single.

Franklin

Mary Baker Eddy Home, 34 South Main Street (private). With her new husband, Daniel Patterson, Mary Baker Eddy spent two unhappy years here before moving to *North Groton,* where she was even more miserable.

Jaffrey

Hannah Davis House, 249 Main Street (private). The first and finest wooden hatboxes in the country were invented and manufactured in this modest white house in the early 1800s. Hannah Davis would trek through the nearby woods to look for the finest spruce trees, which she cut and hauled to her door, neatly sliced with a machine of her own invention, nailed into shape, and finally covered with brightly colored wallpaper. "The Hannah Davis Band Box," priced from twelve cents to the deluxe Easter-bonnet-size fifty-cent model, was a much-coveted treasure for the factory women of Manchester and Lowell, Massachusetts, where Hannah would arrive during their lunch break in an old prairie wagon, a fine selection of boxes piled up all around her. An historical marker near her grave in the Meeting House cemetery celebrates "Aunt Hannah Davis . . . resourceful and beloved spinster" for her unique trademarked boxes, so sturdy they have endured long past her 1863 death. Many can be seen in historical collections here and as far away as Philadelphia, Pennsylvania, and New York City.

Alice Pettee Adams House, Fitzwilliam Road (private). Jaffrey's most famous expatriate, who lived here in her last years, has been called the Jane Addams of Japan for her founding in the 1890s of that country's first social settlement, Hakuaikai Institution in Okayama. Adams was the first woman to receive Japan's Blue Ribbon decoration (1922), and, after thirty-seven years of distinguished service, she was the first American awarded a pension from the Japanese government—330 yen annually for life.

Shattuck Inn, Dublin Road (private). Novelist Willa Cather (see *Gore, Virginia*) came to this rambling old inn, now deserted, every fall for twenty years in search of the privacy and solitude she demanded for her work. Cather was never asked to sign the guest register. She always used the back-door entrance to climb to the third-floor quarters reserved for her—two little rooms with sloping ceilings and a view of her favorite Mount Monadnock—but she would occasionally join other guests by the lounge fireplace. "I never saw anyone to listen so intently," one recalled. "She just drew things out of people—things she could use in her books." During the day, ignoring the autumn chill, Cather would go across the street to her outdoor studio, a tent with a view nestled in the piny woods among the wild flowers. There, she wrote parts of *My Ántonia* (see *Red Cloud, Nebraska*) and her Pulitzer Prize–winning *One of Ours,* whose descriptions of troop movements she gleaned from the diary of a local doctor. Jaffrey was the place Cather "found best to work in," wrote her devoted companion Edith Lewis. "Each day there was like an empty canvas, a clean sheet of paper to be filled. She lived with a simple sense of physical well-being and of country solitude." Cather did not visit Jaffrey again after the hurricane of 1938 knocked down the fir trees that had sheltered her hillside office, but she knew that one day she would indeed return.

Willa Cather Grave, Old Town Burial Ground. Hundreds attended Cather's impressive funeral in New York in April 1947, but, as always, Jaffrey residents respected the loner's privacy, and only a handful of old friends gathered at the service at the grave in the shadow of her beloved Mount Monadnock. A plain marker reads, "The truth and charity of her great spirit will live on in the work which is her enduring gift to her country and all its people," and ends with a quote from *My Ántonia*—"that is happiness, to be dissolved into something complete and great."

Manchester

Stark House, 2000 Elm Street. Elizabeth Page ("Molly") Stark lived here in the oldest house in town from 1760 to about 1765, often converting these elegant rooms into temporary hospital quarters for the wounded compatriots of her husband, Col. John Stark. Molly's woefully uncelebrated life seems to have been replete with courageous responses to last-minute emergencies. When the news came that the British had invaded Boston Harbor, the colonel saddled up so quickly that he left his uniforms behind. Molly, galloping wildly, managed to overtake him a few hours later with the forgotten regimentals. Vermont has honored her name with a trail. (See *Bennington, Vermont.*)

Milford

Carrie Cutter Memorial, Old Cemetery, Elm Street. The heroic Carrie is buried in North Carolina, where she died (see *New Bern, North Carolina*), a humble marker there bearing only her name. But in 1930 the proud citizenry of Milford erected a monument in their native daughter's honor. Near her mother's grave, a bronze tablet on a granite boulder tells Carrie's entire heroic story and pays tribute to her as "the first female to enter the service of her country in the Civil War, the first that fell at her post, and the first to form organized efforts to supply the sick of the army." When she heard that her doctor father was going off to the war, eighteen-year-old Carrie asked what she could do. "You can stay home and keep house. War is no place for women," her father replied. But a determined Carrie petitioned the government for a berth as a nurse on the troopship *Northerner,* arriving at Roanoke Island just in time for a terrible battle where she aided the wounded alongside her astonished but proud father. Carrie, who went to war instead of going abroad to continue her studies of French and German, was the only one on the battlefield who could understand the three young German soldiers who were delirious from typhoid. She cared for them night and day until they were well. Then she died from the vicious fever. Her name is forever immortalized on the Roll of Honor in the Congressional Library in Washington, D.C.

Nashua

Hannah Duston Memorial, Alldst and Fifield Streets. A tablet marks the former location of the cabin of John Lovewell, where Indian captive Hannah Duston (see *Boscawen*) "spent the night after her escape from the Indians at Penacook Island, March 30, 1697."

Newport

Sarah Josepha Hale Memorial, Route 103. An historical marker claims that Hale wrote the famed children's classic "Mary Had a Little Lamb," but recent evidence from historians in *Sterling, Massachusetts,* indicates that in fact someone else—a young boy—wrote the first twelve lines. Hale added twelve more and first published it in 1830. Still, without Hale, the world would not know that beloved ditty at all. There is no dispute however about her other outstanding achievements listed here where she lived for forty years, so happily married that she forever argued that a woman's role was to serve her man. When her husband died in 1822, Hale suddenly realized that such slavish devotion had not prepared her for supporting her five children. She began writing in earnest and was moderately successful with some poems and a novel, *Northwood*. In it, she described her writing room with its yellow floor, blue wainscoting, a giant eagle over the mantelpiece, and the desk where she wrote by the light of the fireplace. Her efforts caught the attention of William Godey who invited her to become the editor of his *Lady's Book* in 1837. "The wish to promote the reputation of my own sex was among the earliest mental emotions I can recollect," she once said. In the pages of that pioneer woman's magazine she enthusiastically promoted higher education for women, female doctors, and legal rights for wives, always reserving a special fondness for women in the home. She unwittingly doomed them to at least one day of enormous cooking chores by her tireless campaigning for a national Thanksgiving Day, which, thanks to her efforts, President Lincoln officially proclaimed in 1863.

North Groton

The five years Mary Baker Eddy spent here (1855–60) with her second husband, Dr. Daniel Patterson, were the most miserable ones of her entire life, fraught with illness, depression, and financial setbacks. Her sister rescued the impoverished Pattersons and brought them to *Rumsey*.

Peterborough

Site of Phoenix Manufacturing Company, Main Street. Twins Elmira and Elvira Fife set a depressing record for continuous underpaid employment with one firm when they retired in 1886 after sixty years, six days a week, eleven hours a day, spinning and weaving in this mill at a daily wage that never went higher than ninety cents and sometimes bottomed out at seven. But who needed money when they had each other? It was said that the identical twins had never been apart for more than seventy hours during their entire long life. At age eighty-three, they posed for a solemn picture as the oldest twins in America. "Neither ever entered a railroad carriage, attended a theater or put on a spectacle, but did lend their voices to the Unitarian choir. . . . No better evidence of strict virginity was ere known in our vicinity," contemporary historians proudly extolled. When Elvira died in 1894, Elmira barely made it through the lonely winter before joining her beloved other half.

MacDowell Colony. Every summer since 1908, dozens of writers, poets, and artists have been coming to this mountain retreat for inspiration and peace. Composer Amy Cheney Beach spent more than twenty summers here, almost up to her death in 1941. Beach, who composed her first waltz at age four, was the first female composer to receive national acclaim for such grand works as her Mass in E-flat, a Gaelic symphony, violin sonatas, and piano concerti. Here in 1938 she worked on her brilliant Opus 150 for piano, violin, and cello. Willa Cather spent a few weeks here in 1926, but the crowds distracted her and she returned to her own mountain retreat in *Jaffrey*.

Rindge

Memorial Bell Tower, Cathedral of the Pines. This huge stone tower honors all American women who died in war service to their country. Murals on its four sides depict women of the armed services, the Sisters of Charity of the War of 1812, Salvation Army "Lassies," riveters, war correspondents, and entertainers. Clara Barton (see *North Oxford, Massachusetts*) is portrayed leading a wounded soldier. The pioneer woman, barefoot, with child at her skirt and a long rifle, stands guarding her home. "At last, long last, you have remembered us," began the poem read at groundbreaking ceremonies in 1963.

Rumsey

Mary Baker Eddy Historic House, Stinson Lake Road. Her health and spirits gradually improved while Mary Baker Eddy and her husband Daniel Patterson lived here from 1860–62. Some of the original furnishings of the house that the poverty-stricken couple had auctioned off have been restored, including the table, chairs, and clock in the front parlor. This was Mary's favorite room, where she began to write down her thoughts on the Bible and spiritual healing that would lead to the founding of Christian Science. (See *Lynn, Massachusetts.*)

Star Island

Vaughn Cottage is a combination library and museum dedicated to poet and author Celia Thaxter, a longtime resident of these Isles of Shoals. Among the memorabilia of the writer are some pieces of furniture from her cottage on nearby *Appledore Island, Maine,* and some pieces of china she painted.

Tilton

Site of Mary Baker Eddy Farm, near School Street. Mary married George Washington Glover, an old friend from *Bow,* on this site in December 1843, but he died less than six months later. A son George was born here shortly afterwards, and Mary moved into town to be with her widowed father. She spent nine years in grieving, restless widowhood, and then she remarried. (See *Franklin.*)

NEW JERSEY

Belleville

Clara Maass Memorial Hospital, 1A Franklin Avenue. This modern 570-bed center is named for a courageous nurse who graduated in 1895 from its predecessor, the Newark German Hospital. The daughter of poor immigrant parents who lived in nearby East Orange, Clara Maass volunteered her medical services with the U.S. Army in Florida, Cuba, and the Philippines. In 1901 she bade adieu to her fiancé in New Jersey to go back to Cuba to work with the experimenters who were trying to discover the origin of yellow fever. As one of those needed to help determine whether the mosquito bred the fever, she voluntarily extended her arm to the winged creature on June 24, 1901. She received one hundred dollars and a mild case of yellow fever, from which she recovered quickly. On August 14 she again submitted to a jab in the arm from the suspected *Stegomyia*. This time the killer disease struck in full force. Ten days later, Clara Maass was dead, the only American and the only woman to die in the experiment. But her death was all that was needed to pin the blame squarely on the mosquito, and thus begin the program to wipe it out. (See *Newark*.)

Bordentown

Patience Wright House, 100 Farnsworth Avenue (private). Before she moved to London in 1772, the nation's first sculptor lived in this three-story red brick house. As a housewife, she is said to have discovered her artistic bent while working with dough on the cookie board. In 1769, a widow and mother of five, she put her talent to professional use, and her wax figures gained fame in leading cities throughout the colonies. When she moved abroad, Wright became a close friend of Benjamin Franklin and of the king and queen of England, whom she casually addressed as George and Charlotte. The plaque on the house here also cites her activities as a "female spy" during the Revolution, an activity she discreetly carried out while sculpting her life-size figure of William Pitt (Lord Chatham), the first American work to be placed in Westminster Abbey.

Clara Barton Schoolhouse, 142 Crosswicks Street. In 1852, in this tiny one-room brick cottage, Clara Barton founded one of the first free schools in the state. Eager to apply the principles she had developed in her hometown of *North Oxford, Massachusetts,* the thirty-one-year-old teacher volunteered her services for three months. Within a year her classroom mushroomed from six pupils to six hundred, and Bordentown officials were persuaded to build a new three-story schoolhouse. When they also decided to install a male principal to supervise Clara Barton's highly successful work, she resigned.

Site of Linden Hall, 49–61 East Park Street (private). This charming cluster of houses known as Murat Row was used as a noted girls' boarding school in the mid-1800s. Caroline Fraser, whose hand had been won by Prince Lucien Murat, nephew of Joseph Bonaparte, turned the graceful homes into the elegant Linden Hall to help pay off debts run up by her extravagant husband.

Burlington

Site of Margaret Morris House, "Green Bank," riverbank west of Wood Street. From a house overlooking the Delaware River on the spot now occupied by the Veterans of Foreign Wars, Quaker widow Margaret Morris was an eyewitness to several key events in the American Revolution. Fortunately, she recorded her observations, and her fascinating journal (found in the local library) is one of the most detailed accounts of the armies' activities. Of special note: her description of the accidental cannonading of Burlington by the patriots in December 1776; and her feelings about the colonists after the Battle of Trenton, as they marched "out of Town in high spirits. . . . My heart sinks when I think of the Numbers unprepared for Death."

Elizabeth

Site of Hannah Arnett House, 1155 East Jersey Street, now occupied by the Elizabeth Carteret Hotel. In the dark days of November 1776, with the Revolutionists despondent over their poor chances of victory, the woman who dwelled in the house once located here nobly advanced the patriots' cause. A group of men had gathered with her husband Isaac to discuss the offer made by generals Richard and William Howe: amnesty to all who would swear allegiance to Great Britain within sixty days. As the male citizenry drew closer to accepting the proposal, Hannah Arnett threw down her knitting and stormed into the parlor. "Shame upon you cowards!" she shouted. "You have forgotten one thing which England has not and which we have—one thing which outweighs all England's treasures, and that is the right. God is on our side, and every volley of our muskets is an echo of His voice." Shunning her husband's efforts to make her return to the spinning wheel and leave the men "to settle affairs," Hannah swore her own allegiance to the country and threatened to leave Isaac if he betrayed it. Later that evening, as the men left, all refused the amnesty offer.

Nearby in the cemetery of the First Presbyterian Church of Elizabeth, a plaque erected by the DAR in 1909 honors Hannah Arnett for keeping the town "loyal to the cause of American Independence."

It was her deed—recounted by Mary Smith Lockwood in a letter to the *Washington Post* in 1890—that helped lead to the formation of the Daughters of the American Revolution. Mrs. Lockwood wrote the letter to protest the "one-sided heroism" and male bias of the Sons of the American Revolution. (See *Washington, D.C.*)

Freehold

Molly Pitcher's Spring, Wemrock Street off Route 522. From this spring, during the fierce Battle of Monmouth (June 28, 1778), the wife of artilleryman John Hays carried water to the hot, thirsty American soldiers. Her name was Mary, or Molly. The cries of the parched fighting men for "Molly!" and her thirst-quenching "pitcher!" soon became her memorable nickname. According to an eyewitness account, when John Hays was shot down, Molly Pitcher took up his post, loaded the cannon, and "like a Spartan heroine fought with astonishing bravery, discharging the piece with as much regularity as any soldier present." Losing only a part of her petticoat to a cannonball, she maintained her post, chewing tobacco and swearing like a trooper, and she helped bolster the American victory. (A second site marked "Molly Pitcher's Well" on Route 522, about two hundred yards west of this spring, has been erroneously identified as the source of the water.)

The Monmouth Battle Monument, opposite the Monmouth County Historical Association at 70 Court Street, is an immense

stone pillar. One of the bronze plaques around its base pictures the barefoot Molly Pitcher in bas-relief. Her water pail rests at her feet while she energetically fires up the cannon. In 1822, Molly who had gone home to *Carlisle, Pennsylvania,* was awarded a pension by the Pennsylvania state legislature.

Gouldtown

The town was named for Elizabeth Adams, who inherited five hundred acres of land from her grandfather, Fenwick Adams, in the seventeenth century, then married a black man named Gould and settled here. That is all the history books record.

Haddonfield

The woman acknowledged as founder and proprietor of the town was a twenty-year-old Quaker, Elizabeth Haddon, who came here from England in 1701 to manage land that her father had purchased. The young settler's romance with missionary John Estaugh has been immortalized by Longfellow in "The Theologian's Tale." According to the poetic legend, Elizabeth announced to the young man on horseback one Sunday, "I have received from the Lord a charge to love thee, John Estaugh." The direct approach worked. They were married in 1702.

Site of Elizabeth Haddon House, 201 Wood Lane (private). Elizabeth Haddon and her husband, John Estaugh, moved here in 1713. A three-story brick house that was rebuilt in 1842 occupies the spot where Elizabeth's two-story yellow brick house stood at the center of the new town bearing her name. Here,

she managed the family property while her husband tended to his missionary journeys. The Brew House she built in 1713, the oldest house in Haddonfield, still stands in the backyard. In this brick structure, the enterprising young woman made medical and chemical preparations, and, it is said, some whiskey. Besides acting as a doctor to many of her neighbors, Elizabeth acted as clerk of the Quaker Women's Meeting for almost fifty years. When John died in 1743, Elizabeth maintained her leading role in the town and managed her own property as well as the estates of others—an unusual responsibility for a woman in colonial times.

Elizabeth Haddon Memorial Tablet, at the old Friends' Burial Ground, Haddon Avenue, was erected in 1913 to celebrate both the town's bicentennial and the woman who made it possible. Attached to a tree facing Haddon Avenue is a plaque indicating that Elizabeth Haddon died in 1762 and is buried "near this tablet." She is recalled as the originator of the Friends' Meeting here in 1721, "A woman remarkable for resolution, prudence, charity."

The Historical Society of Haddonfield, 343 King's Highway East, has a large wooden mortar said to be Elizabeth Haddon's, as well as her marriage certificate and Common Prayer Book.

Hancock's Bridge

Memorial to Cornelia Hancock, Alloway Creek Friends Meeting House. A commemorative flagstone in the yard here perpetuates the memory of the Civil War nurse who was born in nearby *Salem.*

Hillside

Mary Mapes Dodge Grave, Evergreen Cemetery, 1137 North Broad Street. The headstone above the burial place of Mary Mapes Dodge, who died in 1905 (see *Newark*), recalls the sentiments of thousands of readers of *Hans Brinker* and of *St. Nicholas,* the children's magazine she edited. The inscription reads, "Author, Editor, Poet. Lover and Friend of Children and in countless homes beloved."

Hoboken

Hetty Green's Apartment, 1203 Washington Street (private). On the fourth floor of this five-story yellow brick building, still an apartment house, millionaire Hetty Green, who eventually became known as the Witch of Wall Street, shared a bathtub with the other tenants for several years at the turn of the century. Born in 1834 to a rich whaling family in New Bedford, Massachusetts, she said, "I was forced into business. . . . I was taught from the time I was six years old that I would have to look after my property." She shrewdly invested her money and became a millionaire in her own right. She is said to have preferred this location for its quick ferry ride to Wall Street and for its inexpensive rent—under $20 per month. At the time, she was earning some $5,000 a day. Although some called her eccentric, she became the richest woman in America. (See *Bellows Falls, Vermont.*)

Long Branch

Women who wanted to take a swim at this chic seaside resort in the late 1800s had to figure on a hidden cost: the gigolo required to escort them into the water. Even protected by pantalettes, skirts, and long stockings, fashionable female bathers were not considered beach-worthy without a male companion. Resisting the pressure to pair off with just anyone, many of the wealthy women chose to pay for their beach partners, creating a lucrative business (with hourly, daily, or seasonal rates) for some otherwise unemployed young men. The gigolo enterprise

continued until the late 1890s, when it suddenly occurred to the taste makers that a single woman on the beach was acceptable after all.

Morristown

The Seeing Eye, Washington Valley Road. This is the headquarters of the famed school where dogs are trained to guide the blind. It was founded in 1929 by Dorothy Harrison Wood Eustis, a philanthropic dog-fancier interested in the scientific breeding of German shepherds. Inspired by a school in Switzerland where dogs were trained for blind war veterans, she wrote a magazine article about it in 1927. A blind man from Tennessee found the idea exciting and asked her to train such a dog for him. When his experience proved successful, Dorothy Eustis returned to America to open the nation's first Seeing Eye class in Nashville, Tennessee, in 1929. Three years later the school was moved to Whippany, New Jersey, and in 1965 to this Georgian structure in Morristown. Over the years, more than four thousand blind persons have received dogs—many of them the shepherds, Labradors, and golden retrievers that were trained on the streets of Morristown.

National Park

Whitall House, 100 Grove Avenue. This two-story brick house on the grounds of the Red Bank Battlefield was the scene of a heroic—if legendary—story during the fighting of October 22, 1777. While American troops defended Fort Mercer against Hessian advances, Ann Whitall, Quaker wife of James, calmly sat at her spinning wheel upstairs, amidst the hissing and whistling of cannonballs flying past the house. When one shot landed squarely in the wall of her room, she collected her spinning wheel and removed herself to the cellar, where she resumed her work. When the fighting ceased, and wounded Hessian soldiers were brought to the house, Ann scolded them for crossing the ocean to fight the patriots. Her spinning wheel is preserved here with as much care as the legend.

Newark

Mapes Avenue is named for Mary Mapes Dodge, a Newark resident who gained international fame as author of the best-selling children's book *Hans Brinker; or, the Silver Skates* (1865). Using only her vivid imagination and the advice of a few Dutch neighbors, Mrs. Dodge, a widow trying to support her two children, created a children's classic that was translated into foreign languages and published in more than a hundred editions. In 1881 she finally visited Holland and the scenes of her story, where a Dutch bookseller told her son that *Hans Brinker* was the best book on Holland in the store. (See *Hillside*.)

Clara Maass Monument, Fairmount Cemetery, Central Avenue and Eleventh Street. Nearly three decades after she died in Cuba, sacrificing her life for a cure for yellow fever (see *Belleville*), the twenty-five-year-old nurse was honored by a concerned colleague at Newark General Hospital. In 1930, Leopoldine Guinther, superintendent of nurses, spearheaded a drive to place this pink granite headstone on Clara's weed-covered grave, with a bronze plaque retelling the story of her unselfish accomplishment.

Ann and John Plume House, 407 Broad Street. Since 1849, this three-story sandstone building has been the rectory of the House of Prayer, but the current residents—Rev. Harry Grace and his wife Kathryn—eagerly recount the popular legend of colonial days. During the Revolution, Ann Van Wagenen Plume found some Hessian soldiers breaking up her furniture to stoke a warming fire. With exemplary skill, she swiftly imprisoned one of the intruders in the icehouse nearby, delivering him to officers of the Continental army. Legend also has it that a figure from the Hessian's hat was presented to Ann as a reward, and that it was turned into the handsome steel door-knocker. But Mr. Grace told us that careful research on contemporary Hessian uniforms had revealed nothing resembling the lion ornament that is still used to announce visitors.

New Brunswick

Douglass College, originally the New Jersey College for Women, was renamed in 1955 for Mabel Smith Douglass, its founder and dean. Under her strong guidance, the institution was begun in 1918 as the female affiliate of Rutgers. Douglass was installed as the first dean that same year, with fifty-four students in her charge. By the time she retired in 1932, more than a thousand young women were enrolled. Today, that number has more than tripled.

Nutley

Site of Annie Oakley House, 303 and 306 Grant Avenue. Two relatively new houses stand on the site where Annie Oakley and her manager-husband Frank Butler lived from 1893, after their four-year European tour with Buffalo Bill's Wild West Show. The sharpshooters had no closets in their house since they were accustomed to traveling with huge trunks. They chose Nutley after a number of visits on previous tours. Their grand entrance, when they arrived by train, is recalled in the painting, *The Return of Annie Oakley,* on a wall inside the Nutley Post Office. According to Nutley historian Ann Troy, this episode was "chosen over a football theme suggested by those who thought Nutley's winning high school teams were the town's chief distinction." Ann Troy also maintains the Historical Society Museum at 65 Church Street, where several of Annie Oakley's guns and some letters she wrote are town treasures. (See *Greenville, Ohio.*)

Orange

Site of Lucy Stone House, formerly 16 Hurlbut Street. Freeway Drive East has destroyed forever the historic cottage where Lucy Stone and Henry Blackwell (see *West Brookfield, Massachusetts*) moved in 1857. Lucy described it with exuberance: "It is a Gothic cottage, 75 feet from the road, with an acre of ground—young fruit and ornamental trees growing about it, guarded by one venerable old apple-tree . . . I do so enjoy its

quiet." Speeding cars now break the silence where Lucy's daughter Alice was born in 1857. When husband Henry offered to let the infant be called "Stone," since "It is you and not I who have suffered to bring this child into the world," Lucy compromised and gave her both surnames.

In this house, too, Lucy Stone made her famous 1858 protest against taxation without representation. Maintaining that she and other women "will cheerfully pay our taxes" when given the right to vote, she returned her tax bill without payment. The tax collector retaliated by selling off her household goods (including Alice's cradle) for payment; a sisterly neighbor bought them and returned them to Lucy.

More than a half century later, in 1915, long after Lucy Stone's death, suffragists from all over the country joined in a pilgrimage to the cottage to witness the placing of a plaque in honor of the historic tax protest. As one thousand feminists—including an ex-governor of New Jersey—looked on, Alice Stone Blackwell unveiled the bronze tablet that read, "In 1858 Lucy Stone, a noble pioneer in the emancipation of women, here first protested against her taxation without representation in New Jersey." That tablet, like the house, has disappeared. (See *Dorchester, Massachusetts.*)

Perth Amboy

Kearny House, Hayes Park, southeast end of Catalpa Avenue, was the home of Michael Kearny and his wife Elizabeth Lawrence, Revolutionary poet and editor. She taught her half brother, Capt. James ("Don't Give Up the Ship") Lawrence his love of poetry. Her own writings earned her the comment of at least one woman, who wrote, "Oh, why won't Madam stop her scribbling?" The literary world forever after called her Madam Scribblerus. Among her popular prose was a merry war of wits carried on in a magazine with a writer who called himself Duncan Downright.

Site of Eagleswood School, western end of Market Street. From 1853 until about 1861, this was one of the social experiments in the Brook Farm tradition, connected with the Raritan Bay Union, a cooperative community. The school was set up by abolitionist Theodore Weld who, with his noted feminist-abolitionist wife Angelina Grimké and her sister Sarah, formed the nucleus of the teaching community. Angelina taught history; Sarah taught French. The school pioneered in coeducation and impressed one visitor as "the first in which young women were found educating their limbs in the gymnasium, rowing in boats and making 'records' in swimming." Although everyone praised it and helped with the chores, the school was a financial failure and finally had to be run as a private enterprise. Today, all the buildings are gone, replaced by the Philip Carey Roofing Company.

Port Elizabeth

In 1771, Elizabeth Clark Bodly purchased 213 acres of wilderness for 260 pounds sterling and caused this fine town to be laid out. She deeded the first lot on October 1, 1785 to the Methodist Episcopal Church. Elizabeth Bodly was described as a handsome woman with black eyes and above medium size. "She possessed an expanded mind and great benevolence of character," according to a contemporary account. In 1885, at the centennial celebration of Port Elizabeth, her descendants waved flags before a portrait of Elizabeth Bodly that showed her standing in her Quaker costume and holding the deed of the first church plot in her hands. The painting has since disappeared.

Princeton

Annis Boudinot Stockton House, "Morven," Stockton Street. This Georgian mansion, now the official New Jersey governor's residence, was once home to Annis Boudinot Stockton and her husband Richard, a secret signer of the Declaration of Independence. When Annis moved here in 1755, she named the elegant structure for the ancestral home celebrated by the Irish poet Ossian. Annis was an acclaimed and patriotic poet herself, perhaps best known for the song that all the women of Trenton sang to welcome George Washington as he traveled to his first inauguration. It began:

> Welcome mighty chief, once more
> Welcome to this grateful shore,
> Now no mercenary foe
> Aims again the fatal blow.

The music has not been preserved. Another poem Annis wrote to Washington after the fall of Yorktown won his deep appreciation in a generous letter.

Salem

Cornelia Hancock Birthplace, New Bridge Road (private). The Civil War nurse and educator of freedmen was born here in 1839. Her selfless care of the sick and wounded at *Gettysburg, Pennsylvania,* and *Fredericksburg, Virginia,* earned her the title, the Florence Nightingale of America, and army bands struck up the tune "The Hancock Gallop" wherever she went during the war. Not content to rest on her accomplishments after the war, Cornelia Hancock cared for freedmen at a school in *Mount Pleasant, South Carolina,* and worked for the poor in Philadelphia, Pennsylvania. When she died in 1927 her ashes were placed in nearby Harmersville, and a stepping-stone was named in her honor at *Hancock's Bridge.*

Somerville

Wallace House, 38 Washington Place. Martha Washington slept here, along with her husband, the general, the first occupants of this white clapboard residence from December 11, 1778 to June 3, 1779. While the Continental army was encamped at nearby Camp Middlebrook, the future first couple rested tranquilly behind the traditional "witches doors"—their panels shaped like a double cross to bar the entry of whatever witches had not been drowned at *Salem, Massachusetts.*

Trenton

Trenton Psychiatric Hospital, Sullivan Way. Already celebrated for her reforms for the care of the mentally ill in New England, Dorothea Lynde Dix came to New Jersey in 1844 and found a statewide chamber of horrors. In Burlington at the poorhouse: "dreary confined cells, insufficiently lighted, insufficiently warmed, and pervaded with foul air to an intolerable degree." In Morris County: cells that were seven-and-one-half feet high, eight feet square, "dark, damp, and unfurnished, unwarmed and unventilated—one would not hesitate, but refuse to shut up here a worthless dog." She, among few others, understood that the malady of insanity is "ever aggravated by *severity, unkindness, blows and the use of chains.*" Her stirring report, presented to the state legislature in 1845, convinced even the most intransigent lawmakers. Three years later, the New Jersey State Lunatic Asylum, with eighty-six patients, opened its doors on this site—chosen by Dix herself—overlooking the Delaware River. It was the state's first such hospital and, in Dix's heart, her "first-born child."

When she grew ill in 1881, she was provided with an apartment here, and she was treated here until her death in 1887. Today her residence is gone, but the hospital has expanded twentyfold in patient care, thanks to the woman who told the lawmakers of New Jersey, "It is for your own citizens I plead."

Caldwell Parsonage, 886 Caldwell Avenue. While seated either on the porch or in an upstairs bedroom of this parsonage, Hannah Ogden Caldwell, wife of the parson, was felled by a bullet on June 7, 1780. As far as could be determined, the British soldier who pulled the trigger did so without motivation. The outraged citizenry retaliated by driving the Tories out of New Jersey. Today, the parsonage has been restored, and the incident is depicted on the Union County seal. A bronze tablet honors Hannah Caldwell's involuntary martyred entrance into the nation's history.

Vineland

The presidential election of November 1868 provided the opportunity for one of the earliest woman suffrage demonstrations in the country. Fully aware that their votes would not count, 172 women defiantly turned up at the polls here and deposited their ballots in a special rectangular box normally used to hold grapes in this vineyard country. An array of distinguished older women acted as judges, and one young ballot-caster was heard to say, "I feel so much stronger for having voted." An eyewitness wrote in the suffrage journal, *The Revolution,* that the men "said they had never had so quiet and pleasant a time at the polls before." Among the results of this historic event: 164 votes for Ulysses S. Grant, 2 for Elizabeth Cady Stanton.

Washington

Monument to Peggy Warne, Old Mansfield Cemetery, Cemetery Hill Road. A boulder over her grave commemorates the life of "Aunt Peggy" Warne (1751–1840), who was known as the most skilled and accomplished obstetrician of her day. While male doctors were off tending soldiers during the Revolution, Aunt Peggy cared for her own nine children and the newborn of the entire area, spurring her horse across the ridges and rills of two counties in sunshine and storm. A careful physician, she also served the sick of all ages until her death at age eighty-nine.

Wayne

Clara Maass Memorial Window, United Methodist Church, 99 Parish Drive. A stained-glass window presented by Emma Maass on Palm Sunday, 1941, commemorates her older sister Clara, who traded her life to find a cure for yellow fever in 1901 (see *Belleville*). As the inscription recalls, Clara Maass brushed aside perils and "made the supreme sacrifice for Science, that others might live."

Whitesbog

Joseph J. White Company, Lebanon State Forest. The world's only cranberry and blueberry plantation with its own post office owes its commercial success to Elizabeth White, pioneering fruit-grower who cultivated the blueberry to its unprecedented large, tasty, colorful quality. Born into a family that ran cranberry bogs (the springboard for her later honor as the first female member of the American Cranberry Association), she soon turned to experiments with the cranberry's neglected cousin, the blueberry. Constantly searching for a berry that was bluer, bigger, and hardier, she crossbred until she produced the superberry marked first in 1916 as Tru-Blu-Berries. She also added to its enjoyment by becoming the first person to protect her succulent products with cellophane, imported from Europe long before it became a household product here.

At one time yielding up to twenty thousand barrels of berries a year, the company still harvests this important cash crop of New Jersey. At a state-run research center here, students continue the scientific tradition begun by Elizabeth White.

NEW MEXICO

Acoma

Modern tourists with cameras around their necks huff and puff during the hike to the top of this mesa, 357 feet above the flat plain. Hundreds of years ago (the date is unknown), zealous Indian women made the trek carrying soil and building materials on their backs. The result—the San Esteban Rey Mission—is a marvel of adobe construction: walls ten feet thick and sixty feet high, with handsome murals inside. Even the dirt for the mission cemetery was carried up. Acoma, the "sky city," is the oldest continuously inhabited city in the nation.

Albuquerque

Madonna of the Trail Monument, McClellan Park, Fourth and Slate, NW. The sixth of a dozen such statues placed by the DAR is inscribed on its base, "To the pioneer mother of America, thru whose courage and sacrifice the desert has blossomed, the camp became the home, the blazed trail the thoroughfare. Into the primitive west, face upflung toward the sun, bravely she came, her children beside her. Here she made them a home. Beautiful pioneer mother!" (See *Springfield, Ohio.*)

Erna Fergusson Branch, Albuquerque Public Library, 3700 San Mateo, NE, is named for the prominent travel writer who was especially noted as the first female dude wrangler. Her career of taking tourists to see Indian dances—with the Koshare Tours she founded in 1921—was the subject of her first book, *Dancing Gods,* which one critic called "an excellent guidebook and a valuable piece of reporting." In her lifetime of traveling "practically anywhere," Erna Fergusson bypassed prejudice and intolerance with this philosophy: "Even though I speak no foreign language perfectly, one never sounds like gibberish to me; I also realize that there are many religions—I always had good friends who were Catholics, Jews, Quakers, and assorted Protestants. And dark skins neither frighten nor disgust me. All this in my unconscious has doubtless helped me to make friends in the countries I have written about." Her adobe family home at 1801 Central Avenue, NW, is currently the Manzano Day School.

Folsom

Sarah J. Rooke Monument, Folsom Cemetery, south of town off Route 325. A granite boulder in the shadow of towering Mount Capulin honors the memory of Sarah J. ("Sally") Rooke, heroic telephone operator who gave her life in the line of duty in August 1908. Sally came to Folsom on vacation, and she liked it so much she stayed on to operate the town switchboard at age sixty-five. That is where she was working late in the afternoon of August 27 when the rain started. By evening, the dry Cimarron River bed was aflood with driftwood and debris. As the wall of water broke through, Sally Rooke, alerted by Mrs. Ben Own who lived up-creek, telephoned warnings to the townspeople for two hours before the flood peaked. She saved the lives of all but eighteen Folsomites—including her own. Her body was found seven months later, eight miles south of town. At a tearful ceremony here on high ground nearly two decades later, a cortege of townspeople and telephone workers erected this monument, paid for by subscriptions of ten cents each by her friends and coworkers. A Mountain Bell officer eulogized, "Indeed, if we remember that she was no longer young, that she was alone, that it was night time and

that she was contending with one of Nature's most terrible forces, her strength of heart and purpose were superlative." The bronze marker remembers that Sally perished "while at her switchboard."

Hillsboro

Black Range Museum, Route 180. Depending on whose story you trust, this museum either is or isn't the former hotel and restaurant operated by Sadie Orchard, entrepreneur and stagecoach driver when Hillsboro was a wild boomtown. Most accounts agree that the London-born Sadie was a lady. With her cockney accent, her starched riding habit ("I'd not be caught dead in male attire") and high silk hat, she handled a six-horse hitch with kid-gloved hands through the rugged terrain of the beautiful Black Range. The stage operated daily between Kingston and Lake Valley, a thriving sixty-mile line with several horse-drawn wagons (see *Santa Fe*). Museum curator Lydia Key told us there was some question about Sadie's legendary stage-driving business. "It belonged to her husband first and she may have inherited it. I've heard it both ways, that she drove and didn't drive." Undisputed is the story that Sadie had a fierce tongue and a gutsy manner, and that she also ran a bawdy house—called "the house on the hill" and destroyed some time ago in a flood.

Kingston

Until just a decade or so ago, the hills of the Black Range at Sawpit near here were the feeding and grazing grounds for the finest angora mohair goats in the world. The owner of the farm was Margaret McEvey Reid Armer, known as the undisputed Angora Queen of New Mexico. An authority on breeding and flock management, she started from scratch in the late 1800s and built up a thriving business with a flock of four thousand head of the elegant, silky-haired creatures. One rancher attested, "I would take her word on anything pertaining to the mohair business." When Mrs. Armer died a widow in 1933, her children, with inherited fondness for the family livestock, continued to run the ranch until 1962. Her daughter-in-law, Mary Reid, told us that she was shortly going to Carlsbad, where the goats had been sold, for a visit. "I'm lonesome for them!" she confessed. Although the farmhouse is gone, some of its timbers now line the walls of Sue's Antique Store in Hillsboro.

Las Cruces

Amador Hotel, Amador and Water Streets. Once, men lined up regularly outside these thick adobe walls, eager to enter one of the rooms with girls' names, instead of numbers, on the doors. The romance of the 1850s resounded with the names: La Luz, Maria, Esperanza—stopping points for moneyed soldiers and miners. Today, both men and women line up here with their money. The old Amador Hotel is now the Citizens Bank of Las Cruces. The rooms with the women's names are for storage and for a ladies' lounge.

Roswell

The city that today boasts a thriving retirement community barely had a few adobe buildings in 1875 when Sally Wildy Lea moved in. "She was a brave woman!" her granddaughter recalled more than forty years ago. Although accustomed to luxury in her Sartaria, Mississippi home, she told her husband, Capt. Joseph C. Lea, "I want to be with you, even if there be nothing but the stars over my head." For a while, there was little else. But Sally Wildy Lea vigorously whitewashed the walls of her house, bore a daughter, and made the kind of civic and educational improvements that drew other settlers to Roswell in the early 1880s. Before she died in 1884, the village had become an important trading center, largely on land that Sally Wildy Lea had given to entice developers. No monuments in Roswell recall this, although Wildy Street is named for Sally's father.

Santa Fe

Susan Shelby Magoffin arrived in Santa Fe late in the night of August 30, 1846, claiming in her diary to be "the first American lady" to enter the city under the Star-Spangled Banner.

The eighteen-year-old bride had crossed the plains with her husband and their company in comparative luxury, noting during a relentless rainstorm that she was dry in a traveling shelter, wrapped in a buffalo robe with her "books, writing implements, sewing, knitting, somebody to talk with, a house that does not leak and I am satisfied." Her diary, *Down the Santa Fe Trail and into Mexico,* affords one of those treasured glimpses of the old Southwest, and of a newlywed from Missouri as she reacted to it. Near San Miguel, she blushed to see the Indian women bathing topless in a creek. Near the Mexican border, she learned how to make tortillas, and she taught a Spanish woman the simpler American style of knitting. And at Doña Ana, she boldly climbed the rugged cliffs in the heart of Apache country but vowed to be more careful in the future, "as it is really dangerous."

Site of Doña Tules' Casino, Burro Alley, between Palace Avenue and San Francisco Street. More than a century ago, this tiny lane reverberated with the laughter and clinking of glasses from Gertrudis Barcelo's adobe gambling house. Doña Tules, as she was known, ran an elegant popular *sala,* where the city's finest citizens played monte beneath crystal chandeliers and where they bet on the spinning roulette wheels to the strains of violin music. So many prominent Santa Feans, including the governor, regularly enjoyed the luxurious facilities, where smoking and drinking were freely permitted along with faro and poker, that a swarm of legends arose around the beautiful Doña Tules. Naïve young Susan Shelby Magoffin disapprovingly saw her as "a stately dame of a certain age, the possessor of a portion of that shrewd sense and fascinating manner necessary to allure the wayward, inexperienced youth to the hall of final ruin." More serious gossip, according to one historian, hinted that "she carried on sordid affairs with the leading *politicos,* but that kind of gossip has always circulated, and still does today, about men and women in high government circles. Perhaps she did, but there is no contemporary proof." Doña Tules was sufficiently well informed to warn military authorities of a proposed conspiracy and later to lend the United States government a thousand dollars from her considerable earnings at monte. She was buried in 1852 with a funeral that rivaled her gambling house in elegance.

Palace of the Governors, Palace Avenue. A fat-bellied Overland Stage that once was driven by Sadie Orchard of *Hillsboro* is permanently garaged in the center court of the Museum of New Mexico. The red carriage with black trim is painted with its name, Mountain Pride, over the door. It rolled along on big yellow wooden wheels, pulled by a team of horses or mules. Even with its padded seats, the stagecoach seemed to us a most uncomfortable method of travel, no doubt made at least more colorful by the sound of Sadie's cockney-accented commands burning the mules' ears.

Mary Austin House, "Casa Querida," 439 Camino del Monte Sol (private). When she first came to Santa Fe in 1924, author and lecturer Mary Hunter Austin built this adobe house in the center of the Santa Fe artists' colony. Here she continued her prolific writing and her intense interest in American Indian life, and she became involved in the civic and cultural life of the city. Her creative colleague Willa Cather (see *Red Cloud, Nebraska*) wrote the last few chapters of *Death Comes for the Archbishop* in the study here, without telling Austin what she was writing. The fictional portrayal of Santa Fe's Bishop Lamy, interwoven with the city's Spanish and Indian strains, did not entirely please Mary Austin when it was published in 1927. "I was very much distressed to find that she had given her allegiance to the French blood of the Archbishop; she had sympathized with his desire to build a French Cathedral in a Spanish town," Austin wrote in *Earth Horizon.*

Mary Austin herself was best known for her nature writings *(The Land of Little Rain; A Woman of Genius),* sketches of

Sadie Orchard's stagecoach

desert life that, according to Carl Van Doren, "enlarged the national imagination." H. G. Wells called her "the most intelligent woman in America." When Mary Austin died at sixty-five in 1934, she was cremated and her ashes placed in a natural crypt on Mount Pichaco, overlooking Santa Fe. Some say her ashes were scattered. In a noted memorial, Van Doren called her "a matriarch in a desert. . . . I have been told that she was often imperious and arrogant, and that she could be unsparing when her will was crossed. Matriarchs must rule or they are not matriarchs." A decade after her death, a plaster cast of Mary Austin's hand was placed on display at the nearby Laboratory of Anthropology as its Treasure of the Week.

Santa Fe Public Library, 121 Washington Street. The lively frescoes covering the walls of the tiny entrance hall here was painted by Olive Rush, a tribute to the achievements of a group of Santa Fe women. In 1907 the vigorous Women's Board of Trade built this library with funds raised through an energetic round of fiestas, fairs, and dinner parties. When the building was remodeled in 1931, the murals were added. Olive Rush, a transplanted Indianan who became a noted member of the city's art colony, painted the twin trees of knowledge, their outspread branches blooming with books. All the city's rich cultural backgrounds are represented: Indian children, Domin-

ican nuns, burros climbing rugged trails with boxes of books, a tiny Spanish shepherd reading alone, and farmers tending a field of corn. Since Olive Rush created her frescoes largely during library hours, she used many small children as models, reproducing their alert faces as they concentrated on their books. Two simple statements caption the murals: "The Library reaches the people," and *"Con buenos libros no estás solo."*

Taos

Mabel Dodge Luhan House (private), now owned by Hollywood's Dennis Hopper, was once the home of the celebrated patron of artists and writers. Known as Mabel Dodge when she ran her famous salon in New York—a cultural gathering place for such figures as Margaret Sanger, Max Eastman, and Gertrude Stein—she moved here in the 1920s, married Taos Pueblo Indian Antonio Lujan (later Luhan), and helped promote Taos artists. The struggling art colony blossomed under her strong influence, and she described it in books like *Winter in Taos* and *Taos and Its Artists.* She lived here for a quarter of a century. Max Eastman described her: "She has neither wit nor beauty, nor is she vivacious or lively minded or entertaining. She is comely and good-natured, and when she says something it is sincere and sagacious."

HOME OF
HARRIET TUBMAN
"THE MOSES OF HER RACE"
UNDERGROUND RAILROAD
STATION IN SLAVERY DAYS

Auburn

Harriet Tubman Foundation, 180 South Street Road (Route 34). In this two-story white clapboard house on the twenty-six-acre property that once belonged to the remarkable ex-slave, the A.M.E. Zion Church exhibits a fascinating clutter of memorabilia: Harriet Tubman's bed and oversized Bible; yellowed newspaper stories about her; and the builder's plate of the first Liberty ship named for a black woman—the S.S. *Harriet Tubman,* in 1944. The Reverend Guthrie Carter, who runs the site, told us, "I'm all for women. Look at Harriet. She had no education and she liberated men in the 1800s." In the late 1850s, Tubman settled in Auburn, known for its liberal sentiments, in a house near this one. In old age, barely subsisting on a twenty-dollar-a-month pension grudgingly given by the U.S. Congress for her Civil War service, she deeded her land to the church and ran it as a home for poor and elderly blacks.

Harriet Tubman's Grave, Fort Hill Cemetery, Fitch Street off Parker, is near the A.M.E. Zion Church where she worshiped and where her body was viewed by hundreds when she died March 3, 1913 at ninety-three. Her grave is beneath the only evergreen in the cemetry—a towering cedar that dwarfs the neighboring oaks and maples. The inscription on the granite slab—"Heroine of the Underground Railroad. Nurse and Scout in the Civil War"—concludes, "Servant of God, Well Done."

Memorial to Harriet Tubman, Cayuga County Courthouse, Genesee Street. Just to the right of the entrance to this imposing columned structure is the bronze plaque erected in 1914, a year after the death of the Moses of her people. At ceremonies attended by Booker T. Washington and a host of Auburnites, Tubman's grandniece unveiled the plaque that includes the remark Tubman made in the 1880s, when Susan B. Anthony introduced her at a suffrage meeting in Rochester. Said the poorly educated but worldly-wise Harriet Tubman, "On my underground railroad, I nebber run my train off de track and I nebber los' a passenger."

Austerlitz

Edna St. Vincent Millay Home, "Steepletop," off Route 22. The 700-acre farm and white frame house where the poet lived from 1925 until her death in 1950 is currently occupied by her brother-in-law and sister, Charles Ellis and Norma Millay. They plan to convert it to an artists' and writers' colony, in memory of the famed feminist and writer (see *Manhattan, New York City*). Here at Steepletop, named for the showy pink flower (steeplebush) growing wild in the meadows, Edna St. Vincent Millay wrote undisturbed in an upstairs study (under a sign reading SILENCE). Her husband, Eugen Boissevain, managed all the household chores because, he said, "it is so obvious that Vincent is more important than I am."

Beacon

Madam Brett Homestead, 50 Van Nydeck Avenue. Catharyne Brett inherited this 1½-story house with its scalloped shingles when her husband Roger died in the early 1700s. As the marker by the front door claims, the thirty-nine-year-old widow "wisely developed her inheritance" of 85,000 acres of land, building a gristmill nearby which she ran prosperously—along with her house—until her death in 1764.

Bolton Landing

Marcella Sembrich Memorial Studio, Route 9N on Lake George. The famed Metropolitan Opera star gave voice lessons here during the summers from 1924–34. After her death in 1935, the pastoral pink-stucco structure was turned into a memorial to her, filled with memorabilia of operatic history, including scores and costumes, and opened to the public.

Branchport

Jemima Wilkinson Home, Friends Hill (private). From 1790 until her death in 1819, the woman who preferred to be known as the Publick Universal Friend lived and led her religious followers here (see *Penn Yan*). The striking white clapboard mansion with its handsome architectural details and commanding view of the rolling landscape was a fitting headquarters for Jemima Wilkinson, one of the first women to found a religious society in America. Current owners Joseph and Rena Florance, who use the Friend's Home as a summer retreat, told us that "interested individuals" are welcome in their house. One of its most enduring legends is that Jemima Wilkinson is buried in an unmarked grave in the cellar.

Burke

Site of Almanzo Wilder Farm, Stacy Road. Only a state marker commemorates the place where the husband of the famed children's writer, Laura Ingalls Wilder, lived as a child from 1857 until he was seventeen. It is a testimony to her skill that, more than sixty years later, she accurately described the barns and fields she had never seen—the view of the St. Lawrence River and the nearby stream where the boy and his father fished—in her popular book *Farmer Boy.* An authentic portrayal of her husband's boyhood, it was the third of her Little House series and the only one not set in the West. (See *Mansfield, Missouri*.)

Canandaigua

Site of Susan B. Anthony's Trial, Ontario County Courthouse, North Main Street. The courtroom on the second floor of this yellow columned building stirred this peaceful village and the entire nation on June 17, 1873. Susan B. Anthony was on trial for voting in a state election at *Rochester* the previous November. Presiding over the crowded courtroom was federal judge Ward Hunt, described rather ungenerously in Anthony's *History of Woman Suffrage* as "small-brained, pale-faced, prim-looking." For several dramatic hours, Anthony and some of her voting sisters sat in front of the carved wooden balustrade and listened. Anthony's lawyer called the trial "the first instance in which a woman has been arraigned in a criminal court merely on account of her sex." The district attorney sympathized, but he described how she had broken the law. The judge said simply that Anthony was guilty and directed the all-male jury the find her so without a vote. The next day, the judge made the mistake of asking "the prisoner" if she had any presentencing comments. "Yes, your honor, I have many things to say," Susan B. Anthony began, hardly coming up for air throughout an entire list of outrages, despite repeated attempts from the bench to muzzle her. When she finally stopped, Judge Hunt fined her one hundred dollars. "May it please your honor," Anthony declared, "I shall never pay a dollar of your unjust penalty." She never did.

Carmel

Statue of Sybil Ludington, Route 52. A spirited bronze of a young woman on horseback portrays the gallant nighttime ride of the sixteen-year-old known as the female Paul Revere. On the evening of April 26, 1777, alerted by a messenger that British troops were raiding nearby Danbury, Connecticut, young Sybil mounted her horse and rode cross-country along narrow oxcart trails to call out the volunteer militiamen commanded by her father. From her home in the town now renamed Ludington, she rode past this lakeside spot—where the lively statue depicts her riding sidesaddle and clutching the stick she used to knock on the soldiers' doors—then in a circle to Mahopac, Kent Cliffs, Farmers Mills, Stormville, and back home. Her daring mission, which rounded up enough volunteers to help drive the British back, covered twice the distance traveled by Revere.

Castile

Statue of Mary Jemison, Letchworth State Park. This bronze likeness of the diminutive White Woman of the Genesee was erected here in 1910 to mark Mary Jemison's remains. It is several miles from the spot where she tended crops and dispensed advice until she was in her nineties. Captured by Indians as a child (see *Orrtanna, Pennsylvania*), she became so attached to her Seneca "family," who named her Deh-ge-wa-nus, that she ultimately chose to maintain her Indian ways rather than return to white culture. Her first husband, a Delaware chief, was "a comfortable companion . . . I loved him!" Her second, a Seneca warrior named Hiokatoo, gave her "all the kindness and attention that was my due as his wife . . . he uniformly treated me with tenderness, and never offered an insult." These judgments appeared in her popular narrative, *The Life of Mary Jemison,* an account of her adventure as she recalled it in 1824 at age eighty. It was a best seller in more than two dozen editions.

House of Mary Jemison's Daughter, near the statue, was removed to this spot in Letchworth State Park from its location on the Gardeau Flats on the banks of the Genesee River. Mary built the sturdy one-room log cabin herself in about 1800, hauling the foot-thick beams five miles on her back, just as she had carried her daughter, Nancy, with no effort. In her narrative she confessed, "My strength has been great for a woman of my size, otherwise I must long ago have died under the burdens which I was obliged to carry."

Mary's own house was near Nancy's, a log cabin where she lived from about 1762 to 1831. Here Mary was a respected and admired figure, and one of the area's largest landowners, ultimately controlling some thirty thousand fertile acres—to the dismay of white developers.

Dansville

Site of First Local Chapter of American Red Cross, St. Paul's United Lutheran Church, Clara Barton Street. Two decades after she first dressed the wounds of Civil War victims, while recuperating from an illness here in 1881, Clara Barton established the first local Red Cross society in the country. Inspired by the International Red Cross activities she had witnessed on European battlefields, she lobbied continuously for American participation. Her persistence led the U.S. to sign the Geneva Treaty in 1882; eight years later, the federal government chartered the American Red Cross.

Eagle Bridge

Site of Grandma Moses Home, Grandma Moses Road. The Moses Vegetable Stand, run by the grandson and great-grandson of the famed painter of primitives, fronts on the road near the dairy farm where she used to live. It was there, with no formal training, that Grandma Moses created the colorful, delightful pageants of country life that her brother called "lamb scapes" when she was a child. Grandma Moses was "discovered" in nearby *Hoosick Falls* by the art world in 1940, and the first exhibition she ever attended was her own, in New York City, in November of that year. The schoolhouse she attended, located just west of the Vegetable Stand, has been moved to *Bennington, Vermont*.

Elmira

Elmira College, College Avenue at Park Place. When Elmira Female College opened in 1855, its conditions for entrance and graduation were said to be as stringent as those for men. The seventeen women graduated in 1859 were, it is claimed, the first to earn degrees equal to those granted by men's colleges.

One of the college's more notable faculty members in 1877 was Catharine E. Beecher (see *Milwaukee, Wisconsin*), who helped gain respect for domestic science as a profession, to be taught in schools and not just thought of as housework. Catharine Beecher was opposed to woman suffrage—not equal rights—because she believed that men "will gladly bestow all that is just, reasonable, and kind, whenever we unite in asking in the proper spirit and manner." Fortunately, her brother, Henry Ward Beecher, and thousands of determined suffragists disagreed with her.

Park Church, 208 West Gray Street, once the pastorate of Catharine Beecher's brother, Thomas K., was also the pulpit where Annis Ford Eastman preached. A self-taught minister who took over her husband's calling when he fell ill, Annis Ford Eastman wrote the oration for Mark Twain's funeral and preached radical feminism to her four children. Two—Max and Crystal—became ardent feminists themselves, Max helping to found the Men's League for Woman Suffrage in 1909 and Crystal joining Alice Paul's Political Union (see *Washington, D.C.*). Max once recalled his mother's high school graduation essay entitled, "O Femina, Femina." He wrote, "I am sure it expressed the smiling wish that women would buck up and *be something,* and the opinion that it was their own fault and men's loss as well as theirs if they did not."

Grave of Harriet Maxwell Converse, Woodlawn Cemetery, 1200 Walnut Street. Before the body of the well-known defender of Indian rights was shipped home for burial here in 1903, fifty Indian representatives from New York State attended her funeral in New York City. Indian women placed sacred beads around her neck while the men laid moccasins at her feet, and other members of the Six Nations, whose property and privileges she had worked hard to protect, added charms and tokens for the death journey in her bier. When the casket was loaded on the train for Elmira, both whites and Indians piled flowers and trinkets on top. Such was the tribute to the woman who was made a member of the Seneca Nation in 1891 and given the name Ya-ie-wah-noh ("She who watches over us").

Fayetteville

Matilda Joslyn Gage House, 210 East Genesee (private), was the home of the suffrage orator and editor from 1854 until she died in 1898. The fluted columns were added by Matilda Gage and her husband, as were the bay window and the bathroom— the first bathroom in the village. It was in the upstairs study of this busy home that Gage, Susan B. Anthony, and Elizabeth Cady Stanton wrote much of the text of the first three volumes of the *History of Woman Suffrage.* That voluminous record of their pioneering work, paid for with their own money, includes the report that when Anthony was to be tried for the crime of voting (see *Canandaigua*), Gage spoke in sixteen townships on the theme, That the United States Is on Trial, Not Susan B. Anthony.

Grave of Matilda Joslyn Gage, Fayetteville Cemetery, South Manlius Street. "Copy down that motto," the caretaker advised us, pointing to the inspiring words chiseled on the stone marking her grave. We did not have to be told. Matilda Gage's favorite sentiment, part of a suffrage speech she gave in 1873 and the message she signed in autograph books ever after, reads, "There is a word sweeter than Mother, Home, or Heaven—that word is Liberty."

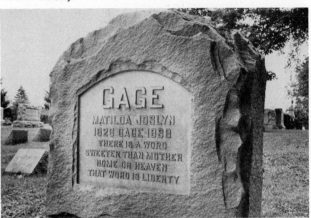

Fishkill

Margaret Sanger Home, "Willow Lake," Van Wyck Lake Road (private). "People still stop outside the gate," current owner Marion S. Land told us, to gaze at the estate once owned by the pioneer of birth control in America (see *Brooklyn, New York City*). Only a few pieces of original furniture remain, though, and the grounds and lake were in "a terrible mess" when Mrs. Land took possession. Margaret Sanger lived in the fieldstone house here from 1924 until the 1940s with her second husband, J. Noah H. Slee. He supported birth control, too, by lending to her cause the business sense that had helped him found the Three-in-One Oil Company, and by smuggling German-made diaphragms (banned in the U.S.) across the border in Three-in-One cartons. Here at Willow Lake, Margaret and her husband, whose name she never took, rode horseback, entertained, and strolled through their garden together, the first hint of luxury and comfort the crusading reformer had known. Here too she wrote *Married Happiness.*

Fonda

Catherine Tekakwitha Memorial, Route 5 west of Fonda. In 1676, in a tiny chapel on this spot, the twenty-year-old Mohawk known as Tekakwitha was baptized a Catholic despite the violent opposition of her Indian family. Choosing the name Catherine—or Kateri in Iroquois—she withstood unceasing persecution from her Mohawk kin who could not tolerate her worship of the white settlers' god. Unable to bear the ridicule, Catherine Tekakwitha slipped out of her village one night and fled by canoe to a friendly Christian settlement in Canada. There she lived a deeply religious existence for four years, until she died at age twenty-four from fever. Her unending piety and voluntary virginity led to her declaration as Venerable by the Church in 1943. The fathers who run this memorial, complete with beatific portraits and touchstone relics, think she ought to be made a saint.

The remains of Caughnawaga, the Mohawk Indian Village where Tekakwitha lived, have been staked out on a hilltop above the memorial. It is the only Iroquois Indian village that has been excavated in this country, rows of stakes indicating the sites of the longhouses where the young convert and her tribespeople dwelled. A bronze plaque points out that when she found refuge in Canada, Tekakwitha was known as the Lily of the Mohawks.

Fort Edward

Grave of Jane McCrea, Union Cemetery, Broadway (Route 4). A slim marble slab, cracked with age, marks the remains of the young Tory woman whose death helped spark the American victory in the Revolutionary War. Jane McCrea was waiting for her fiancé, Loyalist David Jones, to arrive with General Burgoyne's troops. On July 27, 1777, before the lovers could rendezvous, a band of Indians employed by Burgoyne mistakenly attacked the household where Jane was staying, and they removed her scalp. Her unhappy fiancé promptly identified the hairpiece as Jane's, but the real indignation was yet to come. Recognizing the "miserable fate" of the young woman as a rallying cry for the patriots (if a Tory girl was killed, he reasoned, who was safe?), the American commander Horatio Gates spread the word of Jane's scalping. Suddenly, colonists whose sentiments had been tepid, enlisted with rage, greatly expanding the rebel army. The exploited heroine, of course, was dead, unwitting martyr to a cause she had never espoused.

Site of Jane McCrea's Original Grave is further south on Route 4 (Broadway), marked by an iron link fence and six white posts. The body was moved to the Union Cemetery in 1852 by her niece, Sarah Hanna Payne.

Geneva

Site of Geneva Medical College, campus of Hobart and William Smith colleges. A white frame house overlooking Seneca Lake occupies the spot where Elizabeth Blackwell studied to receive the first medical degree conferred upon a woman in the modern world. Born in England and raised in Ohio, Blackwell was inspired in part by a woman suffering from a painful gynecological ailment, who said the suffering might have been relieved if a female physician could have counseled her. But female physicians were neither wanted nor tolerated. Elizabeth was rejected by at least fifteen different medical schools—and she herself turned down the advice of a professor that she don male attire and go to Paris—before tiny Geneva Medical College took her in. The dean had left the decision to the students —"rude, boisterous and riotous" young men—who assumed the application was a hoax and playfully voted to accept it.

On a cold, drizzling, windy November 7, 1847, they learned that their new classmate was real, serious, and determined. Despite official snubs from a doctor's wife and other women, Blackwell found acceptance from her classmates. And although "the professors don't exactly know in what species of the human family to place me," they soon found out. Here is Elizabeth's diary entry for her third day at medical school: "My first happy day; I feel really encouraged. The little fat Professor of Anatomy is a capital fellow; certainly I shall love fat men more than lean ones henceforth."

In 1849 she graduated first in her class, accepting her diploma with the words, "I thank you Sir. It shall be the effort of my life, by God's blessing, to shed honor on this diploma." She did so in *Manhattan, New York City.*

Harrison

Monument to Amelia Earhart, Harrison Railroad Station. At a spot where thousands commute daily to a variety of desk jobs in New York City, a bronze propeller on a granite marker commemorates the somewhat more hazardous trip made by the famed aviator in 1932. On May 21 of that year, Amelia Earhart flew from Harbour Grace, Newfoundland, to Londenderry, Ireland, in a Lockheed Vega (see *Washington, D.C.*), the first woman to make a solo flight across the Atlantic Ocean. The fifteen-hour-and-eighteen-minute flight was planned and prepared at her estate in nearby Rye, where she lived with her husband, publisher George Putnam.

Moments before their 1931 marriage ceremony, Earhart handed Putnam a letter telling of her reluctance to let marriage interfere with her career: "In our life together I shall not hold you to any medieval code of faithfulness to me, nor shall I consider myself bound to you similarly. . . . I may have to keep some place where I can go to be myself now and then, for I cannot guarantee to endure at all times the confinements of even an attractive cage." (See *Atchison, Kansas.*)

Henrietta

Site of Antoinette Brown Blackwell Birthplace, Pinnacle Road (private). A two-story fieldstone house that was her childhood home stands near the site of the log cabin where the nation's first ordained female minister was born in 1825. Accepted into the local Congregational church at the unusually early age of nine, Antoinette Brown attended Oberlin College (see *Oberlin, Ohio*) and was ordained in 1853 in *South Butler*. Three years later, she married Samuel Blackwell, brother of feminists Elizabeth, Emily, and Henry, in this well-proportioned house, a gem among the split-levels sprung up today in this suburb of Rochester. "Nettie" was reluctant to give up her preaching or her woman's rights work and so laid out the ground rules of their marriage for her fiancé: "Only leave me free, as free as you are and everyone ought to be. . . . You may sigh for a more domestic wife. And yet to have me merely go into New York to preach Sundays or gone on a lecturing tour of a few days or weeks won't be so very bad, will it?"

Herkimer

Statue of General Francis E. Spinner, Myers Park, Park Avenue. A seven-foot six-inch bronze likeness of General Spinner, in his familiar military cape and slouch hat, honors the man who first employed women in the offices of the U.S. govern-

ment, a deed now immortalized on this granite base as one that "gives me more real satisfaction than all the other deeds of my life." General Spinner helped liberate the government while holding the office of U.S. treasurer from 1861–75. Faced with the problem of cutting apart newly minted treasury notes that rolled off the presses four to a sheet, Spinner decided that women "with their more nimble fingers could count faster than men." Horrifying male politicians, he selected one Jane ("Jennie") Douglas of *Ilion* to try her mettle at trimming. In the general's words, "I furnished her with a long shears that would cut the length of a sheet at a blow. Her first day's work settled the matter forever." In all, a squad of seven female trimmers of treasury notes was chosen to replace the men. And General Spinner's act opened the way for many more women to come streaming into all government offices.

Unfortunately, the general's achievement was not entirely without flaw. He proudly admitted that one reason for hiring women was that "they could be had at half price." Or even less, in Jane Douglas' case.

Hoosick Falls

Grandma Moses Grave, Maple Grove Cemetery. A series of markers points out the hilly site where the dynamic artist was buried in 1961, aged 101. In a cemetery just outside of a town that looks like her paintings come to life, her epitaph is apt: "Anna Mary Robertson Moses. Her primitive paintings captured the spirit and preserved the scene of a vanishing countryside." (See *Eagle Bridge*.)

Hyde Park

Eleanor Roosevelt Home, Route 9. The humanitarian and stateswoman known as the greatest woman of her generation

never felt entirely comfortable in this, her husband's, family home, since it bore too strongly the imprint of Franklin's mother, Sara Delano Roosevelt. Partly in defense, Eleanor had her own fieldstone cottage built at nearby Val-Kill, a cozy house she shared with Nancy Cook and Marion Dickerman. It was truly the room of her own she required. When she died in 1962, she was buried at Hyde Park, next to her husband, under a single slab of white Vermont marble for both. Perhaps the only appropriate epitaph was Adlai Stevenson's tribute, "She would rather light candles than curse the darkness, and her glow has warmed the world."

Hydesville

Site of Fox Sisters Cottage, Hydesville Road. Atop the original foundations, John Drummond has constructed a replica of the tiny house that is considered to be the birthplace of modern spiritualism. This was the spot where the Fox family, including young daughters Margaret and Katherine, first heard mysterious nighttime rappings in their new home. On the night of March 31, 1848, the spirit "talked" to the girls, responding to their commands with specified numbers of "raps." Margaret and Katherine quickly became celebrities, calling up spirits and raking in a fortune all over the East Coast. Only in 1888 were the skeptics and scientists vindicated, when Margaret—poor, desolate, and taken to the spirits of the bottle—renounced her mystic powers and admitted to an overflow audience at Brooklyn's Academy of Music that it had all been a hoax. The rappings back in Hydesville, she said, were all caused by her big toe.

The revelation, which she retracted a year later, did nothing to shake the already established movement, or the faith of such people as John Drummond. He came here in 1953 from Canada

Rebuilt Fox Sisters' cottage

and built this cluttered cabin that reverberates more from passing cars than from mysterious raps. Drummond pointed out the granite marker, donated in 1927 by the late Mercy Cadwallader of Chicago. Inscribed on it, the rallying cry of the movement begun by the Fox sisters: "There is no death. There are no dead."

Ilion

The first woman employed in an office of the federal government (see *Herkimer*) was described by her employer, U.S. treasurer Francis Spinner, as "a great tall double-fisted girl, that physically and mentally was more than a match for any of the men in the room." Little is known of this pioneer trimmer of treasury notes, except that her salary was a paltry $300 a year compared with the clumsy males' $1,200.

Irvington

Madame C. J. Walker Home, "Villa Lewaro," Route 9 (Broadway). The Anna E. Poth Home for convalescents and the aged is currently housed in the Italianate mansion built in 1917 as a country retreat for the millionaire hairdressing entrepreneur (see *Indianapolis, Indiana*). The Villa Lewaro, named by Enrico Caruso for Madame Walker's daughter, A'Lelia Walker Robinson (see *Manhattan, New York City*), contained oriental rugs, ornate ceilings, sweeping marble staircases and silver and ivory statues. This was where the active Harlem leader entertained her friends. Madame Walker died here in 1919, leaving most of her million-dollar estate to charities and educational institutions. Eleven years later, pressed by taxes and financial problems, her daughter was forced to auction off the priceless treasures. During a two-day sale, the Aubusson tapestry and leather-bound books went to the highest bidders while the caretaker played "The Blue Danube" on Madame Walker's gold-leaf organ.

Ithaca

Helen Hamilton Gardener's Brain, Cornell University, Burt Green Wilder Brain Collection, Zoology Department, Stimson Hall. The brain of the prominent suffragist arrived here in September 1925, about six weeks after her death, "well preserved in a slightly hypertonic solution of formalin," according to the scientific report. Gardener had willed her brain to Cornell for experiments after writing her celebrated book, *Sex in Brain,* refuting a prominent physician's claim that the female brain is inferior to that of the male in nineteen different ways. According to Joseph Papez, who prepared the account in a scientific journal, the feminist brain of the five-foot one-inch Helen Gardener weighed 1,500 grams at removal—"reasonably high for a woman whose normal weight was 106 pounds." But, he went on, "No great value can be assigned to brain weight alone." The study included the observation that her brain had highly developed and finely modeled convolutions in all regions. For the living accomplishments of the Gardener brain, see *Washington, D.C.*

Martha Van Rensselaer Hall, Cornell University. The New York State College of Human Ecology currently occupies the building that was constructed, inspired, and named for the woman who founded Cornell's Department of Home Economics in 1907. Martha Van Rensselaer devoted the first part of her teaching to farm wives, helping to liberate them—as two Cornell faculty members have observed—from a life of "men and mud." Her first two bulletins, "Saving Steps" and "Home Sanitation," were studied by five thousand women. She made the course and the subject matter of home economics so respectable that by 1925 the department became a school of its own, and she was named codirector.

Johnstown

Molly Brant House, "Johnson Hall," Hall Avenue. Superintendent of Indian Affairs Sir William Johnson shared this baronial estate with Mary ("Molly") Brant, a Mohawk Indian who played an influential role during the Revolution. In his papers, Johnson called her his "housekeeper." She bore him nine children. Much later, prudish Victorian writers referred to her as "the Brown Lady Johnson," because, as Johnson Hall historian Col. Charles B. Briggs told us, "they didn't envisage Sir William Johnson shacked up with an Indian woman." For eleven years, "Mrs. Brant," as she called herself, reigned over the house from a second-floor bedroom that is now restored in its original Indian colors of brick red and slate blue.

When she left here after Johnson's death in 1774, Molly moved up the Mohawk Valley about forty miles. There she overheard General Herkimer's plans to relieve the British siege of Fort Stanwix in August of 1777, and she passed the information on to the British general, St. Leger. That enabled him to set up the ambush at Oriskany, killing hundreds of Herkimer's men. According to Colonel Briggs, "after the ambush at Oriskany, the Mohawk Valley wasn't big enough for Molly Brant." She moved to Canada, where she received a lifetime pension from the British crown of one hundred pounds sterling a year for her intelligence activities during the war.

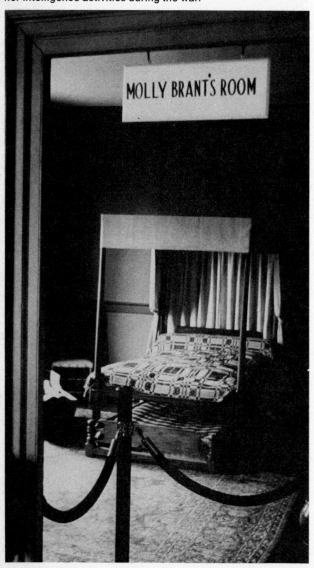

Site of Elizabeth Cady Stanton's Birthplace, Town Square, Main and Market Streets. The State Bank of Albany now occupies the spot where one of the earliest and most effective advocates of woman suffrage was born in 1815. Across the square is the old Tryon County Courthouse (now the Fulton County Courthouse), where the young girl's father, Judge Daniel Cady, dispensed justice. It was in his office that young Elizabeth "heard many sad complaints, made by women, of the injustice of the laws." Informed that such inequities as giving a drunken husband the wife's property or the guardianship of children stemmed from statutes in her father's lawbooks, the ten-year-old reformer "one day marked them with a pencil, and decided to take a pair of scissors and cut them out of the book. . . . I thought that if I could only destroy those laws, those poor women would have no further trouble." Fortunately for his library, her father caught her in time and preserved his books. Elizabeth vowed that when she grew up, she would change the "abominable" laws rather than cut them out. (See *Troy;* see *Seneca Falls.*)

Knox Gelatine, Inc., Knox Road. Rose Markward Knox took over her husband's gelatine business when she became a widow at age fifty, and she was soon recognized as the nation's foremost female industrialist. Her brilliant success began abruptly with the company that gives people jellied salads and hope for weak nails. She later recalled that when her husband died in 1908, "I either had to run the business myself or employ a manager. If I had chosen the latter, as most women would have done in my place, by the time my boys were of age the business would have belonged to the manager." On her own, she raised profits and sanitized the factory. Her advertisements, headed "Mrs. Knox says," dispensed recipes and goodwill. And in 1911 she became the first woman to attend the American Grocery Manufacturer's Association, an organization she had belonged to but never dared participate in. Later she was elected its first female director. When she died in 1950 at ninety-three, she was still actively working as chairman of the board of her multimillion-dollar company.

Lewis

Home of Inez Milholland, "Meadowmount," Lewis-Wadhams Road (private). The older of two sisters raised here, Inez Milholland was a feminist before she entered Vassar (see *Poughkeepsie*) in 1905. As an undergraduate, she radicalized most of her conservative classmates as suffragists; as an alumna, she dazzled the nation by leading a votes-for-women parade down Pennsylvania Avenue, in *Washington, D.C.,* seated on a white charger named Gray Dawn and wearing a white cossack robe. Among her converts to the feminist cause was Eugen Jan Boissevain, a Dutchman who became her husband in 1913. Apparently he enjoyed being the husband of a liberated wife. When Inez Milholland Boissevain died—tragically young—in 1916 during a western suffrage tour, he chose to marry another feminist, Edna St. Vincent Millay (see *Manhattan, New York City*).

Grave of Inez Milholland Boissevain, Congregational Church cemetery, was dedicated at a simple family affair. Weeks later, suffragists from all over the country paid tribute to the dedicated leader in the Capitol building in Washington, D.C. Still later, the citizens of nearby Elizabethtown changed the name of Mount Discovery—along the Lewis-Elizabethtown town line looking down on her home at Meadowmount—to Mount Inez. They do not appear to have told this to the map makers.

Lockport

Ann Eliza Webb Young House, 422 Walnut Street (private). The famed lecturer who had the audacity to divorce Brigham Young and speak out against polygamy (see *Salt Lake City, Utah*) lived here from 1878–80. By then a celebrated lobbyist for the reform of the laws permitting plural wives, Ann Eliza addressed her appeals to the First Lady, Lucy Webb Hayes, and to audiences from Colorado to Indiana. To Mrs. Hayes she wrote of the effects of polygamy: "Women in Utah are but child-bearing slaves." (See *Manistee, Michigan.*)

Middletown

Site of Lydia Hasbrouck House, "Sybil Ridge," 87 Linden Avenue. Memorial Junior School appropriately occupies the site once owned by Lydia Sayer Hasbrouck, the first woman elected to the Middletown School Board in March 1880. In the interests of comfort, she early traded her heavy petticoats and confining corsets for the liberating new costume called "the bloomer" (see *Seneca Falls*). When the shocked faculty of Seward Institute in Florida rejected her admission application because of her radical apparel, the young woman "registered a vow that I would stand or fall in the battle for women's physical, political and educational freedom and equality."

In the famous octagonal stone house she shared here with her husband (whom she married in 1861, dressed in wedding bloomers of white satin with a tunic of white India silk), she published *The Sybil,* a semimonthly journal dedicated to dress and health reform. A victim of taunts and jibes hurled at all women who chose not to wear the outfits men designed for them, Lydia Hasbrouck stuck with her bloomers long enough to read this grudging concession from a Yonkers newspaper: "Her dress sets off her symmetrical and finely developed form to great advantage."

Knox quickly conveyed "his sincere thanks" from West Point. It is not recorded whether the restraining power of the hairnets, keeping Knox's wig neat, contributed to the ultimate American victory.

New Paltz

Mohonk Mountain House, Lake Mohonk. This gabled and turreted mansion just south of the Catskill Mountains was the meeting place (1883–1916) for the Lake Mohonk Conferences of Friends of the Indian, proceedings in which women played an important role. The purpose of the group was to reform the insensitive U.S. Indian policy. Among the female members: Mary Bonney, who in 1879 circulated a petition to keep Indian lands safe from white settlers, garnering thirteen thousand signatures and helping awake the public consciousness; Amelia S. Quinton, who helped Bonney complete her 300-foot-long petition and also coorganized the influential Women's National Indian Association; Alice Cunningham Fletcher; Alice M. Robertson (see *Muskogee, Oklahoma*); and Osia Jane Hiles of *Milwaukee, Wisconsin,* who read Helen Hunt Jackson's *Ramona* (see *San Juan Bautista, California*) and took up the cause of the California Mission Indians. At the 1887 conference Hiles said, "I do not believe there is anything that a woman can't do if she undertakes to do it."

New Rochelle

Carrie Chapman Catt House, 120 Paine Avenue (private). Eight years after she reached her goal, with the passage of the Nineteenth—the woman suffrage—Amendment, the famed feminist and pacifist (see *Ripon, Wisconsin*) moved here with her close

Montour Falls

The Seneca village formerly located here, with its dozens of houses, fine orchards, and plentiful crops, was originally called Catharine's Town by white settlers after its remarkable ruler, Queen Catharine Montour. A "superior woman," according to later accounts, who became the leader of the Senecas after her husband died in the mid-1700s, Queen Catharine was described as possessing "fearless and determined character" and "more than ordinary intellectual powers." Along with her powerful female relatives (see *Wilkes-Barre, Pennsylvania,* and *Sunbury, Pennsylvania*), she was highly respected. Several years after she died in 1804, businessman Charles Cook planned to erect a statue over Queen Catharine's grave. His own death frustrated that monument, and today a barely visible stone marks the remains of the town's namesake.

Newburgh

Hasbrouck House, Liberty and Washington Streets. During her year-and-a-half stay with her husband George, Martha Washington skillfully made two hairnets which she sent to General Knox on March 6, 1783. Their delivery was delayed only by the late arrival of some tape she needed to finish them. General

friend and suffrage lieutenant, Mary Garrett Hay. Shortly afterwards, in 1928, Hay died while waiting for guests to arrive for her seventy-first birthday party (see *Bronx, New York City*). Catt stayed on alone, continuing her international work. She died in this house in 1947, two days after telling her biographer, Mary Gray Peck, that she hoped to live to see the United Nations become a going concern.

New York

Bronx

Site of Anne Hutchinson Home, Boston Road and Hutchinson River, Eastchester. Exiled from *Boston, Massachusetts,* and sheltered temporarily at *Portsmouth, Rhode Island,* the outspoken rebel against Puritanism settled in the Dutch colony here in 1642 with her six children. In August 1643, several neighboring Siwanoy Indians killed Hutchinson and all but one of her children. For many years, historians believed that the site of the house was Split Rock, a glacial boulder in Pelham Bay Park. Recently, though, it has been determined that her cabin was more likely located here, in an area called Hutchinson's Meadow on early maps, on the west bank of the Hutchinson River, also named in her honor. Local map makers were considerably more generous than the Puritan elders whom she had offended in the Massachusetts Bay Colony. According to one report, when the Massachusetts people heard about the massacre that destroyed Anne, they "said it was divine justice and they celebrated the news."

New York Botanical Garden, Bronx Park. This spacious leafy retreat was founded at the suggestion of moss expert and botanist Elizabeth Britton, who was inspired while strolling through the Royal Botanic Gardens at Kew, England. The garden here was incorporated in 1891 thanks to the support and encouragement of Britton and her botanist husband who later became its first director. Without ever acquiring her Ph.D., Elizabeth Britton developed such great expertise in bryology that she was appointed honorary curator of mosses in 1912. Of the many varieties named in her honor, at least one genus, *Bryobrittonia,* a very unusual and distinctive Arctic moss, is a treasured specimen in the garden's herbarium. Another, *Gertrudiella,* a South American moss, was given Elizabeth Britton's middle name.

WOODLAWN CEMETERY, East 233rd Street and Webster Avenue
The first interment here was of a woman, Phoebe E. Underhill, in January 1865. Many others have followed:

Elizabeth Cady Stanton Grave, off Observatory Avenue. On the tall, polished granite column marking the graves of the entire Stanton family (including feminist daughter Harriot Stanton

Blatch), one face of the shaft is devoted to Elizabeth Cady Stanton, "Mother, Author, Orator, Woman Suffrage leader. Called Woman's Right's Convention. . . . Demanded votes for women. Founder National Woman Suffrage Association." Had the monument maker inscribed all of her accomplishments, it might have stretched to *Seneca Falls, New York,* and back. A familiar figure with her white curls crushed beneath her bonnet, the tiny, round woman from *Johnstown, New York,* was described by a contemporary as someone who was "always in high animal spirits, and who, like a ripe grape, carries a whole summer's sunshine in her blood."

Carrie Chapman Catt Grave and Mary Garrett Hay Grave, Laurel Avenue. Two ivy-covered burial places, side by side in death as they were in suffrage parades, are marked by a single monument inscribed in block letters: "Here lie two, united in friendship for thirty-eight years through constant service to a great cause." Both were indefatigable suffrage workers, Catt the general and Hay one of her lieutenants, in the last, successful drive for the vote. They lived together in *New Rochelle, New York,* from 1905, when Catt was widowed for the second time. Catt was the president of the National American Woman Suffrage Association from 1900 to 1904, handpicked by her predecessor, Susan B. Anthony. It was Carrie Catt's brilliant organization and oratory that made the Nineteenth Amendment a reality.

Alva Smith Vanderbilt Belmont Grave, West Border Avenue. Elizabeth Cady Stanton and Carrie Chapman Catt may have been the real leaders for the vote (reflected in their simple but noble graves), but you have to give it to Alva Belmont for style. Like this ornate, gargoyle-adorned chapel where she was buried in 1933, she approached the suffrage cause with pizzazz. A flamboyant socialite who became a feminist in her fifties, she underwrote more than a decade's worth of militant feminist activities. Not only did she pay the bills for office space and for demonstrations, she took part in them. In a 1912 suffrage parade she marched, just a few steps ahead of a sewing machine operator named Rebecca Goldstein, from Washington Square all the way up Fifth Avenue, past the stately mansion at Fifty-second Street where Alva Belmont entertained social royalty. (See *Newport, Rhode Island.*)

Miriam Florence Folline Leslie Grave. When the noted widow of publishing magnate Frank Leslie died in 1914, herself a publishing mogul known internationally as Mrs. Frank Leslie, she left the bulk of her two-million-dollar estate to Carrie Chapman Catt for "the furtherance of the cause of women's suffrage." After the red tape of legalities, Catt put the remaining nearly one million dollars toward the highly respected Leslie Suffrage Commission, a group that helped educate the public about the benefits of votes for women.

Madame C. J. Walker Grave, Butternut Avenue. Groups of black persons frequently make pilgrimages to the huge but simple stone marking the burial place of the successful founder of a beauty business. Madame C. J. Walker (see *Irvington, New York;* see *Indianapolis, Indiana*) died in 1919 at the age of fifty-two, a millionaire who devoted much of her life and fortune to helping others who were less successful. Her last prayer: "Not for me, O Lord, but for my race."

Brooklyn

Lady Deborah Moody House, 27 Gravesend Neck Road, Gravesend (private). This 1½-story Dutch farmhouse is thought to be the house Lady Moody built in 1645. An English widow who fled religious persecution first in her own country, then at settlements at Swampscott and Salem, Massachusetts (where Governor Winthrop wrote of her as "a dangerous woeman"), she became the first female patentee in the New World, carefully establishing her ordered English settlement here in the thriving Dutch colony. Her substantial holdings, unheard of for a woman, extended along what is now Brooklyn's Atlantic shore, and they included Coney Island, Bensonhurst, Sheepshead Bay, and Midwood. The refined and educated Lady Moody, who maintained a fifty-seven-volume library in her house, proved a sensible town planner, laying out her village on a grid system still discernible in the street plan.

opened the nation's first birth control clinic on October 16, 1916. With her sister Ethel Byrne, and coworker Fania Mindell, the pioneering Sanger gave out "safe, harmless information" for ten cents per woman in a two-room, $50-a-month clinic. "We talked plain talk and gave plain facts to about 500 women," Sanger reported, unaware that one patient was really a police officer in disguise. Several days later, the crusading trio was arrested for distributing contraceptive information, and the clinic closed down. Both Sanger and her sister landed in jail for short terms, but the publicity and sympathy they engendered assured the ultimate success of the birth control movement. Sanger never lost her outrage over the police action. "We are not surprised at being arrested," she admitted, "but the shock and horror of it was that a *woman,* with a squad of five plain clothes men, conducted the raid and made the arrest. A woman —the irony of it!" (See *Fishkill, New York.*)

Manhattan

Statue of Liberty, Liberty Island. The world's most famous woman on a pedestal was placed there in 1886 by a Frenchman named Bartholdi, who modeled the figure after his mother. The base was installed by Americans, at precisely the same time that thousands of women were crisscrossing the country

Gravesend Cemetery, Gravesend Neck Road across from Lady Moody's house, is locked inside a chain link fence to keep out the sort of vandals who nearly destroyed it several years ago. A compact (1.6 acres) and charming burial ground, it is said to contain, somewhere among the overgrown headstones, the unmarked grave of Lady Moody, who died in the late 1650s.

Site of Margaret Sanger Birth Control Clinic, 46 Amboy Street, Brownsville. In the midst of a neighborhood where Jews and Italians filled the squalid tenements, Margaret Sanger boldly

to replace their individual pedestals with the vote. At a fundraising campaign for the perch, esteemed poet Emma Lazarus contributed her sonnet "The New Colossus," inspired by the expulsion of Jews and others from their homelands. Her words have greeted arrivals at New York Harbor ever since: "Give me your tired, your poor, your huddled masses yearning to breathe free . . ."

St. Elizabeth Ann Seton Shrine, State Street at Battery Park. America's first native saint lived here in the "Watson House" from 1801–1804. When her husband died in Italy, Elizabeth Ann Seton returned to this elegant columned red brick house to reflect on her decision to become a Catholic. Despite the opposition of relatives and Episcopalian friends, the socially prominent hostess and mother of five not only converted, but she founded the Sisters of Charity of St. Joseph, the first American religious sisterhood. Her generous and holy life was officially sanctioned by Pope Paul VI in September 1975—two hundred years after her birth. A statue of St. Elizabeth Ann Seton stands over the doorway of the church, and, inside, a large stained-glass window over the altar depicts the steps of her life that led to canonization. (See *Emmitsburg, Maryland; Baltimore, Maryland.*)

John Street Methodist Church, 44 John Street, is the oldest Methodist church in America, founded in 1768 at the urging of Barbara Heck. She was known as the mother of American Methodism, and along with Philip Embury she helped spread the new religion with a Wesley Chapel on this site—the first such chapel in the country. The current building is the third erected at this location.

Site of Woodhull, Claflin & Company, 44 Broad Street. The modern office building where financial district workers now labor with predictable regularity, is an inelegant descendant of the spectacular plate-glass and carpeted office that once housed the nation's first female stockbrokers. At least four thousand visitors thronged into the new brokerage on February 4, 1870 to see the dashing Victoria Woodhull and her sister, Tennie C. (for Tennessee) Claflin. The *New York Herald,* which dubbed them "The Queens of Finance" and "The Bewitching Brokers" decided that "their extraordinary coolness and self-possession ... is far more remarkable than their personal beauty and graces of manner, and these are considerable." So many shocked financial wizards came to ogle the handsomely gowned occupants behind the walnut desks that the women were forced to hang a sign reading, "All Gentlemen will state their business and then retire at once."

Henry Street Settlement, 265 Henry Street. Four generations of families on the Lower East Side have enjoyed easier lives because of the agency founded here in 1894 by the remarkable Lillian D. Wald, a trained nurse who received part of her education at Elizabeth Blackwell's medical college, here in Manhattan. In 1893, Wald traded her comfortable uptown residence for the fifth-floor walkup of a Lower East Side tenement when she first observed the sickness and miserable conditions. "We were driven to it. We were driven to everything we did," she later wrote. Among other achievements, she invented the term *public health nurse* and, in 1893, the Visiting Nurse Service that was the seed of the city-wide program now in existence. A year later the service became the Henry Street Settlement which she headed until 1933. It still functions in the shadow of the public housing project named for Lillian Wald. (See *Westport, Connecticut.*)

The Great Hall, Cooper Union, Cooper Square. One of the most notable speeches by a woman at this famous lecture hall was given by Anna Dickinson, "the Joan of Arc of the Civil War," who held five thousand listeners spellbound in May 1863. Fresh from dynamic lecture tours in New Hampshire and Connecticut, where her fiery oratory swept Republican candidates to victory in state elections, the eloquent Quaker brought the house down here with her impassioned plea for the Union. When reporters found themselves unable to capture the swift "magical rapidity of her words," one contented himself with observing, "Applause came often and in long-continued storms, hats were swung and handkerchiefs waved and at times the whole house was like a moving, tumultous sea, flecked with white caps. Never have I seen in New York any speaker achieve such a triumph." When the clapping subsided, emcee Henry Ward Beecher rose and announced, "Let no man open his lips here tonight. Music is the only fitting accompaniment to the eloquent utterances we have heard." Anna Dickinson tucked away her thousand-dollar fee to the strains of "John Brown's Body."

Edna St. Vincent Millay House, 75½ Bedford Street (private). This 9½-foot-wide town house was home to Edna St. Vincent Millay and her new husband, Eugen Jan Boissevain, in 1923. Here the budding feminist and social rebel (see *Camden, Maine*) embarked on the most successful writing period of her career. Her circle of friends included Edmund Wilson and Max Eastman. Her poems included a tribute, "To Inez Milholland," her idol as a Vassar undergraduate whose widowed husband was now married to Millay.

An earlier residence, on the top floor of 25 Charlton Street, was the scene of many Millay soirees in 1918. Dozens of artists, actors, and writers crowded into the apartment every night, where "Vincent" held court in one room, her sisters and mother entertaining friends in three adjoining rooms. (See *Austerlitz, New York.*)

New York Infirmary, Stuyvesant Square East and Fifteenth Street. When no hospital in New York would accept female physicians on its staff, Elizabeth Blackwell, the nation's first woman to receive a medical degree (see *Geneva, New York*), opened her own dispensary in 1854. The clinic, on East Seventh Street, was to serve the poor, the sick, and "medical practicioners of either sex." Several years and many fund-raising drives later, Blackwell bought an old house at 64 Bleecker Street for the enlarged New York Infirmary for Indigent Women and Children. She chose May 12, 1857, as the opening day, to honor the thirty-seventh birthday of her friend Florence Nightingale. Dr. Blackwell was assisted by her younger sister Emily, also a physician, and by Dr. Marie Zakrzewska, a German doctor who would later distinguish herself in *Roxbury, Massachusetts*. This was the nation's first hospital staffed by women, serving women.

In 1868, Dr. Elizabeth joined with Dr. Emily and others in establishing the Women's Medical College of the New York Infirmary, and Elizabeth occupied its first chair of hygiene. Although it was not the first medical school for women, it was among the best, including on the faculty Dr. Mary Putnam Jacobi, who returned from Paris in 1871 after becoming the first female student admitted to the Ecole de Médecine in 1868. The Blackwells' school closed in 1899 when Cornell Medical College admitted women.

Meanwhile, the Infirmary itself, with thirty-five beds, had moved to its present site. One century and considerable expansion later, it still stands, so progressive that male physicians were admitted to the attending staff in the 1960s.

Margaret Sanger Residence, 17 West Sixteenth Street. A marker on the side of the building points out that birth control advocate Margaret Sanger lived here. Her Research Bureau was also here from 1923–73, "the internationally renowned family planning service, education and research organization."

Elsie de Wolfe and Elisabeth Marbury House, 122 East Seventeenth Street (private). Interior decorator Elsie de Wolfe (Lady Mendl) and playwright's agent Elisabeth Marbury lived here from 1887 to 1911, holding court at a lively salon. The transformation of the gloomy Victorian decor into a bright white atmosphere, cotton and muslin replacing velvet and plush, was the beginning of Lady Mendl's career as the first person to turn interior decorating into a profitable profession.

Site of Mary Lindley Murray House, 16 Park Avenue. An eye-level plaque on the Thirty-fifth Street side of this enormous apartment house identifies this spot as the center of the hilltop farm where Mary Lindley Murray is said to have rendered her "signal service in the Revolutionary War." On September 15, 1776, while four thousand of Gen. Israel Putnam's patriot troops beat a hasty retreat northward to the camp of General Washington, Mary Murray entertained three British generals and a governor at her elegant house on Murray Hill. With her gracious hospitality, the shrewd Mrs. Murray so charmed the famed General Howe, plying him with tasty cakes and the fine Madeira

Mrs. Murray's strategy

wine of her absent Loyalist husband, that he let the rebels escape. A surgeon with the retreating Continental forces recorded in his diary, "It has since become almost a common saying, among our officers, that Mrs. Murray saved this part of the American army."

Site of Cary Sisters Home, 53 East Twentieth Street. From 1856, the parlor of the house occupied by poet-authors Phoebe and Alice Cary was a noted cultural center. Their Sunday evening receptions were attended by such cosmopolitan figures as Horace Greeley, Anna Dickinson, Elizabeth Cady Stanton, and John Greenleaf Whittier. Greeley said the house had "one of the best private libraries, with the sunniest drawing-room (even by gaslight) to be found between King's Bridge and the Battery." Both women came to New York from *Cincinnati, Ohio,* enjoying widespread popularity for their verses that were published in contemporary journals. When Alice became the more prolific writer, turning out prose sketches as well (a London critic praised her "unhackneyed grace"), Phoebe elected to attend to domestic chores to leave her sister free for literary pursuits. Both were abolitionists and suffragists. When Alice died here in 1871, followed by Phoebe soon after, Dr. Emily Blackwell bought the celebrated house. It no longer stands.

Town Hall, 123 West Forty-third Street, was the brainchild of six progressive women. All members of the League for Political Education, an 1894 New York suffrage group founded to teach women how to use the vote if they ever won it, these six women planted the idea that ultimately raised the money and opened the auditorium in January 1921. Although the original purpose was to hold continuing lectures on adult education, the Town Hall (which the women insisted should have no socially divisive boxes or seats with obstructed vision) soon was the scene of various cultural activities. The founders were Eleanor Butler Sanders, Catherine Abbe, Adele M. Fielde, Dr. Mary Putnam Jacobi, Lee Wood Haggin, and Laura Day.

Sara Delano Roosevelt House, 47–49 East Sixty-fifth Street. This brick and limestone town house was a gift to her newlywed son and daughter-in-law—Franklin D. and Eleanor—in 1905 from Sara Delano Roosevelt, who conveniently provided a connecting door to her own adjoining residence. Today, clubs and groups connected with Hunter College meet in the rooms where Sara Delano Roosevelt and Eleanor helped nurse Franklin back to health when he was stricken with polio.

Museum of Modern Art, 11 West Fifty-third Street. The outdoor sculpture garden named for Abby Aldrich Rockefeller occupies the site of her eight-story mansion where, in May 1929, she and two other women launched the plans for the world-famous museum. A shrewd art collector who early recognized the value of the moderns, Rockefeller joined with Lizzie Bliss and Mary Quinn Sullivan (both of whom had been influenced by the trend-setting 1913 Armory Show) and decided that a new gallery for works of the modern school should be created. The founding mothers were described by museum biographer Russell Lynes as "women of spirit, vigor, adventurousness, and, not unimportantly, of commanding wealth." That May, over lunch in the Rockefeller brownstone, they persuaded Buffalo art collector A. Conger Goodyear to head up a committee to organize the gallery. Six months later, the Museum of Modern Art opened.

Angel of the Waters Statue, Bethesda Fountain, Central Park. The figures of Purity, Health, Peace, and Temperance frolic in the waters. Emma Stebbins (see *Boston, Massachusetts*) made the sculpture, executed in Paris, and completed in the park in 1873.

Joan of Arc Statue, Riverside Park at West Ninety-Third Street. The first equestrian statue occupying a public site to be fashioned by a woman was sculpted of bronze by Anna Vaughn Hyatt and dedicated in 1915. The artist, who also designed

under her married name, Anna Hyatt Huntington, won the commission in an international competition. A replica of the prize-winning statue is in Blois, France, the town where young Joan was imprisoned.

Bethesda Fountain

Whitney Museum of American Art, Madison Avenue and Seventy-fifth Street. When the Metropolitan Museum of Art rejected sculptor Gertrude Vanderbilt Whitney's collection in 1929, she founded her own museum in Greenwich Village, installing pioneering art collector Juliana Force as its director. An outgrowth of Whitney's earlier studio and gallery for young artists (where she modestly waited eight years to display her own works) the museum grew in stature and moved uptown, finally to this site in the spectacular precast concrete building designed by Marcel Breuer. Whitney also sculpted the statues of Peter Stuyvesant (at Stuyvesant Square) and the Washington Heights Memorial (Broadway and 168th Street) which won the New York Society of Architects' Medal in 1922. (See *Washington, D.C.; Cody, Wyoming.*)

Metropolitan Museum of Art, Fifth Avenue and Eighty-first Street. Art collector and suffragist Louisine Elder Havemeyer died in 1929, willing to this museum her outstanding collection of impressionist art, a priceless bequest that instantly brought the conservative institution into the forefront of exhibitors of contemporary paintings. Mixed in with the treasures she had astutely chosen before they were popular (by Degas, Monet, Cézanne) was El Greco's *View of Toledo.* Previously Mrs. Havemeyer had displayed the collection only once—to raise money for Alice Paul's militant suffrage group, the Congressional Union.

New York Medical College, Fifth Avenue and 106th Street, absorbed the pioneering New York Medical College and Hospital for Women, the first women's medical school in the state. Dr. Clemence Harned Lozier founded the school in 1863, an outgrowth of the series of free medical lectures she gave for women. After lobbying intensively for the state charter, Dr. Lozier became the first president of the college and its dean until 1887. She once undertook a difficult operation rather than entrust it to a male surgeon, saying, "I desire to do this for the sake of the cause, for the credit of woman." She inspired dozens of female physicians, including her own daughter-in-law. When Lozier's school closed in 1918, all its remaining students were transferred here to New York Medical College.

Site of Madame C. J. Walker House, 108–110 West 136th Street. Black businesswoman Madame C. J. Walker built a four-story columned town house on this site in 1914 with $50,000 in profits from the hairdressing business started in *Indianapolis, Indiana.* Considered the wealthiest black woman in the world at the time, she was also a highly respected humanitarian, and the first person voted by readers of *Ebony* magazine to its Hall of Fame in 1956. After Madame Walker's death in 1919 at her *Irvington, New York,* estate, her daughter A'Lelia turned the house into a cultural salon, entertaining bohemians and intellectuals, black and white, during Harlem's literary and artistic renaissance of the 1920s. One of the prominent guests in the popular room of her house known as the Dark Tower was poet Countee Cullen, a black poet whose name is given to the library branch now occupying this site.

Margaret Corbin Monument, Fort Tryon Park, 192nd Street and Broadway. A bronze plaque on a rock in the shadow of the fort commemorates Margaret Corbin, "the first American woman to take a soldier's part in the War for Liberty." Her heroic feat took place here on November 16, 1776, while the Americans tried to defend Fort Washington (later rebuilt and renamed Fort Tryon) from the assault by British and Hessian troops. When Corbin's husband John, a Virginian in the Pennsylvania artillery, was felled by fire, she took over his cannon post, ably discharging the weapon throughout the remainder of the losing battle. "Captain Molly" suffered wounds from three enemy grapeshot that left her without the use of her left arm for the rest of her life. (See *West Point, New York.*)

Eliza Jumel House, West 160th Street and Edgecomb Avenue. The historic house known popularly as the Morris-Jumel Mansion was the residence from 1810–65 of the flamboyant, slightly eccentric woman of whose various names Madame Jumel is the best known. She earned the name by tricking wealthy wine merchant Stephen Jumel into marrying her in 1804, an unsuccessful attempt to gain respectability after being socially ostracized as his mistress for years. When Stephen Jumel learned that the exaggerated tales of her noble upbringing were entirely false, he got angry; many years later, when he was in need of money, she shrewdly but dishonestly transferred title of all his holdings to herself. A year after Jumel died, she married Aaron Burr in the tearoom here. But he didn't stay long. He was a philanderer she described as "that wretch." And after chasing him out of the house with fire tongs when he proposed that he manage her extensive property, she divorced him. Madame Jumel died upstairs in 1865. Her stately fulllength portrait at the top of the stairs still dominates the house, which many say is haunted by her ghost.

Staten Island

Alice Austen House, 2 Hyland Boulevard (private). For threequarters of a century, this once-elegant mansion was the home and darkroom of pioneering photographer Alice Austen. Born here in 1866, owner of her own camera before she was a teenager, the young adventurer washed her plates and prints at a backyard pump and snapped photos of her maids and her bedroom for posterity. Frequently posing in her own shots, using a concealed cable to trigger the shutter, she captured the manners and morals of the Victorian Age with rare insight: on racetracks, at parties, on the newly imported tennis courts, at Ulysses Grant's funeral, and on the ships bearing Admiral Dewey on his return from Manila as they steamed down the Narrows past her front lawn. Never interested in selling her photos, Alice Austen landed in a poorhouse in her old age, having been forced out of this house when the bank foreclosed the mortgage. Fortunately, a picture researcher spotted her fine works, rescuing them from obscurity and selling enough to make Alice Austen's last years more comfortable. She died in 1952, several months after proudly overseeing an Alice Austen Day at the nearby Staten Island Historical Society, where her pictures were displayed. Today, the house suffers from age, termites and the ravages of years of dampness, with little claim on the city's strained budget for needed repairs.

Julia Gardiner Tyler House, 27 Tyler Street. The young socialite, who shocked her East Hampton family in 1839 by allowing her ornately clad figure to appear on a handbill advertising a dry goods store (under the caption, "Rose of Long Island"), lived here during the Civil War, widow of President John Tyler. A Southern sympathizer whose heart was at her abandoned Virginia plantation, Sherwood Forest, she defied local sentiments and displayed a Confederate flag in an upstairs room. Her neighbors found this unpatriotic and hauled it down with force.

Niagara Falls

Horseshoe Falls, Canadian side. Before the turn of the century, the most daring escapade involving these falls was a walk above them on a tightrope. That wasn't enough for Annie Edson Taylor. Eager for a change of career, the forty-threeyear-old schoolteacher from Bay City, Michigan, saw real possibilities in an entirely original vaudeville act starring herself, a wooden barrel, and the Horseshoe Falls. On October 24, 1901, as thousands of spectators cheered her on, she climbed into her barrel and plunged over the edge. The trip was bumpy but swift. Within minutes, the dazed voyager emerged from her battered barrel into the welcoming arms of her admirers. She thus became the first person to navigate—and survive—such a trip. Unfortunately, her act did not lend itself to frequent repetition or reward. Mrs. Taylor died a pauper. Her barrel, however, is preserved at the Niagara Falls Museum.

Ogdensburg

Maria Ameriga de Vespucci House, 303 Washington Street. The Remington Art Museum now occupies the mansion where the chatelaine of wealthy heir George Parish lived for eighteen years. Madame Vespucci so inspired Walter Guest Kellogg that he wrote his popular book *Parish's Fancy* to explain the story.

Oswego

Grave of Dr. Mary E. Walker, Rural Cemetery. An iconoclast to the end, the physician and suffragist who early spurned the confinement of female garments was buried here in 1910, wearing the familiar black frock men's suit in which she was frequently arrested by authorities who disapproved of women in pantsuits. Long denied a commission as an assistant surgeon in the Civil War—despite her proven competence and the urging of a New York senator—in 1864 Dr. Walker finally became the first woman to hold such a commission. She attended the wounded of the Second Corps, Army of the Potomac. Later captured by the Confederates, she achieved the dubious honor of becoming the first female officer war prisoner exchanged for a man of equal rank.

The Congressional Medal of Honor she was awarded in 1865—the first given to a woman—can be seen at the Oswego County

Historical Society, along with her assistant surgeon's medal, her medical diploma, her tattered women's franchise banner, and a sitz tub.

Penn Yan

Only the name of the township—Jerusalem—survives in the promised land named New Jerusalem where Jemima Wilkinson and her band of religious followers settled in about 1790; they were the nucleus of a colony that thrived for three decades (see *Branchport*). Some years earlier, the tall, graceful twenty-three-year-old claimed to have risen from the dead, thence to be known as the Publick Universal Friend. With this title, wearing flowing unisex robes and apparently possessed of a magnetic personal style, she preached a cult of celibacy and piety that at one time attracted nearly three hundred disciples.

One favorite story that was circulated about her miraculous powers had her standing at the edge of nearby Seneca Lake, promising to walk across the waters. "Do you all have faith I can do this?" she asked the multitudes at the shore. "Yes!" they are said to have chorused. "Then," she said, sweeping back into her elegant carriage, "there is no use in further demonstration."

Poughkeepsie

Vassar College opened its doors in 1865. The college was the gift and dream of wealthy brewer Matthew Vassar, who got the idea from his schoolteacher niece, Lydia Booth. "It is my hope," Vassar told the trustees a year before the college opened, "to inaugurate a new era in the history and life of woman. I wish to give one sex all the advantages too long monopolized by the other. Ours is, and is to be, an institution for women—not men." But not forever. Today, the college that boldly began with twenty-two of its thirty faculty members female (including the distinguished Maria Mitchell—see *Nantucket, Massachusetts)* has become coeducational. Some of the illustrious alumnae from the all-women days: feminist Harriot Stanton Blatch, class of 1878; suffrage idol Inez Milholland, 1909; scientist Ellen Swallow Richards, 1911; and poet Edna St. Vincent Millay, 1915.

Prattsburg

Narcissa Prentiss Birthplace. Lace curtains trim the windows and *The Oregon Trail* is among the books on the shelves in this white clapboard house. Narcissa Prentiss, one of the first two women to cross the Rocky Mountains, was born here in 1808. The Fellowship Hall in the Prattsburg Presbyterian Church (which she joined at age eleven) is named for her; a plaque on a geranium-cradled boulder on the lawn of the Franklin Academy recalls that she was a member of its first class of girls. Although early unable to travel on missionary service like all "unmarried females," Narcissa wed Dr. Marcus Whitman in 1836 and set out for the frontier almost immediately (see *South Pass, Wyoming).* A century later, the highway from Prattsburg to Naples, New York (Route 53) was renamed the Narcissa Prentiss Highway, a generous but symbolic gesture for a road that is considerably easier to negotiate than the trails blazed through the rugged Rockies. The garden to the side of the house is comprised of shrubs sent in 1942 by descendants of the Cayuse Indians who turned out to be the Whitmans' unfriendly neighbors in *Walla Walla, Washington.*

Rochester

Susan B. Anthony House, 17 Madison Street. During the last forty years of her life, when she wasn't crisscrossing the country to campaign for the vote; or when she wasn't publishing her suffrage journal, *The Revolution,* in New York; or when she wasn't attending the suffrage conventions of which she was president or popping in at the White House to ask for equal rights, then Susan B. Anthony was probably here, in this three-story red brick house. It was from this cradle of feminism, shared with her sister Mary, that she set out on her historic trip to the polls in November 1872 to test the law and vote in an election. Two weeks later she was arrested by a U.S. deputy marshal in this house and hustled aboard a streetcar to report to the commissioner's office. When the conductor asked Anthony for her fare, she pointed to the deputy and proclaimed, "I'm traveling at the expense of the government. This gentleman is escorting me to jail. Ask him for my fare." (See *Canandaigua.*)

The house is a museum now, filled with the photographs, stuffed Victorian furniture, and faded rugs of its early occupants. Up in the musty attic, where Anthony carefully recorded her memoirs, a spinning wheel from her father's mill huddles under the sloping roof. In her second-floor study, where she penned instructions to her workers, priceless photographs of suffrage leaders cover every inch of the walls. Anthony's familiar wire-frame glasses are delicately laid in a display case near votes-for-women buttons and several locks of her graying hair. We saw the Quaker shawl that kept her warm in drafty lecture halls and the mahogany desk on which Carrie Chapman Catt drafted the final, winning suffrage amendment.

In Susan B. Anthony's bedroom rests the worn alligator traveling satchel she took on her suffrage journeys to Europe. It was in this room that she died, fourteen years before women could vote, on March 13, 1906, her hand in that of her good friend and coworker, Anna Howard Shaw. Several days earlier she had told Dr. Shaw, "Perhaps I may be able to do more for the cause after I am gone."

Susan B. Anthony's Grave, Mount Hope Cemetery, 791 Mount Hope Avenue, is marked on the cemetery map along with that of her close friend, abolitionist Frederick Douglass. Anthony's simple oval marker, near the granite cube marking her parents' grave, is inscribed: "Liberty, Humanity, Justice, Equality." On the day we visited, someone had planted Dainty Marietta marigolds on her burial place and left the identifying seed packet. Anthony's last public utterance, at her eighty-sixth birthday celebration a month before she died, became the rallying cry for the suffrage movement: "Failure is Impossible."

The Rochester Historical Society, 485 East Avenue, celebrates Susan B. Anthony's birthday every February 15 by dressing a papier-mâché mannequin in the garnet velvet costume she wore to meet Queen Victoria. The figure is placed in the Historical Society doorway. "I really do it for my own pleasure," director Mary Shannon told us as she removed the blue plastic bag from the prim outfit. It has a white lace shawl and cuffs, with a tight bodice and full ruffled skirt. Holding it up, we discovered that Anthony was as tall as we are, although perhaps a bit more ample size twelve in view of her frequent seat of honor at the banquet table.

The society also has a weapon labeled the Gun of Mary Jemison (see *Castile*)—a "fowling piece" of the late 1700s with a four-foot barrel. Mrs. Shannon disputes the ownership, however, and told us of the tiny Indian captive, "I doubt she ever carried it. It's heavy as lead."

Gleason Works, 1000 University Avenue. As the boss's daughter, Kate Gleason had an advantage: At the age of twelve, she got to work Saturdays in her father's machine works. Less than five years later, she was back at work, having left her engineering studies at Cornell to help out with the family business. From 1890 to 1901 she was secretary-treasurer of the firm, and she shocked clients as perhaps the world's first female seller of machine tools. Her contributions to the business, along with her suggestion that her father develop a machine for cutting gears, led her to election as first female member of the American Society of Mechanical Engineers in 1914. The fireproof housing she was instrumental in having built—the first such project at low cost—still stands in East Rochester. It made her the first female member of the American Concrete Institute.

Seneca Falls

Elizabeth Cady Stanton House, Washington Street (private). When the thirty-two-year-old feminist and abolitionist arrived here in 1847 with her husband and three children, weeds covered the five-acre lot, and the house desperately needed paint, paper, and a new kitchen. Her father (see *Johnstown*) handed her a check and said with a smile, "You believe in woman's capacity to do and dare; now go ahead and put your place in order." Today the residence she fixed up and lived in for sixteen years has been altered and painted a rather unhistoric bright green, but a marker on the lawn proclaims it as the home of the "promoter of the first woman's rights convention . . . held across the river."

The young mother's first year in Seneca Falls was plagued with the chores of housekeeping, child care, drunken neighbors, and muddy roads. In a plea that predated Betty Friedan by nearly a century, she wrote, "I now fully understood the practical difficulties most women had to contend with in the isolated household, and the impossibility of woman's best development if in contact, the chief part of her life, with servants and children. . . . my only thought was a public meeting for protest and discussion." She soon voiced that thought at *Waterloo*.

Here, too, Stanton met the woman who would become her closest friend and coworker for the next half century: Susan B. Anthony of *Rochester*. It was in this house, seated before an old fireplace, that Stanton and Anthony plotted the strategy for the social revolution known as the suffrage movement. "Here we forged resolutions, protests, appeals, petitions, agricultural reports, and constitutional arguments," Stanton later wrote. She described their lifelong collaboration: "I am the better writer, she the better critic. She supplied the facts and statistics, I the philosophy and rhetoric, and together, we have made arguments that have stood unshaken through the storms of long years."

Site of First Woman's Rights Convention, Fall and Water Streets. The laundromat now on the site of the old Wesleyan Chapel, where the historic meeting took place in 1848, offers a practical lesson in priorities. Women got washing machines long before they got the vote—and it didn't even require a convention. Perhaps that was part of what the courageous feminists who called this meeting that July were talking about when they resolved to remove woman from her "circumscribed limits" to an "enlarged sphere" far beyond kitchen and washtub.

After the *Waterloo* tea party, the planners met at Mary Ann McClintock's house nearby. Huddled around a mahogany table now preserved at the Smithsonian Institution in *Washington D.C.,* they rewrote the Declaration of Independence along feminist lines: "We hold these truths to be self-evident: that all men and women are created equal . . ." Quite as revolutionary as the patriots who had drafted the original, the female rebels listed "the repeated injuries and usurpations on the part of man toward woman"—fifteen inequities, from refusing women the vote to making divorce favor the man. This Declaration of Sentiments was followed by a Declaration of Resolutions.

On the first morning of the convention, a beautiful July 19, some three hundred people, including forty men, from as far as fifty miles away, came in horse-drawn wagons and by foot to the little Wesleyan Chapel for the meeting. On the second day, 100 people signed the combined Declaration of Principles, and by unanimous vote eleven of the twelve resolutions. The twelfth resolution was Elizabeth Cady Stanton's bombshell: "Resolved, that it is the sacred duty of the women of this country to secure to themselves their sacred right to the elective franchise." The first public declaration of women's right to vote barely squeaked by. But the women's movement, a stirring awareness in the minds of many, was alive and growing.

Amelia Bloomer House, 53 East Bayard Street (private). This two-story white clapboard house with its charming cupola and huge lawn was the home of Amelia Bloomer for only one year, sometime after she got married in 1848 (and omitted the word *obey* from the ceremony). Her next home in Seneca Falls was across the river at the corner of Cayuga and Fall streets, where the Masonic Temple now stands. Using the printing press next door to it, she put out her famed temperance paper, the *Lily,* which appeared on January 1, 1849, the first newspaper owned, operated, and edited by a woman for women. Primarily a tool to protest the evils of the grape, the *Lily* soon turned into a suffrage paper.

Once in the early 1850s, Elizabeth Gerrit Smith came to town to visit her cousin, Elizabeth Cady Stanton. Instead of a long skirt, she wore a pair of full long Turkish trousers in black broadcloth, topped by a tunic that reached just below the knee. Amelia Bloomer adopted the new costume and wrote so eloquently about its benefits that it was named for her. When

Elizabeth Cady Stanton and Susan B. Anthony

the ridicule from intransigent males became too much, most reformists abandoned their trousers and slipped back into their skirts without breaking stride in the march for equal rights. Amelia Bloomer also disposed of her bloomers and, back in skirts, became an efficient organizer in *Council Bluffs, Iowa.*

Seneca Falls Historical Society, 55 Cayuga Street, contains a Woman's Rights Room with fascinating memorabilia of the nation's suffrage leaders. The director enthusiastically pointed out her favorite items: a collection of Amelia Bloomer's handwritten speeches ("which are begging to be published"); Elizabeth Cady Stanton's square-shaped piano ("seven of her children took lessons on it"); and a restored rocker in which Stanton claimed her children. From a different era, the society also has a folding fan from the early 1900s with the message "Keep Cool. And Raise a Breeze for Suffrage."

Sherwood

Emily Howland House, State 34B. This was the home of the Quaker abolitionist and educator who spent long years working with young black girls and freed slaves. For a time associated with Myrtilla Miner's school in *Washington, D.C.,* Emily Howland traveled south after the Civil War to run freedmen's villages. Here in her own hometown, Howland founded the Sherwood Select School, whose teachers lived in her own house. An avid suffragist as well, Howland told a convention in 1904, "Our cause came straight from the anti-slavery cause. All its early advocates were also advocates of freeing the despised race in bondage. Let us not forget them now. Neither a nation nor an individual can be really free till all are free."

South Butler

Site of Antoinette Brown Blackwell's Church, Main Street (private). On a rainy September day in 1853, Antoinette L. Brown (see *Henrietta*) was ordained as a minister of the Congregational Church—the first ordained female minister in the nation, and probably in the world. The twenty-eight-year-old preacher accepted the call, for $300 a year, three years after completion of the theology course at Oberlin College (see *Oberlin, Ohio*). Her history-making ordination took place during a raging storm, in the Baptist Church for the Congregationalists' roof was leaking. The regular preacher's sermon was based on the text, "There is neither male nor female; for ye are all one in Christ Jesus," and a contemporary observer wrote, "the arguments were forcible."

Today, the Congregational Church, where Rev. Antoinette Brown preached for one year, has been moved, painted brown, and converted into "just a barn" in the backyard of Helen Gay. The Baptist Church across the street—site of the actual ordination—has fared much better. It is now a cheerful pink residence owned and lived in by Earl Gay, a feisty tombstone salesman whose products decorate the lawn across which a huge crowd walked to witness Brown's ordination. Mr. Gay pointed out the original foot-square beams and carved wooden doors of the church/house, and assured us that the tiny sleepy town used to be "quite a place."

Troy

Site of Troy Female Seminary, Russell Sage College, Second Avenue. On this lawn, in 1821, educator Emma Hart Willard founded the first endowed institution for the education of women. When she could not raise the public funds she needed for her proposed new school (see *Middlebury, Vermont*), she turned to private sources, accepting $4,000 from the citizens of Troy. That September, ninety young women enrolled, willing beneficiaries of Willard's bold new curriculum. Along with geometry and Greek, zoology and French, she taught geography with maps and physiology with drawings (although she did accede to the demands of some shocked parents and preserved the girls' modesty by placing cardboard over the anatomical sketches in their texts). An enormous success that was the model for boarding schools and normal schools of the future, the Troy Female Seminary was internationally respected.

One discontented pupil was Elizabeth Cady Stanton (class of 1832), who only attended school here when the all-male Union College would not admit her. She found the two years the "dreariest of my whole life" and amused herself with such mischievous tricks as kicking the prayer bell down a flight of stairs and waking the entire dormitory. The administrators never caught her.

The statue of Emma Willard here was erected in 1895, twenty-five years after she died, by a committee of her pupils and friends. She is depicted enthroned on her favorite upholstered velvet armchair, a book in her right hand, gazing squarely at the Willard Library across Second Street. Inscribed on the base: "Her most enduring moment, the gratitude of educated Woman." The same year, the school was renamed for her. Today, the Emma Willard School is at Pawling and Elm Grove avenues.

TROY FEMALE SEMINARY.

Russell Sage College, on the original site of the Troy Female Seminary, was founded here in 1916, fifteen years after the Willard School vacated the grounds. Margaret Olivia Slocum Sage, an 1847 graduate of Troy Seminary, used her fortune to finance the college, named for her husband.

Waterloo

Jane Hunt House, Routes 5 and 20, just east of town (private). The gathering that took place in this handsome brick columned house on July 13, 1848 was one of history's most effective business lunches. Mrs. Hunt had invited her good friend, Lucretia Mott (see *Philadelphia, Pennsylvania)* to meet with some other friends, including Elizabeth Cady Stanton (see *Seneca Falls*). Stanton had met Mott in 1840 at the Anti-Slavery Convention in London, where both suffered the indignity of enforced silence behind a partition when the male delegates refused to allow women to participate. Now, at this tea party in Waterloo, the old friendship was rekindled. And Stanton, by then frustrated with housewifery, "poured out, that day, the torrent of my long-accumulating discontent, with such vehemence and indignation that I stirred myself, as well as the rest of the party, to do and dare anything. . . . we decided, then and there, to call a 'Woman's Rights Convention.' " The women drew up an advertisement to be published in the next day's *Seneca County Courier.* The small unsigned notice read, "Woman's Rights Convention . . . to discuss the social, civil and religious rights of women" in *Seneca Falls,* five days hence. A movement was about to be born.

Watervliet

Site of First American Shaker Colony, "Niskayuna," State 155 (Albany-Shaker Road). The pioneering religious order was founded here in 1776 by Mother Ann Lee. Born in England where she joined the newly organized society of Shakers— named for their religious manner of dance—she quickly became the group's leader. Seeking relief from the persecution that had jailed her followers and herself, Mother Ann Lee, the acknowledged spiritual chief of a cult that preached celibacy and racial and sexual equality, sailed for America in 1774. Part of the land they first settled is now the Ann Lee Home, a rest home for the elderly on 787 acres purchased from the Shakers in 1926. Here the growing colony flourished, and, from here, under Mother Ann Lee's supervision, ten other Shaker settlements were established in New England.

The Shaker Cemetery, Route 155 near Albany Airport, is a striking memorial to the principles of simplicity, economy, and order preached by Mother Ann Lee. Neat rows of white marble headstones plainly identify the burial places of early Shakers, a tranquil treat for the eye and the mind despite the airplanes roaring overhead and the cars barreling down the highway inches away. The only distinction for Mother Ann Lee's slab among the symmetrical markers is its height—slightly taller than the rest in the row. It is characteristically modest, announcing just her name and dates (1736–84). Also buried in this historic graveyard is Lucy Wright, who took over the leadership of the colony from after Ann Lee's death until 1821.

West Point

Monument to Margaret Corbin, West Point Cemetery. More than 125 years after she died, the heroine of the Battle of Fort Washington (see *Manhattan, New York City)* was rescued from an obscure grave nearby and reinterred with other old soldiers here behind the Old Cadet Chapel. The bas-relief marking her burial place portrays the strong, energetic fighter at her husband's cannon. The inscription recognizes her as the first woman in the country to receive a U.S. pension (1779)—"half the pay and allowances of 'a soldier in the service.' " The inscription does not point out that the customary order forbidding rum to female camp followers was relaxed to allow the ailing Captain Molly her full alcoholic ration in 1782.

Graves of Susan and Anna Warner, West Point Cemetery. The two sisters were buried with military funerals overlooking Constitution Island—the landmass on the east bank of the Hudson River donated by them to the academy. Directly across from West Point, it was their home from 1836, when they moved into the lovely cottage that now bears their name.

Both sisters made their names as writers. Susan, known under the pseudonym Elizabeth Wetherell, wrote the best seller *Wide, Wide World,* a volume second in popularity only to *Uncle Tom's Cabin.* Anna chose the pen name Amy Lothrop. After her sister died in 1875, Anna maintained the cottage and determined to keep the unspoiled Revolutionary War site from the hands of developers or tourists. At the urging of Margaret Slocum Sage, she sold it to Sage, who then donated it on behalf of both women to the U.S. government in 1908 to be included in the U.S.M.A. Reservation. One of the featured attractions, along with the dirt fortifications studied by West Point cadets, is the Anna B. Warner Memorial Garden, planted with flowers she mentions in *Gardening by Myself.*

Constitution Island

NORTH CAROLINA

Asheville

"Immediately in front of our windows is an open space through which we look at the green hills on which the town is built, rising with gentle, undulating swell in every direction, while afar lie the blue mountains, height over topping height, peak rising behind peak, graceful lines blending, through the gaps more remote ranges to be seen lying so pale and faint on the horizon that it is almost impossible to tell where the mountains end and sky begins." Thus wrote Frances Tiernan—"Christian Reid" (see *Salisbury*)—in her 1875 novel of a pleasant summer trip through the countryside, *The Land of the Sky,* that gave this part of the state the lyrical title by which it is still known.

Allanstand Mountain Crafts, 16 Mountain Street. Frances Louisa Goodrich, a teacher and missionary who came to North Carolina in 1890, almost single-handedly revived the old arts of spinning and weaving among the mountain people. Her primary purpose was to "make less dull and monotonous the lives of my neighborhood women . . . to give [them] a new interest, the pleasure of producing things, the delight of the skilled worker and artist"—work that at the same time would bring in a paying income. She opened this outlet for the women to sell their beautiful handicrafts, and in 1930 she donated it to the Southern Highland Craft Guild which now maintains this shop. Goodrich, who died in 1944, also wrote *Mountain Homespun* (1931), still the most authoritative work on the subject.

Chapel Hill

University of North Carolina. The first state-supported university in the country to open its doors (1795) did not however accept women until more than a hundred years later—and then only if they wore hats and gloves to class and were accompanied by a chaperone. Males backed away in horror and fear; as one pioneer observed, "No matter how crowded the lecture room, a coed always has two benches to herself." In 1901 thirteen female students were not permitted to have their pictures in the yearbook, and, years later, women were still not invited to their own graduation ceremonies. When a residence hall for these valiant scholars was being considered, the college newspaper headlines blared, "Shaves and Shines but no Rats and Rouge . . . Chapel Hill is a place inherently for men and men who desire no women around. . . . women would only prove a distracting influence, could do no possible good, and would turn the grand old institution into a semi-effeminate college." Today, the enrollment of more than 6,000 women out of a total of just under 14,000 makes it slightly less than semieffeminate.

Cornelia Spencer Home, "Widow Puckett House," 501 East Franklin (private). The town's most ardent supporter of its famous university moved here in 1826 when she was a year old. She always pleaded with her mathematics professor father for the same lessons he gave her two older brothers. She moved away in 1855, but she returned to her father's home in 1861 as a widow and began teaching Latin and Greek to the village children. In later years, a student, recalling her impressive personality, said she always gave one the feeling that she ought to be addressed in Latin. Spencer helped establish Chapel Hill's summer teacher-training programs, and she was instrumental in the Normal and Industrial School for Women (1891); it later became the Woman's College at *Greensboro*. Spencer, who had never been allowed to go to the university because she was a woman, now has a building named in her honor at both of the above-mentioned campuses.

Cornelia Spencer House, 410 East Franklin (private). Always loyal to the same street, Spencer nevertheless liked to move around. It is said that here in the gabled white house of her only daughter, June, she wrote her well-documented *The Last Ninety Days of the War in North Carolina* (1866). (See *Raleigh*.)

Cornelia Spencer House, "The Presbyterian Manse," 513 East Franklin Street (private). The dynamic educational reformer lived here occasionally, in the home of her brother Charles, where she wrote numerous newspaper columns in enthusiastic support of higher learning for women.

Harriet Morehead Berry House, 121 South Columbia Street (private). The woman responsible for all the fine roads in North Carolina started out working as a stenographer for the State Geological and Economic Survey in 1901 when she moved here from *Hillsborough*. Shrewdly analyzing all the dictation about roads and money problems she had to record, Berry realized that the only way to get North Carolina "out of the mud" was through a state highway system. Despite heavy opposition from politicians right up to the governor, who referred to her as "that waspish woman," Berry succeeded in the passage of the Good Roads Association Bill in 1921 that authorized millions in state bonds to improve roads, "one of the most stupendous pieces of legislation in the history of the state." (See *Raleigh*.) An eyewitness to the legislative battle wrote, "She was on the ground early, knew what she wanted, knew men well enough to know how to go after them, and she went. . . . She led while appearing to cooperate." Berry lived in this two-story white frame house until her death in 1940.

OLD CEMETERY, Route 54
Cornelia Spencer Grave. "Historian, writer, teacher, friend of the university," died at eighty-three in 1908. Nearby is another grave, noting the less heralded service of a woman:
Dilsey Craig Grave. "Sixty years a slave, chiefly in the house of Dr. James Phillips," reads the inscription of this simple tombstone, erected by a grandchild of Phillips. Phillips was Cornelia Spencer's father.
Grave of Harriet Morehead Berry. Once called "the best politician in the state," Berry is commemorated with a beautiful monument whose inscription reads simply, "She served the Commonwealth."

Currie

MOORES CREEK NATIONAL PARK
Heroic Women of Lower Cape Fear Monument. A garland of flowers in her modestly folded arms, the heroic woman in white marble gazes fondly at the grave of one of her brave sisters. The monument commemorates the hundreds of village women who ably tended the farms while the men fought the Revolutionary War battles.
Polly Slocumb Grave. On the eve of the dreadful Moores Creek Battle in February 1776, Polly (or Molly, or Mary) had a nightmare where she saw "a body wrapped in my husband's guardcloak, bloody dead, and others dead and wounded on the ground about him." Leaping out of bed, she saddled her horse and galloped sixty miles from her home in Goldsboro "through a country thinly settled and poor and swampy; but neither my own spirits nor my beautiful nag's failed in the least." Arriving at Moores Creek in the early morning, Polly found her husband "as bloody as a butcher and as muddy as a ditcher." Undeterred by the gruesome sight, she spent the rest of the day car-

ing for the wounded men. Polly's courageous ride and battle-field devotion here have been disputed, but she is given credit for heroic services elsewhere and at a later date, probably the skirmish at Rockfish Creek about thirty miles to the northeast in 1781. At least she is remembered somewhere, although the simple marker over her grave reads only, "Wife of Ezekiel Slocumb, who departed this life March 6, 1836 aged 76."

Edenton

Site of Edenton Tea Party, Courthouse Green. A large, deco-rated bronze teapot, with a cannon for a table, marks the site where on October 25, 1774, fifty-one of the town's leading fe-male citizens, organized by Penelope Barker, signed a long one-sentence statement. They declared that they were totally in support of the Continental Congress protest against British injustice including the tax on tea and manufactured goods. These women had no need of Indian disguises as did the men of the Boston Tea Party a year earlier, and they openly acknowl-edged their rebellion with their signatures. Their gathering was cruelly satirized in English newspapers: a relative of one of the women, on hearing of their bold actions, wrote sarcastically of "the female artillery" of Edenton.

Penelope Barker House, South Broad Street. The president of the defiant tea-party association lived in this spacious white house several years after yet another courageous and rebel-lious exploit. It is said that when her husband (one of three she outlived) was away in London during the war, she discovered some British soldiers trying to steal her carriage horses from the stable. Grabbing her husband's sword, she confronted the men and sliced the reins from their hands, triumphantly lead-ing the horses back to their stalls as the men fled in fear.

Faison

Mary Lyde Hicks Williams Home, Route 403 (private). This im-posing eighteen-room house, surrounded by towering oak trees, was built in 1853. In it lived the prodigious artist who painted more than five hundred oils of settlers and slaves in the early 1900s. Many of these beautiful portraits still hang on the walls of the house, now owned by Mary's son, Virginius, who told us that she kept on painting right into her eighties. When she lost her sight, a nurse companion told her what colors to use.

Fayetteville

Flora MacDonald Memorial, Cool Springs Street. Near this spot, commemorated by a marker, stood Flora MacDonald waving good-bye to her husband, Allan, and her Scottish countrymen as they marched off to battle the rebellious Whigs at Moores Creek Bridge in 1776. A living legend in Scotland after her 1746 capture and imprisonment while trying to smuggle "Bonnie Prince Charlie" to safety, Flora was revered by her neighbors as a courageous heroine for her past exploits when she moved here from Scotland in 1774. Perhaps if Flora had been at the head of the Tory brigade instead of being left behind, the battle would not have been such a terrible rout for them. Allan Mac-Donald was one of a dozen taken prisoner, and the Loyalists were finished in North Carolina.

Greensboro

Kerenhappuch Turner Monument, Guilford Courthouse Na-tional Military Park, Route 220. When she heard that her son (some say grandson) John had been wounded here in March 1781, Turner rushed to his side, riding more than three hundred miles on horseback from her home in Maryland. She saved John's life by suspending a tub of cold water—from which the constant dripping on his wounds allayed his raging fever. This monument, said to be the first one erected on a battlefield to a woman for services in nursing, as well as the first erected on American soil to a war heroine, was dedicated in 1903. A sweet-faced Kerenhappuch (a biblical name meaning "Horn of Beauty"), whose vital devotion was rewarded by her own life-span of 115 years, is shown here carrying a plate. Unfortu-nately, vandals have desecrated her memorial, firing a bullet through her lovely cheek and pilfering the cup that rested on the saucer. The towel that she used to soothe John's brow has somehow slipped off over the years.

Greensboro College was founded in 1838, through the able efforts of Cornelia Spencer (see *Chapel Hill*), as the first col-lege for women in North Carolina. It became coeducational in 1956, but women here still outnumber men by three to one.

Dolley Payne Madison Birthplace, Guilford College, 5505 West Friendly Avenue. A four-ton boulder with a bronze plaque, mis-spelling Dolley Madison's first name, states "In a house which stood back of this marker was born 'ye 20 of ye 5 mo. 1768'" the wife of James Madison. Dolley was named Dorothea in honor of Dorothea Spotswood Dandridge, who later married Patrick Henry. (See *Ashland, Virginia*.)

Hendersonville

Grave of Lelia Davidson Hansell, Oakdale Cemetery, Sixth Ave-nue. The Sunshine Lady was buried in a custom-designed tomb, three feet above the ground with prisms in the concrete wall so that the sun would forever shine on her skeleton. Hansell, who often said that flowers and sunlight were the greatest gifts of God, and who could not bear the thought of pale bones, built this sunny mausoleum just two weeks before her death from tuberculosis in 1915. Every summer, hundreds of curious tourists peered through the prisms, claiming they could see a three-inch skeleton and even the buttons of her dress. But in 1939, after complaints from relatives of the more-conventionally entombed, the fervid sun worshiper's final solarium was shaded with a concrete plate.

High Point

SPRINGFIELD MEETINGHOUSE CEMETERY
Grave of Hannah Millikan Blair. "I cannot fight with Thee but I can help feed and clothe Thy army," said this gentle Quaker patriot who risked her life many times in support of the Revolution. Hannah once saved two men by hiding them in the corncrib; another time, she bundled up a soldier in the feather tick she was mending and calmly informed the Tory officers, "Thee may search as Thee please." After the war, she was awarded a modest government pension for her courageous service, always in keeping with her simple religious code.
Grave of Tabitha Holton. A simple headstone commemorates Holton's historic achievement: "Granted license to practice law by Supreme Court of North Carolina, Jan. 1878." The state's first female lawyer died in 1886.

Hillsborough

Harriet Morehead Berry House, "Sunnyside," St. Mary's Road (private). The state's champion of speedy, smooth highways spent most of her youth in this four-chimney colonial house. In about 1900 she moved to *Chapel Hill* to begin her epochal career of public service. This house was built by Harriet's grandfather, Capt. John Berry, a noted architect whose name is honored prominently all over town. The local historical society lamented that Harriet "is pretty much unsung in her own home," adding knowingly, "a common fate."

Manteo

Virginia Dare Birthplace, Fort Raleigh National Historic Site, Route 64. The first English child in the New World was born on August 18, 1578, and six days later was christened "Virginia"—the name of the pioneering colony, which mysteriously disappeared three years later along with the nation's tiniest heroine. She has been assured immortality by the dozens of novels, poems, and plays written about her brief life and by the well-traveled Virginia Dare Trail that leads tourists to the Wright Brothers Memorial.

Morganton

Elizabeth Avery Colton Birthplace, Route 40 (private). Colton, born here in 1872, devoted her life to improve female education in the South at a time when colleges trained woman "for such graces as will make·[her] successful as a home getter. . . . and for such solid accomplishments as will be useful to her after the home is got," as summarized by one male president. Such regressive views of woman's capabilities led Colton to publish her influential and controversial survey, "The Various Types of Southern Colleges for Women" in 1916 while she headed the English department at Meredith College in Raleigh. She charged that some finishing schools were masquerading as colleges, and she so enraged one principal of a bogus school that he threatened to shoot her. "Miss Colton looked calmly at him; he dropped his eye and retired before her steady, honest gaze. Shortly after, he closed his so-called college," a contemporary historian recalled. Her devotion to educational honesty led to the founding of the American Association of University Women three years before her death in 1924.

New Bern

Mary Bayard Devereux Clarke House, 519 Easy Front Street (private). Until her death in 1886, the brilliant poet spent the last two decades of her life in this Louisiana-style house that still belongs to her family and contains several of her books, a sofa, and her charming portrait at age twenty, with eyes "so bright, so blue and so full of mischief." Mary, described by her friends as "a highly cultivated and intellectual woman," edited the state's first anthology of local verse (1854) under the pseudonym Tenella (now the name of a street in town). She also wrote several volumes of her own poetry, including *Mosses from a Rolling Stone of Idle Moments of a Busy Woman* and *Reminiscences from Cuba,* where she went in 1855 for a health cure. Settling here in 1868, the industrious Mary wrote to a friend, "I am busy editing my paper, 'The Literary Pastime'; corresponding with others; contributing to two magazines; translating a French novel; added to which I am composing the libretto for an opera, and writing Sunday school hymns at five dollars apiece." Her great-granddaughter Mary Barden proudly told us that critics of her day compared her to Shelley and Keats. One critic wrote, "her poetry in the parlor was what Daniel Webster's speeches were in the Senate." We especially liked these stirring lines from "Clytie and Zenobia":

> In woman's heart there ever lies
> A queenly instinct, which will rise
> At times, however trodden down,
> And claim its right to wear a crown.

Eunice Hunt Memorial, First Presbyterian Church, New Street. Hunt, the great-grandmother of Mary Clarke, was one of the founders (ca. 1819) of this, unusual to the South, weather-boarded meetinghouse with its Ionic portico. Hunt's name is inscribed in a white marble tablet near the pulpit.

Carrie Cutter Grave, New Bern National Cemetery. Grave number 1698 in section 10 is a small, simple marker with her name, the wrong home state (Massachusetts), the date of her death (March 24, 1862), and not a word about her outstanding work (continued until her death) nursing the wounded on the battlefield at Roanoke Island. At least her admirers in her hometown of *Milford, New Hampshire,* have made sure that Carrie's noble deeds will never be forgotten.

Jones House, 231 Eden Street. Emeline Piggott, who used to smuggle Confederate messages in the folds of her velvet skirts, was detained here during the federal occupation of the town. But the resourceful spy found a safer hiding place—she swallowed the incriminating evidence. Eventually released by unsuspecting officials, she continued her stealthy missions.

Raleigh

Women of the Confederacy Memorial, Capitol Square. A bronze statue of a seated woman reading to a sword-carrying youth honors the brave women of the Confederacy, of whom Cornelia Spencer (see *Chapel Hill)* wrote in her book, *The Last Ninety Days of the War in North Carolina:* "When I forget you, O ye daughters of my country, your labors of love, your charity, faith and patience, all through the dark and bloody day, lighting up the gloom of war with tender graces of women's devotion. . . . when I cease to do homage to your virtues and your excellencies, may . . . my voice be silent in the dust."

Harriet Morehead Berry Memorial, Highway Commission Building, Salisbury Street. A plaque was dedicated here in 1962 to honor "The Mother of Good Roads in North Carolina. . . . She loved her state and served it well." (See *Chapel Hill.)*

Delia Dixon Carroll Infirmary, Meredith College, was dedicated in 1962 in honor of the first female doctor in Raleigh. Delia graduated from the Woman's Medical College in *Philadelphia, Pennsylvania,* where she achieved the highest academic average of the class in 1895. She became Meredith College's first physician in 1900 and, until her death in 1934, she gave "breathtakingly dramatic presentations of the simplest principles of health and hygiene"—her own robust physique her best teaching aid.

Salisbury

Elizabeth Maxwell Steele Grave, Thyatira Presbyterian Cemetery. In February 1781, the owner of the popular Steele's Tavern served breakfast to Gen. Nathanael Greene whom she overheard describe himself as "wretched beyond measure, fatigued, hungry, alone, penniless and without a friend." His soldiers were retreating. He had no money to mobilize a militia. Deeply moved by the depressed patriot, Elizabeth brought him two bags of gold and silver coins—her lifetime savings. "Take them for you will need them and I can do without them," the selfless widow insisted. " 'Tis by such patriotic action that revolutions are made," cried the joyous Greene and rode off to victory. A memorial tablet erected over Elizabeth Maxwell Steele's grave in 1948 celebrates her generous deed: "Immortal patriotism—By this gift she being dead yet speaketh."

Grave of Frances Christine Fisher Tiernan, Chestnut Hill Cemetery, South Fulton Street. Under the pen name Christian Reid, which she chose for its ambiguous sex identification, Frances, who died in 1920, wrote more than forty novels, including the popular *The Land of the Sky* (see *Asheville).* A monument on West Innes Street here praises Tiernan for inspiring so many travelers to visit North Carolina "to enjoy scenic beauties so graphically described by her."

Washington

Site of Dr. Susan Dimock Birthplace, East Main Street. North Carolina's pioneer female doctor, born here in 1847, was twice refused admission at Harvard Medical School. She was finally accepted at the more progressive University of Zurich, where she graduated with honors in 1871. She returned to serve as resident physician at the New England Hospital for Women and Children in *Roxbury, Massachusetts,* where the patients were "fascinated by this remarkable union of tenderness, firmness and skill." The secret of her success was in the advice she gave to the nurses, "Treat [every patient] as you would wish your own sister to be treated." In 1875, on her way to Europe for a well-deserved holiday, twenty-eight-year-old Susan was lost in a shipwreck off the coast of England. Her death was a cruel shock in the world of medicine, for, as one male doctor lamented, had she lived she "would have become a great surgeon and would have been sure to stand . . . among those at the head of her profession."

Wilmington

Grave of Rose O'Neal Greenhow, Oakdale Cemetery. Shaded by dogwood, magnolias, and roses, a plain marble cross understates the numerous heroic services of one of the South's boldest spies (see *Richmond, Virginia)* and says only, "Mrs. Rose O'N. Greenhow, a bearer of dispatches to the Confederate Government." Rose, who once proudly said, "I am a southern woman, born with Revolutionary blood in my veins," was buried on a drizzly gray day in October 1864 as hundreds of mourners followed her casket, which was wrapped in a Confederate flag.

Wilson

Grave of Rebecca M. Winborne, Maplewood Cemetery. The Betsy Ross of the Confederacy made her first flag out of flour sacks, a seven-star design, twelve by fifteen inches, which was adopted by the Confederate Congress on March 4, 1861. A more grandiose version, measuring nine feet by twelve, that she sewed through the night while her sister gave momentum to the needle by playing "Dixie" on the piano, was ready to be flown on March 17. Sherman's army was so infuriated by that flying symbol of defiance that they cut it down on their march through Louisburg. Three years after her death in 1918, this simple memorial, engraved with a replica of her flag, was erected as a tribute to the "Maker of the original stars and bars."

Winston-Salem

Sisters' Dormitory, Salem College, Salem Square at West Street. The largest building in town when it was opened in 1786 housed the single sisters of the Moravian Community who were admonished by their elders to close the deep-ochre shutters in the evenings when they lit their candles "because otherwise they will give people the opportunity to all kinds of bad things." Rules of the house where women lived until they were married, stated that only "gentlemen of distinction (or others of whose conduct there can be no doubt)" could be taken through the house. Even then, unmarried women living together were suspect and categorized. The sisters were told that when strangers inquired, "they shall be told that there is no nunnery here and that there is nothing about the few single women who do day work in the families to arouse their curiosity."

NORTH DAKOTA

Beach

This entire town is a thriving memorial to Lydia Richards, "the Mother of Beach." Armed with a civil engineering degree, Lydia found the prejudice against women so bad that, when she came here at the turn of the century, the only job available to her was as a schoolteacher. But the ambitious Lydia soon worked her way up to become superintendent of schools, and then she invested her energy in her first love—land. She planned, built, and developed the town of Beach until in 1910 it had a booming population of 1,500 and was the greatest primary wheat market in the world. When World War I came, Lydia's fortunes reversed, but the shrewd speculator headed south to try her luck with Texas oil and Florida fruit. Richards spent the last years of her life in Wyoming. "She was a woman of her time, gifted with great energy and keyed to an adventurousness which modern days did not afford. Restless, ambitious, capable and optimistic, Mrs. Richards was a road builder for those who followed," the local paper eulogized after her death in 1935 at age seventy-two.

Bismarck

Statue of Sacajawea, State Capitol. Her baby strapped to her back, the brave Shoshoni scout (see *Fort Washakie, Wyoming*) who joined Lewis and Clark near Stanton, North Dakota, gazes hopefully westward. This heroic twelve-foot bronze by Leonard Crunelle was erected in 1910.

Fort Hancock, First and Main Streets. As the town's leading citizen, Linda Slaughter was given the honor of sending the first telegram from the new settlement on August 24, 1872— "greeting to the world!" from the "newly christened child of the Northern Pacific Railroad." Wasting no time, that afternoon she organized the state's first Sunday school. Linda, a "woman of strong personality and decided character," was also the town's first county superintendent of schools, as well as the town's first postmaster and its first writer. Her book *The New Northwest* (1876) was sealed into the cornerstone of the Capitol. And in 1892, the pathbreaking dynamo, in Omaha, Nebraska, as a member of the committee of the People's Party, became the first woman to vote for a presidential candidate in a national convention.

Center

Hazel Miner Memorial, near Log Cabin Museum. A small granite marker commemorates the brave deed of sixteen-year-old Hazel Miner whose ultimate act of sisterly love and devotion caused her death in the raging blizzard of 1920. "The story of her life and of her heroic tragic death is recorded in the archives of Oliver County," says the inscription. "Stranger, read it!" We did as we were told. There, in the annals, Hazel's younger brother Emmet recounted the sad tale: Hazel, Emmet (then eleven), and little Myrdith were at school, waiting for their father to guide them home in the blinding snowstorm. But the horse pulling the children's sleigh started off, tipping the sled. Hazel fastened a robe over the back of the sled and lay down to keep the robe from blowing away. "She kept talking to us and telling us not to go to sleep and . . . [to] keep moving our feet so they wouldn't freeze," Emmet wrote. "The snow would get in around our feet so we couldn't move them but Hazel would break the crust for us. After a while she . . . just laid still and groaned. When she stopped groaning, I knew she was dead." It was twenty-five hours before the children were found—a pathetic huddle—Hazel lying frozen on top of the blanket, the two children sheltered and alive below.

Christine

Even the old-time residents of this small village (population 150) aren't quite sure how it got its lovely female name. Kathleen Moe told us there is still a running controversy about it all. One area resident said that when the railroad came through in about 1884, the Swedish opera singer Christine Nilsson was on the train, waving to the people, so they said, "Let's call it Christine." Two other octogenarians had different theories. "One is positive the town was named after Christine Norby, wife of one of the first settlers," said Mrs. Moe. "Another is just as sure the town was named after its first postmaster, Christine Manger. . . . But another gentleman in a Fargo nursing home who is reported to have a good memory . . . claims it was named for the first infant born here, but he doesn't recall the last name."

Des Lacs

Campaigning for "a bigger, better and cleaner Des Lacs," on March 21, 1922, an all-female ticket of eight won by a landslide in this tiny town (population 190). With a turnout of about forty-five voters, the women captured almost 70 percent of the vote —to make Des Lacs one of the first towns in America totally governed by women. Unfortunately, the matriarchal reign lasted for only a year. Today, the only woman in the government is the city assessor.

Esmond

Minnie Craig, who came to North Dakota from Maine in 1908, was elected to the legislature in 1923 and ten years later became the first woman in the county to be elected speaker of the house in a state legislature.

Mandan

Site of Fort Abraham Lincoln, Route 1806. Elizabeth Custer, traveling across the wild country as the only woman with the regiment, arrived here in 1863, her privileged position assured as Gen. George Custer's wife. The model of the army wife—Elizabeth once recalled how mortified she'd been at dropping her riding whip on the trail, "for I wished to be so little trouble that everyone would be unconscious of my presence"—she nevertheless insisted that she accompany the troops on many of even the most perilous forays (see *Fort Riley, Kansas*). "There never seemed a time when it was not necessary to get accustomed to some new terror," she wrote in *Boots and Saddles: Or Life in Dakota with General Custer,* but she always discovered that "when a woman has come out of danger . . . it is something to know that she is equal to it." For all the trials at this lonely post—rattlesnakes in the fields, a spare diet where the rare onion or cabbage was a delicacy, and five different varieties of merciless mosquitoes—Elizabeth adored her life on the post. Husbands, she discovered, "buttoned our shoes, wrapped us up if we went out, warmed our clothes before the fire, poured water for our bath." The army was less considerate, omitting any mention of officers' wives in the official handbook. Nothing is left of the Custer home today except the cornerstone and an historical marker featuring an old photograph. But the surrounding countryside, bluebonnets scattered in the hills, is unchanged. Elizabeth stood here in the summer of 1876 and waved good-bye to the general "as a premonition of disaster that I had never known before weighed me down." On July 5, 1876 Elizabeth received the news about the Battle of the Little Big Horn. She spent the remaining fifty-seven years of her life defending her husband's memory.

Medora

Chateau de Mores, Route 10. This comfortable twenty-eight-room country place was home for Medora Hoffman, for whom the town is named, who came here in 1883. Her husband, the Marquis de Mores, built up a meat-packing empire while the beautiful titian-haired Medora, an accomplished pianist and brilliant linguist, entertained titled European nobility and such American political notables as Theodore Roosevelt. Medora was an excellent horsewoman who loved to gallop across the plains, a rifle hanging from the saddle, dressed in high boots, a black sombrero with an eagle feather, and trousers. In discarding the bulky riding skirt, Medora was following the influence of her English acquaintance Evelyn Cameron (see *Terry, Montana*).

Pembina

The first white child born here, in December 1807, when Pembina was a fur trading post, was a little boy whose mother had lived among the pioneers for months disguised as "the Orkney lad." "An extraordinary affair occurred this morning . . ." wrote an astonished trader.

Raab

Josephine Grinnell Grave, Queen of Peace Cemetery. A resourceful, patient Indian woman, Josephine Grinnell died in 1945 after a tough, miserable life. Her first husband was a terrible drunk. One day in 1888, he was chasing her to beat her when Josephine, realizing she couldn't get away, turned on him and strangled him with a leather chain he had around his neck. The jury's sympathies were with the long-suffering Josephine. They ruled that Grinnell "met his death through an act of God, thru His agent, Josephine."

Selfridge

Clara Belle Black settled on a ranch here in the 1920s after having operated a successful saloon, gambling house, and brothel in nearby Winona. "She not only ran the brothel, she worked there," one old-time resident told us. Clara was always called Mustache Maude, because, our source patiently explained, "she had more whiskers than most men." She added to her mean image by smoking cigarettes and carrying a six-shooter. A suspected cattle rustler, she was "as fearless as the wildest gunman," the newspapers wrote after her death in 1932 at age fifty-nine, "but she was the only woman who could be called upon when sickness and death came." The papers recalled one incident when Clara rode twenty-five miles across the prairies in a raging northwest blizzard and 28-below-zero temperatures to care for a sick woman.

Washburn

Fort Mandan. This is a reconstructed replica of the fort where Lewis and Clark prepared for their trip west. Here, in April 1805 the explorers met their fate—Sacajawea. She was a pathetic child of sixteen who had been kidnapped by an enemy tribe and was living at the fort with Toussaint Charbonneau. She was also pregnant. When her son Jean-Baptiste was born, the expedition set out for that historic journey that could never have succeeded without the brave Sacajawea (see *Fort Washakie, Wyoming*).

Williston

Hannah Turpin Bell Grave, Riverview Cemetery. "Many brave and daring women came to the West but few have shown more courage, fortitude, honesty and generosity than Hannah Bell," we were told by Marlene Eide, local historian. Hannah, who died in 1939, came with her husband from Nebraska in a covered wagon to hunt buffalo (back in the days when the animal was not an endangered species). She was a skillful tanner, making buffalo-hide shoes and deer-hide shirts, trousers, moccasins, and mittens. Hannah was always on call when needed to help the sick and those in trouble.

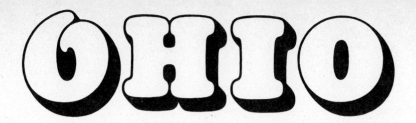

OHIO

Akron

Mary Campbell's Cave, Cuyahoga River Gorge Reservation. Twelve-year-old Mary—the first white child in the area—was brought here from her home in western Pennsylvania by her Indian kidnappers in 1759. She was treated so kindly by the Delaware Indians that she was reluctant to leave five years later when she was retrieved by British troops and returned to her family. A memorial tablet embedded in a boulder here marks the site of her happy days.

Austinburg

Betsey Mix Cowles House, Route 45 (private). One of the earliest graduates of Oberlin College in *Oberlin,* in 1840, Betsey lived here during her early years when she taught in the neighborhood schools and was one of the first in the kindergarten movement. A dedicated abolitionist, called the Maria Weston Chapman of the West for her leadership in antislavery fairs in Ohio, Betsey, with her brother and sister, as "The Cowles Family Singers," rallied others to the cause with spirited hymns and ballads. Later, she added her strong voice to the suffrage cause. She was president of Ohio's historic first convention at *Salem* in 1850, and the following year in Akron she presented "Report on Labor" comparing the woeful inequality of men's and women's wages. Today, her house is owned by Margaret Cowles Ticknow, a great-great-grandniece who told us that at Betsey's request the parlor of her home has been kept exactly as it was in 1850, "and we are happy to show it to anyone who is interested."

Canton

Grave of Ida Saxton McKinley, Seventh Street, NW. Enshrined in this huge mausoleum that is shaped like the Taj Mahal—another living tribute to a wife—is the grave of the Canton native who, despite attacks of epilepsy and other ailments that weakened her all her life, officiated at all important events while her husband served as governor of Ohio (1892–96) and president of the United States in 1897. As remarkable as Ida's capable handling of a full social schedule while she was faced with such suffering was William McKinley's devoted attention to his invalid wife. Ignoring the rules of protocol, he always insisted that she sit by his side during official dinners so he could quickly respond to her attacks. He was the best nurse Ida ever had. On one of their tours, McKinley even canceled an important speech at the Pan-American Exposition in Buffalo to rush back to Washington, D.C., with Ida, who had been close to death while on the road. Ironically, his husbandly loyalty led to his own death. When Ida was well enough to travel again, McKinley rescheduled his speech in Buffalo and there on September 6, 1901 he was assassinated. His last whispered words were "My wife! Be careful . . . how you tell her—oh be careful!" Ida outlived her husband by six years.

Cincinnati

Harriet Beecher Stowe House, 2950 Gilbert Avenue. When she was twenty-one, Harriet (see *Litchfield, Connecticut*) moved here with her family. She taught at her sister Catharine's school (see *Milwaukee, Wisconsin*) and did some writing that hinted at the genius that would immortalize her. Four years later, Harriet married Calvin Stowe and had five children in seven years, but she persisted with her writing, earning just enough money to hire help for the babies. In the 1830s, Harriet journeyed from here into Kentucky (see *Lancaster* and *Washington, Kentucky*) and saw firsthand the desperate life of the slaves on plantations. She often sheltered fugitives in her husband's home. Harriet was a silent but close observer of the tragic events. Often depressed and in ill health, when her right side became mysteriously paralyzed in 1846 Harriet went for ten months to *Brattleboro, Vermont,* for a water cure. In 1850, she moved to *Brunswick, Maine,* where all that she had seen and felt here in Cincinnati was given renewed life in her great novel, *Uncle Tom's Cabin.* The house, a museum now, has relics of the antislavery movement, but there is practically nothing related to Harriet.

Alice and Phoebe Cary Birthplace, "Cary Cottage," 7000 Hamilton Avenue. As teen-agers, by the light from a saucer of lard with a rag wick, Alice and Phoebe, born here in 1820 and 1824 respectively, began writing the verses that would draw praise from such literary giants as Edgar Allan Poe and John Greenleaf Whittier. Whittier once wrote a festive poem to commemorate their visit to his home in Massachusetts. Although Phoebe had many marriage proposals—"Believe me," she once said, "I never loved a man well enough to lie awake half an hour to be miserable about him"—she preferred to devote her life to her work and her sister. Phoebe followed Alice to *Manhattan, New York City* where together they established a brilliant literary salon. Thirty-two years after the deaths of Alice and Phoebe in 1871, another pair of devoted sisters, Georgia and Florence Trader, acquired this cottage and founded the Clovernook Home and School for the Blind, the first home for blind women in Ohio. Vastly expanded, the school still operates today.

Lucy B. Hobbs

Site of Lucy Hobbs Office, 142 West Fourth Street. While waiting to be accepted into the Ohio College of Dental Surgery in Cincinnati, Lucy worked as an apprentice to a dentist here, filling teeth during the day, memorizing the theory behind molars at night, practicing with tiny anvil, hammer, and forceps, and finally winning an award for a smile-proof set of sparkling false teeth. Rejected again and again at the college ("People were amazed when they learned that a young girl had so far forgotten her womanhood as to want to study dentistry") Lucy left for a more liberal Iowa. She returned in 1865 as a resounding success, the first woman accepted in the Iowa State Dental Society. The college now eagerly accepted the practically overqualified Lucy, and on February 21, 1866, at age thirty-three, she became the first woman in the nation to receive a D.D.S. degree. She was enthusiastically praised by her professors: "As an operator she was not surpassed by her associates. Her opinion was asked and her assistance sought in difficult cases almost daily by her fellow students. . . . She is a credit to the profession. . . . A better combination of modesty, perseverance and pluck is seldom, if ever, seen." As Dr. Lucy Hobbs Taylor, she settled in Lawrence, Kansas, in 1867 with her new husband. She patiently and ably trained him in drilling and anesthesia, creating a lucrative partnership.

Grave of Frances Wright, Spring Grove Cemetery, Winton Place. A granite shaft with her likeness in profile, quaint little ringlets carved in the stone, stands over the grave of reformer Frances Wright who died at age fifty-seven in 1852. Two of her characteristic sentiments are inscribed on the monument: "I have wedded the cause of human improvement, staked on it my fortune, my reputation & my life"; and "Human kind is but one family: the education of its youth should be equal and universal." (See *Germantown, Tennessee.*)

Cleveland

Western Reserve University. Emily Blackwell, denied admission at the same college where her sister Elizabeth made history as the nation's first female doctor (see *Geneva, New York*), passed a most searching examination and graduated with the highest honors from the medical school here in 1854. She later joined Elizabeth at the Infirmary for Women and Children in *Manhattan, New York City.* Shortly after Emily left, another hopeful medical student arrived. Marie Elizabeth Zakrzewska, armed with medical books lent to her by Elizabeth Blackwell, was disconcerted to discover there were no lodgings for her. "Alas, nobody wanted to take a female medical student." She hunted several weeks until at last she found a New England woman "willing to brave the criticism of the neighborhood and church." The male students were so hostile they circulated a petition to get rid of the women. But Zakrzewska persisted, graduating in 1856 with a brilliant record. "I prefer to be remembered only as a woman who was willing to work for the salvation of women," she once proposed.

Columbus

Site of Caroline Louisa Frankenburg Kindergarten, Pearl Alley and Rich Street. "An accomplished woman of force and determination . . . in manner and bearing. . . . much of the aristocrat," Caroline started the first kindergarten in Ohio, if not the country (see *Watertown, Wisconsin*) here in 1858. With a little lace cap securely tied under her chin, her shapely hands covered with black lace gloves, Caroline led a small group of German children in creative play with paper birds, boats, and clay. Parents were amused but skeptical of these pioneering efforts, and the school closed shortly after.

Kenyon Hayden Rector House, 878 Franklin Avenue (private). The first licensed woman architect in Ohio designed and built this white stucco Spanish-style house in 1926 on the site where she was married. Her daughter Gilette, who told us the story about her grandmother and the mint juleps (above), lives here now. Gilette recalled that once her mother designed a "Charm House," which was on view in a local department store, "and drew bigger crowds than Pike's Peak." Ms. Rector said that her mother, who died a few years ago, was always a champion of equal rights. "I finally cleared all the National Woman's Party banners out of the attic." They have been generously donated to the party's headquarters in *Washington, D.C.*

Oxley Hall, Ohio State University. The first women's dormitory on campus was designed in 1908 by Florence Kenyon Hayden Rector, who was encouraged by her mother to attend the university and study architecture. When the Southern-born Mrs. Hayden saw the Kentucky colonels sitting on their porches drinking mint juleps while their wives were in the backyards chopping wood, she vowed that her daughters would always be self-supporting and have professional careers. The male trustees of Ohio State University were less liberated, however, and when it was announced that the brilliant twenty-five-year-old Kenyon had received the commission to design the building, they insisted that she be joined by a male associate. After one day of "reasoning" with the assistant, Kenyon locked him out of the office and proceeded alone, completing the plans for this magnificent mansion in twenty-seven days, for less money than had been originally estimated.

Women's Memorial, Ohio State Capitol. At the north entrance to the rotunda, a plaque donated by the League of Women Voters in 1933 commemorates fifty leaders of the feminist movement from all over the country.

Coshocton

Site of White Woman's Village, Route 36. Abducted by the Delaware Indians in 1704 from her home in Massachusetts, ten-year-old Mary Harris settled in this village as the devoted wife of Chief Eagle Feather. Mary quickly adapted to the Indians' way of life and was very much respected by them. She accompanied her husband on his buffalo and bear hunts, and when he prepared to go on raiding parties to the white villages, she would lovingly smear his body with war paint and pack lunches of dried venison and corn, always admonishing him to bring back an attractive selection of scalps that would be styled into the fashionable chignons Mary was so fond of. Perhaps if Mary had had some interests outside the home, she would not have been so upset by Newcomer, a beautiful young white captive that Eagle Feather brought home one day. The next morning Eagle Feather was found with an axe in his head; Newcomer had fled. The Indians suspected Mary, but she eloquently declared her innocence before the council and blamed the "hellish deed" on Newcomer, who was soon captured and killed. Three stone markers here symbolize the tragic love triangle. To the east, there is a village named Newcomertown.

Dayton

Electra C. Doren Library, 701 Troy Street. A memorial plaque in the main reading room here praises Doren as a "creative personality, pioneer in library science and an able executive." She served as Dayton librarian from 1879 to 1905, and she was begged to return in 1913 to restore the collection that had been almost completely destroyed by floods. Doren served devotedly until 1927 and was the first woman to be elected to the American Library Association's publishing board.

Fremont

Site of Elizabeth Foulks Whitaker House, Whitaker Drive. As children, Elizabeth and her husband James were both captured by the Wyandot Indians. They settled here after their release in 1782, thus establishing the first permanent settlement in Ohio, although Marietta claims that honor as well. After James' death in 1804, Elizabeth carried on a successful fur trading business and is credited with introducing the first white beans, beehives, and currant bushes to the area. In a large two-story frame house on the banks of the Sandusky River, the gracious Elizabeth entertained weary travelers. She was the last woman to leave Fort Stephenson before the British attack in 1813 when her home was destroyed by fire.

Greenville

Annie Oakley Grave, Brock Cemetery. In 1868, when she was eight, Phoebe Ann Moses already had such good aim with her father's heavy, rusty rifle that she could shoot squirrels and quail clean through the head, earning enough money from her hunting to pay off the mortgage on her widowed mother's house. In a shooting competition with champion marksman Frank Butler when she was fifteen, Annie beat him by three bull's-eyes, and Butler fell in love. He always liked to say that Annie won so much money from him in sharpshooting bets that he had to marry her to make ends meet. Together, they toured with the Buffalo Bill Wild West Show, where Chief Sitting Bull adopted Annie, naming her *Wantanya Cicilia* ("Little Sure Shot"). Butler sportingly volunteered to be Annie's assistant for her most daring acts, which included knocking a dime out of his finger at twenty paces and shattering swinging balls as they circled his head at the end of a string. During one of their European tours, the kaiser of Germany volunteered to hold a cigarette in his mouth as a target. Annie sometimes mused that she could have changed history if, for that one time, her precise aim had failed her. In 1901, the shock from a terrible train accident turned her hair totally white in seventeen hours and immobilized her for months, but soon she was back in action (see *Cambridge, Maryland*). Another accident twenty years later put her permanently in a brace (see *Nutley, New Jersey*). Some years before her death in 1926, Annie, who had lived in an orphanage in her youth, melted down all her hundreds of gold medals and donated the money to a children's home in the South. "She was a greater character than a rifle shot," Will Rogers said of her. A simple marker over her grave, near Butler's, says only, "At rest."

Garst Museum, 205 North Broadway. Here can be found a complete collection of Annie Oakley memorabilia including her guns, costumes, trophies, and photographs, as well as a gold medal from the people of France, the only medal she did not melt down.

Hillsboro

Mother Eliza J. Thompson House, Willow and East North Street (private). Markers at both ends of the city limits proudly welcome travelers to the home of Mother Thompson, president of one of the first crusading temperance groups in the country that led to the founding of the national WCTU in *Evanston, Illinois*. At age twenty, accompanied by her father, Eliza was the only female in attendance at a stirring temperance meeting in New York in 1836. For the rest of her life she was a convert to the crushing of the grape, but it was not until early 1874 that Eliza took bold action. She organized a committee to plead with the liquor salesmen "in the name of desolate homes, blasted hopes, ruined lives, widowed hearts, for the good name of our town . . . for the sake of our own souls which are to be saved or lost." Rallied by the hymn "Give Wind to Thy Fears," the women marched into saloons where on their knees they prayed with hearty voices. As a result of their zealous entreaties, "the drinking places were reduced from thirteen to one drug store, one hotel and two saloons, and they sold 'very cautiously.' " Mother Thompson's modest, cozy house was for sale when we discovered it, a real find for teetotalers with a sense of history.

Martins Ferry

Betty Zane Statue, Walnut Grove Cemetery. At the entrance to the cemetery where she is buried stands the bronze likeness of Betty Zane, "the Heroine of Fort Henry," her arms firmly clutching a bulging apron. In 1782, "at considerable risk [she] brought a supply of gunpowder to help repulse attackers." (See *Wheeling, West Virginia*.)

McConnelsville

Frances Gage House, 284 North Kennebec Avenue (private). As a child growing up on a farm near Marietta where she was born in 1808, Gage would help her father, a farmer and a cooper. He was so impressed by her skill in making barrels that he could only lament, "Ah Fanny, what a pity you were not born a boy so that you could be good for something," and send her into the house to do some knitting. To the young Gage, it was all too clear. "I was born to make barrels but they would not let me." She moved into this house after her marriage in 1829, and, shortly after, she became the first woman in Ohio to petition for the vote. She had eight children, but despite domestic distractions she traveled all over the state as a gifted speaker arguing for temperance, abolition, and suffrage, especially stirred by the plight of black women, who told her, "You give us nominal freedom but you leave us under the heel of our husbands who are tyrants almost equal to our masters." Described as "large and vigorous. . . . You can see genius in her eyes," Gage was a relentless crusader until she suffered a stroke at age fifty-nine in 1867. Confined to her room, Gage did not despair. She spent the remaining seventeen years of her life writing stories and poems under the pen name Aunt Fanny.

Oberlin

Oberlin College. The first college to make no distinction with regard to color or sex was founded in 1833. One of its foremost objectives was "the elevation of the female character, by bringing within reach of the misjudged and neglected sex all the instructive privileges which have hitherto unreasonably distinguished the leading sex from theirs." On September 6, 1837, the first women entered Oberlin: Mary Hosford, Mary Fletcher Kellogg, Elizabeth Smith Prall, and Caroline Mary Rudd. Four years later—Kellogg the only dropout—the women graduated with Bachelor of Arts degrees that for the first time in history were equivalent to B.A. degrees granted to men. So momentous were the opportunities that one student later wrote, "Our advantages here are great, very great. I heard one of the young ladies remark that when she first came here at almost every recitation her heart was so melted down in view of her great privileges that she could hardly keep from weeping." Other women may have wept from the surly opposition of some unenlightened male students and faculty members. The first year, one of the pioneer coeds recalled, was full of "trials, perplexities and discouragements." Lucy Stone arrived in 1843 and organized a clandestine debating society for the women which brilliantly prepared her to give Oberlin's first public speech by a woman. Her reputation as "a young woman of strange and dangerous opinions. . . . she is always talking about women's rights," instantly attracted her to Antoinette Brown, who would later be ordained as the country's first female minister at *South Butler, New York*, in 1853. The two became great friends, involved for life when they each married a Blackwell brother. It was at Oberlin, according to Antoinette, that Lucy decided never to take her husband's name (see *West Brookfield, Massachusetts*) and resolved "to labor for the elevation of my sex."

Some of Oberlin's famous early graduates include Sallie Holley, noted abolitionist, whose graduation speech in 1851 on "The Ideal of Womanhood" included discussion on the right to vote and preach; Dr. Emeline Cleveland (1853), one of the first female surgeons in the country (see *Philadelphia, Pennsylvania*); Fanny Jackson Coppin (1865), black educator; Margaret Maltby (1882), outstanding physicist; and Mary Church Terrell (1884), one of the charter members of the NAACP (see *Memphis, Tennessee*).

Caroline Mary Rudd,

Mary Hosford,

Mary Fletcher Kellogg,

Elizabeth Smith, Prall,

Ripley

Rankin House. This small red brick house belonging to the Reverend John Rankin, noted abolitionist, was one of the most active stations on the Underground Railroad. Here, according to legend, Harriet Beecher Stowe (see *Cincinnati*) heard the story of a fugitive slave woman who escaped across the melting ice with her baby in her arms—the model for Eliza in her grand work, *Uncle Tom's Cabin* (see *Brunswick, Maine*).

Salem

Site of First Ohio Suffrage Convention, West Second Street. On April 19, 1850, dedicated Ohio feminists gathered for their first meeting at the Second Baptist Church, where a supermarket now stands. Presided over by Betsey Cowles (see *Austinburg*), this was a unique convention, for "it was officered entirely by women; women officiated at all levels and no men were allowed to sit on the platform, to speak, or vote. . . . Never did men so suffer," recalled later suffragists gleefully. "They implored just to say a word; but no, the President was inflexible—no man should be heard. If one meekly arose to make a suggestion, he was at once ruled out of order. For the first time in the world's history, men learned how it felt to sit in silence when questions in which they were interested were under discussion." The men had no choice but to accept this merciless exile, and they gamely founded their own suffrage association where they promptly endorsed all that the women had said and done.

Springfield

Madonna of the Trail Monument, Route 40. On a dozen main streets in cities across the country, this pioneer woman clutches her child to her breast while another child clings to her skirts. She is the symbol conceived by the Daughters of the American Revolution and designed by sculptor August Leim-

bach to mark the Ocean-to-Ocean Highway that carried early settlers across the land. The first of the series (each marking a post where pioneer women again and again demonstrated their courage on the frontier) in the characteristic pinkish-brown Missouri algonite stone, was erected on July 4, 1928, first at Columbia Street Cemetery, but later moved to the present site. The last monument, completing the trails across the continent, was installed at *Bethesda, Maryland,* in April 1929. (See also *Wheeling, West Virginia; Council Grove, Kansas; Lexington, Missouri; Lamar, Colorado; Albuquerque, New Mexico; Springerville, Arizona; Vandalia, Illinois; Richmond, Indiana; Washington, Pennsylvania;* and *Upland, California.*)

Eliza Daniel Stewart House, 215 South Yellow Spring Street (private). When Eliza went south during the Civil War to care for the soldiers, she was deeply stirred by the "drink curse" that afflicted the hapless soldier boys. Shortly after moving here in 1866, Eliza helped organize Springfield's first suffrage organization, but her most zealous work went to save the nation from the evils of whiskey, and she held her first lecture on temperance in January 1872. When her moving appeal to the jury won the case for a drunkard's wife who had sued a saloonkeeper for damages, all of Ohio implored Eliza to "come and wake up the women." Less than a year later, she organized the first Woman's League, the precursor of the WCTU (see *Evanston, Illinois*). Sparing no efforts to ensnare wicked liquor salesmen, Eliza, by now a feared opponent, cleverly disguised herself and purchased a glass of wine in a saloon on Sunday. She had the astonished proprietor prosecuted for violating the sabbath ordinance. Eliza traveled all over the country, even to England, in her enthusiastic, billowing crusade. Age and overwork necessitated periods of rest during which the dedicated Eliza recorded her memoirs. She died here in 1903.

Tiffin

Indian Maiden Monument, Frost Parkway. On the site of the ancient spring that refreshed Indians, soldiers, and pioneer settlers stands this elegant bronze statue, keeping "ceaseless watch where Red Men and sturdy pioneers drank from a spring whose sparkling waters flowed within the stockade of Old Fort Ball."

Toledo

As Ohioans prepared for the centennial celebrations in 1876, the Woman's Suffrage Association was invited to attend a planning meeting. But President Sarah Williams eloquently declined, explaining that the women of Toledo "have no centennial to celebrate . . . we feel it is inconsistent, as a disenfranchised class, to unite with you in the celebration of that liberty which is the heritage of but one-half the people." Newspaper editorials scolded the suffragists for their unpatriotic attitude: "The maids and matrons of 1776 were of a different mold." On July 4, members of the association stayed quietly at home in protest. They had made their point. The entire centennial parade passed under the huge banner they had stretched across the main street; it read, "Woman Suffrage and Equal Rights."

Wilberforce

Site of Hallie Q. Brown Home, "Homewood Cottage," Brush Row Road. The noted black educator and woman's rights leader lived here from the time she was appointed professor of elocution at Wilberforce University in 1893 until her death at age one hundred in 1949. Her voice was said to have "wonderful magnetism and great compass . . . at times she thrills by its intensity; at times it is mellow and soothing. . . . [she] can vary her voice as successfully as a mockingbird." Hallie also used her persuasive speaking skills most brilliantly in the temperance cause, appearing twice before Queen Victoria, one of her admirers, while on a lecture tour in England. One of the first to start clubs for black women, Hallie founded the Colored Woman's League in 1893, a forerunner for the National Association of Colored Women, where she served as president from 1920 to 1924.

Willoughby

Florence Allen House, 7690 Eagle Road (private). The first woman to sit on a court of last resort, when in 1922 she was elected to a six-year term on the Ohio Supreme Court, spent her last years with a companion and died here at age seventy in 1966. Florence Allen was the first woman to get a law degree from New York University (having been refused admission at Western Reserve because she was a woman), and she had a brilliant legal career thickly punctuated with firsts. Seven years after being reelected to the Ohio Supreme Court by an overwhelming 350,000-vote majority in 1935, she was appointed by President Franklin Roosevelt to be the first female U.S. circuit court judge. She could well have been the first female president, but she firmly declined to run in the 1936 campaign.

Yellow Springs

Antioch College. Founded in 1853, Antioch claims to be "the first American college of high rank to grant absolutely equal opportunities to women and men." In a stirring inaugural address, more than a hundred pages long, its first president, Horace Mann, declared that female education must "be rescued from its present reproach of inferiority, and advanced to an equality with that of males." The audience chanted their "Amens" and "swayed before the great orator as a forest yields to a mighty storm." Eleven disillusioned Oberlin students (see *Oberlin*), three of them women, protesting discrimination that forbade women to sit on the platform and read their essays on commencement day, transferred here and were among the first to graduate in 1857—from the platform. Olympia Brown, class of 1860, became the nation's second female minister (see *Racine, Wisconsin*). In 1852, Rebecca Pennell, the first female college professor in the country, was appointed professor of physical geography, drawing, natural history, civil history, and didactics. Despite such a heavy load of teaching duties, Pennell was such a favorite with her students that they pleaded with Mann to have her teach other subjects as well—"for then we can learn."

First graduating class, Antioch, 1857

OKLAHOMA

Anadarko

This outdoor shrine to the nation's American Indian leaders displays nearly two dozen bronze busts in a ten-acre park. Among the women represented: Sacajawea; Alice Brown Davis (see *Wewoka*); and Roberta Campbell Lawson (see *Tulsa*).

Bartlesville

Woolaroc Museum, Route 3, contains an inspiring collection of statues of western women. Along with Jo Mora's *Belle Starr* and *The Squaw,* the eleven runners-up in the *Ponca City* pioneer-woman statue competition of the 1920s are displayed here.

Beaver

Maude O. Thomas, Oklahoma's first newspaperwoman, came to this Panhandle town in a covered wagon with her parents and five brothers and sisters in 1886. She was five years old, and the area was called No Mans Land, Neutral Strip of Indian Territory. By the time she was twenty-one, Maude purchased the *Beaver Herald* and became the state's first female publisher, promoting suffrage and Prohibition with equal gusto. In 1932, after she had sold the paper, Governor William H. ("Alfalfa Bill") Murray appointed her to the State Highway Commission, another first for women. She wrote a letter to her niece, Eleanor Tracy, saying, "I am now having my picture snapped as the First Woman Highway Commissioner in the United States. . . . How do I feel? Just like the grapefruit—too much in the public eye." Eleanor Tracy pointed out to us that, during her brief tenure, her Aunt Maude secured the first permanent improvement to Federal Highway 270 and also planned the diagonal highway across Oklahoma now known as State Highway 3.

Fort Gibson

Vivia Thomas Grave, Fort Gibson National Cemetery. The slender youth who arrived at Fort Gibson sometime in the late 1800s and enlisted in the army turned out to be Vivia Thomas, a young woman from Boston, Massachusetts, who followed to this post the soldier who had spurned her. After making several unsuccessful attempts on his life, one day she shot and killed him. The death was attributed to the Indians. Only on her deathbed in 1870 did Vivia Thomas confess to the priest, "I am a woman and I did kill a man who jilted me." Then she was buried among the officers. Although the details of her life, and the amount of time she served (anywhere from a few months to twenty years), remain a mystery, even less is known of her ungallant lover. His name and his burial place are as anonymous as the graves of two thousand unknown soldiers here.

Fort Sill

Cynthia Ann Parker Grave, Post Cemetery. Beside the towering monument that marks the grave of her son—Quanah Parker, the last Comanche chief—an ornate but humbler granite tombstone commemorates Cynthia Ann Parker. She was captured in 1836 from her home in *Groesbeck, Texas,* and she spent twenty-four happy years with her adopted tribe before being recaptured and unwillingly returned to her white family. In 1910, a year before his own death, Quanah brought his beloved mother from her original burial place in *Poynor, Texas,* to her second grave site near his home in Cache. Both graves were relocated here in 1957 when the U.S. Army extended the military reservation beyond Cache to make room for a missile site.

Guthrie

Site of Carry Nation House, north side of 800 block of West Warner. Several years after drying up most of Kansas (see *Medicine Lodge, Kansas*), Carry Nation moved—with her hatchet, but without her husband—into a house that once stood here. The newly divorced Prohibitionist continued her forays against demon rum in a territory that felt her influence as far away as *Lawton.*

Oklahoma Territorial Museum, 402 East Oklahoma Street, displays the beaded vest that Apache chief Geronimo gave to Lucille Mulhall, the world's first cowgirl, in the early 1900s. The roughriding star of the vaudeville circuit lived on a ranch at nearby *Mulhall,* and old photographs of the sprawling cattle grounds are also on view here.

Lawton

Circumstantial evidence points to another victory for the forces of temperance. Forty-three saloons are listed in the 1902 directory of this frontier town that was created overnight by the land rush. One saloon, at 227 D Avenue, was called Carrie Nation. By the time the 1903 directory was published, the Carrie Nation was no longer listed, and 227 D Avenue was a vacant lot. Such was the penalty for mocking and misspelling the Prohibitionist's name. (See *Guthrie;* see *Medicine Lodge, Kansas*.)

Mulhall

The town is built on the site of the old Mulhall Ranch, the 82,000-acre estate homesteaded by Col. Zack Mulhall in the land run of 1889. It became the training ground for his daughter Lucille, known as the world's first cowgirl. Along with her brother and sisters, Lucille grew up in the saddle and learned to ride and rope as a cowhand across her father's cattle range. She became a cattle owner at age seven when her father innocently promised her all the calves she could tie and brand. Soon "LM" appeared on two-thirds of his stock. By the time she was a teen-ager, Lucille was the star of her father's Wild West Show, hanging a gun alongside her red culottes, busting broncos, and twirling her lariat for adoring audiences from St. Louis, Missouri, to New York City's Madison Square Garden. Once her brother Charlie rescued her from the crowd of fans trying to tear her clothes off at a rodeo, and he explained, "They wouldn't believe that you are really a girl." At another contest, she leaped for joy when she set a new record by roping a steer in twenty-eight seconds flat. She won $1,000 for that speedy feat; in all, she roped in more than $50,000 for her fancy riding. Will Rogers, who was part of the rodeo, said that the word *cowgirl* was coined for her, and Theodore Roosevelt called her the greatest roughrider in the world. Some years after she led Roosevelt's inaugural parade down Pennsylvania Avenue in the nation's capital, Lucille gave up the tiny stages of vaudeville (where she had gone after the rodeos) and retired to the open range of her home. Her niece, Martha Swanson, told us that Lucille was a shy woman, whose last days were sad. "She lived completely in the past. She had no interest in the present." One can understand why. Lucille Mulhall, who had faced wild horses and untamed steers, died here in 1940 of an automobile accident. She was sixty-five.

Lucille Mulhall ropes one in

Muskogee

Site of Alice M. Robertson House, "Sawokla," Agency Hill, Honor Heights Park. A private house now occupies the fifty-five-acre farm where Indian educator and congresswoman Alice M. Robertson built her stone residence in 1910. She named it *Sawokla,* the Creek word for "gathering place," and its cozy fireplaces and wide porches made it a favorite rendezvous spot until it burned down in 1925. (The welcome feelings persist. Today, one neighbor told us, so many warblers congregate on the hill that it is a favorite viewing place for the local bird club.) Alice Robertson moved here in 1913, when she retired from the active Indian mission work she had accomplished at *Okmulgee* and *Tulsa.* She had educated hundreds of Indian children and, an early single parent, she adopted two as her own. She had also just completed five years as U.S. supervisor of Creek schools (in which capacity she drove her horse and buggy through inaccessible plains, in blizzards and rainstorms, to visit schools) and eight years as the postmistress of Muskogee.

While living at Sawokla, Alice Robertson raised a fine herd of Guernsey and Jersey cattle and took their dairy products to open the Sawokla Cafeteria in Muskogee. There "Miss Alice" fed hot meals to more than five thousand World War I soldiers passing through on troop trains.

Although she opposed woman suffrage, Alice Robertson seized advantage of the vote in 1920 and ran for Congress. At age sixty-six, an arch conservative in a Democratic district, she confounded the pollsters by becoming the nation's second congresswoman. Her unimpeachable slogan: "I cannot be bought; I cannot be sold; I cannot be intimidated." Neither, it seems, could she be reelected. After a single term as the only woman in Congress Alice Robertson was returned to Sawokla by a sizable plurality.

Alice Robertson Grave, Green Hill Cemetery. Alice Robertson died in 1931, saved from utter poverty only by the goodwill of old friends. The small stone marking her grave notes that she "gave her life and wealth to mankind." Her good friend Theodore Roosevelt once called her "one of the great women of America." And she probably would not have minded that the statue Oklahomans planned to erect to her honor in the U.S. Capitol in Washington, D.C., was later discarded for one of her good friend Will Rogers.

Carolyn Thomas Foreman House, 1419 West Okmulgee Street. This unpretentious wistaria-covered clapboard house, lined with books, was the home of the prominent Oklahoma historians Grant and Carolyn Thomas Foreman. Their histories of the Five Civilized Tribes and of the early Oklahoma settlers are celebrated for their intellectual approach and attention to detail. Carolyn Thomas Foreman also wrote the unique *Indian Women Chiefs* (1954). Her work in chronicling the diaries and reminiscences of Oklahoma pioneers fills ninety bound volumes. Today, this house where she lived for sixty-nine years— with a male housekeeper to leave her free for writing—has been preserved with equal care.

BACONE COLLEGE

Milly Francis Monument. A granite marker in front of the Art Lodge pays tribute to "Oklahoma's Pocahontas," the Creek woman who saved the life of a Georgia militiaman. In 1817, while her family was living in Spanish Florida, the fifteen-year-old girl stopped a band of Seminole Indians from killing their captive, Capt. Duncan McKrimmon. Her plea on behalf of the doomed white man spared his life and forced him to live among his captors with a shaved head. Some time later, Captain McKrimmon was traded to Spaniards for a barrel of whiskey. When he found Milly at his army post one day and proposed marriage to her, she refused, pointing out that she had not saved his life to wed him. Years later, after Milly's tribe had been decimated by their forced removal to Oklahoma—along the Trail of Tears—she was found living near Muskogee by Maj. Ethan Allen Hitchcock, grandson of Ethan Allen. He heard her story and convinced Congress to grant her a Congressional Medal of Honor and an annual pension of $96. Authorized in 1844, the pension did not come through until much later, doing virtually no good for the poverty-stricken Milly. She died of tuberculosis, unrewarded, in 1848. As the stone monument here reports, she "is buried somewhere in this vicinity."

Sally Journeycake Memorial Building was dedicated in 1937 to honor the first Christian convert among the Delaware Indians. Sally Journeycake chose the white religion over the 'strong objections of her tribespeople, then living in Ohio. They had become embittered over their cruel treatment by whites, and they refused to alter their ways. But Sally had made up her mind. The only Christian Delaware (although not baptized) on the great trek to Kansas—necessitated when the Indian treaties were again broken by whites—she passed her belief on to her young son, Charles. Once in Kansas, the Delawares changed their minds. With Sally as interpreter, missionaries were permitted to preach to the Indians. Charles became the first Delaware baptized in Kansas (1833), and Sally followed two years later. At the dedication ceremony of this building at the Baptist Indian college that was established by Charles Journeycake, Sally Journeycake's great-granddaughter, Roberta Campbell Lawson (see *Tulsa*) said that the new building was "a memorial not only to the noble pioneer Delaware woman, Sally Journeycake, but to every Christian Indian woman in the country."

Norman

University of Oklahoma has named several dormitories for women prominent in the state's history. Included are Alice Brown Davis (see *Wewoka*); Roberta Campbell Lawson (see *Tulsa*); Jane McCurtain (see *Tuskahoma*); and Cynthia Ann Parker (see *Fort Sill*).

Nowata

Nowata County Historical Society preserves the mantelpiece from the razed home of Roberta Campbell Lawson, first Indian woman to become president of the General Federation of Women's Clubs (see *Tulsa*). She began her service career by organizing the first women's club in Nowata when she lived here as a new bride.

Oklahoma City

Grave of Kate Barnard, Fairlawn Cemetery. The unmarked grave of "Oklahoma Kate" Barnard has struck numerous researchers as gross ingratitude to the welfare leader and political reformer who played a leading role when her territory became a state and who became the first Oklahoma woman to win statewide elective office. Appalled by the poverty and child abuse she observed around her, Kate Barnard lobbied and lectured and maneuvered tirelessly to correct them. Largely through her efforts, when Oklahoma reached statehood, its constitution included provisions for child labor laws, compulsory education, and a Department of Charities and Corrections. Barnard ran for the office of commissioner of this department, winning the election in 1907. (Although local historians claim she set a historic first for American women, Estelle Reel of *Fort Washakie, Wyoming,* beat her by thirteen years.) Her first act as commissioner was to cut her own salary from $2,500 to $1,500. As she continued working for prison reform, Indian orphans, and poor immigrants, she never wore jewelry, saying, "How can a woman wear diamonds in a country where little children starve?" When she died in 1930, a governor and several former governors of Oklahoma served as pallbearers, but only a stretch of earth marks her burial spot.

Okmulgee

Nuyaka Mission (private). Only two of the original frame buildings are still standing at the Creek Indian mission that opened in 1885. When the school at Tullahassee, where her parents were working, burned down, Indian educator Alice M. Robertson (see *Muskogee*) went east to raise money for this new venture. With the money she collected, they ordered lumber and nails from St. Louis, Missouri, and had it floated down the river, then freighted across the plains. Alice convinced her sister, Augusta Robertson Moore, to serve as the school's first superintendent. Alice then continued her work elsewhere (see *Tulsa*) as the school flourished until 1921. Today the superintendent's building is occupied by Bill and Oakla Mount Spears, who are restoring the property and setting up a research library. Mrs. Spears, who has become something of an Alice Robertson expert, told us that her home was once occupied by some of the first- and second-grade Creek children, and by faculty members.

Ponca City

Pioneer Woman Statue and Museum, Route 77. The familiar bronze figure of the sturdy sunbonneted mother, striding across the plains in sensible shoes, and clutching her Bible and her son with equal determination, was the gift of an oilman with very specific ideas about women. In the 1920s Ernest Whitworth Marland rejected the suggestion that he finance a statue to the vanishing American Indian. He found the flappers of his day so unappealing, he thought a monument to the vanishing American woman would be more appropriate. In a competition among twelve sculptors, in which 750,000 Americans cast their votes, this design by Bryant Baker was the winner. Marland donated the land and this enduring farewell to the Roaring Twenties. At the unveiling ceremony (which inspired Bess Streeter Aldrich of *Elmwood, Nebraska,* to write *A Lantern in Her Hand,* her own monument to the pioneer women, "not in marble, but through the only medium I could use—the written word") this thirty-foot statue was dedicated to "the women who braved the dangers and endured the hardships incident to the daily life of the pioneer and homesteader in this country." The museum here displays relics and mementos of that daily life.

Sallisaw

Sequoyah's Cabin, Route 101. This one-room log cabin erected by Sequoyah in 1829, along with a statue in the nation's Capitol by Vinnie Ream and the giant trees of California that bear his name, honor the Indian who invented the Cherokee alphabet in 1821. Not even a blade of grass is named after Ahyoka, his seventeen-year-old daughter, the first person to learn and use the new eighty-four-character alphabet. Without her speedy mastery of the signs and symbols (she learned them in less than two weeks), the Cherokees might not have been so eager to read and write.

Tahlequah

Seminary Hall, Northeastern State College, originally housed the Cherokee Female Seminary, one of the earliest institutions to provide full education for Indian girls in accordance with the progressive thinking of their tribe. The imposing three-story brick building, with its turreted towers and arched entryway, was opened in 1889 after the first seminary (opened forty years earlier) had burned to the ground. Here, under the leadership of principal Florence Wilson, the female students followed a rugged schedule that got them out of bed at 5:30 A.M. and insisted on lights out at 9:00 P.M. Along with three-mile walks and ample portions of castor oil, they studied difficult subjects from *The Aeneid* to zoology. Everyone kept the dormitory clean; no one danced or carried a weapon. In time, the pioneering women's Indian school became the coeducational Northeastern State College, where every May 7 the dwindling seminary alumnae return for a homecoming celebration. By tracing its origin to Cherokee legislation of 1846, which first ordered equal education for boys and girls, Northeastern claims to be the oldest public institution of higher learning in the Trans-Mississippi West dedicated to provide a liberal arts education for women. It also claims to be the first in the country to pay equal salaries to men and women professors.

Tulsa

University of Tulsa owes its existence to Alice M. Robertson, the concerned educator of Indian children. After establishing the Nuyaka Mission at *Okmulgee* in 1885, she was put in charge of a Presbyterian Mission School for girls of the Five Civilized Tribes in Muskogee. Once again Alice talked her eastern friends into giving money, and she managed to get the school enlarged and made coeducational. Robertson stayed until 1889, teaching history, English, and civics. The school was renamed Henry Kendall College and was moved to Tulsa in 1907. Alice Robertson also engineered the move, making it possible with money set aside from the Nuyaka Mission. Once the school arrived here, its name was changed for the final time to the University of Tulsa.

Philbrook Art Museum, 2727 South Rockford Road, displays two important collections dealing with noted Oklahoma women. The Indian artifacts of Roberta Campbell Lawson of *Nowata* include costumes, beadwork, and cradleboards collected by her. The granddaughter of the Delaware Indian Sally Journeycake (see *Muskogee*), Roberta Campbell Lawson was born in Indian territory near her friend Will Rogers. She carved out a distinguished career of public service, culminating in her election as president of the General Federation of Women's Clubs from 1935 to 1938.

The Laura A. Clubb Art Collection here was put together by a schoolteacher from Kaw City, whose first purchase in 1922 of a $12,500 Van Marke painting caused her cattleman husband to comment, "I could have bought a trainload of cattle for that." Fortunately, he did not, and the remarkable collection of American impressionist and other paintings is on view today.

Tuskahoma

Choctaw Council House, Route 1 just north of Tuskahoma. When Jackson McCurtain ruled the Choctaw Nation from 1880–

84, his chief adviser was his wife, Jane McCurtain, one of the few Choctaw women prominent in tribal politics. She also wrote a number of his state papers. They moved here in 1883, when Tuskahoma was selected as the tribal capital. After Jackson died in 1885, Jane McCurtain took over the leadership of the Choctaws, ruling in this three-story brick Council House. Later, as superintendent of the new Jones Male Academy, she devoted much of her life to teaching, under the slogan: "Educate the boys and girls for leadership." When she died at eighty-three, still acting as custodian of this Council House, she was buried in the Old Town Cemetery about three-tenths of a mile east. Although Jackson McCurtain's tombstone is ornate and enclosed by a fence, Jame McCurtain's is a simple slab at the head of her husband's, with only her name and dates inscribed. As the Tuskahoma postmistress explained with a resigned sigh, even with all her accomplishments, "she was just a squaw."

Today the Council House is being remodeled as an arts and crafts center in the heart of Choctaw territory. Here, women work on blankets, beads, and rugs in the building where one of the most notable Indian women in the country once ruled.

Vinita

The town was named for sculptor Vinnie Ream by a Cherokee Indian, Col. Elias C. Boudinot, who helped promote the town. He was early smitten with the lovely young artist (see *Iowa City, Iowa*) and saw her frequently in *Washington, D.C.*, where she gained lasting fame for her statues in the Capitol.

Watonga

Elva Shartle Ferguson House and Museum, 521 North Weigel. Elva Shartle Ferguson lived here with her husband, Thompson B., the territorial governor. She first traveled to Oklahoma from Kansas, driving her own covered wagon with the household goods and two small children. An avid writer, she ably carried on the publication of her husband's newspaper, the *Watonga Republican,* when he died in 1921. And it was Elva's life that formed the basis for Edna Ferber's novel *Cimarron.* Ferber (see *Appleton, Wisconsin*) began the book here in the second-floor sitting room in the 1920s. Now that the house is a museum, visitors can see Elva Ferguson's bed, her shoe buttonhook, a crocheted apron, and a copy of her own book *They Carried the Torch,* a story of the early newspapers.

Wewoka

Site of Emahaka Mission, south of the city. In 1908, the superintendent of this well-known school for Indian girls was Alice Brown Davis. She later became the first female chief of the Seminole Indians who had been forced to give up their lands in Florida and move here. She fought vigorously to keep the school under Seminole control, but, with Oklahoma statehood in 1907, the Indians lost both tribal power and their mission school. In 1922, when the federal government decided formally to appropriate the school grounds, President Harding appointed Alice Brown Davis as chief of the Seminoles. When she refused to give away the property without payment, the secretary of interior signed the agreement instead. The building was destroyed by fire in 1927; Alice Brown Davis, last female chief in Oklahoma, died in 1935. A section of the Seminole Museum (524 South Wewoka) is dedicated to her.

Wilburton

Robbers Cave State Park, Route SH-2. Tradition says that the massive boulders and deep shelter of this region provided a sanctuary for every outlaw from the James brothers to Belle Starr. A local historian disputes this with regard to Belle Starr,

pointing out that "she had her own hideout at Hi Early Mountain on her own land [at nearby *Younger's Bend*], and it is known that she did hide some of her gang on her place when the law was after them." He also told us that contrary to popular belief, Belle Starr "did not herself take part in holdups and other crimes, but she is reputed to have been the brains in planning such."

Younger's Bend

Belle Starr Grave (private). When the notorious outlaw and legendary Bandit Queen was shot in the back, her daughter Pearl erected one of the all-time creative tombstones. Beneath a bell, a star, and a drawing of Belle's favorite horse, Venus, is the information that she was born in *Carthage, Missouri,* and died here in 1889. Then comes this heartening poem:

> Shed not for her the bitter tear
> Nor give the heart to vain regret
> Tis but the casket that lies here
> The gem that filled it sparkles yet.

The "gem" inside was buried, it is said, with her hands clutching her six-shooter. This land, deep in the wilderness on the bank of the Canadian River, was Belle Starr's home, or more accurately, her hideout. Although local residents hastened to assure us that she was convicted only once (see *Fort Smith, Arkansas*), on a horse-stealing charge, Belle consorted with a wide band of lawless individuals. Her husbands and intimates included Cole Younger (who sired Pearl), Jim Reed, Cherokee Sam Starr, and Jim July. The outlaws who hid within the Younger's Bend cedar log cabins and nearby caves (see *Wilburton*) included robbers, bootleggers, cattle rustlers, and Jesse James. Belle was not modest about her exploits. In an interview the year before she was ambushed, she told a newspaper reporter, "I regard myself as a woman who has seen much of life."

So many legends and romantic tales followed the Bandit Queen to her grave in 1899 that the original marble headstone was entirely chipped away by souvenir-hunters. A local resident, Claude Hamilton, replaced it with an exact replica in granite, and today his widow preserves the stone, enclosed in an iron fence just below Eufaula Dam.

Belle Starr and Blue Duck

OREGON

Astoria

Site of Fort Astoria, Fifteenth and Exchange Streets. This was a busy fur trading post when in April 1814 Jane Barnes set her tiny foot on the banks of the Columbia River and became the first white woman on the Pacific Northwest Coast. A waitress from Portsmouth, England, in search of adventure, Jane arrived with Territorial Governor Donald McTavish. He drowned a few weeks later, thus clearing the way for Cassakas, son of a Chinook chief, to woo her. Exquisitely decorated with red paint and shiny whale oil, Cassakas promised Jane she would never have to carry wood, draw water, dig for roots, or hunt. She could have all she wanted of salmon, elk, and anchovies to eat and unlimited pipes of tobacco. Jane nevertheless declined such tempting offers until Cassakas threatened to kidnap her, forcing Jane to leave Oregon in September. Apparently heading for home, Jane stopped in China, where it was learned "she was enjoying all the luxuries of eastern magnificence."

Narcissa White Kinney House, 788 Franklin Avenue (private). Calling the saloon "Satan's own back seat in politics," Kinney, president of the Oregon WCTU in 1894, successfully lobbied for strict temperance legislation. "The new woman will demand a new man to walk by her side," she predicted, convincing her husband, the head of the largest salmon cannery in the world, to donate funds for a WCTU meeting hall. Kinney established the Astoria library and aided numerous educational causes. She was dubbed "the good saint of art and literature" when she died in 1901.

Grave of Helen Celiast Smith, Pioneer Cemetery, Clatsop Plains Presbyterian Church. Celiast, daughter of a Clatsop chief, honored with her husband Solomon on the tombstone as Oregon's first schoolteachers, served as heroic mediator between whites and Indians. More than once she single-handedly stopped Indian raids on the villages and hid hunted missionaries at her home. Widowed in 1876, Celiast spent the last twenty-five years of her life living peacefully among her own people again.

Grave of Bethenia Owens-Adair, Ocean View Cemetery. For almost 50 years after her death in 1926, the grave of Oregon's most controversial pioneer doctor was marked with only a tiny cement pauper's marker, overgrown by grass. In July 1975, concerned citizens of Clatsop County finally dedicated this fitting memorial. Bethenia Owens-Adair is praised as "Feminist, Teacher, Physician and Social Reformer." Her much debated book *Human Sterilization* and her outspoken championing of equal rights for women were an outgrowth of one of her favorite creeds, carved into the granite stone: "Only the enterprising and the brave are actuated to become pioneers." (See *Roseburg*.)

Beatty

Grave of Winema, Schonchin Cemetery, Sprague River Road. She was named Winema ("strong-hearted woman") when as a young girl she skillfully guided a canoe through turbulent waters and menacing rocks while her playmates watched in terror and awe. With that same skill and courage, Winema maintained the delicate balance in relations between the white men and the Indians as the cousin of a Modoc chief and the wife of Frank Riddle. But war was inevitable as the whites continued to force the Indians from their lands. During the 1872–73 Modoc uprising, Winema acted as interpreter for the peace commission, saving the life of Col. A. B. Meacham. For her "courageous and loyal service," Winema received a $25 monthly pension from Congress and was honored by President Grant with a parade in Washington, D.C. She then toured the country, starring as the lead in a play about her life. A resident of a nearby town recalled, "Winema, because of her fame for bravery and sagacity, quite overshadowed . . . Frank. However, he seemed content to remain in the background, proud of the respect and recognition that she received from her own people as well as from the whites. She possessed a kind, strong face and a friendly reserved demeanor. To us children, she was a demigod and we regarded her with no little awe." A plaque over her simple grave, where she was buried in 1920 at the age of eighty-four, calls her a "Heroine."

Bend

Klondike Kate House, 231 Franklin Avenue (private). Surrounded by pine trees, its rickety porch overgrown with wild bushes, this brown wooden cottage was once the home of the most famous sweetheart of Alaskan gold rush days. Kate Rockwell, all her fortunes behind her, retired here in the 1920s to work as a short-order cook and dishwasher while proudly wearing diamond rings and necklaces, her Yukon souvenirs. In Dawson, Yukon Territory, in 1900 the nightly showstopper at the Savoy Saloon was Kate's flame dance. In pink tights, swathed in yards of rainbow-colored chiffon, she would spin and whirl as miners wooed her, hurling gold nuggets at her feet. "I'm not trying to put over the idea that we were vestal virgins," she once said when asked about her dance-hall life. "Far from it. We fell head over heels in love and we made mistakes. But primarily we were vendors of laughter and music to men who were starved for beauty and gaiety. And we gave good measure for all the gold the miners showered upon us." The generous heart that won the sourdoughs was as giving as ever in Bend, where Kate took in homeless destitutes, visited prisoners, with pots of homemade stew, and shocked her neighbors with her old Alaskan tricks—such as pulling up her skirts, taking out some papers and tobacco from her garters and rolling a cigarette with one hand.

Cannon Beach

While wintering at nearby *Fort Clatsop* in 1806, Lewis and Clark heard that a whale had been cast ashore here. For the first time during the entire expedition, Sacajawea made a personal request. She wanted to see the whale. "The Indian woman was very impatient to be permitted to go with me and was therefore indulged," wrote William Clark in his diary. "She observed that She had traveled a long ways to See the great waters, and that now that monstrous fish was also to be seen, She thought it very hard that She could not be permitted to See either (She had not yet been to the Ocian." By the time the group got here, all that was left of the whale was a 105-foot skeleton; nevertheless, Sacajawea was thrilled by the sight. Years later, it was said that the "big fish" was the only part of the entire trip she never tired of telling her people about. A plaque marks the site of the beaching.

Columbia Gorge

Marie Dorion Memorial, Vista House, Crown Point State Park. A plaque commemorates "the red heroine of the west, wife of Pierre Dorion, interpreter" who passed this way with the Astoria Overland Expedition in February 1812. (See *Gervais*.)

Enterprise

Mount Sacajawea, Whitman National Forest. At 10,033 feet, the peak named after the guide of the Lewis and Clark Expedition towers above all the other mountains in the park.

Eugene

Pioneer Mother Memorial, near Hendricks Hall, University of Oregon. This heroic bronze statue of a calm, strong-featured woman, sculpted by A. Phimister Proctor, was presented to the university in 1932 by one of its vice-presidents, Burt Brown Baker, in honor of his mother.

Florence

Jessie M. Honeyman State Park, Route 101, was named in honor of Honeyman in 1941, seven years before her death, for her outstanding work to beautify Oregon highways.

Forest Grove

PACIFIC UNIVERSITY
Tabitha Brown Hall. Accompanied by an aged uncle, sixty-six-year-old Tabitha Moffat Brown drove her oxteam across the plains, arriving in Oregon in 1846. Moved by the plight of the hungry and lonely children who had been orphaned on the Oregon Trail, Tabitha founded the Oregon Orphan Asylum, the first such home in the territory where the children could live and study. When the children of the settlers wanted to attend her excellent classes, the home was expanded, renamed Tualatin Academy, and today is a four-year college.
Old College Hall, built in 1850, is "the oldest building in continual educational use west of the Rockies." The building where Tabitha Brown once taught is now a museum containing several items that belonged to her, including her wedding band, some textbooks, and a flag with twenty red stars that she and her students made during the Indian Wars of 1855.

Fort Clatsop

Sacajawea's Quarters. In this precisely reconstructed fort where the Lewis and Clark Expedition wintered in 1805–1806 before their return trip home, Sacajawea and her husband, Toussaint Charbonneau, stayed in the small, dark room, the first to the right as one enters the encampment. During their Christmas celebration, Sacajawea gave the favored Captain Clark two dozen white weasel tails and a precious piece of bread made from real flour that she had been saving for her baby. After a hard winter, with an endless rain that caused a mild influenza epidemic, the group moved out in the middle of March, turning over the fort to the chief of the Clatsop Indians.

Gervais

Site of Marie Dorion Grave, St. Louis Church. The only woman of the 1812 Astoria Expedition—its amazing heroine—is buried somewhere beneath this old white Catholic church. The white-haired pastor of the church told us that hundreds of Marie's devotees come searching for her grave every year. An Iowa Indian, Marie joined the Wilson Price Hunt party heading for the fur post in Astoria from St. Louis when her husband, a half-breed interpreter, refused to leave without her and their two little sons. During the terrible one-year journey, Marie gave birth to a child who lived only eight days (see *North Powder*). After the Indians massacred her husband and several other trappers, Marie set out for the Columbia River with her two children, aged five and seven, and a horse. Within days she was trapped by a raging blizzard in the Blue Mountains. For fifty-three bitter, freezing days, in a hut made from branches, Marie managed to keep herself and her children alive. They fed on berries, twigs, and finally, reluctantly, her horse, until she found her way to an Indian village and later rejoined the Astoria group on its return to St. Louis. When she died in 1850, she was probably about sixty years old, but her painful experience had so worn her face—if not her indomitable spirit—that villagers thought she was one hundred. A small bronze plaque buried in the branches of some fir trees on the corner of the street honors her memory.

La Grande

Mount Emily (6,317 feet) was named in the mid-1800s, some say, by a certain Mr. Leasy as a dubious tribute to his wife—who weighed three hundred pounds and who eventually divorced him for abusive language.

Medford

Clara May Wood House, 31 Geneva Avenue (private). Pioneer settler Wood arrived here with her parents from Wisconsin when she was four years old in 1888. Inching her way up to the job of assistant cashier after twenty-seven years with the National Bank of Medford, Wood was the first woman in Oregon to become a member of the Association of Bank Women.

North Powder

Marie Dorion Memorial, Route 237. A large roadside marker notes that "On December 30, 1811, in this vicinity a son was born to Madame Pierre Dorion 'the Madonna of the old Oregon Trail.' " (See *Gervais*.) Astounded male members of the Astoria Expedition watched her ride twenty miles on horseback and walk another dozen within twenty-four hours after she delivered her child.

Oregon City

Site of Elizabeth Winchell Markham House, Eleventh and Main Streets. In a burst of filial devotion, poet Edwin Markham called his mother Elizabeth "the poet laureate of the new settlement, the earliest woman writer recorded in Oregon." That tribute probably belongs to Anna Lee of *Salem,* although Elizabeth's poems were no doubt among the first, and of more historical import. While managing a general store, planting the peach and apple tree cuttings she had brought from Michigan, and supervising a household of children, in the 1840s Elizabeth wrote poems for the local paper on a variety of local affairs—troubles with the Indians, deaths of pioneers, the flights of strange birds. One of her most clever verses, "A Contrast on Matrimony" came with instructions that if lines one and three, two and four were read together, "the ladies' cause was advocated":

> The man must lead a happy life
> Free from matrimonial chains
> Who is directed by a wife
> Is sure to suffer for his pains.

A plaque at this site notes Edwin Markham's birth here in 1852 with no mention of the mother whose talent he inherited.

Portland

Statue of Sacajawea, Washington Park. The dedication of this monument (sculpted by Alice Cooper Hubbard) to the intrepid scout of the Lewis and Clark Expedition was attended by many notable suffrage leaders who were in town for their national convention in 1905. Susan B. Anthony gave the opening address, encouraging women of Oregon to lead the way to women's liberty like modern Sacajaweas. Abigail Scott Duniway said, "In honoring her we pay homage to thousands of uncrowned heroines whose quiet endurance and patient efforts have made possible the achievements of the world's great men." Dr. Anna Howard Shaw, Carrie Chapman Catt, and hundreds more joined in tumultuous applause after an Indian boy sang the national anthem; the flag "floated away revealing the idealized mother and babe."

Abigail Scott Duniway Grave, Riverview Cemetery, Macadam Street. Oregon's foremost suffrage leader shares a small headstone with her daughter Clara Belle. At Clara's deathbed in 1886, when Abigail tearfully whispered, "I wish I could go with you," Clara replied with failing breath, "You must stay to finish your work, Ma." Ever since Abigail heard her own mother sigh at the birth of another daughter, "Poor baby! She'll be a woman some day!" she vowed to spend her life helping women be more than "general pioneer drudges." In 1871 she began publishing *The New Northwest,* her five children helping to set the type. In this part of the country, where at last women's rights would be treated with "respectful consideration," she toured and lectured on suffrage (see *Grangeville, Idaho*) despite hostile audiences who pelted her with eggs and burned her in effigy. Her sharp wit, definite opinions, and mean stubbornness often strained her relations with other suffrage leaders. Susan B. Anthony always seemed to be hurrying her off to a hotel when Abigail wanted to fight it out with a heckler. David C. Duniway, her grandson, whom we visited in Salem, was only three years old when Abigail died in 1915, but he remembers the talk about her. "Grandmother had a biting tongue. She could come back with such a clever and cruel remark, it could make an enemy of suffrage forever. She had no sense of diplomacy," he said candidly but admiringly. "I think that's why it took so long in Oregon to get the vote." Indeed, the national suffrage association was so concerned about Abigail's effect on Oregon, as much because of her uncompromising stand against temperance as for her barreling personality, that they

sent organizers in from the East. But when women did win the vote in Oregon in 1914, it was Abigail, almost eighty, who was given the credit and the honor of casting the first vote.

Abigail Scott Duniway (center) casts her first vote

Abigail Scott Duniway Memorial, John's Landing, Macadam Street. Her stern, powerful profile gazes down from the top of this glass-paneled elevator tower. The suffrage leader's portrait is among several murals of early pioneers and politicians.

International Rose Test Garden, Washington Park. Internationally recognized Florence Holmes Gerke, the city's official landscape architect who died in 1964, designed this dazzling and heady collection of the most beautiful roses in the world, causing one judge to switch his standard of perfection from the Belfast to the Portland rose.

Port Orford

Site of Minnie Myrtle Dyer House, at the mouth of the Elk River. Two houses have come and gone since the famous poet of Curry County lived here in the 1860s. Her poems published in the Eugene papers attracted the attention of another poet named Joaquin Miller. "I wrote and had replies. . . . her letters grew ardent and full of affection," recalled Joaquin. "I mounted my horse and rode until I came to the sea at Port Orford." And then he saw Minnie—"tall, dark and striking in every respect. In her woody little world there by the sea, the bright and merry girl was brimming full of romance, hope and happiness. I arrived on Thursday. On Sunday next we were married. Oh, to what else but ruin and regret would such romantic folly lead?" The marriage lasted only eight years, doomed by the clashes of competitive careers, when Joaquin conceded, "Much that she wrote was better than any writing of mine."

Roseburg

Site of Bethenia Owens' Dress and Millinery Shop, Northeast Jackson Street. At first, Bethenia didn't know anything about blocking, bleaching, or trimming hats. But with the unwitting help of a competitor whose secrets she learned in 1867 by spying from the rooftop, she soon had one of the most successful shops in town. She was, however, destined for more vital work with scissors and thread. She memorized *Gray's Anatomy* and left for Philadelphia to study medicine. "The delicate and sympathetic office of a physician belongs more to my sex than to the other and I will enter it, and make it an honor to women," she vowed. When she returned to Roseburg in 1874, she was jokingly invited by six male doctors to participate in an autopsy. Although the corpse was a male and a crowd of fifty people were watching, Bethenia skillfully and calmly maneuvered her scalpel. When she had finished, the audience, but not the doctors, gave three cheers for "the woman who dared." In Portland, where she moved shortly after, Bethenia dared to ice-skate, ride astride on a horse, and go around town without a hat, pleasures as forbidden to women as the vote—for which she relentlessly campaigned. But her greatest notoriety came from her fifteen-year effort to pass a law to sterilize the criminally insane. The law was approved in 1925, a year before her death (see *Astoria*).

Salem

State Capitol, Sumner Street Northeast. East of the Capitol entrance, a huge Vermont marble sculpture depicts Sacajawea on foot, pointing the way to Meriwether Lewis and William Clark, comfortably astride their horses.

Inside the rotunda, Sacajawea is commemorated again in a colorful mural: She stands patiently off to the right, watching Lewis and Clark prepare to portage the Celilo Falls on their way to the Pacific in 1805.

The next mural to the right portrays bonneted Narcissa Whitman and Eliza Spaulding, the first white women to cross the Rockies (see *South Pass, Wyoming*), being welcomed by members of the Hudson Bay Company at Fort Vancouver in 1836 as their missionary husbands stand discreetly in the background.

Anna Pittman Lee Grave, Jason Lee Cemetery, D Street, NE. "Beneath this sod the first ever broken in Oregon for the reception of white mother and wife" are the first words of the worn inscription on Anna Pittman Lee's tombstone. The gravestone lies in shattered chunks under the same clump of greenwood trees where she was married—less than one year before her death in childbirth in 1838. Anna left her home in New York when she was thirty-two to assist her fiancé Jason Lee with his missionary work in Oregon. A talented writer of romantic and religious intensity, who was the first poet in Oregon, Anna wrote her last poem when she was six months pregnant as Jason left for a tour of his missions in Washington State:

> Must my dear companion leave me,
>   Sad and lonely here to dwell?
> If 'tis duty thus that calls thee,
>   Shall I keep thee?—No, farewell
> Though my heart aches
>   While I bid thee thus farewell.

Jason Lee Home, Mission Mill Museum, 260 Twelfth Street. The 1841 home of the Methodist Missionaries headed by Jason Lee was being faithfully restored when we visited. No doubt an unwelcome guest in those days was Margaret Jewett Bailey, whose fictionalized autobiography (1854) attacked the hypocrisy and deception of the early missionaries. *The Grains; or, Passages in the Life of Ruth Rover, with Occasional Pictures of Oregon, Natural and Moral,* sometimes called Oregon's first true-confession story, charged that the missionaries were less interested in spreading Christianity than in exploiting the Indians and getting rich through land acquisitions. Besides, Bailey argued, "if Indians were allowed to remain Indians . . . as they were born, with the blessing of God, they [would] become good Indians, and then they [would be] good enough." She demanded equal rights for female missionaries and teachers: "I long my sex should be emancipated from the thraldom of erroneous public opinion, [that] her worth appear

in its true light, her injuries redressed." In its day, *Ruth Rover* was discredited. Margaret Bailey was, after all, a twice-divorced woman, and the men she criticized were revered as brave heroes.

Sisters

This town (population 710) was named for the Three Sisters Mountains to the southwest, whose snow-covered peaks rise in queenly splendor over the bulls in the pastures below. North Sister (10,085 feet); Middle Sister (10,047 feet); and South Sister (10,358 feet) dwarf Bachelor Butte (9060 feet) and The Husband (7520 feet).

The Dalles

Site of Elizabeth Millar Wilson House, 209 Union Street. A gas station now stands where the nation's first female postmaster lived when President Grant appointed her in 1875. A widowed schoolteacher with four children, Wilson got the job in part because her small square frame house was ideally located in the center of town. Her granddaughter, Elizabeth Wilson Buehler, told us that the family lived in a small room in the back while Wilson, whose salary was $75 a month, efficiently dispensed the mail in the front room. There was a steady stream of visitors, and Ms. Buehler's father told her, "it was a marvelous place to grow up."

Walden

Opal Whitely House (private). The friendly proprietors of the general store helpfully directed us to this old, shadowy white house. Opal Whitely claimed that here, when she was five, she wrote the diary that reviewers hailed as "a very remarkable work of genius . . . the most striking human document of the times." It was later discovered to be a hoax. As a grown woman, Opal delivered her diary to the *Atlantic Monthly* in 1920 in five cardboard boxes containing a million pieces of paper, each as small as a postage stamp. She said a jealous sister had shredded the diary. Nine months later she had assembled the 150,000-word story of her fantastic life in the logging camps of Oregon as the secret daughter of the last king of France. The story had a cast of over a hundred characters including a lamb named Menander Euripides Theocritus Thucidides; a pet toad named Lucian Horace Ovid Virgil; Lars Porsena of Clusum, a crow; and a fat little pig called Elizabeth Barrett Browning. The critics marveled at Opal's philosophical insight, childlike innocence, and extraordinary language. As the controversy about the diary's authenticity began to build, Opal disappeared and was said to be in India living with a maharaja. She wrote letters home saying she had married the Prince of Wales, but in fact she spent her last days in an insane asylum where she was always called "Princess." At a nearby farm, we visited eighty-three-year-old Mrs. Glen Scott, Opal's aunt, who said that by now everybody knows Opal didn't write that diary when she was five. "She wrote it when she went to California to college . . . I always knew Opal was a little goofy. She was never satisfied with her life. She always dreamed of being something different and better. Yes, she always wanted to be something more than she was." Who knows what Opal could have been if she had been allowed to be herself?

PENNSYLVANIA

Aliquippa

Historians cannot agree whether the Indian chief for whom this town was named belonged to the Iroquois, Conestoga, Mohawk, or Seneca tribe. In any case, Queen Aliquippa lived here in the late 1740s and ruled this village, formerly known as Logstown, with great authority. She enjoyed good relations with whites, once trading a string of wampum for a cask of powder with which to shoot turkeys. But she insisted on proper respect. A visiting settler described his exchange with the royal leader: "I gave her a shirt, a Dutch wooden pipe and some tobacco. She seemed to have taken a little affront because I took not sufficient notice of her." (See *McKeesport* and *McKees Rocks*.)

Ambler

Mary Ambler House, Main Street and Tennis Avenue. This three-story stone house, the oldest house in town, was the residence of the Quaker Angel of Mercy, heroine of a train wreck in 1856. Mary Ambler was the first to spot the flames when an excursion train from Germantown collided with a regular passenger train on July 17. She fled to the accident site and tended the wounded before any doctors could arrive. Grateful neighbors changed the name of their town from Wissahickon to Ambler in 1869, a year after she died.

Athens

Site of Queen Esther's Town, Route 220. An historical marker identifies the village at the Upper Forks of the Susquehanna River where Esther Montour, granddaughter of Madame Montour (see *Montoursville*) and widow of Chief Eghohowin, ruled the Munsi tribe. Here they built about seventy houses and farmed many acres of fine orchards. Esther's castle stood in the lowlands to the east known as Queen Esther's Flats. Here she maintained her opposition to war, frequently protecting whites from Indian attack although she sympathized with the Indians' hatred of white encroachment on their beloved Wyoming Valley. It was from this village that Queen Esther set out on her distasteful duty to *Wilkes-Barre* on July 3, 1778, to avenge her son's death at white hands. And it was this village that the patriots soon after burned to the ground, to avenge her activities at Bloody Rock. Queen Esther and her people escaped the destruction, and she is thought to have remarried a Tuscarora chief named Steel-Trap.

Bethlehem

Moravian College, West Church Street. This coeducational liberal arts institution is an outgrowth of the first boarding school for girls in the thirteen colonies, founded in 1742 by Benigna Zinzendorf de Watteville. The young Saxon educator originally opened the school in Germantown in May, then moved it to Bethlehem six weeks later. The old Gemein Haus ("Community House") where some of the first classes were held still stands, its original logs covered by a nineteenth-century clapboard facade. After several moves, Benigna de Watteville's school expanded into the Bethlehem Female Seminary, which finally became part of this even larger college.

Bryn Mawr

Bryn Mawr College was the last of the colleges known as the Seven Sister Schools to be founded, opening its doors in 1885 on land donated and endowed by New Jersey physician Dr. Joseph Taylor. Although tradition settled on a male president —James E. Rhoads—the real influence came from the twenty-eight-year-old dean, M. Carey Thomas. She was entirely committed to the higher education of women ("in intellect there is no sex"), and, when she became president in 1894, she solidified the Bryn Mawr image as a high-quality, academically excellent college. Bryn Mawr's entrance exams were said to be as tough as Harvard's. And women were offered the first residential fellowships for graduate work here. A committed suffragist as well, M. Carey Thomas was elected first president of the National College Women's Equal Suffrage League in 1908. At their convention she said, "Now women have won the right to higher education and to economic independence. The right to become citizens of the State is the next and inevitable consequence."

Carlisle

Grave of Molly Pitcher, Old Graveyard, was erected in 1876—as part of the nation's centennial celebrations—to honor the woman who fought at the Battle of Monmouth at *Freehold, New Jersey,* in 1778. Although she was buried with military honors in 1832, there is still some confusion as to her identity. The gravestone and the later Molly Pitcher Monument, a life-sized statue erected in 1916, list Molly's earlier names: born Mary Ludwig, married in succession to John Hays, then to John (or George) McCauley (or McAuley, or M'Kolly). But a recent study maintains that her background was Irish, not German; and there has been some conflict over her birth date. Few, however, dispute her heroism, and her origins do not concern the schoolchildren of Carlisle who blanket her grave with flowers each Memorial Day.

Chambersburg

Wilson College, a liberal arts college for women, was founded in 1869 by two local foresighted ministers. One of them, the

Reverend Dr. Tryon Edwards, at first refused to help organize the proposed "Female Seminary" because he did "not believe in the *female* education of women. . . . If you will agree to organize a first-class college," he said, "affording to young women facilities for a thorough education, such as are now afforded by first-class colleges to young men, I will enter into it, heart and soul." The project took shape when Sarah Wilson, a neighbor with little education but substantial resources, donated $30,000. The college was named in her honor and opened with twenty-six students. One of the first women's colleges to provide physical education for its prim Victorian students, Wilson required each pupil that first year to come with a sense of honor, good grades, and "her own napkin ring . . . overshoes, umbrella, waterproof cloak, and Bible."

Cheyney

Cheyney State College, a four-year liberal arts school, is the modern outgrowth of the Institute for Colored Youth, founded in 1837 by a Philadelphia Quaker. While still located in that cosmopolitan city, the institute hired Sarah Douglass, a tireless worker who had tried to eliminate racial discrimination among her fellow Friends, to run the girls' primary department in 1853. She taught twenty-five young scholars. In 1869, Fanny Coppin Jackson, a freed slave who was recently the first black graduate from Oberlin College, became head principal. Jackson introduced advanced theories to the popular school, instituting a training program for teachers and a much-needed industrial curriculum. Without it, she later wrote, "the only place at the time where a colored boy could learn a trade was in the House of Refuge, or the Penitentiary!" Today, Cheyney State—moved here in the 1900s—has named Coppin Hall after its pioneering principal.

Coatesville

Lukens Steel Company, the nation's oldest steel company, still rolls out ship hulls and railroad parts on the banks of Brandy-

wine Creek—under the management of descendants of Rebecca Pennock Lukens, the nation's first female ironmaster. When the resourceful Quaker woman was widowed in 1825, she was thirty-one, pregnant, and the inheritor of the Brandywine Iron Works. Her husband's dying request: "He wished me to continue and I promised him to comply." Although "the estate shewed an alarming deficiency," Lukens boldly took over. Within nine years she had paid off all her husband's debts, reconstructed the mill into a highly prosperous industry, and earned a reputation as the nation's foremost businesswoman. By the time she died in 1854, Rebecca Lukens' estate was worth more than $100,000. Five years later, the company was renamed for her. Today, the charming Brandywine House, where she lived during her successful rule as ironmaster, has become the Lukens Employees Cooperative Store. When the progressive Rebecca Lukens lived there, she added a porch, an oriental garden, and the first bathtub in Coatesville.

Collegeville

Glenwood Memorial, Main Street, was erected in 1920 on the site of Glenwood Hall, the main building of the Pennsylvania Female Seminary. The seminary was incorporated in 1853 and claims to be the nation's first four-year, degree-granting, legally incorporated liberal arts college for women. That claim has been disputed. A progressive school that granted almost 125 degrees, the seminary closed in 1880 when the Civil War as well as lack of endowments drained it of students and resources. The next year, neighboring Ursinus College admitted women, thus filling the void and becoming one of the early coeducational schools in the country. Fearful of the effect of integration on academic excellence, a vice-president decreed several years later that "the maximum time allowed for visiting and social calls, in our opinion, should not be more than one evening during the week."

Columbia

Site of Susanna Wright House, 36 South Second Street (private). A nineteenth-century relative of the pioneer Quaker settler rebuilt this house on the site of the original mansion that was an intellectual center in the eighteenth century. Susanna Wright was said to have a brilliant mind and a vivacious personality. She was a poet, scrivener, physician, and a good friend to Indians, whom townspeople came to consult for advice. She also raised silkworms here, growing her own mulberry trees and at one time supervising 1,500 worms and producing 60 yards of silk mantua. Here on the banks of the Susquehanna, the celebrated Susanna Wright is credited with making the first pair of silk stockings in the province. She died in 1784, at eighty-seven, and was buried in the Quaker Burial Plot of Mount Bethel Cemetery. Her grave is unmarked, in accordance with the Friends' belief that all lie equal in death.

Ford City

Site of Elizabeth Cochrane ("Nellie Bly") Birthplace, near Crooked Creek Bridge. Only the badly overgrown stone foundation remains of the farmhouse where the daring investigative journalist was born in either 1865 or 1867. In 1887 she stormed into the office of *New York World* publisher Joseph Pulitzer and persuaded him to let her look into the appalling conditions of the New York City's mentally ill. Feigning insanity, she was admitted to the facilities at Blackwell's Island, which she described in a journalistic exposé that made her career. Nellie Bly was also the by-line that traveled around the world in seventy-two days to challenge the trip that took fictional Phileas T. Fogg eight days longer. "Bravo!" cabled Jules Verne appreciatively.

Fort Necessity National Battlefield

One of those present at the Battle of Great Meadows, where

George Washington's first campaign (July 3, 1754) set off the French and Indian War, was the Indian queen Aliquippa (see *Aliquippa*). It is speculated that the aging sachem witnessed her friend, General Washington, confer the title of Colonel Fairfax on her son Canachquasy a month earlier. Soon afterward, Aliquippa died. Her death was confirmed by a note from the Indian agent: "Alequeapy, ye old Quine, is dead."

Fort Washington

Hope Lodge, Bethlehem Pike. The legend surrounding this graceful Georgian mansion is as well preserved as the house itself. Millowner Samuel Morris is said to have constructed the impressive dwelling for his fiancée, whom he'd met on a visit to England. An anonymous poet recalls:

> For her alone, these Lofty Structures rise,
> And Art with Nature, to attract her, vies.

But the prospective bride called off her betrothal when she heard that Morris blurted out intemperately, "Here is the pen. All we need now is the sow." Thus did Morris live here alone, and the poet tells us:

> The hapless Owner sickens at the view,
> In rooms of State his cruel lot bemoans,
>   *   *   *
> And lofty chambers echo to his groans . . .

Morris died here a bachelor in 1770.

Gettysburg

Jennie Wade House, Baltimore Street. The twenty-year-old former resident of this house (now it's a Civil War museum) spent the days before and during the Battle of Gettysburg busily baking bread for the starving Union soldiers. When Confederate troops ordered her to leave, she stuck to her ovens, saying, "Until the battle is over, I wait. I wish to help." On July 3, 1863, the third day of the fighting, a stray Minié ball pierced her heart while she kneaded dough. Jennie Wade became the only Gettysburg resident to be fatally shot during the battle.

Gettysburg National Military Park. The scattered markers pointing out sites of field hospitals serve as the only memorials to the countless Civil War nurses who flocked here in the wake of the fighting to tend the men of both sides. One of the earliest arrivals was Cornelia Hancock of *Salem, New Jersey,* who volunteered her services after Dorothea Dix refused her duty in the Sanitary Commission since she was too young. Hancock arrived on July 6, 1863, three days after the fighting ended; she stayed until September, quieting the pain and the cries of the soldiers. The hospitals where she worked were a converted church, an open-air operating room, and hastily erected tents.

She moved among the men in her torn calico dress, feeding them and dressing their wounds. Late in the summer, the soldiers of Third Division, Second Army Corps, presented her with a silver medal worth twenty dollars as a "Testimonial of regard for ministrations of mercy to the wounded soldiers." (See *Mount Pleasant, South Carolina.*)

Harrisburg

Site of Harris Ferry, River Park, near Washington Street. A marker just downstream from the grave of John Harris is thought to identify a well that was used in connection with the Harris Ferry. In 1719 John Harris came here with his wife Esther Say (or Sey) Harris and settled in a log cabin on the banks of the Susquehanna. Together they pioneered in the uncivilized territory, making friends with the Indians and other settlers. Esther Harris gave birth to six children, one of whom, John, Jr., she is said to have taken by herself to be baptized in Philadelphia. John, Jr. later founded Harrisburg. There are no monuments to Esther Harris, and a local historian has explained, "People didn't bother very much about marking the graves of mere women in those days, and many a pioneer mother is sleeping among the unknown dead today simply because no one took the trouble of keeping a record of where she was buried. Esther Say Harris . . . is one of them."

Kennett Square

Site of Indian Hannah Birthplace, east side of Route 52, about two miles north of Route 1. The last known member of the distinguished Lenni Lenape tribe (also known as Delaware), that flourished on the banks of Brandywine Creek, was born in 1730 in a valley about three hundred yards east of the road. Hannah Freeman, later called Indian Hannah by whites, supported herself and her husband by weaving brooms and multicolored baskets and peddling them from house to house, accompanied by her dogs and, on occasion, her pig. A tall, well-liked woman who also prepared herbs and roots to treat her neighbors, she was said to like cider and tortoises; she disliked thunderstorms. When she grew old and rheumatic, already having outlived all her kinsmen and women, Indian Hannah was cared for in the Chester County Almshouse, where she died in 1802. She is buried there, even though a site at nearby Longwood Gardens contains a mound and a small wooden cross that is popularly, but wrongly, called Indian Hannah's grave. Another marker, erected here in 1925 and unveiled by a descendant of the Quaker on whose land Hannah was born, was stolen in 1941. It has not been replaced.

Lancaster

Site of Ann Wood Henry House, Central Market, King Street. The first female treasurer of Lancaster County lived here with her husband William, a gunsmith, after they were married in 1755. William lost his heart to Ann when she visited one day and picked up a broom that he had purposely strewn on the floor. "Miss Wood loved order, and would make a good wife," William told his sister. "I shall strive to win her." Ann frequently played hostess to the prominent patriots who rendezvoused at this house. One, Thomas Paine, wrote "Crisis," the fifth of his political treatises, here. Ann also filled in for her husband when he traveled, and she did such a fine job on his county treasury work that when he died in 1784, the governor appointed her to the job. A county history reports that she filled the office with credit.

Lititz

Linden Hall, one of the nation's oldest girls' boarding schools, is the modern outgrowth of the coed school founded in 1748 by Moravians. The sisters industriously occupied some of their nonclassroom time with sewing, knitting, weaving, and embroidery, the products of which they sold for their livelihood to customers as far away as Philadelphia. George Washington called them the "first manufactories of the land."

McKeesport

When Indian Queen Aliquippa was living here at the mouth of the Youghiogheny in the winter of 1753, Gen. George Washington went out of his way to pay her a visit. He recorded in his diary, "I made her a present of a watchcoat and a bottle of rum, which latter was thought much the better present of the two." (See *Aliquippa*.)

McKees Rocks

This suburb of Pittsburgh was one of the sites where the Indian Queen Aliquippa lived. It is across from Brunot's Island (formerly Aliquippa Island) which is considered the true home of her tribe. When three Virginia commissioners sailed down the Ohio River in 1752 to sign a treaty with some Indians further west, Queen Aliquippa greeted their fleet with a salute of firearms from her village. The compliment was returned. When the Virginians went ashore to pay their respects, she rewarded them with a strand of wampum and a fine dish of fish. The commissioners presented her a brass kettle and some tobacco. (See *Aliquippa* and *Fort Necessity National Battlefield*.)

Montoursville

The town, like the county to the south, is named for Madame Montour, a woman of French and Indian extraction who roamed up and down the valley interpreting for white settlers and helping to maintain the peace between the English and the Iroquois. She first translated at a conference between the colonial governor and the Five Nations Tribes in Albany, New York, in 1711. Madame Montour lived here after 1727 with her son Andrew, when the village was called Ots-ton-wakin (see *Sunbury*). The town of *Montours Falls, New York,* was named for her granddaughter Catherine, but the citizens of *Wilkes-Barre* have chosen not to memorialize her granddaughter Esther.

Morrisville

Hannah Penn House, "Pennsbury Manor." This forty-acre reconstruction on the site of William Penn's magnificent country plantation suggests the spirit and the daily activities of early eighteenth-century life. This was the house where Hannah, Penn's second wife, spent most of her time during her only visit to Pennsylvania. From 1700–1701 she managed the farm and tended the estate while her husband tended business affairs twenty-five miles away in Philadelphia. She also nursed William and her daughter Letitia through a round of fever and colds. Financial problems sent the family back to England in 1701, where they lived the rest of their lives. There, after 1712, the dignified and sensible Hannah Penn managed her own household with five children, her debt-ridden and invalid husband, and the affairs of Pennsylvania as well. Corresponding by mail with the Philadelphia governors, she took over for the ailing proprietor and, after William's death in 1718, was named sole executrix of his estate. Through skillful and humane management, Hannah Penn kept the province intact.

New Hope

Site of Peg Tuckamony House, Crooks Farm, Upper York Road (Route 263) (private). Once there was a small log cabin here, built shortly after 1705, where one of the last of the Lenape Indians lived. Peg Tuckamony was a highly respected basketmaker who avoided the settlers' roads and traveled along the old Indian paths as she made her way throughout Bucks

County. She died in 1830. The stone that served as her doorstep is now preserved in the eighteenth-century house where the current owner lives. He told us there was no marker to Peg, "although it might be a good idea to have one." He also owns one of the treasured baskets Peg Tuckamony made, and he does not know of any others in existence.

Peg Tuckamony's basket

Orrtanna

Statue of Mary Jemison, Church of St. Ignatius Loyola, near Route 234. Mary Jemison was just fifteen on the morning of April 5, 1758 when a band of Indian warriors and their French colleagues destroyed her family homestead near here at Lower Marsh Creek. Mary and most of her family were taken prisoner; soon she was singled out for survival, and she watched in horror as the scalps of her mother, father, and brothers and sister were dried over the open fire for preservation. Determined to be brave throughout her ordeal, she later recalled in a popular narrative, "My only relief was in silent stifled sobs." In time the young captive was adopted into a Seneca family, given an Indian name, and completely converted to the Seneca way of life. She eagerly took up the Indian woman's duties of hoeing and planting as they moved north, along the Genesee River in New York State. The statue here, erected in 1923, bears little resemblance to the Mary Jemison sculpted in bronze over her grave at *Castile, New York.* In fact, the current parish priest told us that this one is really a likeness of Mohawk Indian Kateri Tekakwitha (see *Fonda, New York*), a Catholic convert, but that Father Will Whalen, who put it up, "chose to call it Mary Jemison."

Penllyn

Sally Wister House, Foulke Mansion, Penllyn–Blue Bell Pike. This neglected farmhouse near the Penllyn Station of the Reading Railroad was abandoned when we visited. Most recently, it served as a tavern called George's. During the Revolution, it was a handsome and well-tended retreat for a sixteen-year-old Quaker girl named Sally Wister and her family. Eager to keep the war away from their doorstep in *Philadelphia*, the Wisters ironically became front-row spectators to the activities of Washington's army encamped at nearby Whitemarsh. Sally decided to record her observations in a diary (written to her friend Deborah Norris), a charming and remarkable account of wartime sentiments. She witnessed General Howe's Redcoats marching out, and she wrote in her journal for December 4, 1777: "Oh gracious Debby, I am all alive with fear. The English have come out to attack (as we imagine) our army. . . . What will become of us, only six miles distant? We are hourly in expectation of an engagement. I fear we shall be in the midst of it. Heaven defend us from so dreadful a sight." Sally Wister could not have known, but Lydia Darragh had already averted the engagement. (See *Philadelphia*.)

Philadelphia

Betsy Ross House, 239 Arch Street. The restored birthplace of the American flag keeps one of our most enduring legends alive and glowing. The story goes that Elizabeth Griscom Ross, a skilled seamstress and upholsterer, first cut her patriotic needle on flags for the state of Pennsylvania. In either 1776 or 1777, a secret committee from the Continental Congress, including Robert Morris and General Washington, called on her to design a flag for the fledgling nation. When she convinced them that five-pointed stars were easier to cut and more appropriate than the six-pointed stars in their sketch, she won the commission. Her historic Stars and Stripes was finished and presented on June 14, now celebrated as Flag Day, and first carried in battle at *Cooch's Bridge, Delaware.* Betsy's story was a well-guarded family secret until 1870, when her grandson, William Canby, modestly relayed it to historians, barely in time for the nation's centennial celebration. With more charm than documentation, it instantly became part of the national heritage. The Betsy Ross grave, which used to be at Mount Moriah Cemetery until vandals stole the flag marking it, was moved here in 1975.

Betsy Ross Grave, Mount Moriah Cemetery, Sixty-second and Kingsessing Streets. The American flag always flew over the grave of the seamstress who may or may not have designed it, until vandals stole it. Her descendants are trying to remove her remains to the garden of the Betsy Ross House.

Site of Lydia Darragh House, "Loxley Hall," 177 South Second Street. Urban renewal has removed without a trace the home of the nurse and midwife who became a Revolutionary heroine during the British occupation of Philadelphia. On the evening of December 2, 1777 Lydia Darragh overheard Gen. William Howe's plans to launch a surprise attack on General Washington, then camped sixteen miles north at *Whitemarsh*. Already an accomplished spy who passed notes hidden in pewter buttons to the army, Lydia, the patriotic Quaker, decided this message called for a more direct approach. Using her empty flour sack as an excuse, she trudged five miles to Pearson's Mill in Frankfort, then walked another few miles towards Whitemarsh, until she encountered an American lieutenant on horseback. She relayed her urgent warning to him, then retraced her steps, picked up her twenty-five-pound sack, and slogged the remaining five miles home. The cavalryman took the message to General Washington, enabling the rebels to repel the invasion and causing Howe's troops to retreat, as one British officer complained, "like a parcel of fools."

Christ Church, Second Street above Market Street. In this historic colonial church you can still see the pews where Martha Washington (pews #56–58) and Betsy Ross (pew #12) worshiped. Here too, in 1738, Anne Catherine Hoof married printer Jonas Green, an event that would have important career consequences for her in *Annapolis, Maryland.* In 1780, Federalist Anne Willing married William Bingham here and lived with him in a splendid mansion on Spruce Street where she introduced the first four-tined eating forks to Philadelphia.

Powel House, 244 South Third Street. This handsome brick town house, built in 1765, was one of the most fashionable centers of colonial Philadelphia. Elizabeth Willing entertained here with her husband Samuel Powel, last mayor of the city under British rule and its first after the Revolution. Elizabeth was an unrivaled hostess, whom Abigail Adams found to be "the best informed, most affable, very friendly and full of conversation; a woman of many charms.'' Abigail's husband John chose to describe one of Elizabeth's distinctive elegant dinners: ''a most sinful feast, curds and creams, jellies, sweetmeats of all sorts, twenty kinds of tarts, truffles, floating-island, sylabubs, etc., in fact everything that could delight the eye or allure the taste.''

Sarah Franklin Bache Grave, Christ Church Burial Ground, Fifth and Arch Streets. Just beyond the wrought-iron fence, the Revolutionary relief worker lies in the family plot next to her famous parents, Deborah and Benjamin Franklin. Sarah contributed to the war by completing the project started by the late Esther de Berdt Reed: raising money and making clothes for the colonial army. She and her legions of swift sewers cut and stitched 2,200 linen shirts for the soldiers in 1780, and George Washington personally thanked her for their ''patriotic exertions.''

Sally Wister House, ''Grumblethorpe,'' 5267 Germantown Avenue. After Quaker Sally Wister returned from her eventful stay in *Penllyn,* she lived in this 2½-story family house built of fieldstone laid over wood from nearby Wister's Woods. In the upstairs chamber still labeled ''Sally's Room,'' we saw the tiny painted chest where she might have kept her hairpins (inscribed ''Sarah Wister'') and her dancing slippers. Her original 1777 diary is also here, handwritten with the same careful attention to penmanship that she gave to the events she recorded. When Sally Wister died here in 1804, her diary was still unknown to any but close family members.

Rebecca Gratz Grave, Mikveh Israel Burial Ground, Ninth and Spruce Streets. A leading charity worker and educator who organized a free Sunday school for Jewish children in her Chestnut Street house in 1838, Rebecca Gratz is best known for yet another accomplishment. She is said to have been the model for Rebecca, the heroine of Sir Walter Scott's *Ivanhoe.* As beautiful and determined as her fictional namesake, Gratz also remained unmarried. She was buried in this cemetery, of the city's oldest Jewish congregation, in 1869.

Dolley Payne Todd House, 153 South Fourth Street. This three-story brick residence became the home of Dolley Payne Todd and her lawyer husband John in November 1791. An outbreak of yellow fever destroyed their happy life here, and Dolley lost both her husband and her infant son. Desolate and lonely, the young widow soon turned the page on a new chapter of her life. Flattered by the attentions of a new man, she scribbled this note to her friend, Eliza Collins, in 1794: ''Thou must come to me—Aaron Burr says that the great little Madison has asked to be brought to see me this evening.'' (See *Charleston, West Virginia.*)

Lydia R. Bailey Grave, Old Pine Street Churchyard, Fourth and Pine Streets. A lacy wrought-iron fence encloses the bright white marble vault of the first woman officially designated as

the city printer of Philadelphia (1830–50). Lydia Bailey learned her trade from her husband and took over his business when he died in 1808 leaving her with four children, numerous debts, and no income. Her first printed accomplishment was two volumes of poetry by Philip Freneau. From then on, she prospered. When she died in 1869, Lydia Bailey was laid to rest in the yard of the church to whose endowment fund she had been the first contributor.

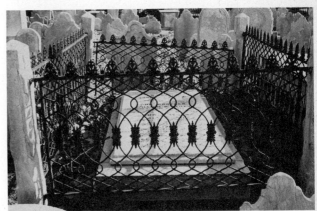

Eliza Lucas Pinckney Grave, St. Peter's Churchyard, Third and Pine Streets. In their efforts to recognize the great southern plantation manager who introduced indigo to America (see *McClellanville, South Carolina*), at whose funeral George Washington was a pallbearer, the local Colonial Daughters of the Seventeenth Century immortalized the wrong accomplishments. The bronze headstone they erected reads: ''Eliza Lucas Pinckney, 1722–1793, lies buried in unmarked grave. Mother of Two S.C. signers of Declaration of Independence.''

Frederika Bremer Room, American Swedish Historical Foundation, 1900 Pattison Avenue, celebrates the accomplishments of women of Swedish origin and, in particular, the accomplishments of Swedish author and feminist Frederika Bremer. During her trip to Philadelphia in 1850, she toured the city with Sarah Josepha Hale as a guide, heard the Quaker Lucretia Mott speak, and was the first to sign the Visitors' Book of old Central High School.

Site of Lucretia Mott House, ''Roadside,'' Old York Road and Township Line Road. The last home of the Quaker preacher, abolitionist, and woman's rights worker has gone the way of her earlier town houses in the center of the city, but the area surrounding her former tree-ringed colonial residence still honors the memory of Lucretia Mott. The adjacent community is named La Mott, in her honor, a tribute from black veterans of the Union army who were offered parcels of land here through Mott's efforts after the Civil War. An early founder of the Philadelphia Female Anti-Slavery Society in 1833, Lucretia Mott nearly had her house burned down by an angry proslavery mob in 1837. It was here at Roadside that she lived the last three decades of her life, and from here she made her last trip to her birthplace in *Nantucket, Massachusetts.* She died here in 1880. She was buried next to her husband James at Friends Fair Hill Burying Ground, and acquaintances recalled that she had once said, ''I am a very much overrated woman—it's humiliating.'' (See *Swarthmore.*)

Germantown Historical Society, 5275 Germantown Avenue, displays a mannequin dressed in the plain garment and shawl that Lucretia Mott probably wore while preaching at a Friends' Meeting. They also have a pocket that the practical and thrifty Quaker wore under her skirt to carry valuables. On one wall hangs the motto she penned: ''Truth for Authority, not Authority for Truth.'' It was, according to her colleague Elizabeth Cady Stanton, ''not only the motto of her life, but it was the fixed mental habit in which she most rigidly held herself." A drawing of the Motts' "Roadside" dining room, and the rocking chair in which she contemplated the rights of women, are placed nearby. Also on display are a small rag rug and potholder she wove out of "free cotton." When she became an abolitionist, Lucretia Mott never knowingly bought a product of slave labor.

The Medical College of Pennsylvania, 3300 Henry Avenue, is the direct descendant of the Female Medical College of Pennsylvania (later the Woman's Medical College), the nation's first medical school for women, established in 1850. It was the gift of progressive Philadelphia businessman William Mullen, who put up $1,500 to rent and equip two rooms at Second and Arch Streets for the first lectures and clinics. At the time, the county medical society called women "unfit for the profession due to their delicate organization and predominance of the nervous system." The first eight graduates in 1851 began a distinguished tradition, proving only that the judgment was "unfit." One member of the class, Hannah E. Longshore, became the first Philadelphia woman to hang out her shingle (at 1116 Callowhill Street), maintaining a prosperous practice despite the crowds who harangued her and the druggists who refused to fill her prescriptions. Another 1851 graduate, Ann Preston, joined the college faculty in 1853 and was instrumental in founding the Women's Hospital in 1861. Dean of the school in 1872 was Dr. Emeline Cleveland, an ovariotomist who in 1875 was the first female physician to perform major surgery. As enrollment increased, the college grew and moved, landing here in 1930 where the radical times and financial pressures led it to admit male students and to remove the word "Woman" from its name. But the commitment is still to the medical education of women.

A huge bas-relief by sculptor Clara Hill, presented by Dr. Rosalie Slaughter Morton ('97) to her alma mater, hangs in the main entrance: Dozens of figures are grouped around the central physician, and all turn to her for aid. The inscription reads, "Daughter of Science, Pioneer. Thy Tenderness Hath Banished Fear . . ." Half a century after the bas-relief was presented, the school learned that the model for the noble central figure was former White House physician to President Kennedy, Dr. Janet Travell.

Moore College of Art, Twentieth and Parkway. The oldest women's professional art college, and the first to teach women industrial arts, was begun in 1844 by Sarah Worthington Peter, a social worker eager to give less fortunate women a means of support. The first few classes were held in her own home, then affiliated with the Franklin Institute. In 1853 it was renamed the Philadelphia School of Design for Women, with a dozen "Lady Managers" in charge of the funds. Although at first men held the leading positions and received the highest salaries, that situation was soon rectified. In 1932 the pioneering school was incorporated into Moore.

Mary Grew Grave, Woodlands Cemetery, Fortieth and Woodland Avenue. The abolitionist and feminist who, with Lucretia Mott, was excluded from the World's Anti-Slavery Convention in London in 1840 was buried here in 1896 beneath a white marble headstone. Although the elements have eroded the inscription on her stone, it is recorded that in 1871 Mary Grew told a suffrage meeting, "What is woman going to do with the ballot? I don't know; I don't care; and it is of no consequence. The right to the ballot does not rest on the way in which they vote." That same year, John Greenleaf Whittier wrote a poem about her that ended,

> The way to make the world anew
> Is just to grow—as Mary Grew!

DAUGHTER OF SCIENCE - PIONEER, THY TENDERNESS HATH BANISHED FEAR, WOMAN AND LEADER IN THEE BLEND, PHYSICIAN, SURGEON, STUDENT, FRIEND.

Pennsylvania Academy of the Fine Arts, Broad and Cherry Streets. The women connected with the oldest institution of its kind in the country disprove the popular cliché that there are no great women artists. Among the finest paintings in the academy's earliest shows were the miniatures of Anna Peale; the still lifes of her sister Margaretta; and the portraits of another sister, Sarah Peale, who became the first female artist in the U.S. to achieve an independent and successful career. Portraitist Cecilia Beaux, foremost woman artist of her time, was the first woman appointed as an instructor here in 1895, following an award-winning array of her work. One of her subjects was Mrs. Theodore Roosevelt; Beaux was quoted as saying, "It doesn't pay to paint everyone." Mary Cassatt also graduated from the academy, but she moved to Paris for more inspiring subjects. She became such an extraordinary painter in the impressionist style that her colleague Degas remarked, "I do not admit that a woman can paint like that."

Pittsburgh

Chatham College, Woodland Road, was founded in 1869 and opened its doors a year later as the Pennsylvania Female College. The earliest liberal arts college (not seminary) for women beyond the Alleghenies, it was supported, as one advocate said, so that "so many of our people may not be subjected to the necessity of sending their daughters to eastern institutions. . . . Why is it none go west?" Later the school was renamed Pennsylvania College for Women, then in 1955 renamed again for the first earl of Chatham, William Pitts, who founded Pittsburgh and championed educational rights for women.

Site of Jane Swisshelm House, Saks Fifth Avenue entrance of Gimbels Department Store, Sixth Avenue. A signpost marks the site of the childhood home of Jane Grey Swisshelm, journalist and reformer who was born in Pittsburgh in 1815 and published the *Saturday Evening Visiter,* an abolitionist and feminist paper, here in 1848. The tablet here points out that she "Secured passage of state law . . . enabling married women to hold and sell property. A Woman of Great moral courage and love for humanity." Jane Swisshelm left Pittsburgh for *St. Cloud, Minnesota,* and returned some time later after becoming the first woman to sit in the press gallery of the U.S. Senate in Washington, D.C.

Quakertown

In 1798 the housewives of Quakertown acted out every taxpayer's fantasy. Irate over a new federal tax to help finance an imminent war with France, the women greeted the unfortunate tax assessors with pans of hot water. The drenched government men responded with military troops, but not before the housewives had poured off a satisfying portion of their boiling tempers.

Sunbury

The island in the Susquehanna River here, formerly known as old Shamokin, was occupied after 1743 by Madame Montour (see *Montoursville*), famous Indian interpreter and peacemaker.

Swarthmore

Swarthmore College was founded in 1864, largely through the help of Quaker Lucretia Mott (see *Philadelphia*). A graduate fellowship bears her name; a portrait of her mother, Anna Coffin of *Nantucket, Massachusetts,* hangs in the Friends Historical Library.

Titusville

Ida M. Tarbell House, 324 Main Street (private). A plaque on the wall identifies the residence of the noted journalist. She lived here for about six years while she was attending Titusville High School (class of 1875). Here she met a number of woman's rights leaders who called on her parents, and here she vowed never to enter into what she considered the imprisonment of marriage. Ida M. Tarbell gained fame first with her stories on President Lincoln for *McClure's* magazine. But it was her critical history of the Standard Oil Company—whose proceedings she had eyed as a youngster in this oil boomtown—that made her reputation as one of the toughest muckrakers in print.

Washington

Madonna of the Trail Monument, east of town on Route 40. The tenth of the series of twelve coast-to-coast trail markers was dedicated December 8, 1928. (See *Springfield, Ohio.*)

Whitemarsh

Emlen House, Pennsylvania Avenue (private). While General Washington was encamped in the stone house here in 1777, he received a timely warning from Lydia Darragh of *Philadelphia* that Gen. William Howe's troops were planning an attack. The Quaker woman's message saved Washington's army.

Wilkes-Barre

Queen Esther's Rock, near Eighth Street Bridge overlooking the Susquehanna River. Protected by an iron picket fence from the chisels of tourists, here squats a piece of the "bloody rock" where an Indian chief is said to have taken her revenge on the citizens of the Wyoming Valley. Queen Esther, granddaughter of diplomat and linguist Madame Montour (see *Montoursville*), had married Chief Eghohowin, and at his death in 1772 she assumed the leadership of his band of refugee Munsee Indians. They lived north of here at present-day *Athens,* where Esther avoided war whenever possible. She particularly avoided the July 2, 1778 attack made by the British and the Indians in their employ here—a violent rout of the colonists that became known as the Wyoming Massacre. The next day, she sent her son down to investigate the event. When he was killed by a white scouting party, the queen had to act. Combining a sense of royal revenge and maternal sorrow, she lined up a group of white Iroquois captives on this rock and methodically executed them with a stone maul. The solemn ritual was carried out to the rhythm of a war chant. Although accounts differ as to the number of victims—anywhere from six to sixteen—all agree that at least one escaped, the one who perpetuated the story. For two centuries, Queen Esther has been represented as a ruthless murderer, "the fiend of Wyoming," who summarized her performance at Bloody Rock by saying, "I was never so tired in my life, killing so many damned Yankees." But at least one modern historian suggests that her action was a duty she had to carry out, and that she may have done the white prisoners a favor by ending their captivity swiftly. By "damned," she means "condemned," the historian says, and "Unquestionably, those dying by her maul escaped a far worse death by fire or torture."

Site of Frances Slocum House, Frances Slocum Playground, North Pennsylvania Avenue and Scott Street. Today children play on the site where five-year-old Frances Slocum was frolicking on November 2, 1778, when she was captured by a band of Delaware Indians. She was taken first to an upstate New York village, then traded to the Miamis, where she was treated so kindly and lived so happily that she refused to return to white ways when found fifty-nine years later. (See *Peoria, Indiana.*)

RHODE ISLAND

Cumberland

Elizabeth Buffum Chace House, 50 Broad Street (private). Elizabeth opened her home as one of the busiest stops on the Underground Railroad in the 1840s, and she spent all her life fighting for equal rights for all, once resigning from the Rhode Island Woman's Club in 1877 because it refused to admit a black applicant. Her first five children died in infancy, so Elizabeth had five more, but she never slowed her efforts to work for suffrage, heeding Lucy Stone's advice to her: "Let the housekeeping take care of itself while you take care of the Republic." Elizabeth served as president of the state suffrage association from 1870 until her death in 1899. She is remembered as "a woman of granite strength and stability of character, with a keen mind . . . and a single-hearted devotion to the great principles of life."

Hope Valley

Prudence Crandall Birthplace, Route 3 (private). In this old 2½-story yellow frame house the courageous abolitionist and teacher was born in 1803. A tiny sign on the house identifies it as the home of her father, Hezekiah Carpenter, who built it in 1770, but Hope Valley has not forgotten Prudence. In 1973 a small granite monument in her honor was erected in the small triangular park in town to commemorate her heroic work on behalf of black children in *Canterbury, Connecticut.*

Site of Prudence Crandall House, Mechanic Street. When she was about two years old, Prudence and her family moved into a small house where now stands this bungalow, whose cornerstone, engraved 1778, was made from the bricks of the original house. The Crandall family moved to Connecticut, the setting of Prudence's great lifework seven years later.

Kingston

Jemima Wilkinson Boulder, North Road, near entrance to Peckham Farm. This huge unmarked rock, large enough for ten picnickers, was in the 1780s the outdoor pulpit of Jemima Wilkinson, whom the president of Rhode Island University called "Jesus Christ in the form of a woman." In her deep-purple flowing robes and her broad-brimmed hat, Jemima stood here majestically preaching the salvation of Faith. Her beliefs would be tested when she left for *Penn Yan, New York.*

Sarah Harris Fayerweather House, Morris Field Road. This cozy cottage was part of the original homestead of Sarah Fayerweather, who lived there until her death at age sixty-six in 1878. As a young mulatto woman, her admission to Prudence Crandall's Select School for Girls in 1832 in *Canterbury, Connecticut,* led to one of the most bitter controversies in the cause of freedom. The result was the closing of the school on September 9, 1834, the very day that Sarah's daughter, whom she named Prudence Crandall, was born. Profoundly influenced by the events of her youth, Sarah worked throughout her life for the liberation of her race, welcoming such noted abolitionists as William Lloyd Garrison and Frederick Douglass to her huge mansion here that was demolished in 1910. She was described as "tall, fine looking, [with] a voice of peculiar sweetness. . . . while her steady gaze seemed to pierce far below the surface of things." A dormitory is named in her honor at the University of Rhode Island in Kingston.

Little Compton

Elizabeth Alden Pabodie Memorial, the Common. A granite monument commemorates the first white girl born in New England (1623), the daughter of the most famous lovers in Pilgrim history, Priscilla and John Alden. At her death ninety-four years later, Elizabeth's friends gave her the highest accolade they could think of—her life had been "exemplary, virtuous and pious."

Narragansett

Winnie Davis Memorial, St. Peter's-by-the-Sea Church. A stained-glass window commemorates the Daughter of the Confederacy who died while vacationing here at the beach in 1898. Born during the Civil War to Jefferson and Varina Davis (see *Natchez, Mississippi*), Winnie was "set apart [by die-hard Southerners] as a kind of shrine at which none but those below the Mason-Dixon line should worship." Her proposed wedding to a Northerner twenty years after the end of the war was so severely criticized that it may have been one of the reasons why she remained single all her life.

Newport

Site of Ann Franklin Printing Shop, Washington Square. When she took over the printing business from her deceased husband in 1735, Ann Franklin became the first female printer of New England. A year later she was named the official colony printer. In addition to her newspapers, almanacs, and her most ambitious effort—the 340-page volume of the laws of the General Assembly—Ann also advertised for printed calicoes and linens "in very lively and desirable colors without the offensive smell which commonly attends linen printed here." Ann was ably assisted by two daughters who were "sensible and amiable women" and more importantly "correct and quick compositors." After twenty-two successful years, Ann retired, but she returned to work in 1762 to publish the *Newport Mercury,* even though her invaluable assistants had died and she was sixty-five years old and in failing health. Her dedication took its toll, for a year later Ann died. The *Mercury* praised her mightily as a woman who "by her Economy and Industry in carrying on the Printing Business supported herself and Family. . . . and would not suffer herself to be detain'd by trivial Family-Concerns: *Herein she excell'd most of her Sex.*"

Abigail Stoneman Coffeehouse, Six Cross Street (private). The Sign of the King's Arms had dancing music six nights a week in the summer, spirits, and "Board and Lodging for Gentlemen," all ably proffered by Abigail Stoneman, the city's first licensed tavern owner (1772). An efficient hotelier with the "genteelest manner," Abigail moved to New York City for the winter and opened another coffeehouse where the gentlemen paid a one-dollar entrance fee and were encouraged to bring their women friends—a discreet forerunner to "dollar-a-dance."

Ida Lewis Yacht Club. For more than fifty years this was the home of the keeper of the lighthouse on Lime Rock. Ida Lewis braved the chilly waters of Newport Harbor dozens of times to save boaters, swimmers, an occasional drunk sailor, and once a sheep belonging to August Belmont. As a young girl, Ida built up her strength, and prepared for her first rescue at age sixteen, by daily rowing her brothers and sisters to school—she herself was deprived of an education so she could support the family—and bringing back supplies, up to her knees in water. Her proud brother said she could "hold a boat to wind'ard in a gale better than any man I ever saw wet an oar. Yes, and do it, too, when the sea is breaking over her." Ida was briefly married to one of the many admirers who had proposed after reading about her heroic exploits, but eventually she returned to the lighthouse and her own name, making her last rescue in 1904 when she was sixty-four. For her countless acts of courage, Ida received the first gold lifesaving medal from the U.S. government in 1880, silver medals from three states, and a very special tribute from Newport—a custom-built boat called *The Rescue* that can still be seen in the Marine Museum of the Newport Historical Society.

Alva Smith Belmont Vanderbilt House, "Marble House," Bellevue Avenue. In 1909, potential suffrage supporters met in this sumptuous two-million-dollar "cottage" to hear lectures by Dr. Anna Howard Shaw (see *Ashton, Michigan*) and Professor Charles Zueblin, who were hopeful in interesting "a new and influential" class that might give as generously as their hostess Alva Belmont to the cause. (See *Bronx, New York City*.)

North Kingston

Joan Barton Smith House, "Updike House," Post Road (private). The finest cheeses in the world came from this house in the 1650s. Joan, who had brought the magic recipe from Gloucestershire and the hefty red cows from Devon, supervised the converting of milk into cheese, adding pints of cream for its extraordinarily rich flavor, and then shipped her Narragansett cheeses (ten dollars per hundred pounds) all over the colony. Drawn by the promise of some tangy Cheshire with their tea,

celebrated guests arrived in droves at the Smith home, making it the social, political, and cultural center of town.

Pawtucket

Slater Mill, Roosevelt Avenue. At this historic site, often called the birthplace of the textile industry, we could find no mention of Hannah Slater, the mill founder's wife. She is generally credited with forever replacing flax sewing threads with the sturdier and more practical cotton thread, after having experimented with the different grades on her spinning wheel. Ignored as well was one of the earliest strikes of women workers that took place here and at other mills in the area in 1824. One hundred and two women held their meetings separately from the male millworkers but joined the men in the strike that lasted several days in protest of a wage cut and long hours.

Peace Dale

Caroline Hazard House, "Lily Pads," 11 North Road (private). This house was part of the huge Hazard estate where Caroline was born in 1856. She developed her strong social conscience when she cared for the children who worked in her father's woolen mills. In 1899, Hazard became the fifth president of Wellesley College (see *Wellesley, Massachusetts*)—its first to have no teaching or administrative experience. Nevertheless, Hazard, who possessed "the ease and breadth of the cultivated woman of the world," during her eleven-year leadership successfully strengthened the financial position of the school, doubling its enrollment and adding a dozen buildings.

Point Judith

Numerous legends surround the naming of this famous mariner's landmark, considered one of the most treacherous spots along the Atlantic Coast during sea storms. It was probably named for someone's wife, although some nagging tongues noting its beastly reputation say it was named for a mother-in-law. The least controversial theory credits the name to the Bible.

Portsmouth

Julia Ward Howe House, "Oak Glen" (private). On soft June afternoons, suffrage leaders of Rhode Island held their meetings here in the home of one of the nation's foremost feminists, Julia Ward Howe (see *Boston, Massachusetts*). She regaled the young neophytes with stories of the early days of the movement when she, Mary Livermore (see *Chicago, Illinois*), and Lucy Stone (see *West Brookfield, Massachusetts*) traveled throughout the countryside, where "the report was sent out that 'three old crows were coming to disturb the town with their croakings.'" Here, "where my days have been precious," Julia died in 1910 at the age of ninety-one.

Founders' Brook, Boyd's Lane. Anne Hutchinson's name is inscribed on the memorial plaque here that commemorates all of the town's first inhabitants who came here in 1638. The courageous religious freethinker, expelled from *Boston, Massachusetts,* lived here until the death of her husband in 1642. Although others called the bold woman a "breeder of heresies" and "the American Jezebel," William Hutchinson to the end called his wife "a dear saint." (See *Bronx, New York City*.)

Providence

Sarah Goddard Home and Office, 21 Meeting Street (private). Sarah lent her son William three hundred pounds to start the *Providence Gazette* in 1762 and then took over as publisher in 1766 for two years, thus becoming Providence's second printer. It was Sarah who taught her daughter Mary (see *Baltimore, Maryland*) the printing trade. The notice of her death in 1770 called it a "public loss" and hailed her "uncommon attainment in literature."

Sarah Helen Whitman Home, 88 Benefit Street (private). A skilled and accomplished poet, a leader of the intellectual circle, Sarah Whitman is also remembered for her stubborn refusal to marry the tempestuous Edgar Allan Poe, who wrote "To

Helen" in her honor. A beautiful woman, who drifted through the Providence Atheneum in floating veils, trailing shawls, always clutching a handkerchief dipped in ether for her weak heart, she captivated Poe with a Valentine's Day poem she sent him half in jest. Their courtship, very Poe-like, with at least one rendezvous in a graveyard, culminated the night she kept him waiting for two hours before he begged her to marry him. "He hailed me as an angel sent from heaven to save him from perdition," Sarah recalled, "and clung to my dress so frantically as to tear away a piece of muslin that I wore." His desperate passion moved her to pity and Sarah consented to marry him on the condition that he stop his depraved drinking. But Poe was so ecstatic about finally winning the beautiful Sarah that he immediately got drunk. Sarah of course broke the engagement, and Poe disappeared, determined "to flee the pestilential society of intellectual females." But Sarah was generous and forgiving, and after his death in 1849 until her own death in 1878 she was one of the most vocal and ardent defenders of his poetry.

Site of Paulina Kellog Wright Davis Home, Davis Park. Young Paulina began to think about woman's rights when, as a religious child, she heard discussions in the churches as to whether women should be permitted to speak in mixed assemblies. She realized that women were often their own worst enemies when in 1844, as one of the earliest proponents of self-help gynecological care, she gave lectures on anatomy to women, using a store dummy she had especially imported from Paris. When the model was unveiled, "allowing to women's ignorance and prejudice, some ladies would drop their veils because of its indelicacy and others would run from the room," recalled Paulina, adding that sometimes the women even fainted. Determined to help her sisters, in 1853 she began publishing *Una* ("a mystical name . . . signifying Truth") which she called "the first pronounced Woman Suffrage Paper" whose purpose was "to discuss the rights, duties, spheres and destiny of woman fully and fearlessly." When she was buried in August 1876 on "a soft, balmy day, just such as our friend would have chosen," Elizabeth Cady Stanton, whom Paulina strongly resembled, with the same soft, white curls, spoke at her funeral, as Paulina had requested.

Pembroke Hall, Brown University. The "prime mover" in the building of this hall, dedicated in 1897, headquarters for "The

Women's College in Brown University," was Sarah Doyle, the noted educator who believed that "women's sphere" should be "of infinite and indeterminate radius." Doyle, suffragist and organizer of the Rhode Island Women's Club in 1876, also helped found the Rhode Island School of Design in 1877. For her numerous efforts on behalf of equality for women, in 1894 Doyle became the first woman to receive an honorary degree from Brown. Her portrait hangs in this hall.

Annie Smith Peck Grave, North Burial Grounds, Branch Avenue. We were surprised to find Annie here. One would have thought that this daring conquistador of South American peaks would have never wanted to be so far beneath the ground. This mountaineer's life was spent leaping from peak to peak, constantly in search of a yet more rarified perch—"some height where no *man* had previously stood." Annie finally found the north peak of Huascarán in Peru (22,205 feet), which she conquered in 1908, making it the highest point in the Western hemisphere that any American man or woman had ever scaled. It was later renamed in her honor. In her chic mountain-climbing outfit of knickerbockers, snug tunic, woolen hose, and a veiled hat, the snowbound suffragist once unfurled a Votes for Women banner on the top of Mount Coropuna (21,250 feet) in Peru in 1911. She was sixty-one years old. Annie was as successful on the stage, giving thrilling accounts of her climbing triumphs, as she was on the cliffs. In 1932, three years before her death, she made her last ascent and conquered Mount Madison in New Hampshire. It was only 5,380 feet but a creditable achievement for someone eighty-two years old. The handsome monument over her grave is inscribed with the words of one of her dear friends on the occasion of her eightieth birthday: "You have brought uncommon glory to women of all time."

Saunderstown

Hannah Robinson House, Boston Neck Road (private). Hannah, the daughter of a wealthy planter who lived here about two hundred years ago, flirted with a French music teacher in these rooms and finally eloped, so angering her father that he renounced her. Hannah's worthless lover left her when he found out there would be no fortune, and Hannah wasted away all alone in Providence, with only one faithful friend, her dog Marcus. Several attempts at a reconciliation were made between father and the by then starving, stricken daughter, but when Hannah refused to tell Robinson who had helped her elope, he abandoned her with the words, "Let the foolish thing die where she is!" He soon repented his cruel words and begged Hannah to come home, but by that time she was so weak she had to be carried back to the family home on a litter, and she died the next day. There is a moral here somewhere, perhaps in the words of Phoebe Cary (see *Cincinnati, Ohio*).

South Kingston

Great Swamp Fight Memorial, Route 2. A pile of stones marks the site of the 1675 battle, but there is no mention of the great warrior Wetamoo, the Wampanoag chief who fought at the head of her three hundred braves in their last desperate stand against the English settlers. Wetamoo camouflaged her warriors with twigs and helped build canoes for the escape. Even though there were only twenty braves left after the bloody battle, Wetamoo fought to the end and escaped, only to be shot several months later. Her head was cut off and sent to Taunton, Massachusetts. There, her loyal followers "made a most horrid and diabolitical lamentation crying out it was their queen's head," wrote one of the cruel desecraters. An admirer remembered her as a proud, magnificent queen who danced at the village ceremonies with "a jersey coat covered with girdles of wampum . . . her arms . . . covered with bracelets. There were handfuls of necklaces about her neck and several sorts of jewels in her ears. She had fine red stockings and white shoes, her hair powdered and her face painted red."

SOUTH CAROLINA

Batesville

Site of Batesville Manufacturing Company, Route 14, on Rocky Creek. Now the Old Mill Stream Inn, this was originally a three-story cotton mill, built in the 1830s, which changed owners several times before being taken over in 1890 by Mary Putnam Gridley. Gridley inherited the mill from her father, and she successfully managed it for more than twenty years as the first female mill president in South Carolina and possibly in the United States.

Camden

Grave of Agnes Glasgow, Quaker Cemetery, Meeting Street. The inscription on this modest headstone tells only that she "departed this life February 12, 1870, age 20." From such spare facts spring a number of romantic legends about the mystery woman. The tourist brochures speculate that she died from fever while following her British lover to Camden; that she was a mistress to Lord Cornwallis; that she was a beautiful camp follower. We wondered why no one has raised the possibility that she may have been a genius, a poet, a hero . . .

Mrs. Joseph Lee's Home, "Greenleaf Villa," 1307 Broad Street (private). When the house was attacked by Union soldiers, a quick-thinking Mrs. Lee mobilized a bucket brigade to put out the flames, thus saving this elegant house for further use as a hospital for Confederate soldiers.

Mary Boykin Chesnut House, "Sarsfield," 136 Chesnut Street (private). The outstanding Confederate diarist spent her last years here—where "there was pure air, large rooms, quiet nights, and literary leisure by day"—revising the 400,000-word manuscript of her *Diary of Dixie,* which was not published until decades after she died in 1886. "Many men have produced narratives of the war between the states and a few women have written notable chronicles of it; but none has given to the world a record more radiant than her or one more passionately sincere," a contemporary historian said of Chesnut. She was appalled by her husband's resignation from the Senate as the Southern states seceded one after the other, and she was filled with "nervous dread and horror" to think of what would be. As she watched the hysterical gaiety of life in Richmond, Virginia, she wrote on New Year's Day in 1864, "God help my country! I think we are like sailors who break into the spirits closet when they find out the ship must be sunk. There seems to be a resolute determination to enjoy the brief hours and never look beyond the day. I now have no hope." (See *Columbia.*)

Central

Cateechee Falls is also called Isaqueena Falls, the Choctaw name of the daring Indian woman who, according to legend, saved the fort at *Ninety-six* from attack and then dramatically leaped over this thundering cataract—with a baby in her arms —when she was being pursued by Indian kidnappers. (See *Keowee.*)

Charleston

Gibbes Art Gallery, 135 Meeting Street. This museum contains five lovely pastel portraits done by Henrietta Deering Johnston, the nation's first woman artist and quite possibly the first female pastelist in Europe or America. She arrived from her native Ireland in the early 1700s and started to paint to help support her incapable minister husband and several children. She was so successful a wage earner that her wretched husband admitted, "Were it not for the Assistance my wife gives me by drawing of pictures . . . I shou'd not have been able to live." Most of her works have disappeared, but there may have been as many as forty—remarkable likenesses of Carolina gentry deftly sketched in chalk on paper slightly larger than this book and signed "Henrietta Johnston Fecit."

Rebecca Motte Home, "Pringle House," 27 King Street (private). British troops during the occupation of Charleston picked Rebecca Motte's house as their headquarters because it was the finest house in the city. Rebecca resigned herself to a patient tolerance of the hated enemy, carefully sending her three daughters up to the attic to protect them from the soldiers. Several years later in *Fort Motte,* she revealed her hostility considerably more overtly.

Grave of Penina Moïse, Beth Elohim Cemetery, Coming Street. The famed and prolific poet is best remembered for her collection of *Hymns Written for the Use of Hebrew Congregations,* published in 1856 when she was fifty-nine years old and described by one critic as "beautiful and stately songs, reminding one in their rhythmic march of the religious verses that Cowper, Pope, Addison and other 18th century poets bequeathed to the world." Blind for the last twenty-five years of her life, Penina still wrote her poems; taught at a small school for girls, sitting in a large rocking chair in a plain calico gown and black woolen scarf; and held gatherings every Friday afternoon for the literary elite of Charleston. She died at eighty-three and is buried here in the oldest Jewish cemetery in the South. Her last words are inscribed on the bronze tablet over her grave: "Lay no flowers on my grave. They are for those who live in the sun and I have always lived in the shadow."

Caroline Howard Gilman House, 11 Orange Street (private). The Boston-born poet moved here in 1820 shortly after her marriage to Gilman, who was the minister at the Unitarian Church. She later wrote, "We associate with just enough fashion to keep us animated in society, just enough mental cultivation to preserve a literary taste, just enough riches and display not to regret that we are limited and receive just enough attention to make us satisfied with our influence." In the almost forty years that she lived here, Caroline wrote letters, essays, romances, and short stories—always stressing the common domestic bond shared by the North and South, dual loyalties and affections that she maintained throughout the war. In a letter to her daughter in the North, her adopted Southern pride was kindled: "We do see all the worst threats of the North in our paper and so are prepared, but you cannot see the calm, indomitable spirit that prevails all over the South."

Timothy House, "Lining House," Chalmers and State Streets (private). With no time for mourning the death of her husband in December 1738, Elizabeth Timothy rushed the *South Carolina Gazette* into print right on schedule, becoming the first female newspaper publisher in the country. She observed that she would, with "the assistance of my Friends," make it "as entertaining and correct as may reasonably be expected," and she humbly asked her readers to "continue their Favours and good Offices to [this] poor Afflicted Widow with six small children and another hourly expected." Elizabeth was such a fine editor that Benjamin Franklin congratulated her. Within a year or two, she generously handed over the paper to her son Peter. He married Ann Donovan in 1745, keeping Ann busy in the nursery with a new baby every other year until there were maybe fifteen little Timothys, while he managed the *Gazette* here. After Peter's death in 1782, with the same determined dedication and discipline that her mother-in-law had, Ann took over publication of the paper for eight years and was the official printer to the state until her death in 1792.

Clemson

Floride Colhoun Calhoun Home, "Fort Hill," Clemson University. "A short, bright brusque woman of tremendous celerity of movement and action," who "knew something about everything and everybody in the world," Floride lived in this fourteen-room mansion with her husband, John C. Calhoun, from 1825 to 1854. Then she moved to *Pendleton*. She was an accomplished musician, as her music book and quaint little spinet still bear witness in the main parlor. She was a talented furniture designer as well, and her handsome wardrobe-bureau and seven-foot walnut bed are on display in the bedrooms.

Clinton

Mary Musgrove Memorial, Musgrove Mill and Battleground, Route 56. A towering block of concrete and stone marks the grave of Revolutionary War heroine Mary Musgrove, who risked her life several times even before the 1780 battle here, never wearied by "the acts of mercy to the wounded and the suffering of those times." Mary was the true heroine of the famous novel *Horseshoe Robinson.* As one admiring historian wrote, John P. Kennedy "could not have chosen a more beautiful character in real life [with] which to adorn . . . his historical novel." In real life when the patriot woodsman Robinson was forced to hide under the Horseshoe Falls to escape the British, Mary daily smuggled him food, supplies, and information about enemy troop movements.

Columbia

Mary Chesnut Cottage, 1718 Hampton Street (private). "Columbia is the place for good living, pleasant people, pleasant dinners, pleasant drives. . . . This is the most hospitable place in the world," an enthusiastic Chesnut wrote in her celebrated diary in 1862 (see *Camden*). It was here in this green-shuttered white frame house that she entertained Jefferson Davis in 1864. Children gathered around, shouting, "Come here and look, there is a man on Mrs. Chesnut's porch who looks just like Jeff Davis on the postage stamps." A fervent defender of the Confederate president, Chesnut could not bear to hear him criticized: "In battering down our administration, these people are destroying our last hope of success."

Site of Wayside Hospital, Gervais Street. An historical marker pays tribute to the group of Columbia women who established the first of the "grand system of Wayside Hospitals," which began as a modest Soldier's Rest house in 1862 and was eventually enlarged to include a soldier's home where more than 75,000 men were sheltered, fed, and given medical treatment before returning to war.

Ann Cunningham Grave, First Presbyterian Church, 1324 Marion Street. A memorial plaque on this simple grave where she was buried in 1876 refers to Cunningham's twenty-year effort to save *Mount Vernon, Virginia.*

Saxon Homes, Seegars Park. This residential area was named in honor of pioneer black educator Celia Saxon, who died in 1935 with a sterling record of never having been absent or tardy for twenty-five years, missing only three days of work in fifty-five years of service in the schools of Columbia. This gentle woman was born a slave in 1857; her heartfelt pleas (often with tears) transformed unruly children into docile and diligent scholars. Saxon started the first working woman's home, which later led to the formation of the first YWCA, named in honor of Phillis Wheatley, the first black female poet (see *Boston, Massachusetts*). After Saxon's death, newspaper editorials observed, "Her place in the school and community was filled so well that there is no need for refilling."

Site of Confederate Printing Plant and Warehouse, Gervais and Pulaski Streets. "While I cannot sign the bills as rapidly as Nanie Gile can, today I finished up four packages of the denomination of fifty dollars. Mr. Tellifier says I am a treasury girl worth having," wrote a pleased twenty-three-year-old Malvina Gist in her diary on February 7, 1865 after a hard day's work making the money that was printed here. With the threat of Sherman's advance, the Confederate Treasury days in Columbia were numbered. "And my father does not consider the track of a great army the safest place for a young woman; hence he wants me to leave. . . . it is frightfully monotonous, just because you are a woman, to be always tucked away in the safe places. I want to stay. I want to have a taste of danger." Instead, Malvina, and the Treasury, were relocated to relatively calm Richmond.

Monument to the Women of the Confederacy, State House. An effusive, lengthy tribute to the women of South Carolina covers three sides of this monument: "Their unconquerable spirit strengthened the thin lines of gray. . . . When reverses followed victories, when want displaced plenty, when mourning for the flower of Southern manhood darkened countless homes, when government tottered and chaos threatened, the women were steadfast and unafraid. . . . At clouded dawn of peace, they faced the future undismayed by problems and fearless of trials, in loving effort to heal their country's wounds. . . ."

Grave of Maria Martin, Ebenezer Churchyard. "Faithful Friend, Gentle Wife, Loving Aunt, and Humble Christian" reads the inscription on Maria Martin's tombstone, but there is not a word about the remarkable achievements of one of the best nature artists of the nineteenth century. Maria, who died in 1863, was an assistant to James Audubon, who often praised her "superior talent" in sketching the lush natural settings for his birds.

As a tribute to her skill in painting bushes, twigs, and trees, thus liberating him to give his full attention to feathers and claws, the naturalist named one of his hairy woodpeckers *Picus martinae*—Maria's woodpecker.

Denmark

Voorhees College. Elizabeth Evelyn Wright, an 1895 graduate of Tuskegee, two years later established the Denmark Industrial School for black girls and boys—with a fine bell and fourteen chairs in a room over an old store. To raise money for new buildings, the frail and sickly but determined Elizabeth walked —often without shoes—along the dusty country roads to small villages where she pleaded in churches for pennies and nickels. The school's survival to this day, as a liberal arts college with an enrollment of five hundred, was assured through the generosity of New Jerseyite Ralph Voorhees, who was so impressed with Elizabeth's dedication that he purchased four hundred acres for the school in 1901 and provided money for new buildings. Poor Elizabeth had exhausted all her strength and died at age thirty, shortly after her dream was realized.

Edgefield

Becky's Pool. Despite her fatal way with husbands, men could not stay away from Becky. She murdered her first unhappy husband by running a mattress needle through his heart "and stilled its aching forever." She weighted his body with chains and dropped it into this pool at the south edge of the city limits, where the headwaters of the reservoir are now located. Soon, another man proposed, and, "too imaginative to fall into a rut," Becky fed him a deadly nightshade herbal potion, then threw his body, tied with bricks, into her favorite pool. Still, the men wanted her. "Suitors were stabbed on the piazza as they grappled with each other" to get her attention. Becky married John Cotton just to get rid of all the other fools and split his head with an ax in 1803. She bewitched the judge and jury at her murder trial and, free again, was no doubt planning another morbid murder when her brother knocked her on the head with a stone in 1807. Becky's grisly deeds were immortalized by Parson Mason Locke Weems in his pamphlet: *God's Revenge Against Cruelty to Husbands Exemplified in the Awful History of the Beautiful but Depraved Mrs. Rebecca Cotton . . . with a Number of Incidents and Anecdotes Most Extraordinary and Instructive,* published in the 1820s. Weems concluded hopefully: "Oh ye Giddy Husbands, see the worth of Religion."

Florence

Grave of Florena Budwin, National Cemetery. Nameless, her only epitaph a soulless number—2480—Florena's tombstone is just like the hundred others here marking the graves of brave soldiers. According to historical records, Florena, wearing a Union uniform, was captured by the Confederates and brought here to Florence where a physical examination put an end to her masquerade. Horrified local women, appalled by her unseemly dress, rushed to bring her female clothing. The soldier Florena, forced to wear skirts again, became Florena the nurse as she generously volunteered to care for sick and wounded prisoners.

Fort Motte

Rebecca Motte Memorial, Route 151 (private). A huge boulder marks the site of old Fort Motte and honors the brave and selfless widow who risked her life and sacrificed her home for the cause of the Revolution (see *Charleston*). When the British seized her beautiful two-story house, in 1781, forcing Rebecca to move into an old farmhouse, the American generals decided their only defense was to burn her home. "Burn it. Burn it," Rebecca insisted. "God forbid that I should bestow a single thought on my little concerns when the independence of the country is at stake. No sir, if it were a palace, it should go." Imbued with patriotic fervor above and beyond the call of duty, Rebecca even provided some inflammable arrows for the job. The fire was so threatening that more than a hundred British soldiers surrendered in time to quell the flames. Rebecca later gave a banquet for the officers of both sides and "by her gentleness and tact, soon had victor and vanquished conversing pleasantly together." Ironically, the house burned down years later, but Rebecca's name has outlasted the flames.

Fountain Inn

Monument to Mother Eve, Town Hall Park. This marble obelisk, inscribed "Eve" and decorated with the figure of an apple, was erected in the 1920s by local journalist Robert Quillen, who explained to curious passersby, "She was a relative of mine—on my mother's side."

Frogmore

Brick Church, Penn Community Services, St. Helena Island, Route 37. This rectangular, gable-roofed, two-story brick church is the only remaining building of the original Penn School, founded in 1862 by two Philadelphia abolitionists, Laura Towne and Ellen Murray. A hundred years ago the school was for newly freed slaves, but the present-day organization continues the commitment to black education and culture. Within six months after the arrival of the two women, more than a thousand children were being taught throughout St. Helena Island in old cotton houses, cabins, and deserted plantations. Laura Towne, a doctor without a degree, traveled in a buggy with her little black bag. The sandy roads she traversed can still be seen today among the moss-covered oak trees, yellow jasmine, and wistaria. The dowry money her father had carefully saved for her marriage was the only financial support she had. Although some Northern teachers left the island, unable to cope with the debilitating malaria, Laura stayed until her death at age seventy-five in 1901. At her funeral, hundreds of devoted islanders chanted her favorite spirituals and followed her coffin, carried on a simple mule cart, along her favorite roads. Soon afterwards, Ellen Murray retired and the school became the Penn Normal, Industrial, and Agricultural School. It has been a community center since the 1960s.

Keowee

Cateechee Trail, which starts at old Keowee Town, now under the lake, and follows the old Indian Trading Path to *Ninety-six,* is named for the Choctaw Indian who rode these ninety-six miles to warn her lover, a young white trader, of an intended Indian raid. Once the area on both sides of the trail was the heart of Cherokee territory and was filled with bear, deer, buffalo, wolf, and wildcats. In the villages, the boys slept on panther skins so they would become strong and cunning; the women were given the soft skins of fawns and buffalo calves to make them gentle and obedient. But Cateechee overcame these passive nocturnal influences to boldly risk her life for a defiant love.

Lexington

Emily Geiger Memorial, Geiger Cemetery. Although the actual site of her grave is unknown, her family cemetery seemed an appropriate place for this sturdy memorial tablet that was erected in 1974 to honor young Emily, who undertook a courier mission no man dared to attempt. In 1781, Gen. Nathanael Greene was desperate to send a message to General Sumter, more than a hundred miles away through Tory-infested territory. Only Emily, a farmer's daughter who happened by, volunteered for the dangerous journey. On her second day out, galloping through the dark woods she was stopped by Tory scouts who

chivalrously sent for a local housewife to search her. Clever Emily read the message she was carrying, tore it up, and swallowed the paper bits, convincing the Tories of her innocence. The eventual union of Greene and Sumter forces, thanks to Emily's courageous trip, led to the crumbling of Tory forces in the South.

Mayesville

Mary McLeod Bethune Birthplace, Route 76. About five miles north of the historic tablet that was dedicated in 1975, the "noted humanitarian and educator" was born on July 10, one hundred years earlier. As the midwife who delivered her exclaimed, "She came with her eyes wide open. She'll see things before they happen." This dedicated visionary, who would give her life to help black women, was the youngest of seventeen children, the first free child of former slaves, whose mother cried at her birth, "Thank God, Mary came under our own vine and fig tree." Mary worked in the fields: "My father's champion cotton picker. When I was only nine, I could pick 250 pounds of cotton a day." Her life suddenly changed when she got the opportunity to go to school. "Every morning I picked up a little pail of milk and bread, and walked five miles to school; every afternoon, five miles home. But I walked always on winged feet." She reached new scholarly heights when she became a teacher at Haines Institute in *Augusta, Georgia,* and then founded her own college in *Daytona Beach, Florida.*

McClellanville

Hampton Plantation, Route 17. Eliza Pinckney came to this plantation to live with her daughter, Harriot Horry. Here, Eliza welcomed such celebrated visitors as George Washington (in 1791), one of her many admirers. Through tireless experimentation, in 1744, Eliza succeeded where all others had failed in the cultivation of indigo, making it the most profitable crop in the Carolinas until the Revolution. Eliza modestly explained her planting triumph: "I have a fertile brain for scheming . . . I love the vegitable world extreamly." She also experimented with hemp, flax, and silk, producing enough fine thread to make three gowns, one of which she gave to a delighted princess of Wales. Eliza was as innovative with her three children as with her plants, and she may have been one of the first in the country to try radical techniques of child rearing. She once asked a friend in England to send some new toys so she could teach her son Charles "his letters by the time he can speak, you perceive we begin by times for he is not yet four months old." (Charles grew up to be a leading statesman and a candidate for president.) After her death in 1791, when she was in her seventies, Eliza was buried in *Philadelphia, Pennsylvania.*

Mount Pleasant

Laing Middle School, Route 17. Now part of the public school system, Laing was founded in 1866, as a school for freed slaves, by Cornelia Hancock, a young Quaker who had served as a nurse at *Gettysburg, Pennsylvania,* and *Fredericksburg, Virginia.* In a bullet-riddled old church, working under primitive conditions at first, Cornelia stuck with it for ten years as the school's principal, educating several hundred blacks. When friends from her home in *Salem, New Jersey,* criticized her unchaperoned and self-sufficient life, Cornelia wrote her parents, "They cannot expect everyone to be satisfied to live in as small a circle as themselves in these days of great events." A marker at the front entrance of the school pays tribute to its noble founder.

Ninety-six

Cateechee Trail ends in this small town, once a busy fort and trading post where Cateechee's lover, Allen Francis, a silversmith, traded his goods with the Indians for animal skins, corn, and tobacco. A breathless Cateechee, who had galloped through the night for ninety-six miles from *Keowee* to warn the settlers of an Indian attack, arrived just in time to bolt the stockade gates. The thwarted Indians rode away, but they returned later to kidnap Allen Francis and their traitor, Cateechee. (See *Central.*)

Kate Fowler Branch. This little stream is named after a young heroine who in 1781 broke through American lines on her speedy horse Bullet to bring a message that help was on the way to her young lover, one of a besieged British garrison. At Kate's news, the boisterous cheers of relief from inside the surrounded fort frightened the Americans into retreating. But the British and her lover eventually left too, leaving behind a sorrowful Kate. According to legend, she pined away to dimensions tiny enough to be carried on a handkerchief by four weeping maidens and was then buried in a clump of white oaks beside the river.

Pendleton

Floride Calhoun Home, "Mi Casa," 430 South Mechanic Street (private). After leaving her home in *Clemson* in 1834, in a huff, it is said, because her daughter-in-law served her tea in a cracked cup, Floride Calhoun supervised her own kitchen here until her death in 1866. She was joined during the Civil War by her daughter Anna Maria who was active in helping the poor who had lost their property through the ravages of the war.

Plantersville

Elizabeth Allston Pringle House, Chicora Wood Plantation, Route 701 (private). When in 1885 Elizabeth Pringle decided to take over the management of her deceased husband's rice fields miles away on the banks of the Pee Dee, her brother "seemed much shocked and surprised and said it was impossible; how was it possible for me, with absolutely no knowledge of planting or experience to do anything?" But, as she wrote in her best-selling account, *A Woman Rice Planter* (1913), "It proved to be a great success!" The novice planter was so encouraged that, when her mother died ten years later, she easily took over the rice fields of Chicora as well, commuting between the two homesteads. "I went through the burning suns all that summer, twice a week, five miles in a buggy and six in a boat. I who had always been timorous drove myself the five miles entirely alone . . . and walked around the 200 acres of rice in all stages of beauty and awfullness of smell." When the fortunes of the plantations began to dwindle, not from mismanagement on Elizabeth's part, but from several seasons of storms and the competition from mechanized rice plantations, Elizabeth adapted her unique experiences into newspaper articles and served as the state vice-regent for the restoration at *Mount Vernon, Virginia.* She died here at seventy-six in 1921.

Spartanburg

Margaret Catherine Barry Moore Home, Walnut Grove Plantation, "Manor House," Route 1. Built in 1764, this was the home of "Kate," the heroine of the Battle of Cowpens. When she heard news of an impending Tory attack and was unable to find proper child-care facilities, she secured her little daughter to a bedpost and rode off to warn the neighborhood.

Converse College, East Main Street, was founded in 1889 by Dr. D. E. Converse, who believed that "the well-being of any country depends on the culture of the women." One of the college's prominent early graduates was Lily Strickland, South Carolina's greatest composer, best known for such songs as "Lindy Lou" and "Honey Chile." In May 1930, her grand oratorio, *St. John the Beloved,* premiered here.

Union

Site of Grimké Plantation, "Belmont," Route 49. Sarah Grimké learned the horrors of slavery in 1796 when, at age four, she saw the whipping of a slave woman at her father's plantation here. "Slavery was a millstone around my neck, and marred my comforts from the time I can remember myself," she once wrote. Further, Sarah was constantly bothered by the slights she had to endure as a girl. Her father would not teach her Latin; unlike her brother, she was not allowed to go away to college: "With me, learning was a passion." Despite the sanctions against teaching slaves to read, every night when Sarah was supposed to be having her hair combed out, she shared her books with the servant girl she always treated as a sister. During a trip to Philadelphia, Pennsylvania, in 1819, Sarah met some Quakers, and she left South Carolina forever in 1821 to devote her life to abolition, and later, inevitably, suffrage. Her sister Angelina, thirteen years younger, joined her. "The discussion of the rights of the slave has opened the way for the discussion of other rights and the ultimate result will most certainly be the breaking of *every* yoke. . . . an emancipation far more glorious than any the world has ever yet seen," said Angelina. Sarah wrote in her *Letters on the Equality of the Sexes* (1838), "I ask no favors for my sex. . . . All I ask of our brethren is that they will take their feet from off our necks, and permit us to stand upright on that ground which God deigned us to occupy." The sisters traveled all over the Northeast giving lectures, often in the face of hostile, angry crowds. In later, more peaceful, years they settled in *Perth Amboy, New Jersey.*

SOUTH DAKOTA

Custer

Annie Tallent Monument, Gordon Stockade. On the long trek from the Missouri River to the land of the Sioux Indians, propelled by dreams of gold, Annie Tallent's shoes gave out. She wrapped her feet in gunnysacks and kept pushing on. With her husband, her young son, and twenty-five exhausted men, Annie, a hardy forty-six year old, entered the Black Hills in December, 1874. She was the first female trespasser in that forbidden territory. Annie settled on the banks of the French Creek in a cabin made from hemlock boughs and earth. She used the sheerest flour sacks she could find for the windows and a large coffee bag as a door. It was a miserable winter: "the very remembrance causes ague chills to creep rapidly along the spinal column," Annie wrote in her memoirs, *The Black Hills* (see *Sturgis*). The following spring, because the region was considered still too remote and dangerous for settlers, the cavalry ejected the group at the Gordon Stockade. Annie, the first woman to leave the Black Hills, rode out more comfortably than she came in—on a government mule. A towering granite spire here at the stockade honors her memory.

Deadwood

Most of the old dance halls have burned or fallen apart. Annie Tallent (see *Sturgis*) wrote of some of the notorious women: "The big voiced Monteverde nightly entertained and enchanted hundreds of men with ribald songs and dance and wine and smutty jests.... All this I was told and much more, over which it is better to draw the veil." In addition to being blessed by those talents that Annie discreetly bypassed, Monteverde, a lusty, quick-fingered blackjack dealer, was once a famous Confederate spy, as clever behind the front lines as behind a hand of cards. Monteverde arrived in Deadwood in a bright yellow mobile home that was furnished with curtains, a comfortable bed, and a shelf of books, but she rolled out again when her lover, the head of a road gang, was lynched. Arrested during an opium raid in San Francisco, California, Monteverde died of cancer in prison in 1881.

Kitty Le Roy, "a starry beauty" with eyes and teeth that outshone her huge diamond earrings, an ace at faro, and an expert handler of her seven revolvers and five husbands, managed the Gem Theater in town in the mid-1800s. Her last husband wanted her to give up her career to become a housewife. When she insisted on earning her own income, he shot her dead in a jealous rage and then killed himself. She was twenty-eight when she died, dressed according to one witness "in silks and dainty fluffs and furbelows ... like a bride preparing for her wedding."

Grave of Calamity Jane, Mount Morris Cemetery. Born Martha Cannary in *Princeton, Missouri,* Calamity Jane always claimed she had been secretly married to Wild Bill Hickok (see *Billings, Montana*), the dashing frontier marshal who was shot in a poker game in Deadwood on August 2, 1876. A heroine in town for her devotion to the miners during a smallpox epidemic, she returned to Deadwood in May 1903 after years roaming the West as a scout, bullwhacker, and notorious hooligan. She told friends she was "ailing," and on August 2, she announced, "It's the 27th anniversary of Bill's death. Bury me next to Bill." Ten thousand mourners marched in her cortege, and Calamity was buried here in a black skirt and dainty white blouse, closer to Wild Bill in death than she probably ever was in life. Matching monuments mark their graves. Mistrustful of her claim to be Bill's wife, the townspeople labeled her grave "Mrs. M. E. Burke," for one of her traditionally accepted husbands. But her famous nickname is carved in bold white letters on the stone wall above.

De Smet

Laura Ingalls Wilder Home. De Smet was *The Little Town on the Prairie* and the setting for four other books about her pioneer childhood that Laura Ingalls Wilder wrote when she was well past retirement age (see *Mansfield, Missouri*). A marker locates the site of the original homestead shanty where her parents were the first family to settle in 1880. The cottonwood trees towering over the boulder were planted by her father to stake his claim. When Laura was eighteen she married Almanzo Wilder. Their early married life on a nearby farm was beset with problems and tragedy—their crops were ruined by hailstorms and drought; both were ill with diphtheria; Almanzo suffered a stroke and was partially paralyzed. Laura wrote about these difficult years but hid the book away. Her daughter Rose did not publish *The First Four Years* until 1971, fourteen years after Laura's death.

Huron

Site of Emma Smith DeVoe House, 347 Kansas Avenue, SE. The South Dakota Suffrage Association was founded here in 1889 by the indefatigable Emma who opened up her home for its headquarters. A talented lecturer, praised by her coworkers as "a most forcible and logical advocate of the equality of sexes," she was often called on to help out flagging associations in other states (see *Helena, Montana*). Emma was fond of embellishing her speeches with catchy suffrage songs composed by her husband. Emma moved on to Illinois in 1891 before the vote was won here, but the first thing she did in her new home was to organize another suffrage society which soon became the largest local organization in Illinois. The education offices of the First Methodist Church now occupy this historic site.

Keystone

Holy Terror Gold Mine was discovered in June 1894 by a Mr. Franklin and his daughter Cora. When Mrs. Franklin chided her husband for naming his mining claims after distant relatives, maiden aunts, and anything else under the sun except her, Franklin agreed and quixotically called it the Holy Terror in her honor. His wife took it all with good humor, for gold valued at $70,000 was being carried out of the mine every week. The mine has been idle since 1942, but a local mining engineer told us that "with the change in the outlook for gold prices, the mine may be reopened in the not too distant future." Whether or not it will have the same name will no doubt depend on the new owner's degree of liberation.

Marty

St. Paul's Indian Mission. The first community of Indian nuns in the country was established here in 1935 by Father Sylvester, O.S.B. The six Oblate Sisters of the Blessed Sacrament who taught at the mission school formed an independent community in 1951 which now includes several white candidates for the sisterhood. "While the community is not a large one due chiefly to its remote location," the nuns told us, "we feel sure that it has done remarkably well in the few years of its existence."

Mobridge

Monument to Sakakawea, Dakota Memorial Park. The chief clerk at Fort Manuel wrote on December 20, 1812, "This evening the wife of Charbonneau, A Snake Squaw died of a putrid fever. She was a good and the best woman in the Fort, aged about 25 years." Based on his entry and the brief notation, "Dead," near her name in Capt. William Clark's diary of 1828, South Dakota claims to be the burial home of Sacajawea, thoroughly appropriating her as their special heroine by changing the conventional spelling of her name. Other accounts record her death, after many lost years, as a centenarian at *Fort Washakie, Wyoming.* But, as one Dakota historian wrote, "I, for one, am much better pleased, with a feeling that this truly great woman died at Fort Manuel. . . . rather than try to follow the vague and nebulous wanderings of a woman who had many husbands, followed the hard life of a drudge among the fur traders and died wholly unrecognized," This graceful cement shaft, paid for by the pennies of devoted schoolchildren, was erected in 1929 to commemorate her lost grave.

Pierre

Site of Fort Sully, Route 34, Farm Island State Park. Only a marker remains of the fort where the Indian captive, nineteen-year-old Fanny Wiggins Kelly, made her daring escape to freedom. Fanny, along with Sarah Larimer, was captured by the Oglala Sioux near *Fort Laramie, Wyoming,* in July 1864. Fanny became the servant of Chief Ottawa. She was fairly treated, and she learned how to speak the language and tended the wounded Indians after their battles with whites. The Blackfeet Sioux borrowed this magnolia-skinned booty as a barter to break into Fort Sully in December, but the alert Fanny darted through the gates and was rescued. Seventeen years later, in the wake of Sarah Larimer's successful account of her own thirty-six-hour captivity, Fanny published an illustrated *Narrative of My Captivity among the Sioux Indians,* which gave, in addition to her own exciting adventures, a concise and scientific portrayal of Indian life. The book stayed on the best-seller list for more than twenty years.

Verendrye Plate Monument, Verendrye Hill. The strange-looking lead plate that established French territorial rights on the American continent in 1741 and is the first written record of the visit of white men to South Dakota, was found in 1913.

Hattie Foster, her sister Blanche, George O'Reilly, and several other school children were walking up this hill on a warm Sunday afternoon in February. It was Hattie who first saw the odd plate with the Latin printing and pulled it out of the ground. But after the plate's authentication, it was George who was given the $500 reward while Hattie received only $200.

Sturgis

Annie Tallent House, 1603 West Main Street (private). The state's first pioneer (see *Custer*) moved to town in 1897 from Rapid City where she had served as superintendent of public instruction and as president of the board of education. She wrote the spirited story of her early days, *The Black Hills; or, the Last Hunting Grounds of the Dakotahs,* shortly before her death at age seventy-three in 1901. "Her life was beset with many of life's bitterest trials and sorrows, but instead of making her hard and pessimistic, they but served to increase her sympathy," an editorial eulogized. The local historian here told us that plans are underway to officially designate the home of "this great woman."

Poker Alice House, North Junction Avenue (private). In her day, this gentle cigar-chomping poker player figured that half a million dollars slipped through her fingers, "but very little stuck." Born in England, Alice settled with her first husband

in Colorado where she carefully watched the gamblers, asked them to explain a straight flush, and practiced, keeping an inscrutable face as she dealt cards in front of a mirror. When her husband died, Alice began gambling for a living, moving about the mining camps all over the West, where her skill and luck at faro and stud poker soon became legend. "We were all gamblers," she once reminisced, and explained about her luck, "Some staked theirs in mines, some on goods, some in cattle, some with a pan at a stream. I took mine at a table with a deck of cards." She retired briefly after a second marriage, but, widowed again, she opened up her own gambling house, where she added some female entertainment. The tables were always shut down on Sunday so that Alice could read the Bible aloud to the staff. Despite her careful observance of the sabbath, she was arrested for "running a disorderly house," found guilty, and convicted. The governor, mindful that he was jailing a Dakota institution, pardoned her, and Alice settled into this clapboard house to spend her last years raising chickens instead of stakes and smoking her favorite fat black cigars. She died here in 1930 at seventy-nine and is buried in St. Francis Cemetery as "Poker Alice."

Valley Springs

Adeline Jenney Home, 812 Sunnyside Avenue (private). On Route 16 at the outskirts of town, a large white sign with yellow and red letters proudly announces that this was the home of the state's poet laureate. A folksy bard all her life, Adeline Jenney was named to the state's highest literary post in 1968 when she was eighty-four years old.

TENNESSEE

Bakersville

Hattie Wyatt Caraway Birthplace. One mile south of town, near the Buffalo River, Hattie Caraway, the nation's first woman to be elected to the United States Senate, was born in February 1878. (See *Jonesboro, Arkansas*.)

Benton

Nancy Ward Grave, Route 411. "Princess and Prophetess of the Cherokee Nation. The Pocahontas of Tennessee" is inscribed on the marker that is embedded in a pyramid of quartz fieldstones over Nancy Ward's grave. As "Beloved Woman" of her Cherokee tribe and the head of the Woman's Council, with a voice of authority as formidable as a chief's, Nancy intervened many times to help the whites. "The white men are our brothers . . . the same sky covers us all," she said. When she rescued a pioneer woman from being burned at the stake, the grateful homemaker taught Nancy how to make cheese and butter. Nancy was so impressed that she soon bought her own cows and introduced dairying to her people. Described as "queenly and commanding . . . tall, erect and beautiful with . . . an imperious yet kindly air," Nancy was too old to attend the Cherokee Council in 1817. She sent her sacred walking cane instead and wrote, "Your mothers and sisters beg of you not to part with any more of our lands . . . for it is our own country for if it was not they [whites] would not ask you to put your hands to paper for it would be impossible to remove us all." Mercifully, the wise, brave leader died five years later and did not live to see her people's humiliation when they were forced to move, dying by the hundreds along the Trail of Tears. (See also *Grainger County*.)

Chattanooga

Site of Bessie Smith Birthplace, "Blue Goose Hollow," West Sixth Street. The great blues singer was at the height of her fame in the 1920s; some of the 160 recordings of her songs sold as many as 100,000 copies a week. It all started here, where she was born thirty years earlier, when as a little girl she sang in front of her broken-down shack until she was discovered by Ma Rainey (see *Columbus, Georgia*), who gave her the advice she followed all her life. "Let your soul do the singing." Billed as the Empress of Blues, Bessie put the pain of life—her draining affair with alcohol, her early poverty—into her songs, some of which she wrote herself. A handsome, robust woman, Bessie was once stabbed during a performance at the old Liberty Theater in Chattanooga. She chased her attacker for three blocks with the knife still in her side, then she returned to continue singing. Although her popularity waned somewhat during the depression, she was making a successful comeback when she was killed in an automobile accident at age forty-one in 1937. She was buried near Philadelphia, Pennsylvania, and her epitaph reads, "The Greatest Blues Singer Will Never Stop Singing."

University of Tennessee. When this school was called the University of Chattanooga in 1910, the school paper, *The Echo* (still being published), interviewed some students for a column on "Women's Idea of Woman's Suffrage." It was not difficult for us to spot which one of the following was the woman who made the first suffrage speech in town:

—"Woman's suffrage is simply a spark set aglow by only old maids and fanned into flame by wives of henpecked husbands."—Ruby Wolfe.

—"I am so busy with my thesis that I have not time to consider woman's suffrage."—Hellen Hellerstedt.

—"A woman who studies politics knows enough to stay out of it."—Margaret Aull.

—"Woman's suffrage will improve the world sooner than some people expect."—Margaret Ervin.

—"If we had woman's suffrage, what would happen if Miller Bros. should have a mill-end sale on election day?"—Lili Nagler.

Clarkrange

Kate Bradford Stockton House, Route 1, one mile west of junction routes 62 and 127 (private). The first woman to run for governor lived here from 1884, when she was four, until her marriage some twenty years later. As the Socialist candidate in the 1936 campaign, Stockton, queried on her chances in an interview, replied with candor unusual for a politician. "I am not saying it is impossible, but I admit that it is rather improbable." While Stockton stomped all over Tennessee urging those radical reforms that were later taken up by the Democratic party, her husband stayed home with their daughters, one of whom, Mabel Stockton Merchant, told us that her mother lost by a large majority—"but even to have entered the race as a woman in those years was something. Mother was impractical to live with but very interesting to know." Merchant recalled that her mother was an early advocate of birth control and an outspoken feminist. "We were fed equal rights along with our milk."

Clarksville

Site of First Woman's Bank, South Second Street. Every officer, director, and staffer was female—the secretary-treasurer doubled as janitor—when the first Woman's Bank opened for business on October 6, 1919. President Brenda Runyon had decided to keep the idea of the bank a secret until the opening day. "It was this fact that won us the confidence of many people," said Runyon in an interview that year. "They are now

assured that we can keep our affairs to ourselves which proves to them that theirs too will be taken care of in like manner." The women had no trouble in disposing of their stock, which they shrewdly limited to two shares per customer, although many men were eager to have as many as ten. To Runyon, this meant that men knew that "women can develop into efficient business women; that we can succeed in the big and worth-while things in life; that we are no longer clinging vines." The bank, which was located in the old Arlington Hotel, was razed in 1973 for a parking lot. It operated successfully until its merger in 1926 with the First Trust and Savings Bank. Runyon always modestly and correctly disclaimed the honor of being the first female bank president. (See *Richmond, Virginia*.)

Columbia

Site of Antoinette Polk House, "Ashwood Hall," Route 43. While visiting her uncle six miles away, young Antoinette overheard federal troops planning to raid her mansion where several Confederate officers were visiting. She quickly saddled a game bay mare and galloped away to Ashwood "like a winged angel on a beam of sunlight." The federals were left "as though tied to a fence," with only the sight of a purple plume from Antoinette's bonnet drifting a farewell in the air. By the time the raiders reached her home, the Confederates were gone. Ashwood Hall smoldered for two weeks after a fire destroyed it in 1874. A wheat field is all that remains of "the grandest house in the county."

Elizabethton

Mary Patton Memorial, Carter County Courthouse. Among the names of soldiers who served in wars from the Revolution to Vietnam, inscribed on this granite monument is the name of Mary Patton, "who made the powder that fought the King's Mountain Battle." In September 1780, she helped the Overmountain men of East Tennessee as they prepared to go across the mountains to meet the Redcoats.

Germantown

Site of Nashoba. This entire town stands on the grounds where in 1825 Frances Wright, the controversial reformer, established her settlement, Nashoba—"wolf" in Chickasaw—where she envisioned training slaves so they could free themselves by working on this plantation. Enthusiastic about her project, Fanny wrote, "We have also laid down for ourselves a plan of life where temperance, exercise . . . with I hope eternal peace of mind, will have their usual beneficial results. Even I am beginning to find an unaccustomed joy in life." Fanny expounded her ideas on the colony in a Memphis paper, adding a few words against marriage: "The marriage law existing without the pale of the institution [Nashoba] is of no force within that pale. No woman can forfeit her individual rights or independent existence, and no man assert over her any rights or power whatsoever beyond what he may exercise over her free and voluntary affection." As for sex: "Let us not teach, that virtue consists in the crucifying of the affections and appetites. . . . Let us not attach ideas of purity to monastic chastity, impossible to man or woman without consequences fraught with evil." Religion "occupies no place in this institution." The scandalized reactions of neighbors, coupled with financial problems and malaria, eventually led to Nashoba's collapse in 1828, but the undaunted Fanny left for her utopian inspiration, *New Harmony, Indiana.*

Grainger County

Nancy Ward Statue, Arnwine Cemetery, Route 41. This haunting granite sculpture of the brave Indian chief (see *Benton*) stands guarding the grave of Mrs. Ben Farmer. Made in the 1930s by Elbert Walker, the statue of Nancy, with eyes burning bright, is shown holding a tiny calf, symbolic of the cattle trade she introduced to the Cherokee. A huge medallion at her knees is inscribed with her name and "Watauga 1776," the Tennessee River Valley where she helped white settlers. No one is quite sure how this magnificent statue found its way here, but for years Nancy's admirers have tried unsuccessfully to relocate it to her grave at *Benton,* where it was originally supposed to be placed.

Greeneville

Eliza McCardle Johnson House, West Main Street. After more than twenty years of marriage to the man who would become America's seventeenth president, Eliza moved here with Andrew Johnson in 1851. It was this tall, clever woman who taught him how to write, and add and subtract, and who read aloud to him from her collection of philosophy books while he sewed in his tailor shop. She thus ably prepared him for his political career while she herself was wasting away as a consumptive.

Hermitage

Emily Donelson House, "Tulip Grove," When Rachel Jackson, the wife of President Andrew Jackson, died in 1828, Emily, whose husband was Jackson's nephew and personal secretary, became the official White House hostess. There, only twenty-one years old, her very unsisterly, snobby behavior toward Peggy Eaton, the secretary of war's wife—a woman of great charm but controversial personal character—led to Emily's banishment back to Tennessee. "It required no small courage for this young woman, living the gay life of the capital with the prestige of high official position to give it all up for a matter of principle and to stand like a rock against the President of the United States," wrote a biographer. But Emily followed her conscience regardless of consequence and returned here to supervise the construction of this beautiful house in 1834. She died at age twenty-nine shortly after its completion.

Jellico

Grace Moore House, Route 25. "Everything in my life has been a long way from Jellico, yet everything starts there," wrote the actress and opera star in her autobiography recalling her first years in this large white house, now a funeral home, where she lived in the early 1900s. "A skinny long-legged ugly girl, good at sports, much disliked by the other girls, but a pal to all the boys in the neighborhood," Grace roamed the mountains, playing hooky from school on warm spring days and when the circus came to town. "I was . . . a public scandal (and definitely no lady)." Grace began singing at the First Baptist Church, which still stands, and she begged her reluctant father to send her to music school in Nashville, as much to learn how to sing as to escape the prejudices of a small town. When she heard the sound of her own high, clear voice, "I felt that I could, perhaps, sing myself out of the narrow restrictions of my life into a bigger, more generous world. I was determined to try." She dazzled audiences all over the world in musical comedy, operas, and films, until her death in a plane accident after entertaining American troops in Europe in 1947.

Knoxville

Barbara Blount Hall, University of Tennessee. Erected in 1890, this building was named in honor of "the nation's first coed." Barbara, the daughter of the territory's first governor, was only twelve in 1804 when she and three friends enrolled for such courses as philosophy and Virgil—which few other women were studying in those days. Instead of being given grades, the women were rated as "attentive," "diligent," or "ingenious."

Barbara was all three. Other women did not enter the college until their official acceptance in 1893 when forty-eight promptly enrolled. The president of the university reported the following year that the decision to admit women was a "wise, just and much needed one." Female students made off with all the honors, winning top prizes in three classes out of four. Unprepared for this clean sweep and outstanding display of intellect, the president wondered if it might be explained by "the intense determination of the women . . . to make a record for themselves fully equal to that of men." The first master's degree to a woman of any southern college was granted here in 1898.

Livingston

Catherine Sevier Memorial, Route 52. It was said that "she could outrun or outleap any woman; walk more erect and ride more gracefully than any other female in the mountains," which was why the widowed John Sevier, first governor of Tennessee, married Catherine in 1780; although his motherless ten children may also have had something to do with his decision. But Catherine, a woman with her own ideas, insisted on accompanying her husband on his Indian raids, declaring, "The wife of John Sevier knows no fear. I neither skulk from duty nor from danger." When John brought home thirty prisoners he didn't know where to put, Catherine treated the Indians with such kindness and care that they remained on her homestead for years. Once, when the Tories stormed into her house, she refused to flinch when a pistol was put to her head. "Such a woman is too brave to die," said the soldier, putting his gun away. In 1815, after her husband died, Catherine settled eleven miles north of the historical marker here. A visitor described her as "remarkably neat in her person, tidy, and particular," sitting on a hearth rug in front of the fire, "erect as a statue—no stooping of the figure, so often acquired by indolence and careless habit, or from infirm old age." (See *Russellville, Alabama.*)

Madison

Maria Thompson Daviess House, Hillcrest Drive (private). Maria Daviess, who lived here in the 1920s, was a photographer, a sculptor, a prize-winning miniature painter, and a jeweler. She was also a farmer, a suffragist, and an author who combined all three experiences in her best-selling novel *Equal Franchise*, about a rooster she raised by that name. As a young woman, she and her good friend Anne Dallas (Dudley) made a vow with their hands on volumes of John Stuart Mill and Olive Schreiner to "do something about the to-be-a-woman question. . . . I began to read all I could find about woman suffrage movements in my native land and then to rage over it all with Anne. . . . We didn't know exactly what to do until [we got] a message from Dr. Anna Howard Shaw—'Organize.' " Daviess helped found the Nashville Equal Suffrage League and tirelessly toured the state for the cause, although author and feminist were sometimes in collusion. "I was standing on the curb or rostrum or running board of a flivver . . . telling women that they must throw off the yoke of male dominion . . . and in between such outbursts I was writing impassioned romances in which tender gallants wooed beautiful maids into eternal happiness." But *The Melting of Molly,* which was made into a successful Broadway play, had a very modern and apt moral. It was the story of a plump young woman who wanted to become thin for her fiancé. By the time Molly had melted away those ugly pounds, he had become obese.

Memphis

Site of Memphis Free Press Offices, 379 Beale Street. The forerunner of Rosa Parks (who in 1954 refused to give up her seat on the bus, thus starting the civil rights movement), Ida Wells Barnett defied a railroad conductor's demands that she move back to the "colored" section, and was forcibly ejected from a train. She sued but eventually lost her case before the Tennessee Supreme Court in 1887. As a teacher in the black schools of Memphis, Ida was so relentless in her criticisms of the unsatisfactory educational system that she was laid off in 1891. Ida began working for the *Memphis Free Speech,* and, when she saw three of her friends lynched, she determined to devote her life to freedom for her black brothers and sisters. Her investigative articles in the *Free Speech* about other lynchings were merciless: "More than ten thousand Negroes have been killed in cold blood, without the formality of judicial trial . . . and for all these murders only three white men have been tried, convicted, and executed." As for the charge of rape that was used to justify lynchings, "White men of [the South] . . . to justify their own barbarism . . . assume a chivalry which they do not possess. True chivalry respects all womanhood, and no one who reads the record, as it is written in the faces of the million mulattoes in the South, will for a minute conceive that the southern white man had a very chivalrous . . . respect for the womanhood which circumstances placed in his power." In 1892, Ida's offices here on the site of the First Baptist Church were plundered and demolished, her life was threatened, and she was forced to move to *Chicago, Illinois.*

Site of Mary Church Terrell Birthplace, 384 South Lauderdale. Born here in 1863, Terrell, who would become a charter member of the NAACP, like Ida Wells Barnett crusaded against the evils of lynching, pleading with her white sisters: "What a tremendous influence for law and order and what a mighty foe to mob violence Southern white women might be if they would arise in the purity and power of their womanhood to improve their fathers, husbands, and sons no longer to stain their hands with the black man's blood!" The famed black educator received her college degree in *Oberlin, Ohio.*

Sisters of St. Mary Memorial, St. Mary's Episcopal Church, 692 Poplar Avenue. Five nuns arrived from New York in August 1873 to start a school for young girls. Within days, the devastating yellow fever epidemic struck the city. Although the sisters had no experience in nursing care, they ventured selflessly out to the stricken areas. Five years later, the epidemic struck again and this time took four of the five sisters in its deathly wake. To commemorate the heroic work of the sisters, their names are inscribed here on the steps leading to the high altar; a beautiful stained-glass window honors "The Sisters Who Labored in 1873."

Annie Cook Memorial, Elmwood Cemetery. Annie Cook's name is not inscribed on the five-foot-tall marker of the Howard Association—which also contributed help during the raging yellow fever epidemic of 1878. But Annie Cook is buried here, herself a victim of the fever when she sent away her assistants and turned her palatial Mansion House on Gayoso Street into a hospital. The leading men of town had once paid for shelter and loving attention in her house. At her death on September 12, the newspaper announced, "Annie Cook, the woman who after a long life of shame, ventured all she had of life and property for the sick, died . . . while nursing her patients. . . . Her faith has made her whole."

Murfreesboro

Site of Mary Noailles Murphree Birthplace, "Grantlands," Route 41. Under the pen name Charles Egbert Craddock, Mary wrote more than twenty books about life in Tennessee. That such fine, bold writing "that moved men mightily over the years" could come from the pen of such a "petite, cultured, reticent woman" astounded the nation when, after the publication of her best-selling *In the Mountains of Tennessee* (1884) when she was thirty-four, her identity was revealed. In all, Mary wrote twenty-five novels, and she was so renowned that when Theodore Roosevelt came through town in 1894, the first question he asked was "Where is Craddock? She's the person I want to see." He then stated in his speech that no honor or praise could express his appreciation of her literary achievements.

Nashville

Site of Hetty McEwen House, 117 Eighth Avenue. In true conciliatory spirit during the Civil War, Hetty McEwen erected a flagpole and raised the Stars and Stripes in the front yard of her house, but she spent her nights and days baking cakes and knitting socks for the Confederate soldiers.

Monument to Women of the Confederacy, War Memorial Building. In 1909, sculptor Belle Kinney was the only female among eighty competitors to design a series of monuments to the Women of the Confederacy. The selection of Kinney as the winning sculptor caused a near riot by the rejected, disappointed males. The commission was said to be the first such ever given for the making of a monument to a group of women. Kinney's bold design shows Fame in the center with a dying soldier struggling to raise the flag; to the right a strong Confederate woman, clasping the palm of victory to her breast, is being crowned by Fame. The only other existing monument in the series is in *Jackson, Mississippi.* Belle started her brilliant career when, as a youngster, fascinated by an exhibit of a petrified man, she made her own mummy out of mud. She won her first gold medal—for a bust of her father—at the Tennessee Centennial Exhibition when she was ten. She and her husband Leopold Scholz designed a series of friezes at the Parthenon in Nashville, and several of her works can also be seen here inside the War Memorial Building. One of her most famous works is her statue of Governor John Sevier which stands in Statuary Hall in *Washington, D.C.*

Site of Suffrage Headquarters, Hotel Hermitage, 231 Sixth Avenue North. By March 1920, thirty-five states had ratified the Nineteenth Amendment. Only one more state's signature was needed to enfranchise the women of America. At the "very earnest" urging of President Woodrow Wilson, on August 9 a special session of the Tennessee Legislature was called to consider the amendment. Troubleshooter Carrie Chapman Catt arrived here to assist with the last-minute efforts to combat such saboteurs as the Men's Anti-suffrage Association and other reactionary groups who were determined to use any means to subvert the amendment. (Later Carrie Chapman Catt would write, "Never in the history of politics has there been such a nefarious lobby as laboured to block the ratification in Nashville. In the short time that I spent in the capital I was more maligned, more lied about, than in the 30 previous years I worked for suffrage [see *New Rochelle, New York*]. I was flooded with anonymous letters, vulgar, ignorant, insane . . . Even tricksters . . . appropriated our telegrams, tapped our telephones, listened outside our windows and transoms.") Passionate speeches rang throughout the legislature, climaxing on August 18 in the House. One representative, recovering from a serious operation, was brought from the hospital to vote. Another, on his way home to see his dying baby, turned around mid-route to place his (affirmative) vote. And twenty-four-year-old Harry Burn changed his vote in favor of ratification "because I believe in full suffrage as a right. I believe we had a moral and legal right to ratify." But most touchingly, he confessed, "I know that a mother's advice is always safest for her boy to follow and my mother wanted me to vote for ratification." On August 26, the victory was assured, with Tennessee claiming the glory of that last, most important, yes.

Edward Ward Carmack Statue, State Capitol, Cedar Street. This heroic bronze was made by Nancy Cox-McCormack, the gifted sculptor whose many works were exhibited all over the country. She was the only sculptor for whom Mussolini ever posed.

Nancy noted that the pronounced bump on the back of Napoleon's head (denoting egoism) was missing in Mussolini, whom she misguidedly called "the greatest man in Europe." With a more worthy subject, Nancy also designed the Jane Addams memorial portrait medal at Hull House in *Chicago, Illinois.*

Sewanee

Sarah Barnwell Elliott House, University Avenue (private). When Sarah Elliott lived in this house and held informal gatherings, called "Mondays," for university students, she was already famous for her novel *Jerry* (1891), which one reviewer noted "along with the words of Charles Craddock [see *Murfressboro*] turned the eyes of America toward the Southern mountains." Elliott moved to New York in 1895 (where she was called Jerry in the literary salons—and loved it) and spent several productive years there, writing her last novel, *The Making of Jane,* before returning to Sewanee in 1902 when she was fifty-four. In her unenlightened youth she once wrote to her brother, "Do you not realize that I, having reached the age of 22, have 'quit struggling' and 'quite sneer matrimony down.' . . . When a woman gives up all ideas of matrimony, she either turns saint or womans rights, and as the name of Elliott has never yet been disgraced, I do not propose to find my vocation in the Forum." However, Miss Sada, as she now was called, energetically took up the suffrage cause. As president of the Tennessee State Equal Suffrage Association in 1913, she was the first woman ever to address the legislature—with a resounding speech on woman's rights that did not disgrace her in the least.

Shelbyville

Site of Evans House, Dixie Hotel, the Square. Union spy Pauline Cushman, posing as an exiled actress searching for an older brother in the Confederate army, moved into this hotel where many rebel officers stayed in 1863. She quickly struck up a friendship with the captain of the engineers. He was so infatuated with the ravishing Pauline that he forgot about the plans and drawings of defense fortifications lying about the room. Pauline stole them, smuggling some out in the handles of butcher knives, stuffing others into the craw of a chicken that was then carried across the lines by a female farmer. When Pauline's stealthy moves were discovered, she was put in jail to await a military court martial. The verdict was guilty, but, before she could be hanged, the federal forces appeared and freed her. Pauline was later commissioned as a major in the Union army in gratitude for her courageous help. She moved on to *Casa Grande, Arizona,* for a different kind of hotel work.

TEXAS

Austin

Site of Eberly House, Lavaca and Sixth Streets. The capital of Texas might well be Houston if it had not been for the noted innkeeper Angelina B. Eberly, whose determined claim on the state's files were motivated as much by shrewd business logic as hometown loyalty. Described as "one of the handsomest and most queenly women ever born in the valley of the Mississippi," Angelina defied Republic President Sam Houston's armed Texas Rangers one midnight in December 1842, when they snuck into town to remove the government archives. She fired a six-pound cannon, awakening the town. Irate citizens recaptured the precious records and put them into safekeeping on the second floor of Angelina's inn. The town's triumph in the "War of the Archives" thus assured Austin's status as state headquarters, and it insured a steady stream of visitors that would keep Angelina's hotels thriving.

At the time of her death in 1869, the estate of this feisty hotelier, known for the "excellent collations" of her tables, was valued at more than $50,000. The Claudia Taylor (Lady Bird) Johnson Hall now stands on the site of Angelina's popular hotel.

Elisabet Ney Museum, 304 East Forty-fourth Street. In 1892, the brilliant, flamboyant sculptor camped in a nearby tent to supervise the construction of this elegant studio, which she named "Formosa," after her studio in Spain. For years afterwards, visitors flocked to watch the artist at work in her daring costume—a smock that reached only to her knees with buttoned serge leggings or high-laced boots. Relaxing here in the afternoons, Elisabet liked to paddle about in a canoe on the pond, and she welcomed such distinguished admirers as Paderewski, Caruso, and the ballerina Pavlova for tea and clabber (curdled milk) under the oak trees. Here, Elisabet made the clay casts for her famous statues of Houston and Austin (see *Washington, D.C.*). Thoroughly dedicated to her work, the spartan Elisabet once said, "Women are fools. They are fools to be bothered with housework. Look at me. I sleep in a hammock, which requires no making up; I break an egg for my breakfast and sip it raw from the shell; I make lemonade in a glass and then rinse the glass—and my housework is done for the day!" Elisabet lived here for the last two years of her life, until 1907, making occasional visits in her rig to her home—"Liendo"— in *Hempstead*. Today, the studio, preserved as a memorial, contains forty of her most famous sculptures, including Bismarck, Garibaldi, the plaster patterns of Houston and Austin, and a larger-than-life Lady Macbeth.

Laguna Gloria, 3809 West Thirty-fifth Street. This beautiful Italian villa was constructed in 1916 by Clara Driscoll, who was often called the Savior of the Alamo (see *San Antonio*). She donated this home to the Texas Fine Arts Association for use as an art gallery in 1943, two years before her death. Driscoll brought the wishing well from Tuscany and the statues, which grace the Garden of the Four Seasons, from Venice. The fireplace wall panel was especially carved for her from an old rafter of her beloved Alamo. Forever generous with her enormous wealth, Driscoll donated thousands of dollars to numerous causes, including the Texas Federation of Women's Clubs and later became governor of Texas (see *Temple*).

Grave of Joanna Troutman, State Cemetery. Just inside the gates of the cemetery stands a towering bronze statue of Joanna Troutman. Her raised right hand holds a needle, as if the last stitch were finally in place, the thread snapped, and the famous Lone Star Flag that is gathered in the folds of her skirt were finished. The sixteen-year-old Georgian (see *Knoxville, Georgia*) designed the banner and presented it to a Macon battalion as they left to assist Texas in its fight for independence in December 1835. The flag, a single azure five-pointed star (symbolic of the state's lonely struggle) on a white silk field, inscribed with the words *"Ubi Libertas Habitat, ibe nostra patria est,"* was first raised at Velasco on January 8, 1836 and later carried to the fortress at Goliad. By the time the bitter fight against Mexico came to its bloody end in March, only tattered shreds of Joanna's patriotic token remained. She died in Georgia in 1880 and was buried in an obscure grave until 1913 when the Texas legislature claimed her as its adopted heroine and decreed that her body should rest here in the state's most hallowed burial ground.

Belton

Miriam A. Wallace Home, Route 2 (private). Miriam, born in 1875, lived here until 1899 when she married James Ferguson and later became governor of Texas (see *Temple*).

Brownsville

Fort Brown. During the heavy bombardment of this historic fort on May 3, 1846, Sarah Bowman, "the Great Western" (see *Yuma, Arizona*), chief cook for the Fifth Infantry, a six-foot ebullient Irishwoman, "with the utmost coolness and disdain of Mexican copper shot and cannon balls that banged about in all directions," kept right on with tasty preparations for the officers' mess.

Columbus

Dilue Rose Harris House, 602 Washington Street (private). Intimately acquainted with the leaders of the Texas Revolution and of the Republic, Dilue Rose Harris, who died in 1914, was able to gather extensive material which she published in 1900–1904 as *Reminiscences.* Today they are considered a primary source of Texas history. This charming cottage, built around 1859, is of unusual tabby construction.

Corpus Christi

Charlotte M. Sidbury House, Bayfront Science Park. A local historian called Sidbury "an early prototype of the successful businesswoman." At her death in 1904, she had amassed a fortune of several hundred thousand dollars from shrewd management of a lumberyard with branches in several Texas towns, and as a director of the Corpus Christi National Bank. Sidbury "was interested in nearly every public improvement that has given substantial promise to developing the resources of southwest Texas." It was she who worked tirelessly to insure the deep harbor that Corpus Christi is famous for today. When her home is restored, it will serve as headquarters for the Junior League.

Dallas

Site of St. Nicholas Hotel, Broadway. The Dallas County Courthouse stands where, in 1859, the finest hotel in northern Texas, built by pioneer settler Sarah Cockrell, once welcomed weary travelers. Her career as an entrepreneur began when she became a widow, in 1858, Sarah, who had helped her illiterate husband with his accounts and letters, easily took over the management of his lucrative toll bridge and ferry across the Tunry River and completed the building of the St. Nicholas Hotel. It was destroyed less than a year later, but, undaunted, Sarah soon built another fine hotel and added a prosperous flour mill to her growing enterprises.

Margo Jones Theater, Grand and First Avenues. Called the Dallas Dynamo for her boundless creative energy, Margo Jones introduced the world's first "theater in the round," in 1947, acclaimed by dramatists all over the world as a major theatrical innovation. A grateful citizenry said, "Theatrically speaking, Margo put Dallas on the map." Originally it was called Theater '47; Margo changed the name every New Year's Eve during a ceremony atop the arena building at Fair Park. It was Theater '55 when she died at age forty-three. Margo, whom Thornton Wilder called "a Divining Rod for American Drama. . . . a fighter, builder, explorer, a mixer of truth and magic," was devoted to discovering new talent. Her theater was a showcase for many promising young dramatists and actors whom she encouraged with the words of her own life code: "The important thing is your own individuality, your own beliefs and your own convictions. You must have a capacity for tremendous amount of hard work and joy in doing so."

Denton

Pioneer Woman Monument, Texas Woman's University. Unarmed, childless, the prairie breezes whipping her long skirt against her hiking boots, the pioneer woman portrayed in this heroic thirteen-foot marble monument, dedicated in 1938, represents the "unsung sainted of the nation's immortals. . . . with unswerving courage she met each untried situation with a resourcefulness equal to the need. . . . she illumined the dullness of routine and loneliness of isolation with beauty and love abundant. And withal she lived with casual unawareness of her value to civilization." This last line was a favorite of Eleanor Roosevelt, who wrote, "There we have the secret which should be driven home to every woman. In countless homes in this country today there are women who are 'casually unaware' of the great accomplishments which are theirs. . . . We forget them because they do their daily tasks so casually that their heroism and the vital place which they fill in our world passes almost unnoticed and certainly unsung in the present."

El Paso

After her bold defiance of polygamy in *Salt Lake City, Utah,* and her brief days of sweet triumph in *Manistee, Michigan,* Ann Eliza Webb Young Denning, Brigham Young's rebel bride, moved here in 1902. She changed addresses four times in five years in El Paso, and today all that stand on the sites of this restless runaway's residences are a laundromat on Magoffin Street; Interstate 10; a parking lot at San Antonio Street; and a remodeled apartment house at 602 Myrtle. No one knows where or when she died.

Groesbeck

Old Fort Parker, Route 14, Park Road 35. On May 19, 1836, this fort was attacked by hundreds of Comanche warriors who killed five members of the Parker family. A mounted warrior carried nine-year-old Cynthia Ann away in his arms. For twenty-four years Cynthia lived happily with the wild Indian tribe, married the great Chief Nacona, and had two children. Her son Quanah became the greatest Comanche chief in history. Her daughter's name was Topsannah, or Prairie Flower. Cynthia was captured in a raid by the Texas Rangers in 1861 and reunited with her family. But she could never forget her glorious free life with her Indian family, and she futilely tried to escape and return to them several times. She died a few years later from the most bitter loneliness and despair. (See *Poynor*.)

Hamilton

Ann Whitney Memorial, Courthouse Lawn. During yet another Comanche Indian attack in 1867—this one led by a renegade white man with red hair—Massachusetts-born Ann Whitney sacrificed her life to insure the escape of her students from her small log cabin schoolhouse. As the arrows whizzed through the cracks in the logs, Ann hurriedly pushed the children out the tiny back window to safety. Weighing more than 230 pounds, Ann gave up all hope for her own escape and heroically sacrificed herself to shield the children from the deadly arrows, more than a dozen of which horribly impaled her. She was buried in nearby Graves-Gentry Cemetery where thankful children have erected a marble pillar over her grave. Here in the heart of town, shiny granite blocks commemorate her courageous deed.

Hempstead

Elisabet Ney House, "Liendo," Addie Gee Road (private). When she first saw this seventeen-room Greek revival house in 1873, the delighted sculptor declared, "This is where I shall live and die." Although her favorite studio in *Austin* claimed her last days, Elisabet is buried here under a large oak tree. In this beautiful countryside, Elisabet lived exuberantly, riding through the glens in her cool Grecian gown with a pair of six-shooters hanging from her belt. Providing the nervous neighbors with even more gossip, Elisabet consistently denied that the man she was living with was her husband. He was, but when Elisabet consented to marry Edmund Montgomery in 1863 (only because he wished it; to her, marriage was a "Great Social Lie") it was on the condition that their marriage would always be kept a secret. He called her Miss Ney, and she referred to him as her best friend. She never admitted the fact of her marriage to her own son. Already famous in her native Germany for her magnificent statues of Bismarck and Garibaldi, Elisabet was invited to design statues of Texas figures. She moved to her studio in Austin in 1879.

Houston

Site of Mansion House, Congress and Milam Streets. Pamela Mann's tough, independent reputation preceded her when she came to this rough frontier town as one of its first settlers shortly after her historic confrontation with Sam Houston in 1836. Pamela generously lent Houston some oxen to pull his two cannons, "Twin Sisters," stipulating that he use the beasts only as far as Nacogdoches. When the general steered the oxen off in another direction, Pamela pursued him. Blocking his path with a pair of pistols and a long knife, she accused him of telling her "a damn lie." She cut the oxen yoke and brought her tired team home. She was called "a most notorious character" when she opened the Mansion House hotel—itself notorious for its turbulent brawls, duels, and police raids, until Pamela got everything under control. (Today, easier-to-manage parking lots and a burlesque house stand on this site.) Pamela was so respected that when she was sentenced to death on charges of forgery, the governor hastily granted her clemency. A Methodist minister wrote after her death in 1840 that she was "a woman who, perhaps under happier environments might have been an honor to her sex. . . . a widow, forced perhaps from the injustices of others to step forward in her own defense and meet lawless men on their own grounds."

Grave Site of Sarah Emma Edmonds, Washington Cemetery. When she heard of the start of the Civil War, Sarah Edmonds recalled, "It was not my intention or desire to seek my own personal ease and comfort while so much sorrow and distress filled the land. But the great question to be decided was, what can I do? What part am I to act in this great drama?" So the fearless twenty-year-old disguised herself as a man, called herself Frank Johnson, and joined an infantry regiment from Michigan. Several times she served as a spy behind the Confederate lines. "I felt just as happy and as comfortable as it was possible for anyone to be . . . I am naturally fond of adventure, a little ambitious, and a good deal romantic, and this together with my devotion to the Federal cause . . . made me forget the unpleasant items and not only endure, but really enjoy, the privations connected with my perilous positions." Her account, *Nurse and Spy in the Union Army* (1865), was enormously popular. Almost twenty years after the war, her comrades testified on behalf of her heroics, and Congress honored her with a pension of twelve dollars a month. Just before her death in 1898, she was the first woman enrolled in the GAR. She is said to be buried in their section of this cemetery but even with the help of officials we were unable to locate the grave.

Hortense Malsch Ward House, 6024 Fordham Road (private). Hortense started out as a secretary in a cigar factory. She studied law through a correspondence course and became the first woman in Texas to pass the bar (1910) and be admitted to practice before the U.S. Supreme Court. She consistently battled for equal legal rights for women, and the married woman property rights act, passed in 1913, bore her name. She died here in 1944.

Independence

Margaret Moffette Lea Houston Home, two blocks east of the intersection of Routes 50 and 390 (private). The intelligent and charming Margaret of the "placid violet eyes" married Sam Houston in 1839 when she was only twenty. He was forty-six, already a famous general. Hailed in the wedding toasts as "Conqueress of the Conqueror," Margaret expended a lot of her energy taming the impetuous and headstrong Houston, whom friends described as "totally unfit for domestic happiness." She insisted on making time for her poetry and prose writings, and she ably managed the plantations while Houston was in Washington. After his death in 1863 she moved to this "sweet village. . . . loveliest spot on earth to me," and she died four years later after an attack of yellow fever. "The world will take care of [Sam] Houston's fame," his good friend Andrew Jackson once said. Neglected Margaret was not eulogized until ninety-eight years after her death when the pink granite monument was erected at her grave located two blocks away near the Independence Baptist Church.

Moody

Mother Neff Memorial State Park was named for Isabella Eleanor Neff who was born in Roanoke, Virginia, in 1830 and "gave up a life of comfort, of congenial associations, to pit herself against, or rather with, primitive raw pioneering." The park ranger here, quoting from a history of the area, told us that "while her husband fought back the Indians on the frontier, she fought the battles of frontier life in the home. . . . the refinements of culture were transplanted by Mrs. Neff into this wild raw country where they took root, and spread to the everlasting benefit of Texas."

Poynor

Site of Grave of Cynthia Ann Parker, Old Fosterville Cemetery, Route 315. Brokenhearted and bereft, mourning the death of her daughter Prairie Flower ten months earlier, and still lonely for the Comanche life she had shared for twenty-four years (see *Groesbeck*), Cynthia Ann Parker died a virtual prisoner in her sister's home in 1864. She was originally buried in this cemetery. Almost fifty years later, famous Chief Quanah Parker sought to have the grave of his mother moved to his home in Oklahoma. He had not seen her since she had been abducted by Texas Rangers and taken back to her family in 1861. "They took my mother away.... They would not let me see her. Now she dead. Her boy want to bury her. Sit by her mound.... Comanches had much land.... No more Texas. Few Indians, little land. Lonesome.... Me bury her, you keep her, she mine." In 1910, his heartfelt wish was granted, and today mother and son are buried side by side in *Fort Sill, Oklahoma*. The marker here was dedicated in 1969 with dozens of Parker descendants in attendance.

Richmond

Site of Jane Long House, River Road. One of the very first settlers of the state—the Mother of Texas—died here at age eighty-two in 1880. In the 1820s, when her husband left to fight in the revolution for Texas independence, Jane was left alone at Bolivar (across from Galveston on the coast) where for more than two months she endured isolation that would have been fatal for one less dedicated and strong. Stranded without food or supplies, Jane shot birds and caught fish to feed herself and her children. On the coldest night of the year, when the wind blew the roof off the house and the snow tumbled onto her bed, Jane delivered her baby. When she was finally rescued, she learned that her husband had been killed. Undaunted, she opened a small hotel in Brazoria which became famous for its celebrated social functions that included such guests as Sam Houston and Mirabeau Lamar, both of whom reputedly asked her to marry them. She preferred to devote her time to management of her plantation near here, one of the richest in Texas.

Site of Carry Nation's Boardinghouse, Morton and Fourth Streets. Carry Nation didn't find much fulfillment in being a housewife while her husband David (see *Holden, Missouri*) practiced law. In the 1880s, she started a string of boardinghouses in Columbia, Texas, and she expanded to an even bigger inn here. When she had a fight with the town, she put seats in the dining room and held Sunday-school classes there after lunch. The people of Richmond called her a religious fanatic, but it was not until the Nations moved on to *Medicine Lodge, Kansas,* that anyone understood just how fanatic Carry Nation could be. The Fort Bend County Museum at 500 Houston Street has some interesting Nation memorabilia.

San Antonio

The Alamo. Few people who remember the Alamo remember the woman whose moving account of the dreadful 1836 siege inspired those historic words. Eighteen-year-old Suzanna Dickerson, her fifteen-month-old daughter Angelina toddling at her heels, cared for the sick and wounded during the battle. She finally took refuge in a cramped room at the back of the chapel, from where she watched the last of the brave defenders mercilessly slaughtered. After her release by Santa Anna, Suzanna rode to Sam Houston's headquarters to tell him the sad news. "They all died fighting for liberty as every true Texan should die," she said. Houston wept when he heard the tragic details. It is said that it was Suzanna's conversation with Houston that resulted in the rallying cry, "Remember the Alamo," which impelled the Texans to fight so boldly at the Battle of San Jacinto.

Another unheralded heroine of the Alamo siege is Andrea Candelaria, a hotelier. Sam Houston asked Andrea to care for his good friend James Bowie, who was suffering from tuberculosis. When the battle erupted, Andrea staunchly refused to

leave her entrusted charge. Andrea recalled in her diary that during the terrible fighting, she threw herself in front of Bowie and was bayoneted through the arm and chin. At the end of the twelve-day rout, with more than one hundred seventy dead, Andrea remembered that when she "stepped on the floor of the Alamo blood ran into my shoes." The Texas legislature granted her a pension of one hundred dollars a year for her courageous stand with the men of the Alamo. When she died at age one hundred thirteen in 1898, military men served as her pallbearers.

Clara Driscoll Memorial, Old Chapel. Concerned that "the grandest monument in the History of the World" was going to crumble from neglect and vandalism, Clara Driscoll (see *Austin*) donated close to $100,000 of her own money and almost twenty years of her life to insure the faithful preservation of this historic shrine, earning for herself the title, Savior of the Alamo. A memorial plaque inside the chapel commemorates her patriotic efforts that transformed the "blood-stained lands" into a "park of blooming flowers—a benison of peace to myriads who come with homage for the heroic defenders of the Alamo ... the accomplishment of her dream."

Marion Koogler McNay Art Institute, 6000 North Braunfels. During Marion McNay's lifetime, this Spanish-Mediterranean house was the cultural and art center of town. When she died in 1950, McNay donated her house, her priceless collection of sculptures and paintings, and the bulk of her estate for this splendid museum of modern art that welcomes more than one hundred thousand visitors a year. In addition to works by Picasso, El

Greco, Cézanne, and Van Gogh, we were pleased to find some beautiful watercolors by McNay herself, including her *Navajo Women Weaving,* located in the New Mexican Arts and Crafts Room.

Tascosa

Grave of Frenchy McCormick, Casimero Romero Cemetery. When the last of the Girls of the Golden West died in 1941, Elizabeth McCormick's grave was marked with only a crudely inscribed tin sign, a pathetic contrast to the handsome monument she had erected over the grave of her gambler husband, Mickey. Elizabeth left her home in Louisiana in the 1870s to become a dance girl in Dodge City, Kansas, where she picked up her saucy nickname—Frenchy. Whenever she was asked about her past, Elizabeth always replied vaguely, "No one ever knows or ever shall know who I am." She married McCormick in 1881, and the two vowed they would never leave Tascosa or each other. When he died in 1912, Elizabeth kept her word. By 1917, she was the only resident in the small, rough town, refusing to leave her adored husband. During the years before her death, she was blind, deaf, and withdrawn, and she finally died peacefully in 1941. Laura Graham, a resident of nearby Vega, told us that Elizabeth's funeral was attended by some well-known French aristocrats from New Orleans. "But there were always stories about her, how true, no one ever knew"— exactly as the mysterious woman wished. A devoted friend of Elizabeth's finally raised enough money to put a sturdy stone over her grave in 1965.

Temple

Miriam Ferguson Home, 518 North Seventh Street (private). The nation's second female governor (see *Belton*), elected in 1924 by a landslide victory of more than eighty thousand votes, took the governor's oath just a few days after Nellie Tayloe Ross took a similar oath in *Cheyenne, Wyoming.* A controversial and colorful figure, Ferguson (who always detested the nickname, "Ma," she was burdened with) was—perhaps unfairly—considered merely a figurehead for her husband, former Governor Jim Ferguson, "Pa." He had been impeached in 1917. The clever couple turned the rumors into a campaign slogan— "Two Governors for the Price of One"—when she ran for another term and won in 1933. Ferguson said she was not happy as governor, and would have preferred to stay home and work in the garden here. But she was a devoted friend of the poor and underprivileged, and she did her job so ably that, at her death in 1961, a Texas senator said, "She left a record that will inspire people in the future to elect some other woman as governor."

Waco

Armstrong Browning Library, Baylor University. The world's largest collection of Elizabeth Barrett and Robert Browning's letters, books, manuscripts, and memorabilia are preserved here, along with Harriet Hosmer's (see *Watertown, Massachusetts*) sculpture of the famous literary couple's lovingly *Clasped Hands.*

Governor Miriam Ferguson

Bicknell

Thurber Relief Society Hall, Main Street, Highway 24. For three years, the women of Bicknell (formerly named Thurber) sewed quilts, peddled butter and cheese, and squirreled away profits from the sale of Sunday eggs to raise money for the construction of this first public building in the ward. When it was determined that the bricks were not colorful enough, they were dipped into a dye made from red clay from Redmond, Utah. The red brick building was dedicated in 1899.

Corinne

Site of Corinne Opera House. The plaque erected here by the Daughters of Utah Pioneers calls it "the largest recreation center in Utah outside of Salt Lake City." Built in 1870 of red pine with square nails, the Corinne Opera House had a grand auditorium that attracted leading companies bound for California on the Central Pacific Railroad. Maude Adams, for whom James Barrie created *Peter Pan,* played here, too. Perhaps it was the curved circle of footlights behind the red velvet curtains illuminating the stage that helped inspire Adams to develop her own inventive stage lighting techniques.

Huntsville

Mary Dilworth Hammond Monument, Valley School grounds. Born a Pennsylvania Quaker and converted to a Utah Mormon, Mary Dilworth, the state's first schoolteacher (see *Salt Lake City*), was later one of this town's finest. After a hazardous trip to the Sandwich Islands with her husband on missionary work, she returned to the more sedate life of teaching here in Huntsville in 1865. The monument is a slab of red stone bearing a bronze plaque showing the teacher with two children, a tent, and the Conestoga wagon of her transcontinental journey.

Mary Heathman Smith Monument, Public Square. Among the pines and picnic tables, a tall white concrete shaft pays tribute to Mary Heathman Smith, "lovingly known as 'Granny' Smith," an English-born "doctor, surgeon, midwife and nurse." For thirty years after she came to Utah in 1862, "in storm or sunshine, during the bleakest winters or the darkest night, with little or no remuneration, she attended the people of Ogden valley with a courage and faithfulness unexcelled. In addition to rearing her own family of nine . . . she brought into the world more than 1,500 babies." A likeness of "Granny" in bas-relief peers across the street at the Valley School, populated no doubt by numerous descendants of the babies she delivered.

Jensen

Josie Morris Cabin, Cub Creek, Dinosaur National Monument. The log cabin built by this child of the wild and woolly West still sits among the poplars, walnuts, and cottonwood trees she planted in 1913. Josie Morris was a toddler when her cattleman father brought her to the remote corner of Brown's Park (across the border in Colorado) in the 1870s. A childhood witness to hangings and shootings in the vicinity of the hideouts of Butch Cassidy, Josie left Brown's Park and homesteaded here. After three husbands, she continued to live in this cabin until she died in 1964. She was a spunky, independent cowpuncher who won first prize in a calf-roping contest when she was past eighty.

Josie Morris

Josie's sister, Ann, was born in 1878, the first white baby in Brown's Hole. Sent to prep school in Boston, Massachusetts, Ann disdained Eastern etiquette, donned buckskin breeches, and returned here. Somewhere along her rifle-shooting, cigarette-rolling trail, she was nicknamed Queen Ann. She went to forestry school and passed all the tests, then was barred from working as a forest ranger "for the slapdash reason that I happened to be a female." Both women are buried in Brown's Park, just over the ridge from the school.

Kanab

The undefiled streets here are in no small measure attributable to the all-woman council who cleaned up Kanab in 1912. Mayor Mary Woolley Chamberlain Howard and her four victorious board members comprised the first all-female government of an incorporated town in America. When they took office, one of their first official acts was to ban livestock from the sidewalks and thoroughfares. Careless owners of loose cows and horses were fined twenty-five cents per head. Another early act was the prohibition of slingshots within the town limits, "thus protecting our feathered friends," according to the mayor. The female governors, each a mother with from two to seven children, ran Kanab efficiently until 1914, when they modestly stepped down to share the honors of office with a new slate. Although their meetinghouse has gone the way of the troublesome livestock, town history books report that the women were "a very able body of lawmakers, and . . . put over a splendid program for city improvements."

Knolls

Donner-Reed Trail Monument, on U.S. 40, in Cedar Mountains commemorates the crossing of the Great Salt Desert by the ill-fated Donner party. (See *Truckee, California*.)

Park City

Park City Pioneers Monument, Route 248. The first family to settle in this mining-town-turned-ski-resort were the Snyders: Rhoda and husband George, and three children. They arrived by wagon in 1872, chopping down trees to clear a path to the spot then known as Upper Parleys and Upper Kimballs. Two months later they celebrated their arrival by renaming the town and holding festivities. From a bed sheet, a red flannel baby blanket, and a blue silk handkerchief, Rhoda Snyder and her daughters Sylvia and Lillian made the first flag to fly over Park City.

St. George

Site of Emma Lucy Gates Birthplace, First West and First North. Utah's most popular coloraturo soprano was born here November 5, 1880, to Susa Young Gates, one of Brigham Young's wives. She once wrote, "my whole soul seems to be brought out more when I sing," and embarked on her operatic career. Always loyal to her home state, she organized the Lucy Gates Opera Company in Salt Lake in 1915—the first such company organized by a prima donna.

Salt Lake City

This Is The Place Monument, Pioneer Monument State Park. Three women formed a small minority among the 143 men, 70 wagons, 93 horses, 52 mules, 66 oxen, and 19 cows who arrived here with Brigham Young on July 24, 1847. Clarissa Decker Young, Ellen Saunders Kimball, and Harriet Page Wheeler Decker Young are memorialized here in bronze, trudging alongside the wagons by foot, clad in sunbonnets to block the harsh plains heat, and dragging two children behind.

Beehive House, 67 East South Temple. This sturdy yellow building with its bright white trim was the executive mansion where Brigham Young was tended by one of his plural wives and several sons and daughters. To learn poise, the young girls lived in bedrooms with lace curtains. To learn hard work, the boys slept in sparsely furnished rooms with no heat. It was here on the "sacred sofa" in the Mormon leader's office that Mrs. Frank Leslie interviewed him about the great curiosity, polygamy. "How can women share a husband?" she asked the bearded president. He answered that "our women are content in trying to make their husbands happy and their homes pleasant. . . . For my own part I always endeavor to show perfect impartiality." "Then do Mormon husbands feel no preference?" "Well, perhaps; human nature is frail, but our religion teaches us to control and conceal those preferences as much as possible, and we do—we do."

Lion House, 63 East South Temple. This yellow and green mate to Beehive House, now a church social center, was home to more of the wives whom Brigham Young claimed to treat with "perfect impartiality." The stone lion guarding the portico struck one anti-Mormon visitor as "a sad misapplication . . . as that royal brute is ever content with *one mate.* The bull would have been more appropriate." For a time it was believed that the number of gables on the house represented the number of wives, each peak crowning a Mrs. Young's apartment. But the Mormons point out that "only" seven wives lived here; the rest —a never-counted total—were dispersed around the state. To Mrs. Frank Leslie, Lion House resembled the "closely guarded seraglios of a Turkish Prince." Other descriptive accounts make it sound more like a girls' dormitory, where communal living was interrupted only by the prophet's unannounced visit to a wife after dark. Brigham never stayed the night in a wife's room; it is said he always returned to his austere bedroom in Beehive House to get his presidential sleep.

Eliza R. Snow Monument and Grave, Brigham Young's Private Cemetery, First Avenue between North State and A Streets. The mother of Mormonism, the Presidentress, was, after Emma Smith, the most influential woman in the Mormon community

in *Nauvoo, Illinois.* Also after Emma Smith, Eliza Snow married Joseph Smith, the original prophet. A year after Smith and his brother were murdered by hostile anti-Mormons, Eliza wrote the most popular work of her career, the hymn, "O My Father," which is reproduced here—a giant sheet of bronzed music. Then she moved to Salt Lake, marrying Brigham Young "in name only" and devoting her life to the church. She was said to be an inspiration to Mormon women, steadfastly defending polygamy and insisting that Mormon women did not live in a state of subjection. When she died in 1887 in her Lion House apartment, "Aunt Eliza" was buried in the rear of this grassy plot along with the other Mrs. Youngs.

Eliza R. Snow Statue, grounds of Daughters of Utah Pioneers Museum, 300 North Main. This bronze statue portrays the young Eliza Snow, looking skyward for inspiration and holding the small gold pencil given her by Joseph Smith, with which she wrote the poem that became the hymn "O My Father." Not all critics share the Latter-Day Saints' regard for Eliza Snow's poetic talents. One wrote, "Miss Eliza R. Snow's poems belong to that middling class which Horace says, 'Gods and men despise.' They never rise high, and rarely sink low enough to be ridiculous: their style is a dead level of mediocrity."

Brigham Young's Forest Farm Home, 732 Ashton Avenue, Pioneer Monument State Park. From 1870–72, the mistress of this adobe and pine cottage on the hundred-acre working farm that supplied butter, milk, and cheese for the residents of Lion and Beehive houses was Ann Eliza Webb Young. She would leave a lasting mark on Mormon history. Ann Eliza said later that she married Brigham in 1869 because he threatened to bankrupt her brother. She became either wife #19, by her own count, or wife #27 by later reckonings—in either case, an ultimately unhappy, bitter member of the harem. Her two-year tour of duty in this house (previously located at 732 Ashton Avenue) made her increasingly disillusioned with her husband. The farm itself, with thirty workers to feed and hours of work to be done, was, she wrote, "by no means a desirable place of residence."

Site of Ann Eliza Webb Young House, 180 East South Temple. Ann Eliza was overjoyed at first with her new two-story gabled cottage. It stood on the corner here, where a clothing store and tire shop stand today. But when she finally moved in that August of 1872, she disliked the interior of the house and complained that Brigham treated her poorly. Her frail physique deteriorated as quickly as the marriage. One night she read a book by Mrs. T. B. H. ("Fanny") Stenhouse called *Exposé of Polygamy in Utah,* one woman's account of "the suffering and sorrowing of women in Polygamy." It was the catalyst she needed. On July 15, 1873, Ann Eliza Webb Young moved out of her cottage and into a hotel, and she announced the unthinkable: She would divorce Brigham Young. The shock waves reverberated far beyond Beehive House. With the help of friends, the runaway Mormon wife was spirited out of Utah in the dead of night, and she embarked on a nationwide lecture tour, delivering a passionate plea against polygamy that helped stir public opinion and the laws finally prohibiting it. She even spoke in Salt Lake City, where Brigham sent as surrogates his daughters and daughters-in-law, who sat in the front row and made faces at Ann Eliza.

Her bold crusade also resulted in a book, *Life in Mormon Bondage,* an instant best seller that we could not locate in Utah bookstores. (See *Lockport, New York.*)

Site of Women's Industrial Home, 145 South Fifth East. Not all women objected to polygamy, as some well-meaning reformists soon found out. In part aroused by Ann Eliza Webb Young's lectures, in part by Methodist do-gooder Angelia Newman from Nebraska, the federal government erected the Women's Industrial Home here in 1889 to provide a refuge for women and children fleeing from the victimization of polygamy. The building was three stories high, with splendid furnishings. To the government's surprise, the only people who showed up to accept their munificent offer were a few female transients and three men. After several changes of ownership, it seemed more practical to convert the building into the Ambassador Athletic Club.

Site of Deseret Hospital, 50 South Fifth East. In 1882, eager for a hospital of their own, the Mormons took over the vacated premises of St. Mary's Hospital and organized the Deseret Hospital. Eliza R. Snow served as president of a board of directors consisting entirely of women. One staff member was Dr. Romania B. Pratt, the first woman to leave Utah to study medicine (1873), then the first female specialist in the state (eye and ear surgery), and the first to perform a cataract operation. A board member was Dr. Ellis Shipp, the pioneering doctor who founded a school of obstetrics and nursing in 1879. Dr. Shipp crisscrossed the country to coordinate her medical education in the East with her family in the West. Her personal items, including the black lace dress she wore when inducted into Utah's Hall of Fame, are at the Pioneers Museum in Salt Lake City. Brigham Young urged Mormon women to study medicine, no doubt to handle polygamy's unusually high birthrate.

Site of First Utah School, Pioneer Park, Third South and Third West Streets. In a military tent pitched here in October 1847, Mary J. Dilworth taught at the state's first school, some three months after the first pioneers had arrived. The Quaker-born young woman had taught Mormon children during their trip across the country. When they settled in the Old Fort here, now a park, Utah's first schoolteacher gave her lesson from an old army campstool, while some fifteen to twenty children sat on rough logs. They gathered around a fire of sagebrush, learned to write with charcoal, and read from the Bible or some Lindley Murray readers she had thoughtfully provided. (See *Huntsville.*)

Emmeline B. Wells Bust, State Capitol. In a niche in the lobby sits the bust of Emmeline B. Wells, donated by the women of Utah in 1928, the centenary of her birth. The likeness is inscribed, "A fine soul who served us." Emmeline B. Wells was a plural (seventh) wife who worked tirelessly for both woman suffrage and polygamy. Although she lost the fight against the Women's Industrial Home, she was instrumental in helping Utah women achieve the franchise along with Utah's statehood in 1896. Elected Salt Lake County treasurer in 1878, she was not permitted to serve because women could not hold public office. When Emmeline Wells died in 1921, flags flew at half-staff, the first time a woman was so honored in Utah.

Site of First Nursing School in Utah, South Temple and State Streets. The Alta Club occupies the site where in 1886 Dr. Martha Hughes Cannon established the first training school for nurses in the state. A colorful feminist who combined three apparently disparate passions—medicine, politics, and polygamy—"Mattie" defended woman's right to partake in all three. In 1896 she was elected to the Utah state senate—the first woman in the nation to become a member of a state legislature. And on polygamy, she said, "A plural wife isn't half as much of a slave as a single wife. If her husband has four wives, she has three weeks of freedom every single month."

Maude Babcock Theater, University of Utah. The little theater on the lower level is named for the first female professor at the university, a champion of woman's rights. A strict devotee of physical culture and elocution who improved her own frail health with calisthenics, Maude Babcock organized a gymnastics exhibition for students in 1893 because she believed young girls should grow up to be more than "ladies."

Springville

Pioneer Mother Monument, City Park. This bronze tribute to "the noble women who braved the wilderness" portrays a sunbonneted woman, gazing out atop an image of her wagon train. Famed sculptor Cyrus E. Dallin, who also did likenesses of Julia Ward Howe and Anne Hutchinson in Boston, Massachusetts, executed the statue for the town where he was born. For some time it was mistakenly believed that Dallin's own mother posed for the statue, which would have been tricky since she died in 1919, before it was commissioned.

Tooele

Grave of Dr. Emily Atkins, Tooele City Cemetery. A carved lamb adorns the white marble gravestone of Emily Atkins, a promising young doctor who died in 1889 at the tragically young age of thirty. She embarked on her medical career at the encouragement of Dr. Romania Pratt in *Salt Lake City.*

Torrey

Capitol Reef National Monument. A hiking trail near Capitol Dome leads into the high and narrow hideaway known as Cohab—for Cohabitation—Canyon. Legend has it that this difficult-to-reach perch in the cliffs above Fruita (whose entryway is still classed as moderately strenuous) was sought by polygamous Mormons in the 1880s as a refuge when Congress passed laws forbidding the collection of plural wives. It is not known if any federal officers chased them, or if any Mormons actually cohabited here, but it is considered a pleasant scenic surprise for today's trail hikers.

VERMONT

Arlington

Martha Canfield Library, Route 7. Donated to the town by Dorothy Canfield Fisher, one of the state's most beloved writers, this library was named for her favorite aunt who had an informal library here when it was her home. Dorothy, a lifelong resident of Arlington, wrote dozens of children's books and "forthright and courageous novels." In *The Home Maker,* published in the 1920s, she attacked the then accepted notion that it was degrading for a man to do "woman's work." "What is homemaking?" she asked. "Good housekeeping or a capacity to understand children and their needs."

Barnard

Dorothy Thompson House, "Twin Farms," Sonnenberg Ski Area (private). Graduating from Syracuse University in 1914, Dorothy Thompson spent three years touring New York State for suffrage, and, when that was won, she tackled the world as a foreign correspondent. When she came to central Europe in the turbulent 1920s, John Gunther called her "a Blue-eyed Tornado . . . she was brimful of excitement and freshness and saw stories that were not stories to more experienced correspondents." "While other women got to interview Mussolini via the famous Palazzo Chigi couch . . . Dorothy was different," recalled one of her Berlin colleagues years later. "She was the only 'newspaper man' of our time. That was a very high compliment in the pre women's lib days." Sinclair Lewis proposed to her the night he met her, but he had to pursue her on various assignments in Vienna and Moscow before she agreed to marry him in 1928. His wretched caricature of feminists in his novel *Ann Vickers* was just one of the problems that led to their divorce in 1942. During the Hitler years, Dorothy entertained distinguished refugees at this huge, comfortable white house, persuading so many of them to stay that Gunther called the Barnard area "Sudeten Vermont." Dorothy was the only woman to address the Harvard Club, and she was the first woman to speak at the New York State Chamber of Commerce in its 169-year history. But the praise she was accorded for her unique accomplishments rankled her at times. "I am tired of being told I have the brains of a man. What man? . . . My strength is altogether female."

Bellows Falls

Bellows Falls, which were turned off to a trickle when we visited, were originally called the Great Falls, a treacherous fifty-foot plunge to the threatening rocks below. An eighteenth-century Englishman recalled with amazement that he saw "timber and trees strike on one side or the other, splintered like a broom." The same writer repeated the incredible story of the first person to survive a plunge over the falls. An Abnaki Indian woman, realizing her desperate plight when her canoe got caught in the current, downed an entire bottle of rum, and, pleasantly fortified, relaxed, and lived.

Site of Hetty Green House, School and Westminster Streets. The Witch of Wall Street, notorious for her shrewd money management, shabby clothes, and other harmless eccentricities, liked to sit on the floor of a bank vault, shuffling her stocks and bonds. She would perhaps be not entirely displeased to find that the house where she lived in the 1870s is now occupied by a bank. The red brick mansion—where Hetty, garbed in black, posed for picture postcards as "the richest woman in the world"—belonged to the family of her husband, Edward Green. Although he was wealthy enough in his own right for the careful Hetty to trust, Edward turned out to be a bungler in the bull market when he ignored Hetty's accurate hot tips. "My husband is of no use to me at all. I wish I did not have him," she said, and soon the two were living apart. (See *Hoboken, New Jersey.*)

Bennington

Site of Marcy Leonard Robinson House, Monument Avenue. In the first log cabin in town, built in 1761, Marcy waved firebrands to chase away the wolves that came howling at the door. That's all the history books say about this fearless pioneer, but friends recall her as "a superior sort, intellectual in her tastes, and a great reader of history." In the mid-1800s, her granddaughter remembered her as "quite a businesswoman. She was accustomed . . . to ride to Albany on horseback, transact business, make her purchases, and return. I believe she would be gone for several days, for she usually attended meetings." The nature of her business has not been recorded.

Battle of Bennington Monument. A huge stone monolith commemorates the celebrated 1777 victory of the colonists over the British, with no mention of the local heroic women who converted the town church into a hospital, shredded their linens to make bandages for the wounded, and kept a prayerful vigil all day on Harwood Hill. The most popularized woman of the battle was never even there, earning her fame from the sacrificial words of her husband, Gen. John Stark: "There are Red Coats and they are ours, or this night Molly Stark sleeps a widow." But Molly warrants attention for her own celebrated deeds (see *Manchester, New Hampshire*), and Vermont has honored her with the Molly Stark Trail that extends along Route 9 from Bennington to Brattleboro and passes Molly Stark Park in *Marlboro*.

Grandma Moses Schoolhouse, Bennington Museum. The one-room schoolhouse used by the primitive painter and three generations of her descendants was moved to the grounds of this museum from its original location in *Eagle Bridge, New York,* the artist's home. The schoolhouse contains memorabilia—dresses, dolls, papers, and the art supplies with which she created her famed scenes of country life. A connecting gallery to the museum contains more than eighty of her original lively paintings. One of her life creeds: "Idle hands make mischief."

Brattleboro

When Clarina Howard Nichols joined her husband's newspaper, the *Windham County Democrat,* here in 1843, she became its real editor, helped raise its circulation, and then used it as a platform for the cause of woman's rights. Earlier she had established her reputation for rebellion by walking through the streets of Brattleboro in bloomers of buff calico. Her 1847 editorial urging property rights for married women inspired a state senator to introduce a bill giving married women their own real estate as well as the right to make up a will. Nichols later called this "the first breath of a legal civil existence to Vermont wives." In 1850 she was invited to address the state legislature on behalf of her petition to secure the vote for women in school elections, and she traveled to Montpelier—against one committee member's protest of her "scramble for the breeches." In a tremulous voice that choked from anxiety, Nichols pled her case with passion, beginning with an answer to the antifeminist legislator. She said that although she had earned the dress she wore, her husband owned it by law, adding that it would be "time enough for them to taunt us with being after their wardrobes when they shall have restored to us the legal right to our own." The speech was greeted with a profound hush, then feet-stomping approval. A crowd of women told her, "We did not know before what Woman's Rights were, Mrs. Nichols, but we are for Woman's Rights." Although the petition failed, the speech was considered a triumph. Clarina continued her work in *Kansas City, Kansas.*

Site of Wesslhoeft Water-Cure, Water Court. When her right side became mysteriously paralyzed in 1846, Harriet Beecher Stowe left her husband Calvin and her children in *Cincinnati, Ohio,* and came to this popular "Hydropathic Establishment." For ten months she strictly adhered to the regimen prescribed for the cure. At 4:00 A.M. she was wrapped in thick woolen blankets until she perspired, then covered with cold compresses, dipped into a cold bath, and sent out to walk and to drink the pure springwater. She wrote Calvin faithfully every day. "Not for years have I enjoyed life as I have here . . . I could tell you worlds . . . of heaven begun on earth as I walk through these beautiful mountains." The cure was helpful, but nothing quite revived her like her writings, and an exhausted but optimistic Harriet left for her creative work in *Brunswick, Maine.* Julia Ward Howe visited the establishment that same year and left, feeling "well and happy." Today, on the site of the main lodge are a fire station, private homes, and a laundry, whose owners are thinking of bottling the therapeutic springwater for sale.

Bridport

Grave of Rhoda Farrand, Central Cemetery, Middle Road. While living in New Jersey in 1777, Rhoda Farrand, remembered here with a plain marble slab, received a letter from her soldier husband lamenting what a "sorry sight are our men. No socks or shoes. By dropping blood you can trace their tracks." Stirred by these pathetic words, Rhoda drove in a wagon with her son to dozens of farms and settlements, knitting all the way, and rallying other purlers to make socks as rapidly as possible. By the end of the week, she carried 133 pairs of socks to the joyous soldiers in Jersey. Rhoda moved to Bridport as a forty-seven-year-old widow, but her husband certainly did not die of cold feet.

Enosburg Center

Susan Tolman Mills Birthplace, State Aid Road #1 (private). A cousin of hers recalled Susan, who was born in this big white farmhouse on November 18, 1825, as a lively little girl with "snapping black eyes . . . as spry as a cricket," unafraid of anything except perhaps the snorting cattle in the rock pasture. More than seventy years later, Susan wrote about her school days in Enosburg. "Once a week we girls sewed patchwork while the boys declaimed; and we girls wished we could go onto the little platform and say: 'On the Grampian hills my father feeds his flocks' [a popular oratory exercise]. We knew we could do it better than the boys, but we were girls only." Susan grew up to found her own lecture platform—Mills College in *Oakland, California.*

Ludlow

Grave of Abby Maria Hemenway, Ludlow Cemetery. Her plan to write a definitive history of Vermont was criticized as "unsuitable for a woman," but when the first edition of the *Vermont Quarterly Gazetteer* appeared in 1860, it was hailed as "an historic monument to the Green Mountain State such as no other state has." Abby devoted thirty years of her life to compiling four million words in five volumes about every county but one to "preserve a past too rich . . . too unique or romantic to lose." Soliciting dozens of contributions from each town, Abby was an unmeddling editor whose only bit of revision was an occasional "oaths are omitted." Constantly underfinanced and in debt, Abby peddled each volume to raise money for the next. Eventually she had to flee to Chicago to escape her nagging creditors. Tragically, a fire destroyed three-quarters of volume 5 in 1886. Although Abby was able to resurrect her notes and put the volume back together, she died in 1890, the history of one county—Windsor, her home—still unwritten. A simple granite monument marks her grave in the Hemenway family plot, bordered by four giant maple trees.

Marlboro

Molly Stark State Park, Route 9, named for the modest Revolutionary heroine (see *Bennington*), is noted for its panoramic views, especially from the top of Hogback Mountain.

Middlebury

Emma Willard House, Middlebury College Campus. In this two-story brick building, across from the men's college campus where she was denied the opportunity to study, Emma Hart Willard (see *Berlin, Connecticut*) opened her own school in 1814. The Middlebury Female Seminary (designed to help her financially shaky husband) pioneered in educating young women above the secondary school level, introducing new subjects that Emma herself had to learn. In 1819, Emma delivered her famous *Plan for Improving Female Education* to New York's Governor Clinton, an address, written here in Middlebury, that has been called the Magna Carta of female education. Although the brilliant speech went unheeded, Emma found a private means of teaching young women (see *Troy, New York*). The house named for her is now used as an admissions building, and a plaque on the upper Village Green and a marble monument on the lower green honor her memory. On the monument, opposite a low relief of the famous educator penning her *Plan* is a quotation from it: "Education should seek to bring its subjects to the perfection of their moral, intellectual and physical nature in order that they may be of the greatest possible use to themselves and others."

Plymouth

Victoria Moor Coolidge House, "Wilder House." Little is known of the romantic, ethereal Victoria who died here in 1885, thirteen years after the birth of her son who would grow up to be president. In his autobiography, Calvin remembered the "touch of mysticism and poetry in her nature which made her love to gaze at the purple sunsets and watch the evening stars. Whatever was grand and beautiful in form and color attracted her." His peculiar personality and those long conversational pauses have been traced to the traumatic sense of loss he felt after her sudden death, probably from tuberculosis—"the greatest grief that can come to a boy," he wrote. After his own death, it was revealed that the old pocket watch he carried over his heart contained a picture of Mother.

Shelburne

Electra Havemeyer Webb Memorial Building, Route 7, contains paintings by Mary Cassatt. Next door, the Webb Gallery of American Art has some fine works by Grandma Moses (see *Bennington*).

South Royalton

Hendee Memorial Arch, Village Green. Carved into the granite on the left side of this arch in the park is a tribute to the heroine of the Tory and Indian raid on this village in 1780. Hannah Hendee (not Handee as the inscription reads), pleading for the release of her little son who had been snatched away by the Indians, noticed several of the neighbors' children among the captives. She petitioned with such passion that she won freedom for all the children. She brought them all home by swimming twice across a treacherous river, each time with a child on her back and several others clinging to her neck, saving nine children in all. "The boldest hero of the other sex could never have effected what she accomplished," wrote an eyewitness.

Vergennes

Philomen Daniels House, 50 McDonough Drive (private). In her fleet of five sturdy steam vessels, all named after men, Philomen Daniels cruised along Lake Champlain as the world's first female licensed steamboat captain. She was forty-two in 1890 when she got her license, and when her husband died thirteen years later she took over the management of the Daniels Steamboat line, carrying grist, iron ore, and dozens of passengers who were impressed by her skillful navigation. Her great-granddaughter-in-law, Lydia Daniels, told us that Philomen always wore the most beautiful dresses with bustles, bows, and beads; hats with flowing ribbons; and a parasol. "You'd think she was going to a ball," said Ms. Daniels. But Philomen took her job very seriously: "Once, during a bad storm on the lake, a dapper young man in a brown derby came up to the pilot house. Philomen ordered him to go back down on deck. But the brown derby was a little slow in moving, so Philomen gave him a poke and he fell into the lake. That's the kind of woman she was," said an admiring Ms. Daniels.

West Salisbury

Ann Story Memorial, near Shard Villa (private). A granite shaft buried in a clump of trees, invisible from the main road, marks the site of Ann Story's house. When everyone else in town had fled because of the intense fighting, the widow lived here with her many little children—in spite of great danger from the British and Indians. In the 1780s her house was a favorite rest stop for the Green Mountain Boys, to whom Ann passed on information she had gleaned by spying on the Royalists. Once, when she was caught snooping, a Royalist threatened to kill her. "But to all his threats I bid defiance, and told him I had no fears of being shot by so consummate a coward as he," Ann said boldly, and the traitor slouched off. Abby Hemenway (see *Ludlow*) described Ann in her *Gazetteer* as one who "entered in person into all the labors of the farm, and had a hand in the political moves of the community." There are plans to build a log cabin replica of her house here. Meanwhile, another monument honors her on an island in Otter Creek.

Winhall

Pearl Buck House, "Mountain Haunt" (private). Buck came for a visit to satisfy her curiosity about maple sugaring "and fell in love with the snow, the woods, the mountains . . . I was enchanted . . . and made up my mind I wanted to own a piece of land here." In her first home in Vermont, the celebrated author of life in China (see *Hillsboro, West Virginia*) cooked on fireplaces, used oil lamps and candles, and showered with buckets of water—to teach her four children about life without modern conveniences. This second house—in a Chinese style that she designed herself in the 1950s—was more comfortable. It had a living room forty feet wide and sixty feet long with flagstone floors of red Vermont slate, a huge walk-in fireplace, and an inside rock garden. Her writing desk was at the window overlooking Stratton Mountain.

Alexandria

Grave of the "Female Stranger," St. Paul's Cemetery. The husband of this twenty-three-year-old typhoid victim was determined that his wife remain eternally anonymous. A handsome, six-pillared marble tomb is engraved—not "wife" or "mother" or even "beloved"—simply, "Female Stranger whose mortal suffering terminated on the 14th day of October, 1816." But the "disconsolate husband" used the leftover space on the tomb for a pithy bit of philosophizing:

> How loved, how valued once avails thee not
> To whom related, or by whom begot.
> A heap of dust alone remains of thee
> 'Tis all thou art and all the proud shall be.

Grave of Anne Brunton Merry Wignell Warren, Christ Churchyard. A white marble tabletop tombstone capsulizes the many achievements of Warren's theatrical career: "By her loss the American stage has been deprived of one of its brightest ornaments. The unrivall'd excellence of her theatrical talents was only surpassed by the many virtues and accomplishments which adorned her private life." Warren, born in England in 1773, in the derangement of her last days would recite passages from some of her favorite characters; for example, Juliet: "in such a pathetic strain . . . as would draw tears from . . . witnesses of the sad spectacle." She died ten days after delivering a stillborn child in 1908.

Arlington

ARLINGTON NATIONAL CEMETERY

Jane Delano Memorial, section 21, Memorial Drive and McPherson Avenue. A stylized marble statue of the famed Red Cross nursing corps organizer (see *Washington, D.C.*) watches over that section of the cemetery occupied by the nurses who served the country during World War I. Jane Delano was superintendent of the Army Nurse Corps from 1909–1912, and later, working with the Red Cross, she was responsible for the enlistment of some twenty thousand of her sisters in white—on the battlefields and at home during the war. Typically concerned about her women, she sailed to France in 1919 for a postwar inspection of nursing facilities. Already weak from illness, she died there, aged fifty-seven.

Grave of Anita McGee, section 1, Humphreys Drive. A shield-shaped headstone, beneath which Anita McGee was buried with full military honors in 1940, marks the grave of the founder of the Army Nursing Corps. A tireless worker who possessed both a medical degree and an extraordinary talent for organizing, Dr. McGee helped shatter the bias against female nurses in the post–Civil War army during the Spanish-American War. She was a key factor in the official establishment of the nursing group in 1901, many of whom lie buried in section 21 beneath Jane A. Delano's watchful eye.

Vinnie Ream Hoxie Monument, section 3, Miles Drive. In memory of the wife he had met while she sculpted Admiral Farragut's memorial, Brig. Gen. Richard Hoxie commissioned a bronze replica of Vinnie Ream's marble Sappho to mark her grave in 1915. The grieving husband, whose major contribution to history has been this memorial to Vinnie, also installed a bas-relief portrait with the inscription, "Words that would praise thee are impotent." A trail-blazing sculptor who opened the doors of artistic achievement to countless other young artists, Vinnie is best known for her bust of Lincoln in *Washington, D.C.*

Jane Delano Memorial

Ashland

Dolley Payne Madison Home, "Scotchtown," Route 685. When she was seven years old, Dolley Payne moved to this enormous mansion, at that time of unpainted wood set on a huge brick basement. Young Dolley would walk to the nearby country school shrouded with a white linen mask, a sunbonnet sewed on her head, and long gloves to protect her from the sun's damaging rays. A little bag of wicked baubles, given to her by her grandmother, was hidden under her plain Quaker dress so that her parents would not discover them. Dolley no longer had to disguise her secret taste for finery after she moved to *Philadelphia, Pennsylvania,* in 1783.

Buckland

Martha A. Moss House, Buckland Mill Road (private). Although little is known of her life, Martha Moss will never be forgotten for retrieving the original copy of George Washington's will from the county clerk's office when the federal army was advancing toward Fairfax in 1861. She tucked the will in her stocking and hid it in the house until it could be safely brought to Richmond. Historians have often wondered why it never occurred to Martha's husband, the county clerk, to bring home the will himself.

Charlottesville

Mary Cooke Branch Munford Memorial, Alderman Library, University of Virginia. The university finally admitted female undergraduates in September 1970, more than fifty years after Mary Munford started her campaign to introduce coeducation. At that time, there was no state college for women in Virginia. "Education has been my deepest desire from my girlhood, beginning with an almost passionate desire for the best education for myself, which was denied," Munford, who was born in 1865, once explained. The admission of women was violently opposed by male alumni in a bitter struggle with "the kind of forces which are roused when a new idea collides with the entrenched conservatism of an old society." Although at her death in 1938 the issue still had not been resolved—women were only accepted at the graduate level in 1920—those who fought alongside Munford said, "When [the battle is won] . . . the laurels will belong to Mrs. Munford." There is a building named after her here, and the plaque near the library reference desk honors Munford, "who carried the devotion of a great mind and a flaming spirit into unselfish service to public education throughout Virginia. Her memorial is in numberless young lives set free."

Sacajawea Monument, Ridge and Main Streets. Perhaps because the brave Lewis and Clark guide never passed through Virginia (or perhaps because both explorers were born in Virginia) the sculptor has mistakenly portrayed Sacajawea in a most unlikely pose. She is crouched behind the two explorers rather than boldly pointing the way—as depicted in her likeness in *Portland, Oregon.*

Covington

Ann Bailey Memorial, near Falling Spring waterfall, Route 220. A plaque commemorates the site of "Mad Ann" Bailey's rude hut where the brave scout (see *Point Pleasant, West Virginia*) spent the last years of her life.

Danville

Site of Nancy Witcher Langhorne Birthplace, Main and Broad Streets (private). An apartment house stands on the site where the first woman in the world to sit in the British Parliament

Sacajawea Monument

(1919) was born in 1879. An historical marker praises Lady Astor for her wit, her commitment to woman's rights, and her "articulate affection for her native state." When she returned home in 1922 for this memorial's dedication ceremonies, Lady Astor remarked, "It is a strange thing that England's first Member of Parliament should have come from England's first colony." She was presented with a loving cup engraved "Behold, Virginia gives a daughter to her old Mother." Her election to the House of Commons caused Winston Churchill to admit that he felt "as though a woman had burst into my bathroom and I had nothing to defend myself with but a sponge." To which Lady Astor replied, "Don't worry, Winston, you're not handsome enough to have worries of that kind." A tireless worker for birth control and equal rights, Lady Astor was repeatedly reelected to Parliament until her retirement at age sixty-five in 1945. She predicted that one day there would be a female U.S. president and a woman at No. 10 Downing Street. "It will come, for women have the greatest opportunity in the world. Their future in politics is bright and there is no post they can't have if they go out and fight for it."

Fairfax Station

With three railroad cars full of supplies, two assistants, and a dogged determination, Clara Barton was the first volunteer to reach Fairfax Station during the second Battle of Bull Run, August 1862. Refusing to ally herself with Dorothea Dix's nurses (see *Hampden, Maine*), Barton independently maneuvered through red tape and army security, bringing needed supplies and comfort to the stricken soldiers. She drove her own mule-pulled wagon to countless field hospitals while shells burst around her. She fed three thousand soldiers, and she loaded the wounded onto wagons, her long skirt dragging in the muddy battlefield. Several weeks earlier, at the Battle of Cedar Mountain, she worked five solid days and nights with but three hours of sleep. It was her first venture to the front lines, and, as she would later write, "When our armies fought at Cedar Mountain, I broke the shackles and went to the field." For the future founder of the American Red Cross, it was ominous: "And so began my work." (See *Fredericksburg*.)

Falls Church

Antonia Ford House, 3977 Chain Bridge Road. During the Civil War, the clever Antonia Ford lived in this large brick house, now used as an office building, where she lavishly entertained federal troops, secretly gathering information for the Confederates. She was responsible for the capture of Gen. Edwin Stoughton, for which she was honored with a commission as an army lieutenant. Major Willar, the provost marshal, arrested her, but he later worked for her release so that he could marry her.

Farmville

Longwood College, founded in 1839 as the Farmville Female Seminary Association, is the fifth oldest private educational institution for women in continuous operation in the United States and the oldest such school in Virginia. Female education in Virginia could have started much earlier if Thomas Jefferson, from whom the state received its inspiration for popular education, had thought to include women in his planning. But "a plan of female education has never been a subject of systematic contemplation with me," Jefferson admitted in 1818. "It has occupied my attention so far only as the education of my own daughters required."

Fredericksburg

Mary Washington House, 1200 Charles Street. Even though she insisted, "My wants are few and I feel perfectly competent to

take care of myself," Mary's son George insisted that she move here from her nearby farm. With her two horses, a cow, and a dog, Mary lived here until her death in 1789, a few months after her son's inauguration. When the war started, she is said to have sighed, "Oh, these men. Must they always be fighting and killing each other?" But patriotically she knit socks for the soldiers as the other women were doing. Here in these gardens, Mary, described as "dignified and imposing . . . courteous though reserved," was said to have greeted Lafayette with a mint julep and some of her famous gingerbread, whose recipe has been handed down over the generations. Although George once said, "All that I am I owe to my mother," he apparently only found time to write six letters to her over a period of fifty years.

Mary Washington Monument, Washington Avenue at Pitt Street. This fifty-five-foot granite shaft stands on the site where Mary used to meditate and pray and where she is now buried. The inscription says simply, "Mary, the Mother of Washington." A hundred years after her death, the Mary Washington Monument Association was founded, and five years later in 1894 this monument was erected—the first such tribute to a woman organized by women. Mrs. Levin J. Houston, "directress"—as she requested to be called—of the Mary Washington Branch of the Association for the Preservation of Virginia Antiquities, agreed with us that if Mary had not had a son who became the first president, certainly no tribute would ever have been paid her. "She was a plain Virginia woman. She did not seek a place in history and was probably not conscious of her place. She was not great, but neither was she callow as some have de-

scribed her. She raised her children, managed her farm, and did what she had to do."

Lacy House, "Chatham," east side of Rappahannock River (private). In the bitter December Battle of Fredericksburg in 1862, Clara Barton displayed her characteristic courage and devotion to the care of the wounded. She converted this house into a hospital where she relieved the suffering of countless soldiers, including at least one rebel officer whose death from a thigh wound was made considerably less painful by Barton's attention. Then she crossed the flimsy pontoon bridge to serve the besieged Union soldiers of the Ninth Army Corps, making the courageous crossing, as she later said, with "the water hissing with shot on either side. . . . An officer stepped to my side to assist me over the debris at the end of the bridge. While our hands were raised in the act of stepping down, a piece of an exploded shell hissed through us, just below our arms, carrying away a portion of both the skirts of his coat and my dress, rolling along the ground a few rods from us like a harmless pebble in the water." (See *Andersonville, Georgia.*)

Wilderness Battle Site. The first nurse to arrive here after the Battle of the Wilderness in May 1864 was Cornelia Hancock (see *Salem, New Jersey*), who began her indefatigable labors by preparing soup and farina for the crowds of injured soldiers. Receiving no wages for her soothing and much-loved activities, she gave what one eyewitness termed her "unwearied attention. . . . She commanded respect, for she was lady-like and well educated; so quiet and undemonstrative, that her presence was hardly noticed, except by the smiling faces of the wounded as she passed." (See *Mount Pleasant, South Carolina.*)

Front Royal

Belle Boyd Cottage, near Strickler House Apartments. In her boldest and most famous spying mission, in May 1862, Belle Boyd (see *Martinsburg, West Virginia*) hurried to her room in this two-story frame house to jot down all that she had heard through a knothole in the floor of an upstairs closet where she was hiding in the hotel next door. The information about troop locations had to be delivered to Stonewall Jackson, so Belle, ignoring the obviousness of her white sunbonnet, dark blue dress, and fancy apron, raced to reach the rebel forces as bullets from Union rifles whistled in her ears and pierced her clothes. Jackson, who launched his brilliant attack on Front Royal on the basis of Belle's facts, sent her an effusive thank-you note for her "immense service to the country." More than twenty years later, Belle returned to Front Royal (which she once described as "a picturesque village, which nestles in the bosom of the surrounding mountains and reminds one of a young bird in its nest") to talk about her Civil War experiences. The lecture was held at the Old Presbyterian Church on Chester Street. It was just before one of these dramatic presentations that she died at *Wisconsin Dells, Wisconsin,* in 1900.

Gore

Willa Cather Birthplace, "Willowshade Farm," Route 50W (private). In her grandmother's house, a two-story red brick no longer shaded by willow trees, the author of *My Ántonia* was born December 7, 1873. Her early life here has been described as "one of great richness, tranquil and ordered and serene." In *Sapphira,* the only book she wrote that reminisces about Virginia, she described this house and the "high hills which shut the winter sun. . . . early." In this peaceful area, Willie—as the sturdy little girl liked to be called—learned how to read and write from her grandmother, spent the afternoons roaming the fields with her father, and tended the sheep with the family dog, Vic, who wore leather booties to protect his feet from the sharp rocks. Cather's family left for *Red Cloud, Nebraska,* when she was nine. When Cather returned for a visit here twelve years later, she found her rabbit traps exactly where she had left them in the woods.

Hollins College

Hollins College, founded in 1842 as the Roanoke Female Seminary, was the first chartered school in Virginia for the higher education of women. Its name was changed to Hollins Institute in 1855 in honor of Mr. and Mrs. John Hollins, the college's first benefactors. Its most famous early graduate (1854) was Civil War heroine Molly Tynes from *Tazewell,* whose watercolor sketch of pink tulips is still owned by the college.

Hopewell

Site of Susanna Bolling Home, Mansion Hill (private). In 1781, while Lord Cornwallis wined and dined at the Bolling Home (which was located here until it burned about fifty years ago), young Susanna listened carefully to his plans for capturing the French hero Lafayette. In the night, Susanna crept through an underground passage from the house to the Appomattox River, which she crossed, and then raced to the Half-way House (now a restaurant on the present-day Richmond-Petersburg Turnpike), warning Lafayette of the British plans.

Jamestown

Pocahontas Statue, near Old Church Tower. Capt. John Smith was to write that Pocahontas was "the instrument to prusurve

this colonie from death, famine and utter confusion." The daughter of Chief Powhatan, she was ten years old when the Jamestown colonists arrived in 1607. She brought food to the ill-prepared settlers and intervened on their behalf when tensions between Indians and whites arose. Smith taught Pocahontas English and gave her small presents of beads and chains. Pocahontas taught him her language and so respected him that when Smith was about to be executed by the Powhatans, she stepped forward, took Smith's "head in her armes and laid her owne upon his to save him from death." Impressed by his daughter's courageous gesture, the chief spared Smith and subsequently adopted him into the tribe, naming Pocahontas as his life guardian. In 1614, settler John Rolfe decided he wanted to marry Pocahontas, "to whom my hartie and best thoughts are, and have been a long time so intangled, and inthralled in so intricate a labrinth." In view of such passionate sentiments, Pocahontas accepted. On April 5, in a church decorated with wild flowers, Pocahontas walked up the aisle in a "tunic of Dacca muslin, a flowing veil and a long robe of rich material" with a chain of freshwater pearls given to her by her father, who had refused to attend the ceremony.

She was buried at St. George's Church in Gravesend, England, where she died in 1617. This statue in Jamestown was erected in her honor in 1922. A memorial plaque inside the church reads, "Gentle and humane, she was the friend of the earliest struggling English colonists whom she nobly rescued, protected and helped."

Lynchburg

Randolph-Macon Women's College, founded in 1891, was the first accredited college for women in Virginia and the first south of the Potomac to receive a charter for a Phi Beta Kappa chapter (1916). "In those early years it had to be demonstrated that the girls could do as much work as the boys," recalled one early graduate. "To do this, work was piled on us. In addition to the heavy work for class, about double ordinarily given, we had to read one thousand pages to meet language requirements." At the first commencement exercises in June 1894, the class orator spoke on "Higher Education for Women" and "The Dignity of Toil"; the main speaker, the college president, "condensed into less than an hour a volume of wit and wisdom" on "Woman's Rights."

Elizabeth Langhorne Lewis House, 104 Oakwood Place (private). At her death here at age ninety-four in 1946, Elizabeth Lewis was hailed as a pioneer in the state's suffrage movement, one of the first to fight for legislation to improve working conditions for women. She was as honored and famous as her niece, Lady Astor (see *Danville*). Lewis was the founder of the local Unitarian church, which has placed a bronze plaque on her favorite organ there in appreciation for more than a half century of her inspirational hymn playing.

Marion

Hungry Mother State Park, Route 16. According to legend, this 2,180-acre park was named in memory of the sad story of a pioneer mother and her child. Molly Marley, a prisoner of the Indians just north of this area, managed to escape with her little son, but after subsisting on wild berries for a few days, she died at the foot of a mountain that is now known as Molly's Knob. The child crawled to the safety of a village, where his first words were, "Hungry—Mother!"

Mathews

Grave of Sally Tompkins, Christ Church yard. At the time of her death in 1916, the devoted "hospital organizer, provider, superintendent and nurse" (see *Richmond*) was more than eighty years of age, "shrunken and bent and piteously feeble. . . . But to those who knew her history, she passed with fluttering banner, still lifted high, all armored and panoplied in bravery and beauty. So might Joan of Arc have passed," wrote a contemporary historian. Sally was buried with full military honors, and years later this huge gravestone was dedicated in her honor by the Daughters of the Confederacy.

Mount Vernon

The Mount Vernon Ladies Association, which owns and maintains this most popular of all historic shrines (visited by more than a million people every year), was founded in 1856 by Ann Pamela Cunningham. It is considered the first women's patriotic society in the U.S. Despite a debilitating and painful spinal

handicap, criticisms that her work was inappropriate for her sex, and the enormous difficulties in raising the $200,000 purchase price, in 1860 Cunningham managed to secure the elegant mansion for her association. In the following years, Cunningham formed a board of vice-regents from every state—women who had wealth, social position, leisure, patriotism, and energy, the characteristics Cunningham specifically required. She then began the long task of refurnishing the house with Washington's possessions, many of which Martha Washington had in spontaneous generosity given away to celebrated visitors from all over the world. Upon her resignation from the regency in 1874, a year before her death, Cunningham left her lasting command: "Ladies, the home of Washington is in your charge. . . . Let no irreverent hand change it; let no vandal hands desecrate it with the fingers of progress. . . . Let one spot in this grand country of ours be saved from change." Devoted followers first hung her portrait in Mount Vernon's dining room. But, remembering Cunningham's strict policy of authentic restoration—"Keep it the home of Washington!"—and knowing how she would disapprove of finding her nineteenth-century face in George's eighteenth-century home, they have since relocated it to the administration building. A bronze plaque commemorating Cunningham's work hangs on the wall of the Mount Vernon museum.

Norfolk

Margaret Douglass started Virginia's first school for free black children in June 1852 in a four-room house in "a quiet, respectable neighborhood." History has lost all trace of both the house and the neighborhood. Within a year she had twenty-five students. She was brought to trial for her defiance of a law that prohibited "the instruction of all colored persons by means of books or printed papers." She later wrote, "I am happy to say, although I was afterwards cruelly cast into prison and otherwise unjustly dealt with, I have the satisfaction of knowing that I suffered in a good and righteous cause. . . . I shall be only a single sufferer under the operation of one of the most inhuman and unjust laws that ever disgraced the state book of a civilized community."

Orange

Montpelier, Route 20 (private). Dolley Madison and her husband James retired here to their beloved estate in 1817 after his second term as president. They spent the next twenty years graciously entertaining celebrated visitors from all over the world. The lavish hospitality that Dolley had been famous for in the White House was brought to this elegant mansion for as many as one hundred guests every day of the year. As one habitual visitor put it, "There has seldom, even in the hilarious land of Old Virginia, been a house kept—especially by elderly people—at which it was pleasanter to be a sojourner. They always made you glad to have come and sorry that you must go." A visiting Englishwoman saw Dolley as "a strong-minded woman, fully capable of entering into her husband's occupations and cares, and there is little doubt that he owed much to her intellectual companionship, as well as to her ability in sustaining the outward dignity in his office." Dolley died on July 12, 1849. She is buried beneath a walnut tree in the family cemetery —which can be visited here—next to her husband, whose huge granite monument dwarfs Dolley's simple marble obelisk. It is inscribed "Wife of James Madison" with the date of death inexplicably four days too early.

Petersburg

Nora Fontaine Maury Davidson House, 126 South Adams Street (private). On the first anniversary of the federal attack on Petersburg on June 9, 1864, Nora Davidson, the school principal, began taking her students to decorate the graves of the Confederate soldiers. In 1866, Mrs. John Logan, the wife of a Union general, noticed the touching scene at the cemetery and encouraged her husband to designate an official Memorial Day, which he did. Petersburg thus lays its claim as the originator of the day that, in turn, inspired the national Decoration Day. Several other cities appropriate the honor: *Columbus, Georgia,* and *Columbus, Mississippi.* James Bailey, the local historian, told us he was well aware of the other contenders for the title, "but I believe Petersburg's claim has at least as much backing as any. The probable truth is that the idea sprang up spontaneously in several localities."

Pocahontas

Such names as Marymoore and Powell's Bottom were considered for this town, but a gentleman from Philadelphia, Pennsylvania, decided he wanted it named for his favorite heroine (see *Jamestown*) and in June 1882 the town was officially named Pocahontas.

Radford

Mary Draper Ingles Monument, City Cemetery, Fifth and Pendleton Streets. Constructed from the stones of the chimney from her old house, this grand obelisk commemorates the daring escape of Mary Draper Ingles, a young pioneer captured by the Indians in 1755. "No greater exhibition of female heroism, courage and endurance are recorded in the annals of frontier history," reads the inscription with enthusiastic local pride. Mary, her two little sons, and several members of the settlement at Draper's Meadow were captured by the Shawnee Indians in July 1755, after a massacre that left many pioneers dead. Mary, who gave birth to a little girl shortly after her capture, was treated kindly by the Indians, especially when they saw the elegant checked shirts that Mary sewed from cloth purchased from French traders. But when she was brought to dig salt at Big Bone Lick (southwest of present-day Cincinnati, Ohio), separating her from her children, she was so miserable that she planned her escape with another prisoner, an old Dutch woman. For forty days the women subsisted on berries, roots, and, once, the head of a deer they found floating in a creek. They stumbled along the banks of the Ohio River for eight hundred miles. Aside from the lack of clothing and food, the cold, the merciless insect bites, and the constant fear of recapture, Mary had to contend with her companion's failing spirits and latent cannibalism. Mary ran away from the woman (who was rescued a few days later) and, after an excruciating cliff climb in the falling snow, her limbs frozen and swollen, she arrived very near the place she had started out from a half a year earlier, a true heroine.

Radford College, the largest woman's college on the East Coast, with more than four thousand female students, started its classes in 1913 at a time when female education was so unpopular in the South that the school's first president, Dr. John Preston McConnell, received commiserations from a friend "seeing so scholarly a mind being thrown away in the education of women."

Richmond

Site of Robertson Hospital, northeast corner Third and Main Streets. A plaque marks the site of the private house that Sally Tompkins rented to set up a twenty-two-bed infirmary in 1861. Because of her tireless, solicitous care and her insistence on spotlessly clean wards, of one thousand three hundred cases she treated in four years, only seventy-three did not survive. When all private hospitals were ordered closed, Jefferson Davis commissioned her as a captain in the cavalry so that she could proceed with her invaluable work. Even after the end of the war, having rejected numerous marriage proposals, Sally continued her nursing and other good works that depleted her purse and her health. She died in 1916 at the Home for Confederate Women. (See *Mathews.*)

Site of Elizabeth Van Lew House, 2311 East Grace Street. An abolitionist since her youth, Elizabeth declared her loyalty to the North during the Civil War and, despite threats on her life from her neighbors, she began visiting Union soldiers in the local prisons and hospitals, providing them with food, books, clothing, and, occasionally, escape to freedom. To allay mounting suspicion about her espionage work, Elizabeth took to wearing bizarre clothing and affecting such weird manners that the Confederates mistakenly figured they could safely ignore "Crazy Bet." Meanwhile, Elizabeth sent messages written in invisible ink and tucked in the soles of her servants' shoes. She clinched the ultimate link in her spy network when one of the slaves she had freed years before managed to get a position in the Confederate White House. Elizabeth's relay system was so effective that Gen. Grant, camped on the outskirts of Richmond waiting to launch his attack, every evening received flowers cut that morning from her garden, notes on troop movements mingled in with the blossoms. When the Union troops raided Richmond in April 1865, Elizabeth's was the first house displaying the thirty-four-star American flag, and Grant came personally to thank her for her courageous work. His first post-inaugural act in 1869 was to appoint Elizabeth postmaster of Richmond. She delivered the mail until 1877 as capably as she had delivered her secret wartime ciphers. Richmond society never really forgave Elizabeth for her fearless lonely stand for liberty, and she was further shunned for her outspoken support of equal rights. She died all alone in 1889 at age eighty-two. The house where Elizabeth hid Union soldiers in secret panels was demolished in 1911 to make way for the Bellevue School.

Grave of Elizabeth Van Lew, Shickhoe Cemetery. Although spurned by the South, the Union spy was lovingly remembered by Massachusetts friends who donated this 2,000-pound monument as a tribute to the woman who "risked everything that is dear to man—friends, fortune, comfort, health, life itself for the one absorbing desire of her heart, that slavery be abolished and the Union be preserved."

Site of Ballard House, Franklin and Fourteenth Streets. After almost a year under federal arrest, Confederate spy Rose O'Neal Greenhow, the rebel flag smuggled under her skirts, was released with the warning never to return to the North. She arrived at the capital of the Confederacy in June 1862. Newspapers joyfully welcomed her: "If the tyrant has released her, it was because that even he quailed before the might of her power." President Lincoln himself was to have said that "Wild Rose" did more to damage and to bring his government into disrepute than "all the rest of the darned rebels together." In the moment that Rose recalled as the proudest of her life, Jefferson Davis came to the hotel, Ballard House, (now nothing more than a turnpike exit) the evening after her arrival to say, "But for you there would have been no Battle of Bull Run." He later sent her $2,500 for her "valuable and patriotic service." "A tall brunette with slumberous eyes . . . with gaunt beauty, education, manners and resourceful speech," Rose remained Davis' confidante for the remainder of her stay in Richmond. She sailed for England in August 1863 to get her prison diary published and to gather support for the Confederate cause. A year later, she was heading home with a report for Davis. Off the coast of North Carolina, a federal gunboat in pursuit, a storm came up and a huge wave knocked over her boat. Rose, weighted down with a purse of gold sovereigns—the royalties from her successful book—drowned and her secret dispatches disintegrated into the sea. (See *Wilmington, North Carolina*.)

Rose O'Neal Greenhow and her daughter

Lila Valentine Memorial, House of Delegates, State Capitol. A marble bas-relief portrays the "Leader in Virginia for the Enfranchisement of Women." Lila Valentine was elected in 1909 as the state's first president of the suffrage league because she was "the only woman who combined the requisite courage and intelligence." Valentine argued for the vote as a "world-wide protest against the mental subjection of woman," and further gave generously of her time for educational reforms—she introduced kindergartens and vocational training—and better conditions for the city's blacks. Lady Nancy Langhorne Astor (see *Danville*) attended the dedication of the plaque here on October 20, 1936, fifteen years after Valentine's death.

Site of Chimborazo Hospital, Chimborazo Park. Phoebe Yates Levy Pember was the first female administrator of the army hospital that stood here during the Civil War; more than fifteen thousand soldiers came under her attentive care. Although at that time it was the largest military hospital in the world, conditions were often deplorable. As recorded in her diary, *A Southern Woman's Story* (1879), Phoebe had to put up with "a thousand miseries"—fighting for control of the whiskey rations that besotted doctors drank up, depriving their suffering patients; and coping with the rats and filth and tragic instances of incompetence. Once a tipsy surgeon mistakenly set the wrong, unbroken leg of a soldier, who died as a result. From the first day of her arrival in November 1862, when a surgeon stage-whispered "in a tone of ill-concealed disgust, that 'one of them

had come,'" Phoebe never let the criticisms of her sex and position overcome her courage and determination. "In the midst of suffering and death," she wrote, "a woman *must* soar beyond the conventional modesty considered correct under different circumstances."

Office of Maggie Lena Walker, Consolidated Bank and Trust Company, North First Street. In 1903, Maggie Walker, the daughter of a kitchen slave, became the first female bank president in the country when she took over the management of St. Luke Penny Savings Bank. It later merged with several other banks to form the present company, where Maggie served as chairman of the board until her death in 1934. Despite the double handicap of being black and female, Maggie left a safe teaching position to study business and accounting, and in 1889 she took a position paying eight dollars a month as executive secretary-treasurer of the fraternal Order of St. Luke. She started out with thirty dollars in the treasury and left it twenty-five years later as a multimillion-dollar enterprise—with 700 branches in 28 states—that provided insurance and death benefits for poor black people. Loved and respected by the citizens of Richmond, Maggie compounded her interests to include a variety of black causes in the city. A street, a theater, and a school in Richmond are named in her honor. Although during the last twenty years of her life she was a paraplegic confined to a wheelchair, her shrewd business judgment was never impaired. At her death, the board of directors mourned that "this institution has sustained a loss which it never expects to be able to similarly fill."

Ellen Glasgow House, 1 West Main Street (private). Ranked with Edith Wharton and Willa Cather as one of the foremost novelists of her day, Ellen Glasgow lived, worked, and, in 1945, died in this two-story brick town house. Although she did not attend school, Glasgow read books voraciously. While all her seventeen-year-old friends were making their debuts, she finished writing her first full-length novel. It was followed by nineteen others throughout her life, all dealing with the southern experience, that were well received by the public, if not always the critics. In her last years, which she called "perhaps my richest and fullest," her prolific output was showered with numerous honors, including the Pulitzer Prize in 1942, following the publication of *In This Our Life*.

Smithfield

Elizabeth Bennett Young Memorial, Old Courthouse Building. Elizabeth Young, through careful diligence, assured Isle of Wight County of its place in history. She deserves more than the brief mention of her name—as the wife of Francis Young—on this bronze plaque embedded in a large round stretcher table inside the courthouse. While her husband, the deputy county clerk, was away during the Revolutionary War, Elizabeth packed up all the precious records in a hair trunk which she buried on her farm to prevent their capture by raiding British armies. After the war, the records were recovered in good condition, and, thanks to Elizabeth's foresight, Isle of Wight County now has some of the oldest records in the state, dating back as far as 1629.

Staunton

Mary Baldwin College, founded in 1842 as the Augusta Female Seminary, the second oldest Presbyterian College for women in the United States, was renamed in honor of one of its most beloved early principals.

Stratford

Site of Hannah Lee Corbin Birthplace, Machodac Plantation. The woman often called Virginia's first suffragist, born here in

1728, made her historic bid for equal rights when as a young widow she protested being heavily taxed for her estate when she had no voice in framing the laws. She implored help for "poor, desolate widows" from her politician brother, Richard Henry Lee. Pondering such discrimination at the polls, Lee speculated, "Perhaps 'twas thought rather out of character for women to press into those tumultuous assemblages of men where the business of choosing representatives is conducted," but he added sympathetically, "[though I] would at any time give my consent to establish their right of voting." However, such noble sentiments did not solve Hannah's problem for the moment. Her status as a widow was further complicated by her husband's will, which stated that if she were to remarry, "my said Wife shall be deprived of the Bequest already made her and in lieu thereof shall only have one-third of my Estate." Hannah, at thirty-four, desirous of marrying again but unhappy about losing such a large chunk of her estate, took the revolutionary step of inviting her lover to move in with her without those costly matrimonial banns. They had two children and lived for more than fifteen years as respected members of the community—a tribute, according to a local historian, to Hannah's independence of spirit, force of character, courage, and, he might have added, good business sense. Her birthplace has burned, and its site is appropriately named Burnt House Field.

Surry

Rolfe-Warren House, Route 31. The land here was a dowry gift from Chief Powhatan to John Rolfe after his marriage in 1614 to the chief's daughter, Pocahontas (see *Jamestown*). The Indian heroine never had a chance to live here though, for she died in England in 1616 (or 1617). Her son Thomas laid claim to the property and then sold it in 1652 to Thomas Warren, who built a "fifty foot Brick House," which has been restored today.

Sweet Briar

Sweet Briar College, chartered in 1901, was one of the first southern institutions for women to begin with a four-year academic program at the college level. Founded by Indiana Fletcher Williams in memory of her only daughter, young Daisy, whose angel-decorated grave is located on campus, its purpose was to provide young women with "such education in sound learning, and such physical, moral and religious training as shall in the judgment of the Directors best fit them to be useful members of society."

Tazewell

Molly Tynes Grave, Jeffersonville Cemetery. This courageous equestrian was an unheralded heroine for almost a hundred years. She had no Longfellow to immortalize her brave ride—from Tazewell to Wytheville in July 1863—to warn the households along the treacherous forty-mile mountainous route that the Yankees were coming. But in 1968, several markers were erected to commemorate Molly: "slender, graceful, bruised and bleeding, [she] will not be forgotten while Tazewell's mountains stand." Over the last twelve years, the Tazewell riding club has annually reenacted the Molly Tynes ride—a three-day celebration with as many as ten thousand spectators and a thousand riders galloping thirty miles along almost the same dirt road that Molly traveled. (The last ten miles are a too-treacherous highway.) A city woman, a graduate of *Hollins College*, Molly was in her mid-twenties that summer when a thousand federal cavalrymen were camped outside the city in preparation for an attack on Wytheville, the railroad, the lead mines, and the saltworks. Leaping onto her favorite horse, Fashion, Molly set out in the early afternoon and rode over four mountains and rough wooded trails, shouting her warning. The enemy was routed; the town and the railroad were saved. According to a relative, Molly "thought nothing of [the ride]."

Virginia Beach

Witchduck Road leads to the spot on the Lynnhaven River where in 1706 Grace Sherwood was tried for being a witch after a neighbor blamed Sherwood—instead of her own inept gardening—for a weed-infested cotton crop. The robust and hardy Sherwood did not drown during the traditional "trial by ducking," when she was trussed "thumb of right hand to big toe of left foot and thumb of left hand to big toe of right foot." She was then searched by a jury of women, "ancient and knowing" and no doubt frail and unathletic, who declared "she was not like them or any other woman that they knew of" and condemned her to prison.

Statue of "the Norwegian Lady," Twenty-fifth and Oceanfront Streets. Donated by the citizens of Moss, Norway, this nine-foot bronze statue of a wistful sea-gazer commemorates the loss of the Norwegian ship *The Diktator* in 1891. The captain's wife and son drowned off the coast of Virginia. Originally, the ship's wooden figurehead stood here, but it was replaced by this serene figure bearing the inscription, "I stand here as my sister before me, to wish all men of the sea safe return home." *The Norwegian Lady* was erected in 1962 at the same time as her bronze twin in Moss Harbor, Norway. The two statues face each other fondly across the wide Atlantic.

Williamsburg

Clementina Rind House, Duke of Gloucester Street (private). This handsome brick house served as the printing offices of the *Virginia Gazette* and as the home of its publisher, Clementina Rind, who, when her husband died in 1773, took over the business as a means of support for her five "dear infants." Within weeks, Clementina was embroiled in controversy. She was accused of reneging on the paper's motto—"Open to all but influenced by none"—when she refused to print a scandalous anonymous letter about some powerful men termed "the guilty Great." Clementina correctly insisted on a signed letter, which she promised to publish even though "repugnant to her inclinations." In May 1774, Clementina's fine editorial judgment won her the position of official public printer, but she died just a few months later, eulogized by her competitors as a "Lady of singular merit and universally esteemed"; a woman "with manly sense, and fortitude of mind/The softer graces of her sex combin'd."

WASHINGTON

Bellingham

Site of Ella Higginson Home, 605 High Street, Western Washington State College. The state's illustrious poet laureate, who died here in 1940, wrote her first poem when she was eight. Even though her older brother made fun of it and, years later, her husband criticized her literary ambitions, Ella would spend sixteen hours a day perfecting her poems. Her work became so popular that many of her lyrics were set to music and sung by such concert stars as Emma Calvé and Enrico Caruso. Her best-known poem is the ever-popular "Four Leaf Clover," which she was inspired to write on "one of the heaviest-hearted days of my life" in 1890 when she found one of the lucky little herbs by the village post office while she was waiting for the mail.

> One leaf is for hope, and one is for faith
> And one is for love, you know.
> And God put in another for luck,
> If you search you will find where they grow.

Ella championed the clover's cause as the official state flower, but it lost out to the rhododendron. Viking Union stands in the place of Ella's home, but Higginson Hall on campus is named in her honor.

Federation Forest

Catherine Montgomery Interpretive Center was named for the pioneer educator and conservationist who died in 1958 and left part of her fortune to the state for park improvements.

Ford

Site of Tshimakin Mission, Route 231. A large monument north of town marks the home of Mary Richardson Walker, one of the first white women to cross the Rockies (1838). She was on a honeymoon trip with her husband Elkanah to their mission home in the land of the Spokane (or Flathead) Indians. Throughout fifty years of her life, Mary kept an extraordinary diary, reflective of her humor and intelligence. In it she described her first home at Tshimakin, "the place of springs": a fourteen-foot square log hut with a sod roof that dripped mud in the rain, a dirt floor covered with pine needles, and windows that were covered with deerskin, scraped as thin as possible to permit light. She helped her husband with mission work, and she must rank as the paragon of the working mother. One diary entry reads, "Rose about five. Had early breakfast. Got my house work done about nine. Baked six loaves of bread. Made a kettle of mush and have now a suet pudding and beef boiling. . . . I have managed to put my clothes away and set my house in order. May the merciful be with me through the unexpected scene. Nine o'clock p.m. Was delivered of another son." Mary was an amateur botanist, geologist, taxidermist, carpenter, and a mother of eight, who in a rare weak moment conceded, "Sometimes I wish there was a way to live easier." Despite the teachings of St. Paul, Mary never compromised her independent spirit and once signed a letter to Elkanah, "Your loving but not always obedient wife." After the massacre of their friends the Whitmans (see *Walla Walla*), the Walkers abandoned their mission and moved to Oregon. The harsh, repressed life of a missionary wife soon took its toll. Mary slowly lost her mind and spent her last widowed years, before her death in 1897, sitting on a saddle in a rocking chair, dressed in a traveling cape with nowhere to go.

Home

Now a rather quiet and tame Tacoma suburb, this small town used to be a haven for the daring dropouts of the late 1800s. They meant it when they said, "There is no place like Home." Socialists, political dissenters, nudists, sexual libertines, and others eager to break away from traditional sex roles lived here in chaotic bliss. Some of the more notorious residents included Lois Waisbrooker, who expounded her theories on how to liberate the world from the "disease of sex" and published an interesting periodical called *Clothed with the Sun,* which landed her in jail; Laura Wood, who tried living in a wigwam for a while; and a Professor Thompson, who arrived in 1886 with his beard, cane, and long skirts to promote his questionable theory that there would be true progress in the world only if everyone wore women's clothing—which he found much more "aesthetic and comfortable." Emma Goldman, foremost anarchist of the day (see *Forest Park, Illinois*), came to lecture and visit her many little namesakes.

When the local paper, *Discontent, the Mother of Progress,* appeared, trouble began at Home. Such articles as "The Rights of Woman in Sexual Relations" (which one reviewer found "many and interesting") led to the paper's banishment from the federal mails. But it was "The Great Nude Sunbathing Case" of 1910 that finally finished off the colony. Though some Home residents had been walking around "clothed with the sun" for years, the arrest of four women and one man made national headlines, and naturalists, feminists, and anarchists were forced to move to more liberated territories.

Maryhill

Maryhill Museum of Fine Arts. This huge white mansion, set on a spectacular bluff overlooking the Columbia River, was dedicated in 1926 by Queen Marie of Romania, a good friend of Samuel Hill, the Museum's founder. She was the first woman to receive an award from the Royal Literary Society in London (1934) for her three-volume autobiography, and she donated gowns, jewels, and many other items to the museum.

Pasco

Sacajawea State Park. Today, vacationers swim, fish, and go boating near the spot where Sacajawea, heroine of the Lewis and Clark Expedition, camped in 1805. (See *Fort Washakie, Wyoming.*)

Seattle

Louisa Boren Park, Interlaken Boulevard, was named for the only unmarried woman in the small boatload of settlers that arrived at historic Alki Point in September 1851—Seattle's first white inhabitants. Life on the barren point was so depressing that some of the married women wept, but the curious Louisa Boren spent her time exploring the land, collecting shells, and studying the shrubbery and the cedar trees that were soon chopped down to make her first home.

Site of Catherine Blaine's School, First Avenue, between Columbia and Cherry. A tablet marks the location of the first school in town, a tiny frame house where Seattle's first teacher taught from 1854–56, when Indian troubles forced it to close. Since it wasn't considered safe to spend the nights in town, every evening after classes Blaine would row back to her husband in the gunboat *Decatur* in the harbor, with her baby son in her arms. "The babe is a month old today and I guess has been tossed about as much as a child of his age ever was. He stands it pretty well," she once wrote in a letter to her family in New York. She added, with candid objectivity that few mothers would dare, "though he cries considerably from wind on his stomach, is as fat as a pig and dreadfully homely."

Site of Home of Catherine Maynard, 1223 Cherry Street. Catherine Maynard is credited with saving the entire town of Seattle more than a century ago, although her own home was later unappreciatively replaced by the offices of a refrigeration company here.

One dark, stormy night in 1856, she rowed out to the gunboat *Decatur* in the harbor to warn her husband and Chief Sealth of an impending attack by some Klickitat warriors. She was accompanied by Sally, daughter of Chief Kitsap, but other accounts of the brave mission also mention Princess Angeline (see below). At dawn, the women returned to shore before the Klickitats missed them, and the attack was successfully thwarted.

Few northwest gardeners are aware that Catherine Maynard also introduced the ubiquitous dandelion to the area. Instead of cursing the hardy weed, they should consider its medicinal uses, as Maynard, a very practical nurse, did. Also, in her more sedate years, Maynard started the first reading room in Seattle, which led to the founding of the local YMCA after her death in 1906.

Grave of Princess Angeline, Lakeview Cemetery. When she died in 1896, the entire town turned out to honor the old Suquamish Indian woman they had treated less than royally in her last years. The daughter of Chief Sealth, for whom Seattle is named, was buried in her familiar checked shawl and scruffy bandana. Her coffin was canoe shaped, a paddle resting on the

stern. It was in a canoe that Angeline rowed out to the *Decatur* to warn the white men of an Indian attack, and she became known as the Pocahontas of the Northwest. But it was Catherine Maynard (see above), her brave white counterpart on the stealthy mission, who gave her the title she is best remembered by. Her Indian name was Kick-is-om-lo Sealth, but once Maynard told her she was beautiful enough to be a princess, "and I now christen you Angeline." A well-intentioned but misguided Maynard also taught Angeline to do the washing for white women, but in her later years she was too feeble for such work. She would sit on the wooden sidewalks downtown and sell trinkets and baskets. Pictures of her craggy, noble face were sold as souvenir postcards. Not surprisingly, someone else made the profits, and soon Angeline had to beg to keep alive. Schoolboys chased after her and taunted the old woman as she hobbled along with her cane. Today, her grave is marked by a rough granite block paid for by nickels and dimes donated by the city's schoolchildren—whose fathers may have been the very children who were so cruel to this proud woman before she died.

Methodist Protestant Church, Second Avenue and Madison. This old brown church was the setting for Asa Mercer's most successful love match; his own. He was the brains behind an ambitious scheme to marry off the rugged men of the pioneer West with fine, genteel women of the East—called "Mercer Girls." Mercer succumbed to the charms of Annie Stephens of Baltimore, Maryland, one of his recruits. They were married here on July 15, 1886, a few weeks after the arrival of Seattle's most famous charter group. "Never in the history of the world was an equal number of women thrown together with a higher average of intelligence, modesty and virtue," said Mercer of the ten widows and thirty-six unmarried women who had been lured to the West by the promise of work in Seattle with wages "adequate for their support without recourse to marriage." After a tedious three-month 7,000-mile sea voyage (see *Whideby Island* for Flora Engle's reminiscences), the women arrived in Seattle, where almost a thousand men greeted them with something less than job offers.

> "Ain't you Miss K. of B., Ohio?" asked the youth with a look of agony.
> "No, I am L. from New York," answered the young woman rather coldly.
> "All I want is a wife and if you are willing I would as soon take you as the other woman."
> "I do not wish to marry, sir," she said with some asperity in her voice.
> "Well, if yer didn't come to get married, what the deuce did yer come for?"
> "To make pants, coats and vests," she laughingly replied.

But some marriages were inevitable. Mary Morford, over forty, married Mr. Tallman, one of the ship's crew, a "frisky youth (aged twenty-five) who was overpowered with her charms." Libbie Peebles married a Mr. MacIntosh and then became the first female clerk of the state legislature. Today, hundreds of Seattlites can trace their matriarchal lineage to those extraordinary pioneers whom we prefer to call "Mercer Women."

Site of Seattle's First Public School, Second Avenue, between Spring and Madison. The school, which was started in 1870, and the commemorative marker are long gone, but Elizabeth Ordway, the city's first public school teacher, is still remembered for her timeless words as the only Mercer woman who did not marry: "Nothing could induce me to relinquish the advantages of single blessedness."

Eliza Ferry Leary House, 1551 East Tenth Street. The construction of this impressive stone mansion was supervised by Eliza after the death in 1901 of her husband, John J. Leary, "the first mayor of Seattle to keep regular business hours." Eliza, the founder of the Seattle Children's Home and Orthopedic Hospital, graciously lent her house for various charitable functions and did most of her work in the den, which was furnished with Indian artifacts, including baskets of the Attu and Yakitat tribes. When she died in 1935, she willed the house to her favorite charity, the American Red Cross. In 1949, the house became the headquarters for the Episcopal Diocese of Olympia.

Seattle Symphony Hall, 305 Harrison Street. Today's symphony audiences don't have the pleasure and privilege of hearing the first female symphony conductor in America and possibly the world. Mary Davenport-Engberg, who ruled with her baton from 1921–24 in the since-demolished Metropolitan Theater, was also a composer, a teacher, and a violin virtuoso. Critics from New York as well as the West called her "a notable figure in the musical world, a splendid artist . . . who deserved the big ovations she received."

Site of Bertha Landes Home, 4710 University Way. Seattle's first female mayor—the first female mayor of a major American city—lived at this location, now an apartment house, after she was elected in 1926. As City Council president in 1924, she boldly ousted the chief of police and began a block-busting campaign to clean out the gambling dens. Having made her point on law and order, she won the mayoralty handily and earned a reputation as an able and respected administrator. Keenly aware of her unique status, she was always available for official ceremonies, good-naturedly posing for pictures with shovels, locomotives, and with such visiting celebrities as Charles Lindbergh and Will Rogers. But her nonpartisan approach to civic affairs and her firm stand on public morality, combined with her uncompromising femaleness in a tough city with an "open town" tradition, brought on her defeat in 1928. She is still remembered as one of Seattle's best chief executives.

Spokane

May Arkwright Hutton Grave, Fairmont Park. Only half of this large monument for Washington's most colorful suffrage leader is polished smooth and trimmed with ivy. When May Arkwright Hutton died at age fifty-five in 1915, her grieving husband said that her death was premature, her lifework yet unfinished, and so instructed that the monument over her grave be left unfinished too. May was schooled in suffrage work in Idaho, where she ran a boarding house and married Levi W. Hutton who struck it rich in the Hercules Mine (see *Wallace, Idaho*). Settled in Seattle, with monthly dividends of $4,000 coming in, her husband said, "May, spend anything that is reasonable on your suffrage campaign and do what you please without making a holy show of yourself." Weighing in at 225 pounds, with a penchant for zebra-striped coats and huge hats with ostrich plumes, May usually ignored the latter part of her husband's advice. In recognition of her work for equal rights, which won the vote for the women of Washington in 1910, May was one of the first two women in Spokane County to be called for jury duty. She was also the first female delegate to a Democratic National Convention, which she attended in Baltimore in 1912, thoroughly shocking the city by hanging her wash out the front window of its most expensive exclusive hotel. Such thrift-minded measures enabled her to donate thousands of dollars for suffrage and numerous charities.

Site of Old Opera House, Main and Post Streets. When Emma Abbott first sang in Spokane in 1887, her stage was an old warehouse cleared of its plows and wagons for the night. The cowboys, miners, and rough mountaineers were "so responsive, sympathetic . . . prompt in applause, just at the right moment," said a delighted Emma after her performance of *The Bohemian Girl.* "The people's prima donna"—she always sang in English—returned four years later to the fabulous new opera house, more than seven stories tall, that has now been replaced by a drugstore. Here, she appeared as Eliva in *Rose of Castile,* in one of the dazzling costumes she was most famous for—an ermine mantle over a purple velvet gown with hand-embroidered trailing vines and bunches of grapes made from precious stones.

Sacred Heart Medical Center, 101 West Eighth Avenue. The city's first hospital, opened in 1886, was designed and built by Mother Joseph of the Sacred Heart who learned her carpentry skills from her carriage-maker father. With a sturdy apron pinned over her habit, she worked right alongside the builders, climbing ladders to test the beams and peeking under floors to check the foundation. Mother Joseph and five sisters from Montreal began their vital work at Fort Vancouver, where in 1857 they established the first permanent school in Washington; a year later, they opened St. Joseph's Hospital, the first hospital in the Northwest—one tiny room with four beds, benches, and tables carved by Mother Joseph. When the sisters relocated to Spokane, the original thirty-bed hospital was soon filled to capacity. One admiring doctor said, "The sisters did more by their assiduous care than the surgeons and apothecaries did by their bleeding, sweat baths and drastic remedies."

Tacoma

Home of Blanche Funk Miller, 301 North Fourth Street (private). The first female city clerk in Tacoma (1918) and its first female justice of the peace (1920) lived and worked in this white stucco, red-tile-roofed house overlooking Puget Sound. Blanche Miller ran for reelection as judge several times and always won. During one campaign, she capitalized on being the only female in the race: "I have tried to serve you faithfully and seek re-election not only because of long years of experience but because I am convinced that one of the four justices to be selected should be a woman."

Home of Alice Maud Smith, 4309 Park Avenue (private). Doctor, teacher, author, poet, Alice started her varied career at age sixteen when she left home to study nursing in Boston. With a degree in both nursing and medicine, in the 1920s she became the first female to be appointed to the Washington State Board of Medical Examiners. But by then, living in this house, she had gained a creditable reputation as a short story writer and poet, and one of her plays, *The Strength of the Weak,* was made into a film. When asked to explain her boundless energy and assorted interests, she once said, "A steady monotonous grind, even though one be interested in the work involved, is bad mental hygiene; and so I have my profession as my substitution for marriage and authorship as a compensation for being an 'old maid.' "

Home of Alice D. Engley Beek, 1310 North Fifth Street (private). A highly creative artist who was taught how to draw by her mother, Alice lived here when not touring Europe to exhibit her lovely paintings. She believed that watercoloring could surpass oil painting in strength and beauty, and she proved it by winning the Cross of Honour, the gold medal and the silver medal at the Expositions Internationales in France in 1896. The next year she made a clean sweep of the honors by also winning the grand prix, which meant that her work was "above competition" at subsequent expositions. Critics all over the world hailed her for establishing a new standard for watercolors.

Vancouver

Esther Short Park, Colonial and Eighth Streets. The founder of Vancouver arrived in 1845, saw beyond the wilderness to lay out and plot the town, and then generously donated this block-square park to the public in 1855. At first, British authorities of the Hudson Bay Company refused to let Esther and her husband—unwanted American citizens—settle in. They tore down Esther's carefully constructed fence and then sent a surly squad of French Canadians to evict the couple. Esther strode up to the group's leader and slapped him in the face. The Shorts were never bothered again. As the territory's governor conceded, "We can never hope to win against such a brave woman as that."

The park, identified by a huge boulder on the corner, contains a heroic bronze sculpture of a pioneer mother with her rifle at the ready and three frightened children clutching at her skirts. The statue is merely symbolic of Esther Short, who guarded her turf with ten children.

Vancouver Barracks, West Reserve Street. Mary Williams earned the title Barbara Fritchie of Vancouver town (see *Frederick, Maryland*) when, in July 1913, a stranger of uncertain origin stopped at her house located near here and asked for something to eat. According to scanty accounts of the day, he pointed to the American flag, shook his fist, called it a "dirty rag," and tried to stamp on it. Mary, her patriotic sentiments duly incensed, grabbed a dish of water reserved for her dog and doused the vile man.

Walla Walla

Whitman Mission, U.S. 12. In 1836, after her historic trip with the Spaldings across the Rockies, Narcissa Prentiss Whitman (see *South Pass, Wyoming; Prattsburg, New York*) settled here among the Cayuse Indians with her missionary husband, Marcus. She supervised the school and taught hymns in her lilting voice. Life at Waiilatpu ("the place of the rye grass") was a constant struggle, and the accidental drowning of her adored three-year-old daughter Alice Clarissa added to Narcissa's loneliness. The Cayuse whispered among themselves that she was "haughty and very proud," and that Marcus was an evil sorcerer who was poisoning the tribe to make way for the white emigrants. On November 29, 1847, a small band of warriors

took their revenge and killed thirteen whites, including the Whitmans. It was Henry Spalding's (see *Spalding, Idaho*) painful duty to write Narcissa's parents about her death: "Sister Whitman in anguish now bending over her dying husband and now over the sick, now comforting the flying, screaming children, was passing by the window, when she received the first shot in her right breast and fell to the floor. She immediately rose and kneeled by the settee on which lay her bleeding husband, and in humble prayer she commended her soul to God." Today, at this beautiful historic park, the rye grass still shudders in the wind, but nothing remains of Narcissa's home. Probable sites of the various houses are marked, and tape recordings tell the story of the mission's life and destruction. The museum here has a lock of Narcissa's thick straw-colored hair. Her remains are buried in "The Great Tomb." Off in the distance a memorial shaft towers on the hill where Narcissa used to sit in the cool, peaceful afternoons.

Wenatchee

Home of Adelaide Clark, "Wells House," 1300 Fifth Street (private). This huge Gothic house of wood and hand-squared rock was designed by Adelaide Clark, who should probably be called the Mother of Wenatchee Valley. Her husband, W. T. Clark, who built the house in 1909, was called the Father of Wenatchee Valley. He started the irrigation of the valley that helped make Wenatchee the world's apple capital. Adelaide incorporated her favorite fruit in the unique design for the magnificent stained-glass window in the entrance hall here.

Whideby Island

Fort Casey Lighthouse. Flora Pearson Engle settled on this rocky point as the assistant lighthouse keeper a few years after her arrival in *Seattle* with Asa Mercer's group. Though a male *New York Times* reporter had come along for the exclusive story of that historic trip, he wrote more about such exotic ports of call as Rio de Janeiro than about his fascinating shipmates. It is thanks to Flora's observant eye and memory that today we know their ship was definitely not in a class with the *Queen Elizabeth II.* "Nothing had been done to the steamer since it was last used for transporting soldiers, except, possibly a partial fumigation," she wrote. The food was "disgraceful" and everyone managed to get seasick, including one woman who lost her false teeth while leaning over the rail and was called "toothless" all the way to Seattle. Flora brought her precious piano with her from her home in Massachusetts so she could teach music. Her piano lessons were so popular that some of the keys soon became concave.

WEST VIRGINIA

Buffalo

Mary Meek Atkenson Birthplace, "Lawnvale" (private). The noted author and lecturer on country life was born in this two-story brick house in 1884. Her two most popular books were *Shining Hours* and *Woman on a Farm.* Her fine history, *Pioneers of Agriculture,* was written in collaboration with her father.

Charleston

"Harewood," RFD 2 (private). On September 15, 1794, the day James Madison often called the most fortunate of his life, he married Dolley Payne (see *Philadelphia, Pennsylvania*) in a quiet unannounced ceremony in this two-story Georgian house, the home of Dolley's sister, Mrs. George Steptoe Washington. Dolley was dressed in silver satin; Madison wore ruffles of Mechlin lace that the bridesmaids later cut up for mementos. While the small gathering of guests were still dancing in celebration, the newlyweds slipped away in their coach to their mountain retreat, "within a squirrel's jump of heaven," "Montpelier," in *Orange, Virginia.*

Clarksburg

Graves of Mary Coles Payne and Mary Payne Jackson, Jackson Cemetery, East Pike Street. These women are honored in this small cemetery with markers over their graves recognizing them as the mother and sister of the famous Washington hostess Dolley Madison. Mary Jackson's death at twenty-seven in 1808 was a tragic loss to her husband, who inscribed a long, loving tribute on the six-foot slab covering her grave: "It requires not this marble slab to perpetuate her memory. It is embalmed in the heart of a husband who adored her. . . . the noblest spirit that ever adorned her sex in all the endearing attributes of wife, mother and friend."

Core

Elizabeth Bozarth Memorial, Route 7. Already widowed by the Indian raids of 1778, Elizabeth Bozarth defended her homestead a year later in a hand-to-hand fight with a new band of attackers. An historical highway marker commemorates Elizabeth's self-defense. Armed only with an ax, she killed three Indians and chased off the others. The more tranquil and industrious part of her life has been lost to history.

Grafton

Mothers Day Shrine, East Main Street. Anna M. Jarvis, who established a Mothers Friendship Day in 1868 to help ease postwar tensions between the blue and the gray, died in 1905 with the hope that someone would establish a day of national tribute to mothers everywhere. "I went directly from the grave to my room and began to plan for Mothers Day," remembered her adoring daughter, Anna. Its purpose would be "to revive the dormant love and filial gratitude we owe to those who gave us birth . . . to brighten the lives of good mothers." Three years later, after numerous meetings and appeals, more than four hundred people gathered here in Andrews Methodist Episcopal Church to honor their mothers. Anna gave out hundreds of white carnations, the symbol of purity—one each to the sons and daughters and, in token of their excess of virtues, two flowers for every mother. To make the tribute truly universal,

Anna worked six more years, resigning her position as an insurance clerk, lecturing, and writing so many letters that she was forced to buy two additional houses for storage purposes. In 1914, President Woodrow Wilson proclaimed that the second Sunday of May be forever known as Mothers Day. Anna's most loyal benefactor, John Wanamaker, once said, "I would rather have the honor of establishing this Mothers Day than I would be King of England." But by the time of her death in 1948, Anna was almost sorry she had ever started the movement in the first place when she saw how grossly commercialized her simple tribute had become. In 1962, this church was declared the International Mothers Day Shrine. Visitors can buy special Mothers Day cards and brass plates that will be engraved with a mother's name and dates of birth and death and installed in the large bronze plaque in the vestibule.

Hillsboro

Pearl S. Buck Birthplace, Route 219. "I remember when I was born. I am sure I remember. How else can I account for the intimate knowledge I have always had of my mother's house," Pearl Buck wrote many years after she was born here on June 26, 1892. "I see the dressing table between the windows. . . . There were white ruffled curtains at the windows, and from those windows one sees the broad lawn and the big maple trees." Three months after her birth, Pearl was brought to China where her parents, Hermanus and Carrie Sydenstricker, were missionaries, and where the author found a lifetime of inspiration for the many celebrated works that won her the Nobel Prize for literature in 1938. Pearl returned here when she was nine—"a time of pure delight in which I learned to ride horseback, ate quantities of grapes and other fruits, and took part in every activity about the place from . . . watching great lumps of butter washed and shaped . . . to riding in hay wagons. Life was one day of joy after the other, and those weeks did much to wipe away the memories of a changed China." In her book *My Mother's House,* Pearl spoke of her wish to restore her home and open it to the public: "I would like it to belong to everyone. . . . From that house there has come so much life that it ought never to die or fall into ruin. . . . For me it was a living heart in the country I knew was my own but which was strange to me until I returned to the house where I was born. For me that house was a gateway to America." In May 1974, the "goodly, twelve-room house of wood with smooth floors and plastered and papered walls, a city house," was officially dedicated as a museum. (See *Winhall, Vermont.*)

Martinsburg

Site of Belle Boyd House, South Queen Street. A plaque marks the site of the notorious Confederate spy's first heroic exploit. On July 4, 1861, a Union soldier insisted on raising the Stars and Stripes over her house here. Belle wrote that he "addressed my mother and myself in language as offensive as it is possible to conceive. I could stand it no longer; my indignation was roused beyond my control; my blood was literally boiling in my veins; I drew out my pistol and shot him." Belle was seventeen. In the next years, the fearless spy constanly defied danger and death for the cause (see *Front Royal, Virginia*) until she was finally captured and, with an armed escort of 450 cavalrymen, put into prison. Even in jail Belle kept up her defiant, spunky ways—reading *Harper's,* eating peaches, and singing every night in a loud voice, "Maryland, My Maryland," so movingly that it brought tears to the eyes of other Confederate prisoners. After the war, Belle published her memoirs—which a New York paper called "a valuable contribution to our war literature"—and she went on stage lecturing about her thrilling career.

Site of Fort Evans, Big Spring. When the Indians attacked this old fort in 1756, all the men were gone. But Polly Evans, wife of the fort's builder, rallied the women. In the deepest, loudest voice she could muster, she shouted orders as if a thousand men were preparing for a counterattack. Frightened by this clever ploy, the Indians retreated.

Morgantown

West Virginia State College. Coeducation at this college, founded in 1867, was roundly voted down year after year on the grounds that women were simply not suited for the rigors of higher education; and, besides, where would they live? When student enrollment slipped from one hundred fifty-nine in 1882 to ninety-six the next year, suddenly women were decreed eminently qualified, even though there were still no residence dormitories for them. The first ten women were finally admitted in 1889, and a year later the college president filed his report: "The admission of ladies seems to have been a successful experiment. . . . They have demonstrated their ability to do as thorough work as the young men. Their influence has been wholesome on the young men."

Point Pleasant

Grave of "Mad Ann" Bailey, Tu-Endie-Wei Park. The neighbors started calling her "mad" when Ann Bailey "abandoned all her feminine employments and no longer sewed, spun or attended to household or garden concerns, but practiced with the rifle, slung the tomahawk and rode about the country attending every muster of soldiers." Ann Hennis, born in Liverpool, England saw her first husband Richard Trotter killed by the Indians during the Battle of Point Pleasant in 1774. As a thirty-two-year-old widow, "strange and wild spirits" seemed to possess her, the neighbors feared. The adventurous, athletic Ann found peace and happiness at last, riding for hundreds of miles on her black horse named Liverpool, nibbling on venison jerky and johnnycake, and sleeping alone in the woods with a huge bonfire to keep the wolves away. Although she married John Bailey in 1785, she kept on with her fearless exploits. The most celebrated was her two-hundred-mile ride in 1791 to bring gun-

powder to a garrison besieged by Indians. Ann died in 1825. She is buried near the site where her first husband died—the occasion that marked the start of her "madness." Her gravestone is made from a granite block from the top of Battle Monument that was knocked down by lightning in the 1920s.

Pratt

Site of "The Lock-up," Washington Avenue. "From out the military prison walls of Pratt, West Virginia, where I have walked over my eighty-fourth milestone in history, I send you the groans and tears and heartaches of men, women and children as I have heard them in this state," read the telegram that union organizer Mother Jones—called "the most dangerous woman in America" by one state prosecutor—smuggled out to congressmen in Washington in 1913 to plead for her beloved miners. She was getting ready to start serving a twenty-year sentence for conspiracy to commit murder and to dynamite a train when the governor of West Virginia wisely freed her. For more than thirty years Mother Jones fought her toughest unionizing battles in this state. When a judge in Parkersburg said of her, "It seems to me that it would have been better far . . . to follow the lines and path which the Allwise Being intended for her sex to pursue . . . the true sphere of womanhood," Mother Jones called him a scab. This "impious Joan of Arc, an industrial Carry Nation" kept up her fight with more legal hatpins, mops, and language as colorful as the red and purple dresses she liked to wear, right up to the very end of her life. (See *Mount Olive, Illinois.*)

Sistersville

The only town in the United States with this most hospitable name (although *Sisters, Oregon,* is equally welcoming) was built on land bequeathed in 1815 to sisters Sarah and Delilah, the seventeenth and eighteenth children of Charles Wells, one of the area's first settlers. At the height of the oil boom, the town's population was thirteen thousand, but the memory of the two fine women proved to be more lasting than the petroleum. Today, the population is only two thousand three hundred.

Summersville

Nancy Hart Memorial, Courthouse Lawn, Route 19. When the Union troops captured this town in 1862, they took no chances. They arrested twenty-year-old Nancy Hart, the daring rebel fighter who forayed in the hills and provided Confederate guerrillas with information she had charmed out of Union soldiers. That charm was deadly. One day, Nancy struck up a conversation with the young guard at her cell door, inquiring sweetly whether she could hold his gun. When the naïve, smitten guard handed it over, Nancy shot him and, with furious soldiers in pursuit, escaped on the Union colonel's favorite horse. A week later, on July 25, Nancy rode back into town at the head of two hundred Confederate cavalryman who recaptured the town. An historical marker notes the site of her brief captivity. It is the only memorial left in her honor after her unmarked grave was bulldozed to make way for a beacon tower. The Revolutionary heroine Nancy Hart (no relation) has been considerably more honored in *Elberton, Georgia.*

Sweet Springs

Site of Anne Royall Home, Route 3. An historical highway marker pays tribute to "America's first woman journalist." Anne Royall lived here, first as Maj. William Royall's servant, then as his wife, and then as a widow, until about 1820. Without money or property after a bitter will dispute, Anne decided to leave home. "They look well but nothing wears worse than mountains," she wrote, and then took off on a tour of the country that resulted in her first literary success, *Sketches of History Life* and Manners in the United States. It was published in 1826 when she was fifty-seven years old, and it was followed by ten other entertaining travel journals. Readers adored her tangy critiques and her chatty, intimate style. Innkeepers were terrified of her scathing reviews. No place was sacred to Royall's mighty pen. She inveigled her way into convents to ask nuns about their life's intimacies, and she once eavesdropped on a parson and his female companion in an adjoining hotel room. "I wish to write books that people will read, and I find that there is nothing like throwing in plenty of spice," she said. She then headed for fertile reporting territory in Washington, D.C.

Wheeling

Madonna of the Trail Monument, Wheeling Park. Dedicated in 1928, this is another in the series of twelve DAR monuments (see Springfield, Ohio) honoring the pioneer women "whose courage, optimism, love and sacrifice made possible the National Highway that united the East and the West."

Site of Fort Henry, Main Street. Betty Zane was the heroine of the last battle of the Revolutionary War. The battle took place here in September 1782 when the fort was under an Indian attack instigated by the British. When the supply of gunpowder ran out, young Betty insisted that she be the one to try to retrieve more from a storage cabin that was some hundred yards away. Through a blazing cross fire, Betty ran to the cabin and scooped up as much powder as she could carry in a tablecloth that she had slung around her like a bulging apron. As the bullets zipped through her dress, Betty raced back and saved the day. Her proud descendant Zane Grey celebrated her courageous deed in his 1903 novel Betty Zane. (See Martin's Ferry, Ohio.)

Lydia Boggs Shepherd Cruger House, "Monument Place," Routes 40 and 88. In this huge, handsome stone house, built in 1798 (called the city's most valuable historic building), lived the intrepid Lydia. She was a legendary figure. When she was sixteen, during an attack at Fort Henry, she "beat out the flames of British and Indian firebrands with moccasin clad feet and blistered her hands with molten lead as she shaped bullets." Here, in the lavishly decorated rooms, she entertained such celebrated visitors as Andrew Jackson, Daniel Webster, and Henry Clay. Clay was such a frequent guest that a special bedroom was set aside for his permanent use. Lydia, "a small, little figure [with] a haughty grace of carriage," is most revered for using her influence with Kentucky Senator Henry Clay to reroute the National Road (now I-70) in 1818 so that it passed right by her house, bringing prosperity and an occasional traffic jam to Wheeling.

At her death in 1867, Lydia was more than one hundred years old. She asked to be buried between the two husbands she had outlived and her huge granite shaft towers over their monuments on the highest point of Stone Church Cemetery in nearby Elm Grove.

Site of Rebecca Harding Davis House, Twentieth Street, near Second Presbyterian Church (private). As a young girl in the 1830s, Rebecca would look out the windows of her house and see "the slow stream of human life creeping past, night and morning, to the great mills. Masses of men with dull, besotted faces bent to the ground, sharpened here and there by pain or cunning . . . breathing from infancy to death an air saturated with fog and grease and soot, vileness for soul and body." Those childhood memories were recalled in the opening passages of Life in the Iron Mills, published anonymously in 1861 when Rebecca was thirty. The story showed the contrast between the lives of the rich millowners and the lives of a tubercular ironworker, who should have been a sculptor, and his hunchbacked sister, who worked in the cotton mills (although, for her, the infirmity of being female would have been tragedy enough). "I want to make it real for you. . . . You busy making straight paths for your feet on the hills," she wrote. So successful were her vivid portrayals that the book has become a literary landmark. It broke with the romantic, sentimental writing tradition of the day and preceded Emile Zola by a number of years in its grim realism. Although Rebecca continued writing essays, short stories, and novels, when she died in 1910 at seventy-nine, no literary journal made note of her death. Today, the steel mills have been moved a few miles away from Rebecca's home. No one walks to work, and the air may or may not be cleaner, but the contrasts between rich and poor, male and female, remain.

White Sulphur Springs

Kate's Mountain, Route 60. Kate Carpenter and her little daughter hid in these mountains during Indian raids here in the 1750s and found it to be such a beautiful place they returned again and again when there was no more danger. The area is filled with interesting, rare shrubs, including the box huckleberry, one of the longest-living plants known, with some specimens as old as six thousand years, and a hardy unique species of the mountain clover, named for Kate.

WISCONSIN

Appleton

Edna Ferber House, 218 North Street (private). In 1897, ten-year-old Edna and her family moved here from Iowa. While her father operated a general store, Edna shone as the leading star of high school plays, won prizes in debating contests, and dreamed of a stage career. But her father's illness forced her to take a job, and, instead of going to college, she became the first female reporter for the *Appleton Daily Crescent.* Her salary was three dollars a week. She wrote, "In love with my job, I was the town scourge, a plump seventeen, my hair tied back in a bunch of wiry black corkscrew curls, I daily ranged the news spots from jail and courthouse to Pettibone's Dry Good Store." The author who would one day win a Pulitzer Prize was fired after eighteen months because the editor, it seems, did not like her writing style. But the *Journal* in *Milwaukee* did. She stayed there four exhausting years before returning here, where she bought a battered old typewriter and, in her peculiar four-finger style, banged out her first successful novel, *Dawn O'Hara* (1911), the story of a daring Milwaukee newspaperwoman. That was the start of a sixty-year writing career that produced twenty-five books, including such best sellers as *Giant* and *Show Boat.*

Avoca

Dr. Bertha E. Reynolds Home, Fourth Street (private). In 1940, after forty years as one of Wisconsin's first female doctors, Dr. Reynolds came here from *Lone Rock* to retire at age seventy-two. But when World War II broke out, leaving the town without a physician, she took up her stethoscope again and practiced for another thirteen years.

Dr. Bertha Reynolds House, "Wanek House," Main Street (private). Here, in what was once a harness shop, Avoca's beloved doctor spent the last years before her death in 1961 at age ninety-three. Her tombstone in Bear Valley says simply, "She served her community well."

Berlin

Lucy Smith Morris House, 209 East Park Avenue (private). Such noted suffrage leaders as Susan B. Anthony, Julia Ward Howe, and Elizabeth Cady Stanton stayed in this impressive house when they came to town for their lectures, always delighted to visit their dear friend Lucy Morris. She was known affectionately throughout the state as Little Mother for her founding work with the Wisconsin Federation of Women's Clubs and for her dedication to political equality for women as organizer of the League of Women Voters. At Lucy's death at age eighty-three in 1935, a coworker summarized her influence in the community: "She was actful without effusion. She was dominant without being overbearing. . . . She was a leader who never assumed command."

Columbus

Hattie Griswold House, 310 South Ludington (private). Poet and suffrage leader Griswold lived here in the 1860s. A contemporary biographer effusively noted that "none of the women poets of America have written anything more widely known or popular of its class than [her] short poem, 'Under the Daisies.'" Gris-

wold's other outstanding works include *Waiting on Destiny* and *Lucille and Her Friends,* published several years after she served as president of the Wisconsin's Women's Suffrage Association in 1884.

Fond du Lac

Pier Family Home, 681 South Main Street (private). In this rambling white frame house, one of the oldest in town, reigned a remarkable dynasty of female lawyers. Kate Hamilton Pier gave her maiden name (Hamilton) to each of her three daughters—Kate, Caroline, and Harriet—along with her indomitable pioneering feminist spirit. Mother Kate got her business training as sole manager of her parents' estate. Knowing the loneliness and hardships of that singular struggle, she supportively enrolled at the University of Wisconsin law school with her daughter Kate in 1886. "Their companionship was evidently so pleasant, their manners were so perfect and their aims so high and womanly, that they met with general kindness and pronounced courtesy," a contemporary biographer recalled. The two Piers completed the two-year course in the record time of less than a year, graduating on June 22, 1867. Mother Kate received her law degree as a thirty-second birthday present. They opened a law firm in Milwaukee where four years later, in 1891, they were joined by Caroline and Harriet, creating a most formidable legal quartet. That same year, the elder Kate was appointed the first female circuit court commissioner in the country, and, shortly after, inspired by her mother's path-breaking precedent, daughter Kate became the first female attorney to practice before the U.S. Circuit Court of Appeals.

Green Bay

Baird Law Office. In 1824, as the fourteen-year-old bride of lawyer Henry Baird, when Elizabeth arrived in what was once a desolate and wild land, she quickly discovered that, "My husband thought he could be both a farmer and a lawyer, but it turned out as I had predicted; he would be the lawyer, and I the farmer's wife." She proceeded to learn how to make bread, prepare venison, and manage the house. Part French, part Indian Elizabeth was unable to speak or understand English. She was often lonely, with only the companionship of "a dear little cow. . . . Many was the time I coaxed her to remain by the kitchen doorway by feeding her that I might have some breathing thing near me." But the talented, energetic Elizabeth later learned enough English to write *Reminiscences of Early Life in Territorial Wisconsin* (1886–87), one of the most valuable historical accounts of pioneer settlers. Earlier, when Henry Baird moved into these law offices in 1842, Elizabeth was an able assistant as recorder of deeds.

Deborah Beaumont Martin House, "Hazelwood," 1008 South Monroe Avenue. Taking over where Elizabeth Baird (see above) left off, Deborah Martin, who died here in 1931, was eulogized for her historical works written about this region. She was a "treasure house of information, a source book for other historians . . . with her intimate knowledge of [the area's] colorful and interesting past." Thanks to her tireless efforts, several historic homes in Green Bay, such as the Porter Tank Cottage and the Fort Howard Hospital Building, have been restored. A grateful city has preserved her own unique house, virtually unchanged since it was built in 1837.

Green Bush

Wade House. Although Ruth Kohler died in 1953 before this historic house was dedicated, it was through her commitment that this old Half Way house was preserved and restored. A plaque in the house commemorates her "vision and devotion."

Janesville

Site of Carrie Jacobs Bond Birthplace, 1806 West Court Street. In a cluster of oak trees in the parking area of a shopping center, a monument marks the place where the noted composer was born on August 11, 1862. By the time she was nine, Carrie could play ("by ear") Liszt's Hungarian Rhapsody on the piano, and she dreamed of becoming a famous songwriter.

Site of Carrie Bond Home, 402 East Milwaukee Street. On this site, now a used-car lot, Carrie wrote her famous song "I Love You Truly," which was published in 1901 in her modestly titled collection *Seven Songs as Unpretentious as the Wild Rose.* One of the first female composers to write and publish, as well as design the covers of, her songs, Carrie celebrated her greatest triumph with "A Perfect Day," nine years later in *Riverside, California.*

Frances Willard House, "Forest Home," 1816 South River Road (private). In 1846, when she was seven years old, the famous temperance leader and her family settled on "a beautiful farm, half prairie, half forest on the banks of the Rock River." (The original location of this house was actually north of here and is marked at 1720 South River Road.) Her early years here were "intellectual, yet . . . most healthful," Frances remembered. She romped outdoors in simple flannel suits, her hair cut short, answering only to the name of "Frank" as she tried to keep up with her older brother Oliver. Frances received most of her schooling at home, but when Oliver left to attend school in Beloit, she was so despondent about not being able to go to college that she considered running away from home. Her mother finally agreed to send her to a female seminary in *Evanston, Illinois,* where she later settled.

Frances Willard Schoolhouse, 1401 East Craig Avenue. During her summer vacation from Northwestern University in 1858, Frances taught here for six weeks. It was the start of a busy teaching career that would take her to six schools over the next sixteen years—before she launched her spirited lifework as a temperance reformer.

Rhoda Lavinia Goodell House, 29 South Academy (private). Wisconsin's first female lawyer lived here when she was admitted to the bar of Rockland County Circuit Court in 1874. When one of her cases was appealed to the supreme court, she applied for the right to go with it, but she was refused. In 1877 she fought successfully for a passage of a law to give women the right to practice before the state's highest court. She then joined up with her friend Angie King for a dynamic partnership in their firm, Goodell and King.

Johnstown

Site of Ella Wheeler Wilcox Birthplace, Scharine Road. A memorial tablet marks the first home, since rebuilt, of the famous poet. The inscription inexplicably slices five years off her age with an incorrect birth date of 1855. "My literary career was in a large measure begun before my birth through prenatal influences," Wilcox wrote in her autobiography. Her mother had always been "a devotee at the shrine of literature." Wilcox wrote constantly in her teens, ignoring numerous rejection slips. One story, on its tenth attempt at a magazine, was returned with the heartless memo, "This is a dead dog . . . better bury it." But Wilcox hopefully sent it off again, and it was published. "I found my way into favor of editors by sheer persistence," Wilcox recalled. Such dogged determination paid off, for it was yet another rejection slip that catapulted her into lifelong fame. When a Chicago publishing house refused to print her "immoral" *Poems of Passion,* Milwaukee newspaper headlines blared, "Scarlet City by the Lake shocked by Badger Girl," and the book was eagerly snatched by another publisher. Such lines as "convulsive raptures of a kiss" and "your shoulders nude" sent the public clamoring to the bookstores for more, and nothing she wrote was ever rejected again. (See *Short Beach, Connecticut.*)

Kenosha

Mary D. Bradford House, 6028 Third Avenue (private). At her death in 1943, this pioneer teacher, acclaimed as one of the three leading educators in the country, was called "one of Kenosha's Immortals," whose "undying beneficial influences [continue] to enrich the life of the community." As superintendent of schools from 1910–21, the first woman to hold the position in the state, Bradford established dozens of "firsts"— kindergartens, the open-air school, a vocational school, a school for the deaf, the PTA, a Girl Scout group, and other important innovations. For all this, it was a fitting tribute that she be the first person to be granted an honorary M.A. from the University of Wisconsin in 1938. Her portrait hangs in the Mary D. Bradford Central Senior High School.

Ladysmith

From Flambeau Falls to Corbett to Warner, during a festive venison dinner in 1900, the town's name was finally elevated to Ladysmith in honor of the fiancée of one of the guests, Charles Smith. Despite the tribute, the couple settled on the other side of the state.

Lone Rock

Home and Office of Dr. Bertha Reynolds, Main Street. Although her family advised her to go into nursing, Bertha boldly enrolled as the only woman in her medical school class in Chicago, Illinois. As her good friend Anna Cooper told us, sympathetic male classmates smuggled out cadavers that Bertha, being female, was forbidden to see. She secretly practiced dissecting in an old barn, a lantern lighting her studies.

Working out of this office from 1902 on, Dr. Bertha traveled through tornadoes and floods for hundreds of miles by horse, buggy, boats, and handcars (and once in 1923 in a plane piloted by a young barnstormer named Charles Lindbergh) to reach her patients. "For a mild-mannered woman, she had the most stubbornness when there was a sick person to reach," neighbors recalled. She retired to *Avoca* in 1940, but not for long. Her house is now used as a tavern, but a more healthful landmark in her honor can be found at the Dr. Bertha Reynolds Memorial Forest just east of town.

Madison

Site of Cordelia Harvey's Hospital, Spaight and Brearly Streets. After an official trip to the South during the Civil War, where she was repelled by the overcrowded, unsanitary Union hospitals and the inadequate supplies for hundreds of suffering soldiers, Cordelia Harvey realized the urgent need for a fine military hospital in the North. Armed with a petition of eight thousand signatures, she went straight to President Lincoln who at first opposed the idea, arguing that a hospital near the soldiers' homes would encourage defection. But after months of Cordelia's persistent appeals, Lincoln authorized the construction of three army hospitals in Wisconsin. The largest was located on this block, and Lincoln wanted to name it for Cordelia, but she humbly requested it be called simply Harvey, in honor of her husband, a former governor. Wisconsin has not forgotten her courageous work, however, and today there is a Cordelia Harvey School in Kenosha.

Site of Rosaline Peck Home, South Butler Street. Madison's first settlers moved here in 1837, and, soon after, a baby girl named Wisconsiana was born—the first white child born in the town. The site is marked by a plaque in the back of the Capitol Hotel here. Years later, Robert Lee Ream rented the log cabin, and in 1841 (not 1847 as usually assumed) the noted sculptor Vinnie Ream was born here (see *Washington, D.C.*). One of her beautiful sculptures, *Spirit of the Carnival,* can be admired at the Wisconsin Historical Museum in Madison.

"Genius of Wisconsin," Capitol Building. This dramatic sculpture of a young woman, her right breast bared, her left arm fondly clutching the head of an eagle that is preparing to fly away, was executed by Wisconsin's other genius sculptor, Helen Farnsworth Mears of *Oshkosh.*

Milwaukee

Site of Laura R. Wolcott Home and Office, 462–471 North Milwaukee Street. One of the first women to practice medicine in the West lived and worked here. Laura Wolcott arrived in 1858, after graduating with the highest honors from the Woman's Medical College in *Philadelphia, Pennsylvania.* One of the state's pioneer suffrage leaders as well, Wolcott was described by Elizabeth Cady Stanton as "a remarkable woman of rare intelligence, keen moral perceptions and most imposing presence.... Her graceful figure, classic face, rich voice and choice language make her attractive in the best social circles, as well as in the laboratory and lecture room."

Site of Edna Ferber Home, 760 North Cass Street. The budding novelist lived here during her four years as a reporter for the *Milwaukee Journal.* Edna wrote that she "worked like a horse, happily galloping the city from Lake Michigan to West Allis."

She finally collapsed from exhaustion. Edna returned home to *Appleton* in 1910 to start her famed career as a novelist. In late 1974, after an architectural historian declared that the house she lived in here in Milwaukee had "no historical value," it was razed to make way for a parking lot.

Site of Milwaukee Female Seminary, University of Wisconsin. In 1848, New York schoolteacher Lucy Parsons opened the doors of the Seminary and invited Catharine Beecher (see *Litchfield, Connecticut*) to implement her Great Plan for the education of young women. Beecher's idea was basically to prepare women for their roles as wives and mothers with classes in child care, teaching, nursing, and homemaking. As reactionary as it may seem today, Beecher's concept was revolutionary then, for she insisted on thorough professional training—albeit for housework—while many other schools treated women as dilettantes. Although Beecher herself never taught, never held an administrative position, and did not stay more than a few weeks at the college, her ideas dominated the spirit of the school, and hers was a valuable name to assist in the very necessary fund raising. Beecher's good friend, noted poet Lydia Sigourney (see *Norwich, Connecticut*), was persuaded to donate a substantial fund which she suggested be used for a grove of trees. Six hardy spruces—the "Mrs. Sigourney Memorial"—were planted in 1856 with the heartfelt dedication that "although they are long-lived evergreen trees, we know that they will perish long before the memory of your name and good works is obliterated from the minds of the wise and good." Indeed, the trees perished even before Sigourney died in 1865—they were cut down to make way for new buildings. Deploring this casual obliteration of the Sigourney memorial, the class of 1911 planted another tiny forest in her honor, but today no one seems to remember its location.

Sabin Science Hall, University of Wisconsin, was named for Ellen Sabin, the president in 1890 of Downer College (a forerunner of this university). Sabin began her career as the first female high school principal in Portland, Oregon, in the 1870s. She loved her profession so much that she once remarked she "could never pass . . . a school without wanting to go right in and begin teaching."

Woman's Club, Atheneum Building. Osia Jane Hiles, one of the charter members of the Woman's Club, founded in 1876, devoted her life to Indian reform after reading Helen Hunt Jackson's impassioned plea in *Ramona* (see *Colorado Springs, Colorado*). Hiles participated in the Lake Mohonk Conference of Friends of the Indians (see *New Paltz, New York*) in 1887, and, using all her financial resources, social connections, and energy, fought against plans to destroy Indian reservations. She helped start an association to care for the Oneidas in Wisconsin, and was responsible for the defeat of a measure that would have cheated the Indians out of their lands. Despite her sincere concern for Indians as an oppressed minority, Hiles fell victim to the misguided notions of her era. Like other "friends of the Indians," she saw the ultimate solution in "civilizing" and "Christianizing" the Indians into exact replicas of the white Americans. But at least like her inspirational soul mate, Helen Hunt Jackson, Hiles publicized the need for reforms. Without her dynamic leadership, after her death in 1902, the Wisconsin Indian Association dwindled away.

Site of Josette Juneau Cabin, 110 East Wisconsin Avenue. In the early 1820s, Josette and her husband Solomon lived on this site in a small cabin with a packed-earth floor, bearskin blankets, and boards for beds. Three-sixteenths Ottawa Indian, Josette always kept barrels of flour and sugar outside her house for Indians who were too shy to ask for food. Several times she interceded with the Indians to save the tiny community from massacre. This brave pioneer is honored today as one of the founders of Milwaukee.

Grave of Mathilde Anneke, Forest Home Cemetery, 2405 Forest Home Avenue. Preceded by the notoriety of her famous tract *Das Weib in Konflikt mit den sozialen Verhältnissen* (Woman in Conflict with Social Conditions), published in Germany in 1847, the militant suffragist came to Milwaukee in 1849. She soon launched a monthly German journal advocating the total emancipation of women. Anneke—whom Elizabeth Cady Stanton described as "a German lady of majestic presence and liberal culture"—exulting in her newfound freedom of speech after oppression in her own country, traveled to suffrage conventions all over the states. Her powerful, spirited lectures excited listeners even before the words were translated from German. For, as she explained, if she could not speak the English language she could at least speak the language of the heart. Representing Wisconsin at an 1869 meeting in New York, Anneke argued persuasively (in translation): "Whether it be prudent to enfranchise women is not the question—only whether it be right. What is positively right, must be prudent, must be wise, and must, finally, be useful." She died in Milwaukee at age sixty-seven in 1884.

Grave of Louise Phelps Kellogg, Forest Home Cemetery. At her death in 1942 at age eighty, the first female president of the Mississippi Valley Historical Society (now the Organization of American Historians) was eulogized: "For a generation . . . the best known woman historian of the West."

Mary Belle Austin Jacobs Statue, Kosciusko Park, Ninth and Lincoln Streets. Erected in 1931, two years after her death, this statue of Mary Belle Jacobs—shown gently leading a child by the hand—commemorates her founding of organized social work in Wisconsin. Mary Belle and her husband Herbert operated a settlement house not far from this site, helped establish a workingman's camp, and promoted home nursing branch libraries along with numerous other important social efforts.

New Berlin

Theodora Winton Youmans Home, 19485 West National Avenue (private). As press secretary for the Woman's Suffrage Association in 1912, Theodora Youmans, who was raised in this house, sent out weekly news releases to more than six hundred papers in the state. As president of the association, she led the suffrage campaign to victory in 1919. "Some may think," she later wrote, "that woman suffrage just happened, that it was 'in the air,' but we know . . . changes . . . are the result of ceaseless, unremitting toil. Stones wear away with constant dripping. So do prejudices, which are much tougher."

Oshkosh

Helen Farnsworth Mears House, 222 Parkway Avenue (private). Helen was born here in 1872 into an exceptionally talented family—her mother was Wisconsin's first poet, one sister was a writer, the other an illustrator. With such creative energies around her and with the encouraging support of her father, who gave her anatomy lessons and turned his woodshed into a studio, Helen began her celebrated career as a sculptor at an early age. She started by molding bread into figures of dogs and horses and by cutting out paper dolls that looked remarkably like the neighbors. At age nine she displayed a head of Apollo at the county fair. When she was twenty, her *Genius of Wisconsin,* exhibited at the Chicago Exposition, was nationally acclaimed. With her prize money, Helen went to New York to study with Augustus Saint-Gaudens, and she became his first female assistant. One of her greatest honors was her commission to make a nine-foot statue of Frances Willard (see *Washington, D.C.*), which was dedicated in 1905. But her outstanding masterpiece—on which she worked five years—is probably *The Fountain of Life.* (Tragically that plaster mold has disap-

peared since it was last seen about twenty years ago on its way to a museum in Illinois.) It was a fourteen-foot-high bas-relief in the Grecian mode that "tells the truth about life," she explained to an interviewer on the day before she died suddenly of overwork and exhaustion. The year was 1916 and Helen was forty-three.

Pepin

Site of Laura Ingalls Wilder Birthplace, Route 183. The beloved author of the "Little House" books, who began her writing career when she was sixty-five and wrote ten best-selling books about her childhood memories, was born here on February 7, 1865. *The Little House in the Big Woods,* a one-room cabin where Laura climbed a ladder to reach her tiny niche in the attic, has been torn down, but a marker commemorates the site. (See *Mansfield, Missouri.*)

Pickett

Anne Pickett House (private). Anne and her husband Armine settled here in 1849, leaving behind the first dairy cooperative in the United States at nearby Lake Mills. There, the couple and their three children arrived in 1838 on oxcarts from their native Ohio. They found "a boundless expanse of grass growing over beautiful openings and lower marsh ground," recalled their son James. "The material from which butter and cheese could be made was growing in almost tropical luxuriance all over the country." Anne's ten cows were not enough, she figured, to make plentiful amounts of cheese, so she originated the brilliant idea of recruiting the neighbors' cows for help. In 1841, in the kitchen of her log cabin, Anne produced the first tangy cheeses, the result of a cooperative effort where the cows' owners drew their shares in nourishing cheese instead of cash. Pickett cheese became so famous that when Anne moved to Winnebago County in 1845, this town was named in its honor.

Portage

Juliette Kinzie House, "Agency Hill." One of Wisconsin's first settlers, Juliette, a linguist and an accomplished pianist, lived in this huge, elegant house for only a year—shortly after it was built in 1832. Her thrilling and descriptive narrative, *Wau-Bun,* which she illustrated with six of her drawings, is one of the most important records of early Wisconsin history.

Zona Gale House, 506 West Edgewater. From her second-story study in this white-pillared house on the banks of the Wisconsin River, the Pulitzer Prize–winning author wrote her numerous homespun tales about life in Portage. Starting out in 1901 as a reporter in Milwaukee and later in New York, where she was considered the most ambitious female reporter in the city, Zona persisted with her fiction writing despite hundreds of rejections. She finally returned to Portage in 1912 to live among the people she knew and loved best. Town residents revere Zona for her loving portrait of her hometown: "Portage, Wisconsin—What Only a Native Knows." The Woman's Club is now headquartered here.

Prairie du Chien

Jane Dousman House, "Villa Louis." Considered "probably the truest and most complete example of mid-nineteenth century style to be found not only in Wisconsin, but in the United States," the "House on the Mound" was the home of the redoubtable hostess Jane Fisher Dousman until her death in 1882. One of Wisconsin's first millionaires, Dousman was loved and revered for her countless acts of charity and service, especially during one severe smallpox epidemic. But she is probably more heralded today for the lavish parties she and her husband gave for celebrated personalities of the day. Guests were weighed upon their arrival and, after an evening of gorging and feasting, were weighed as they left—"to determine their appreciation of the food."

Racine

Olympia Brown Hall, Universalist Church of the Good Shepherd, Seventh Street and College Avenue. After serving for six years as pastor of a parish in Massachusetts, according to a friend, Olympia "said characteristically, the church was then on so admirable a footing she could safely entrust it to a man's management." Olympia Brown, the nation's second female minister (after her good friend and inspiration, Antoinette Brown Blackwell in *South Butler, New York*), arrived in 1880 at a Universalist church (the original building has been destroyed) that had been given up as a lost cause by her male predecessors. Her amazing four-month stomp for suffrage through Kansas in 1867—at Lucy Stone's urgent request— where she spoke three and four times a day, even on Sunday, established her power as an orator. Her arguments were so tenacious and rational that one of her opponents once felt compelled to join in the standing ovation after her speech, but he restrained himself for the sake of appearances. Here in Racine, Olympia's rousing, succinct sermons "interested the indifferent, called many of the wanderers back and furnished food for thought to the most advanced thinkers. Her addresses were always to the point," recalled one parishioner. Olympia was sorely missed when she resigned in 1887, but the sinners' loss was suffragists' gain. She served as president of the Wisconsin Suffrage Association for twenty-eight years until 1912, adding her powerful preacher's voice to stirring opening prayers and clinching last points that left her opponents "powerless and overcome." When the Nineteenth Amendment was passed in 1920, Olympia was the only living pioneer suffragist who had witnessed the entire movement from the early days in *Seneca Falls, New York*. At her death six years later at age ninety-one, her daughter proudly recalled, "All of it she saw and part of it she was."

Richland Center

Ada James House, 383 East Haseltine (private). A founder of the Political Equality League and an enthusiastic suffragist, Ada, who died here in 1952 at age seventy-six, traveled all over the state for the cause. Deaf from an early age, and a great experimenter with every new hearing device on the market, Ada employed a most effective debating technique. She removed the trumpet from her ear or disconnected the little machines right after she presented her side of the argument, thus eliminating the replies of her sputtering, angry opponents. She knew she was right. And when the Nineteenth Amendment was passed, Ada knew her home state should have the glory as the

Ada James (wearing Votes for Women sash) campaigns for suffrage

first ratifier, so she speedily mobilized her seventy-six-year-old father. A state legislator, who with his brother had introduced Wisconsin's suffrage bill, he was also the courier for the governor. Ada lent him her suitcase so he could jump on the first train to Washington with the official ratification papers. The sprightly Mr. James touched out the competing representative from Illinois for the momentous honor of being the first state to ratify the amendment. Ada devoted her last years to advocating pacifism and birth control, and to helping the youth of the town by opening the entire upper floor of her house, which is now divided into apartments, for activities of the Girl Scouts and the High School Hornets' Lodge.

Ripon

Carrie Chapman Catt Birthplace, 324 Spaulding Avenue (private). From her birth in 1859 until she was seven years old, Carrie Lane lived in this house which still has its original door and at least one original window pane. As a schoolgirl, the future suffrage leader (see *Bronx, New York City*) quickly outdistanced her classmates, winning a penny prize for learning the multiplication table of two's better than anyone else in class. A year later, when the boys in school started giggling at an unfortunate blushing girl whose hoopskirt had slipped to the ground, Carrie confronted the rude leader and slapped his face. "They had more respect for the girls after that!" she recalled later in an interview. The budding young feminist and her family next moved to *Charles City, Iowa.* Once, in her seventies, the white-haired celebrity revisited her old house, but she refused to go inside to see how time had changed it.

Sun Prairie

Grave of Ada Bird, Sun Prairie City Cemetery. "She wakens to heavenly music," reads the inscription on the grave of the founder of the Wisconsin School of Music (1909). Beneath Ada Bird's name is the insignia of the medal that the French Academy awarded her in 1914 for her outstanding contribution to the music world. The medal was pinned to her burial dress when she died, just two months after she received it. A museum in Sun Prairie, built on the site of her 1859 birthplace, contains a plaque that commemorates her four brothers who served in the Civil War and remembers Ada for her gentler, more lasting contributions to music.

Viroqua

Lucy Stone Memorial, 400 block, North Rock Avenue. In the summer of 1857, Lucy Stone and her husband, Henry Blackwell (see *West Brookfield, Massachusetts*), drove from Chicago to Viroqua in a horse and buggy, stopping for dinners of bread and fresh milk at the homes of friendly farmers, encountering old acquaintances. Ohio-born Henry wrote, "I knew all the Westerners, Lucy all the Easterners. She was profound east of Pittsburgh; I was deeply saturated with Ohio, Indiana and Illinois." At a Fourth of July celebration here, a platform was quickly constructed in a shaded grove where Lucy delivered "the first Women's Rights address and Anti-slavery speech ever given by a woman in the great Northwest." During her rousing speech, the platform suddenly crumbled, and Lucy fell. Struggling to her feet, the clever Lucy ad-libbed, "So will the nation fall unless slavery is abolished!" The memorial tablet on the site, erected by Lucy's daughter, Alice Stone Blackwell, concludes the story of the episode by recalling that through Lucy's efforts, "the world for women has been revolutionized."

Watertown

First Kindergarten in the United States, Octagon House grounds. One hot summer day in 1856, in the parlor of her house, Margarethe Meyer Schurz decided to occupy her two daughters Agathe and Marianne and four German-speaking little cousins by playing with brightly colored balls, blocks of wood, and shiny papers, and by singing songs to the accompaniment of the piano. The little ones were so happy and clever that, by the autumn, Margarethe's neighbors were asking if she could teach their children as well. The first officially recognized kindergarten in the country, despite claims from *Columbus, Ohio,* and *St. Louis, Missouri,* was started in a tiny vacant store (see below) that has been relocated here and restored with period furnishings and mannequins portraying the happy class in action. In Hamburg, in 1849, Margarethe had been a student of Friedrich Froebel, the noted German pioneer of infant education. She practiced his theories—basically, letting children teach themselves through creative play—when she came to Watertown as the wife of Carl Schurz, the famed statesman. Schurz described his wife, after their first meeting, as "of fine stature, a curly head, something childlike in her beautiful features and large, dark truthful eyes."

Site of First Kindergarten, North Second and Jones Streets. Margarethe Meyer Schurz is honored here on this memorial marker as the founder of the first kindergarten in America. Although the kindergarten only lasted two years, the school was an important influence for Elizabeth Peabody. The two women met by chance in Massachusetts, in 1859, and Peabody was so inspired by Margarethe's enthusiasm and experience that she opened her own school in Boston a year later, generally considered the first English-speaking kindergarten in the country.

Wisconsin Dells

Belle Boyd Grave, Spring Grove Cemetery, Route 23. Surrounded by a three-sided redwood fence, beneath a blooming snowball bush lies a small red granite marker for "Confederate Spy" Belle Boyd (see *Martinsburg, West Virginia*), who died at fifty-six, in 1900, of a heart attack while on a lecture tour in Wisconsin. As usual, the dynamic Belle had captivated her audiences with dramatic accounts of her espionage adventures and endeared them with her concluding entreaty for a new unity between North and South. So sincere was her plea that after her death, four Union veterans asked to carry her coffin to the grave—which was sprinkled with soil from Virginia. Her tombstone was originally marked with the words "One flag, one country," but a tenacious rebel from Mississippi was said to have replaced it some years later with this simple stone, noting only her birth and death, "Erected by a friend."

Woodruff

Lakeland Memorial Hospital. Thanks to the persistent efforts of Dr. Kate Newcomb, this modern hospital was opened in 1953. Although Dr. Newcomb had practiced in Detroit as early as 1917, when she came to Wisconsin in the 1920s, she quit medicine to care for her ailing husband and her children. But when a doctor friend, well aware of the need for doctors in this remote area, told her that she was wasting her education on housework, she resumed her practice, recalling, "Before the ink was dry on my license, my telephone began to ring all hours of the day and night." She had a special car fitted out with skis on the front wheels and tractor treads on the rear, a pair of snowshoes in the trunk so that she could always be sure to reach the sick on the inaccessible trails. The Angel on Snowshoes soon became a familiar and dear figure throughout the countryside where households tied red rags on branches and fence posts as a sign that the doctor was needed. In 1956, at age seventy, Dr. Newcomb was still aiding the sick, when she fell, broke her hip, and died.

Alcova

Site of Lynching of Cattle Kate, Route 220. The waters of the Alcova Dam have flooded the place where the state's first and last woman was brutally lynched in 1889. Born Ella Watson in Kansas, she was nicknamed Cattle Kate in Wyoming for her matchless skill in ranching. Her "crime" was her adventurous and uninhibited life-style. The *Cheyenne Sun* called her "a holy terror, [who] rode straddle and always had a vicious bronco for a mount and seemed never tired of dashing across the range." Her tragic misfortune was her choice of a local address, next door to the real target of the murderers, Jim Averill. Ella had married Averill secretly, for as a "wife" she would not have been able to file on a homestead, and together they managed their ever-growing herd of cattle, neatly branded "EW." Five jealous ranchers warned the pair to get out of town and, on July 20, decided to hasten their departure. There was hardly time for a struggle as Averell and Ella were tied up and the ropes flung over the limb of a scrub pine. Their sun-scorched bodies were found several days later. The murderers went free, and there was little public sympathy for the senseless death of Cattle Kate. By then, she was being described in the papers as a rustler and a prostitute, "slouchy and filthy . . . an arrant coward . . . who could not ride horseback." We tried to find out more about Ella's life, but all that old-time residents of the area remembered was her unjust death, and no one wanted to talk about that.

Buffalo

Crazy Woman Creek. Indian men can be blamed for this unkind title, though there are more versions of its naming than there are forks in this busy river (three). Some say the creek was named for a white woman who was captured by the Indians, went insane, and was abandoned on the riverbanks. Others say the crazy woman was an Indian who, spurned by her tribe, wandered up and down the creek for many years.

Casper

Grave of Ada Magill, Route 26, near Old Deer Creek Station. The unmarked grave of a three-year-old Kansas pioneer, who died on the Oregon Trail in 1864, was discovered in the early 1900s by two young boys, who lovingly enshrined it with rocks and flowers. When construction of the new road began, Maud Dawes, the county superintendent of schools had the grave moved to its present site for undisturbed recall of the memory of that brave little traveler. No one knows why or how young Ada died, but we did learn that her parents barely had a chance to recover from their grief when Ada's brother died after eating a poisonous weed.

Cheyenne

Site of Old Capitol Building, Sixteenth and Warren. On December 10, 1869, in two small rooms located on this corner, the men of Wyoming gave their women the first right to vote in the history of the world. No monuments or plaques celebrate the site, and the old building has long since been cleared away for familiar symbols of progress and Americana—a gas station, a used-car lot, and a hamburger joint. The twenty-two legislators met in these rented rooms to consider the suffrage bill that had been introduced—after the persuasive appeal of Esther Morris (see below)—by William H. Bright in the senate. There, the bill passed easily on November 27, but, in the house, there was some nonsensical opposition. One man moved that the word *ladies* be used in place of *women*. Another proposed that the age requirement be changed from eighteen to thirty, figuring that no woman would want to vote if she had to admit to being that old. However, the bill was signed and sent to Governor John A. Campbell, a bachelor and the sole Republican in power. He was momentarily undecided about the bill. But then Campbell remembered a time when, as a young boy in Ohio, he snuck into a woman's rights convention and watched with fascination as the women handled all their business efficiently while the men in the audience sat silent. Surely women deserved their fair share. With a flourish, leaving a tiny inkblot under his middle initial, Governor John A. Campbell signed "An Act to Grant to the Women of Wyoming the Right to Suffrage, and to Hold Office."

Statue of Esther Morris, Capitol Avenue. The heroine of the Wyoming suffrage movement (see *South Pass City*) is honored at the Capitol entrance by this shiny bronze statue, erected in 1963. A youthful and forceful Esther Morris, carrying flowers and a portfolio, is described simply as the "Proponent of the legislative act in 1869 which gave distinction to the Territory of Wyoming." A larger version of the statue is in Statuary Hall in *Washington, D.C.*

Esther Morris Home, 2114 Warren Avenue (private). After her triumphant suffrage work and her historic service as justice of the peace in *South Pass City,* Esther Morris lived in this modest white house until her death at eighty-seven in 1902. She was honored several times over the years in Cheyenne as the Mother of Suffrage, and in 1895 she welcomed Susan B. Anthony, who called her first visit to Wyoming one of the proudest moments of her life. A plaque on the front lawn here was installed in 1950, and the home's present owner, Mrs. Nickie Lepas, who interrupted her vacuuming to welcome us inside, said she had been delighted by the honor. The three-bedroom house, bought in 1938 by Mrs. Lepas and her now-deceased husband, both Greek immigrants, has been considerably remodeled. Guiding us through the cozy rooms, Mrs. Lepas recalled that the house had very small windows and high ceilings; a fire years ago destroyed some old papers, and Mrs. Lepas worried that they may have belonged to Morris. Always pleased to have visitors, Mrs. Lepas said she looked forward to the summer months when many stop by to admire her historic house.

Nellie Tayloe Ross Home, 902 East Seventeenth Street (private). The nation's first female governor lived in this elegant two-story white house during her term of office, 1925–27. When her husband, Governor William Ross, died suddenly in 1924, Nellie was asked to run on the Democratic ticket. Though a reluctant campaigner, she won easily by eight thousand votes. A most efficient and intelligent executive, during her one term she reduced the state debt by more than a million dollars and made great gains for public education. Known for her graciousness, tact, and eloquent speeches, this dignified woman was very popular throughout the state, but she alienated some crucial voters by her positions on Prohibition (for) and professional prizefighting (against). Trying to discount Ross' considerable achievements, her opponent claimed that it was a court of male advisers who ran the government. She lost the 1926 election—most probably because she was a Democrat in a Republican state—but she made history again when she was named the first female director of the U.S. Mint in 1933.

Cody

Buffalo Bill Statue, Buffalo Bill Historical Center, Sheridan Avenue. This huge bronze sculpture of the old scout on his favorite horse, Smoky, is considered one of the best-known equestrian statues in the U.S. It is the magnificent work of Gertrude Vanderbilt Whitney (see *Manhattan, New York City*), who also donated the surrounding forty-acre plot to the historical center. Whitney, who finished the statue in 1924 after Buffalo Bill's death, worked from his photographs. But since Smoky was still available as a model, she had the horse shipped to her New York studio where, in her habitual pursuit of artistic realism, she carefully studied its prances and gallops. Her work successfully captures the high-spirited adventurous style of the famous showman. And his horse.

Fort Laramie

Fort Laramie National Historic Site. This military post that operated from 1849–90 was a favorite rest stop for thousands of weary travelers heading west. Narcissa Whitman and Eliza Spalding stopped here in 1836 to lighten their wagonloads in preparation for their historic trip as the first white women across the Rockies (see *South Pass*). A marker in front of Sutler's store informed us that once Calamity Jane (see *Sheridan*) visited with a girl friend. They borrowed cavalry uniforms and roamed around the fort saluting puzzled officers.

One of the fort's responsibilities was to warn the pioneers of any Indian movements in the area, but at least once it seems the forward observers didn't do their job. In the summer of 1864, Sarah Larimer and Fanny Kelly were among eleven travelers in five wagons heading for Idaho who stopped here to inquire about Indian activity. "Renewed pledges of safety on the road" brought instead a band of 250 mounted and war-painted Oglala Sioux who surrounded the party near Little Box Elder River, about eighty miles past the fort. According to Sarah Larimer, at first the Sioux were friendly, as they rode along with the wagons and said they would leave after they were fed. "Though to prepare a meal for two hundred and fifty Indians was not a small undertaking, the work was soon in progress. When all the men were busily engaged, the savages deeming it a favorable opportunity, threw off their mask of friendship, and displayed their true character and intentions." The Indians, fugitives from white retaliation for the Minnesota Sioux massacre in 1862, broke into the wagons and killed several of the men. Larimer and her eight-year-old son, Frank, and Fanny Kelly and her five-year-old niece, Mary, were taken as captives, but, thirty hours later, Larimer and Frank escaped. The others were not so lucky. Kelly spent seven months as a captive and little Mary was scalped. Larimer's story, *The Capture and Escape; or, Life among the Sioux,* which she published five years later, was such a success that she tried to get a second book out about her friend's experiences, but Kelly slapped her with a lawsuit and wrote her own best seller (see *Pierre, South Dakota*).

Mary E. Homsley Grave. On the way out of Fort Laramie, the first narrow road to the left bears a sign pointing to Mary Homsley's grave site, a white obelisk marker enclosed by a white fence on the banks of the North Platte River. Here in 1852, a heartbroken Benjamin Homsley wrapped the body of his twenty-eight-year-old wife in a feather tick and buried her beneath a crude sign bearing her name. The Homsleys and their two daughters had been traveling to Oregon when poor Mary died from measles. Her life and death might have remained a mystery, as did the stories of countless other victims of the rugged trip west (see *Guernsey*). However, newspaper accounts of the grave's discovery in 1925 reached Mary Homsley's daughter, Mrs. Laura Gibson in Portland, Oregon, who long since had given up her search for her mother's grave. Shortly afterwards, the present marker was erected as a memorial. Dr. Grace Hebard (see *Laramie*) delivered a eulogy to "The Pioneer Mothers on the Oregon Trail," at the memorial service which was attended by more than five hundred people, many of whom were descendants of such brave mothers.

Fort Washakie

Grave of Sacajawea, Wind River Reservation. The gateway to the cemetery bears her name, and the most magnificent monument on the hill belongs to the brave Shoshoni guide of the Lewis and Clark Expedition. The grave is surrounded by red, yellow, and blue plastic flowers, worn paths leading to it from all directions. Although there is considerable evidence that this might not be the real grave of the real Sacajawea (see *Mobridge, South Dakota*), it seemed to us a worthy pilgrimage on the cold, rainy day when we visited. Flanking her grave are smaller markers to her son, Jean-Baptiste Charbonneau, "Papoose" and to her nephew, Bazil. To some historians, Sacajawea was little more than "a well-behaved youngster who didn't get underfoot" and was hardly indispensable to the success of the 1805–1806 explorations. But Lewis and Clark in their own diaries tell of the countless times Sacajawea helped them. She rescued valuable equipment from flooded canoes; she taught them about the wild vegetation; she cared for the sick travelers; and, most important, her presence assured their safety as well as a grand welcome when she led them to the land of her people. As Clark wrote, "A woman with a party of men is a token of peace." After completion of the expedition in 1806, the "Wind River Sacajawea" virtually disappears from historical record. Though for almost two years her every footstep was duly noted and is today commemorated throughout four states with markers and monuments, suddenly Sacajawea is lost for more than three-quarters of a century. She is said to have wandered from tribe to tribe, returning here to the Shoshonis where she died on April 9, 1884, when she was almost one hundred years old.

Estelle Reel was a frequent visitor to the Wind River Reservation after her appointment as national superintendent of Indian schools in 1898, the first time a woman had been unanimously approved by the Senate for a national position. This honor came four years after she was elected state superintendent of public instruction in Wyoming, a landslide victory that made her the first woman in the United States to win a state office.

Grand Teton National Park

The Grand Tetons. Those spectacular, snow-covered mountains in the distance include Grand Teton (13,770 feet); Mount Owen (12,928 feet); and Mount Teewinot (12,325 feet)—"the Cathedral Group"; or, as they were named by French trappers more than 150 years ago, *Trois Tetons* ("the Three Breasts")— a monumental tribute to the sexual fantasies of men in the wilderness. For a less modest view, see *Ashton, Idaho.*

Jenny Lake and the **Jenny Lake Museum** (which contains a fine geology and mountaineering exhibit) were named for the Shoshoni woman Jenny Leigh, whose marriage to "Beaver Dick" Leigh was the first wedding ceremony between an Indian woman and a white man in the area. Jenny and her six children died in 1876 during the smallpox epidemic that swept Snake River Valley.

Green River

County Courthouse, 50 West Flaming Gorge. On May 8, 1950, for the first time since women first served on a jury in 1870 in *Laramie*, women were jurors again in Wyoming. Because of a legal technicality, it was eighty years before the Wyoming Supreme Court ruled that women were indeed permitted to serve on juries. Shortly after that decision in 1950, six women joined

Grand Tetons

six men in the courtroom, which was later replaced by this modern building. Aware that they were making history, the jurors added another distinctive note by selecting Louise Spinner Graf as the first woman in the world to be named a jury foreman. Graf and the other women did their job so well, returning a verdict of second-degree murder against a man accused of shooting a coal miner, that the defense attorney complained he never would have lost the case if it hadn't been "for those damn women."

Guernsey

Grave of Lucinda Rollins, on the banks of the North Platte River. The engineers who stumbled on the old stone grave marker in 1934 had to use a magnifying glass to decipher the crudely etched words. All we know is that her name was Lucinda, that she was from Ohio, and that she was twenty-four years old when she died on July 11, 1849. Today the grave, encircled with smooth white stones, is marked with a chalkwhite obelisk, similar in style and spirit to that of Mary Homsley (see *Fort Laramie*). The grave stands alone off the tourist track that leads to Registry Cliff, where thousands of emigrants carved their own names into the high rocks instead of leaving the job to grieving relatives.

Kemmerer

Annie Richey, who lived on a nearby ranch, narrowly avoided the questionable distinction of being the only woman in Wyoming to serve time for cattle rustling. In 1922, she swallowed strychnine with her coffee instead of waiting out her sentence behind bars.

Lander

Pioneer Museum of Fremont County, 636 Lincoln Street. The grand treasure here, visible the minute you enter the door, is a weather-beaten high-backed wooden chair made in 1869. Esther Morris supposedly relaxed in it when she was living in *South Pass City.*

Laramie

The site of the most historic event in Wyoming, when the first woman cast her vote for the first time anywhere in the world, is not marked and has never been located. T. A. Larsen, the state's foremost historian, told us unhappily, "There is *not* any place in Laramie to commemorate Mrs. Swain's casting the first equal suffrage vote. In fact, there seems to be no record of where the polling place was." We do know that, very early in the morning on September 6, 1870, seventy-year-old Louisa Ann Swain arrived at the polls wearing a tidy apron, shawl, and hat and carrying a little bucket for some yeast she was planning to pick up at Mrs. Luther Fillmore's house on her way home. Although the polls were still closed, the gentle Quaker was permitted to cast her vote; then she convinced Mrs. Fillmore to do likewise. Later in the day, more women gathered at the polls. "I saw the rough mountaineers maintaining the most respectful decorum whenever the women approached . . . and heard the timely warning of one of the leading canvassers as he silenced an incipient quarrel with uplifted finger, saying, 'Hist! Be quiet! A woman is coming!' " wrote an eyewitness of that memorable day.

Site of the first woman jury, Garfield and First Streets. Just three months after women got the vote in Wyoming, they were summoned to serve on a jury, yet another historic first for the Equality State. On March 7, 1870, a packed courtroom in the Laramie Grocery Building (the site is now occupied by the Smith Furniture Store) heard the memorable words, "Ladies and gentlemen of the Grand Jury . . ." Judge John Howe, who had empaneled five women as an experimental solution to the increasing lawlessness and low number of convictions brought about by men, assured them, "You shall not be driven by the sneers, jeers and insults of a laughing crowd from the temple of justice as your sisters have from medical colleges of the land. The strong hand of the law will protect you." But newspaper cartoons cruelly caricatured the women who were too

Site of First Women's Jury

busy with murder and cattle-rustling cases to pose for photographs, and editorial writers cynically asked, "Is it possible for a jury of women, carrying with them all their sensitiveness, sympathies, predilections, jealousies, hatreds, to reach an impartial verdict?" Such a foolish question was answered by Judge Howe who, when the grand jury recessed three weeks later, commented, "In eighteen years experience I have never had as fair, candid, impartial and able a jury in court as in this term." A small stone marker in the women's honor stands near the railroad parking lot.

Grace Hebard Home, 318 South Tenth Street (private), is not far from the University of Wyoming where for more than twenty-five years beginning in 1891, this formidable woman was a teacher (of history and sociology), a member of the board of trustees, and head librarian. She also found the time to win the state golf and tennis championships. Hebard also wrote several volumes on Wyoming history, including the definitive and scholarly *Sacajawea* (1933), which builds a strong case for the validity of the Wind River Sacajawea (see *Fort Washakie*). Hebard lived here (until her death in 1936) with her dear friend, poet Agnes Matilda Wergeland. The brown two-story building, now converted into four apartments, was familiarly called "the Doctors' House" for its two Ph.D. occupants.

Green Hill Cemetery, Fifteenth Street. From one house to one grave, the two Ph.D.'s, Grace Hebard and Agnes Wergeland, inseparable to the end, are buried under one large marker. Another university colleague, June Downey, remembered for her bold experimentation in the psychological interpretation of handwriting, is also buried in this cemetery along with Mary Godot Bellamy, the first woman elected to the Wyoming state legislature (1910). Lake Marie in the Snowy Range west of Laramie was named in her honor by her adoring husband.

Site of Root's Opera House, Third Street near Grand Avenue. Helen Root, "Sissy" to her friends, was the manager of an elegant theater that stood on this site in the 1890s. As many as six hundred theater lovers thronged the halls to watch popular plays; afterwards, the chairs were cleared for dancing. Sissy insisted on supervising every phase of the theater's operation, and she could often be seen perched on a ladder pasting down ads for coming attractions. She was known in show business as the country's first "Woman Bill Poster." Where once Sissy's handiwork advertised the plays and the stars, today the Chef Cafe boasts its breakfast specials.

Newcastle

Anna Miller Museum, East Newcastle. This museum for pioneer articles and wildlife exhibits was named for an early resident of the area who died in 1951. Anna Miller had been a schoolteacher when she was married, but as a widow she rose to the position of county superintendent of schools, and she also became the first county librarian.

Sheridan

"It was on Goose Creek, Wyo., where the town of Sheridan is now located," wrote Martha Jane Cannary in her diary, published in 1931, explaining where and how she was christened Calamity Jane. It was during the Big Horn Campaign of 1872 and "Captain Egan was in command of the post. We were ordered out to quell an uprising of Indians and were out for several days and had numerous skirmishes during which six of the soldiers were killed and several severely wounded when on returning to the post we were ambushed about a mile and a half from our destination. When fired upon, Capt. Egan was shot. I was riding in advance when hearing the shot, turned in my saddle and saw the captain reeling in his saddle as though about to fall. I turned my horse and galloped back with all haste to his side and got there in time to catch him as he was falling. I lifted him onto my horse in front of me and succeeded in getting him safely to the fort. Capt. Egan on recovering, laughingly said: 'I name you "Calamity Jane." The heroine of the plains.' I have borne that name until the present time."

From the beginning (see *Princeton, Missouri*) to the end (see *Deadwood, South Dakota*), the legend is larger than the life of this bawdy, boisterous cowboy, scout, and traveling woman who always did exactly as she pleased.

South Pass

Parting of the Ways Monument, Route 28. Narcissa Whitman and Eliza Spalding are unceremoniously referred to as "and wives" on this white marble marker that commemorates the 1836 journey of their missionary husbands along the Oregon Trail. The historic sites planner of Wyoming told us that the monument has the wrong legend and is in the wrong location. Another monument, geographically and historically more accurate, names the women and gives them credit for their accomplishments. Unfortunately, it robs them of full glory, for it defies tourist detection, isolated three miles to the east of the highway in the middle of a barren plain. Since you may be as unsuccessful as we were in finding it, we provide this description: a neatly-chiseled boulder singling out Narcissa Prentiss Whitman and Eliza Hart Spalding as the "first white women to cross this pass, July 4, 1836" on their way to mission work in *Walla Walla, Washington,* and *Spalding, Idaho.*

South Pass City

Home and Office Site of Esther Hobart Morris. Down past the souvenir shops of this restored ghost town, a small fence-enclosed tablet honors Esther Morris as "the first woman Justice of the Peace" and "author with W. H. Bright of the First Equal Suffrage Law." Here Esther gave the legendary tea party for Wyoming legislative candidates on September 2, 1869, when she extracted a promise from both Democrats and Republicans to give women the vote. Bright, the husband of a determined suffragist, won. Though some historians insist that Esther didn't meet Bright until after the election, the story endures of her persuasive appeal over tea and cookies.

Esther, a mighty contender, almost six feet tall and weighing close to two hundred pounds, was the perfect candidate for justice of the peace of this rugged mining town that once boasted a population of two thousand. She was appointed on February 14, 1870, and, though she served for only a few months, she handled as many as seventy cases. None of her decisions were overturned by a higher court, not even her charge of assault and battery against her husband. She slapped him with a fine and abandoned him when she moved to *Cheyenne.* The bare frame of a wooden foundation of her office was all that could be seen on the unusual snowy summer day we visited, but perhaps by now the two-room replica of her cabin is finished, with Esther's favorite chair in its rightful place. (See *Lander.*)

South Pass City, 1870

Bibliography

Books

Aikman, Duncan. *Calamity Jane and the Lady Wildcats.* New York: Blue Ribbon Books, 1937.

Allen, Opal Sweazea. *Narcissa Whitman.* Portland, Oregon: Binfords & Mort, 1959.

Alley, Reuben E. *Frederic W. Boatwright.* Richmond: University of Richmond, 1973.

Ambler, Charles H. *A History of Education in West Virginia.* Huntington, West Virginia: Standard Printing and Publishing Co., 1951.

Anderson, Peggy. *The Daughters.* New York: St. Martin's Press, 1974.

Armstrong, Margaret. *Fanny Kemble, A Passionate Victorian.* New York: Macmillan, 1938.

Atherton, Gertrude. *California.* New York: Harper and Bros., 1914.

Augur, Helen. *Anne Hutchinson: An America Jezebel.* New York: Brentano, 1930.

Avery, Mary W. *Washington—A History of the Evergreen State.* Seattle: University of Washington, 1965.

Banning, Evelyn I. *Helen Hunt Jackson.* New York: Vanguard Press, 1973.

Barnum, P. T. *Barnum's Own Story.* New York: Dover Publishing Company, 1961.

Barr, Pat. *A Curious Life for a Lady.* Garden City: Doubleday, 1970.

Barzman, Sol. *The First Ladies.* New York: Cowles Book Co., 1970.

Bassett, Margaret. *Profiles and Portraits of American Presidents and Their Wives.* Freeport, Maine: The Bond Wheelwright Co., 1969.

Bateman, Newton and Paul Selby (editors). *Historical Encyclopedia of Illinois and History of Ogle County,* Vol. II. Chicago: Munsell Publishing Co., 1909.

Beach, Cora M. (editor). *Women of Wyoming.* Casper: S. E. Boyer & Co., 1927.

Beasley, Delilah L. *The Negro Trail Blazers of California.* Los Angeles: Times Mirror Printing and Binding House, 1919.

Bede, Elbert. *Fabulous Opal Whitely.* Portland: Binfords & Mort, 1954.

Belden, L. Burr. *Death Valley Heroine.* San Bernardino: Inland Printing Co., 1954.

Bell, Margaret. *Women of the Wilderness.* New York: E. P. Dutton & Co., 1938.

Bernikow, Louise (editor). *The World Split Open.* New York: Vintage Books (Random House), 1974.

Biddle, Gertrude Bosler and Sarah Dickinson Lowrie. *Notable Women of Pennsylvania.* Philadelphia: University of Pennsylvania Press, 1942.

Bigelow, Gorden E. *Frontier Eden, The Literary Career of M. K. Rawlings.* Gainesville: University of Florida Press, 1966.

Bingham, Hiram, A. M. *A Residence of Twenty-One Years in the Sandwich Islands, or, The Civil, Religious, and Political History of Those Islands.* New York: Sherman Converse, 1847.

Binheim, Max (editor). *Women of the West.* Los Angeles: Publisher's Press, 1928.

Bird, George F. and Edwin J. Taylor. *History of the City of Bismarck.* Bismarck: Bismarck Centennial Association, 1972.

Bird, Isabella. *A Lady's Life in the Rocky Mountains.* New York: Ballantine, 1960.

Bishop, Harriet E. *My Floral Home.* New York: Shelden Blakeman & Co., 1857.

Blackwell, Alice Stone. *Lucy Stone.* Norwood, Massachusetts: Alice Stone Blackwell Committee, 1930.

Boatner, Mark M., III. *Encyclopedia of the American Revolution.* New York: David McKay Co., Inc., 1974.

Bolton, Reginald Pelham. *A Woman Misunderstood—Anne, Wife of William Hutchinson.* New York, 1931. (Privately Printed.)

Booth, Sally Smith. *The Women of '76.* New York: Hastings House, 1973.

Bradburne, E. S. *Opal Whitely.* London: Putnam, 1962.

Breckenridge, Sophonisba. *Madeline McDowell Breckenridge.* Chicago: University of Chicago Press, 1921.

Britten, Norman A. *Edna St. Vincent Millay.* New York: Dwayne Publishers Inc., 1967.

Brockett, L. P. and Mary C. Vaughan. *Woman's Work in the Civil War.* Philadelphia: Zeigler, McCurdy & Co., 1867.

Brooks, Geraldine. *Dames and Daughters of Colonial Days.* New York: Thomas Y. Crowell, 1900.

Brooks, Van Wyck. *Helen Keller.* New York: E. P. Dutton, 1956.

Brown, Dee. *The Great Tamers: Women of the Old Wild West.* Lincoln: University of Nebraska Press, 1958. Paperback: Bantam Books, 1974.

Brown, E. K. *Willa Cather.* New York: Alfred A. Knopf, 1953.

Brown, Harriet Connor. *Grandmother Brown's 100 Years.* Boston: Little, Brown & Co., 1929.

Buck, Pearl. *The Exile.* New York: John Day, 1936.

Burke, John. *Duet in Diamonds.* New York: G. P. Putnam's Sons, 1972.

————. *Winged Legend: The Story of Amelia Earhart.* New York: G. P. Putnam's Sons, 1970.

Burke, Pauline. *Emily Donelson of Tennessee.* Richmond, Virginia: Garret and Massic Inc., 1941.

Cabaniss, Allen. *The University of Mississippi: Its First Hundred Years.* Hattiesburg, Mississippi: University and College Press of Mississippi, 1971.

Cameron, Mabel Ward (compiler). *Biographical Cyclopedia of American Women.* New York: Halvard Publishing Co., 1924.

Carey, Naomi. *Mountain Men to Astronauts.* Lodi: Lodi Centennial Citizens Advisory Committee, 1969.

Carleton, Hiram (editor). *Genealogical and Family History of the State of Vermont,* Vol. II. New York: Lewis Publishing Co., 1903.

Carr, James (compiler). *Mantle Fieldings Dictionary of American Painters, Sculptors and Engravers.* New York: James Carr Publishers, 1965.

Carter, Morris. *Isabella Stewart Gardner and Fenway Court.* Boston: ISG Museum, 1925.

Catt, Carrie Chapman and Nettie Rogers Shuler. *Woman Suffrage and Politics.* Seattle: University of Washington Press, 1969.

Ceram, C. W. *The First American.* New York: Harcourt Brace Jovanovich, 1971.

Chamberlain, Hope Summerall. *Old Days in Chapel Hill.* Chapel Hill: University of North Carolina Press, 1926.

Chamberlin, Hope, *A Minority of Members, Women in the U.S. Congress.* New York: Praeger, 1973.

Chesnut, Mary. *A Diary from Dixie.* New York: D. Appleton & Co., Peter Smith, 1929.

Chester, Giraud. *Embattled Maiden: The Life of Anna Dickinson.* New York: G. P. Putnam's Sons, 1951.

Chester, Laura and Sharon Barba (editors). *Rising Tides: Twentieth Century American Women Poets.* New York: Washington Square Press, 1973.

Chevigny, Hector. *Russian America, The Great Alaskan Venture 1741-1867.* New York. The Viking Press, 1965.

Clark, Sydney. *All the Best in Hawaii.* New York: Dodd, Mead & Co., 1961.

Clarke, Robert. *Elen Swallow: The Woman Who Founded Ecology.* Chicago: Follett Publishing Co., 1973.

Clayton, W. Woodford. *History of Davidson County, Tennessee.* Philadelphia: J. W. Lewis & Co., 1880.

Coffin, Levi. *Reminiscences.* New York: Augustus Kelley, 1876.

Cole, Doris. *From Tipi to Skyscraper, a History of Women in Architecture.* Boston: i press Incorporated, 1973.

Colman, Gould P. *Education and Agriculture: A History of the New York State College of Agriculture at Cornell University.* Ithaca, New York: Cornell University, 1963.

Conant, Roger. *Mercer's Belles.* Seattle: University of Washington Press, 1960.

Connelley, William. *History of Kansas,* Vol. II. Chicago: Lewis Publishing Co., 1918.

Cooper, Courtney Ryley. *Annie Oakley.* New York: Duffield & Co., 1927.

Coratheru, Alice T. *In Detroit . . . Courage Was the Fashion: The Contribution of Women to the Development of Detroit from 1701 to 1951.* Detroit: Wayne State University Press, 1953.

Cornelius, Roberta D. *The History of Randolph-Macon Woman's College.* Chapel Hill: The University of North Carolina Press, 1951.

Cott, Nancy F. (editor). *Roots of Bitterness.* New York: E. P. Dutton, 1972.

Coues, Elliott (editor). *The Manuscript Journals of Alexander Henry,* Vol. I. New York: Francis P. Harper, 1897.

Crawford, Lewis. *History of North Dakota.* Chicago and New York: The American Historical Society, Inc., 1931.

Custer, Elizabeth B. *"Boots and Saddles" or, Life in Dakota with General Custer;* with an introduction by Jane R. Stewart. Norman: University of Oklahoma Press, 1961.

————. *Following the Guidon.* Norman: University of Oklahoma Press, 1966.

————. *Tenting on the Plains, or General Custer in Kansas and Texas.* Norman: University of Oklahoma Press, 1971.

Cyclopedia of Eminent and Representative Men of the Carolinas Nineteenth Century. Madison, Wisconsin: Brant and Fuller, 1892.

Dabbs, Edith. *Face of an Island.* New York: Grossman Publisher, 1971.

Daniell, L. E. *Personnel of the Texas State Government.* San Antonio: Maverick Printing House, 1892.

Dash, Joan. *A Life of One's Own.* New York: Harper and Row, 1973.

Davenport, William W. *Fodor's Hawaii 1973.* New York: David McKay Co., Inc., 1973.

Davis, Curtis Carroll (editor). *Belle Boyd in Camp and Prison.* South Brunswick and New York: Thomas Yoseloff, 1968.

Davis, Dorothy. *History of Harrison County, West Virginia.* American Association of University Women, Parsons, West Virginia: McClain Printing Co., 1970.

Davis, George Wesley. *Sketches of Butte.* Boston: The Cornhill Company, 1921.

Davis, Jean. *Shallow Diggin's.* Caldwell, Idaho: The Caxton Printer, 1962.

Davis, Rebecca Harding. *Life in the Iron Mills.* Old Westbury, New York: The Feminist Press, 1972.

Day, A. Grove. *Hawaii and Its People.* New York: Duell, Sloan and Pearce, 1955.

——— and Carol Carl Stroven (editors). *A Hawaiian Reader.* New York: Appleton-Century Crofts, Inc., 1959.

Defenbach, Byron. *Idaho,* Vols. I, II, III. The American Historical Society, 1933.

De Gasmo, Mrs. Frank. *Pathfinders of Texas, 1836-1846.* Austin: Press of Von Boeckman-Jones Co., 1951.

Denny, Emily Inez. *Blazing the Way.* Seattle: Rainier Printing Co., 1909.

Dexter, Elisabeth Anthony. *Career Women of America.* Clifton, New Jersey: Augustus M. Kelley, 1972.

———. *Colonial Women of Affairs.* Clifton, New Jersey: Augustus M. Kelley, 1972.

Douglas, Emily Taft. *Margaret Sanger: Pioneer of the Future.* New York: Holt, Rinehart & Winston, 1970.

Douthit, Mary Osborn (editor). *The Souvenir of Western Women.* Portland: Anderson & Duniway, 1905.

Dowling, M. P., S.J. *Creighton University Reminiscences.* Omaha: Burkley Printing Co., 1903.

Drago, Henry Sinclair. *Notorious Ladies of the Frontier.* New York: Dodd, Mead & Co., 1969.

Drake, Samuel Adams. *Old Landmarks and Historic Personages of Boston.* Rutland, Vermont: Charles E. Tuttle Co., 1971.

Drinnon, Richard. *Rebel in Paradise: A Biography of Emma Goldman.* New York: Bantam, 1973.

Dryden, Cecil. *Give All to Oregon.* New York: Hastings House, 1968.

DuBroca, Isabelle. *Good Neighbor Eleanor McMain of Kingsley House.* New Orleans: Pelican Publishing Co., 1955.

Duffus, R. L. *Lillian Wald.* New York: Macmillan, 1938.

Duniway, Abigail Scott. *Path Breaking.* New York: Schocken Books, 1971.

Dunlop, Richard. *Rand McNally Vacation Guide.* Chicago: Rand McNally & Co., 1970.

Dysart, Laberta. *Chatham College: The First Ninety Years.* Pittsburgh: Chatham College, 1959.

Eagle, Mary Kavanaugh Oldham. *The Congress of Women . . . World's Columbian Exposition, Chicago, USA, 1893.* New York: W. W. Wilson, 1894.

Edgar, Betsy Jordan. *Our House.* Parsons, West Virginia: McClain Printing Co., 1965.

Edwards, Lee R. and Arlyn Diamond (editors). *American Voices, American Women.* New York: Avon Books, 1973.

Elfer, Maurice. *Madam Andrea Candelaria.* Houston: The Rein Co., 1933.

Ellet, Elizabeth F. *The Pioneer Women of the West.* Philadelphia: Porter and Coates, 1873.

———. *The Women of the American Revolution,* Vols. I, II, III. New York: Baker and Scribner, 1848.

Elzas, Dr. Barnett. *The Jews of South Carolina.* Philadelphia: J. B. Lippincott, 1905.

Faber, Doris. *The Mothers of American Presidents.* New York: New American Library, 1968.

Farmer, Margaret Pace. *History of Pike County, Alabama.* Troy, Alabama: Adwards Bros. Inc., 1950.

Fearn, Anne. *My Days of Strength.* New York: Harper and Bros., 1939.

Fetherling, Dale. *Mother Jones, The Miners' Angel.* Carbondale: Southern Illinois University Press, 1974.

Filler, Louis. *The Unknown Edwin Markham.* Yellow Springs, Ohio: The Antioch Press, 1966.

Finley, Ruth E. *The Lady of Godey's.* Philadelphia: J. B. Lippincott, 1931.

Flexner, Eleanor. *Century of Struggle.* New York: Atheneum, 1970.

Foner, Philip S. (editor). *Helen Keller: Her Socialist Years.* New York: International Publishers, 1967.

Forrester-O'Brien, Esse. *Art and Artists of Texas.* Dallas: Tardy Publishing Co., 1935.

Fortune, Jan and Jean Burton. *Elisabet Ney.* New York: Alfred A. Knopf, 1943.

Fowler, W. W. *Woman on the American Frontier.* Hartford: S. Scranton & Co., 1877.

French, Hiram T. *History of Idaho,* Vol. II. Chicago: The Lewis Publishing Co., 1914.

Gem State Author's Guide. Starlight and Syringa. Boise: Gateway Printers Inc., 1959.

Gentry, Curt. *The Dolphin Guide to San Francisco and the Bay Area.* Garden City: Doubleday, 1962, 1969.

———. *The Last Days of the Great State of California.* New York: G. P. Putnam's Sons, 1968.

———. *The Madams of San Francisco.* New York: Ballantine, 1971.

Giffin, Frederick C. (editor). *Woman as Revolutionary.* New York: New American Library, 1973.

Goode, James M. *The Outdoor Sculpture of Washington, D.C.* Washington, D.C.: Smithsonian Institution Press, 1974.

Goodsell, Charles True and Willis Frederick Dunbar. *Centennial History of Kalamazoo College.* Kalamazoo: Kalamazoo College, 1933.

Goodwin, Maud Wilder. *Dolley Madison.* New York: Charles Scribner's and Sons, 1896.

Gould, Jean. *The Poet and Her Book.* New York: Dodd, Mead & Co., 1969.

Goulianos, Joan (editor). *By a Woman Writt.* Baltimore: Penguin Books, 1974.

Graham, Jory. *Chicago, an Extraordinary Guide.* Chicago: Rand McNally & Co., 1967.

Great Historic Places. By the Editors of *American Heritage.* New York: American Heritage Publishing Co., 1973.

Green, Norma Kidd. *Iron Eye's Family: The Children of Joseph La Flesche.* Lincoln, Nebraska: Johnsen Publishing Co., 1969.

Gridley, Marion E. *American Indian Women.* New York: Hawthorn Books, 1974.

———. *America's Indian Statues.* Chicago: The Amerindian, 1966.

Griswold, Mary Hoadley. *Yester-Years of Guilford.* Guilford, Connecticut: Shore Line Times Pub. Co. Inc., 1938.

Gruening, Ernest. *The State of Alaska.* New York: Random House, 1968.

Guinn, J. M. *A History of California,* Vols. I, II, III. Los Angeles: Historical Record Co., 1915.

Gurko, Miriam. *The Ladies of Seneca Falls.* New York: Macmillan, 1974.

Hahn, Emily. *Once Upon a Pedestal.* New York: Thomas Y. Crowell Co., 1974.

Hale, Will T. *A History of Tennessee and Tennesseans.* Chicago: The Lewis Publishing Co., 1913.

Hanaford, Phebe A. *Daughters of America; or, Woman of the Century.* Augusta, Maine: True and Company, 1883.

Hansen, Kaye Welch. *Hearst San Simeon Castle.* Minneapolis: T. S. Denison, 1962.

Harper, Ida Husted. *History of Woman Suffrage,* Vols. V and VI. New York: J. J. Little & Ives Company, 1922.

——— and Susan B. Anthony. *History of Woman Suffrage,* Vol. IV. Indianapolis: The Hollenbeck Press, 1902.

Harris, Theodore F. *Pearl S. Buck.* New York: The John Day Co., 1969.

Havighurst, Walter. *Annie Oakley of the Wild West.* New York: Macmillan Co., 1954.

Haviland, Laura S. *A Woman's Life-Work, Labors and Experiences.* Chicago: Pub. Assoc. of Friends, 1889.

Hawaii, A Holiday Magazine Travel Guide. New York: Random House, 1971.

Hawk, Grace E. *Pembroke College in Brown University.* Providence: Brown University Press, 1967.

Hawthorne, Jolian. *History of Washington,* Vol. II. New York: American Historical Publishing Co., 1893.

Hays, Elinor Rice. *Those Extraordinary Blackwells.* New York: Harcourt, Brace and World, 1967.

Historic Houses of America. New York: American Heritage Publishing Co., 1971.

Holdridge, Helen. *Mammy Pleasant.* New York: Ballantine Books, 1953.

Horan, James D. *Desperate Women.* New York: Bonanza Books, 1952.

Howard, Harold P. *Sacajawea.* Norman: University of Oklahoma Press, 1971.

Howe, A. De Wolfe. *Who Lived Here?* New York: Bramhall House, 1952.

An Illustrated History of San Joaquin County, California. Chicago: Lewis Publishing Co., 1890.

Ingham, Mrs. W. A. *Women of Cleveland and Their Work*. Cleveland: W. A. Ingham, 1893.

Jackson, Grace. *Cynthia Ann Parker*. San Antonio, Texas: Naylor Co., 1959.

James, Bessie Rowland. *Anne Royall's U.S.A.* New Brunswick, New Jersey: Rutgers University Press, 1972.

James, Edward T., Janet Wilson and Paul S. Boyer (editors). *Notable American Women 1607-1950*. Cambridge: Belknap Press of Harvard University, 1971.

James, Elias Olan. *The Story of Cyrus and Susan Mills*. Stanford: Stanford University Press, 1953.

Jensen, Oliver. *The Revolt of American Women*. New York: Harcourt Brace Jovanovich, 1971.

Johannesen, Eric. *Selected Landmark Architecture of Alliance, Ohio*. Alliance: Alliance Historical Society, 1971.

Johnson, Gerald. *Mount Vernon: The Story of a Shrine*. New York: Random House, 1953.

Johnson, Mary Lynch. *A History of Meredith College*. Raleigh, North Carolina: Meredith College, 1972.

Jones, Katherine M. (editor). *Heroines of Dixie: Spring of High Hopes*. New York: Ballantine, 1974.

———. *Heroines of Dixie: Winter of Desperation*. New York: Ballantine, 1974.

Jones, Nard. *Seattle*. New York: Doubleday, 1972.

Josephson, Hannah. *The Golden Threads*. New York: Duell, Sloan and Pearce, 1949.

———. *Jeannette Rankin, First Lady in Congress*. New York: Bobbs-Merrill Co., Inc., 1974.

Kallir, Otto (editor). *Grandma Moses, American Primitive*. New York: The Dryden Press, 1946.

Kaplan, Beverly S. *Daniel and Agnes Freeman, Homesteaders*. Lincoln, Nebraska: Johnsen Publishing Co., 1971.

Keller, Helen. *Teacher*. New York: Doubleday, 1955.

Kemble, Frances Anne. *Journal of a Residence on a Georgian Plantation in 1838-1839*. Edited with an introduction by John A. Scott. New York: Alfred A. Knopf, 1961.

Kennedy, David. *Birth Control in America: the Career of Margaret Sanger*. New Haven: Yale University Press, 1970.

Kirkland, Caroline. *A New Home or Life in the Clearings*. New York: G. P. Putnam's Sons, 1953.

Kohn, August. *The Cotton Mills of South Carolina*. Charleston: Daggett Print Co., 1907.

Kolb, Carolyn. *New Orleans*. Garden City: Doubleday, 1972.

Kraditor, Aillen S. *The Ideas of the Woman Suffrage Movement 1890-1920*. Garden City: Doubleday, 1971.

———. *Up from the Pedestal*. New York: Quadrangle, 1968.

Krauss, Bob. *Bob Krauss' Travel Guide to the Hawaiian Islands*. New York: Coward-McCann, Inc., 1956, 1965–66.

Lander, Ernest McPherson. *The Textile Industry in Antebellum South Carolina*. Baton Rouge, Louisiana: Louisiana State University Press, 1969.

Larimer, Sarah. *The Capture and Escape; or, Life Among the Sioux*. Philadelphia, 1871.

Lash, Joseph. *Eleanor and Franklin*. New York: W. W. Norton & Co., 1971.

Lathrop, Elise. *Historic Houses of Early America*. New York: Tudor Publishing Co., 1946.

Laubim, Reginald and Gladys. *The Indian Tipi, Its History, Construction and Use*. Norman: University of Oklahoma, 1957.

Laufe, Abe (editor). *An Army Doctor's Wife on the Frontier*. Pittsburgh: University of Pittsburgh Press, 1962.

Lee, Bourke. *Death Valley*. New York: Ballantine, 1974.

Lee, Howard. *Bloodletting in Appalachia*. Morgantown: West Virginia University, 1969.

Leonard, Eugenie Andruss. *The Dear-Bought Heritage*. Philadelphia: University of Pennsylvania Press, 1965.

Lerner, Gerda (editor). *Black Women in White America*. New York: Pantheon, 1972.

———. *The Grimke Sisters*. New York: Schocken Books, 1971.

———. *The Woman in American History*. Menlo Park, California: Addison-Wesley Publishing Co., 1971.

Long, E. John. *America's National Monuments and Historic Sites*. Garden City: Doubleday & Co., 1960.

Lucia, Ellis. *Klondike Kate*. New York: Ballantine Books, 1972.

Lutz, Alma. *Emma Willard, Daughter of Democracy*. Boston: Houghton Mifflin, 1929.

———. *Susan B. Anthony: Rebel, Crusader, Humanitarian*. Boston: Beacon Press, 1959.

Lutz, Francis Earle. *The Prince George-Hopewell Story*. Richmond: William Byrd Press Inc., 1957.

Lyford, James Otis. *History of Canterbury*. Concord, New Hampshire: Rumford Press, 1912.

Lynes, Russell. *Good Old Modern*. New York: Atheneum, 1973.

McCarty, John L. *Maverick Town—The Story of Old Tascosa*. Norman: University of Oklahoma Press, 1946.

McDonald, Lucille and Werner Lenggenhager, *Where the Washingtonians Lived*. Seattle: Superior Publishing Co., 1969.

McGlashan, C. F. *History of the Donner Party*. Stanford, California: Stanford University Press, 1940.

McGroarty, J. S. *Los Angeles from the Mountains to the Sea*. Chicago: American Historical Society, 1921.

McGuigan, Dorothy Gies. *A Dangerous Experiment: 100 Years of Women at the University of Michigan*. Ann Arbor: Center for Continuing Education of Women, 1970.

McKay, Claude. *Harlem: Negro Metropolis*. New York: E. P. Dutton & Co., 1940.

Magoffin, Susan Shelby. *Down the Santa Fe Trail and Into Mexico*. Edited by Stella M. Drumm. New Haven and London: Yale University Press, 1962.

Marsh, Kenneth Frederick and Blanche Marsh. *The New South*. Columbus, South Carolina: R. L. Bryan Co., 1965.

Massey, Mary Elizabeth. *Bonnet Brigades*. New York: Alfred A. Knopf, 1966.

Merriam, Eve. *Growing Up Female in America*. Garden City: Doubleday, 1971.

Merrille, Arch. *Bloomers and Bugles*. New York: American Book-Stratford Press, 1958.

———. *From Pumpkin Hook to Dumpling Hill*. New York: American Book-Stratford Press, 1969.

———. *Pioneer Profile*. New York: American Book-Stratford Press, 1957.

Millard, Bailey. *History of the San Francisco Bay Region*. Chicago: American Historical Society, 1924.

Miller, Emma Gene. *Clatsop County, Oregon*. Portland: Binfords and Mort, 1957.

Miller, Joaquin. *An Illustrated History of the State of Montana*. Chicago: The Lewis Publishing Co., 1894.

Miller, Ronald Dean. *Shady Ladies of the West*. Los Angeles: Westernlore Press, 1964.

Moody, Ralph. *The Old Trails West*. New York: Thomas Y. Crowell Co., 1963.

Moore, Grace. *You're Only Human Once*. Garden City: Doubleday, Doran & Co., Inc., 1944.

Moulder, George B. *The Parthenon at Nashville, Tenn. USA*. Nashville: George B. Moulder, 1930.

Mullens, P. S., S.J. *Creighton Biographical Sketches*. Omaha: Creighton University, 1901.

Murray, Janette Stevenson and Frederick Gray Murray. *The Story of Ada Raynds*. New York: Stratford House, 1950.

National Register of Historic Places, Washington, D.C.: U.S. Dept. of Interior, National Park Service, USGPO, 1971, 1972.

National Register of Historic Places Supplement 1974. Washington, D.C.: U.S. Dept. of Interior, National Park Service, USGPO, 1974.

Neely, Ruth (editor). *Women of Ohio*. S. J. Clarke Publishing Co. (no date).

New Hampshire Women Legislators 1921-1971. Concord, New Hampshire: New Hampshire Savings Bank, 1971.

Noyes, Ethel J. R. C. *The Women of the Mayflower and Women of Plymouth Colony*. Ann Arbor: Gryphon Books, 1971.

O'Neill, William. *The Woman Movement*. New York: Quadrangle, 1971.

Owens-Adair, Dr. Bethenia. *Dr. Owens-Adair, Some of Her Life Experiences*. Portland, Oregon: Mann and Beach, 1905.

Palmer, Edwin O. *History of Hollywood*, Vol. II. Hollywood: Arthur Cowston, 1937.

Park, Maud Wood. *Front Door Lobby*. Boston: Beacon Press, 1960.

Parker, Gail (editor). *The Oven Birds*. New York: Doubleday, 1972.

Parker, Robert A. *Yankee Saint*. New York: G. P. Putnam's Sons, 1935.

Parkhill, Forbes. *The Wildest of the West*. New York: Henry Holt & Co., 1951.

Parton, James, Horace Greeley and others. *Eminent Women of the Age*. Hartford, Connecticut: S. M. Betts & Co., 1868.

Parton, Mary Field (editor). *The Autobiography of Mother Jones*. Chicago: Charles H. Kerr Publishing Co., 1974.

Patterson, Ada. *Maude Adams*. New York: Benjamin Blom, Inc., 1971.

Pember, Phoebe Yates. *A Southern Woman's Diary*. Edited by Bill Wiley. New York: Ballantine Books, 1959.

Pennington, Patience. *A Woman Rice Planter*. Cambridge: Harvard University Press, 1961.

Perkins, Mary E. *Old Houses of Ancient Town of Norwich*. Norwich, Connecticut: Press of Bulletin Co., 1895.

Peterson, Emil. *A Century of Coos and Curry.* Portland: Binfords and Mort, 1952.

Peterson, William J. *The Story of Iowa,* Vol. I. New York: Lewis Historical Publishing Co., Inc., 1952.

Poetical Works of Alice and Phoebe Cary, The. With a Memorial of their lives by Mary Clemmer. New York: Hurd and Houghton, 1876.

Prosch, Thomas. *David S. Maynard and Catherine T. Maynard.* Seattle: Lawman and Harford, 1906.

Pruitt, Olga Reed. *It Happened Here.* Holly Springs, Mississippi: South Reporter Printing Co., 1950.

Putnam, Emily Jane. *The Lady.* Chicago: University of Chicago Press, 1970.

Quarles, Benjamin. *The Negro in the American Revolution.* Chapel Hill: University of North Carolina Press, 1961.

Ranck, Glenn N. *Legends and Traditions of Northwest History.* Vancouver, Washington: American Printing and Stationery Co., 1914.

Ray, Grace Ernestine. *Wily Women of the West.* San Antonio: The Naylor Company, 1972.

Raymer, Robert George. *Montana: The Land and the People,* Vols. I, II, III. The Lewis Publishing Co., 1930.

Rice, Alice C. Hegan. *Mrs. Wiggs of the Cabbage Patch.* New York: Century Co., 1901.

Rittenhouse, Mignon. *The Amazing Nellie Bly.* New York: E. P. Dutton, 1956.

Robbins, Phyllis. *Maude Adams, An Intimate Portrait.* New York: G. P. Putnam's Sons, 1956.

Robinson, Elwyb B. *Heroes of Dakota,* Part I. Grand Forks, North Dakota: University of North Dakota, 1947.

Roger, John Williams. *The Lusty Texans of Dallas.* New York: E. P. Dutton, 1960.

Rogers, Lou. *Tar Heel Women.* Raleigh, North Carolina: Warren Publishing Co., 1949.

Ross, Ishbell. *Charmers and Cranks—Twelve Famous American Women Who Defied the Conventions.* New York: Harper & Row, 1965.

———. *Crusades and Crinolines.* New York: Harper and Row, 1963.

———. *Ladies of the Press.* New York: Harper and Row, 1936.

———. *The President's Wife, Mary Todd Lincoln.* New York: G. P. Putnam's Sons, 1973.

———. *Rebel Rose.* New York: Ballantine, 1973.

———. *Silhouette in Diamonds.* New York: Harper and Bros., 1960.

———. *Sons of Adam, Daughters of Eve.* New York: Harper and Row, 1969.

———. *The Uncrowned Queen.* New York: Harper and Row, 1972.

Ross, Nancy. *Westward the Women.* New York: Alfred A. Knopf, 1945.

Rossi, Alice S. (editor). *The Feminist Papers.* New York: Bantam, 1974.

Ruggles, Rowena Gidding. *The One Rose.* Branson, Missouri: School of the Ozarks and Shepherd of the Hills Museum, 1964.

Ruttenber, E. M. and L. H. Clark. *History of Orange County, N.Y.* Newburgh, New York: E. M. Ruttenber and Son, 1875.

St. Amand, Mary Scott. *A Balcony in Charleston.* Richmond, Virginia: Garrett & Massie, Inc., 1941.

Sammak, Dr. Emil G. and Don O. Winslow. *Dover: The First Two Hundred and Fifty Years, 1717–1967.* City of Dover, Delaware, 1967.

Sanders, Marion K. *Dorothy Thompson, A Legend in Her Time.* Boston: Houghton Mifflin Co., 1973.

Sandoz, Mari. *Hostiles and Friendlies, Selected Short Writings of Mari Sandoz.* Lincoln: University of Nebraska Press, 1959.

Sanger, Margaret. *Woman and the New Race.* New York: Brentano's, 1920.

Sargent, Shirley. *Pioneers in Petticoats.* Yosemite, California: Flying Spur Press, 1966.

Schneir, Miriam (editor). *Feminism: The Essential Historical Writings.* New York: Random House, 1972.

Scott, Anne Firor (editor). *The American Woman, Who Was She?* Englewood Cliffs, New Jersey: Prentice-Hall, Inc., 1971.

———. *The Southern Lady.* Chicago: University of Chicago Press, 1970.

Scrugham, James. *Nevada,* Vols. I, II, III. Chicago: American Historical Society, Inc., 1935.

Seaver, James E. *A Narrative of the Life of Mrs. Mary Jemison.* New York: The American Scenic and Historic Preservation Society, 1963.

Shepherd, Henry L. *Litchfield, Portrait of a Beautiful Town.* Collinsville: Guy Wilson, 1969.

Sherwood, Morgan B. (editor). *Alaska and its History.* Seattle: University of Washington Press, 1967.

Shuck, Oscar T. *History of the Bench and Bar of California.* Los Angeles: Commercial Printing House, 1901.

Silverberg, Robert. *Ghost Towns of the American West.* New York: Ballantine Books, 1968.

Simkins, Francis B. and James Welch Patton. *The Women of the Confederacy.* Richmond and New York: Garrett and Massie, Inc., 1936.

Sinclair, Andrew. *The Emancipation of the American Woman.* New York: Harper and Row, 1965.

Smith, Helen Krebs. *The Presumptuous Dreamers: A Sociological History of the Life and Times of Abigail Scott Duniway,* Vol. I (1834–1871). Lake Oswego, Oregon: Smith, Smith & Smith Publishing Co., 1974.

Smith, Helena H. *The War on Powder River.* New York: McGraw-Hill, 1966.

Smith, Page. *Daughters of the Promised Land.* Boston: Little, Brown & Co., 1970.

Snow, Edward Rowe. *Women of the Sea.* New York: Dodd, Mead & Co., 1962.

Snyder, Charles McCool. *Dr. Mary Walker.* New York: Vantage Press, 1962.

Sochen, June. *Movers and Shakers.* New York: Quadrangle, 1973.

———. *The New Woman in Greenwich Village, 1910–1920.* New York: Quadrangle, 1972.

Speer, Allan. *Black Chicago.* Chicago: University of Chicago Press, 1967.

Spruill, Julien. *Women's Life and Work in the Southern Colonies.* New York: W. W. Norton and Co., Inc., 1972.

Stanton, Elizabeth Cady. *Eighty Years and More.* New York: Schocken Books, 1971.

———, Susan B. Anthony and Matilda Joslyn Gage. *History of Woman Suffrage,* Vols. I, II, III. New York and Rochester: Fowler & Wells, Publishers, 1881, 1882, 1886.

Steadman, Melvin Lee. *Falls Church by Fence and Fireside.* Falls Church, Virginia: Falls Church Public Library, 1964.

Steegmuller, Frances (editor). *"Your Isadora."* New York: Random House and the New York Public Library, 1974.

Steele, Roberta Ingles and Andrew Lewis Ingles (editors). *The Story of Mary Draper Ingles and Son Thomas Ingles.* Radford, Virginia: Commonwealth Press, 1969.

Stember, Sol. *The Bicentennial Guide to the American Revolution.* New York: Saturday Review Press/E. P. Dutton and Co., 1974.

Stern, Madeleine B. *Purple Passage.* Norman: University of Oklahoma Press, 1953.

———. *We, the Women.* New York: Schutte Publishing Co., 1963.

Stewart, George. *Ordeal by Hunger.* New York: Pocket Books, Simon and Schuster, 1971.

Stiles, Henry R. *History of Ancient Wethersfield, Conn.* New York: Grafton Press, 1904.

Suhl, Yuri. *Ernestine Rose and the Battle for Human Rights.* New York: Reynal & Co., 1959.

Summerhayes, Martha. *Vanished Arizona, Recollections of My Army Life.* Philadelphia: J. B. Lippincott Co., 1963.

Taggard, Genevieve. *Origin: Hawaii.* Honolulu: Donald Angus, 1947.

Tardy, Anne. *Living Female Writers of the South.* Philadelphia: Claxton, Remsen and Haffelfinger, 1872.

Taylor, A. Elizabeth. *The Woman Suffrage Movement in Tennessee.* New York: Bookman Associates, 1957.

Taylor, V. F. *Davy Crockett.* San Antonio: The Naylor Co., 1955.

Temple, Sarah Blackwell Gober. *The First Hundred Years: A Short History of Cobb County in Georgia.* Atlanta: Walter W. Brown Publishing Co., 1935.

Terkel, Studs. *Giants of Jazz.* New York: Thomas Y. Crowell Co., 1957.

Tharp, Louise Hall. *The Peabody Sisters of Salem.* Boston: Little, Brown and Co., 1950.

Thompson, Erwin N. *Whitman Mission.* Washington, D.C.: National Park Service Historic Handbook Series No. 37, 1964.

Thompson, Ray. *Betsy Ross: Last of Philadelphia's Free Quakers.* Fort Washington, Pennsylvania: The Bicentennial Press, 1972.

———. *Washington at Whitemarsh: Prelude to Valley Forge.* Fort Washington, Pennsylvania: The Bicentennial Press, 1974.

Tiernan, F. C. *The Land of the Sky.* New York: D. Appleton and Co., 1876.

Underwood, Rev. J. L. *The Women of the Confederacy.* New York and Washington: The Neale Publishing Co., 1906.

von Briesn, Martha and Dorothy S. Vickery. *Sweet Briar College Seven Decades 1901–1971.* Sweet Briar, Virginia: Sweet Briar College, 1972.

Wagenknecht, Edward. *Chicago.* Norman: University of Oklahoma Press, 1964.

Waite, Frederick Clayton. *Western Reserve University Centennial History of the School of Medicine.* Cleveland: Western Reserve University Press, 1946.

Wallace, Irving. *The Twenty-Seventh Wife.* New York: New American Library, 1962.

Waller, William (editor). *Nashville in the 1890's.* Nashville: Vanderbilt University, 1970.

We, the People, The Story of the U.S. Capitol. Washington, D.C.: U.S. Capitol Historical Society in Cooperation with the National Geographic Society, 1974.

Webb, Walter Prescott (editor). *The Handbook of Texas,* Vol. II. Austin, Texas: Texas State Historical Association, 1952.

Westmore, Alphonso. *Gazetteer of the State of Missouri.* St. Louis: C. Keemle, 1837.

White, Norval and Elliot Willensky (editors). *AIA Guide to New York City.* New York: Macmillan, 1967, 1968.

White, Ruth Young (editor). *We Too Built Columbus.* Columbus: Stoneman Press, 1936.

Wickham, Gertrude Van Rensselaer. *The Pioneer Families of Cleveland 1796-1840,* Vol. II. Cleveland: The Evangelical Publishing House, 1914.

Willard, Frances E. and Mary A. Livermore. *A Woman of the Century.* Buffalo: Charles Wells Moulton, 1893.

Wilson, Dorothy Clarke. *Bright Eyes: the Story of Susette La Flesche, an Omaha Indian.* New York: McGraw-Hill, 1974.

Wister, Sarah. *Sally Wister's Journal.* Philadelphia: Ferris & Leach, 1902.

Wood, Edwin. *Historic Mackinac.* New York: Macmillan, 1918.

Woodward, Grace Steele. *Pocahontas.* Norman: University of Oklahoma Press, 1969.

Woolson, Constance Fenimore. *East Angels.* New York: Harper and Bros., 1886.

Wooten, Mattie Lloyd (editor). *Women Tell the Story of the Southwest.* San Antonio: The Naylor Co., 1940.

Wright, Bob and Kathryn. *Montana, Territory of Treasures.* Billings: The Gazette Printing Co., 1964.

Wright, Richardson. *Forgotten Ladies.* Philadelphia: J. B. Lippincott, 1928.

Yarber, Esther. *Land of the Yankee Fork.* Salt Lake City: Publishers Press, 1970.

Yates, Elizabeth. *Pebble in a Pool.* New York: E. P. Dutton, 1958.

Young, Agatha. *The Women and the Crisis.* New York: McDowell, Oblensky, 1959.

Young, Ann Eliza. *Wife No. 19.* Hartford: Dustin, Gilman and Co., 1876.

Also see the state guides of the American Guide Series of the Federal Writers' Project of the Works Progress Administration and the travel guides of the American Automobile Association and the Mobil Oil Company.

Pamphlets

"Acceptance and Unveiling of the Statue of General John Sevier." Washington, D.C.: U.S. Congress, Senate Document #101, Government Printing Office, 1932.

Adams, Mildretta. "Historic Silver City." Nampa, Idaho: Schwartz Printing Co., 1969.

Addenbrooke, Alice B. "The Mistress of the Mansion." Palo Alto: Pacific Books.

Aldous, Rea Bryant. "Caroline Howard Gilman." Charleston, South Carolina: The Archives Committee of the Woman's Alliance, 1960.

Anderson, Leon W. "Hannah Duston." Evans Printing Co., 1973.

Andrews, Edward Deming. "The Hancock Shakers." Hancock, Massachusetts: Shaker Community, Inc., 1961.

Arter, Bill. "Columbus Vignettes IV." Columbus: Nida-Eckstein Printing, Inc., 1971.

Bancroft, Caroline. "Historic Central City." Boulder: Johnson Publishing Co., 1970.

————. "Silver Queen, the Fabulous Story of Baby Doe Tabor." Boulder: Johnson Publishing Co., 1973.

————. "Six Racy Madams." Boulder: Johnson Publishing Co., 1973.

Barnett, Franklin. "Viola Jimulla, The Indian Chieftess." Prescott, Arizona: publication sponsored by Prescott Yavapai Indians, 1968.

Belden, L. Burr. "Goodbye Death Valley." Publication No. 5, Death Valley '49ers, Inc. San Bernardino: Inland Printing, Inc., 1956.

Best, Hillyer. "Julia Bulette and Other Red Light Ladies." Sparks, Nevada: Western Printing and Publishing Co., 1971.

Blair, Kay Reynolds. "Ladies of the Lamplight." Leadville: Timberline Books, 1971.

Bluemel, Elinor. "One Hundred Years of Colorado Women." Denver: published by the author, 1973.

Bonfanti, Leo. "Biographies and Legends of the New England Indians,

Volume I." Wakefield, Massachusetts: Pride Publications, Inc., 1971.

————. "The Witchcraft Hysteria of 1692." Wakefield, Massachusetts: Pride Publications, 1971.

Brent, William and Milarde. "The Hell Hole: The Yuma Prison Story." Yuma: Southwest Printers, 1962.

Caldwell, May. "Historical and Beautiful Country Homes Near Nashville, Tennessee." Nashville: 1911.

Carmichael, Virginia. "Mary Ball Washington." Woodbridge, Virginia: Mary Washington Branch of the Association for Preservation of Virginia Antiquities, 1967.

Carter, Kate B. (compiler). "Eliza R. Snow—Pioneer, 1847." Salt Lake City: Daughters of Utah Pioneers, 1974.

————. "Monuments Erected by Daughters of Utah Pioneers." Salt Lake City: Daughters of Utah Pioneers, April, 1953; September, 1953; May, 1957; April, 1962.

————. "Pioneer Women Doctors." Salt Lake City: Daughters of Utah Pioneers, 1963.

"Celia and Winnie Mae Murphree." Blant County Historical Society: 1964.

Churchill, Stephanie D. (compiler). "Utah: A Guide to 11 Tours of Historic Sites." Salt Lake City: Utah Heritage Foundation, 1972.

"Churchyard of Trinity Parish." New York: Trinity Church, 1948.

"Civil War Battlefield Parks of Virginia." Richmond: Virginia State Travel Service.

Clewes, Carolyn M. "Wheaton Through the Years, 1835-1960." Norton, Masachusetts: Wheaton College.

"Crossroads of the West." Lander, Wyoming: Crossroads of the West, Inc., 1965.

Crump, Bonnie Lela. "Carry A. Nation: Hatchet Hall." Eureka Springs, Arkansas: Echo Press, 1959.

Cunningham, John T. "Capsules of New Jersey History." Trenton: Manufacturers Insurance Co., 1974.

DePauw, Linda Grant. "Four Traditions: Women of New York During the American Revolution." Albany: New York State American Revolution Bicentennial Commission, 1974.

Edwards, Elbert. "Maude Frazier—Nevadan." Las Vegas: Southern Nevada Retired Teachers Association, 1970.

Eisensohn, Sister M. Alfreda. "Idaho Chinese Lore." Caldwell, Idaho: Caxton Printers, 1970.

Elliott, Sarah Barnwell. "Sewanee Life." Sewanee, Tennessee: Fraternities of the University of the South.

"Famous Wisconsin Women, Volumes I–IV." Madison: Women's Auxiliary, State Historical Society of Wisconsin, 1971-74.

Feitz, Leland. "Cripple Creek." Colorado Springs: Little London Press, 1967.

Finley, Louise. "Sarah Barnwell Elliott." Written for the Fortnightly Club, 1944.

"First Hundred Years: Brief Sketches of the History of the University of Richmond." Richmond: Published on the occasion of the Centennial Celebration of the University, 1932.

"Five Historic Houses." Brookline, Massachusetts: Longyear Historical Society, 1974.

Flowers, Charles Vernon. "The Fiction of Sarah Barnwell Elliott." Unpublished thesis submitted to the University of Tennessee, 1950.

Foote, Don C. and Stella. "Calamity Jane's Diary and Letters."

Force, Juliana. "Memorial Exhibition of Gertrude V. Whitney." New York: 1943.

Foreman, Carolyn Thomas. "Indian Women Chiefs." Muskogee: Hoffman Printing Co., 1954.

Fradin, Morris. "Follow the Cannon: The Story of Clara Barton." Cabin John, Maryland: See-and-Know Press. Reprinted from *Valleys of History* (Summer, 1967).

Frohman, Louis H. "The Abigail Adams Smith House."

Galland, Bess Innes. "Some Recollections of Louise Caldwell Murdock." Wichita: Wichita Art Museum, 1963.

Garwood, Ellen. "Early Austin Inns—A Study in Social Relationships." Paper delivered at the State Conference of the Texas Historical Commission. Austin: April, 1956.

" 'Gone With The Wind' and Its Author Margaret Mitchell." New York: The Macmillan Co., 1961.

Gressinger, A. W. 'Florence Tour Guide." Florence, Arizona: Pinal County Historical Society.

Hale, Laura Virginia. "Belle Boyd, Southern Spy of the Shenandoah." Sponsored by Warren Rifles Chapter, United Daughters of the Confederacy.

Halliburton, Rudia, Jr. "Northeastern's Seminary Hall." Tahlequah, Oklahoma: Oklahoma State University.

"Harriet Beecher Stowe's House." Hartford: The Stowe, Beecher, Hooker, Seymour, Day Foundation, 1970.

"Historical Handbook of Smith College." Northampton: Smith College, 1932.

"Historical Sign Program in the State of Idaho." Boise: Idaho Department of Highways, 1972.

"Historical Sketch of Rockford Seminary." Rockford, Illinois: Register Co. Printers and Readers, 1876.

"Historic Houses and Museums of New England." Boston: New England Council.

"Historic Places in the South Carolina Appalachian Region: A Survey." Greenville, South Carolina: South Carolina Appalachian Council of Governments, 1972.

Howard, Virginia. "Then and Now—Niagara Falls, N.Y., 1892–1967." Niagara Falls: Niagara Falls Area Chamber of Commerce, 1967.

Howland, William S., Norman S. Berg and Susan Myrick. "Margaret Mitchell." Atlanta: Atlanta Public Library, 1954.

Huber, Leonard V. and Samuel Wilson, Jr. "Baroness Pontalba's Buildings and the Remarkable Woman Who Built Them." New Orleans: The Friends of the Cabildo, Inc., 1964.

"In Memory of Harriet Chalmers Adams." Washington, D.C.: The Society of Woman Geographers, 1938.

"Jane Addams." Chicago: University of Illinois—Jane Addams Hull House, 1968.

Jeffrey, John Mason. "Adobe and Iron: The Story of the Arizona Territorial Prison." La Jolla: Prospect Avenue Press, 1969.

Johnson, Mary Lynch. "Elizabeth Avery Coltun: an Educational Pioneer in the South." North Carolina Division and South Atlantic Section of American Association of University Women.

Johnson, Robert Neil. "California-Nevada Ghost Town Atlas." Susanville, California: Cy Johnson & Son, 1967.

Jones, Jack M. "Early Coal Mining in Pocahontas." 1969.

Judd, Laura Fish. "Honolulu—Sketches of the Life—Social, Political and Religious." Honolulu: Honolulu Star-Bulletin, 1928.

Ke Mo Ha (Patrick Patterson). 'Woolaroc Museum." Bartlesville, Oklahoma: The Frank Phillips Foundation, Inc., 1965.

Klotz, Esther H., Harry W. Lawton and Joan H. Hall (editors). "A History of Citrus in the Riverside Area." Riverside, California: Riverside Museum Press.

Lester, Caroline F. "Mrs. Bloomer and Mrs. Stanton in Seneca Falls." *Centennial Volume of Papers of Seneca Falls Historical Society.* Seneca Falls, New York: Seneca Falls Historical Society, 1948.

Luder, Hope Elizabeth. "Women and Quakerism." Wallingford, Pennsylvania: Pendle Hill, 1974.

McCord, David. "An Acre for Education." Cambridge, Massachusetts: Radcliffe College, 1958.

McCormack, Mrs. Arthur Thomas. "Our Pioneer Heroine of Surgery—Mrs. Jane Todd Crawford." Harrodsburg, Kentucky: Daniel M. Hutton. Reprinted from *The Filson Club History Quarterly,* Vol. VI, No. 2. Louisville: April, 1932.

McCracken, Harold and Richard Frost. "The Buffalo Bill Story." Salt Lake City: Intermountain Tourist Supply.

McGill, Frederick T., Jr. "Insularity and the Isles of Shoals." Printed for members of the Isles of Shoals Association.

Martin, Mary-Paulding. "The Flag House Story." Baltimore: The Star-Spangled Banner Flag House Association, Inc.

Martinez, Raymond J. "The Immortal Margaret Haughery." New Orleans: Hope Publications.

————. "Mysterious Marie Laveau, Voodoo Queen, and Folk Tales Along the Mississippi." Jefferson, Louisiana: Hope Publications, 1956.

"The Marty Story." Marty, South Dakota: St. Paul's Indian Mission, 1954.

Mazzulla, Fred and Jo. "Brass Checks and Red Lights." Denver: published by the authors, 1966.

Merrick, Judge John J. "History of Malibu." From *The Malibu,* published by Robert Lever and James Hill.

Merritt, Evelyn B. "Arizona's First Capitol." Prescott, Arizona: Sharlot Hall Historical Society.

Mills, Bary B. and Elizabeth S. "Melrose." Natchitoches, Louisiana: The Association of Natchitoches Women for the Preservation of Historic Natchitoches, 1973.

Mims, Nancy C. *Devil in Petticoats.*

Mitchell, Rebecca Brown. Glimpses from the Life of Rebecca Brown Mitchell." Idaho Falls: Idaho Falls Public Library, 1934.

Moore, Idora McClellan. "Christmas on the Old Time Plantation." Talladega: Talladega County Historical Association, 1974.

"Nampeyo, Hopi Potter: Her Artistry and Her Legacy." Fullerton, California: Muckenthaler Cultural Center, 1974.

"Nebraska Women Through the Years, 1867–1967." Prepared under the direction of the Governor's Commission on the Status of Women. Lincoln, Nebraska: Johnsen Publishing Co., 1967.

"One Hundred Twenty-Five Years of Methodism in Keokuk." Keokuk: Keokuk Methodist Historical Societies.

Peare, Catherine Owens. "William Penn's Dream House." Reprinted for the Pennsylvania Historical and Museum Commission from the *Bucks County Traveler,* May, 1957.

"Pensacola Historic Landmarks." Pensacola: Pensacola Historic Preservation Society, 1968.

"Pioneering in Child Welfare: A History of the Iowa Child Welfare Research Station 1917–1933." Iowa City: State University of Iowa, 1933.

"Pioneer Nevada." Reno: Harolds Club, 1951, 1956.

"Pioneer—Pacesetter—Innovator: The Story of the Medical College of Pennsylvania." New York, Downington, Princeton, Portland: The Newcomen Society in North America, 1971.

"Pioneer People of Douglas and Converse County [Wyoming], 1886." July, 1962.

Pollard, Lancaster. "Lewis and Clark at Fort Clatsop." Clatsop County Historical Society: Seaside Publishing Co., 1962.

"Proceedings of the Tenth Annual Meeting of the Lake Mohonk Conference of Friends of the Indian, 1892." Ulster County: Lake Mohonk Conference, 1892.

Prock, Barbara (editor). "The Honolulu Academy of Arts: Its Origin and Founder." Honolulu: Honolulu Academy of Arts, 1967.

Rambo, Ralph. "Lady of Mystery." San Jose, California: The Rosicrucian Press, 1967.

Reid, Courtland T. "Guilford Courthouse." Washington, D.C.: National Park Service Historic Handbook Series No. 30, 1959.

Rich, Everett (compiler). "A Memorial to a Great American." Emporia, Kansas: The Teachers College Press.

Riggs, Leila Sloan (compiler). "Calico Memories of Lucy Bell Lane." (manuscript) San Bernardino, California: Glen Helen Regional Park.

Rivette, Barbara S. "Fayetteville's First Woman Voter—Matilda Joslyn Gage." Fayetteville, New York: The League of Women Voters of Fayetteville- Manlius, 1970.

Scripps, Ellen Browning. "A Sampling from Travel Letters, 1881–1883." Claremont, California: Scripps College, 1973.

Secrest, William B. "Juanita." Fresno, California: Saga-West Publishing Co.

"Seeing Providence." Publication of the Providence, Rhode Island, *Journal-Bulletin.*

Shattuck, Mary L. P. "The Story of Jewett's Bridge." Pepperell, Massachusetts: published by the author, 1964.

Sherwood, Herbert F. "The Story of Stamford." New York: The States History Co.

Sillanpa, Capt. Tom. "Annie Wittenmyer, God's Angel." Hamilton, Illinois: Hamilton Press, Inc., 1972.

Simpson-Poffenbarger, Livia. "Ann Bailey." Point Pleasant, West Virginia, 1907.

Skala, Helen and Dora Krocesky. "Leadville's Tales from the Old Timers." Leadville: published by the authors, 1972.

Smith, Bertha Jenny. "Clovernook Home and School for the Blind." Cincinnati, Ohio.

Smith, Goldie Capers. "Joanna Troutman: The Lady of Goliad." Austin: Chamber of Commerce, from the Dallas *Morning News,* Jan. 8, 1928.

Smith, Samuel Stelle. "A Molly Pitcher Chronology." Monmouth Beach, New Jersey: Philip Freneau Press, 1972.

Somerville, Mollie (compiler). "Women and the American Revolution." Washington, D.C.: National Society, Daughters of the American Revolution, 1974.

Sprague, Waldo Chamberlain. "The President John Adams and President John Quincy Adams' Birthplaces." Quincy, Massachussets: Quincy Historical Society, 1959.

"Stanford: A Man, a Woman . . . and a University." Stanford: Board of Trustees of the Leland Stanford Jr. University, Publications Service, 1962.

Stark, Dolores. "The Story of the Historic Jackson House." Colorado Springs: O'Brien Typesetting and Printing Co., 1969.

"The Story of Children's Hospital." San Francisco: Children's Hospital.

"The Story of Hannah Duston" (revised). Haverhill, Massachusetts: The Duston-Dustin Family Association, 1959.

"The Story of Mary and Her Little Lamb, as told by Mary and Her Neighbors and Friends." Sudbury, Massachusetts: Longfellow's Wayside Inn.

Swanson, Roger. "A History of the Children's Mercy Hospital." Kansas City, Missouri: The Lowell Press, 1961.

Sykes, Robert H. "Proud Heritage of West Virginia." A Bethany College Benedum Foundation—Regional American Studies Publication.

Taft, Eleanor Gholson. "The Cary Cottage." Cincinnatti.

"Tennessee Historical Markers Erected by the Tennessee Historical Commission (6th Edition). Nashville: State Historical Commission, 1972.

Thompson, Erwin N. "Shallow Grave at Waiilatpu: The Sagers' West." Portland: Oregon Historical Society, 1973.

Townsend, George Alfred. "The Entailed Hat or Patty Cannon's Times." Cambridge, Maryland: Tidewater Publishers, 1955.

Traywick, Ben T. "Tombstone's Immortals." Tombstone, Arizona: Ben T. Traywick, 1973.

"United Daughters of the Confederacy: Minutes of the . . . Annual Convention." Nashville: United Daughters of the Confederacy, 1930–1939.

Wallace, Paul A. W. "Historic Hope Lodge." Reprinted for the Pennsylvania Historical and Museum Commission from the Pennsylvania Magazine of History and Biography, Vol. LXXXVI, No. 2, April, 1962.

"War Reminiscences of Columbus, Mississippi." Compiled by Columbus Chapter, United Daughters of the Confederacy. West Point, Mississippi: Stephen D. Lee Chapter #34, U.D.C., 1961.

Weber, Carl J. (compiler). "Maine—Poets' Corner of America." Augusta, Maine: Department of Economic Development.

Weiser, Francis X., S.J. "Kateri Tekakwitha." Montreal: Kateri Center, 1971.

"White River Ute Commission Investigation." Washington, D.C.: 46th U.S. Congress, 2nd Session, House Executive Document 83, 1880.

Wilson, Robert H. "Philadelphia—Official Handbook for Visitors." Philadelphia: Independence Hall Association, 1972.

Wolcott, Robert W. "A Woman in Steel—Rebecca Lukens (1794–1854)." New York: The Newcomen Society of England, American Branch, 1949.

Wold, Gladys B. "Benicia." Benicia, California: Chamber of Commerce, 1971.

Wright, Caroline E. "Tribute to Kate Baker Curley." Unpublished address to Idaho Falls Round Table Club, April 21, 1947.

Periodicals

Adams, Sally Aldrich. "Aroostook Posy Lady." Down East XX:8 (May, 1974).

Alderson, William T. and Robert McBride (editors). "Landmarks of Tennessee History." Tennessee Historical Quarterly (1965).

And So It Began. . . . Reprint of Bulletin of Wesleyan College, 38:3 (April, 1958).

Bailey, Margaret Emerson. "Dove and Raven." Atlantic Monthly (November, 1923).

Boder, Bartlett. "Miss Mary Alicia Owen." Museum Graphic XI:3 (Summer, 1959).

———. "The Three Owen Sisters . . . Famous Scientists." Museum Graphic VIII:2 (Spring, 1956).

Braithwaite, Debra. "Double Gallows: The Potts Murder Case." The Northeastern Nevada Historical Society Quarterly IV:2 (Fall, 1973).

Branham, Bud. "Gold-Rush Mother." The Alaska Sportsman (August, 1940).

Brimlow, George. "The Life of Sarah Winnemucca." Nevada Historical Society Quarterly (June, 1952).

The Bulletin of Miss Porter's School XXI:2 (Summer, 1968; Fall, 1973).

Burnham, Howard J. "Vancouver, Washington Land Grants." Oregon History Quarterly (June, 1947).

Chavez, Fray Angelico. "Doña Tules, Her Fame and Her Funeral." El Palacio 57 (August, 1950).

Clark, J. Stanley. "Carolyn Thomas Foreman." Chronicles of Oklahoma 45 (Winter, 1967–68).

Clough, Wilson O. "Mini-Aku, Daughter of Spotted Tail." Annals of Wyoming XXXIX:2 (October, 1967).

Coates, Gladys Hall. "The Seventy-Fifth Anniversary of the Coming of Women to the University of North Carolina." University of North Carolina Alumni Review (May, 1973).

Cole, Martin. "Pio Pico Mansion: Fact, Fiction and Supposition." Journal of the West II:3 (July, 1963).

Colorado Prospector.

Confederate Veteran.

Coulter, E. Merton. "Nancy Hart, Georgia Heroine of the Revolution." Georgia Historical Quarterly XXXIX:2 (June, 1955).

Dangberg, Grace. "Carson Valley." The Carson Valley Historical Society. Minden, 1972.

DeBartolomeo, Robert. "Lydia's Sage." West Virginia State Magazine (January 16, 1972).

"Dr. and Olive Mann Isbel." The Ventura County Historical Society Quarterly I:1 (November, 1955).

Duncan, Janice K. " 'Ruth Rover'—Vindictive Falsehood or Historical Truth?" Journal of the West XII:2 (April, 1973).

Duniway, David C. "Dr. Luke A. Port, Builder of Deepwood." Marion County History X (1969–71).

"Dust on Their Petticoats." American Scene XII:1. Tulsa: Thomas Gilcrease Institute of American History and Art, 1972.

Dykshorn, Jan M. "The Verendrye Plate." South Dakota State History 1 (1973).

Earl, Phillip. "Nevada's Suffragettes Battle for the Vote," Nevada Highways and Parks (Fall, 1974).

"Eskimo Belle at Point Barrow and Her Catch," Pioneer Magazine I:1 (May, 1911).

Eyres, Lawrence E. "Ya-le-Wa-Noh (She Who Watches Over Us), Harriet Maxwell Converse." Chemung Historical Journal 3:2 (December, 1957).

Farr, Elsie S. "Pearl Rivers." Dixie Rotogravure Magazine (1951).

Fenex, Jim. "Little Ada Magill." Annals of Wyoming 43:2 (Fall, 1971).

"First Ladies of South Dakota." South Dakota State History 3:2 (Spring, 1973).

Floe, Beverly Brooks. "The Abbot Academy Heritage." The Andover Bulletin 67:2 (August, 1973).

Freeman, Anne Hobson. "Mary Munford's Fight for a College for Women Co-ordinate with the University of Virginia." Virginia Magazine of History and Biography 78 (July, 1970).

Gallaher, Ruth A. "Annie Turner Wittenmyer." Iowa Journal of History and Politics 29:4 (October, 1931).

Gilman, Isabel Ambler. "The Alaska School Service." The Granite Monthly XI:8 (August, 1916).

Graham, Eleanor. "Nashville Home of Adelicia Acklen." Tennessee Historical Quarterly 30 (1971).

Green Bay Historical Bulletin: 6:3 and 4 (July-December, 1931).

Greene, Janet. "The Woman Who Told Everything." Vermont Life (Winter, 1960).

Greve, Harriet. "The Women's Department in the University of Tennessee." Tennessee Alumnus (April, 1922).

Griffith, Vonnie Rector. "The First Woman President of the First Woman's Bank in the U.S." Ladies' Home Journal (June, 1920).

Haley, J. Evetts. "The Last Great Chief." The Shamrock (Spring, 1957).

Hall, Clarence J. "Whitesbog, New Jersey." Cranberries (February, 1939).

Hall, Robert F. "Inez Milholland, Women's Lib Leader." Adirondack Life II:1 (Winter, 1974).

Hancock, Harold B. "Mary Ann Shadd: Negro Editor, Educator, and Lawyer." Delaware History XV:3 (April, 1973).

Harkness, David James (compiler). "Legends and Lore: Southern Indians, Flowers, Holidays." The University of Tennessee Newsletter XL:2 (April, 1961).

———. "Northeastern Heroines of the American Revolution." University of Tennessee Continuing Education Series XLIX:2 (January, 1974).

———. "Southern Heroines of the American Revolution." University of Tennessee Continuing Education Series XLIX:1 (June, 1973).

Harrison, Francis Burton. "Footnotes Upon Some XVII Century Virginians." The Virginia Magazine of History and Biography L:4 (October, 1942).

Haselmayer, Louis A. "Belle A. Mansfield: August 23, 1846–August 1, 1911." Women Lawyers Journal 55:2 (Spring, 1969).

Hebard, Grace Raymond. "The First Woman Jury." The Journal of American History VII:4 (1913).

Hempstead, Alfred G. "The Legends of Jonathan Buck." Down East VIII:4 (November, 1961).

Hill, Lee. "Grave of a Southern Spy." Wisconsin Week-End (October 16, 1974).

"Historical News and Notices." Tennessee Historical Quarterly V (June, 1946) and VII (June, 1949).

"History of an Idea." Wilson College Bulletin XXXII:5 (April, 1969).

"The Hon. Alice M. Robertson." Chronicles of Oklahoma X:1 (March, 1932).

Hooker, Kenneth Ward. "A Stowe Memorial." Florida Historical Quarterly XVIII (January, 1940).

Horner, John B. "Mrs. Ella Higginson." Oregon Native Son I:5 (September, 1899).

Hulse, Dr. James and Jan Frank. "Virginia City—The Queen." Nevada Highways and Parks (Fall, 1971).

"In Memoriam." (Annie Jump Cannon.) The Telescope (May–June, 1941).

Iowa Bulletin 4:9 (September, 1924).

"Jane Long, Mother of Texas." Humble Way Magazine (May–June, 1955).

"The Jane Todd Crawford Memorial." Supplement to the Kentucky Medical Journal 33:9 (September, 1935).

Johnson, Claudius O. "George Turner Washington Territory." Oregon Historical Quarterly 44 (1943).

Journal of the Schuyler County (New York) Historical Society.

"The Kate Sessions Issue." *California Garden* 44:3 (Autumn, 1953).

Kay, Lee. "Josie Morris, Brown's Park Pioneer, Tells of Early Day History." *Vernal Express* (August 1, 1974).

Keen, Dora. "First Up Mount Blackburn." *World's Work* 27 (November, 1913).

Kieckhefer, Grace Norton. "The History of Milwaukee-Downer College 1851–1951." *Milwaukee-Downer College Bulletin* 33:2 (November, 1950).

Klamath Echoes 12 (1974), published by Klamath County, Oregon, Historical Society.

Langhorne, Elizabeth. "Nancy Langhorne Astor." *Virginia Cavalcade* (Winter, 1974).

Larson, Gustive O. "An Industrial Home for Polygamous Wives." *Utah Historical Quarterly* 38:3 (Summer, 1970).

Larson, T. A. "Dolls, Vassals, and Drudges—Pioneer Women in the West." *Western Historical Quarterly* III:1 (January, 1972).

———. "Idaho's Role in America's Woman Suffrage Crusade." *Idaho Yesterdays* 18:1 (Spring, 1974).

———. "Montana Women and the Battle for the Ballot." *Montana, the Magazine of Western History* XXIII:1 (January, 1973).

———. "The Woman's Rights Movement in Idaho." *Idaho Yesterdays* 16:1 (Spring, 1972).

Lewis, Ann E. "Martha Berry—Her Heirs and Legacies." *Georgia Magazine* X:3 (October–November, 1966).

Lewis, Naomi. "The Domestic Bard: Ella Wheeler Wilcox." *Harper's Magazine* 204:1222 (March. 1952).

Liljeblad, Dr. Sven. "Indian Peoples of Idaho." *Idaho State University Journal* (August, 1957).

McCarthy, Nancy. "Queen Ann's Revenge." *Colorado* X:2 (September–October, 1974).

McClary, Ben Harris. "Nancy Ward: The Last Beloved Woman of the Cherokees." *Tennessee Historical Quarterly* XXI:4 (December, 1962).

McCormick, John. "Was She a Bluebeard?" *The Birmingham News Magazine* (January 9, 1955).

McDonald, John J. "Vinnie Ream Hoxie at Iowa and Elsewhere." *Books at Iowa* 22 (April, 1975).

McKay, Blythe. "Margaret Mitchell in Person." *Atlanta Historical Bulletin* IX:34 (May, 1950).

Martin, George Madden. "The Dawn of Abdominal Surgery." *Kentucky Medical Journal* XI:4, Part II, Woman's Auxiliary Section (October, November, December, 1942).

"Mary Musgrove, Patriot in Petticoats." *The Joanna Way* (July, 1958).

The Mirror V:2 (Summer, 1966). Publication of Westbrook, Maine, Junior College.

"The Missionary's Daughter." *The University of Tulsa Alumni Magazine* I:4 (April, 1964).

Monroe, Mary Barr. "Pioneer Women of Dade County." *Tequesta* 9 (1949).

Morrissey, Charles T. "Green Mountain Girls." *Vermont Life* (Summer, 1973).

Morrow, Sara Sprott, "A Brief History of Theater in Nashville 1807–1970." *Tennessee Historical Quarterly* XXX:2 (Summer, 1971).

"Northeastern's Seminary Hall." *Chronicles of Oklahoma* LI:4 (Winter, 1973–74).

Nowell, Elizabeth Davis. "At Home with the Eskimos of the Far North." *The Pioneer Magazine* I:1 (May, 1911).

O'Steen, Neal. "Barbara Blount: The First Coed." *The Tennessee Alumnus* (December, 1973; Winter, 1974).

The Palimpsest XLIII:10 (October, 1962). Special edition on Spirit Lake Massacre.

"Pamela Mann." *Southwest Review:* 20 (1935)

Papez, Joseph. "The Brain of Helen H. Gardener (Alice Chenoweth Day)." *American Journal of Physical Anthropology* (October–December, 1927).

Parsons, William T. "Pennsylvania Female College." *Ursinus College Bulletin* LX:3 (Spring, 1962).

Passariello, Jo. "Trail Blazer for Women's Rights." *Bostonia* 48:3 (September, 1974).

Perkins, Angie Warren. "Report of the Dean of the Women's Department." *University of Tennessee Record* (January, 1899).

Petersen, William J. "Equal Rights for All!" *The Palimpsest* 51:1 (January, 1970).

"Phillis Wheatley Poetry Festival." *Jackson State Review* VI:1 (Summer, 1974).

Porter, Kenneth W. "Jane Barnes, First White Women in Oregon." *Oregon Historical Quarterly* 31 (1930).

Pratt, Theodore. "Zora Neale Hurston." *Florida Historical Quarterly* 40 (July, 1961).

Prucha, Francis Paul. "A 'Friend of the Indian' in Milwaukee: Mrs. O. J. Hiles and the Wisconsin Indian Association." *Historical Messenger of the Milwaukee County Historical Society* 29:3 (Autumn, 1973).

"'Queen Ann' of Brown's Park." *The Colorado Magazine* XXIX:2, 3 and 4; XXX:1 (April, July and October, 1952; January, 1953).

Reckard, Gardner Arnold. "Ella Wheeler Wilcox and the Bungalow." *The Connecticut Quarterly* 1 (1895).

Reinstedt, Randall. "The West's Greatest Stage Driver Was a Gal!" *The West* (November, 1973).

Robinson, Corinne H. "Early Days of Central College." *Faulkner Facts and Fiddlings* VIII:3 (Fall, 1966).

Robinson, Winifred J. "History of the Women's College of the University of Delaware, 1914–1938." *Delaware Notes* (1947).

Rogers, Cameron. "The Irresistable Montez." *Pictorial Review* (July, 1927).

Rolfsrud, Erling Nicolai. "The Top Drawer." *The North Dakota Teacher* (January, 1946).

Rosenberger, Homer T. "Montgomery County's Greatest Lady: Lucretia Mott." *Bulletin of Historical Society of Montgomery County* VI:2 (April, 1948).

Scott, Leslie M. "Indian Women as Food Providers." *Oregon Historical Quarterly* 42 (1941).

Sinise, Jerry. "Tascosa: Portrait of a Cowtown." *Southwest Heritage* 3 (Summer, 1967).

Skeffington, Florence V. "Report of the Dean of the Woman's Department." *University of Tennessee Record* (February, 1901).

"Sketch of the Life of Miss Hallie Quinn Brown." *A.M.E. Church Review* 6:3 (January, 1890).

Speare, Elizabeth G. "Abbie, Julia and the Cows." *American Heritage* VIII (June, 1957).

Stanley, J. A. "South Dakota's State Park." *The Pahasapa Quarterly* 10:4 (June, 1921).

Stockley, Tom. "Seattle's Woman Mayor." The Seattle *Times* (July 14, 1974).

Stutter, Boyd B. "Anne Royall—A Militant Free-lance." *The West Virginia Review* (November, 1931).

Sullivan, B. P. "Cinderella of the Comstock Lode." *True West* (December, 1956).

Taft, Bertha. "She Said She'd Walk on Water." *The Narragansett Times* (June 28, 1973).

Taggard, Genevieve. "Hawaii, Washington, Vermont." *Scribner's Magazine* (July–December, 1934).

"A Tender Tale of Love in Laurens." *The Joanna Way* (December, 1962).

Tharp, Louise Hall. "Bonnet Girls." *New England Galaxy* I:3 (Winter, 1960).

Tobias, Thomas J. "The Cemetery We Rededicate." *American Jewish Historical Quarterly* LIII:4 (June, 1964).

Townley, Carrie Miller. "Helen J. Steward: First Lady of Las Vegas." *Nevada Historical Society Quarterly* XVI:4 (Winter, 1973) and XVII:1 (Spring, 1974).

Utah Historical Quarterly 38:1 (Winter, 1970). Special issue on Women in Utah.

Walker, Alice. "In Search of Zora Neale Hurston." *Ms.* Magazine III:9 (March, 1975).

Wernick, Robert. "Glamorous Actress Found No Glamour in Georgia Slaver." *Smithsonian Magazine* (November, 1974).

"The Wesselhoeft Water-Cure." *Annals of Brattleboro.*

Western Womanhood 3:1 (July, 1896).

"What Women Are Doing in the West." *The Great West* (July, 1911).

White, Jean Bickmore. "Woman's Place Is in the Constitution: The Struggle for Equal Rights in Utah in 1895." *Utah Historical Quarterly* 42:4 (Fall, 1974).

Wi-iyohi, Bulletin of the South Dakota Historical Society (1954–1974).

"Wisconsin Historic Sites." *Badger History* XXV:2 (November, 1971).

"Wisconsin Women." *Badger History* XXII:3 (January, 1969).

Wittke, Dr. Carl F. "Dr. Marie Elizabeth Zakrewska—Class of 1856." *Voice of Reserve* (July, 1951).

"A Woman's Place." *Wellesley Alumnae Magazine* (Winter, 1974).

"Women and the American West." *Montana, the Magazine of Western History* XXIV:3 (July, 1974).

"Women in the University." *University of Tennessee Record* (December, 1905).

"Women in the University of Tennessee." *University of Tennessee Record* (March, 1898).

"Women in the West." *Journal of the West* XII:2 (April, 1973).

"Women's Idea of Woman Suffrage." *The Echo* 4:11 (March 15, 1910).

Woodward, Carl R. "A Profile in Dedication: Sarah Harris and the Fayerweather Family." *The New England Galaxy* XV:1 (Summer, 1973).

Yates, Elizabeth. "Required Reading . . ." *New Hampshire Profile* (December, 1955).

Zeidler, Frank P. "Some Women of Good Influence in Milwaukee County." *Historical Messenger of the Milwaukee County Historical Society* 29:2 and 3 (Summer, 1973).

Acknowledgments

Countless numbers of generous and able people assisted us with our research and we apologize if we have inadvertently omitted any in the list below. We wish to thank our researcher, Kate Sharp, whose skill in uncovering and cataloguing reams of information was surpassed only by her enthusiasm. Also, our deepest thanks to our editors at Bantam: Nancy Hardin, who believed in the project from the very beginning and then showed even further confidence by delivering us over to Jean Highland, our responsible and enormously supportive editor and friend.

Alabama

ATHENS: Mrs. Thomas Edwards; BIRMINGHAM: Chamber of Commerce; Catherine Lockmond; Dick Mueller; CLAYTON: Betty Caraway; W. Oates Caraway; DECATUR: Chamber of Commerce; S. Wallace Harper; FAIRHOPE: Eastern Shore Chamber of Commerce; FORT PAYNE: Elizabeth Howard; GADSDEN: Margaret Rouse; GUNTERSVILLE: Virginia Hooper Barton; Mrs. Porter Harvey; HUNTSVILLE: Huntsville-Madison County Chamber of Commerce; Bessie K. Russell; JACKSONVILLE: Larry Smith; JASPER: Chamber of Commerce; MOBILE: Historic Mobile Preservation Society; Mrs. E. S. Sledge; MONTGOMERY: Department of Archives and History (Milo B. Howard); Huntingdon College; ONEONTA: Eugene A. Maynor; RUSSELLVILLE: Kenneth R. Stuart; SPANISH FORT: Alice K. Helms; TALLADEGA: V. M. Scott; TUSCALOOSA: Marvin Harper; Tuscaloosa County Preservation Society; TUSCUMBIA: Helen Keller Property Board; WETUMPKA: Elaine Moores.

Alaska

JUNEAU: Alaska Historical Library (Jennie Riggen); Susan Stevens.

Arizona

FLORENCE: Pinal County Historical Society Museum; FORT APACHE: Fort Apache; White Mountain Apache Culture Center; KINGMAN: Kingman Area Chamber of Commerce; PHOENIX: Arizona Museum; Gaye and Sid Fillmore; PRESCOTT: Rev. Donald Watkins (Trinity Presbyterian Church); Sharlot Hall Museum; SPRINGERVILLE: White Mountain Chamber of Commerce; TEMPE: Carl T. Hayden Archive, Hayden Library, Arizona State University (Charles C. Colley); TUCSON: Arizona Historical Society; YUMA: Century House; LOS ANGELES, CALIFORNIA: Southwest Museum.

Arkansas

ALICIA: Lana Phillips; CONWAY: Faulkner County Historical Society; EUREKA SPRINGS: Louis Freund; FAYETTEVILLE: University of Arkansas (James H. Clark); Arkansas Historical Association; FORT SMITH: Chamber of Commerce; HOPE: Mrs. S. H. Smith; JONESBORO: Chamber of Commerce; LITTLE ROCK: Arkansas History Commission; Arkansas Department of Parks and Tourism; Pope County Historical Association (Elaine Weir Cia); Arkansas Historic Preservation Program (Gene Richardson); MARKED TREE: Chamber of Commerce; PINE BLUFF: Chamber of Commerce; STATE UNIVERSITY: Arkansas State University (Elizabeth G. Wittlake).

California

BERKELEY: University of California (Ray Colvig, William Roberts); BRIDGEPORT: Steven Moore; CLAREMONT: Scripps College (Helen Eisworth); COLOMA: Marshall Gold Discovery State Park (Evon G. Till); DEATH VALLEY: Death Valley Natural History Association; GRASS VALLEY: Chamber of Commerce; Ron Gallucci; HEALDSBURG: Chamber of Commerce; HEMET: The Ramona Pageant Association; HOLLYWOOD: Chamber of Commerce; JACKSON: Amador County Chamber of Commerce; LA JOLLA: Museum of Contemporary Art (Janet Larrabee); LODI: Stanley J. Matli; LOS ANGELES: El Pueblo de Los Angeles State Historic Park (Mary Louise Custer); William Hall; International Church of the Foursquare Gospel (June Kronquist); Municipal Arts Department; Mary S. Pratt; Southern California Visitors Council; Michael Kazickas; MALIBU: Serra Retreat; MINERAL: Lassen Volcanic National Park (Lewis Albert); MONTEREY: Monterey History and Art Association (Amelie Elkinton); NEVADA CITY: Nevada County Historical Society (Doris Foley); OROVILLE: Butte County Library; Ehmann Olive Company; PLEASONTON: Chamber of Commerce; RIVERSIDE: Chamber of Commerce; Mission Inn; ROUGH AND READY: Fay Dunbar; SACRAMENTO: California State Library; SAN BERNARDINO: John Scull; SAN DIEGO: Historical Collection and Title Insurance Company (Larry Booth); San Diego Floral Association; SAN FRANCISCO: California Historical Society; Children's Hospital; Kate Kennedy School; San Francisco Examiner; San Francisco Convention and Visitors Bureau (Gwynn O'Gara); San Francisco National Cemetery; SAN JACINTO: Chamber of Commerce; SANTA CLARA: Diane Malm; The University of Santa Clara (Peggy Major); SANTA PAULA: Linda Spink; STANFORD: Stanford University (Relly Weiner); STOCKTON: Raymond Hillman; TRUCKEE: Donner Memorial State Park (Judy Kelso); UPLAND: Chamber of Commerce; VENTURA: Ventura County Historical Society; WATSONVILLE: Mrs. Monte Lewis; WEST COVINA: Chamber of Commerce; WHITTIER: Claudia Moiseve, Whittier Historical Society (Claire Redford); YOSEMITE: Shirley Sargent; YREKA: Siskiyou County Historical Society (Eleanor Brown); Mrs. Norman Cooley; WASHINGTON, D.C.: National Geographic Society (Newton Blakeslee); The Society of Woman Geographers (Helen Loerke); NEW YORK, N.Y.: Joan Whitman; SCARSDALE, N.Y.: Carol Schneider.

Colorado

AURORA: Colorado Prospector (Elaine Steele); BOULDER: Boulder Historical Society; COLORADO SPRINGS: Chamber of Commerce; Colorado Springs Fine Arts Center; Pioneers Museum; CREEDE: John LaFont; CRIPPLE CREEK: Cripple Creek District Museum (Dayton M. Lummis, Jr.); The Old Homestead; DENVER: Colorado State Museum; Molly Brown House; Emily Griffith Opportunity School; Western History Collection, Denver Public Library; Rocky Mountain News; Historic Denver, Inc.; Colorado Department of Health; National Jewish Hospital and Research Center (Dave Martin); ESTES PARK: Elaine A. Hostmark; FAIRPLAY: Chamber of Commerce; FORT COLLINS: Fort Collins Pioneer Museum; GREELEY: Greeley Museums (Florence Clark); LAMAR: Chamber of Commerce; MONTROSE: Ute Indian Museum; SYRACUSE, N.Y.: Maxwell Brace.

Connecticut

BRANFORD: Chamber of Commerce; BRIDGEPORT: Bridgeport Public Library; FAIRFIELD: Fairfield Historical Society (Charlotte Amelung); FARMINGTON: Miss Porter's School; GLASTONBURY: Catherine Bagdon; GUILFORD: Mrs. E. P. Hubbell, Edith B. Nettleton; HARTFORD: Antiquarian and Landmarks Society (Mrs. G. P. Burgess); Connecticut Historical Commission (Richard Kuns); Connecticut Historical Society (T. R. Harlow, Melanchton W. Jacobus); Edmond Tofeldt; HIGGANUM: T. C. Dunham; LEBANON: Mary Barlow; LITCHFIELD: Litchfield Historical Society (L. Ford Ballard); MERIDEN: Cecilia Caneschi; Greater Meriden Chamber of Commerce; Meriden Historical Society (Bernice Morehouse); NEW HAVEN: Albertus Magnus College; New Haven City Burial Ground; New Haven Colony Historical Society; Troup Middle School (W. R. Beatty); Yale University (George Vaill); NEW LONDON: New London County Historical Society (Elizabeth Knox); Elizabeth Whitten; NORWALK: Norwalk Historical Society (Mr. Harold Martin); NORWICH: Elvira Jordan; Society of Founders of Norwich, Inc. (Philip A. Johnson); OLD LYME: Lyme Historical Society (Ann Smith); PLEASANT VALLEY: A. Carl Stamm; STAMFORD: Thomas Kemp; STONINGTON: Stonington Historical Society (Roger Williams); WATERBURY: Rosemarie A. D. Chiara; Silas Bronson Library; WESTPORT: Westport Public Library (E. Ruth Adams); WETHERSFIELD: Wethersfield Historical Society (Ronna Reynolds); Wethersfield Public Library (Marjorie Buck); NEW YORK, N.Y.: Joe McCusker; John and Liz Wheeler.

Delaware

DOVER: Dover Public Library (Delma H. Batton); State Division of Historical and Cultural Affairs; Delaware State Visitors Service; George B. Carroll, Sr.; Wesley College (Ethelwyn Worden); LEWES: Virginia Layton Orr; MILFORD: Milford Historical Society (Catherine Downing); NEWARK: University of Delaware (John M. Clayton, Jr.); WILMINGTON: Historical Society of Delaware; Emily P. Bissell Hospital; NEW YORK, N.Y.: American Lung Association.

District of Columbia

Architect of the Capitol; Library of Congress; National Woman's Party (Elizabeth Chittick); Smithsonian Institution; Washington Cathedral; The American National Red Cross (Edwin H. Powers); Moorland-Spingarn Research Center, Howard University; Washington College of Law (Office of Alumni Affairs); Trinity College; National Society, Daughters of the American Revolution; Congressional Cemetery (Fritz Lehman); Ann Blackman; Mike Putzel.

Florida

APALACHICOLA: John Gotrie Statue Museum (Charles A. Browne); DAYTONA BEACH: Bethune-Cookman College; FERNANDINA BEACH: Chamber of Commerce; FORT GEORGE ISLAND: Kingsley Plantation State Historic Site (Mrs. Frances Duncan); FORT PIERCE: St. Lucie-Okeechobee Regional Library; GAINESVILLE: University of Florida; HAWTHORNE: Marjorie Kinnan Rawlings State Museum; JACKSONVILLE: Dena Snodgrass; MIAMI: Dade County Aviation Department, Miami International Airport; Historical Association of Southern Florida; Miami-Metro News Bureau; PENSACOLA: Pensacola Historical Society; ST. AUGUSTINE: St. Augustine Historical Society; TALLAHASSEE: Chamber of Commerce; State Division of Archives, History and Records; TAMPA: Florida Historical Society; Tampa-Hillsborough County Public Library System; WINTER PARK: Rollins College (George E. Larsen); GREENWICH, CONN.: Joseph P. Kazickas.

Georgia

ANDERSONVILLE: Andersonville National Historic Site; ATHENS: Chamber of Commerce; Athens-Clarke Heritage Foundation, Inc.; University of Georgia (Jan H. Collins); Mrs. J. Lund; ATLANTA: State Department of Archives and History; Atlanta Historical Society; Georgia Historical Commission; Georgia Institute of Technology (Library); Atlanta Public Library (Margaret Mitchell Room); BRUNS-WICK: Brunswick-Golden Isles Chamber of Commerce; CARTERS-VILLE: Chamber of Commerce; Mrs. John F. Collins, Jr.; COLUMBUS: Historic Columbus Foundation; Confederate Naval Museum; Bradley Memorial Library; FAYETTEVILLE: Margaret Mitchell Library; HART-WELL: Chamber of Commerce; LA GRANGE: Chamber of Commerce; MACON: Middle Georgia Historical Society (John J. McKay, Jr.); Wesleyan College; MARIETTA: Cobb County Chamber of Commerce; MOUNT BERRY: Martha Berry Museum and Art Gallery; ROYSTON: Victoria Bryant State Park; SAVANNAH: Juliette Gordon Low Birth-place; Colonial Dames of America; SEA ISLAND: The Cloister; TOCCOA: Chamber of Commerce; WASHINGTON: Wilkes-Taliaferro-Greene Regional Library; Wilkes County Chamber of Commerce; NEW YORK, N.Y.: Girl Scouts of the U.S.A.

Hawaii

HILO: Hawaii Volcanoes National Park; Hawaii Visitors Bureau; HONAUNAU: City of Refuge National Park; HONOLULU: Department of Land and Natural Resources, State Parks Division; Daughters of Hawaii; Hawaii Visitors Bureau; Honolulu Academy of Arts; Bernice P. Bishop Museum; Kamehameha Schools; Pat Kelley Shearer; State Archives (Agnes C. Conrad); Queen Emma Summer Palace; Queen Liliuokalani Children's Center; The Queen's Medical Center; Rev. Abraham K. Akaka, Kawaiahao Church; KAILUA: Hotel King Kame-hameha; LIHUE: Coco Palms Resort Hotel (Grace Buscher Gus-lander); WAILUKU: Hawaii Visitors Bureau.

Idaho

BOISE: Idaho State Historical Society (James Davis); State of Idaho Division of Tourism (Dorine Goertzen); CLAYTON: Dan Pence; COEUR D'ALENE: Museum of North Idaho (Carl Kruger); COTTON-WOOD: Sister Mary Alfreda; IDAHO FALLS: Idaho Falls Public Library (Noreen Aboutok); Mr. and Mrs. Mac McAndrew; LEWISTON: Luna House Historical Society (Toni Earl); MERIDIAN: Ira W. Kistler; MOUNTAIN HOME: A. Hicks; MURPHY: Owyhee County Historical Complex (Julie Hyselop); OSBURN: Donald Springer; PRESTON: Preston Carnegie Library; Mrs. Vera Nelson; SALMON: Salmon National Forest (Ronald Averill); Lemhi Historical Society (Rose Carum); TWIN FALLS: Twin Falls Public Library (Elaine Nesbitt).

Illinois

ALTON: Chamber of Commerce; ANDOVER: Andover Historical Society; AURORA: Aurora Historical Museum; CHARLESTON: Sally Lincoln Chapter, D.A.R.; CHICAGO: Chicago Historical Society; Alfreda Duster; Jane Addams Hull House (Mary Ann Johnson); Palmer Estates (William B. Colvin); Provident Hospital; University of Chicago; Visitors Bureau; CRETE: Chicago Heights Historical Society; EVANSTON: National Woman's Christian Temperance Union (Grace Storer); Evanston Historical Society; FOREST PARK: Forest Home Cemetery; FREEPORT: Stephenson County Historical Society Museum (Frances Woodhouse); GALESBURG: Chamber of Commerce; Gales-burg Public Library (Kathleen M. Ferrer); Knox College; GODFREY: Monticello College Foundation; HARVEY: Thornton Township Histori-cal Society (Karl Treen); JACKSONVILLE: Jacksonville State Hospital (Lois E. Wells); Illinois College; JOLIET: Chamber of Commerce; LOCKPORT: Will County Historical Society; MENDOTA: Jessica Nashold, The Mendota *Reporter;* NAUVOO: Joseph Smith Historic Center (Kenneth Stobaugh); OREGON: Ogle County Historical Society (Donald Black); PARK RIDGE: Park Ridge School for Girls; PEORIA: Peoria Historical Society (Mrs. E. Neal Claussen); PETERSBURG: Chamber of Commerce; ROCKFORD: Rockford College; SOUTH HOLLAND: South Suburban Genealogical and Historical Society (Edith Degenhart); SPRINGFIELD: State Historical Library; Lincoln Home National Historic Site; URBANA: University of Illinois at Urbana-Champaign; VANDALIA: Vandalia Historical Society; WILMETTE: Wilmette-Kenilworth Chamber of Commerce.

Indiana

BEECH GROVE: Lloyd Bolton Mann, Jr.; EVANSVILLE: Deaconess Hospital; Evansville Public Library; GREENCASTLE: DePauw Uni-versity; GREENFIELD: Riley Old Home Society; INDIANAPOLIS: Indiana Historical Society and Library; Indiana State Museum; Indianapolis Propylaeum; Madame C. J. Walker Manufacturing Com-pany; LAFAYETTE: Spring Vale Cemetery; Tippecanoe County His-torical Association; LINCOLN CITY: Lincoln Boyhood National Memorial; NEW HARMONY: New Harmony Tourist Council; NORTH VERNON: Jennings County Public Library (Edna Hyder); RICHMOND: Chamber of Commerce; Earlham College; ROCKPORT: Lincoln

Pioneer Village; SULLIVAN: Sullivan County Public Library; TERRE HAUTE: Vigo County Historical Society; VEVAY: Switzerland County Public Library; VINCENNES: George Rogers Clark National Historic Park (Robert L. Lagemann); WEST LAFAYETTE: Purdue University.

Iowa

AMANA: Amana Society; AMES: Iowa State University; ARNOLDS PARK: Iowa Great Lakes Area Chamber of Commerce; BURLINGTON: Burlington Public Library; CEDAR FALLS: Cedar Falls Public Library; CEDAR RAPIDS: Dave Kirkpatrick and Bill Lenway; Linn County Heritage Society; CHARLES CITY: Chamber of Commerce; Floyd County Historical Society; CLARINDA: Chamber of Commerce; CLINTON: Doris N. Pilgram; COUNCIL BLUFFS: Katherine Schlott; DAVENPORT: Putnam Museum; DES MOINES: Annals of Iowa; Iowa State Department of History and Archives; FAIRFIELD: Ben J. Taylor (Jefferson County Historical Society); FORT MADISON: Thelma and S. T. Shepherd; IOWA CITY: Old Capitol Restoration Committee; State Historical Society; University of Iowa; KEOKUK: William L. Talbot; Merlin J. Ackerson (Trinity United Methodist Church); LE MARS: Chamber of Commerce; MOUNT PLEASANT: Thomas W. Clayton (Iowa Wesleyan College); NEWTON: Maytag Company; Newton Public Library; SIGOURNEY: District Court Clerk; SIOUX CITY: Sioux City Public Library; WAPELLO: Louisa County Historical Society.

Kansas

ARGONIA: Argonia & West Sumner County Historical Society (Grace Handy and Ruth Harper); ATCHISON: Chamber of Commerce; Paul and Winney Allingham; CHANUTE: Martin & Osa Johnson Safari Museum (John C. Awald); DELPHOS: State Bank of Delphos; EMPORIA: Chamber of Commerce; Emporia *Gazette;* FORT RILEY: U.S. Cavalry Museum (Henry B. Davis, Jr.); GIRARD: Henry Haldeman; Chamber of Commerce; HAYS: Hays Public Library (Dorothy Richards); Mrs. Douglas Philip; HIAWATHA: Keith M. Brock; INDE-PENDENCE: Chamber of Commerce; KANSAS CITY: Chamber of Commerce; LIBERAL: Coronado Museum; MEDICINE LODGE: Mr. and Mrs. John N. Ford; PITTSBURG: Kansas State College (Gene DeGruson); ST. PAUL: Fr. Wilfrid Flanery, Saint Francis Church; TOPEKA: Kansas State Historical Society; WICHITA: Wichita Art Museum; Wichita Public Library; WASHINGTON, D.C.: Supreme Court of the United States (Edward G. Hudon); ROSWELL, GA.: Alice De-Loach.

Kentucky

DANVILLE: McDowell House and Apothecary Shop; FRANKFORT: Department of Public Information; GREENSBURG: Sam W. Moore, Green County Historical Society; HARRODSBURG: Old Fort Harrod State Park; HINDMAN: Hindman Settlement School; LANCASTER: Nancy S. Little; LESLIE COUNTY: Frontier Nursing Service; LEXING-TON: Henry Clay Memorial Foundation; Rita R. Allen; Bettye Lee Mastin, Lexington *Herald-Leader;* University of Kentucky; LONDON: Sue Bennett College; LOUISVILLE: Cave Hill Cemetery; Chamber of Commerce; Louisville Visitors Bureau; PARIS: Duncan Tavern Historic Center; PEWEE VALLEY: Vivien Hoskins Reinhardt; PIPPA PASSES: Alice Lloyd College; RICHMOND: White Hall State Shrine (Jouette Walters); SPRINGFIELD: Chamber of Commerce.

Louisiana

BATON ROUGE: Louisiana State Library; State Tourist Development Commission; CLOUTIERVILLE: Bayou Folk Museum (Mildred L. McCoy); LAKE CHARLES: Blair Foster Clark; Imperial Calcasieu Museum; MONROE: Chamber of Commerce; Sherry Freeland Walker; Better Business Bureau; NATCHITOCHES: Robert DeBlieux; Joseph M. Henry, Jr.; NEW ORLEANS: Louisiana State Museum; New Orleans Public Library; Sara Mayo Hospital; Tulane University; Metairie Cemetery Association (Henri A. Gandolfo); Ursuline Academy; Stuart H. Brehn, Jr.; Sewerage and Water Board of New Orleans; Old Town Praline and Novelty Shop; Voodo Museum; Albert D'Orlando (First Unitarian Church); ST. MARTINVILLE: City of St. Martinville; Acadian House Museum; NEW YORK, N.Y.: Dee Wedemeyer.

Maine

AUGUSTA: Lipman Brothers, Inc. (Norman Vear); BANGOR: Bangor Historical Society; BAR MILLS: Olive W. Hannaford; BRUNSWICK: Stowe House; Pejepscot Historical Society; CAMDEN: Whitehall Inn; DOVER-FOXCROFT: Madelyn C. Betts; ELLSWORTH: Stanwood Wild-life Foundation (Chandler S. Richmond); FARMINGTON FALLS: Ben Stinchfield, Nordica Association; GARDINER: John Richards; KENNEBUNKPORT: Kennebunkport Historical Society (Joyce Butler); KITTERY POINT: Dorothy Corey; Rosamond Thaxter; NORRIDGE-WOCK: Chamber of Commerce; POLAND SPRING: United Society of Shakers, Sabbathday Lake; PORTLAND: Westbrook College (Dorothy Healy); Maine Historical Society; ROCKLAND: Chamber of Commerce; SOUTH BERWICK: Jewett House; THOMASTON: Gertrude N. Rowe; WATERFORD: Margaret M. Sawyer; WINTHROP: Town Office;

BOSTON, MASS.: Barbara E. Jornensen, Star Island Corporation; EXETER, N.H.: Exeter Historical Society (Nancy C. Merrill); SHORT HILLS, N.J.: Frederick T. McGill, Jr.

Maryland

ANNAPOLIS: Historic Annapolis Inc. (Norma Groverman); BALTIMORE: Maryland Historical Society (Romaine Somerville); S. A. Lauver; The Star Spangled Banner Flag House; The Peale Museum (Paul Amelia); Commission for Historical and Architectural Preservation (Barbara Hoff); Eastern High School (Betty Williams); The Johns Hopkins University (Kathryn Jacob); Enoch Pratt Free Library (Morgan Pritchett); DENTON: Caroline County Public Library; Dr. Christian Snyder; EASTON: The Talbot County Free Library (Mary Starin); ELKTON: Cecil County Library (Linda Brammer); ELLICOTT CITY: Patapsco Middle School (Peter McIntosh); Howard County Historical Society (Anita Cushing); EMMITSBURG: St. Joseph's Provincial House (Mrs. Valli Ryan); FREDERICK: Barbara Fritchie Museum; Mr. and Mrs. Ray Grudois; GLEN ECHO: Clara Barton House (Ruth Bonzer); HAGERSTOWN: Washington County Historical Society (Howard Spessard); LADIESBURG: Ethel V. Sharrer; LEONARDTOWN: St. Mary's County Economic Development Committee (Arthur Briscoe); MIDDLETOWN: George Roderick; ST. MARY'S CITY: St. Mary's City Commission (Mary C. Barber); SHARPSBURG: Antietam National Battlefield Site (A. W. Anderson); SMITHSBURG: Smithsburg Library (Marie Funk); STEVENSON: The Alumnae Association of St. Timothy's School (Marion Jervey); TOWSON: Hampton National Historic Site (John Franklin Miller); WESTMINSTER: Historical Society of Carroll County; NEW YORK, N.Y.: John Wheeler.

Massachusetts

ADAMS: Chamber of Commerce (Clarence R. Scott); ANDOVER: Andover Phillips Academy; BOSTON: Isabella Stewart Gardner Museum; New England Historic Genealogical Society; The Boston Athenaeum; Boston University; Margaret and Diarmaid Douglas-Hamilton; Ellen Goodman; BROOKLINE: Longyear Historical Society; BUCKLAND: Buckland Historical Society; CAMBRIDGE: Mount Auburn Cemetery; Lyle G. Boyd; University Archives, Harvard University Library; Mount Auburn Hospital; Massachusetts Institute of Technology; Radcliffe College; Schlesinger Library; DANVERS: Danvers Archival Center; DORCHESTER: Dorchester Historical Society; DUXBURY: Alden Kindred of America, Inc.; EVERETT: Woodlawn Cemetery; FALL RIVER: Fall River Historical Society; FALMOUTH: Falmouth Historical Society; FRAMINGHAM: Framingham Historical Society (Stephen D. Pratt); GARDNER: Chamber of Commerce; GLOUCESTER: Sargent-Murray-Gilman-Hough House (Helen M. Farnum); GROTON: Groton Historical Society; HAMILTON: Janice E. Pulsifer; HANCOCK: Shaker Community, Inc.; HAVERHILL: Dr. Arnold P. George; Haverhill Historical Society; HINGHAM: Julian C. Loring; LENOX: Foxhollow School; LOWELL: Lowell Historical Society; Lowell Technological Institute (Martha Mayo); LYNN: Lynn Historical Society; MEDFORD: Medford Public Library; NANTUCKET: Nantucket Maria Mitchell Association; Nantucket Historical Association; NORTHAMPTON: Smith College; The Clarke School for the Deaf; NORTH ANDOVER: North Andover Historical Society; NORTH WEYMOUTH: Abigail Adams House; NORTON: Wheaton College; PEPPERELL: Beatrice Parker; PLYMOUTH: Plymouth Antiquarian Society; QUINCY: John Quincy Adams Birthplace; REHOBOTH: Robert S. Trim; ROXBURY: Dimock Community Health Center; SALEM: Salem Witch Museum; Essex Institute; SOUTH HADLEY: Mount Holyoke College; STOUGHTON: Stoughton Historical Society (Edward N. Meserve); TAUNTON: Old Colony Historical Society; WATERTOWN: Perkins School for the Blind; Watertown Free Public Library; Historical Society of Watertown; WAYLAND: Wayland Historical Commission (Helen F. Emery); WELLESLEY: Wellesley College; Mary R. Lefkowitz; WEST BROOKFIELD: West Brookfield Historical Commission (Archie Jay); WESTFIELD: Western Hampden Historical Society; WEST ROXBURY: West Roxbury Historical Society; WESTWOOD: Chamber of Commerce; Allen Baker; WORCESTER: Worcester Historical Society; Rural Cemetery; KANSAS CITY, MO.: American Nurses' Association.

Michigan

ADRIAN: Adrian Public Library; ANN ARBOR: Historical Society of Michigan; BATTLE CREEK: Kimball House Museum; Willard Library; Battle Creek Seventh-Day Adventist Tabernacle (Mark L. Bovee); BEAR LAKE: Virginia Stroemel; BIG RAPIDS: Mecosta County Historical Society (Marie Brophy); DEARBORN: Dearborn Historical Museum; DETROIT: Detroit Public Library (Burton Historical Collection); Detroit Historical Commission; The Merrill-Palmer Institute; Mariners' Church; Pewabic Pottery (Roger Ault); Wayne State University; GRAND RAPIDS: Grand Rapids Historical Society; Elaine Smith; Ruth L. Evans; Woodlawn Cemetery; Ladies Literary Club; HOWELL: Livingston County Historical Society; JACKSON: Ella Sharp Museum; Margaret Tinkham; KALAMAZOO: Ladies Library Association; Kalamazoo College; Chamber of Commerce; Kalamazoo Public

Museum; LANSING: Department of Education, State Library Services; Department of Natural Resources, Mackinac Island State Park Commission; Michigan History Division, Michigan Department of State; Jack T. Crosby; LITCHFIELD: Chamber of Commerce; MANISTEE: Manistee Bank and Trust Co.; PONTIAC: Gertrude Miller-Long; PORT HURON: Museum of Arts and History; North American Benefit Association; REED CITY: Osceola County Historical Society; YPSILANTI: Ypsilanti Historical Museum.

Minnesota

AUSTIN: Mower County Historical Society; DETROIT LAKES: Becker County Historical Society; FERGUS FALLS: Otter Tail County Historical Society; HUTCHINSON: McLeod County Historical Society; MINNEAPOLIS: Hennepin County Historical Society and Museum; University of Minnesota; General Mills, Inc.; Minneapolis Park and Recreation Board; NEW ULM: Brown County Historical Society Museum; NORTHFIELD: R. R. Warn; OWATONNA: Chamber of Commerce; PIPESTONE: Pipestone National Monument; RED WING: Goodhue County Historical Society; Chamber of Commerce; ROCHESTER: Olmsted County Historical Society; Mrs. Robert W. Morrein; ST. CLOUD: St. Cloud State College; ST. PAUL: Minnesota Historical Society; ST. PETER: Niccolet County Historical Society; SPRING VALLEY: Spring Valley Community Historical Society (M. J. Dathe); WILLMAR: Kandiyohi County Historical Society; WINONA: Winona Heritage Association; Winona County Historical Society, Inc.; College of St. Teresa; NEW YORK, N.Y.: Nancy Smith Bate.

Mississippi

ABERDEEN: Patsy Clark Pace; Evans Memorial Library (Lucille Peacock); BILOXI: Jefferson Davis Shrine (William Stigler); Visitors Bureau; CALHOUN CITY: Claude Johnson; CANTON: Madison County Library; CLEVELAND: William Cash; Lucy Somerville Howorth; CLINTON: Mississippi Baptist Historical Commission (R. A. McLemore); Jimmy Hartfield; COLUMBUS: Columbus and Lowndes County Historical Society (Mrs. George Hazard); Historic Columbus, Inc.; Mississippi University for Women (Gerald Weaver, Margaret Henry); GREENVILLE: G. F. Archer; Mary L. Merideth; GRENADA: Elizabeth Jones Library (Ann H. Manscoe); GULFPORT: Gulfport Area Chamber of Commerce; Mr. M. James Stevens; HOLLY SPRINGS: Marshall County Historical Society (Mrs. John Williamson); JACKSON: Jackson State College (Rubye Hughes); Mississippi State Department of Archives and History (Carl A. Ray, Michelle Hudson); MERIDIAN: Meridian Public Library; Rose Hill-Magnolia Cemetery Association (Ralph Lewis); NATCHEZ: Natchez-Adams County Chamber of Commerce; Mrs. A. C. Tipton, Sr.; OXFORD: Oxford-Lafayette County Chamber of Commerce; PASS CHRISTIAN: Chamber of Commerce; PICAYUNE: Chamber of Commerce; PORT GIBSON: Port Gibson-Claiborne County Chamber of Commerce; Elizabeth S. McLendon; RED BANKS: Marie Jenkins; TUPELO: North Mississippi Methodist Historical Society (J. W. Carroll); UNIVERSITY: The University of Mississippi (Edward Moore); VICKSBURG: Historical Society of Vicksburg (Anne G. McGuffee); WASHINGTON: Methodist Historical Research (J. B. Cain); WINONA: Montgomery County Chamber of Commerce.

Missouri

BELTON: Chamber of Commerce; BRANSON: Shepherd of the Hills Farm; CANTON: Culver-Stockton College (Dr. T. L. Pittenger); CARTHAGE: Chamber of Commerce; COLUMBIA: State Historical Society of Missouri; EL DORADO SPRINGS: A. D. Dale; FARMINGTON: Chamber of Commerce; HANNIBAL: Becky Thatcher Book Shop; KANSAS CITY: Dr. Sterrett S. Titue; Children's Mercy Hospital; LEXINGTON: Jerre K. Cullom; MANSFIELD: Laura Ingalls Wilder Home and Museum; MARYVILLE: Northwest Missouri State University; ST. CHARLES: St. Charles County Historical Society; The Lindenwood Colleges; STE. GENEVIEVE: Foundation for Restoration of Ste. Genevieve, Inc.; ST. JAMES: Alice Smallwood; ST. JOSEPH: St. Joseph Historical Society; ST. LOUIS: The Principia; Convention and Tourist Board; Jefferson National Expansion Memorial; Missouri Historical Society; Bellefontaine Cemetery Association; The Mercantile Library; St. Louis Public Schools; Washington University School of Law; Maryville College; WARRENSBURG: Mildred Adams.

Montana

ANACONDA: Jerry Biggs; BILLINGS: Billings Public Library (Myrtle Cooper); Frank Quinn; Western Heritage Center (Thomas Posey); BOZEMAN: Dr. R. C. Bellingham; Montana State University Library (Minnie Paugh); CASCADE: Murry S. Moore; EKALAKA: Chamber of Commerce; GREAT FALLS: Great Falls Public Library (Kay H. Courtnage); HELENA: Montana Historical Society (Marriet C. Meloy); Montana Travel Publicity (Lois McBride); Gordon Warren; LEWISTON: Chamber of Commerce; Central Montana Historical Association (Bobbie Deal); LIVINGSTON: Livingston Public Library; PLENTYWOOD: Sheridan County Historical Association; TEIGEN: Ann Teigen; THREE FORKS: William Davis; VIRGINIA CITY: Harvey Romey;

WHITE SULPHUR SPRINGS: Jean B. Ellison; WASHINGTON, D.C.: The Anacostia Neighborhood Museum (Carolyn Margolis); FAIRFAX, VA.; Joyce Litz.

Nebraska

BEATRICE: Ruth Schleif; Homestead National Monument; ELMWOOD: Village Clerk (Sandra Leroy); GORDON: Caroline Sandoz Pifer; GRAND ISLAND: Charlotte E. Abbott; Edith Abbott Memorial Library; Grand Island Public Library; HASTINGS: Dorothy Weyer Creigh; Adams County Historical Society; LINCOLN: Nebraska State Historical Society; Norma Kidd Green; First-Plymouth Congregational Church; Governor's Commission on the Status of Women; Wyuka Cemetery; OMAHA: Omaha Public Library; Joslyn Art Museum Library; Creighton University; Prospect Hill Cemetery Association (W. T. Fuller); RED CLOUD: Willa Cather Pioneer Memorial and Educational Foundation; WALTHILL: Marguerite D. Langenberg.

Nevada

AUSTIN: Molly Knudsen; Archie Albright; CARSON CITY: Nevada State Park System (Marshall Humphreys); Department of Highways (Frank Smyth); Bob Frank; ELKO: Northeastern Nevada Museum (Howard Hickson); Antoine Primeaux; FALLON: Churchill County Library; Helen Millward; LAS VEGAS: University of Nevada Special Collections Department (Susan Anderl); Helen J. Stewart School; The Mesquite Club; LOVELOCK: Pershing County Chamber of Commerce; MINDEN: Carson Valley Historical Society (Marie Wallis); PIOCHE: Chamber of Commerce; RENO: Getchell Library, University of Nevada (Carrie Townley); Karen Shilts; Nevada Historical Society (L. James Higgins, Jr.); Daughters of the American Colonists (Phyllis Walsh); VIRGINIA CITY: Louis Beaupre; C. E. Pollock; Neal Longshaw.

New Hampshire

CANTERBURY: Shaker Village, Inc.; CHARLESTOWN: Old Fort No. 4 Associates (Donald Galbraith); CONCORD: New Hampshire Historical Society (Arthur McAllister); DOVER: Chamber of Commerce; Dover Public Library (Alice Manock); Roland Jenkins; FARMINGTON: Roger Nutter; HAMPTON: Meeting House Green Historical Association (John M. Holman); JAFFREY: Robert A. MacCready; Evelyn Ruffle; LITTLETON: Littleton Public Library (Elsie Riley); MANCHESTER: Manchester City Library (Gerald Rice); Mrs. William L. John; MARLBOROUGH: Frost Free Library (Corrine Nash); MILFORD: Chamber of Commerce; NASHUA: Chamber of Commerce; NEWPORT: Chamber of Commerce; PETERBOROUGH: Peterborough Historical Society (Elizabeth Greenie); Jonathan W. Strong; The MacDowell Colony; PORTSMOUTH: Portsmouth Public Library (Dorothy Vaughan); RINDGE: Cathedral of the Pines Trust (Lorraine Hill); WEST SWANZY: Mrs. Clair E. Wyman; WINCHESTER: E. W. Atkins; BOSTON, MASS.: Committee on Publications, The First Church of Christ, Scientist.

New Jersey

BELLEVILLE: Chamber of Commerce; BORDENTOWN: Bordentown Historical Society; BRIDGETON: Addie Gould Lloyd; BROWNS MILLS: Conservation and Environmental Studies Center, Whitesbog; BURLINGTON: Burlington County Historical Society; Henry H. Bisbee; ELIZABETH: First Presbyterian Church; FREEHOLD: Monmouth County Historical Association; HADDONFIELD: Historical Society of Haddonfield; HILLSIDE: Evergreen Cemetery; NEWARK: New Jersey Historical Society; NEW BRUNSWICK: Douglass College; NUTLEY: Nutley Branch, U.S. Post Office; ORANGE: The Orange Public Library; PORT ELIZABETH: Port Elizabeth Free Public Library; PRINCETON: Historical Society of Princeton; SALEM: Salem County Historical Society; TRENTON: State of New Jersey, Office of the Governor; Trenton Psychiatric Hospital; State Department of Environmental Protection; The State Museum; UNION: Chamber of Commerce; UPPER MONTCLAIR: Montclair State College; WASHINGTON: Chamber of Commerce; Helen Peyrek; WAYNE: United Methodist Church; WOODBURY: Gloucester County Historical Society; NEW YORK, N.Y.: The Seeing Eye, Inc.

New Mexico

ALBUQUERQUE: Chamber of Commerce; Erna Fergusson Branch, Albuquerque Public Library; DEMING: Mary Reid; HILLSBORO: Lydia Key, Black Range Museum; Margaret Vetter; LAS CRUCES: Citizens Bank of Las Cruces; ROSWELL: Chamber of Commerce; Josephine B. Rohr; SANTA FE: Santa Fe Public Library; Museum of New Mexico; TAOS: Chamber of Commerce; DENVER, COLO.: Mountain Bell.

New York

AUBURN: Cayuga Museum of History and Art; Harriet Tubman Foundation (Rev. Guthrie Carter); AUSTERLITZ: The Millay Colony for the Arts, Inc.; BRANCHPORT: Joseph and Rena Florance; BUFFALO: Buffalo and Erie County Historical Society; CORNING: Valentine B. Pratt; ELMIRA: The Park Church; Herbert A. Wisbey, Jr. (Elmira College); Chemung County Historical Society; FISHKILL: Willa Skinner; Marion S. Land; FONDA: Fonda Tekakwitha Shrine; FREDONIA: Darwin R. Barker Library; GENEVA: Hobart College;

HERKIMER: Herkimer County Historical Society; Hazel C. Patrick; HYDE PARK: Franklin D. Roosevelt Library; HYDESVILLE: John Drummond; IRVING: Seneca Indian Historical Society; ITHACA: Cornell University (Department of Manuscripts and University Archives); JOHNSTOWN: Chamber of Commerce; John B. Knox, Knox Gelatine; Johnson Hall (Col. Charles B. Briggs); LOCKPORT: Niagara County Historical Society; MALONE; Franklin County Historical and Museum Society; MIDDLETOWN: Historical Society of Middletown and the Walkill Precinct, Inc.; Orange County Chamber of Commerce; NEW PALTZ: Lake Mohonk Mountain House; NEW ROCHELLE: Alexandra Kazickas, John Kazickas; Mr. and Mrs. Joseph K. Valiunas; NEW YORK: Henry Street Settlement; Town Hall; New York Medical College; Landmarks Preservation Commission; Bronx County Historical Society; Galerie St. Etienne; The Cooper Union; Abigail Adams Smith House; City of New York Parks, Recreation and Cultural Affairs Administration; Morris-Jumel Mansion; New York Infirmary; Lois Sherr; Betty Lane; OGDENSBURG: Remington Art Museum; OSWEGO: Oswego County Historical Society; PENN YAN: Frank Swann; POUGHKEEPSIE: Vassar College; ROCHESTER: Gleason Works; Susan B. Anthony Memorial, Inc. (Agnes and Joseph Hilbert); Rochester Historical Society (Mary Shannon); SAVANNAH: Helen Wright; SENECA FALLS: Seneca Falls Historical Society (Mrs. George Patterson); SOUTH BUTLER: Helen Gay; Earl Gay; STATEN ISLAND: Staten Island Historical Society; SYRACUSE: Onondaga County Historical Association; TROY: Russell Sage College; Emma Willard School; WATKINS GLEN: Schuyler County Historical Society; WEST POINT: U.S. Military Academy; NORTH PLAINFIELD, N.J.: George Cornwell.

North Carolina

ASHEBORO: Randolph Public Library; ASHEVILLE: Southern Highland Handicraft Guild (Carol R. Smith); Henry Colton; Biltmore Industries, Inc.; CHAPEL HILL: Roger B. Foushee; CHARLOTTE: Chamber of Commerce; Queens College; CHEROKEE: Mary Chiltoskey; CURRIE: Moores Creek National Military Park (Terry E. Maze); DURHAM: Jean Anderson; EDENTON: Historic Edenton, Inc. (Louis Hafermehl); FAISON: Virgil F. Williams; FAYETTEVILLE: Chamber of Commerce; GOLDSBORO: Chamber of Commerce; GREENSBORO: Greensboro College; Guilford Courthouse National Military Park (Donald Long); Guilford College; Greensboro Historical Museum (William J. Moore); HENDERSONVILLE: Chamber of Commerce; HIGH POINT: Mary Browning; HILLSBOROUGH: Historical Society of Hillsborough; MAGGIE: Maggie Valley Chamber of Commerce; MANTEO: Dare County Tourist Bureau; Cape Hatteras National Seashore (Norman Messinger); MOCKSVILLE: Mocksville-Davie Chamber of Commerce; MOUNT OLIVE: Mount Olive College; NEW BERN: Mary Moulton Barden; New Bern Historical Society (Charles T. Barker); Tryon Palace Restoration (Donald Taylor); RALEIGH; State of North Carolina Division of Archives and History (Thornton W. Mitchell); Duplin County Historical Society (W. D. Herring); RED SPRINGS: Chamber of Commerce; SALEM: Salem College; SALISBURY: Rowan Public Library (Patricia Rosenthal); Frances C. Beaver; SEAGROVE: Nancy Sweezy; WASHINGTON: Chamber of Commerce; WILMINGTON: Mrs. Willie Mae Sawyer; WILSON: Wilson County Chamber of Commerce; WINSTON-SALEM: Old Salem, Inc. (Frances Griffin); NEW YORK, N.Y.: Liz Colton.

North Dakota

BEACH: Golden Valley County Library (Frances Kress); BISMARCK: State Historical Society (Lyle S. Nelson); Chamber of Commerce; Barbara Baskerville; Deanie O. McMahon; North Dakota Highway Department; CENTER: Mrs. Kenneth Johnson; CHRISTINE: Mrs. Thomas W. Moe; DES LACS: Gladys Dixon; FARGO: Chamber of Commerce; HURON: Leitha·A. Henegar; MEDORA: Chateau de Mores; PEMBINA: Mrs. Albert Christopher; VALLEY SPRINGS: Judy Lovenmuehler; WILLISTON: Marlene Edie.

Ohio

AKRON: Chamber of Commerce; Akron-Summit County Public Library (Jean Wiedemer); ALLIANCE: Mount Union College (Yost Osborn); ATHENS: Ohio University Library (Robert McDonnell); AUSTINBURG: Margaret Ticknor; CANTON: Stark County Historical Society (Gervis Brady); CINCINNATI: Cincinnati Historical Society (Laura Chace); Public Library (Donna S. Monnig); Cemetery of Spring Grove; Clovernook Home and School for the Blind; CLEVELAND: Public Library (Ethel Robinson); Case Western Reserve University Library (Ruth W. Helmuth); Western Reserve Historical Society (Virginia Hawley); CLYDE: Thaddeus B. Hurd; COLUMBUS: Ohio Historical Society (Thomas Hartig); Gillette H. Rector; Elaine A. Black; Columbus Public Library (Sam Roshon); Ohio State University; COSHOCTON: Raymond Hay; DAYTON: Montgomery County Historical Society (Susan Tomlin); ELYRIA: Lorain County Historical Society (Mary Hillier); GALLIPOLIS: Mary Allison; GREENVILLE: Garst Museum (Gertrude Holzapfel); Darke County Historical Society; Darke County Chamber of Commerce; HILLSBORO: Nellie Fenner; Mrs. Elouise W. Postle; MCCONNELSVILLE: Kate Love Simpson Library (Joy Mazza); MOUNT

VERNON: Chamber of Commerce; OBERLIN: Oberlin College; OXFORD: Miami University; PAINESVILLE: Morley Library (Josephine Sheffer); RIPLEY: Edna McKenzie; SALEM: Chamber of Commerce; SPRINGFIELD: Clark County Historical Society; TIFFIN: Seneca County Historical Society (M. E. Distel); TOLEDO: Chamber of Commerce; Toledo-Lucas County Public Library (Morgan J. Barclay); WILBERFORCE: Carnegie Library, Wilberforce University (Frank Moorer); YELLOW SPRINGS: Antioch College.

Oklahoma

ANADARKO: The National Hall of Fame for Famous American Indians; BARTLESVILLE: Woolaroc Museum; Chamber of Commerce; BEAVER: Beaver County Historical Society; ENID: Chamber of Commerce; FORT GIBSON: Fort Gibson National Cemetery; FORT TOWSON: Fort Towson Historic Site; GUTHRIE: Martha Swanson; Chamber of Commerce; Oklahoma Territorial Museum; LAWTON: Museum of the Great Plains; Chamber of Commerce; MUSKOGEE: Bacone College; Five Civilized Tribes Museum; Foreman Home (Fannie Little); NORMAN: University of Oklahoma; NOWATA: Nowata County Historical Society; OKLAHOMA CITY: Oklahoma Historical Society; Bill Burchardt (Oklahoma Today); OKMULGEE: Oakla Mount Spears; Creek Indian Museum and Council House; PONCA CITY: Pioneer Woman Museum; PORUM: J. D. Graves; SALLISAW: Sequoyah's Home Historic Site; SHAWNEE: Chamber of Commerce; TAHLEQUAH: Northeastern Oklahoma State University; TULSA: Philbrook Art Center; TUSKAHOMA: Ruth Screws; VINITA: Chamber of Commerce; WATONGA: Mrs. Max Shaw; WEWOKA: Chamber of Commerce; WILBURTON: Eastern Oklahoma Historical Society (I. C. Gunning); Robbers Cave State Park; DOWNEY, CALIF.: Eleanor Tracy.

Oregon

ASTORIA: Bruce Berney; CENTRAL POINT: Clara Beth Doe; FLORENCE: Public Library (Beverly Stafford); GRANTS PASS: Josephine County Library (Jean Smith); KLAMATH FALLS: Helen Helfrich; LA GRANDE: Walter M. Pierce Library, Eastern Oregon College (John W. Evans); Helen Bliss; Chamber of Commerce; MEDFORD: Jackson County Library System (Helen Mills); OREGON CITY: Clackamas County Historical Society (Maxine Stroup); PORTLAND: Oregon Historical Society (Susan Sudduth, Richard Engeman); John Gumert; Stuart Mechlin; Clarence Phillips; Library Association of Portland (Leon T. Decker); Joan Salisbury; University of Oregon Library (Heather G. Rosenwinkel); PORT ORFORD: Public Library (Wilma MacNamara); ROSEBURG: Douglas County Museum (George Abdill); SALEM: David Duniway; THE DALLES: Elizabeth Wilson Buehler; The Dalles-Wasco County Library (Richard Wagner); WALDEN: Mrs. Glen Scott; Mrs. Robert Davies; SAN FRANCISCO, CALIF.: Margery Hoffman Smith.

Pennsylvania

ALIQUIPPA: Ralph Rubino; Chamber of Commerce; BETHLEHEM: Moravian College; BRYN MAWR: Bryn Mawr College; CARLISLE: Chamber of Commerce; CHAMBERSBURG: Wilson College; CHEYNEY: Cheyney State College; COATESVILLE: Chamber of Commerce; Lukens Steel Company; COLLEGEVILLE: Ursinus College; COLUMBIA: Chamber of Commerce; FALLSINGTON: Rev. Raymond R. Taylor; FORT WASHINGTON: Historical Society of Fort Washington; Hope Lodge; GETTYSBURG: Gettysburg National Military Park; Adams County Historical Society; HARRISBURG: Chamber of Commerce; Historical Society of Dauphin County; KENNETT SQUARE: Southeastern Chester County Chamber of Commerce; Longwood Gardens (Leslie J. Spraker); KITTANNING: Armstrong County Historical Society; LANCASTER: Chamber of Commerce; LITITZ: Linden Hall School for Girls; MEADVILLE: Allegheny College (Reis Library); MORRISVILLE: Pennsbury Manor; NEW HOPE: Forrest C. Crooks; ORRTANNA: Church of St. Ignatius Loyola; PHILADELPHIA: The Franklin Institute (Albert D. Hollingsworth); Presbyterian Historical Society; Pennsylvania Academy of the Fine Arts; The Congregation Mikveh Israel; Shirley and Louis Sherr; The Historical Society of Pennsylvania; The Medical College of Pennsylvania (Anna Insinger); St. Peter's Church; Joseph and Alexander Kazickas; The Costume Museum of the Germantown Historical Society; Independence National Historical Park; Grumblethorpe; Woodlands Cemetery; Christ Church; PITTSBURGH: The Historical Society of Western Pennsylvania; Chatham College; SUNBURY: Central Susquehanna Valley Chamber of Commerce; Northumberland County Historical Society; SWARTHMORE: Swarthmore College; TITUSVILLE: Chamber of Commerce; WASHINGTON: Washington County Historical Society; Washington-Greene County Tourist Promotion Agency; WEST CHESTER: Chester County Historical Society; WESTTOWN: Westtown Alumni Association; WILKES-BARRE: Chamber of Commerce; WORTHINGTON: Mildred D. Thomas.

Rhode Island

BRISTOL: Bristol Historical and Preservation Society (Charlotte Young); EAST GREENWICH: Col. Vernon S. Allen; NEWPORT: Newport Historical Society (Gladys Bolhouse); Aaron J. Slom; E. W.

Connelly; Newport Restoration Foundation (Benjamin Reed); R. Sullivan; Ida Lewis Yacht Club (W. H. D. Jones); The Preservation Society of Newport (Mrs. Leonard Panaggio); NORTH KINGSTOWN: Chamber of Commerce; PAWTUCKET: Old Slater Mill Museum; PEACE DALE: Raymond Schwab; PORTSMOUTH: Portsmouth Historical Society (Richard Long); PROVIDENCE: The Rhode Island Historical Society (Nancy Chudacoff); Providence Preservation Society (Frederic L. Chase, Jr.); Robert Cool; The Providence Athenaeum (Sylvia Moubayed); Brown University; TIVERTON: Essex Public Library (E. W. Reed); WAKEFIELD: South Kingstown Chamber of Commerce; WARWICK: Warwick Historical Society (Lewis A. Taft); WESTERLY: Sallie E. Coy; Great Westerly-Pawtucket Area Chamber of Commerce; Mrs. Charles F. Hickox; WEST KINGSTON: James Myers; WOONSOCKET: Chamber of Commerce; BOSTON, MASS.: Frances Howard.

South Carolina

ALLENDALE: Ray B. Edenfield; ANDERSON: Anderson County Library (B. Diane Brockman); Marjorie Young; BEAUFORT: Mary Clyde Huskey; Historic Beaufort Foundation; BELTON: Allen Burgess; CAMDEN: Mrs. Alfred H. Ehrenclou; Kershaw County Historical Society (Priscilla Oliver); CHARLESTON: South Carolina Historical Society (Martha Matheny); Gibbes Art Gallery (Virginia Hall); Charleston County Library (Jan Buvinger); M. Maxine Larisey; Kahal Kadosh Beth Elohim; CHESTER: Mrs. F. O. Mayes; COLUMBIA: Historic Columbia Foundation (Rodger Stroup); First Presbyterian Church; Arthur St. Julian Simons; South Carolina Department of Archives and History; South Carolina Confederate Relic Room (LaVerne H. Watson); Felix Walker; DENMARK: Voorhees College; EDGEFIELD: Main Library; FLORENCE: Horace Fraser Rudisill; FROGMORE: Penn Community Services; GEORGETOWN: Great Myrtle Beach Chamber of Commerce; Elizabeth Ashford; GREENVILLE: Greenville County Library (Mary Morris); GREENWOOD: Louise Watson; LAURENS: Betty Irwin; MCCLELLANVILLE: Hampton Plantation; MOUNT PLEASANT: William Gilden; MURRELLS INLET: Gurdon Tarbox, Jr.; PENDLETON: Pendleton District Historical Commission; ST. MATTHEWS: Calhoun County Museum (Mable Brandenburg); SUMTER: J. E. Eldridge; Sumter County Historical Commission (Myrtos G. Osteen); Catharine Bass.

South Dakota

ABERDEEN: Brown County Museum and Historical Society (Peg Stiles Lamont); CUSTER: Melvin J. Gibbs; DEADWOOD: Chamber of Commerce; K. M. Tjormby; Deadwood Public Library (Marjorie Pontius); DE SMET: Laura Ingalls Wilder Memorial Society, Inc.; KEYSTONE: Arthur Johnson; LEAD: Hearst Free Library (Carroll Bedsaul); MARTY: St. Paul's Indian Mission; MOBRIDGE: Chamber of Commerce; PIERRE: South Dakota Historical Resources Center (Janice Fleming); South Dakota Department of Economic and Tourism Development; St. Mary's Hospital; STURGIS: Richard Williams; YANKTON: Dorothy Jencks.

Tennessee

CHATTANOOGA: Chamber of Commerce; University of Tennessee (W. O. P. Dorsey, Jr.); Chattanooga Public Library (Patricia Bennett); CLARKSVILLE: Ursula S. Beach; Clarksville and Montgomery County Chamber of Commerce; Frank J. Runyon; CLEVELAND: Cleveland State Community College (Roy Lillard); COOKEVILLE: Dorrie Norwood; Mrs. Bryan Hill; ELIZABETHTON: George Dugger; ERWIN: Unicoi County Library (Maxine Jones); GREENVILLE: Andrew Jackson National Historic Site (Hugh Lawing); HERMITAGE: The Ladies' Hermitage Association (Ada Whisenhunt); JAMESTOWN: Fentress County Historical Society (Mr. Ruble Upchurch); KNOXVILLE: The University of Tennessee (Neal O'Steen); Knoxville-Knox County Public Library (Martha C. Johnson); Knoxville Tourist Bureau; MADISON: Chamber of Commerce; Mrs. Joe McGregor; MEMPHIS: Memphis Public Library (Katherine Embury); Elmwood Cemetery; St. Mary's Cathedral; West Tennessee Historical Society (Elsie M. Ballard); MILLINGTON: Chamber of Commerce; MURFREESBORO: Middle Tennessee State University (Homer Pittard); NASHVILLE: Tennessee State Library and Archives (Max Mendelsohn); Scarritt College; The Nashville Room, Public Library of Nashville and Davidson County (Janita Rose); Tennessee Arts Commission (Jeannie Donaldson); Tennessee Historical Commission (Ilene J. Cornwell); Stanley Horn; SEVIERVILLE: Chamber of Commerce; SEWANEE: Jessie Ball duPont Library, The University of the South (Trudy Mignery); SHELBYVILLE: Shelbyville and Bedford County Chamber of Commerce; Margie Cooper Public Library; WAVERLY: Myrtle Baker; Humphreys County Library (Davis Crane); COCHRAN, GA.: Ben Harris McClary; DARLINGTON, PA.: Mrs. Richard Douthitt; ARLINGTON, VA.: Mabel Stockton Merchant.

Texas

ATHENS: Mrs. W. C. Perryman; AUSTIN: Elisabet Ney Museum (Mary Diane Harris); Texas Highway Department (Richard Pierce); Daughters of the Republic of Texas Museum (V. Blomquist); Laguna Gloria Art Museum; Austin-Travis County Collection (Mary Schmidt); W. T.

Phillips; BEAUMONT: The Texas Gulf Historical Society (William Adams); BELTON: Carroll Neighbours; BROWNSVILLE: Chamber of Commerce; COLUMBUS: Chamber of Commerce; CORPUS CHRISTI: La Retama Public Library (Mary Kaye Donahue); DALLAS: Dallas Public Library (Lucile A. Boykin); Southern Methodist University; DEL RIO: Whitehead Memorial Museum; DENTON: Texas Women's University (Eloise Mordecai); EL PASO: El Paso County Historical Society (Conrey Bryson); GROESBECK: Old Fort Parker State Park (Ronald L. Holland); HAMILTON: Genevieve Clark; HASKELL: Chamber of Commerce; HOUSTON: Houston Public Library (Marion Brown); INDEPENDENCE: Texas Baptist Historical Center (Eddis Smith); LUBBOCK: Chamber of Commerce; LUFKIN: Tim Jones; MOODY: Mother Neff State Park (Kenneth Pollard); NACOGDOCHES: Hoya Memorial Library (Mrs. T. G. Gilford); PARIS: Chamber of Commerce of Lama County; RICHMOND: Fort Bend County Library (Lillian Stavinoha); Fort Bend County Museum Association (Mark E. Price); SAN ANTONIO: Greater San Antonio Chamber of Commerce; Daughters of the Republic of Texas (C. J. Ling); Marion Kooglar McNay Art Museum; TEMPLE: Chamber of Commerce; VEGA: Laura Graham; WACO: Baylor University; WICHITA FALLS: Wichita Falls Board of Commerce; GREENWICH, CONN.: Joseph M. Kazickas; FORT SILL, OKLAHOMA: Field Artillery Museum Association (Linda Shaw); LAWTON, OKLAHOMA: Lawton Public Library.

Utah

KANAB: Chamber of Commerce; MONTICELLO: The San Juan Record; PARK CITY: Chamber of Commerce; ST. GEORGE: Chamber of Commerce; SALT LAKE CITY: Utah Historical Society (Miriam Murphy); Ambassador Athletic Club; University of Utah; The Lion House; Hotel Utah; Daughters of Utah Pioneers; Church of Jesus Christ of Latter-Day Saints (Historical Department); SPRINGVILLE: Chamber of Commerce; TORREY: Capitol Reef National Park; PAGE, ARIZ.: Glen Canyon National Recreation Area; DINOSAUR, COLO.: Dinosaur National Monument.

Vermont

ARLINGTON: Martha Canfield Memorial Free Library (Gerald Rafferty); BELLOWS FALLS: Rockingham Free Public Library (Muriel Thomas); BENNINGTON: Bennington College (Gail Thain Parker); Bennington Museum (Charles Bennett); BRATTLEBORO: Brooks Memorial Library (Eva Leich); BRIDPORT: Anna T. Howlett; BROWNINGTON: Orleans County Historical Society (Edward S. Alexander); BURLINGTON: Bailey Library, University of Vermont (T. Bassett); Fletcher Free Library (Marjorie Zunder); ENOGSBURG: Enogsburg Public Library; HINSDALE: Rosetta B. Lowe; LUDLOW: Black River Academy Museum (Milyon G. Moore); MIDDLEBURY: Middlebury College (Max Petersen); Sheldon Art Museum; MONTPELIER: Vermont Historical Society (Mrs. Reidun Nuquist); PUTNEY: Putney Public Library (Eleanor Carey); SHELBURNE: Shelburne Museum; VERGENNES: Mrs. Matt Daniels; WETSON: Mrs. Ralph Boothby; WINDSOR: Historic Windsor, Inc.; WOODSTOCK: Woodstock Historical Society, Inc. (Nancy Campbell).

Virginia

ALEXANDRIA: Historic Alexandria Foundation (Mrs. Hugh B. Cox); ARLINGTON: Ruth Rose; BIG STONE GAP: Lonesome Pine Arts and Crafts, Inc.; BLACKSBURG: Virginia Polytechnic Institution (Agnes Davis); CHARLOTTESVILLE: University of Virginia Library (Linda Sundholm); Charlottesville and Albemarle County Chamber of Commerce; Albemarle County Historical Society (Charles Moran); CLIFTON FORGE: Mrs. Guy B. Persinger; Chamber of Commerce; R. Eva Tatum; COVINGTON: Covington-Alleghany County Chamber of Commerce; DANVILLE: Danville Historical Society (George B. Anderson); DUBLIN: Mary Kegley; FAIRFAX: The Historical Society of Fairfax County (Joan Butler); FALLS CHURCH: Falls Church Public Library (Mrs. A. W. Rupps); FALMOUTH: Historic Falmouth Towne, Inc. (George Taylor); FARMVILLE: Longwood College; FREDERICKSBURG: Mary Washington College; Association for the Preservation of Virginia Antiquities (Betty Houston); Historic Fredericksburg Foundation, Inc.; Fredericksburg and Spotsylvania National Military Park (Stuart Vogt); City of Fredericksburg Information Center; FRONT ROYAL: Laura Virginia Hale; GREENWOOD: Langhorne Gibson; HAGUE: Blake Tyler Newton; HANOVER: Hanover County Historical Society; HOLLINS: Hollins College (Nancy Raley); HOPEWELL: A. Robbins, Jr.; LA CROSSE: Verna Bracey; LANCASTER: Mary Ball Memorial Museum (Ann Lewis Burrows); LYNCHBURG: Lynchburg Public Library (Mary Douglas Boldrick); Jones Memorial Library (Josephine Wingfield); MANASSAS: Manassas Historical Society (Edgar Conner, III); MOUNT VERNON: Woodlawn Plantation (George Smith); The Mount Vernon Ladies' Association (Charles Wall); NORFOLK: Norfolk Public Library System (Lucile B. Portlock); PEARISBURG: Pearisburg Public Library; PETERSBURG: Blandford Church Interpretation Center (James Bailey); QUANOCK: Eastern Shore of Virginia Historical Society (Helen Fosque); RICHMOND: Association for the Preservation of Virginia Antiquities (Patricia Capsanes); Virginia State Library (Milton C. Russell); Virginia State Library;

Valentine Museum (Betty Gray Gibson); Virginia State Travel Service; University of Richmond; ROANOKE: Patrick Henry Memorial Foundation (Mabel Olver Bellwood); Roanoke Valley Historical Society (Donna Ware); SMITHFIELD: Mrs. Harry G. Dashiell; STAUNTON: Martha S. Grafton Library (Alice G. Simpkins); Staunton-Augusta County Chamber of Commerce; STRATFORD: Stratford Hall Plantation (Edith Healy); SURRY: Rolfe-Warren House; SWEET BRIAR: Sweet Briar College; VIRGINIA BEACH: Mrs. L. V. Kyle; Chamber of Commerce; WILLIAMSBURG: Colonial Williamsburg Foundation (Edward M. Riley); Thomas L. Williams; WYTHEVILLE: Wythe County Historical Society (Helen Umberger); YORKTOWN: Colonial National Historical Park (James Haskett).

Washington

ADDY: J. C. McMillan; BELLINGHAM: Chamber of Commerce; Western Washington State College; BREMERTON: Kitsap Regional Library (Jeanne Blair); MARYHILL: Maryhill Museum of Fine Arts; PASCO: Chamber of Commerce; SEATTLE: Chamber of Commerce; Office of Urban Conservation; Seattle Public Library (Phoebe Harris); Seattle Historical Society (Bertha Stratford); Diocese of Olympia Episcopal Church; Seattle Symphony Orchestra (Karen R. Donnelly); University of Washington (Andrew F. Johnson); SPOKANE: Spokane Opera House and Convention Center; Spokane Public Library (Mary C. Johnson); TACOMA: Tacoma Public Library (Edith Ohlson); Frederic D. Beek; VANCOUVER: Fort Vancouver National Historical Site (David Hansen); WENATCHEE: Wenatchee Valley College (Donna Allen); ONTARIO, CALIF.: Harry D. Clark.

West Virginia

BUCKHANNON: Upshur County Historical Society (H. Gene Starr); BUFFALO: Caroline H. Frazier; CHARLESTOWN: John A. Washington; Jefferson County Historical Society (N. Watson); Department of Archives and History (Jane Brand); GRAFTON: Mothers Day Shrine; Charles Roth; HILLSBORO: Pearl Buck Birthplace Foundation; KEYSER: Keyser Mineral County Chamber of Commerce; MARLINTON: Jane Price Sharp; MARTINSBURG: Don C. Wood; MORGANTOWN: Antiquities Commission, West Virginia University; Earl Core; POINT PLEASANT: Mason County Bi-Centennial Commission (Jack Burdett); SALEM: Dorothy Dabis; SISTERSVILLE: Tyler County Historical Commission; WHEELING: Chamber of Commerce; Beverly Fluty; Florence Crittenden Home; Mrs. Harry Renshaw; WHITE SULPHUR SPRINGS: Chamber of Commerce.

Wisconsin

APPLETON: Chamber of Commerce; Leland D. Ester; AVOCA: Ann Cooper; BERLIN: Mrs. N. D. Secora; COLUMBUS: Chamber of Commerce; FLORENCE: Mrs. R. R. Yehle; FOND DU LAC: Mrs. Kenneth Worthing; Fond du Lac Public Library (Kay Conrad); GREEN BAY: Brown County Historical Society (Dorothy Strauble Wittig); GREENFIELD: Esther Fisher; JANESVILLE: Rock County Historical Society (R. Hartung, N. B. Douglas); JEFFERSON: Lake Mills-Aztalan Historical Society; KENOSHA: Kenosha County Historical Society; LADYSMITH: Rusk County Information Center; MADISON: Chamber of Commerce; State Historical Society, Division of Archives (George Talbot, Melodie Knisely, Dr. Josephine Harper); Walter E. Scott; MERRILL: T. B. Scott Free Library (Ramon Hernandez); MILWAUKEE: Jill Sherry; Marquette University; The University of Wisconsin (Elizabeth Devitt); Metropolitan Milwaukee Association of Commerce; Milwaukee Public Library (Mina Hoyer); Milwaukee County Historical Society (Robert Carroon); Frank P. Zeidler; NEENAH: Neenah Historical Society (Mrs. C. Hedges); NEW BERLIN: Mrs. Donald Hermann; OSHKOSH: June Ives; Chamber of Commerce; Oskosh Public Library (Helen Simpson); PORTAGE: Dorothy McCarthy; RACINE: Racine County Historical Museum (Janet Nielsen); RICHLAND CENTER: Margaret H. Scott; Chamber of Commerce; RIPON: Ripon College; SUN PRAIRIE: Ardin D. Laper; VIROQUA: Constance Stephen; Chamber of Commerce; WATERTOWN: Watertown Historical Society (Gladys Mollark); WAUKESHA: Waukesha County Museum (Nancy K. Fleischmann); WAUPUN: Waupun Historical Society (Thelma Kaiser); WAUWATOSA: Wauwatosa Public Library; WEST ALLIS: Margaret Jane Park; WINDSOR: Virginia Sorenson.

Wyoming

BUFFALO: Stuart D. Frazier; CASPER: Chamber of Commerce; CHEYENNE: Wyoming Recreation Commission; Wyoming State Archive and Historical Department (Katherine Halverson); Mrs. Nickie Lepas; FORT LARAMIE: Fort Lamarie National Historic Site (Richard Maeder); FORT WASHAKIE: Shirley Keith; Ted Bell; Herb Higg; GREEN RIVER: Sweetwater County Historical Museum (Henry Chadey); KEMMERER: Jacob Antilla; Gertrude A. Lewis; LANDER: Fremont County Pioneer Museum (Bertha Coghill); Minnie Woodring; LARAMIE: University of Wyoming (T. A. Larson); MOOSE: Grand Teton National Historic Site (Linda Olson); NEWCASTLE: Weston County Historical Society (Mary Capps); Gene Gressky; Rusell Jairell; Kathy Wright; Mrs. Ray Sell; WASHINGTON, D.C.: The Honorable Nellie Tayloe Ross.

Index

Lynn Sherr

Lynn Sherr and Jurate Kazickas created the highly acclaimed *Liberated Woman's Appointment Calendar,* which is now entering its seventh edition. In the course of unearthing landmarks of American women for this book, Jurate Kazickas discovered she had grown up four houses away from the home of suffragist Carrie Chapman Catt in New Rochelle, New York. Lynn Sherr turned up no such surprise neighbors on her block in Merion, Pennsylvania, but is determined to find a way to include her hometown in a future edition. Currently both women have put aside their treks to libraries, unmarked houses and gravesites and returned to New York City and the twentieth century to resume their careers in print and television journalism.   photos: Lois Sherr

Jurate Kazickas